CLYMER® MANUALS

SUZUKI

GS550 • 1977-1986

More information available at Clymer.com

Phone: 805-498-6703

Haynes Publishing Group
Sparkford Nr Yeovil
Somerset BA22 7JJ England

Haynes North America, Inc
859 Lawrence Drive
Newbury Park
California 91320 USA

ISBN 10: 0-89287-664-6
ISBN-13: 978-0-89287-664-8

Cover: *Mark Clifford Photography at www.markclifford.com.*

Printed in the UK

M373, 10U1, 17-352 **ABCDEFGHIJKLMNOPQRST**

Common spark plug conditions

NORMAL

Symptoms: Brown to grayish-tan color and slight electrode wear. Correct heat range for engine and operating conditions.
Recommendation: When new spark plugs are installed, replace with plugs of the same heat range.

WORN

Symptoms: Rounded electrodes with a small amount of deposits on the firing end. Normal color. Causes hard starting in damp or cold weather and poor fuel economy.
Recommendation: Plugs have been left in the engine too long. Replace with new plugs of the same heat range. Follow the recommended maintenance schedule.

CARBON DEPOSITS

Symptoms: Dry sooty deposits indicate a rich mixture or weak ignition. Causes misfiring, hard starting and hesitation.
Recommendation: Make sure the plug has the correct heat range. Check for a clogged air filter or problem in the fuel system or engine management system. Also check for ignition system problems.

ASH DEPOSITS

Symptoms: Light brown deposits encrusted on the side or center electrodes or both. Derived from oil and/or fuel additives. Excessive amounts may mask the spark, causing misfiring and hesitation during acceleration.
Recommendation: If excessive deposits accumulate over a short time or low mileage, install new valve guide seals to prevent seepage of oil into the combustion chambers. Also try changing gasoline brands.

OIL DEPOSITS

Symptoms: Oily coating caused by poor oil control. Oil is leaking past worn valve guides or piston rings into the combustion chamber. Causes hard starting, misfiring and hesitation.
Recommendation: Correct the mechanical condition with necessary repairs and install new plugs.

GAP BRIDGING

Symptoms: Combustion deposits lodge between the electrodes. Heavy deposits accumulate and bridge the electrode gap. The plug ceases to fire, resulting in a dead cylinder.
Recommendation: Locate the faulty plug and remove the deposits from between the electrodes.

TOO HOT

Symptoms: Blistered, white insulator, eroded electrode and absence of deposits. Results in shortened plug life.
Recommendation: Check for the correct plug heat range, over-advanced ignition timing, lean fuel mixture, intake manifold vacuum leaks, sticking valves and insufficient engine cooling.

PREIGNITION

Symptoms: Melted electrodes. Insulators are white, but may be dirty due to misfiring or flying debris in the combustion chamber. Can lead to engine damage.
Recommendation: Check for the correct plug heat range, over-advanced ignition timing, lean fuel mixture, insufficient engine cooling and lack of lubrication.

HIGH SPEED GLAZING

Symptoms: Insulator has yellowish, glazed appearance. Indicates that combustion chamber temperatures have risen suddenly during hard acceleration. Normal deposits melt to form a conductive coating. Causes misfiring at high speeds.
Recommendation: Install new plugs. Consider using a colder plug if driving habits warrant.

DETONATION

Symptoms: Insulators may be cracked or chipped. Improper gap setting techniques can also result in a fractured insulator tip. Can lead to piston damage.
Recommendation: Make sure the fuel anti-knock values meet engine requirements. Use care when setting the gaps on new plugs. Avoid lugging the engine.

MECHANICAL DAMAGE

Symptoms: May be caused by a foreign object in the combustion chamber or the piston striking an incorrect reach (too long) plug. Causes a dead cylinder and could result in piston damage.
Recommendation: Repair the mechanical damage. Remove the foreign object from the engine and/or install the correct reach plug.

CONTENTS

QUICK REFERENCE DATA

TORQUE SPECIFICATIONS

Item	mkg	ft.-lb.
Front axle nut	3.6-5.2	26-38
Front axle pinch bolt	1.5-2.5	11-18
Front master cylinder bolts	0.5-0.8	4-6
Caliper mounting bolts		
(front and rear)	2.5-4.0	18-29
Caliper housing bolts (1983-on)	3.0-3.6	22-26
Front caliper axle bolt (1977-1982)	4.0-5.5	20-40
Rear master cylinder bolts	1.5-2.5	11-18
Steering stem pinch bolt		
(except LD, LF & LG models)	1.5-2.5	11-18
Steering stem pinch nut (LD models)	1.2-2.0	9-15
Steering stem head nut or bolt		
1980-1982	3.6-5.2	26-38
All others	2.0-3.0	15-22
Fork cap bolts	1.5-3.0	11-22
Handlebar clamp bolts (1977-1982)	1.2-2.0	9-15
Handlebar fasteners (1983-on)		
Set bolt (except LD)	1.5-2.5	11-18
Holder bolt (except LD)	5.0-6.0	36-44
Holder bolt (LD models)	1.5-2.5	11-22
Holder bolt (LF & LG models)	1.2-2.0	8.5-14.5
Holder nut (except LD)	2.0-3.0	15-22
Holder nut (LD models)	1.0-1.5	7-11
Upper fork pinch bolt		
1977-1980	2.0-3.0	15-22
1981-1982	3.5-5.5	26-40
1983-on	2.0-3.0	15-22
Lower fork pinch bolt		
1977-1980	2.0-3.0	15-22
1981-on (except LD models)	1.5-2.5	11-18
LD models	1.2-2.0	9-15
LF-LG models	1.5-2.5	11-18
Brake disc mounting bolt	1.5-2.5	11-18
Rear sprocket nut		
1977-1982	4.0-6.0	29-43
1983-on	2.5-4.0	18-29
Swing arm pivot bolt		
1977-1982 and LD models	5.0-8.0	36-58
All others	5.5-8.8	40-64
Shock absorber nut (1977-1982)	2.0-3.0	15-22
Rear axle nut		
1977-1982	8.5-11.5	62-83
1983-on	5.0-8.0	36-58
Torque link nut	2.0-3.0	15-22
Engine mounting bolts (1977-1982)		
8 mm	1.3-2.3	10-17
10 mm	2.5-4.5	18-33
Engine mounting bolts (1983-on)		
Upper bolts	6.0-7.2	44-52
Lower bolts	6.7-8.0	49-58
Footrest mounting bolts	2.7-4.3	20-31
Exhaust pipe flange bolts		
and clamp bolts		
TSCC models	0.9-1.2	6.5-8.5
All others	0.9-1.4	6.5-10.0
Muffler mounting bolt		
TSCC models	2.2-3.5	16.0-25.5
All others	1.8-2.8	13.0-20.0

TUNE-UP SPECIFICATIONS

Recommended spark plugs	
1977-1982	NGK B-8ES or ND W24ES
1983-on	NGK D9EA or ND X27ES-U
Spark plug gap	0.6-0.8 mm (0.024-0.03 in.)
Breaker point gap	0.3-0.4 mm (0.012-0.016 in.)
Ignition timing	
1977-1979	17° BTDC below 1,500 rpm
	37° BTDC above 2,500 rpm
1980-1982*	15° BTDC below 1,400-1,600 rpm
	40° BTDC above 2,250-2,450 rpm
1983-on*	11° BTDC below 1,550-1,750 rpm
	31° BTDC above 2,900-3,100 rpm
Valve clearance	
1977-1982	0.03-0.08 mm (0.001-0.003 in.)
1983-on	0.08-0.013 mm (0.003-0.005 in.)
Idle speed	
1977-1982	1,000-2,000 rpm
1983-on	900-1,100 rpm
Firing order	1, 2, 4, 3**

* Timing on 1980-on models is pre-set and is not adjustable.
** No. 1 cylinder is on the left-hand side of the engine.

CAPACITIES

	Fuel tank		
	Liters	U.S. gal.	Imp. gal.
1977-1978	17	4.5	3.7
E models			
1979-1981	16	4.2	3.5
1985-on			
49-state	18	4.8	3.9
California	17.5	4.2	3.5
L models			
1979-1980	13	3.4	2.9
1981-on	12	3.2	2.6
1982 M models	23	6.1	5.0
All others	16	4.2	3.5
	Engine/transmission oil		
	Liters	**U.S.qt.**	**Imp. qt.**
Without filter change			
1983-on L models	2.6	2.7	2.3
All others	2.4	2.5	2.1
With filter change			
1983-on L models	3.1	3.3	2.7
All others	2.6	2.7	2.3
After overhaul			
1983-on L models	3.3	3.5	2.9
All others	2.7	2.9	2.4

(continued)

CAPACITIES (continued)

Fork oil capacity	cc	U.S. oz.	Imp. oz.
E models			
1977-1980	165	5.6	5.8
1983-1984	321	10.8	11.3
1985-on	345	11.6	12.14
ES models			
1983	321	10.8	11.3
1984	330	11.2	11.6
L models			
1979-1980	217	7.3	7.6
1981	249	8.4	8.8
1982	239	8.0	8.4
1983	288	9.7	10.1
1985	276	9.3	9.7
1986	248	8.4	8.8
1981 T model	190	6.4	6.7
1982 M model	223	7.5	7.9
All others	165	5.6	5.8

Fork oil level*	mm	in.
E models		
1977-1980	204	8.0
1983-1984	125	4.9
1985-on	114	4.5
ES models		
1983	125	4.9
1984	119	4.7
L models		
1979-1980	229	9.0
1981	201	7.9
1982	144	5.7
1983	190	7.5
1985	179	7.05
1986	181	7.1
1981 T model	201	7.9
1982 M model	140	5.5
All others	204	8.0

* The maximum allowable difference between the right and left fork tubes is 1 mm (0.04 in.). Remove the spring and measure the oil level from the top of each fork leg held vertical and fully compressed.

COMPRESSION PRESSURE

	Standard compression kg/cm² (psi)	Service limit kg/cm² (psi)
1977-1980	9.0-12.0 (128-171)	6.5 (92)
1981-1982	9.0-13.0 (128-185)	7.0 (100)
TSCC models	10.0-14.0 (142-199)	8.0 (114)
Maximum difference between cylinders	2.0 (28)	

RECOMMENDED TIRE PRESSURE*

Tire	psi	kg/cm²
Front tire (normal riding)		
Solo (1977-1982)	25	1.75
Solo (1983-on)	28	2.00
Dual (L models)	28	2.00
Dual (1983-on)	28	2.00
Front tire (continous high-speed riding)		
Single and dual	28	2.00
Rear tire (normal riding)		
Solo (1977-1982)	28	2.00
Solo (1983-on)	32	2.25
Dual (LN, LX, LZ)	32	2.25
Dual (LD & LF)	36	2.50
Dual (ED, ESC, EE, EE, ESE)	40	2.80
Dual (all others)	36	2.50
Rear tire (continous high-speed riding)		
Solo (L models)	36	2.50
Solo (all others)	40	2.80
Dual	40	2.80

* Inflation pressure for factory equipped tires.

RECOMMENDED FUEL AND LUBRICANTS

Fuel	Unleaded or low-lead; 85-95 octane
Engine/transmission oil	SAE 10W/40, SE rated
Fork oil	SAE 15 fork oil
Brake fluid*	Rated DOT 3 or DOT 4

* Use only glycol-based brake fluid rated DOT 3 or DOT 4. Mixing silicon- or petroleum-based fluids can cause brake component damage leading to brake system failure.

TAPPET SHIM SIZES (1982 AND EARLIER)

No.	Thickness (mm)	Part No.	No.	Thickness	Part No.
1	2.15	12892-45000	11	2.65	12892-45010
2	2.20	12892-45001	12	2.70	12892-45011
3	2.25	12892-45002	13	2.75	12892-45012
4	2.30	12892-45003	14	2.80	12892-45013
5	2.35	12892-45004	15	2.85	12892-45014
6	2.40	12892-45005	16	2.90	12892-45015
7	2.45	12892-45006	17	2.95	12892-45016
8	2.50	12892-45007	18	3.00	12892-45017
9	2.55	12892-45008	19	3.05	12892-45018
10	2.60	12892-45009	20	3.10	12892-45019

CLYMER®

SUZUKI

GS550 • 1977-1986

INTRODUCTION

This detailed, comprehensive manual covers all 1977-1986 Suzuki GS550's. The expert text gives complete information on repair, maintenance and overhaul. Hundreds of photos and drawings guide you through every step. This book includes all you need to know to keep your bike running right.

Where repairs are practical for the owner/mechanic, complete procedures are given. Equally important, difficult jobs are pointed out. Such operations are more economically performed by a dealer or indepenent garage.

A shop manual is a reference. You want to be able to find information fast. As in all Clymer books, this one is designed with this in mind. All chapters are thumb tabbed. Important items are indexed at the end of the book. All the most frequently used specifications and capacities are summarized on the *Quick Reference* pages at the beginning of the book.

Keep the book handy. Carry it in your tool box. It will help you to better understand your Suzuki, lower repair and maintenance costs, and generally improve your satisfaction with your bike.

1

CHAPTER ONE

GENERAL INFORMATION

The troubleshooting, maintenance, tune-up, and step-by-step repair procedures in this book are written specifically for the owner and home mechanic. The text is accompanied by helpful photos and diagrams to make the job as clear and correct as possible.

Troubleshooting, maintenance, tune-up, and repair are not difficult if you know what to do and what tools and equipment to use. Anyone of average intelligence, with some mechanical ability, and not afraid to get their hands dirty can perform most of the procedures in this book.

In some cases, a repair job may require tools or skills not reasonably expected of the home mechanic. These procedures are noted in each chapter and it is recommended that you take the job to your dealer, a competent mechanic, or a machine shop.

MANUAL ORGANIZATION

This chapter provides general information, safety and service hints. Also included are lists of recommended shop and emergency tools as well as a brief description of troubleshooting and tune-up equipment.

Chapter Two provides methods and suggestions for quick and accurate diagnosis and repair of problems. Troubleshooting procedures discuss typical symptoms and logical methods to pinpoint the trouble.

Chapter Three explains all periodic lubrication and routine maintenance necessary to keep your motorcycle running well. Chapter Three also includes recommended tune-up procedures, eliminating the need to constantly consult chapters on the various subassemblies.

Subsequent chapters cover specific systems such as the engine, transmission, and electrical system. Each of these chapters provides disassembly, inspection, repair, and assembly procedures in a simple step-by-step format. If a repair is impractical for the home mechanic it is indicated. In these cases it is usually faster and less expensive to have the repairs made by a dealer or competent repair shop. Essential specifications are included in the appropriate chapters.

When special tools are required to perform a task included in this manual, the tools are illustrated. It may be possible to borrow or rent these tools. The inventive mechanic may also be able to find a suitable substitute in his tool box, or to fabricate one.

The terms NOTE, CAUTION, and WARNING have specific meanings in this manual. A NOTE provides additional or explanatory information. A

CAUTION is used to emphasize areas where equipment damage could result if proper precautions are not taken. A WARNING is used to stress those areas where personal injury or death could result from negligence, in addition to possible mechanical damage.

SERVICE HINTS

Time, effort, and frustration will be saved and possible injury will be prevented if you observe the following practices.

Most of the service procedures covered are straightforward and can be performed by anyone reasonably handy with tools. It is suggested, however, that you consider your own capabilities carefully before attempting any operation involving major disassembly of the engine.

Some operations, for example, require the use of a press. It would be wiser to have these performed by a shop equipped for such work, rather than to try to do the job yourself with makeshift equipment. Other procedures require precision measurements. Unless you have the skills and equipment required, it would be better to have a qualified repair shop make the measurements for you.

Repairs go much faster and easier if the parts that will be worked on are clean before you begin. There are special cleaners for washing the engine and related parts. Brush or spray on the cleaning solution, let stand, then rinse it away with a garden hose. Clean all oily or greasy parts with cleaning solvent as you remove them.

WARNING

Never use gasoline as a cleaning agent. It presents an extreme fire hazard. Be sure to work in a well-ventilated area when using cleaning solvent. Keep a fire extinguisher, rated for gasoline fires, handy in any case.

Much of the labor charge for repairs made by dealers is for the removal and disassembly of other parts to reach the defective unit. It is frequently possible to perform the preliminary operations yourself and then take the defective unit in to the dealer for repair, at considerable savings.

Once you have decided to tackle the job yourself, make sure you locate the appropriate section in this manual, and read it entirely. Study the illustrations and text until you have a good idea of what is involved in completing the job satisfactorily. If special tools are required, make arrangements to get them before you start. Also, purchase any known defective parts prior to starting on the procedure. It is frustrating and time-consuming to get partially into a job and then be unable to complete it.

Simple wiring checks can be easily made at home, but knowledge of electronics is almost a necessity for performing tests with complicated electronic testing gear.

During disassembly of parts keep a few general cautions in mind. Force is rarely needed to get things apart. If parts are a tight fit, like a bearing in a case, there is usually a tool designed to separate them. Never use a screwdriver to pry apart parts with machined surfaces such as cylinder head or crankcase halves. You will mar the surfaces and end up with leaks.

Make diagrams wherever similar-appearing parts are found. You may think you can remember where everything came from — but mistakes are costly. There is also the possibility you may get sidetracked and not return to work for days or even weeks — in which interval, carefully laid out parts may have become disturbed.

Tag all similar internal parts for location, and mark all mating parts for position. Record number and thickness of any shims as they are removed. Small parts such as bolts can be identified by placing them in plastic sandwich bags that are sealed and labeled with masking tape.

Wiring should be tagged with masking tape and marked as each wire is removed. Again, do not rely on memory alone.

Disconnect battery ground cable before working near electrical connections and before disconnecting wires. Never run the engine with the battery disconnected; the alternator could be seriously damaged.

Protect finished surfaces from physical damage or corrosion. Keep gasoline and brake fluid off painted surfaces.

Frozen or very tight bolts and screws can often be loosened by soaking with penetrating oil like Liquid Wrench or WD-40, then sharply striking the bolt head a few times with a hammer and punch (or screwdriver for screws). Avoid heat unless absolutely necessary, since it may melt, warp, or remove the temper from many parts.

Avoid flames or sparks when working near a charging battery or flammable liquids, such as gasoline.

No parts, except those assembled with a press fit, require unusual force during assembly. If a part is hard to remove or install, find out why before proceeding.

Cover all openings after removing parts to keep dirt, small tools, etc., from falling in.

When assembling two parts, start all fasteners, then tighten evenly.

Wiring connections and brake shoes, drums, pads, and discs and contact surfaces in dry clutches should be kept clean and free of grease and oil.

When assembling parts, be sure all shims and washers are replaced exactly as they came out.

Whenever a rotating part butts against a stationary part, look for a shim or washer. Use new gaskets if there is any doubt about the condition of old ones. Generally, you should apply gasket cement to one mating surface only, so the parts may be easily disassembled in the future. A thin coat of oil on gaskets helps them seal effectively.

Heavy grease can be used to hold small parts in place if they tend to fall out during assembly. However, keep grease and oil away from electrical, clutch, and brake components.

High spots may be sanded off a piston with sandpaper, but emery cloth and oil do a much more professional job.

Carburetors are best cleaned by disassembling them and soaking the parts in a commercial carburetor cleaner. Never soak gaskets and rubber parts in these cleaners. Never use wire to clean out jets and air passages; they are easily damaged. Use compressed air to blow out the carburetor, but only if the float has been removed first.

Take your time and do the job right. Do not forget that a newly rebuilt engine must be broken in the same as a new one. Refer to your owner's manual for the proper break-in procedures.

SAFETY FIRST

Professional mechanics can work for years and never sustain a serious injury. If you observe a few rules of common sense and safety, you can enjoy many safe hours servicing your motorcycle. You could hurt yourself or damage the motorcycle if you ignore these rules.

1. Never use gasoline as a cleaning solvent.
2. Never smoke or use a torch in the vicinity of flammable liquids such as cleaning solvent in open containers.
3. Never smoke or use a torch in an area where batteries are being charged. Highly explosive hydrogen gas is formed during the charging process.
4. Use the proper sized wrenches to avoid damage to nuts and injury to yourself.
5. When loosening a tight or stuck nut, be guided by what would happen if the wrench should slip. Protect yourself accordingly.
6. Keep your work area clean and uncluttered.
7. Wear safety goggles during all operations involving drilling, grinding, or use of a cold chisel.
8. Never use worn tools.
9. Keep a fire extinguisher handy and be sure it is rated for gasoline (Class B) and electrical (Class C) fires.

EXPENDABLE SUPPLIES

Certain expendable supplies are necessary. These include grease, oil, gasket cement, wiping rags, cleaning solvent, and distilled water. Also, special locking compounds, silicone lubricants, and engine and carburetor cleaners may be useful. Cleaning solvent is available at most service stations and distilled water for the battery is available at supermarkets.

SHOP TOOLS

For complete servicing and repair you will need an assortment of ordinary hand tools (**Figure 1**).

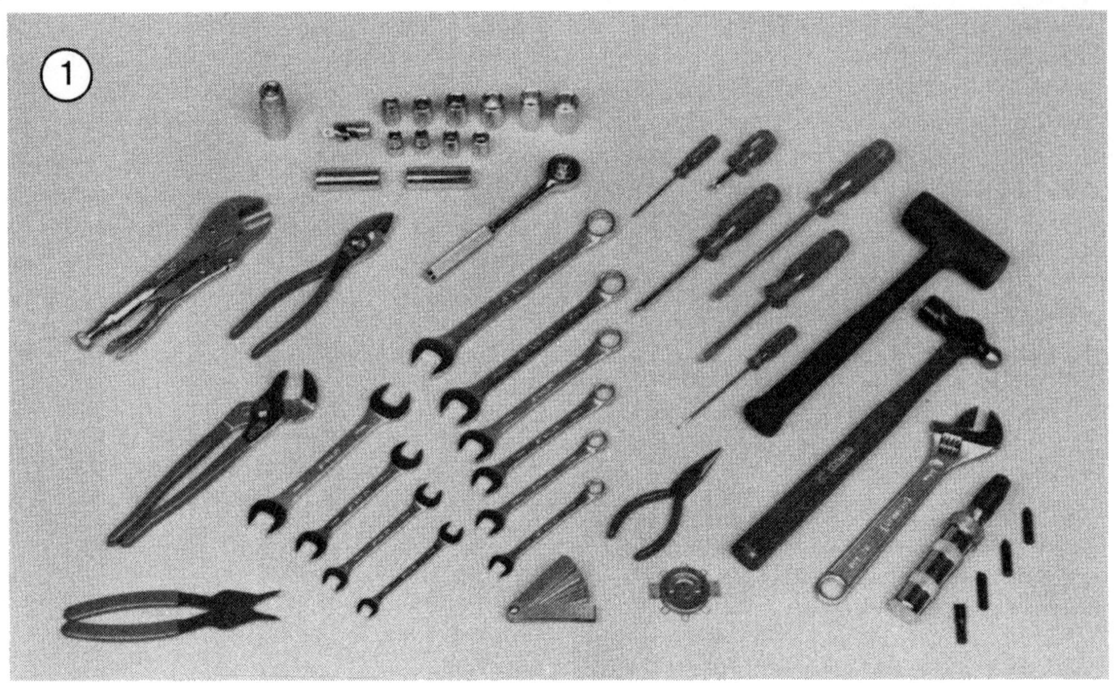

As a minimum, these include:

a. Combination wrenches
b. Sockets
c. Plastic mallet
d. Small hammer
e. Impact driver
f. Snap ring pliers
g. Gas pliers
h. Phillips screwdrivers
i. Slot (common) screwdrivers
j. Feeler gauges
k. Spark plug gauge
l. Spark plug wrench

Special tools required are shown in the chapters covering the particular repair in which they are used.

Engine tune-up and troubleshooting procedures require other special tools and equipment. These are described in detail in the following sections.

EMERGENCY TOOL KITS

Highway

A small emergency tool kit kept on the bike is handy for road emergencies which otherwise could leave you stranded. The tools and spares listed below and shown in **Figure 2** will let you handle most roadside repairs.

a. Motorcycle tool kit (original equipment)
b. Impact driver
c. Silver waterproof sealing tape (duct tape)
d. Hose clamps (3 sizes)
e. Silicone sealer
f. Lock 'N' Seal
g. Flashlight
h. Tire patch kit
i. Tire irons
j. Plastic pint bottle (for oil)
k. Waterless hand cleaner
l. Rags for clean up

Off-Road

A few simple tools and aids carried on the motorcycle can mean the difference between walking or riding back to camp or to where repairs can be made. See **Figure 3**.

A few essential spare parts carried in your truck or van can prevent a day or weekend of trail riding from being spoiled. See **Figure 4**.

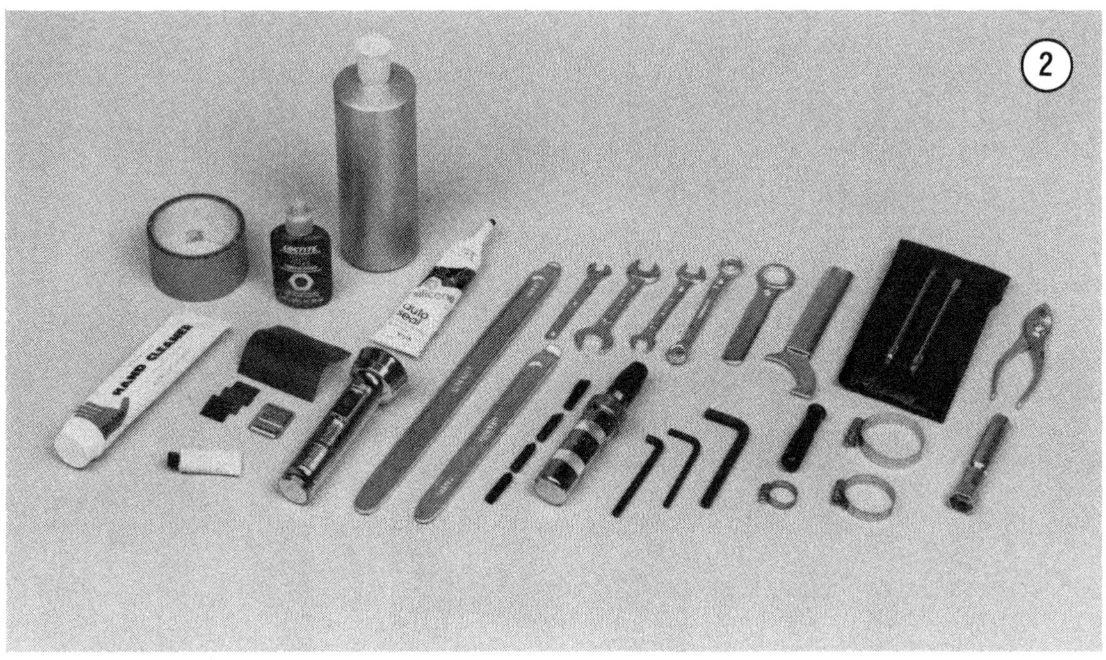

(2)

On the Motorcycle

a. Motorcycle tool kit (original equipment)
b. Drive chain master link
c. Tow line
d. Spark plug
e. Spark plug wrench
f. Shifter lever
g. Clutch/brake lever
h. Silver waterproof sealing tape (duct tape)
i. Loctite Lock 'N' Seal

In the Truck

a. Control cables (throttle, clutch, brake)
b. Silicone sealer
c. Tire patch kit
d. Tire irons
e. Tire pump
f. Impact driver
g. Oil

WARNING

Tools and spares should be carried on the motorcycle — not in clothing where a simple fall could result in serious injury from a sharp tool.

TROUBLESHOOTING AND TUNE-UP EQUIPMENT

Voltmeter, Ohmmeter, and Ammeter

For testing the ignition or electrical system, a good voltmeter is required. For motorcycle use, an instrument covering 0-20 volts is satisfactory. One which also has a 0-2 volt scale is necessary for testing relays, points, or individual contacts where voltage drops are much smaller. Accuracy should be ± ½ volt.

An ohmmeter measures electrical resistance. This instrument is useful for checking continuity (open and short circuits), and testing fuses and lights.

The ammeter measures electrical current. Ammeters for motorcycle use should cover 0-50 amperes and 0-250 amperes. These are useful for checking battery charging and starting current.

Several inexpensive VOM's (volt-ohm-milliammeter) combine all three instruments into one which fits easily in any tool box. See **Figure 5**. However, the ammeter ranges are usually too small for motorcycle work.

Hydrometer

The hydrometer gives a useful indication of battery condition and charge by measuring the

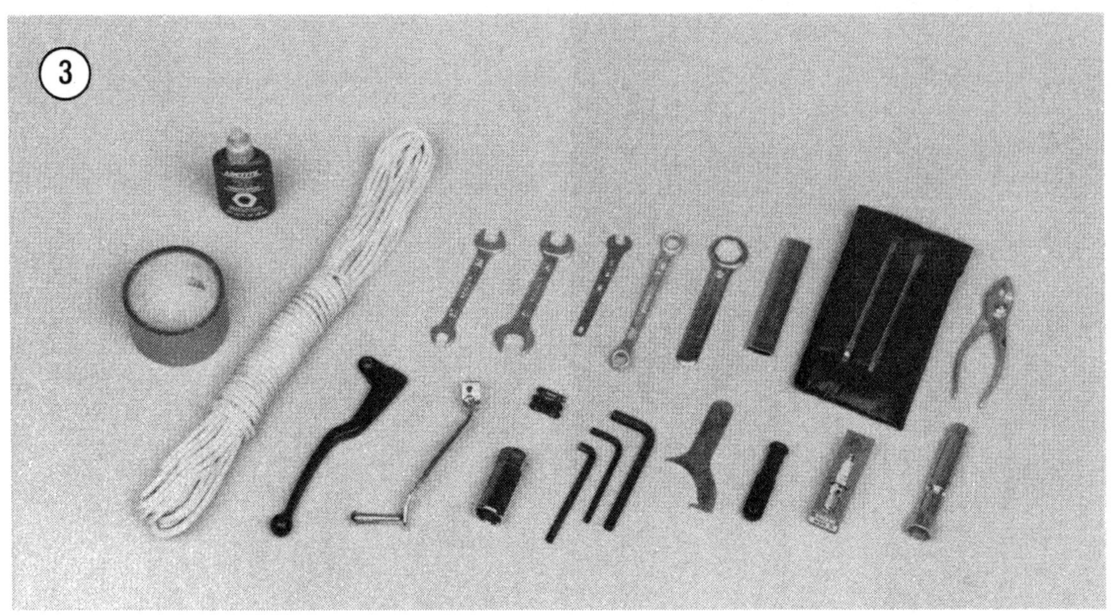

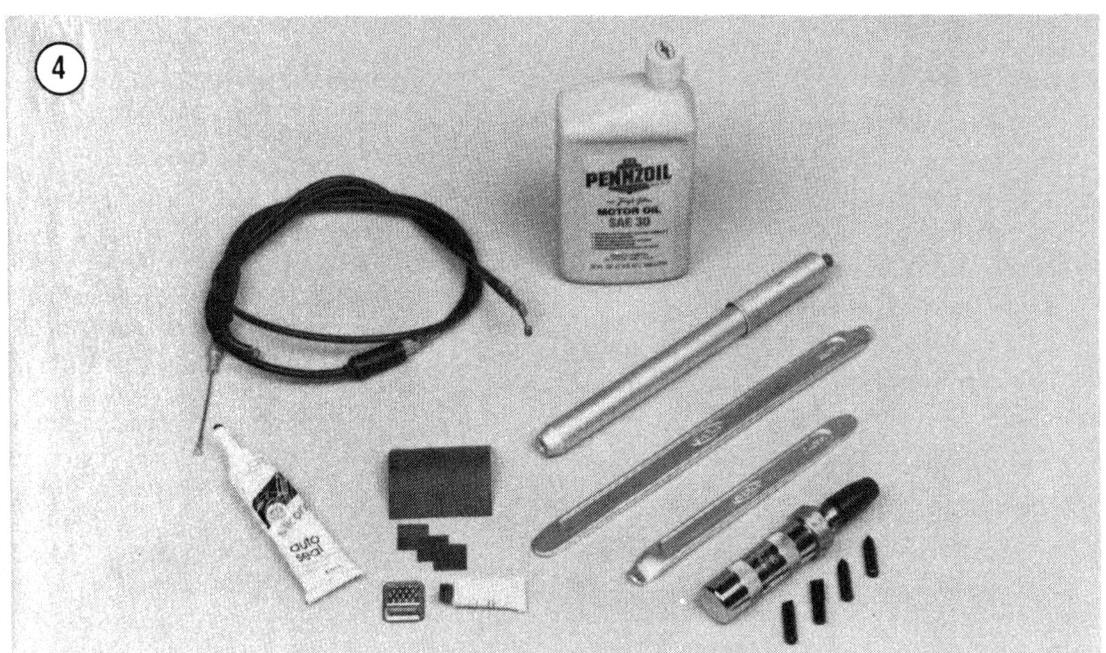

specific gravity of the electrolyte in each cell. See **Figure 6**. Complete details on use and interpretation of readings are provided in the electrical chapter.

Compression Tester

The compression tester measures the compression pressure built up in each cylinder. The results, when properly interpreted, can indicate general cylinder, ring, and valve condition. See **Figure 7**. Extension lines are available for hard-to-reach cylinders.

Dwell Meter (Contact Breaker Point Ignition Only)

A dwell meter measures the distance in degrees of cam rotation that the breaker points remain closed while the engine is running. Since

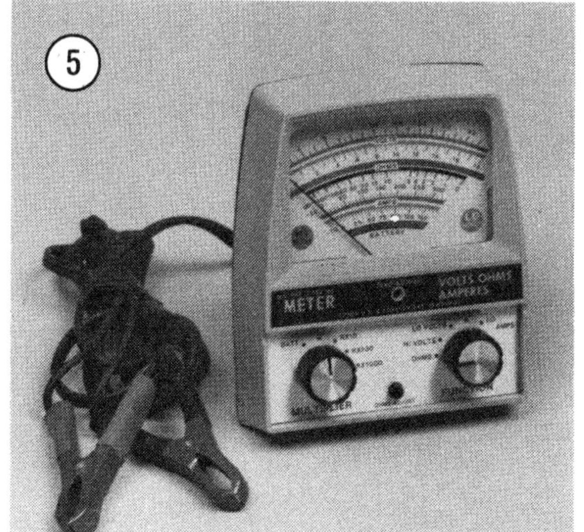

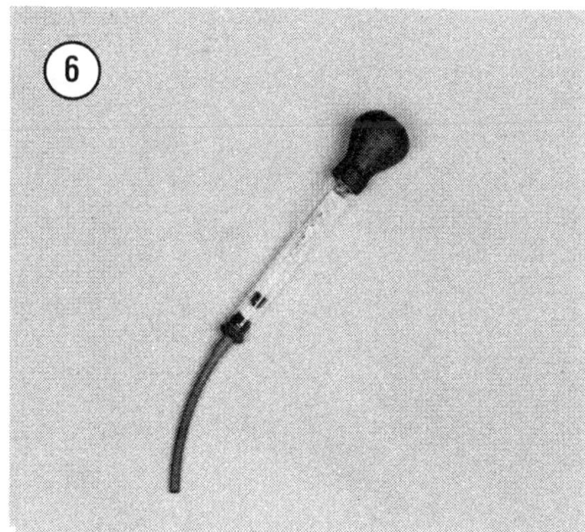

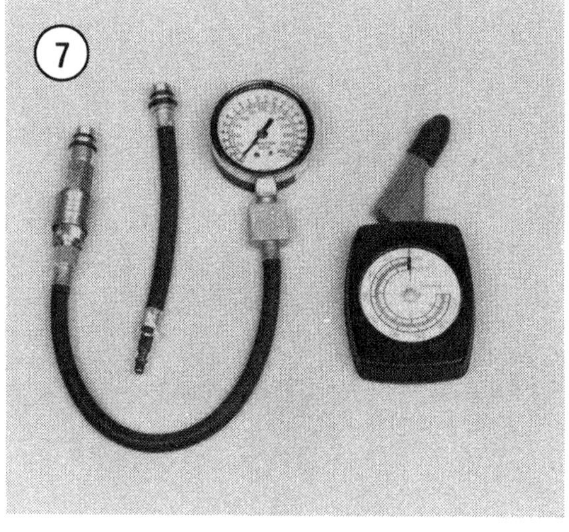

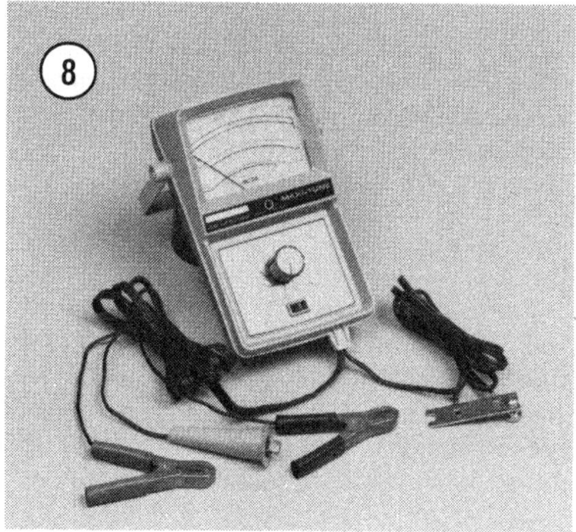

this angle is determined by breaker point gap, dwell angle is an accurate indication of breaker point gap.

Many tachometers intended for tuning and testing incorporate a dwell meter as well. See **Figure 8**. Follow the manufacturer's instructions to measure dwell.

Tachometer

A tachometer is necessary for tuning. See **Figure 8**. Ignition timing and carburetor adjustments must be performed at the specified idle speed. The best instrument for this purpose is one with a low range of 0-1,000 or 0-2,000 rpm for setting idle, and a high range of 0-4,000 or more for setting ignition timing at 3,000 rpm. Extended range (0-6,000 or 0-8,000 rpm) instruments lack accuracy at lower speeds. The instrument should be capable of detecting changes of 25 rpm on the low range.

NOTE: *The motorcycle's tachometer is not accurate enough for correct idle adjustment.*

Strobe Timing Light

This instrument is necessary for tuning, as it permits very accurate ignition timing. The light flashes at precisely the same instant that No. 1 cylinder fires, at which time the timing marks on the engine should align. Refer to Chapter Three for exact location of the timing marks for your engine.

Suitable lights range from inexpensive neon bulb types to powerful xenon strobe lights. See **Figure 9**. Neon timing lights are difficult to see and must be used in dimly lit areas. Xenon strobe timing lights can be used outside in bright sunlight.

Tune-up Kits

Many manufacturers offer kits that combine several useful instruments. Some cone in a convenient carry case and are usually less expensive than purchasing one instrument at a time. **Figure 10** shows one of the kits that is available. The prices vary with the number of instruments included in the kit.

10

Manometer (Carburetor Synchronizer)

A manometer (**Figure 11**) is essential for accurately synchronizing carburetors on multi-cylinder engines. The instrument detects intake pressure differences between carburetors and permits them to be adjusted equally. The cost of a suitable manometer varies.

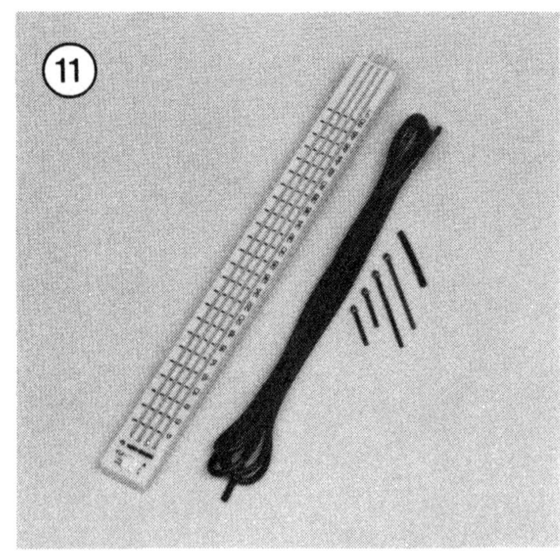

11

Fire Extinguisher

A fire extinguisher is a necessity when working on a vehicle. It should be rated for both *Class B* (flammable liquids – gasoline, oil, paint, etc.) and *Class C* (electrical – wiring, etc.) type fires. It should always be kept within reach. See **Figure 12**.

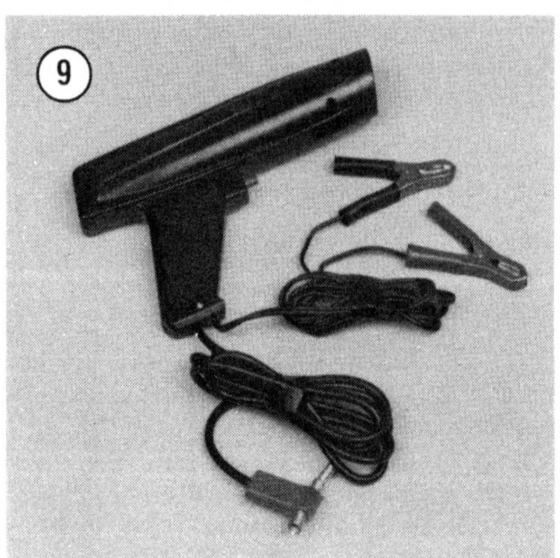

9

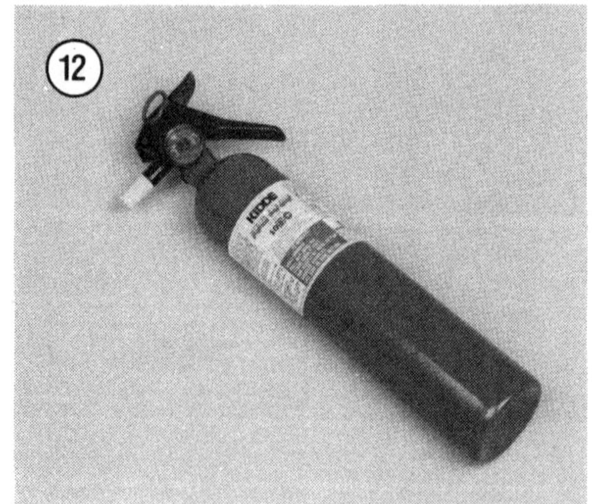

12

CHAPTER TWO

TROUBLESHOOTING

Troubleshooting motorcycle problems is relatively simple. To be effective and efficient, however, it must be done in a logical step-by-step manner. If it is not, a great deal of time may be wasted, good parts may be replaced unnecessarily, and the true problem may never be uncovered.

Always begin by defining the symptoms as closely as possible. Then, analyze the symptoms carefully so that you can make an intelligent guess at the probable cause. Next, test the probable cause and attempt to verify it; if it's not at fault, analyze the symptoms once again, this time eliminating the first probable cause. Continue on in this manner, a step at a time, until the problem is solved.

At first, this approach may seem to be time consuming, but you will soon discover that it's not nearly so wasteful as a hit-or-miss method that may never solve the problem. And just as important, the methodical approach to troubleshooting ensures that only those parts that are defective will be replaced.

The troubleshooting procedures in this chapter analyze typical symptoms and show logical methods for isolating and correcting trouble. They are not, however, the only methods; there may be several approaches to a given problem, but all good troubleshooting methods have one thing in common — a logical, systematic approach.

ENGINE

The entire engine must be considered when trouble arises that is experienced as poor performance or failure to start. The engine is more than a combustion chamber, piston, and crankshaft; it also includes a fuel delivery system, an ignition system, and an exhaust system.

Before beginning to troubleshoot any engine problems, it's important to understand an engine's operating requirements. First, it must have a correctly metered mixture of gasoline and air (**Figure 1**). Second, it must have an airtight combustion chamber in which the mixture can be compressed. And finally, it requires a precisely timed spark to ignite the compressed mixture. If one or more is missing, the engine won't run, and if just one is deficient, the engine will run poorly at best.

Of the three requirements, the precisely timed spark — provided by the ignition system — is most likely to be the culprit, with gas/air mixture (carburetion) second, and poor compression the least likely.

STARTING DIFFICULTIES

Hard starting is probably the most common motorcycle ailment, with a wide range of problems likely. Before delving into a reluctant or non-starter, first determine what has changed

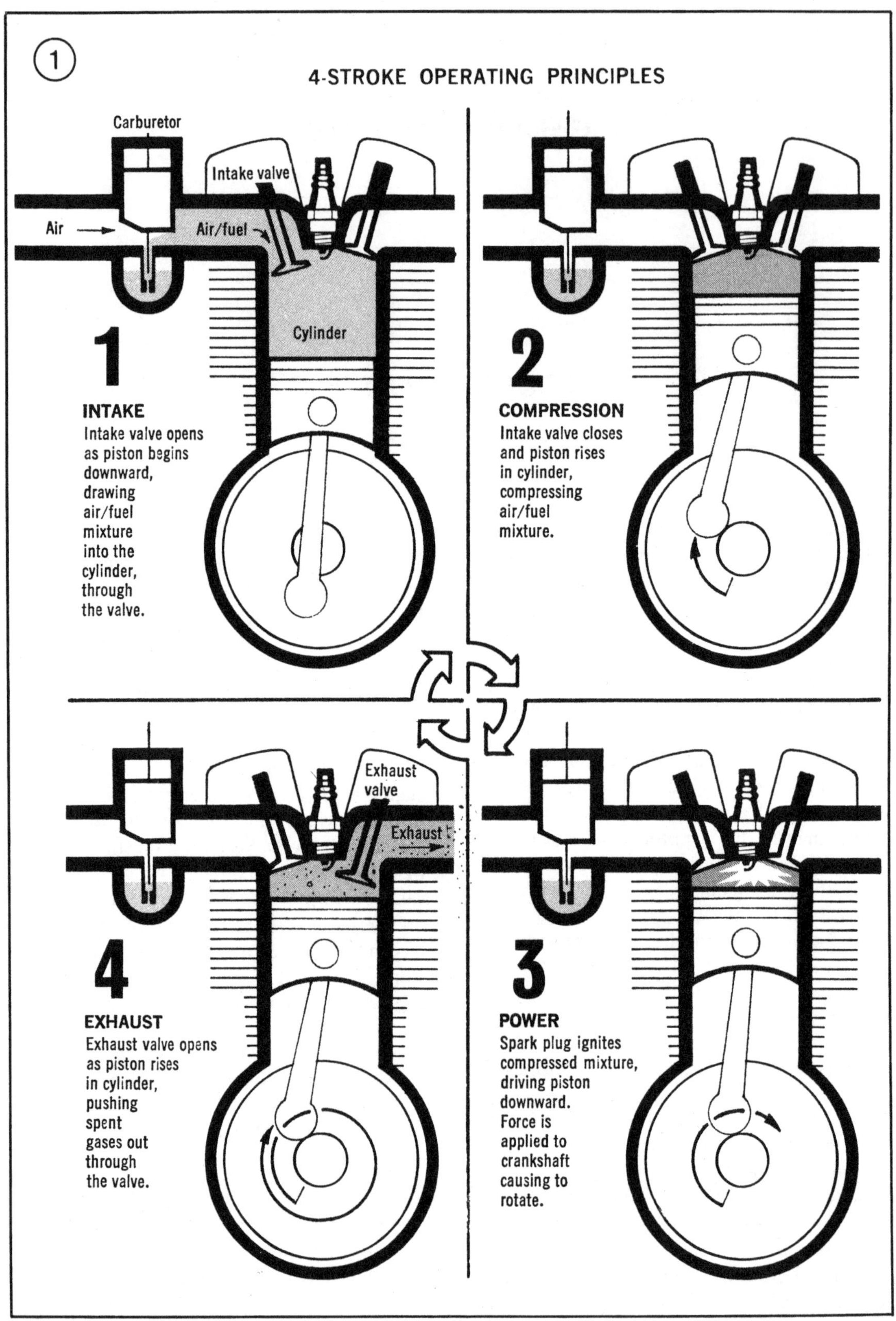
1
4-STROKE OPERATING PRINCIPLES
Carburetor
Intake valve
Air
Air/fuel
Cylinder
1
INTAKE
Intake valve opens as piston begins downward, drawing air/fuel mixture into the cylinder, through the valve.
2
COMPRESSION
Intake valve closes and piston rises in cylinder, compressing air/fuel mixture.
Exhaust valve
Exhaust
4
EXHAUST
Exhaust valve opens as piston rises in cylinder, pushing spent gases out through the valve.
3
POWER
Spark plug ignites compressed mixture, driving piston downward. Force is applied to crankshaft causing to rotate.

since the motorcycle last started easily. For instance, was the weather dry then and is it wet now? Has the motorcycle been sitting in the garage for a long time? Has it been ridden many miles since it was last fueled?

Has starting become increasingly more difficult? This alone could indicate a number of things that may be wrong but is usually associated with normal wear of ignition and engine components.

While it's not always possible to diagnose trouble simply from a change of conditions, this information can be helpful and at some future time may uncover a recurring problem.

Fuel Delivery

Although it is the second most likely cause of trouble, fuel delivery should be checked first simply because it is the easiest.

First, check the tank to make sure there is fuel in it. Then, disconnect the fuel hose at the carburetor, open the valve and check for flow (**Figure 2**). If fuel does not flow freely make sure the tank vent is clear. Next, check for blockage in the line or valve. Remove the valve and clean it as described in the fuel system chapter.

If fuel flows from the hose, reconnect it and remove the float bowl from the carburetor, open the valve and check for flow through the float needle valve. If it does not flow freely when the float is extended and then shut off when the flow is gently raised, clean the carburetor as described in the fuel system chapter.

When fuel delivery is satisfactory, go on to the ignition system.

Ignition

Remove the spark plug from the cylinder and check its condition. The appearance of the plug is a good indication of what's happening in the combustion chamber; for instance, if the plug is wet with gas, it's likely that engine is flooded. Compare the spark plug to **Figure 3**. Make certain the spark plug heat range is correct. A "cold" plug makes starting difficult.

After checking the spark plug, reconnect it to the high-tension lead and lay it on the cylinder head so it makes good contact (**Figure 4**). Then, with the ignition switched on, crank the engine several times and watch for a spark across the plug electrodes. A fat, blue spark should be visible. If there is no spark, or if the spark is weak, substitute a good plug for the old one and check again. If the spark has improved, the old plug is faulty. If there was no change, keep looking.

Make sure the ignition switch is not shorted to ground. Remove the spark plug cap from the end of the high-tension lead and hold the exposed end of the lead about ⅛ inch from the cylinder head. Crank the engine and watch for a spark arcing from the lead to the head. If it's satisfactory, the connection between the lead and the cap was faulty. If the spark hasn't improved, check the coil wire connections.

If the spark is still weak, remove the ignition cover and remove any dirt or moisture from the points or sensor. Check the point or air gap against the specifications in the *Quick Reference Data* at the beginning of the book.

If spark is still not satisfactory, a more serious problem exists than can be corrected with simple adjustments. Refer to the electrical system chapter for detailed information for correcting major ignition problems.

Compression

Compression — or the lack of it — is the least likely cause of starting trouble. However, if compression is unsatisfactory, more than a simple adjustment is required to correct it (see the engine chapter).

An accurate compression check reveals a lot about the condition of the engine. To perform this test you need a compression gauge (see Chapter One). The engine should be at operating temperature for a fully accurate test, but even a cold test will reveal if the starting problem is compression.

Remove the spark plug and screw in a compression gauge (**Figure 5**). With assistance, hold the throttle wide open and crank the engine several times, until the gauge ceases to rise. Normal compression should be 130-160 psi, but a reading as low as 100 psi is usually sufficient for the engine to start. If the reading is much lower than normal, remove the gauge and pour about a tablespoon of oil into the cylinder.

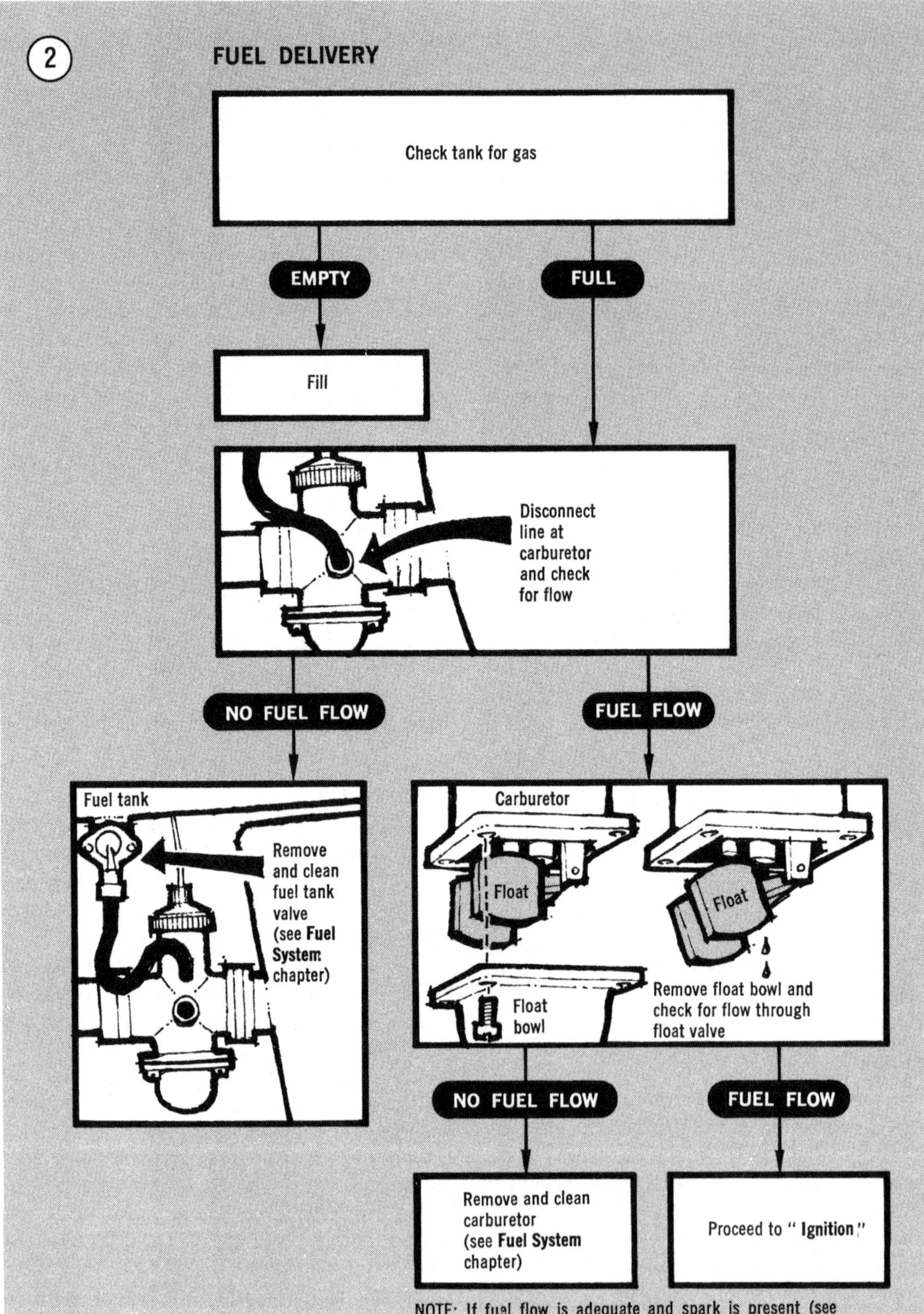
2
FUEL DELIVERY
Check tank for gas
EMPTY
FULL
Fill
Disconnect line at carburetor and check for flow
NO FUEL FLOW
FUEL FLOW
Fuel tank
Remove and clean fuel tank valve (see Fuel System chapter)
Carburetor
Float
Float
Float bowl
Remove float bowl and check for flow through float valve
NO FUEL FLOW
FUEL FLOW
Remove and clean carburetor (see Fuel System chapter)
Proceed to " Ignition."
NOTE: If fuel flow is adequate and spark is present (see Ignition which follows), increase fuel ratio with idle screw.

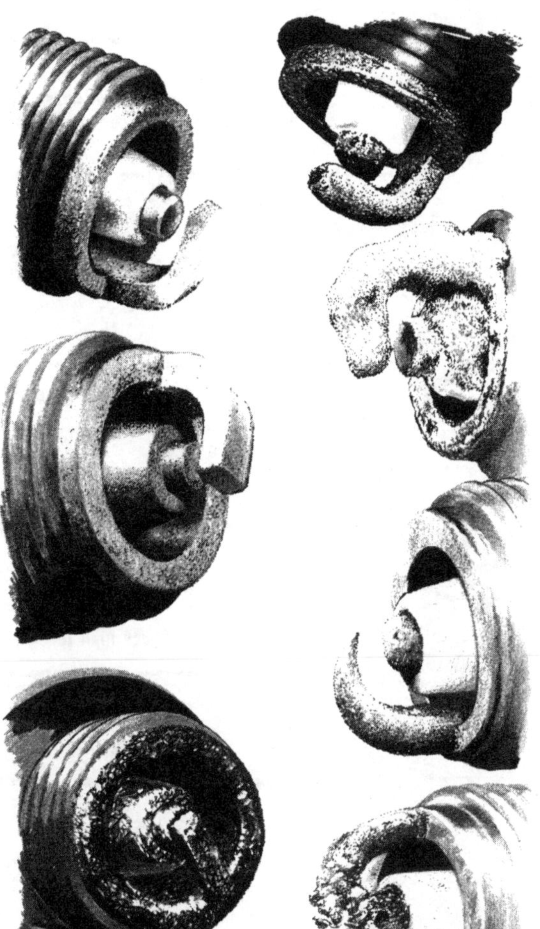

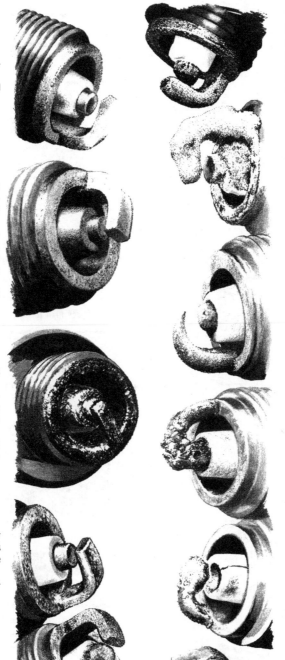

NORMAL
- Appearance—Firing tip has deposits of light gray to light tan.
- Can be cleaned, regapped and reused.

CARBON FOULED
- Appearance—Dull, dry black with fluffy carbon deposits on the insulator tip, electrode and exposed shell.
- Caused by—Fuel/air mixture too rich, plug heat range too cold, weak ignition system, dirty air cleaner, faulty automatic choke or excessive idling.
- Can be cleaned, regapped and reused.

OIL FOULED
- Appearance—Wet black deposits on insulator and exposed shell.
- Caused by—Excessive oil entering the combustion chamber through worn rings, pistons, valve guides or bearings.
- Replace with new plugs (use a hotter plug if engine is not repaired).

LEAD FOULED
- Appearance — Yellow insulator deposits (may sometimes be dark gray, black or tan in color) on the insulator tip.
- Caused by—Highly leaded gasoline.
- Replace with new plugs.

LEAD FOULED
- Appearance—Yellow glazed deposits indicating melted lead deposits due to hard acceleration.
- Caused by—Highly leaded gasoline.
- Replace with new plugs.

OIL AND LEAD FOULED
- Appearance—Glazed yellow deposits with a slight brownish tint on the insulator tip and ground electrode.
- Replace with new plugs.

FUEL ADDITIVE RESIDUE
- Appearance — Brown colored hardened ash deposits on the insulator tip and ground electrode.
- Caused by—Fuel and/or oil additives.
- Replace with new plugs.

WORN
- Appearance — Severely worn or eroded electrodes.
- Caused by—Normal wear or unusual oil and/or fuel additives.
- Replace with new plugs.

PREIGNITION
- Appearance — Melted ground electrode.
- Caused by—Overadvanced ignition timing, inoperative ignition advance mechanism, too low of a fuel octane rating, lean fuel/air mixture or carbon deposits in combustion chamber.

PREIGNITION
- Appearance—Melted center electrode.
- Caused by—Abnormal combustion due to overadvanced ignition timing or incorrect advance, too low of a fuel octane rating, lean fuel/air mixture, or carbon deposits in combustion chamber.
- Correct engine problem and replace with new plugs.

INCORRECT HEAT RANGE
- Appearance—Melted center electrode and white blistered insulator tip.
- Caused by—Incorrect plug heat range selection.
- Replace with new plugs.

2

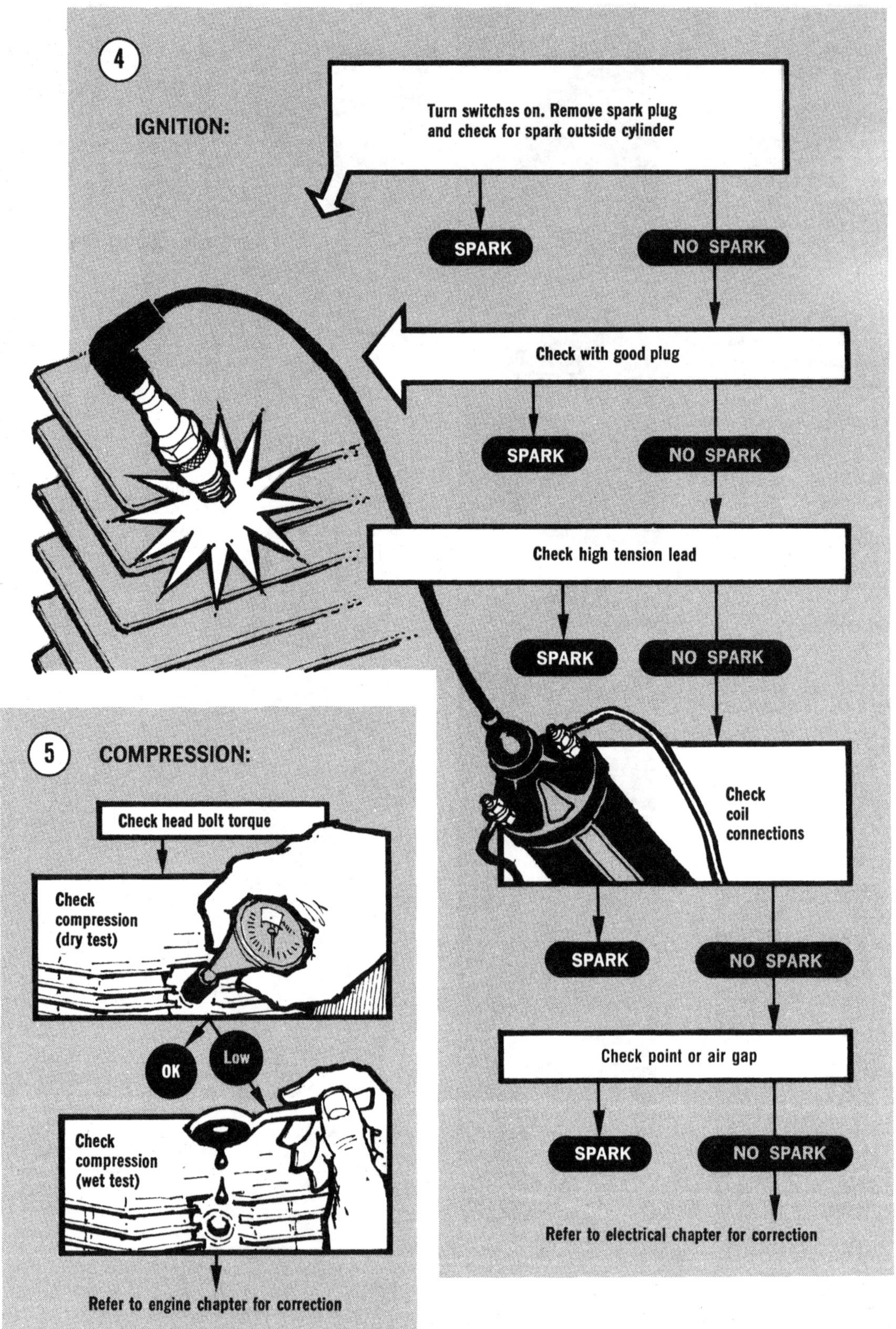
4
IGNITION:
Turn switches on. Remove spark plug and check for spark outside cylinder
SPARK
NO SPARK
Check with good plug
SPARK
NO SPARK
Check high tension lead
SPARK
NO SPARK
Check coil connections
SPARK
NO SPARK
Check point or air gap
SPARK
NO SPARK
Refer to electrical chapter for correction
5
COMPRESSION:
Check head bolt torque
Check compression (dry test)
OK
Low
Check compression (wet test)
Refer to engine chapter for correction

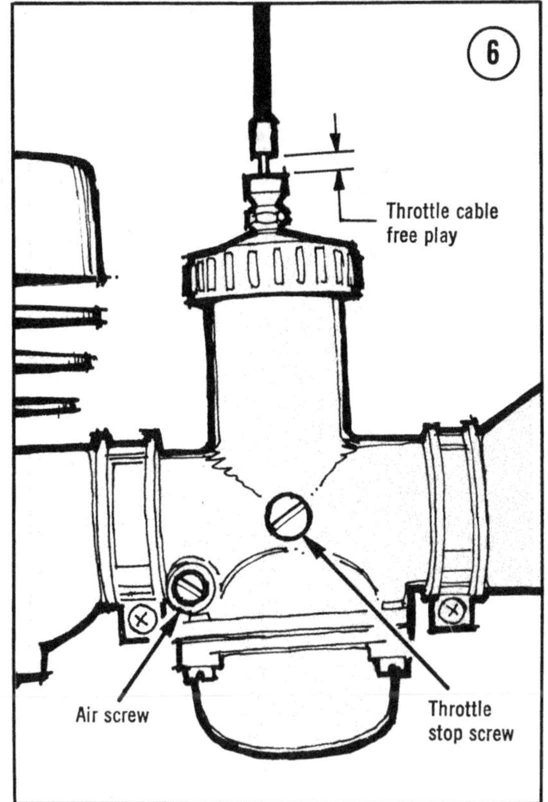

Crank the engine several times to distribute the oil and test the compression once again. If it is now significantly higher, the rings and bore are worn. If the compression did not change, the valves are not seating correctly. Adjust the valves and check again. If the compression is still low, refer to the engine chapter.

NOTE: *Low compression indicates a developing problem. The condition causing it should be corrected as soon as possible.*

POOR PERFORMANCE

Poor engine performance can be caused by any of a number of things related to carburetion, ignition, and the condition of the sliding and rotating components in the engine. In addition, components such as brakes, clutch, and transmission can cause problems that seem to be related to engine performance, even when the engine is in top running condition.

Poor Idling

Idling that is erratic, too high, or too low is most often caused by incorrect adjustment of the carburetor idle circuit. Also, a dirty air filter or an obstructed fuel tank vent can affect idle speed. Incorrect ignition timing or worn or faulty ignition components are also good possibilities.

First, make sure the air filter is clean and correctly installed. Then, adjust the throttle cable free play, the throttle stop screw, and the idle mixture air screw (**Figure 6**) as described in the routine maintenance chapter.

If idling is still poor, check the carburetor and manifold mounts for leaks; with the engine warmed up and running, spray WD-40 or a similar light lube around the flanges and joints of the carburetor and manifold (**Figure 7**). Listen for changes in engine speed. If a leak is present, the idle speed will drop as the lube "plugs" the leak and then pick up again as it is drawn into the engine. Tighten the nuts and clamps and test again. If a leak persists, check for a damaged gasket or a pinhole in the manifold. Minor leaks in manifold hoses can be repaired with silicone sealer, but if cracks or holes are extensive, the manifold should be replaced.

A worn throttle slide may cause erratic running and idling, but this is likely only after many thousands of miles of use. To check, remove the carburetor top and feel for back and forth movement of the slide in the bore; it should be barely perceptible. Inspect the slide for large worn areas and replace it if it is less than perfect (**Figure 8**).

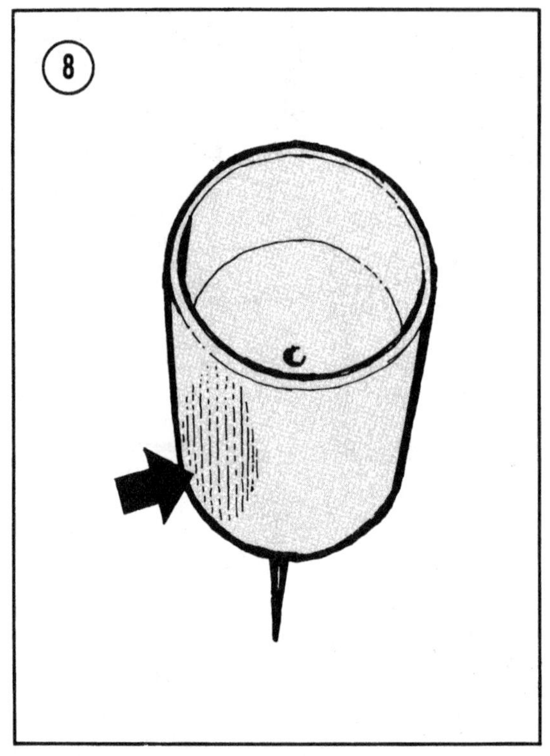

If the fuel system is satisfactory, check ignition timing and breaker point gap (air gap in electronic ignition). Check the condition of the system components as well. Ignition-caused idling problems such as erratic running can be the fault of marginal components. See the electrical system chapter for appropriate tests.

Rough Running or Misfiring

Misfiring (see **Figure 9**) is usually caused by an ignition problem. First, check all ignition connections (**Figure 10**). They should be clean, dry, and tight. Don't forget the kill switch; a loose connection can create an intermittent short.

10

Handlebar (kill) switch

Main switch

Coil

Battery

Spark plug

Breaker points or electronic module

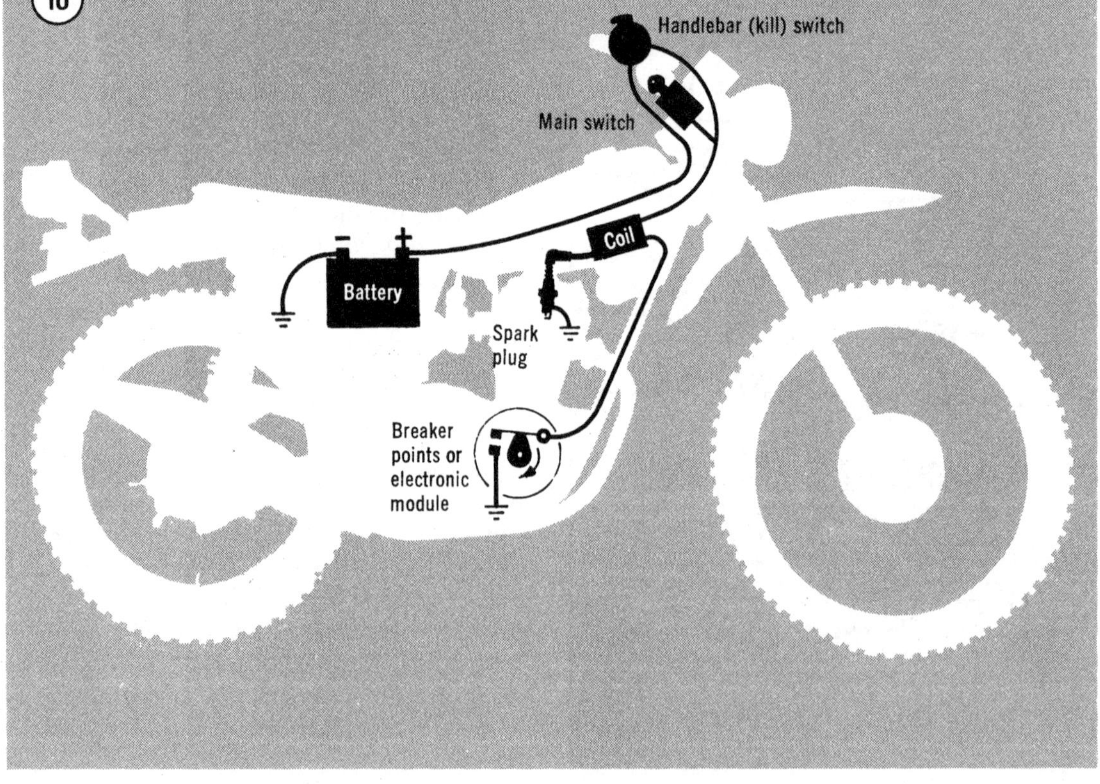

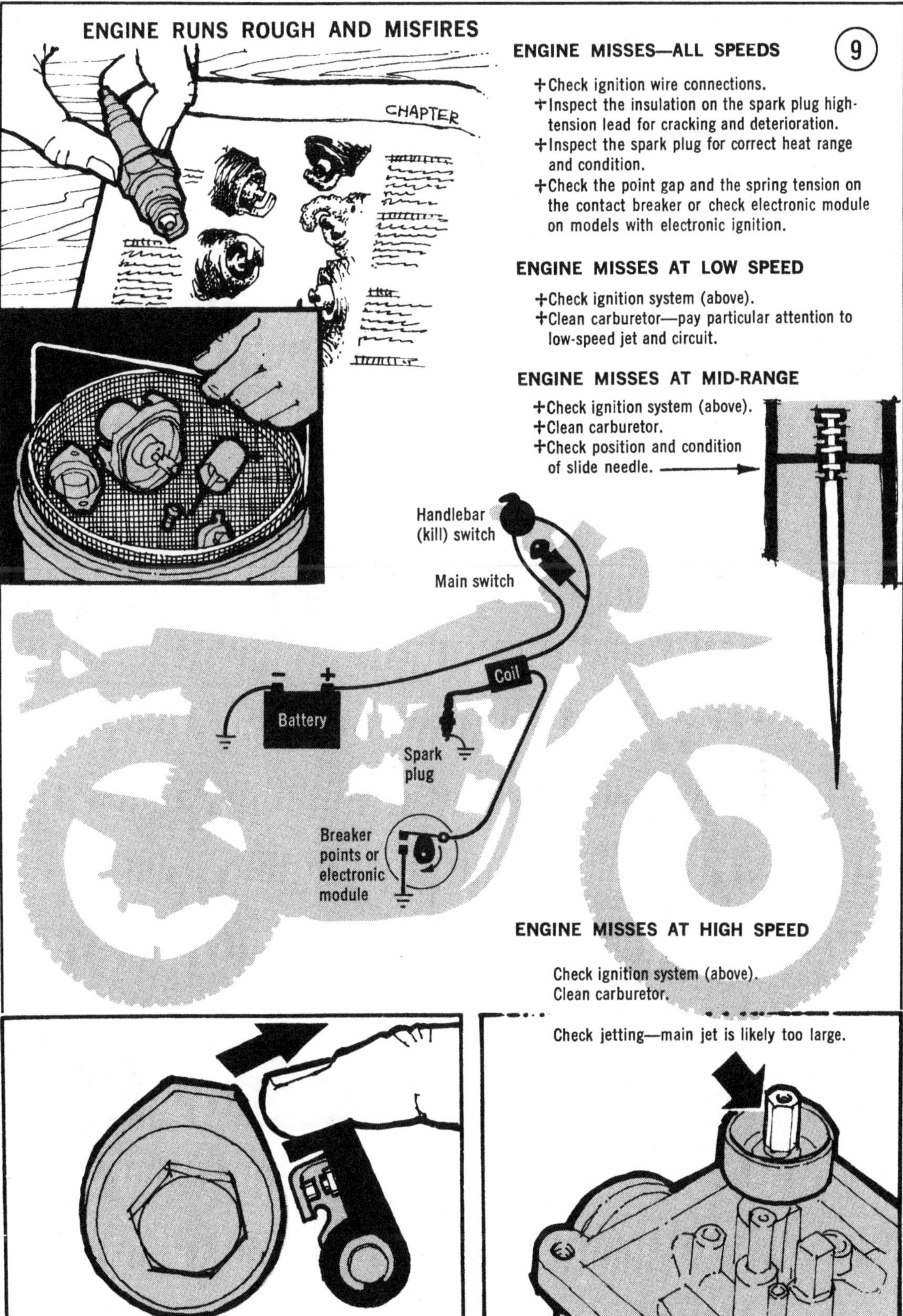
ENGINE RUNS ROUGH AND MISFIRES
CHAPTER
ENGINE MISSES—ALL SPEEDS
9
+Check ignition wire connections.
+Inspect the insulation on the spark plug high-tension lead for cracking and deterioration.
+Inspect the spark plug for correct heat range and condition.
+Check the point gap and the spring tension on the contact breaker or check electronic module on models with electronic ignition.
ENGINE MISSES AT LOW SPEED
+Check ignition system (above).
+Clean carburetor—pay particular attention to low-speed jet and circuit.
ENGINE MISSES AT MID-RANGE
+Check ignition system (above).
+Clean carburetor.
+Check position and condition of slide needle.
Handlebar (kill) switch
Main switch
Coil
Battery
Spark plug
Breaker points or electronic module
ENGINE MISSES AT HIGH SPEED
Check ignition system (above).
Clean carburetor.
Check jetting—main jet is likely too large.

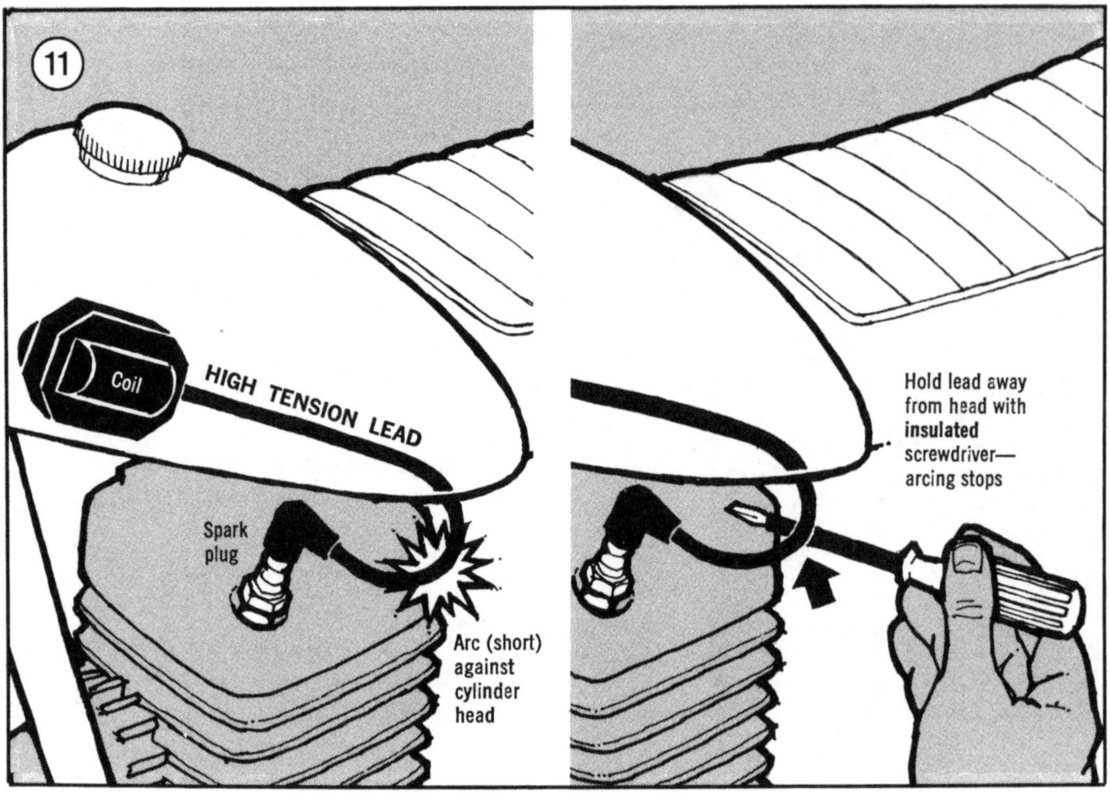

11

Coil

HIGH TENSION LEAD

Spark plug

Arc (short) against cylinder head

Hold lead away from head with **insulated** screwdriver— arcing stops

Check the insulation on the high-tension spark plug lead. If it is cracked or deteriorated it will allow the spark to short to ground when the engine is revved. This is easily seen at night. If arcing occurs, hold the affected area of the wire away from the metal to which it is arcing, using an insulated screwdriver (**Figure 11**), and see if the misfiring ceases. If it does, replace the high-tension lead. Also check the connection of the spark plug cap to the lead. If it is poor, the spark will break down at this point when the engine speed is increased.

The spark plug could also be poor. Test the system with a new plug.

Incorrect point gap or a weak contact breaker spring can cause misfiring. Check the gap and the alignment of the points. Push the moveable arm back and check for spring tension (**Figure 12**). It should feel stiff.

On models with electronic ignition, have the electronic module tested by a dealer or substitute a known good unit for a suspected one.

If misfiring occurs only at a certain point in engine speed, the problem may very likely be

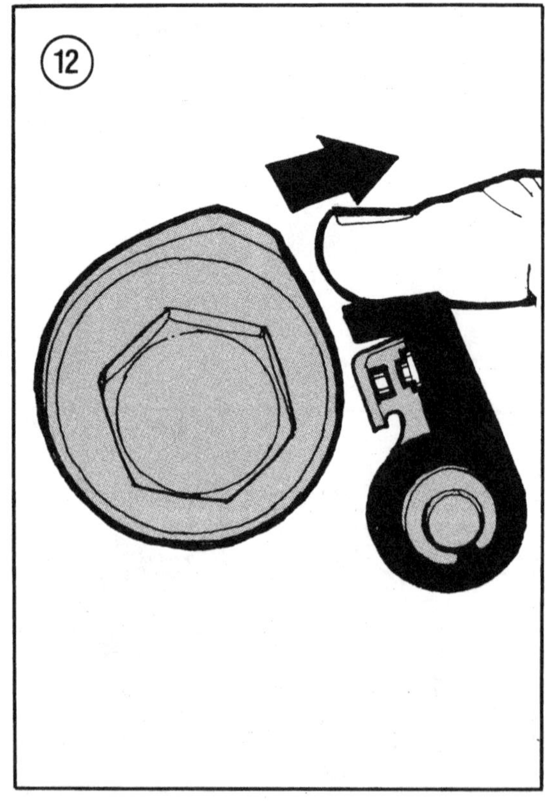

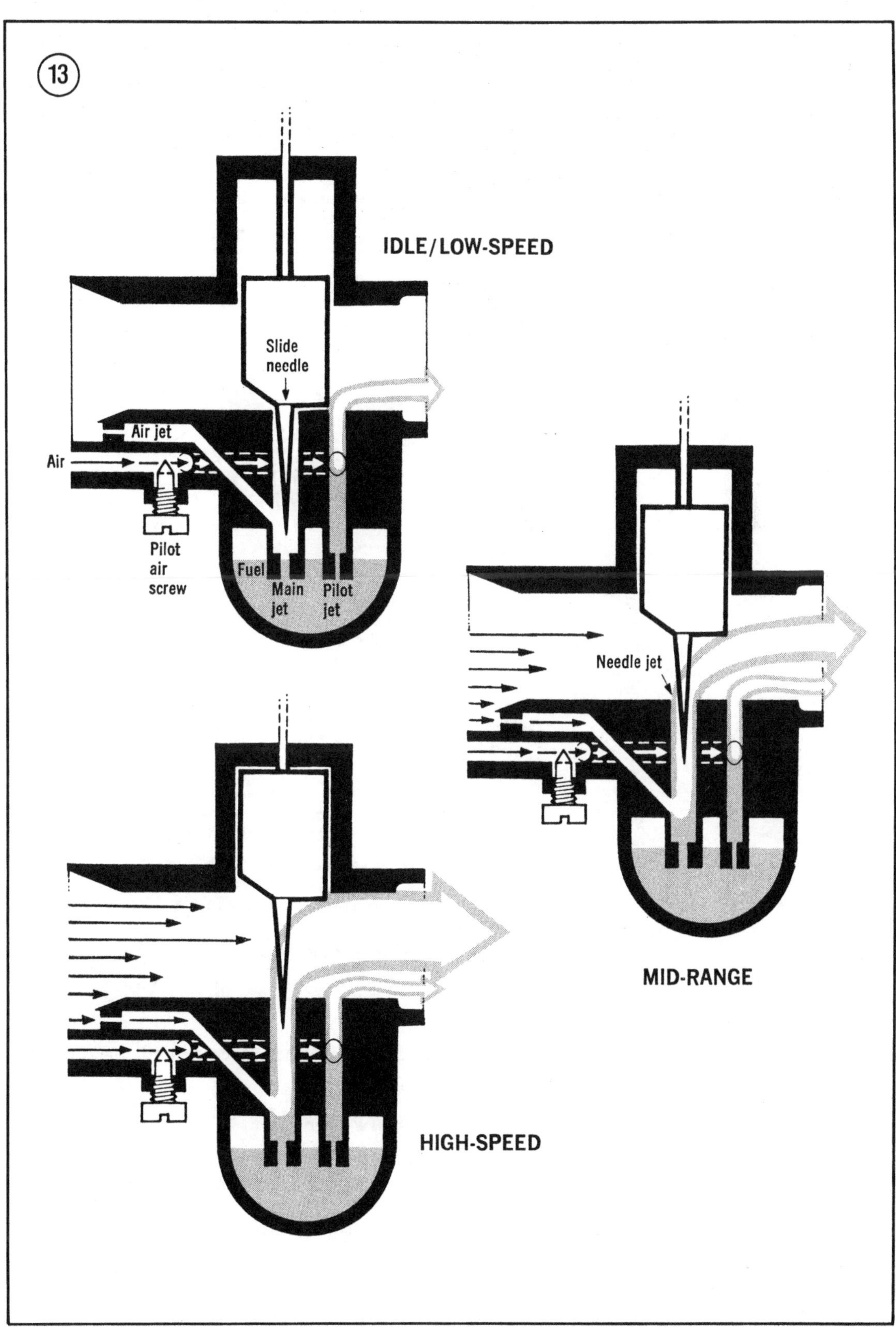
13
IDLE/LOW-SPEED
Slide
needle
Air jet
Air
Pilot
air
screw
Fuel
Main
jet
Pilot
jet
Needle jet
MID-RANGE
HIGH-SPEED

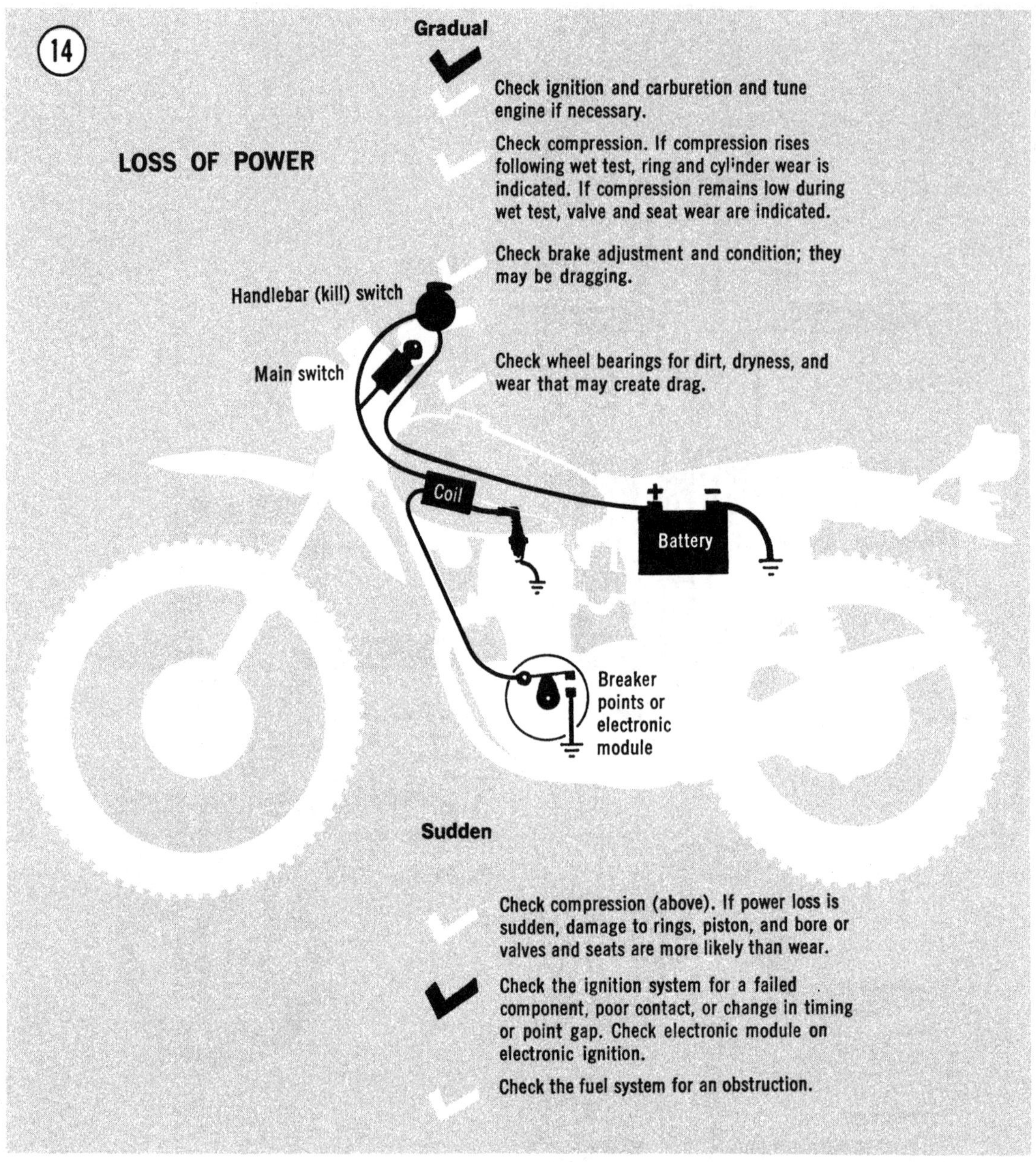

carburetion. Poor performance at idle is described earlier. Misfiring at low speed (just above idle) can be caused by a dirty low-speed circuit or jet (**Figure 13**). Poor midrange performance is attributable to a worn or incorrectly adjusted needle and needle jet. Misfiring at high speed (if not ignition related) is usually caused by a too-large main jet which causes the engine to run rich. Any of these carburetor-related conditions can be corrected by first cleaning the carburetor and then adjusting it as described in the tune-up and maintenance chapter.

14
LOSS OF POWER
Gradual
Check ignition and carburetion and tune engine if necessary.
Check compression. If compression rises following wet test, ring and cylinder wear is indicated. If compression remains low during wet test, valve and seat wear are indicated.
Check brake adjustment and condition; they may be dragging.
Check wheel bearings for dirt, dryness, and wear that may create drag.
Handlebar (kill) switch
Main switch
Coil
Battery
Breaker points or electronic module
Sudden
Check compression (above). If power loss is sudden, damage to rings, piston, and bore or valves and seats are more likely than wear.
Check the ignition system for a failed component, poor contact, or change in timing or point gap. Check electronic module on electronic ignition.
Check the fuel system for an obstruction.

Loss of Power

First determine how the power loss developed (**Figure 14**). Did it decline over a long period of time or did it drop abruptly? A gradual loss is normal, caused by deterioration of the engine's state of tune and the normal wear of the cylinder and piston rings and the valves and seats. In such case, check the condition of the

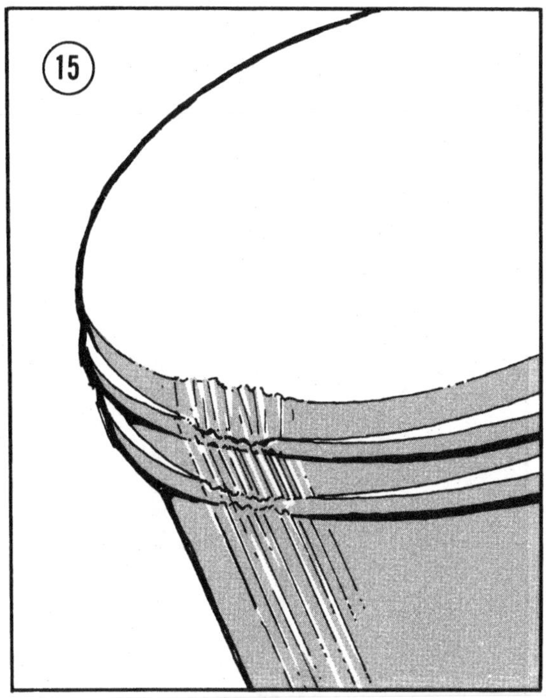

ignition and carburetion and measure the compression as described earlier.

A sudden power loss may be caused by a failed ignition component, obstruction in the fuel system, damaged valve or seat, or a broken piston ring or damaged piston (**Figure 15**).

If the engine is in good shape and tune, check the brake adjustment. If the brakes are dragging, they will consume considerable power. Also check the wheel bearings. If they are dry, extremely dirty, or badly worn they can create considerable drag.

Engine Runs Hot

A modern motorcycle engine, in good mechanical condition, correctly tuned, and operated as it was intended, will rarely experience overheating problems. However, out-of-spec conditions can create severe overheating that may result in serious engine damage. Refer to **Figure 16**.

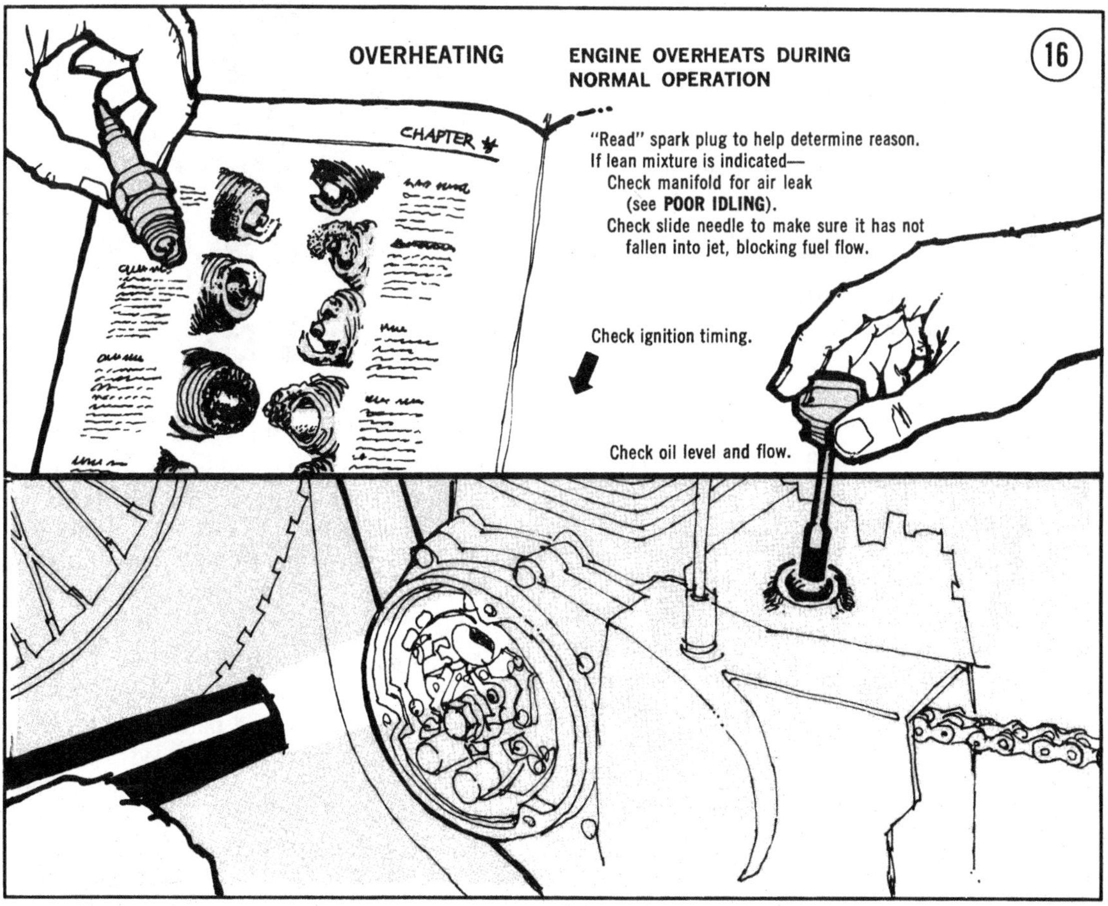

16

OVERHEATING

ENGINE OVERHEATS DURING NORMAL OPERATION

"Read" spark plug to help determine reason.
If lean mixture is indicated—
Check manifold for air leak (see **POOR IDLING**).
Check slide needle to make sure it has not fallen into jet, blocking fuel flow.

Check ignition timing.

Check oil level and flow.

CHAPTER 4

Overheating is difficult to detect unless it is extreme, in which case it will usually be apparent as excessive heat radiating from the engine, accompanied by the smell of hot oil and sharp, snapping noises when the engine is first shut off and begins to cool.

Unless the motorcycle is operated under sustained high load or is allowed to idle for long periods of time, overheating is usually the result of an internal problem. Most often it's caused by a too-lean fuel mixture.

Remove the spark plug and compare it to **Figure 3**. If a too-lean condition is indicated, check for leaks in the intake manifold (see *Poor Idling*). The carburetor jetting may be incorrect but this is unlikely if the overheating problem has just developed (unless, of course, the engine was jetted for high altitude and is now being run near sea level). Check the slide needle in the carburetor to make sure it hasn't come loose and is restricting the flow of gas through the main jet and needle jet **(Figure 17)**.

Check the ignition timing; extremes of either advance or retard can cause overheating.

Piston Seizure and Damage

Piston seizure is a common result of overheating (see above) because an aluminum piston expands at a greater rate than a steel cylinder. Seizure can also be caused by piston-to-cylinder clearance that is too small; ring end gap that is too small; insufficient oil; spark plug heat range too hot; and broken piston ring or ring land.

A major piston seizure can cause severe engine damage. A minor seizure — which usually subsides after the engine has cooled a few minutes — rarely does more than scuff the piston skirt the first time it occurs. Fortunately, this condition can be corrected by dressing the piston with crocus cloth, refitting the piston and rings to the bore with recommended clearances, and checking the timing to ensure overheating does not occur. Regard that first seizure as a warning and correct the problem before continuing to run the engine.

CLUTCH AND TRANSMISSION

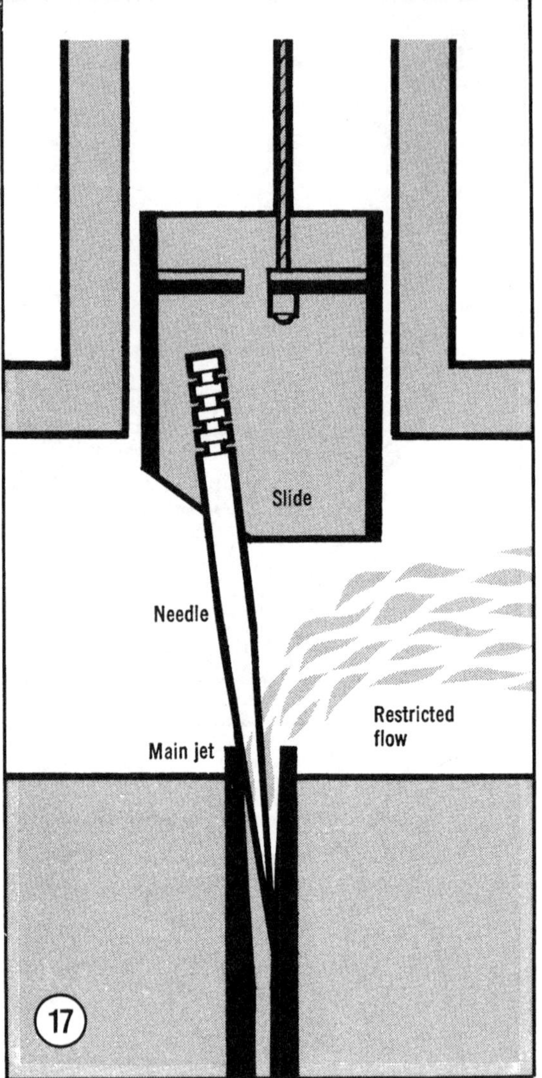

1. ***Clutch slips***—Make sure lever free play is sufficient to allow the clutch to fully engage **(Figure 18)**. Check the contact surfaces for wear and glazing. Transmission oil additives also can cause slippage in wet clutches. If slip occurs only under extreme load, check the condition of the springs or diaphragm and make sure the clutch bolts are snug and uniformly tightened.
2. ***Clutch drags***—Make sure lever free play isn't so great that it fails to disengage the clutch. Check for warped plates or disc. If the transmission oil (in wet clutch systems) is extremely dirty or heavy, it may inhibit the clutch from releasing.
3. ***Transmission shifts hard***—Extremely dirty oil can cause the transmission to shift hard.

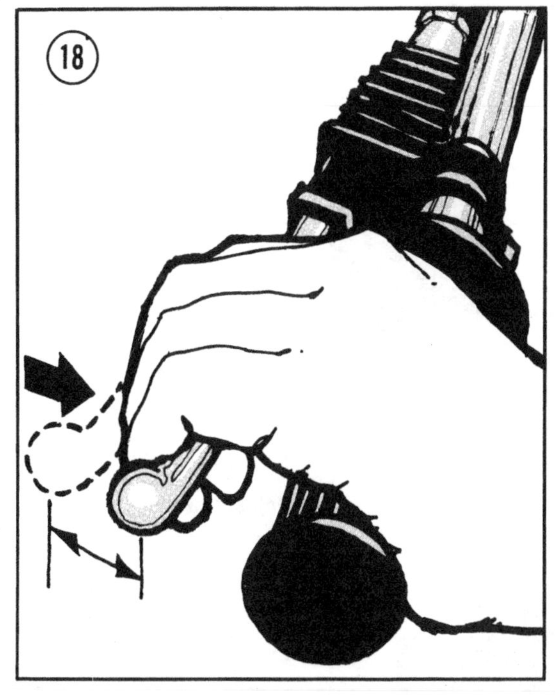

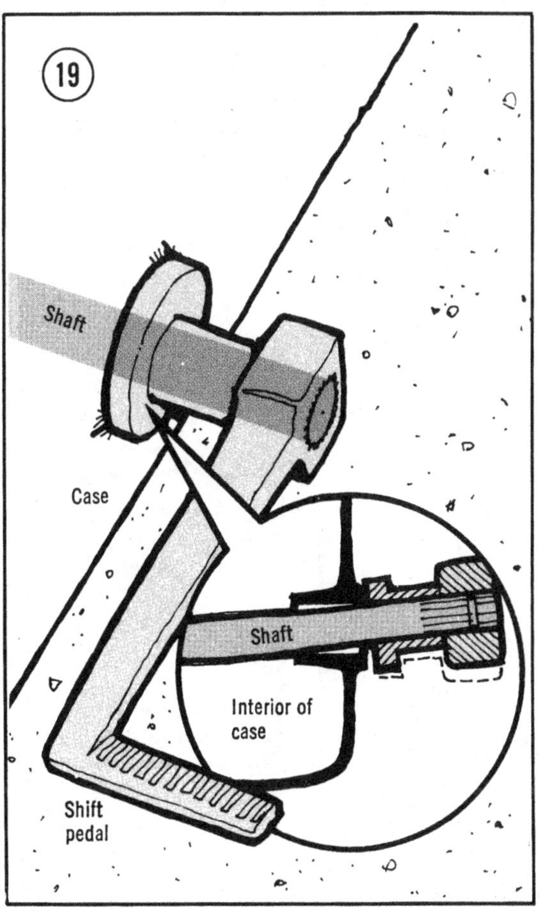

Check the selector shaft for bending (**Figure 19**). Inspect the shifter and gearsets for wear and damage.

4. ***Transmission slips out of gear***—This can be caused by worn engagement dogs or a worn or damaged shifter (**Figure 20**). The overshift travel on the selector may be misadjusted.

5. ***Transmission is noisy***—Noises usually indicate the absence of lubrication or wear and damage to gears, bearings, or shims. It's a good idea to disassemble the transmission and carefully inspect it when noise first occurs.

DRIVE TRAIN

Drive train problems (outlined in **Figure 21**) arise from normal wear and incorrect maintenance.

CHASSIS

Chassis problems are outlined in **Figure 22**.

1. ***Motorcycle pulls to one side***—Check for loose suspension components, axles, steering

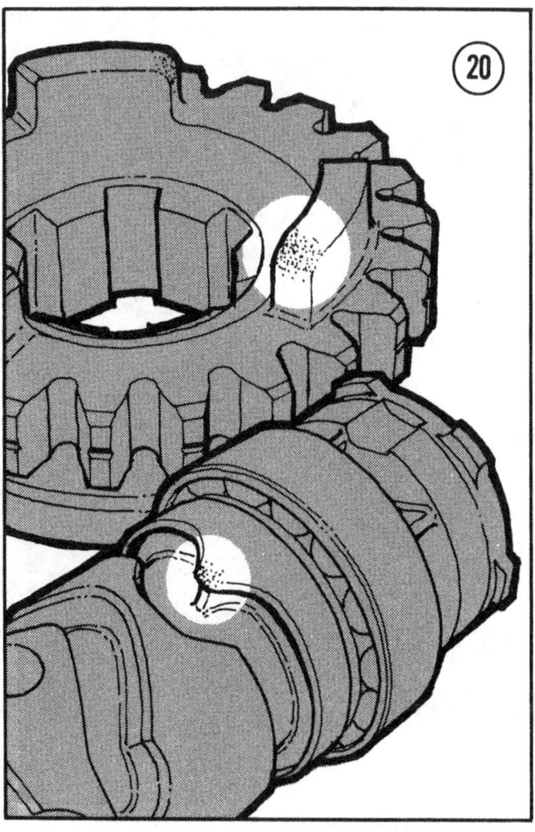

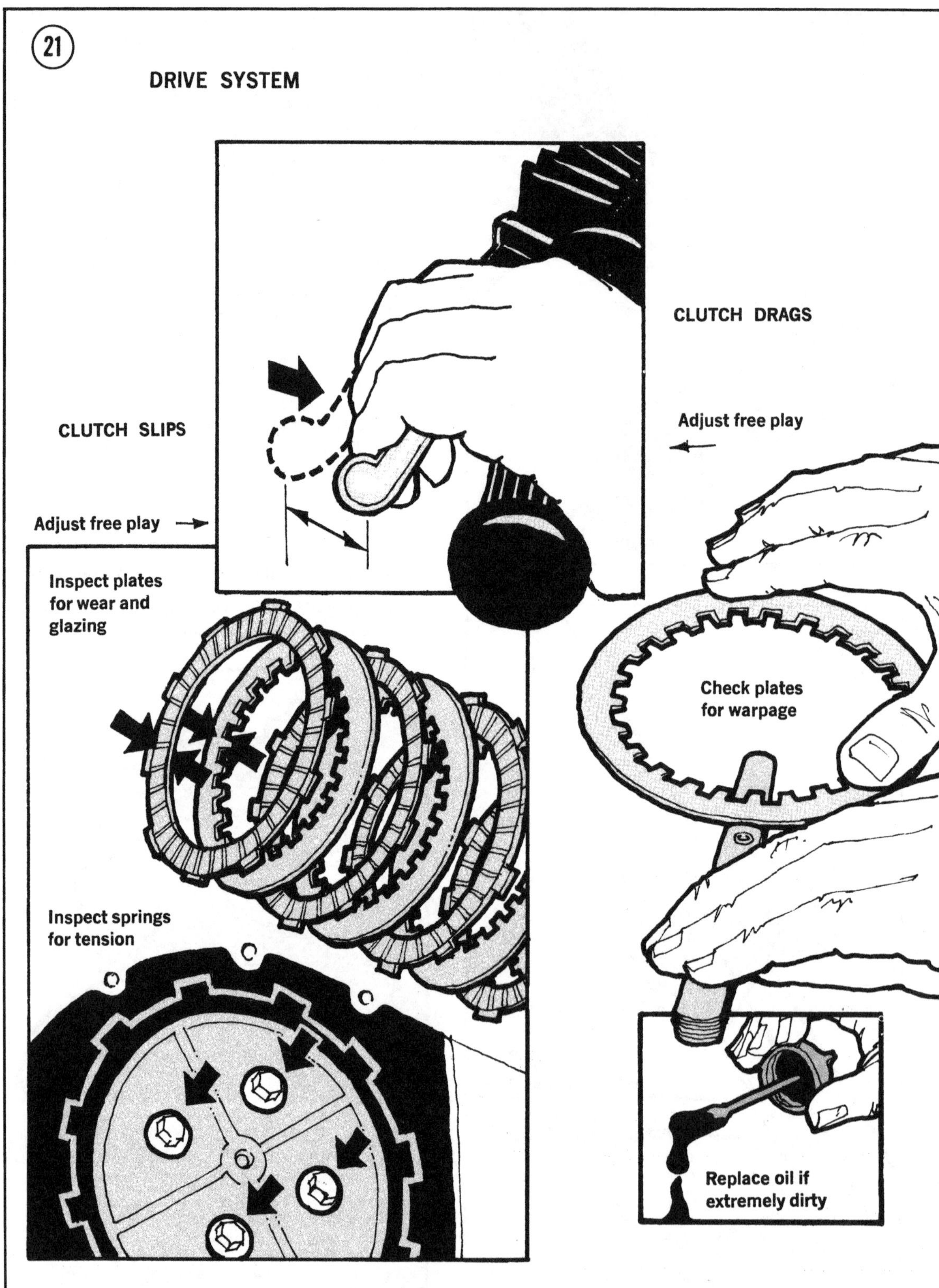
21
DRIVE SYSTEM
CLUTCH DRAGS
Adjust free play
CLUTCH SLIPS
Adjust free play
Inspect plates
for wear and
glazing
Check plates
for warpage
Inspect springs
for tension
Replace oil if
extremely dirty

2

TRANSMISSION SLIPS OUT OF GEAR

TRANSMISSION SHIFTS HARD

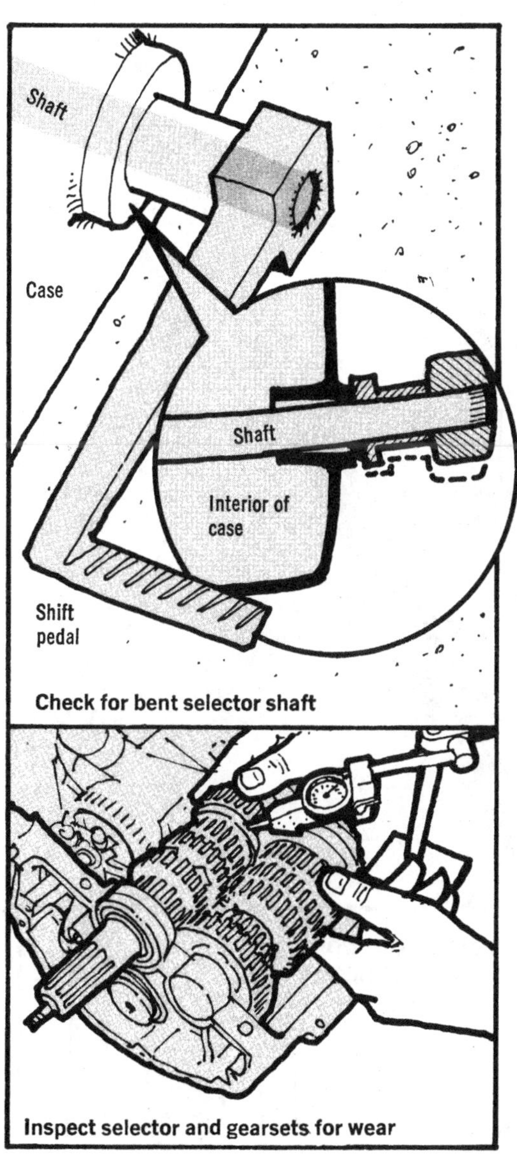

Check for bent selector shaft

Inspect selector and gearsets for wear

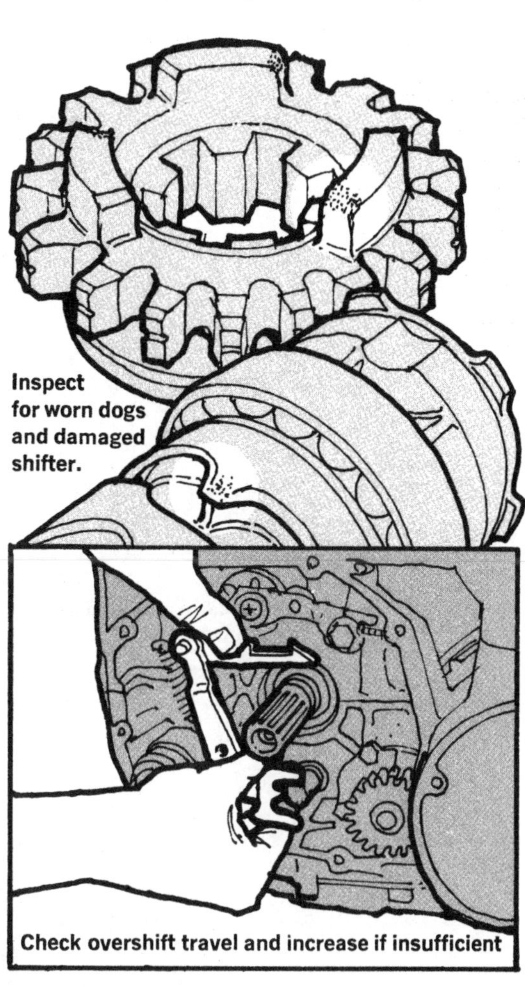

Check overshift travel and increase if insufficient

TRANSMISSION IS NOISY

Check oil level

Disassemble and inspect (see Transmission chapter)

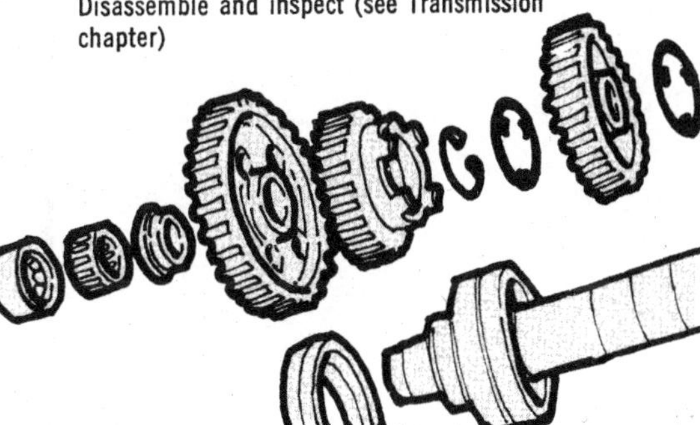

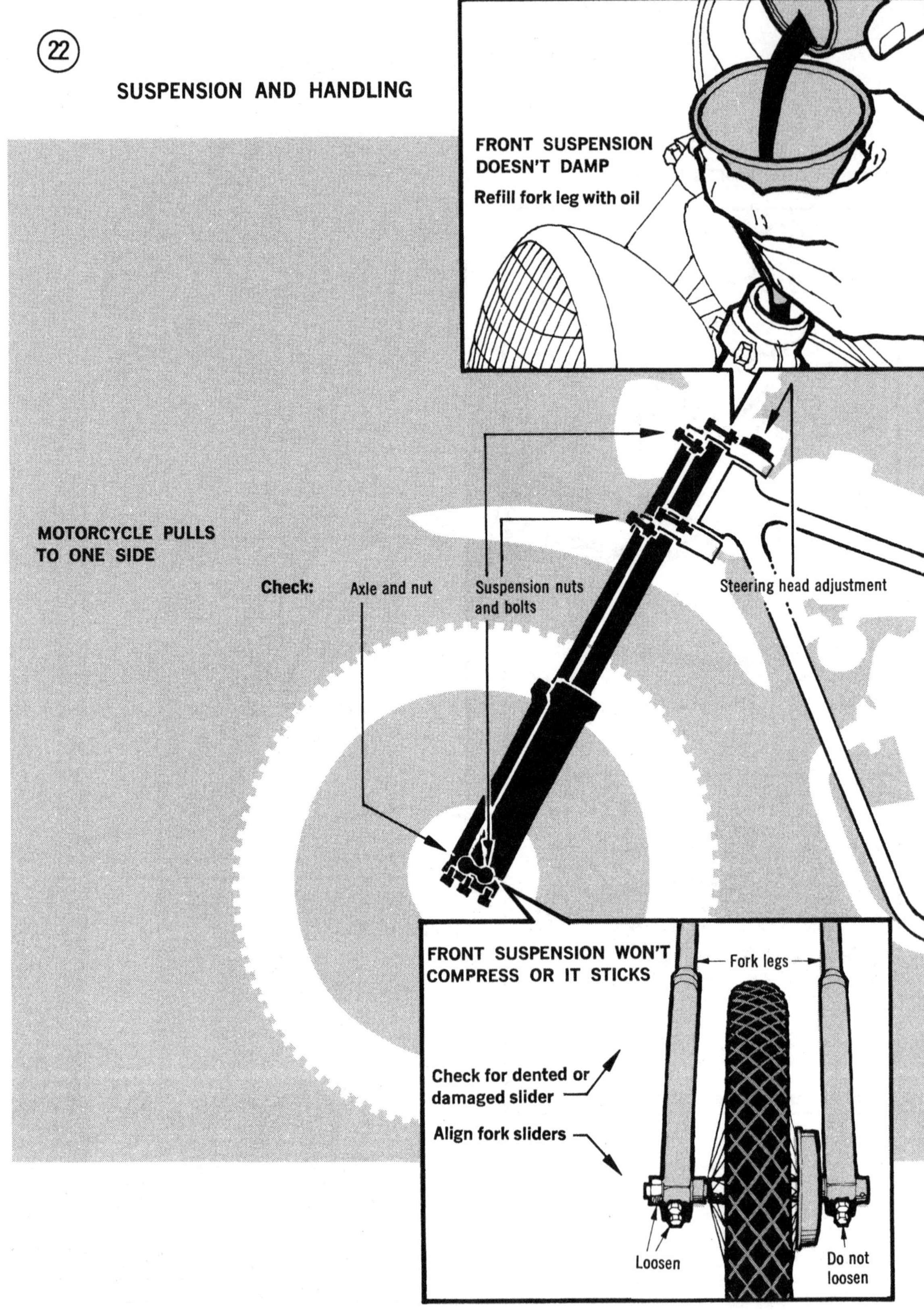
22
SUSPENSION AND HANDLING
FRONT SUSPENSION
DOESN'T DAMP
Refill fork leg with oil
MOTORCYCLE PULLS
TO ONE SIDE
Check:
Axle and nut
Suspension nuts
and bolts
Steering head adjustment
FRONT SUSPENSION WON'T
COMPRESS OR IT STICKS
Fork legs
Check for dented or
damaged slider
Align fork sliders
Loosen
Do not
loosen

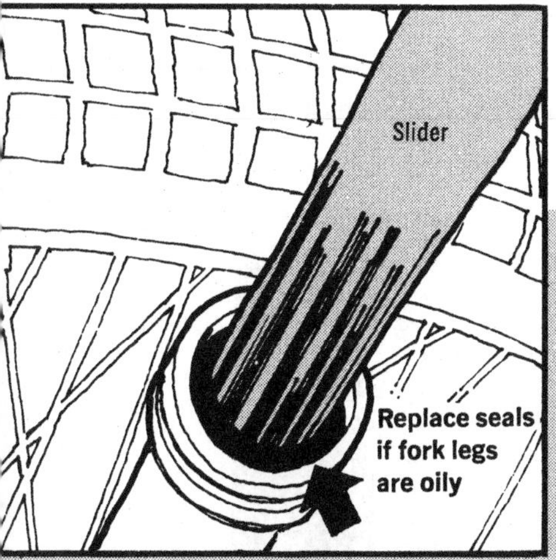
Slider
Replace seals if fork legs are oily

SUSPENSION AND HANDLING CONTINUED

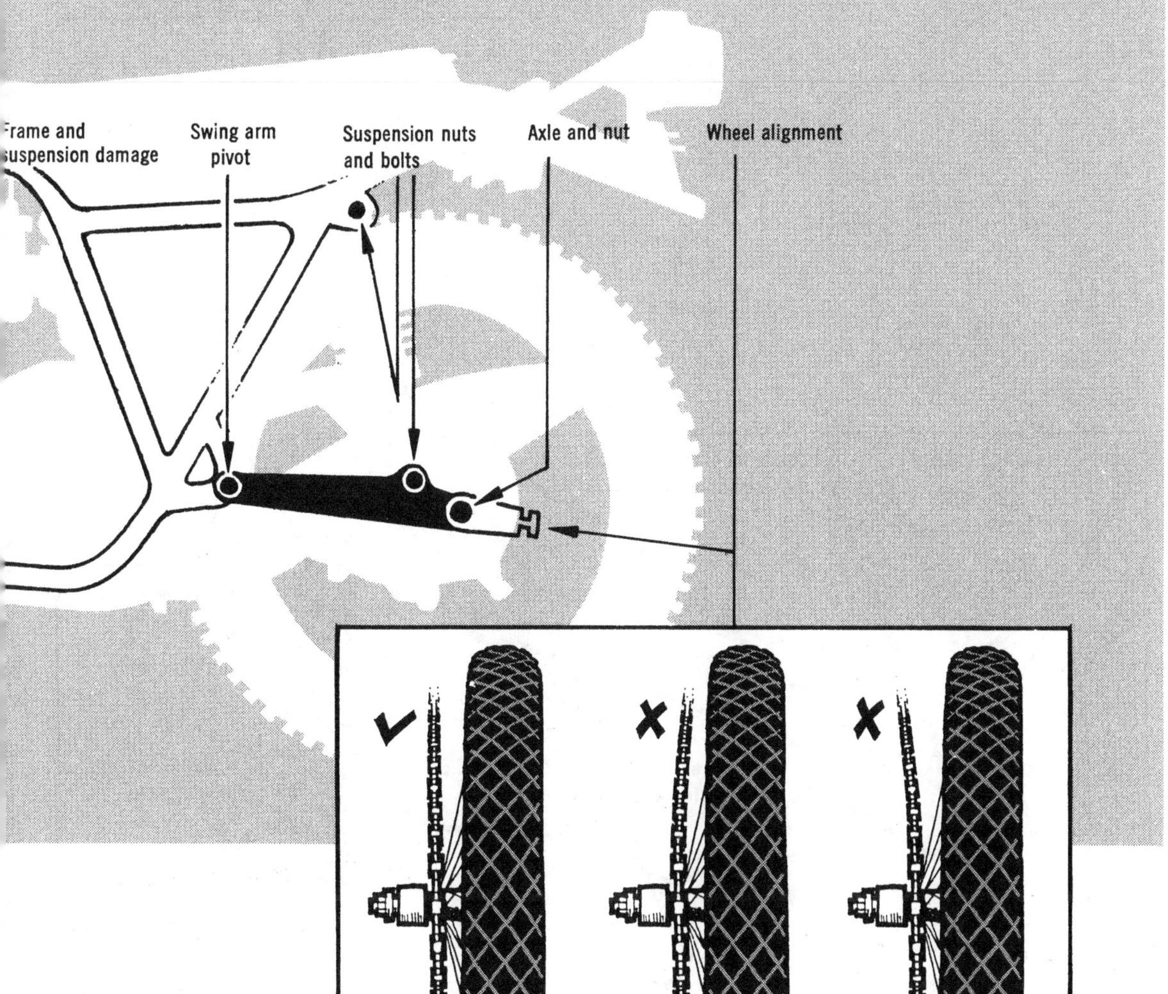

Frame and suspension damage

Swing arm pivot

Suspension nuts and bolts

Axle and nut

Wheel alignment

SUSPENSION AND HANDLING CONTINUED

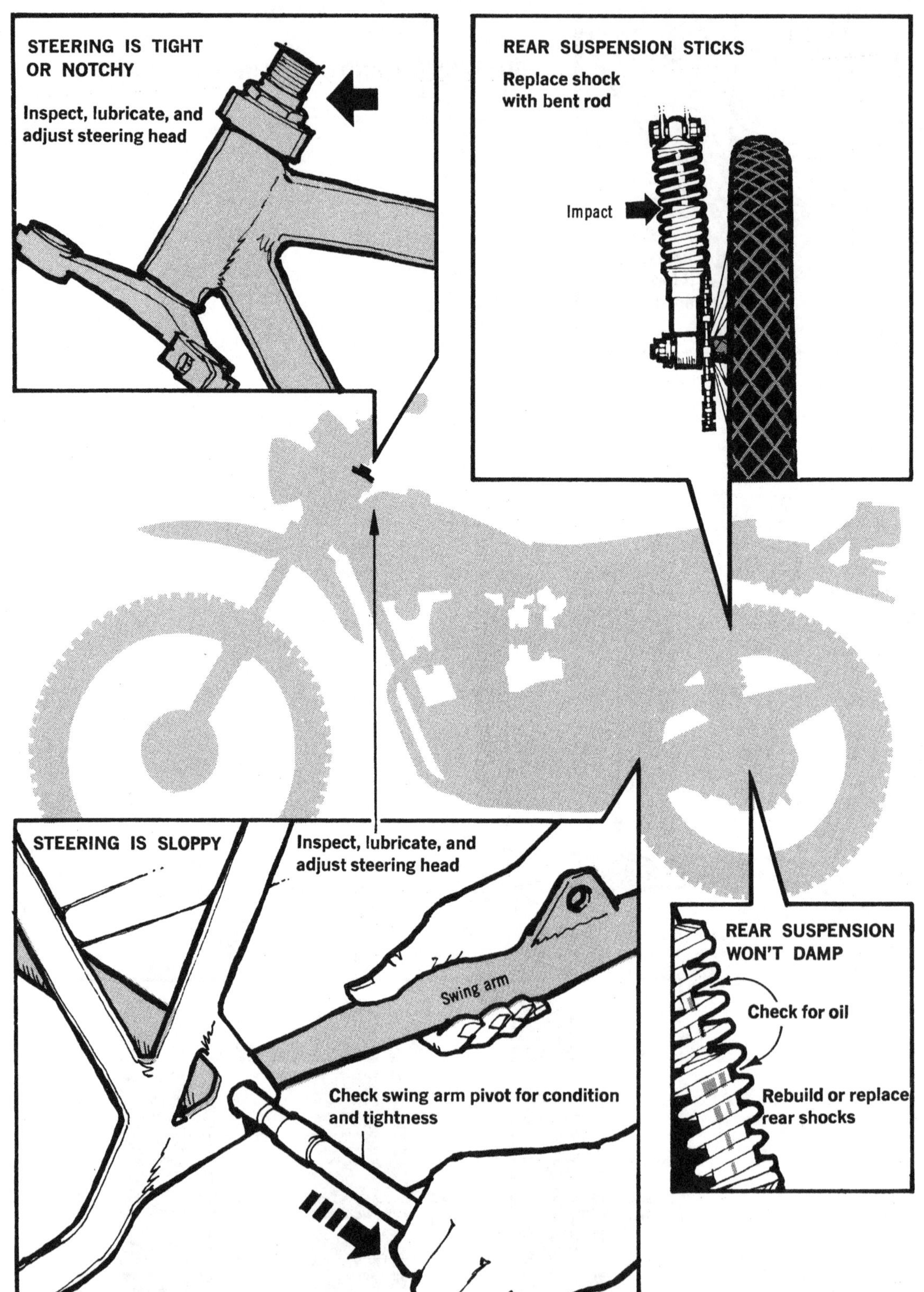
STEERING IS TIGHT OR NOTCHY
Inspect, lubricate, and adjust steering head
REAR SUSPENSION STICKS
Replace shock with bent rod
Impact
STEERING IS SLOPPY
Inspect, lubricate, and adjust steering head
Swing arm
Check swing arm pivot for condition and tightness
REAR SUSPENSION WON'T DAMP
Check for oil
Rebuild or replace rear shocks

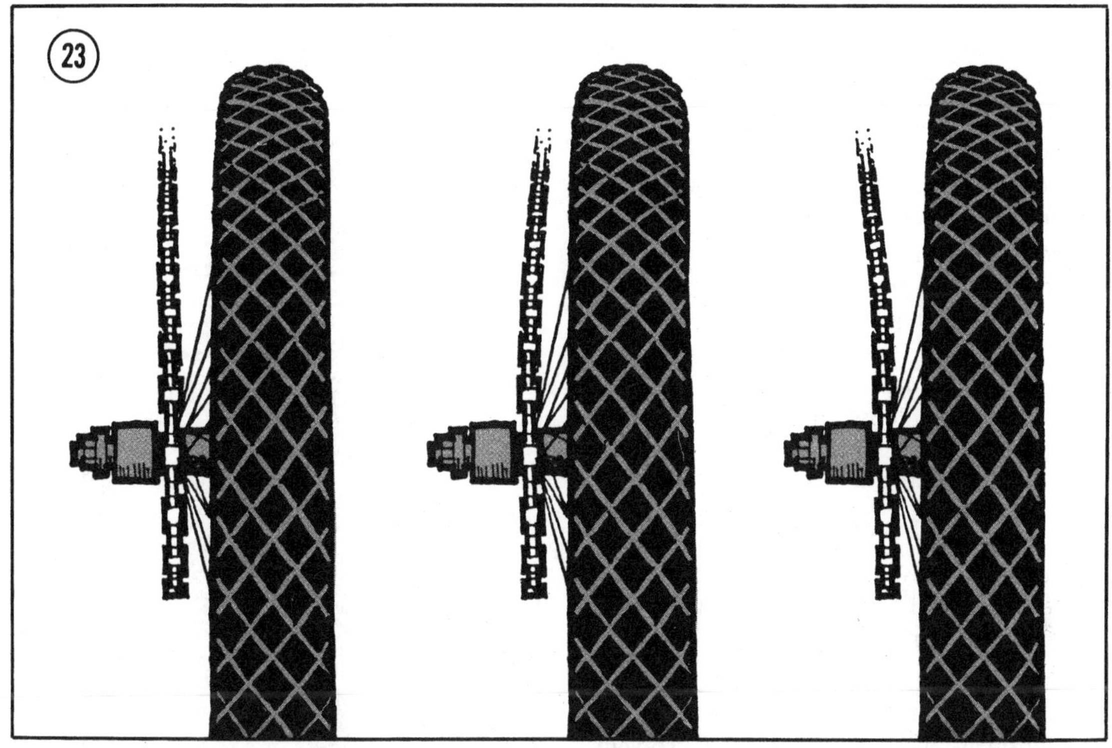

head, swing arm pivot. Check wheel alignment (**Figure 23**). Check for damage to the frame and suspension components.

2. ***Front suspension doesn't damp***—This is most often caused by a lack of damping oil in the fork legs. If the upper fork tubes are exceptionally oily, it's likely that the seals are worn out and should be replaced.

3. ***Front suspension sticks or won't fully compress***—Misalignment of the forks when the wheel is installed can cause this. Loosen the axle nut and the pinch bolt on the nut end of the axle (**Figure 24**). Lock the front wheel with the brake and compress the front suspension several times to align the fork legs. Then, tighten the pinch bolt and then the axle nut.

The trouble may also be caused by a bent or dented fork slider (**Figure 25**). The distortion required to lock up a fork tube is so slight that it is often impossible to visually detect. If this type of damage is suspected, remove the fork leg and remove the spring from it. Attempt to operate the fork leg. If it still binds, replace the slider; it's not practical to repair it.

4. ***Rear suspension does not damp***—This is usually caused by damping oil leaking past

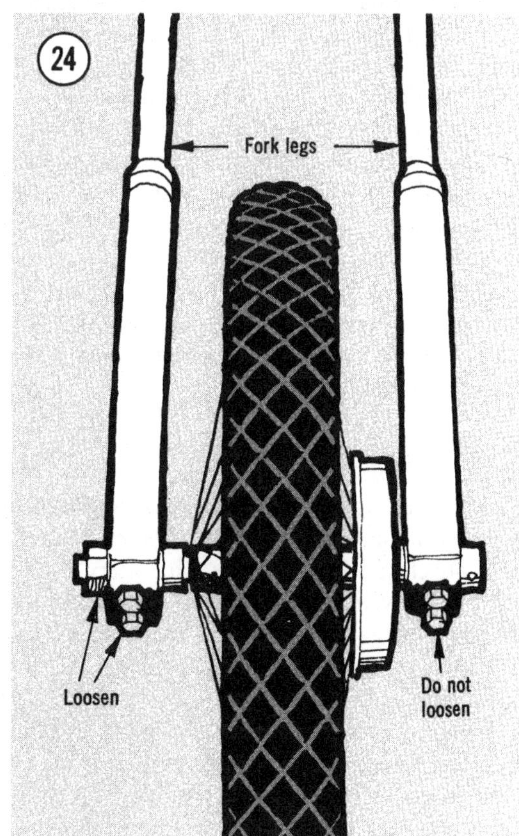

worn seals. Rebuildable shocks should be refitted with complete service kits and fresh oil. Non-rebuildable units should be replaced.

5. ***Rear suspension sticks***—This is commonly caused by a bent shock absorber piston rod (**Figure 26**). Replace the shock; the rod can't be satisfactorily straightened.

6. ***Steering is tight or "notchy"***—Steering head bearings may be dry, dirty, or worn. Adjustment of the steering head bearing pre-load may be too tight.

7. ***Steering is sloppy***—Steering head adjustment may be too loose. Also check the swing arm pivot; looseness or extreme wear at this point translate to the steering.

BRAKES

Brake problems arise from wear, lack of maintenance, and from sustained or repeated exposure to dirt and water.

1. ***Brakes are ineffective***—Ineffective brakes are most likely caused by incorrect adjustment. If adjustment will not correct the problem, remove the wheels and check for worn or glazed linings. If the linings are worn beyond the service limit, replace them. If they are simply glazed, rough them up with light sandpaper.

In hydraulic brake systems, low fluid levels can cause a loss of braking effectiveness, as can worn brake cylinder pistons and bores. Also check the pads to see if they are worn beyond the service limit.

2. ***Brakes lock or drag***—This may be caused by incorrect adjustment. Check also for foreign matter embedded in the lining and for dirty and dry wheel bearings.

ELECTRICAL SYSTEM

Many electrical system problems can be easily solved by ensuring that the affected connections are clean, dry, and tight. In battery equipped motorcycles, a neglected battery is the source of a great number of difficulties that could be prevented by simple, regular service to the battery.

A multimeter, like the volt/ohm/milliammeter described in Chapter One, is invaluable for efficient electrical system troubleshooting.

See **Figures 27 and 28** for schematics showing

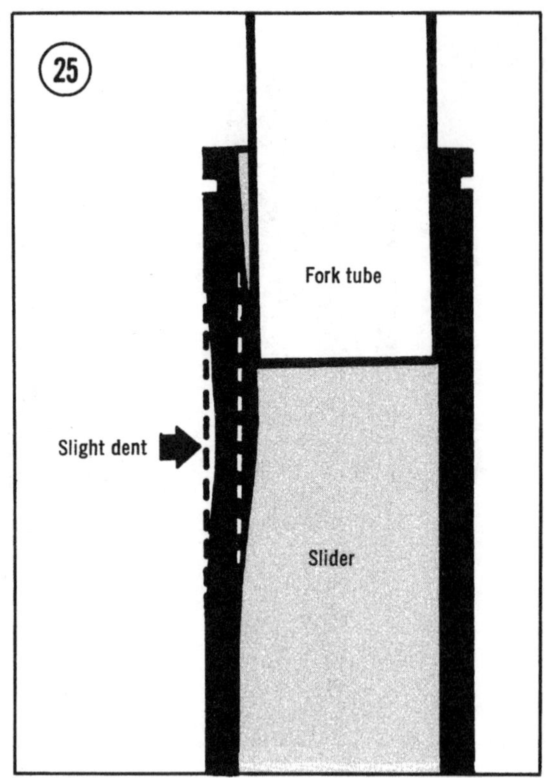

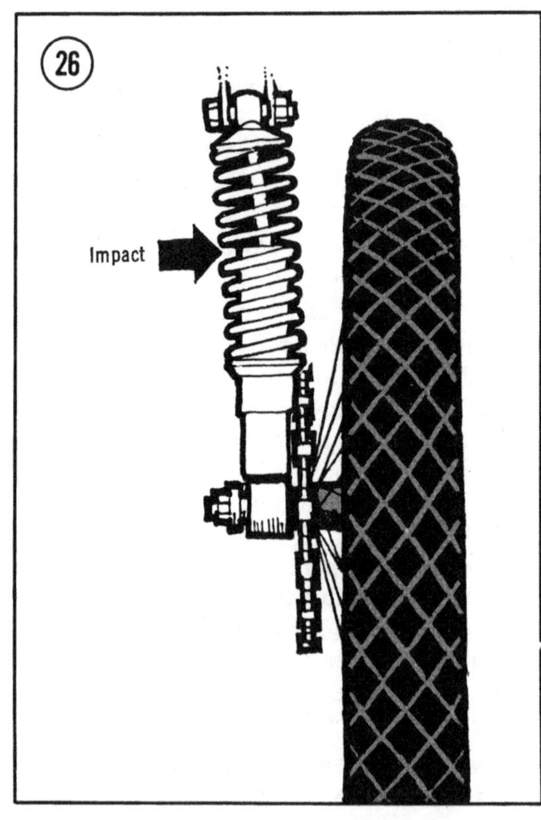

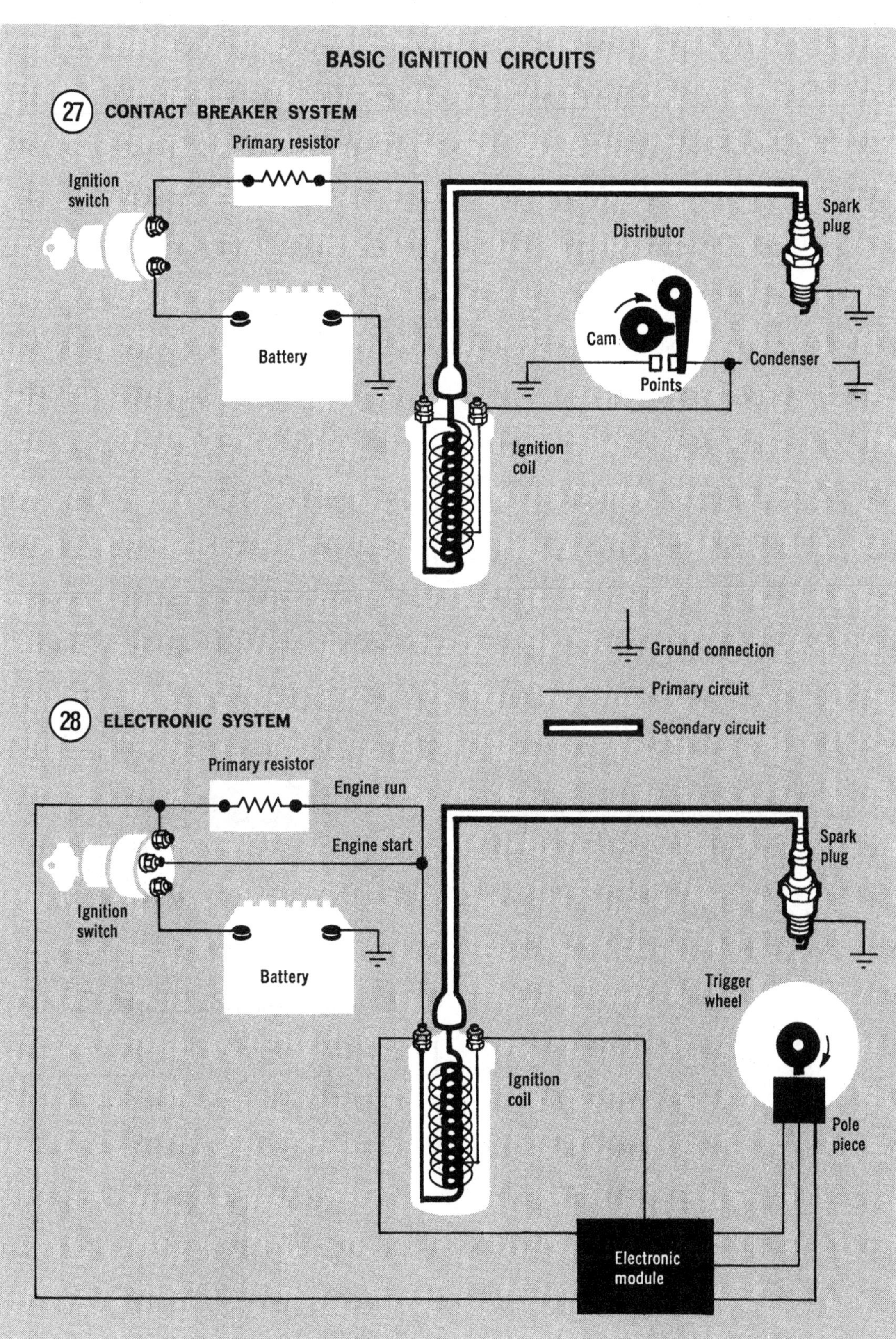
BASIC IGNITION CIRCUITS
27 CONTACT BREAKER SYSTEM
Primary resistor
Ignition switch
Battery
Distributor
Spark plug
Cam
Condenser
Points
Ignition coil
Ground connection
Primary circuit
Secondary circuit
28 ELECTRONIC SYSTEM
Primary resistor
Engine run
Engine start
Ignition switch
Battery
Spark plug
Trigger wheel
Ignition coil
Pole piece
Electronic module

simplified conventional and electronic ignition systems. Typical and most common electrical troubles are also described.

CHARGING SYSTEM

1. ***Battery will not accept a charge***—Make sure the electrolyte level in the battery is correct and that the terminal connections are tight and free of corrosion. Check for fuses in the battery circuit. If the battery is satisfactory, refer to the electrical system chapter for alternator tests. Finally, keep in mind that even a good alternator is not capable of restoring the charge to a severely discharged battery; it must first be charged by an external source.
2. ***Battery will not hold a charge***—Check the battery for sulfate deposits in the bottom of the case (**Figure 29**). Sulfation occurs naturally and the deposits will accumulate and eventually come in contact with the plates and short them out. Sulfation can be greatly retarded by keeping the battery well charged at all times. Test the battery to assess its condition.

If the battery is satisfactory, look for excessive draw, such as a short.

LIGHTING

Bulbs burn out frequently—All bulbs will eventually burn out, but if the bulb in one particular light burns out frequently check the light assembly for looseness that may permit excessive vibration; check for loose connections that could cause current surges; check also to make sure the bulb is of the correct rating.

FUSES

Fuse blows—When a fuse blows, don't just replace it; try to find the cause. Consider a fuse a warning device as well as a safety device. And never replace a fuse with one of greater amperage rating. It probably won't melt before the insulation on the wiring does.

WIRING

Wiring problems should be corrected as soon as they arise — before a short can cause a fire that may seriously damage or destroy the motorcycle.

A circuit tester of some type is essential for locating shorts and opens. Use the appropriate wiring diagram at the end of the book for reference. If a wire must be replaced make a notation on the wiring diagram of any changes in color coding.

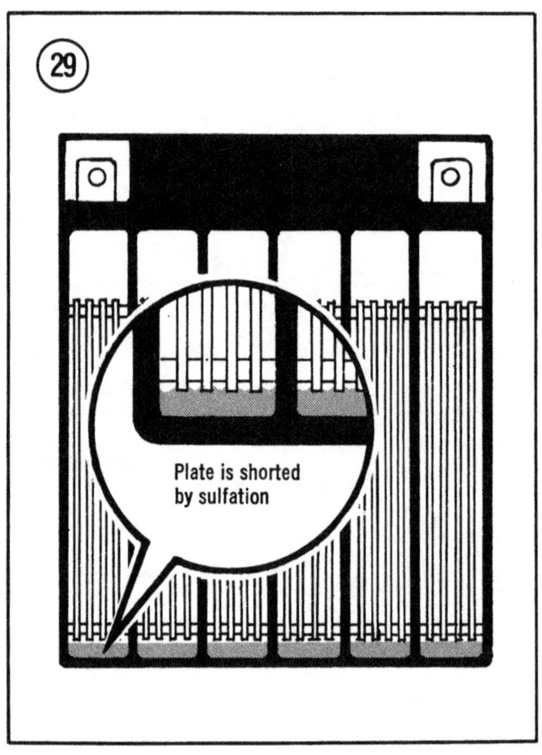

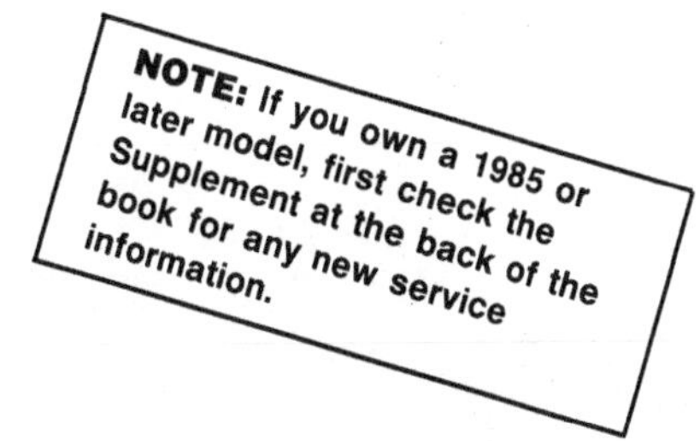
NOTE: If you own a 1985 or later model, first check the Supplement at the back of the book for any new service information.

CHAPTER THREE

LUBRICATION, MAINTENANCE AND TUNE-UP

A motorcycle, like any other precision machine, requires a certain amount of routine and preventive maintenance to ensure its safety, reliability and performance.

The maintenance and lubrication intervals specified in **Table 1** are recommended by Suzuki for the average rider. Harder than average riding may require more frequent service to maintain peak reliability and performance.

If you ride less than 500 miles per month, the engine oil should be changed every 3 months regardless of miles.

If the motorcycle is used mostly in stop-and-go traffic, it is a good idea to change the oil more often than is recommended. This is also true for frequent short trips. Acids tend to build up rapidly under these conditions and, if allowed to remain in the engine, they will accelerate engine wear.

This chapter describes all periodic maintenance and lubrication required to keep your bike running properly. Routine checks are easily performed at each fuel stop. Other periodic maintenance appears in the order of frequency.

Engine tune-up is treated separately from other maintenance tasks because the various tune-up procedures interact with each other. All tune-up procedures should be performed together and in the specified order.

Plan ahead for all servicing and tune-ups. Make sure you have all the supplies such as engine and fork oil, chain lubricant and spark plugs before starting the service work. Nothing is more aggravating or time-consuming than having to stop in the middle of a job and pick up some forgotten item. This is particularly important when performing a valve adjustment. The engine must be dead cold, that is, not run for at least 12 hours prior to adjustment.

MODEL DIFFERENCES

The following procedures cover 2 types of GS550 machines. All 1982 and earlier models share one style engine as well as most frame and suspension components. Minor changes and improvements have been added to these models during the years of production and where necessary these changes are covered with special procedures.

All 1983 and later GS550 machines are fitted with a TSCC (Twin Swirl Combustion Chamber) engine and a single-shock rear suspension. Throughout this manual these models are identified by year and/or the "TSCC" designation. All TSCC models share components that differ from earlier machines.

Most maintenance and repair procedures are very similar for motorcycles with both engine types. All minor differences, where applicable, are specified within the procedure. Where significant differences exist, a separate procedure is provided for each type of motorcycle. Before starting any repair or maintenance work, read completely all applicable procedures and note the differences between the models.

Tables 1-9 are located at the end of this chapter.

ROUTINE CHECKS

Develop a habit of making the following basic checks at each fuel stop. A few minutes spent may prevent personal injury or damage to the motorcycle. Correct any problem found before riding.

Engine Oil Level

Place the motorcycle on the centerstand and check the engine oil level through the inspection window (**Figure 1**). Maintain the oil level between

the "F" and "L" marks. Use the appropriate oil recommended in **Table 2**.

General Inspection

1. Examine the fuel line and the fuel valve for signs of leakage.
2. Check the control cables for fraying or kinks. All controls must operate smoothly.
3. Inspect the tires and wheels for damage.
4. Check the engine and frame for loose bolts and nuts, wiring, etc.
5. Check the drive chain slack and ensure that the chain is properly lubricated.
6. Ensure that both front and rear brakes operate correctly.
7. Make sure that the lights work properly and that the engine kill switch will shut off the engine.

Battery and Connections

Check the electrolyte level in the battery; it should be between the upper and lower level marks on the battery case (**Figure 2**). Top up, if necessary, with distilled water. To reach the battery, perform the following:

a. On 1982 and earlier models, remove the left side cover to gain access to the battery (**Figure 3**). It may be necessary to remove the rubber

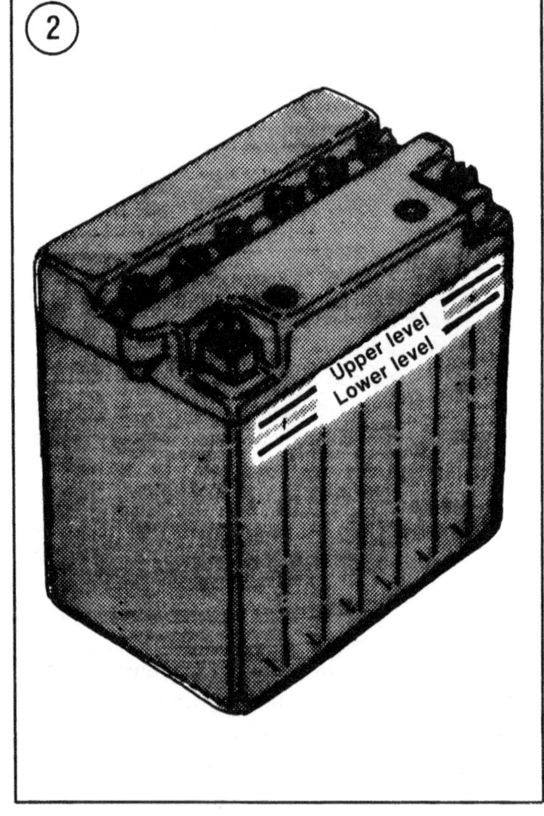

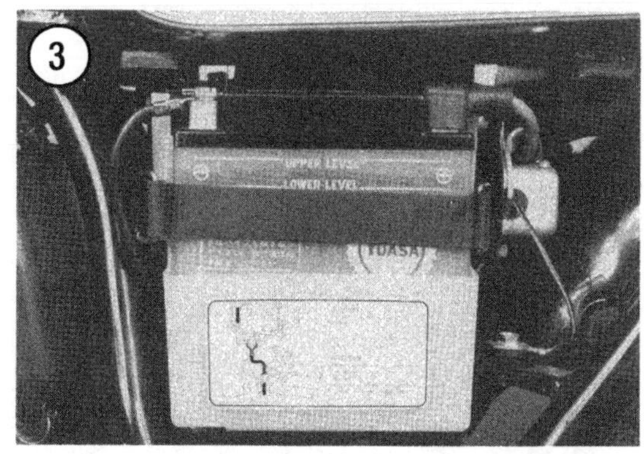

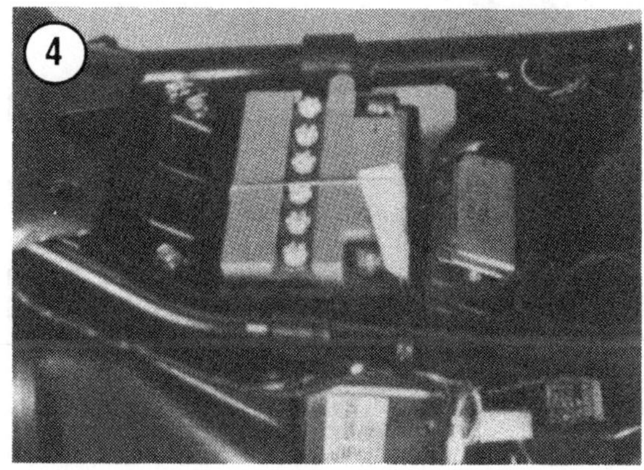

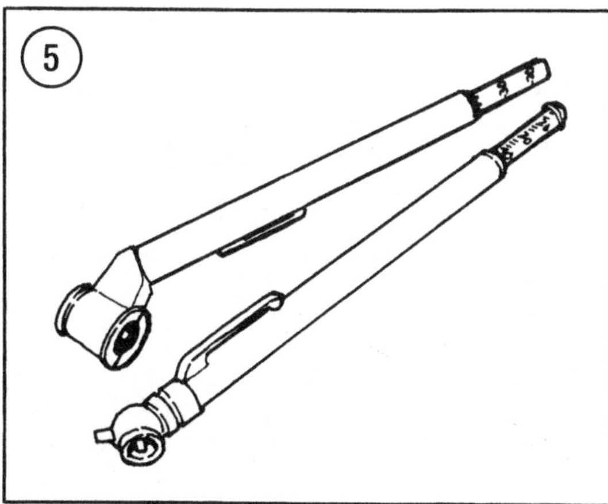

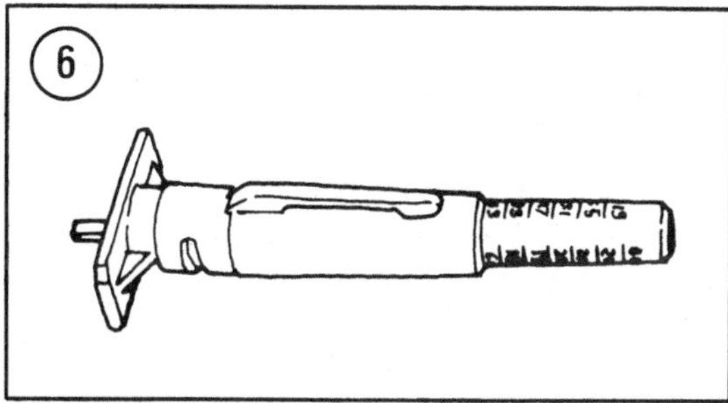

strap and plastic cover from the battery to view the level marks.

b. On 1983-on models, remove the seat (**Figure 4**).

If battery connections are dirty and corroded they must be cleaned with baking soda. To clean the battery connections and check the specific gravity of the electrolyte, refer to *Battery* in Chapter Seven.

3

Tire Pressure

Tire pressures should be checked and adjusted when the tires are cold. A simple, accurate guage (**Figure 5**) can be purchased for a few dollars and should be carried in your motorcycle tool kit. Refer to **Table 3** for the recommended tire pressures.

Tire Inspection

Check the tread for excessive wear, deep cuts and imbedded objects such as nails or bits of broken glass. If you find a nail in a tire, mark its location with a light-colored crayon before pulling it out. This will help locate the hole in the inner tube.

Check local traffic regulations concerning minimum tread depth. Measure with a tread depth gauge (**Figure 6**) or a small ruler. Suzuki recommends tire replacement when the tread depth is less than 1.6 mm (1/16 in.) in the front and 2.0 mm (3/32 in.) in the rear. Tread wear bars or indicators appear across the tire when the tread reaches the minimum safe depth. Replace the tire at this point.

Wheels

On spoke wheels, check the wheel hubs and rims for bends and other signs of damage. Check for broken or bent spokes. Damaged spokes must be replaced immediately to prevent possible wheel failure or further wheel damage. Tap each spoke lightly with a small hammer or wrench. All spokes should emit approximately the same tone or sound. A too-tight spoke will have a higher pitch than the others. A too-loose spoke will have a lower pitch. If only one or two spokes are slightly out of adjustment, adjust them with a spoke wrench as outlined in Chapter Eight. If more spokes are affected, the wheel should be removed and trued as outlined under *Spoke Adjustment* in Chapter Eight.

On models equipped with alloy wheels, carefully examine the wheels for cracks, bends or warpage. These wheels cannot be serviced, except for balancing. If the wheels are damaged they must be replaced.

Refer to Chapter Eight for wheel balancing.

PERIODIC MAINTENANCE

The following maintenance items are summarized in **Table 1**. A good way to ensure that all necessary items are covered during a periodic service is to make a check list and use it each time you service the motorcycle. Keep an up-to-date record of all items serviced and when the service was performed; otherwise it is too easy to forget what was done and when.

Drive Chain Adjustment and Lubrication

WARNING
Always keep the drive chain correctly adjusted and lubricated. A badly worn chain or a chain with excessive slack can easily become a thrown or broken chain. Such an occurance can result in a locked-up rear wheel and a serious spill.

The drive chain should be carefully inspected and lubricated at least every 600 miles (1,000 km). Lubricate and adjust the chain more frequently if necessary. The importance of proper drive chain maintenance cannot be overemphasized. Accelerated drive chain wear as a result of neglect can prove very costly. A drive chain is an expensive item to replace and a failed chain may cause engine or transmission damage.

CAUTION
*Do not use a specially compounded chain oil on the drive chain unless the oil is specifically recommended for O-ring chains. The drive chain is permanently lubricated with O-ring seals around the pins as shown in **Figure** 7. The penetrants in non-approved chain lubricants may damage the O-rings or thin the permanent lubrication. If approved oil is not available, keep the outside of the chain well lubricated with heavy motor oil.*

1. Measure the chain deflection (slack) halfway between the sprockets as shown in **Figure 8**. Normal deflection is 20-30 mm (13/16-1 3/16 in.). If the chain requires adjustment, proceed to the next step.

NOTE
When checking drive chain adjustment, check the slack in several places along the length of the chain by rotating the rear wheel. The chain will rarely stretch uniformly and as a result will be tighter in some places than others.

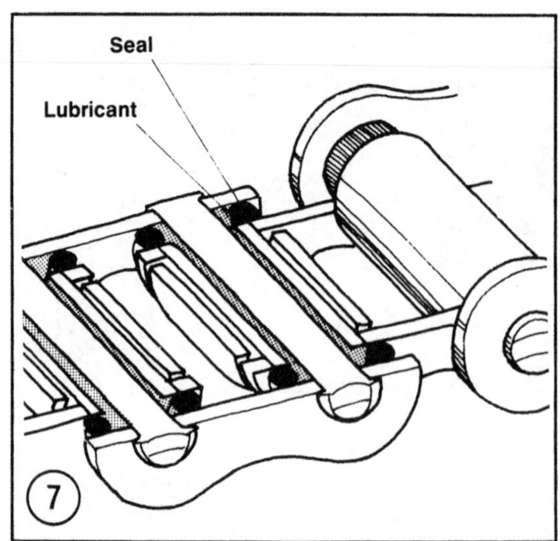

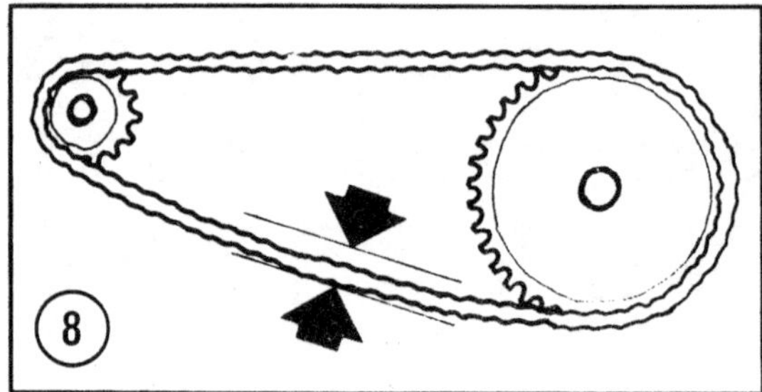

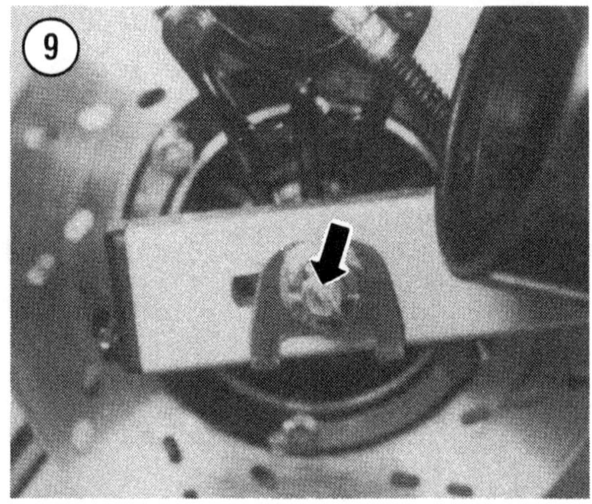

2. Remove the cotter pin or lynch pin securing the rear axle nut (**Figure 9**).
3. Loosen the axle nut (**Figure 10**). It may be necessary to use a Phillips screwdriver shaft inserted in the axle head to keep the axle from turning.

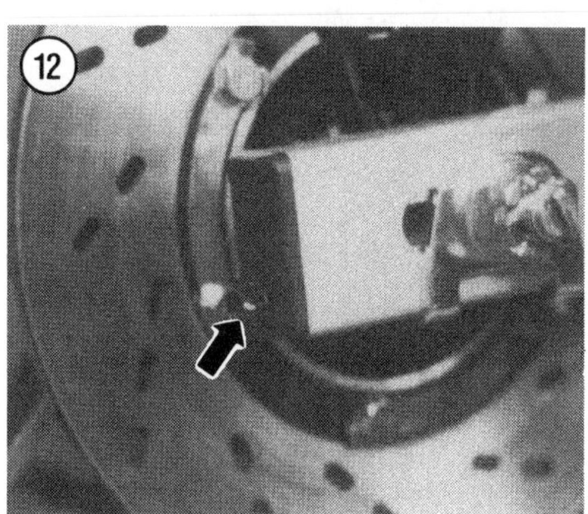

NOTE
On most 1982 and earlier models, the muffler/rear footrest bolt can be removed on each side and the mufflers pulled away slightly from the frame to provide additional clearance around the rear axle.

4. On 1982 and earlier models, loosen the locknuts securing the axle adjuster bolts on each side (**Figure 11**).

5. Turn the adjuster bolts equally on each side until the chain deflection is 20-30 mm (13/16-1 3/16 in.). See **Figure 12** for TSCC models. Make sure the index mark on each adjuster aligns with

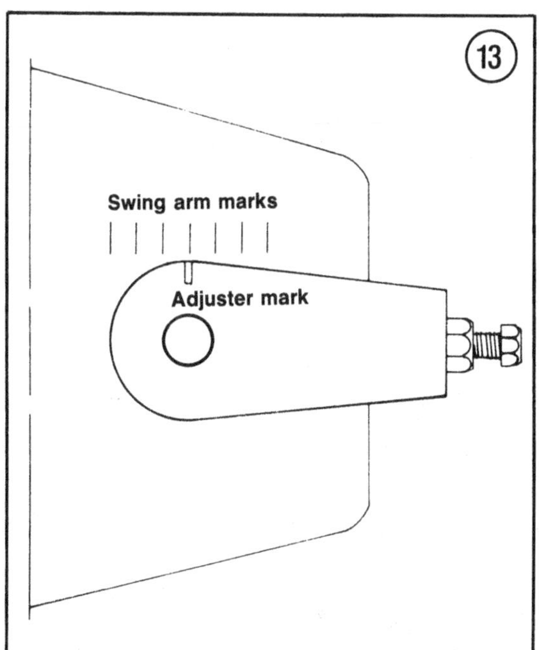

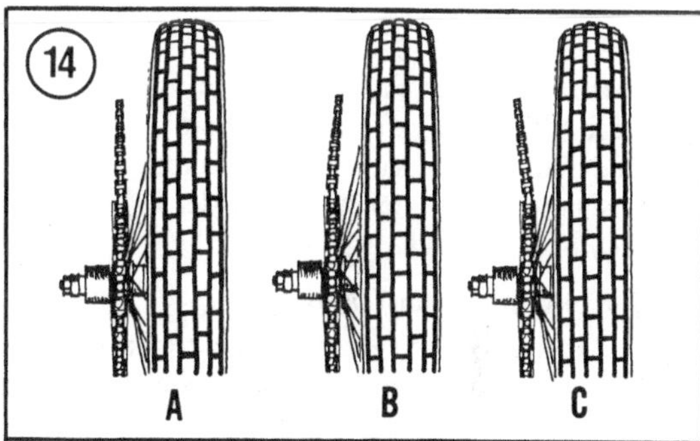

the same mark on each side of the swing arm (**Figure 13**).

6. On 1982 and earlier models, tighten the adjuster bolt locknuts. Rotate the rear wheel a few revolutions and recheck the chain deflection. Readjust if necessary. If the chain cannot be adjusted within the specified limits, it is excessively worn and must be replaced.

7. When the adjustment is correct, sight along the chain from the rear sprocket and check that the rear wheel is correctly aligned. The chain should leave the top of the rear sprocket in a straight line as shown in A, **Figure 14**. If the chain is cocked to one side or the other as shown in B and C, **Figure 14**, the rear wheel is incorrectly aligned. Loosen the locknuts (if so equipped) and turn the adjusters until the chain alignment is correct. When the alignment is correct, recheck the chain deflection and readjust if necessary.

NOTE

It may be necessary to remove the chain guard to obtain a clear view of rear wheel alignment.

8. Torque the axle nut as specified in **Table 4**. Secure the nut with a new cotter pin.
9. Install the muffler/rear footrest bolt, if removed. Torque the bolt to 2.7-4.3 mkg (19.5-31 ft.-lb.).
10. Lubricate the chain with an approved O-ring chain lubricant according to the manufacturer's instructions. If chain lubricant is not available, perform the following:
    a. Soak a clean rag in engine oil.
    b. Wrap the rag around the drive chain and hold it in place.
    c. Slowly turn the rear wheel to allow the chain to run through the oil-soaked rag. Rotate the wheel until the chain is completely coated with a light film of oil.
11. Inspect the sprockets for signs of wear and undercutting (**Figure 15**). Refer to Chapter Four for drive sprocket replacement and Chapter Nine for rear sprocket replacement.

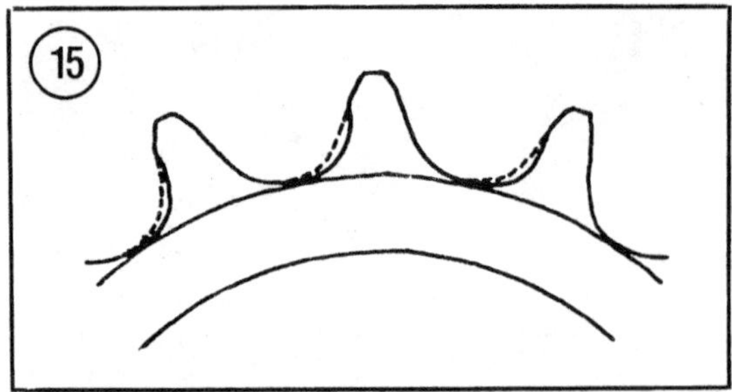

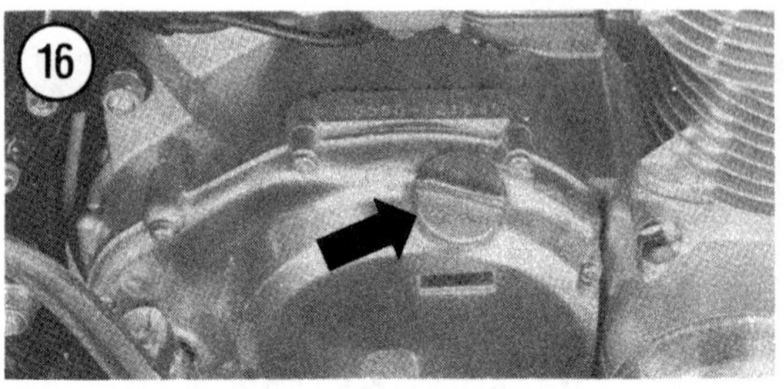

Engine and Frame Fasteners

Constant vibration can loosen many fasteners on a motorcycle. Refer to **Table 4** and torque all the engine and frame fasteners as specified. Torque the cylinder head nuts and bolts as outlined under *Valve Clearance Adjustment* in this chapter.

Engine Oil and Filter Change

Regular oil and filter service will contribute more to engine longevity than any other single factor. Change the oil and clean the oil filter at least as often as specified in **Table 1**. Change both oil and filter more often if the motorcycle is used in dusty areas or primarily on short trips.

CAUTION

Never add STP or similar friction reducing oil additives to the engine oil. These products will destroy the friction properties of the clutch, requiring a complete flushing of the engine and replacement of the clutch plates.

To change the engine oil and filter you will need the following items:

a. Drain pan.
b. Funnel.
c. Can opener or pour spout.
d. 4 quarts of oil.
e. A new oil filter element.

There are a number of ways to discard the used oil safely. The easiest way is to pour it from the drain pan into a gallon plastic bleach, juice or milk container for disposal.

NOTE

Never dispose of motor oil in the trash, on the ground, or down a storm drain. Many service stations accept used motor oil and waste haulers provide curbside used motor oil collection. Do not combine other fluids with motor oil to be recycled. To locate a recycler, contact the American Petroleum Institute (API) at www.recycleoil.org.

1. Warm up the engine and place the motorcycle on the centerstand.
2. Remove the oil filler cap (**Figure 16**).
3. Place a drain pan under the engine. Use a socket to remove the drain plug (**Figure 17**). Allow several minutes for the oil to drain completely.

WARNING

Get your hand out of the way as soon as the plug is ready to come out. Hot oil drains very rapidly and could cause painful burns.

4. Remove the bolts, nuts or Allen screws securing the oil filter cover and remove the cover (**Figure 18**). Remove the oil filter (**Figure 19**).
5. Clean the filter cover and drain plug in solvent. Inspect the gasket on the drain plug and the O-ring on the filter cover. Replace the gasket or O-ring if they are not in good condition. Use a little grease to help hold the O-ring in the filter cover.
6. Install the filter (open end in) into the engine as shown in **Figure 19**.
7. Apply a thin layer of grease to the O-ring on the filter cover (**Figure 20**). Install the cover with the spring positioned as shown in **Figure 20**.

17

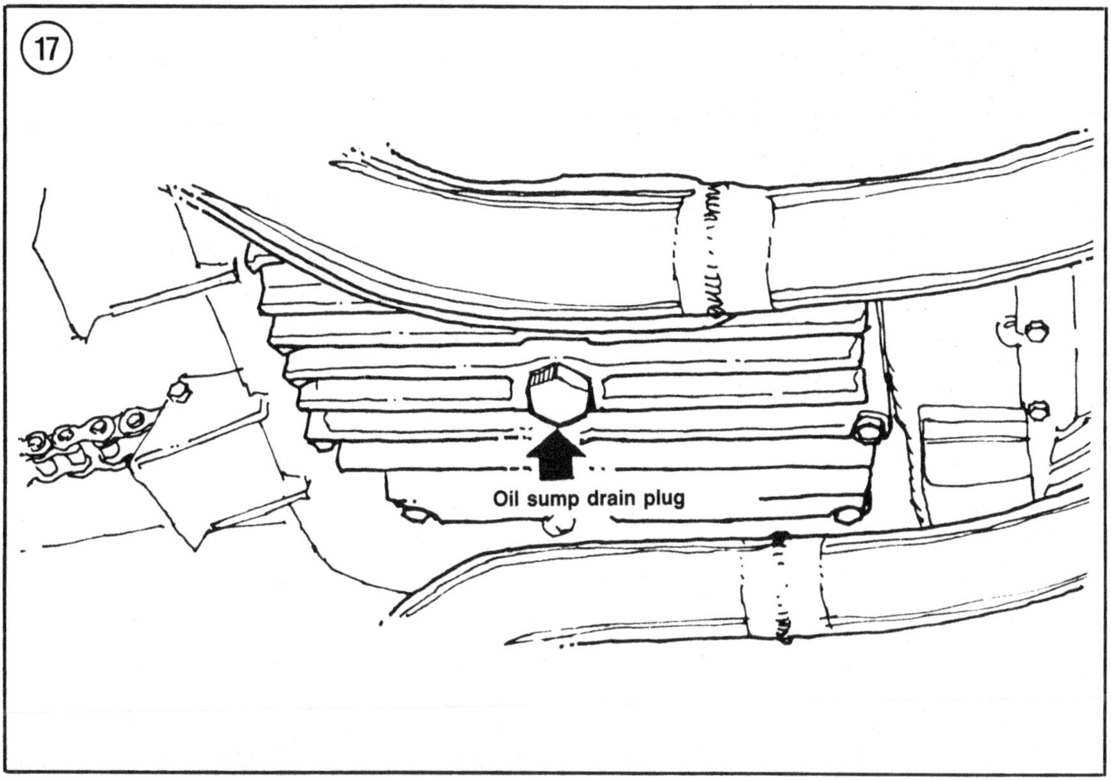

Oil sump drain plug

8. Push in against the spring tension of the cover and install the washers and nuts securing the cover.

9. Tighten the fasteners securing the filter cover gradually and evenly in a crisscross pattern. Take care not to overtighten.

10. Install the drain plug and torque to 1 mkg (7 ft.-lb.).

11. Add the recommended quantity and type of oil to the crankcase through the filler opening. Refer to **Table 2** and **Table 5**.

CAUTION

Never start and run the engine without adding oil or the engine will be seriously damaged.

12. Start the engine and allow it to idle so the oil will circulate completely. When the engine has warmed up, shut it off and wait at least 2 minutes. Check the oil level through the oil level window. If the level is below the "L" mark, add oil until the level is correct.

NOTE

When checking the engine oil level, the motorcycle must be on the centerstand.

13. Check carefully for leaks around the filter cover and the drain plug.

Air Filter Service (1982 and Earlier Models)

The air filter element on 1982 and earlier models is a foam unit that should be cleaned and reoiled at least as often as recommended in **Table 1**.

If the motorcycle is subjected to abnormally dirty conditions, the filter element should be checked and cleaned more frequently.

CAUTION

Do not carry clothing or rags under the seat or the air flow to the air cleaner will be restricted and engine performance will be affected.

1. Remove the seat and pull the carburetor vent hoses out of the filter cover.
2. Remove the screws securing the filter cover (**Figure 21**) and remove the cover.
3. Remove the screw securing the filter assembly to the air box and remove the assembly (**Figure 22**).
4. Remove the retaining band and separate the foam element from the metal frame (**Figure 23**).
5. Wash the foam filter element in solvent, then in hot, soapy water. Rinse the element in clean water and squeeze it between your palms to remove as much water as possible. The element can be pressed between several layers of paper towels to speed up the drying process. Allow the element to dry completely.

CAUTION

Never wring or twist the foam element during the cleaning or reoiling process, as the foam can easily be damaged.

6. Carefully examine the foam element for any splits or tears. Replace the element if it is damaged in any way.
7. Apply engine oil or special air filter oil to the element and gently work the foam in your hands until the element is completely saturated with oil. Squeeze the element between your palms to remove all the excess oil.

NOTE

Place the filter element and filter oil in a plastic bag to eliminate most of the mess of the job.

NOTE

A good grade of special air filter oil provides better protection against dirt and moisture than plain engine oil.

8. Thoroughly clean the inside of the air box and the filter sealing flange.

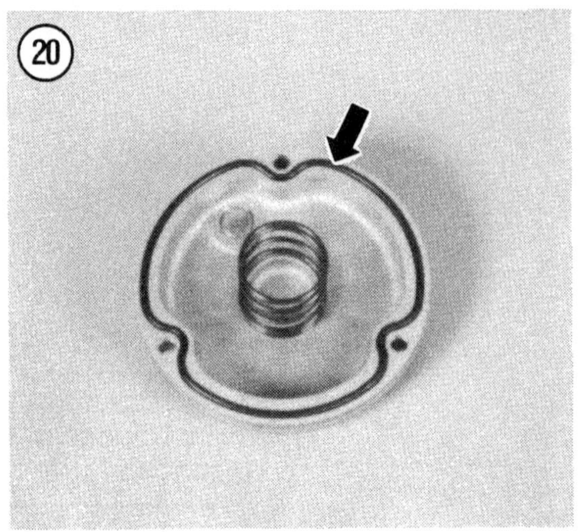

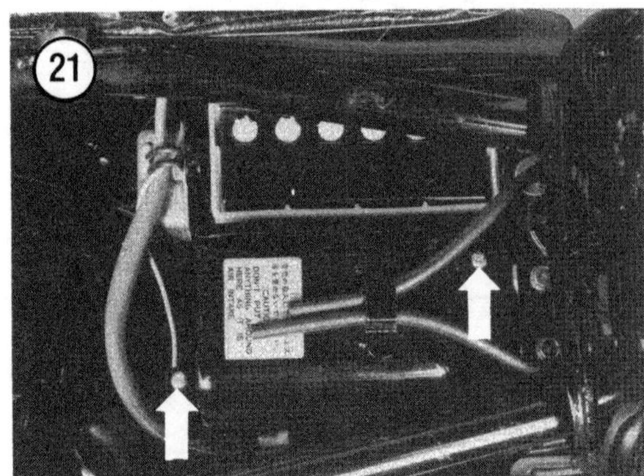

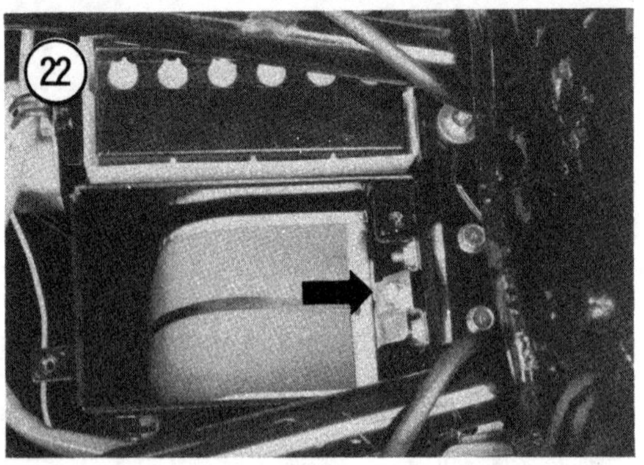

9. Secure the foam element to the metal frame and install the filter assembly into the air box.
10. Make sure that the lip on the metal frame engages the clip in the air box (**Figure 22**).
11. Secure the filter assembly with the screw and install the filter cover.
12. Route the vent hoses through the slot in the cover and install the seat.

Air Filter Service (TSCC Models)

The filter element on TSCC models is made of a treated paper material. It can be blown clean once, but should be replaced at least as often as recommended in **Table 1**.

If the motorcycle is subjected to abnormally dirty conditions, the filter element should be checked and cleaned more frequently.

1. Remove the seat and the right side cover.

2. Slide back the metal retaining clips securing the air box cover (**Figure 24**) and remove the cover.
3. Remove the screw securing the filter element (**Figure 25**).
4. Slide the filter element out of the air box (**Figure 26**).
5. Blow out the air filter with compressed air from the inside.

CAUTION
Direct compressed air from the inside of the element toward the outside. Air pressure applied to the outside will force the dirt back into the pores of the treated paper material and destroy the filtering ability of the air cleaner.

6. Slide the filter element into the air box as shown in **Figure 26**.
7. Secure the filter element to the air box with the screw (**Figure 25**).
8. Install the air box cover. Install the right side cover and seat.

Clutch Cable Adjustment

1. Pull back the rubber boot and loosen the locknut securing the cable adjuster. See **Figure 27**

for 1982 and earlier models and **Figure 28** for TSCC models.

2. Loosen the large knurled locknut and screw in the cable adjuster on the clutch handlebar lever (**Figure 29**).

3. Remove the screws securing the clutch adjustment cover and remove the cover. See **Figure 30** for 1982 and earlier models and **Figure 31** for TSCC models.

4. Loosen the locknut securing the adjuster screw and back out the screw 2 or 3 turns (**Figure 32**).

5. Slowly turn the adjuster screw in until resistance is felt as the adjuster screw contacts the clutch pushrod. Back out the adjuster screw 1/4-1/2 turn (**Figure 33**).

6. Hold the adjuster screw and tighten the locknut to secure the adjustment. Install the clutch adjustment cover.

7. Turn the cable adjuster on the engine until 2-4 mm (1/16-1/8 in.) of free play exists in the cable at

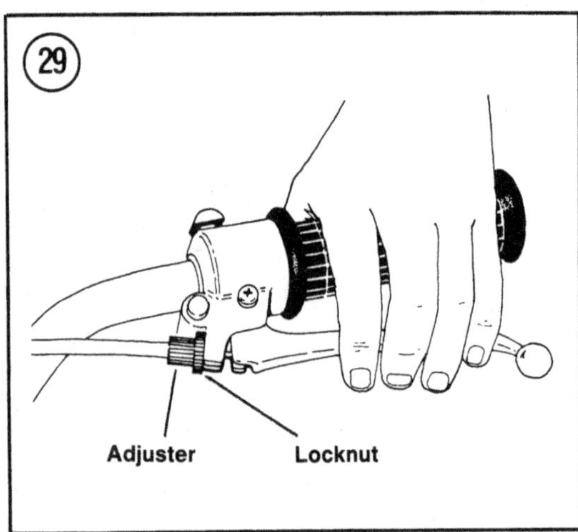

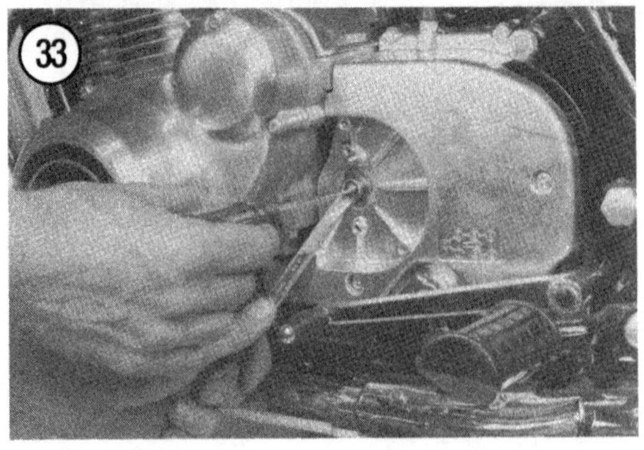

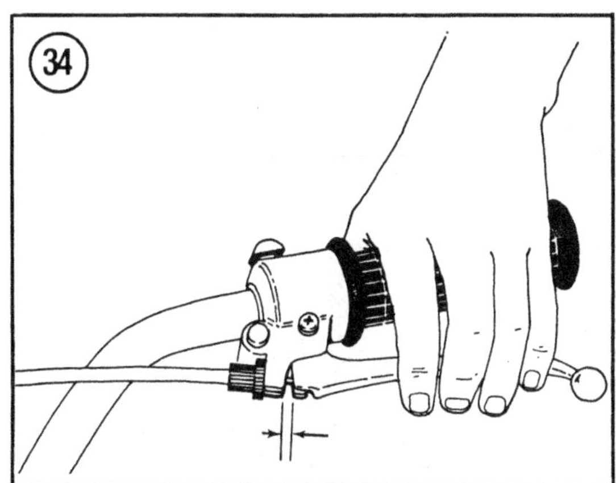

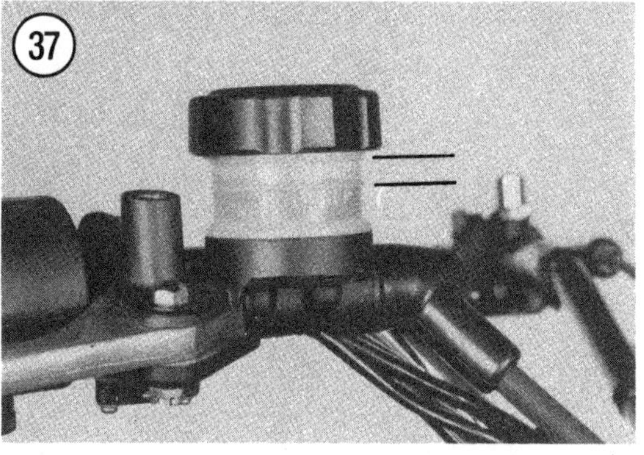

the handlebar lever (**Figure 34**). Secure the cable adjuster with the locknut. Pull the rubber boot over the adjuster.

8. Future clutch cable adjustments can be made at the handlebar adjuster until the cable stretches enough that you must readjust the clutch at the engine.

Brake Fluid Level

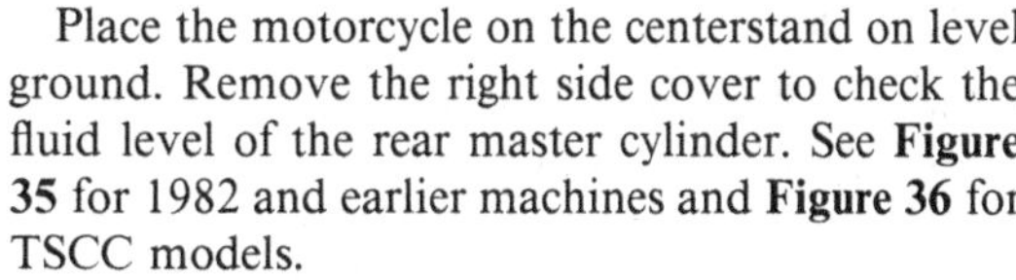

Place the motorcycle on the centerstand on level ground. Remove the right side cover to check the fluid level of the rear master cylinder. See **Figure 35** for 1982 and earlier machines and **Figure 36** for TSCC models.

Refer to **Figure 37** or **Figure 38** for the front master cylinder. Maintain the fluid level above the lower level mark. If fluid must be added to either reservoir, wipe the area around the filler cap with a clean rag before removing the cap.

WARNING

The brake system on all models uses a glycol-based brake fluid. If fluid must be added to the reservoirs, use only a glycol-based brake fluid rated DOT 3 or DOT 4. Mixing silicone or petroleum-based fluids into the brake system can cause brake component damage leading to brake system failure.

CAUTION

When adding brake fluid to the master cylinder reservoirs, make sure that no fluid is spilled on any painted surfaces or the paint will be damaged.

Brake Pad Inspection

Brake pad wear depends on a number of factors including riding conditions and rider habits. If most of your riding is in mountainous areas or stop-and-go traffic or if you know you are heavy on the brakes, check them more frequently than recommended in **Table 1**. On all machines, replace the pads as a set when they are worn down to the red line as shown in **Figure 39** for front pads and **Figure 40** for rear pads.

On 1977-1979 models, the front brake pad wear lines are usually visible before pad wear is beyond limits. If there is any question about the condition of the pads, remove them as outlined in Chapter Ten.

On 1980-1982 models, the front brake calipers have a small window to check brake wear as shown in **Figure 41**. If the inside of the window is covered with brake dust, carefully pry it out to check the pad wear.

On all TSCC models, snap off the plastic caliper cover (**Figure 42**). Check pad wear on the exposed edge of the pads (**Figure 43**).

On all models with rear disc brakes, to view the rear pads snap off the plastic caliper cover (**Figure 44**). Check the wear on both rear pads and replace them as a set when the shoulder on the pads is worn off as shown in **Figure 39** or **Figure 40**.

To inspect rear drum brakes, see Chapter Ten.

Brake Pedal

Lightly oil the rear brake pedal pivot shaft and linkage. Work the oil in by moving the pedal up and down. To adjust rear drum brakes, see *Rear Wheel Removal/Installation* in Chapter Nine.

Brake Hoses

Check the brake hoses between both master cylinders and the front and rear calipers. If any

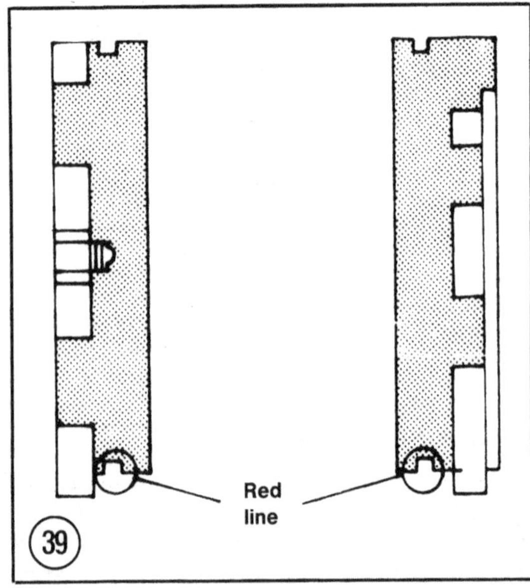

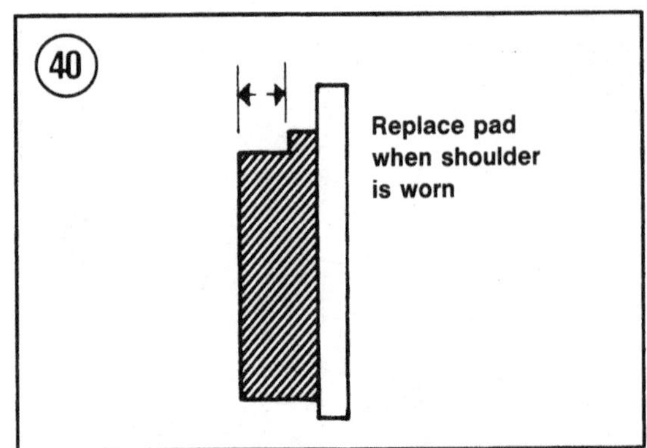

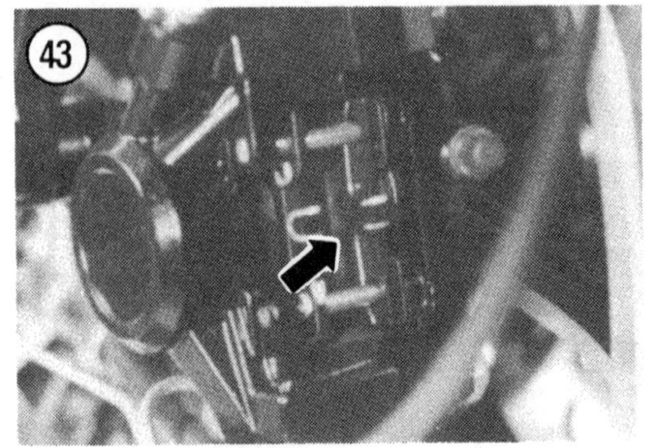

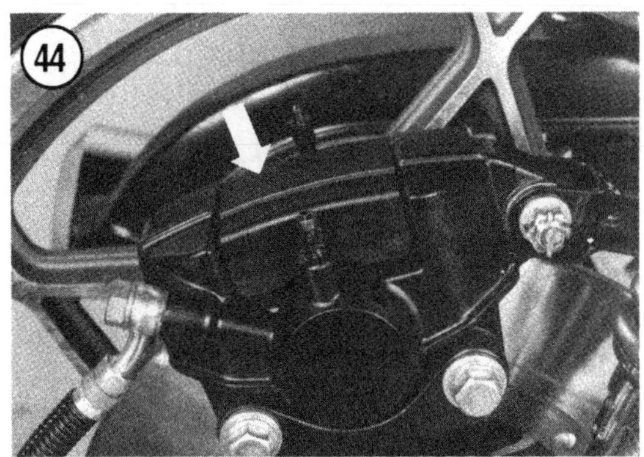
44

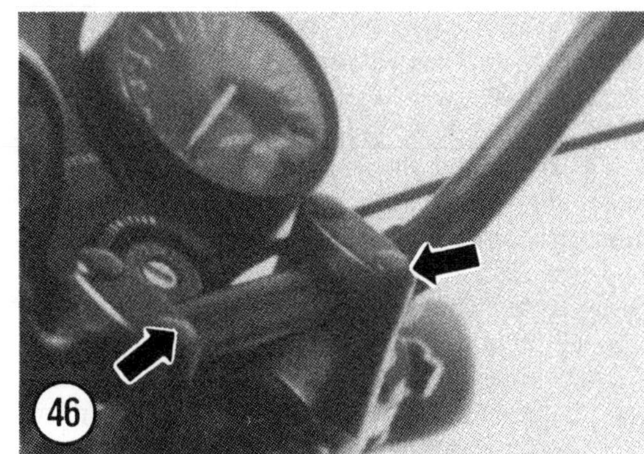
46

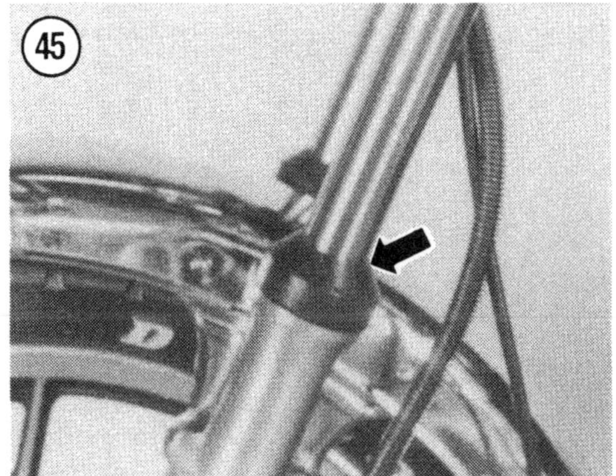
45

47

leakage is present, tighten the connections or replace the leaking hoses. Top off the brake fluid and refer to *Bleeding* as outlined in Chapter Ten.

Suzuki recommends that the brake fluid be changed every year and all brake hoses be replaced every 2 years. Refer to *Changing Brake Fluid* in Chapter Ten.

Front Fork Oil

The front suspension requires the correct amount of damping oil in each fork leg if it is to perform correctly. Damping characteristics depend greatly on oil viscosity, so the handling of the motorcycle can be changed by a change from one viscosity oil to another. Only personal experience will enable you to find the oil that is best for you and your style of riding. Generally, thinner oils are better suited to lighter riders and thicker oils are usually best for heavier riders or machines that are equipped with heavy touring gear. Thicker oils might also be used if most of your riding is done with a passenger. Refer to **Table 2** for the oil recommended by Suzuki.

It is impractical to add oil to a fork leg that has lost oil due to a leaky seal. The forks should be drained, flushed and refilled with the proper amount of oil after the leaky seal has been replaced. Seal leakage is indicated by oil oozing out around the fork wiper boots (**Figure 45**). Refer to Chapter Eight to replace the fork seals.

The following procedure describes how to change fork oil with the forks installed. The tubes can be flushed more completely by removing both fork tubes as outlined in Chapter Eight.

On models equipped with air valves in the fork tubes, refer to *Suspension Tuning* in this chapter to pressurize the front forks.

1. Remove the rubber plugs covering the handlebar bolts on models so equipped (**Figure 46**). Remove the 4 bolts securing the handlebars (**Figure 47**). Place a few rags on the fuel tank and carefully lay the handlebars back on the fuel tank.

NOTE
If desired, refer to Chapter Six and remove the tank to keep it from being damaged.

NOTE
On TSCC models, the fork caps can be removed with the handlebars in place.

2. On models equipped with air valves, remove the rubber fork cap (**Figure 48**) or protection cap (A, **Figure 49**) from the air valves and carefully bleed off the fork air pressure.
3. On models with screw-type fork cap bolts, loosen the upper fork pinch bolt (B, **Figure 49**) and unscrew the cap bolt (**Figure 50**).
4. On models without screw-type fork cap bolts, perform the following:
   a. Remove the rubber cap from the top of each fork tube (**Figure 48**).
   b. Carefully press down against the spring stopper and remove the snap ring securing the stopper (**Figure 51**).
   c. Remove the spring stopper with the spring collar.
5. Remove the upper and lower fork springs with the spring guides from each fork tube. Have a few rags ready as the fork springs are quite oily.
6. Place a drain pan under each fork leg and remove the fork drain screw (**Figure 52**). Allow several minutes for the forks to drain completely. Compress the forks a few times to help force the oil out.
7. Flush each fork tube with clean solvent. Allow several minutes for the forks to drain thoroughly. Install the drain screw.
8. Refer to **Table 2** and **Table 5** and add the specified amount and type of fork oil to each fork

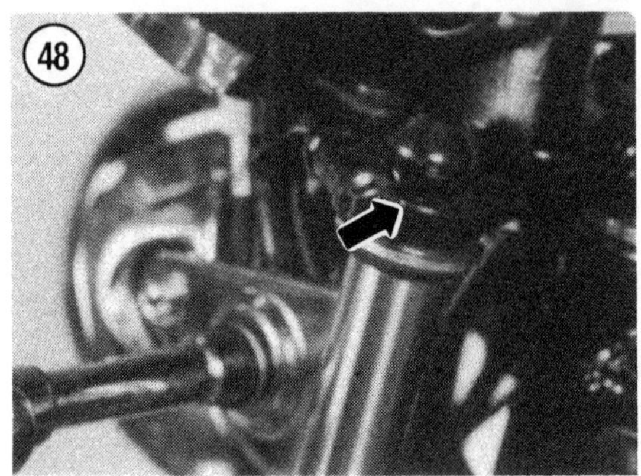

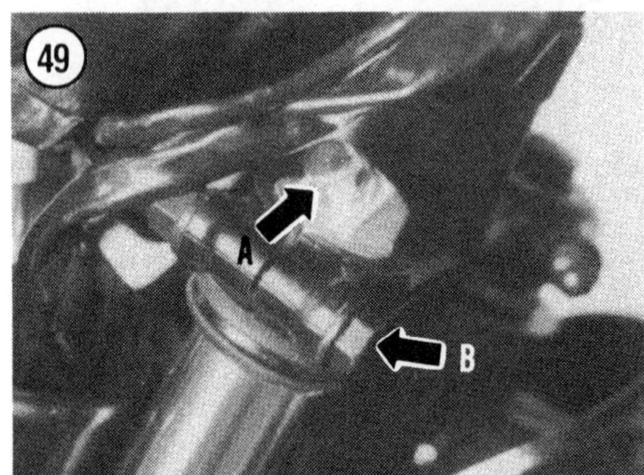

tube. Use a baby bottle to make sure the oil amount is correct for each fork tube.

NOTE
Suzuki recommends that the fork oil level be measured, if possible, to ensure a more accurate filling of each fork tube. Proceed to Step 9 to correctly set the fork oil level.

9. Compress the forks completely and raise the rear of the motorcycle until the fork tubes are perfectly vertical. If it is inconvenient to raise the rear of the motorcycle, it will be necessary to remove both fork tubes. Refer to Chapter Eight.

10. Use an accurate ruler or the Suzuki oil level gauge (part number 09943-74111) to ensure the oil level is as specified in **Table 5**. An oil level measuring device can be locally fabricated as shown in **Figure 53**. Fill the fork with a few cc's more than the required amount of oil. Position the hose clamp on the top edge of the fork tube and draw out the excess oil. Oil is sucked out until the level reaches the small diameter hole. A precise oil level can be achieved with this simple device.

11. Allow the oil to settle completely and recheck the oil level measurement. Adjust the oil level if necessary.

12. Install the fork springs with the closer wound coils pointing up and the smaller diameter coils pointing down. Make sure that the spring guide is installed between the upper and lower springs. On models without the screw-type fork cap, install the collar on top of the upper spring.

13. Check the condition of the O-ring on the fork cap or the spring stopper (**Figure 54**). Replace the O-ring if it is damaged or distorted.

52

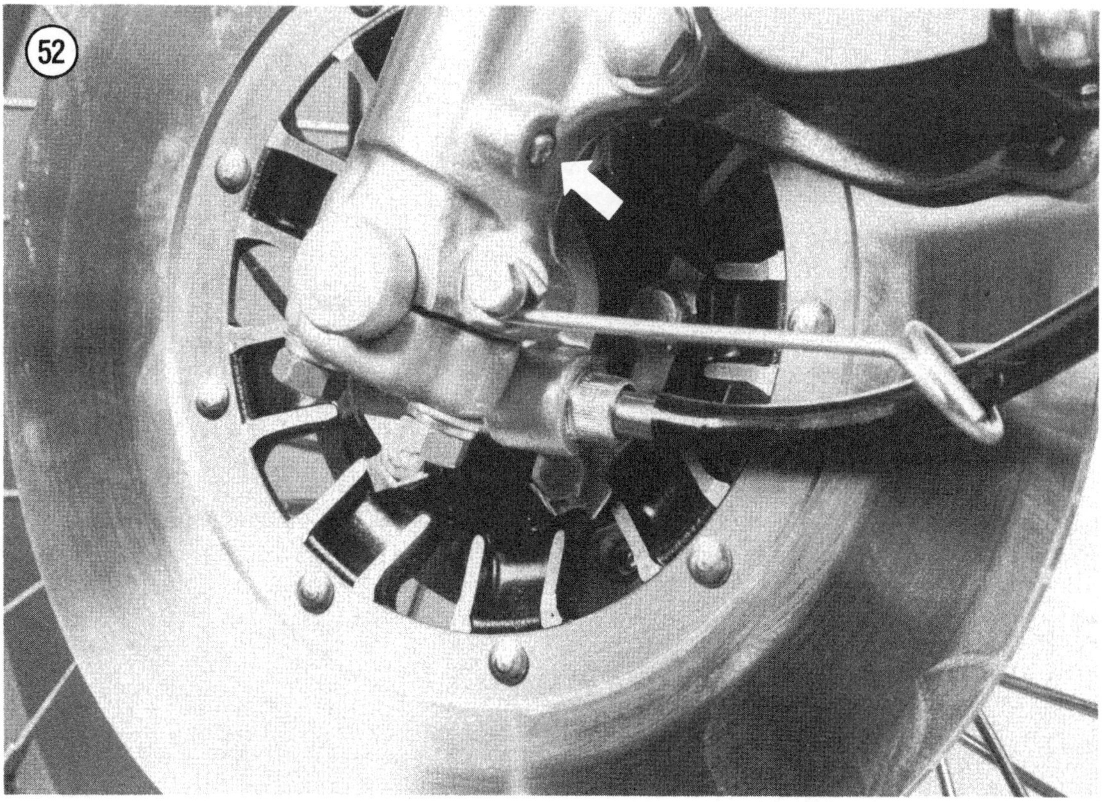

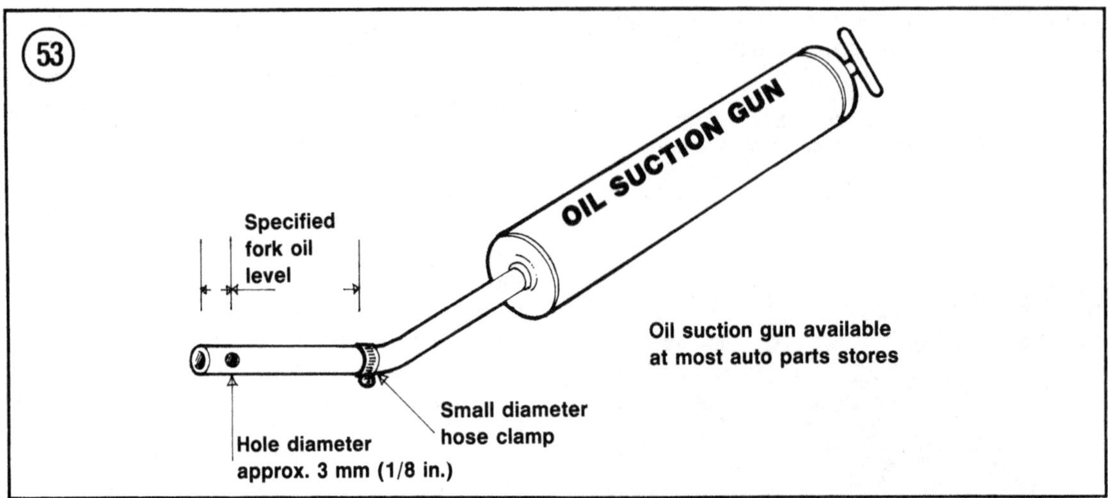

14. On models with screw-type fork cap bolts, install the fork caps. Torque the fork caps and the upper fork pinch bolt as specified in **Table 4**.
15. On models without screw-type fork cap bolts, install the spring stopper and press down on the stopper until the snap ring groove is exposed. Install the snap ring to secure the spring stopper. Make sure the snap ring is fully engaged in the groove in the fork tube. Install the rubber caps in the ends of the fork tubes.
16. Refer to **Figure 55** and install the handlebars. Make sure the punch mark is properly aligned and equal clearance is present on both sides of the handlebar holders. Torque the handlebar clamp bolts as specified in **Table 4**. Install the rubber plugs over the handlebar bolts on models so equipped.
17. On models with air valves, refer to *Suspension Tuning* in this chapter to pressurize the front forks.

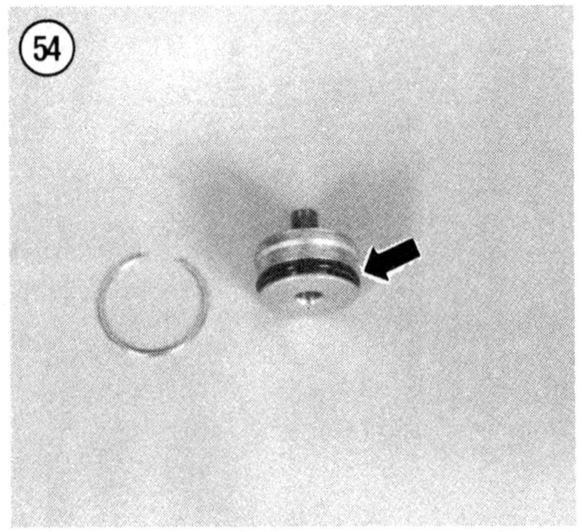

Steering Head Check

The steering head is fitted with 2 tapered roller bearings. The steering head should be checked for looseness at least as frequently as specified in **Table 1**.

Jack up the motorcycle so that the front wheel is clear of the ground. Hold onto the front fork tubes and rock the fork assembly back and forth (front to rear). If any looseness can be felt, refer to *Steering Head Adjustment* in Chapter Eight.

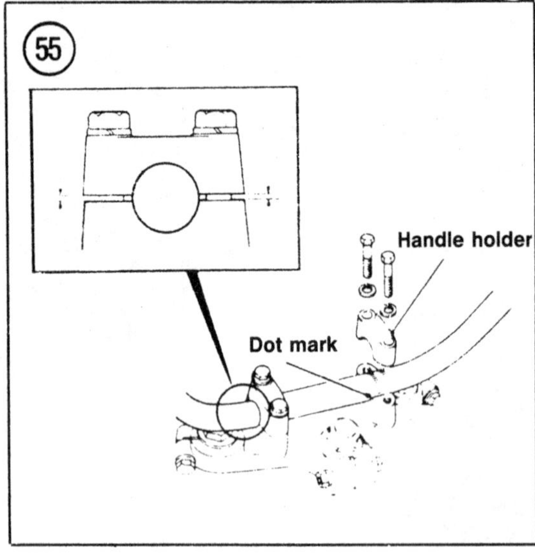

Throttle Grip

1. Loosen, but do not remove, the screws securing the throttle grip and switch housing to the handlebar (**Figure 56**).
2. Slide the throttle grip assembly off the handlebar.

3. Clean the end of the handlebar with a solvent-soaked rag. Dry the handlebar with a clean rag.
4. Apply a light coat of grease to the handlebar and slide the throttle grip assembly back into position.
5. Tighten the screws securing the throttle grip assembly. Check the action of the throttle. It should turn freely and snap back when released.

Swing Arm

Use a good grade of chassis grease or marine wheel bearing grease to lubricate the swing arm. Remove the pivot bolt as outlined under *Swing Arm, Removal/Installation* in Chapter Nine and inject grease directly into the swing arm bearings.

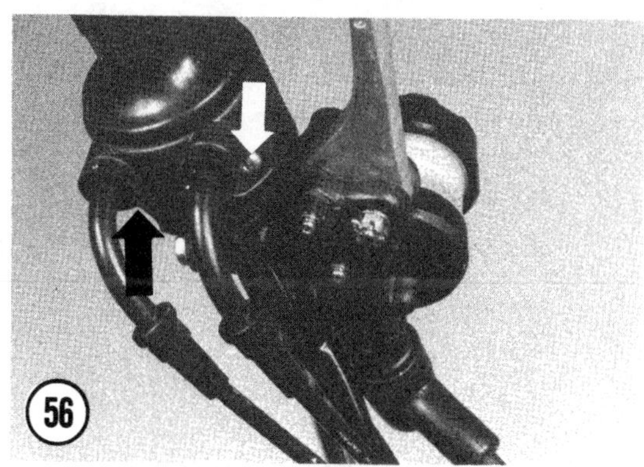

Oil Pressure Check

A special gauge is required for checking the oil pressure. Have the task performed by a dealer. Keep a record of pressure checks to determine if oil pressure decreases as engine wear increases.

The engines on all 1982 and earlier models are equipped with a high-volume, low pressure oil pump. Normal oil pressure is greater than 0.1 kg/cm^2 (1.42 psi) and less than 0.5 kg/cm^2 (7.11 psi) at 3,000 rpm.

The engines on all TSCC machines are equipped with a high pressure oil pump. Normal oil pressure is greater than 2.5 kg/cm^2 (35 psi) and less than 5.5 kg/cm^2 (78 psi) at 3,000 rpm.

Speedometer Drive

The speedometer drive (**Figure 57**) should be removed, cleaned and greased when the front wheel bearings are serviced. When installing the speedometer drive, ensure that the 2 dogs on the drive unit engage the slots in the front wheel hub. The embossed "UP" must be located as shown in **Figure 58**.

SUSPENSION TUNING

Proper suspension adjustment and tuning is necessary to provide optimum handling and comfort. Most late-model machines are equipped

3

with air valves in the fork tubes (**Figure 59**). Air valves allow air pressure to be pumped into the fork tubes to change the handling characteristics of the motorcycle as well as help support the weight of any touring gear or accessories that may be installed.

On the rear suspension, increase the spring pre-load as necessary to compensate for an additional passenger or touring equipment.

WARNING

All suspension components must be adjusted the same on both sides of the motorcycle; for example, the preload for each rear shock absorber spring must be set the same. Unequal adjustments of the forks or rear suspension components may cause handling instabilities.

Front Fork Air Pressure

It is necessary to maintain proper air pressure in the forks to obtain the best possible performance and to prevent premature fork tube wear.

Pressurizing the air forks is easiest with the Suzuki air gauge (part number 09940-44110) as shown in **Figure 60**. This gauge allows air to be pumped into or bled from the fork tubes in a very precise manner. No pressure is lost from the fork tube when the gauge is removed.

If the Suzuki special gauge is not available, air pressure can be set reasonably accurately with the small air gauge supplied with the motorcycle (**Figure 61**). When using the small gauge make sure it is placed squarely on the air valve and removed quickly to prevent as much air loss as possible. Normal air loss when the gauge is removed is 0.7-1.4 psi (0.05-0.10 kg/cm²).

1. Place the motorcycle on the centerstand and jack up the machine until the front wheel is clear of the ground.

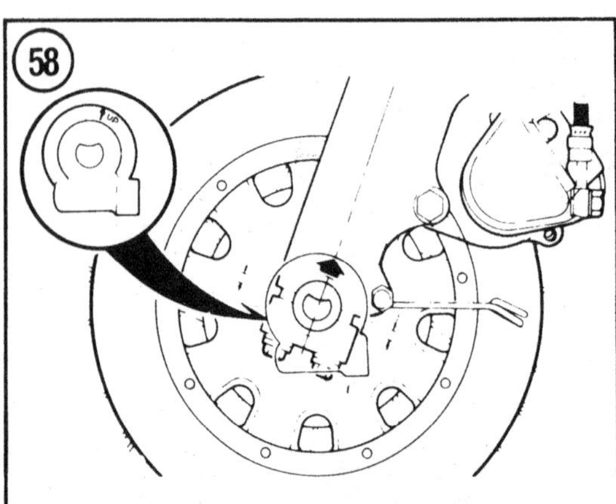

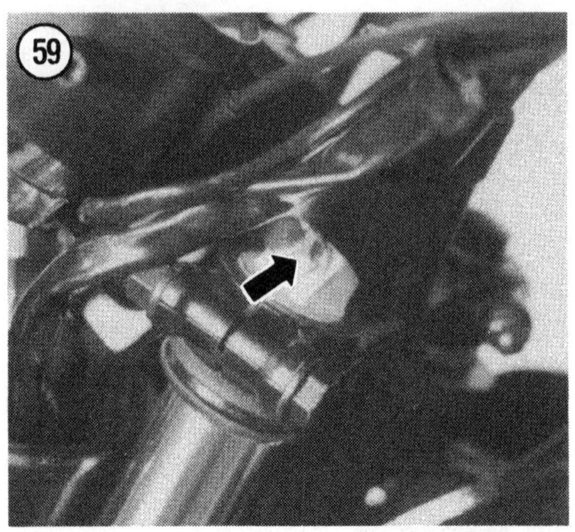

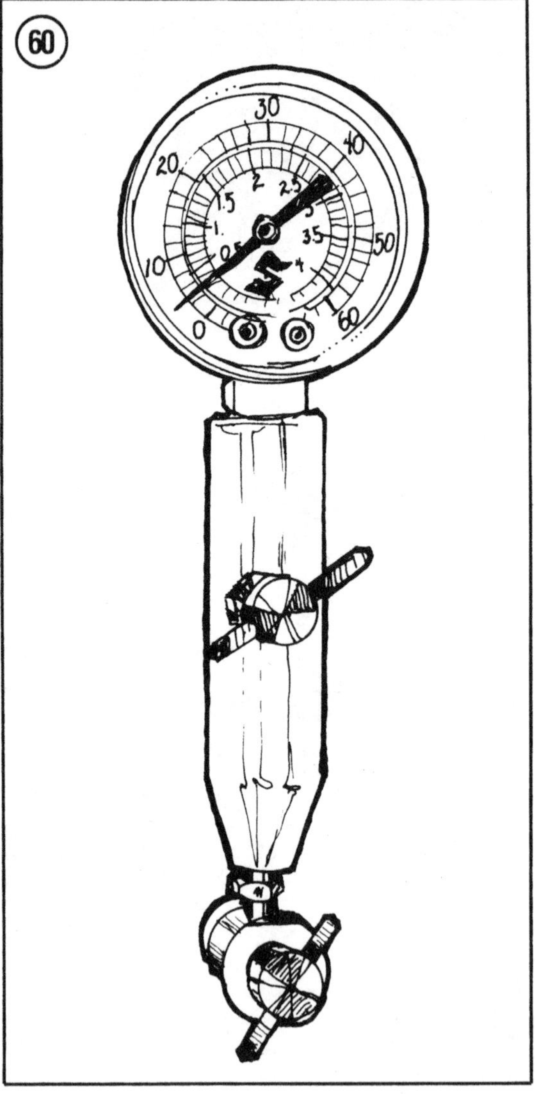

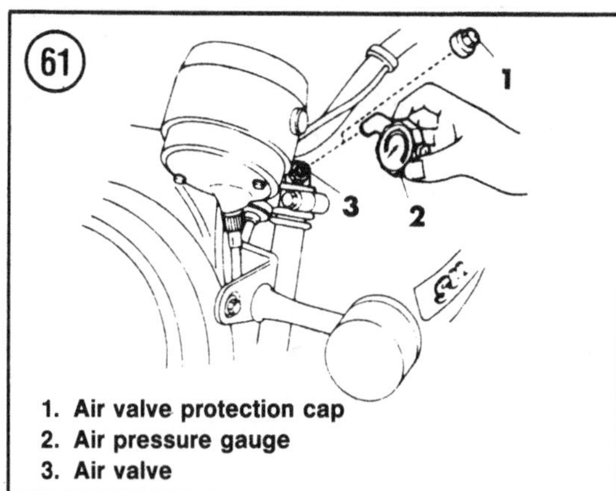

1. Air valve protection cap
2. Air pressure gauge
3. Air valve

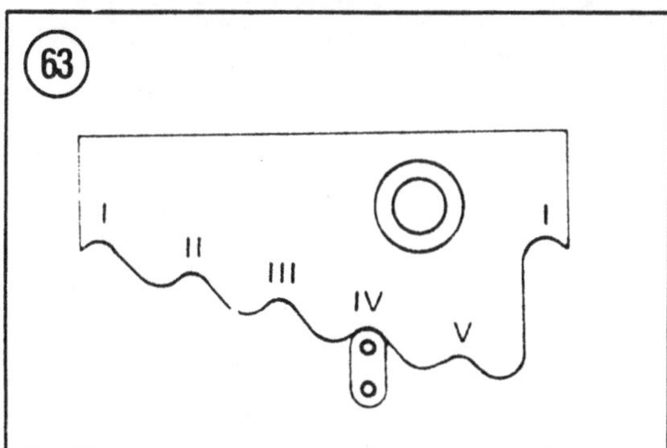

2. Remove the rubber fork cap (**Figure 62**) or protection cap (**Figure 59**) from the air valves and bleed off any remaining air pressure.
3. If using the Suzuki special air gauge, perform the following:
   a. Close the center valve on the air gauge.
   b. Back out the stem on the end valve.
   c. Carefully install the gauge on the air valve.
   d. Screw in the end valve stem. This opens the gauge chamber to the fork tube.
4. Connect a bicycle tire pump to the fork air valve or the center valve on the special air gauge.

CAUTION
Never use a high-pressure air supply (such as a service station air hose) to pressurize the fork tubes or the fork seals will be damaged. Use only a hand-operated tire pump for the best results.

5. Pump up pressure in the fork tube to approximately 1.8 kg/cm^2 (25 psi).

CAUTION
Do not exceed 2.5 kg/cm^2 (35 psi) or the fork seals may be damaged.

6. Slowly bleed air from the fork tubes until 0.3 kg/cm^2 (approximately 4 psi) is achieved. Use the center valve on the special air gauge to bleed off the excess air pressure. Maximum allowable difference between fork tubes is 0.1 kg/cm^2 (1.4 psi).
7. Remove the special air gauge as follows:
   a. Close the center bleed valve.
   b. Back out the stem on the end valve.
   c. Carefully unscrew the gauge from the fork air valve.
8. Install the air valve protection caps. Remove the jack from under the motorcycle.

Rear Spring Pre-load Adjustment

The rear shock absorbers on 1982 and earlier models have an adjustable spring pre-load mechanism as shown in **Figure 63**. The standard pre-load position is "I" (softest). Make sure that the pre-load is the same for both rear springs.

On TSCC models, the rear spring pre-load is adjusted with a remote mounted knob (**Figure 64**). The knob can be positioned in any one of 5 settings; "1" is softest, "5" stiffest. To adjust the pre-load place the machine on the side or centerstand and turn the knob to the desired setting.

ENGINE TUNE-UP

An engine tune-up consists of accurate and careful adjustments made to maintain maximum engine performance and efficiency. Because different systems in the engine interact to affect the overall performance, tune-ups must be carried out in the following order:

a. Valve clearance adjustment.
b. Ignition adjustment and timing (1977-1979 models).
c. Spark plug cleaning or replacement.
d. Carburetor synchronization.

Perform engine tune-up procedures at least as frequently as specified in **Table 1**. Refer to **Table 6** for all tune-up specifications.

All U.S. models manufactured after January 1, 1978 are engineered to meet stringent EPA (Environmental Protection Agency) regulations. All tune-up specifications must be strictly adhered to, whether the work is performed by the owner, dealer or an independent repair shop. Modifications to the ignition system, exhaust system and carburetion are forbidden by law unless modifications (aftermarket exhaust systems, etc.) have received written approval from the EPA. Engine idle speed and carburetor float level adjustments are permissable. Carburetor air screw adjustments are preset and must not be altered. Failure to comply with EPA regulations may result in heavy fines.

Valve Clearance Adjustment (1982 and Earlier Models)

CAUTION

Valve clearance adjustments must be performed when the engine is completely cold—not run for at least 12 hours. If the engine is not completely cold, the adjustments will not be accurate and engine damage may result.

1. Remove the fuel tank as outlined in Chapter Six.
2. On early models, remove the screws securing the end covers to the cylinder head and remove the covers (**Figure 65**).
3. Spring open the clamp securing the breather hose to the breather cover (**Figure 66**) and disconnect the hose from the cover.
4. Remove the bolts securing the breather cover and remove the cover (**Figure 67**).
5. Disconnect the horn wires (**Figure 68**). Remove the bracket securing the horn to the frame and remove the horn.
6. Disconnect the tachometer drive cable (**Figure 69**).
7. Remove each spark plug lead by pulling on the cap. Do not pull on the wire lead or it may be

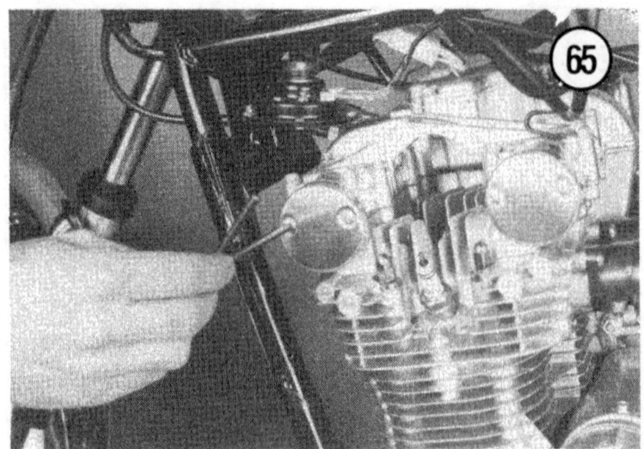

65

66

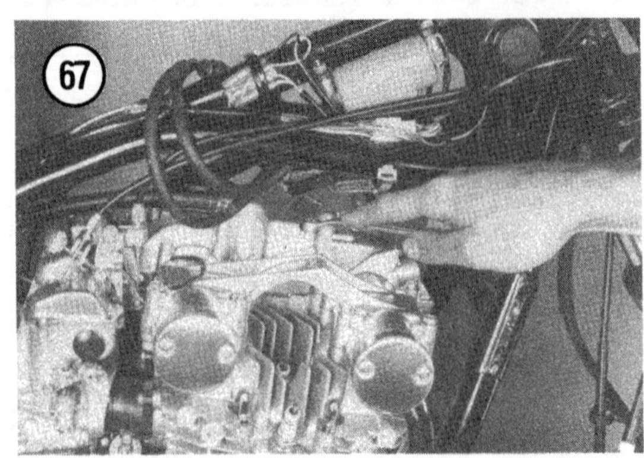

67

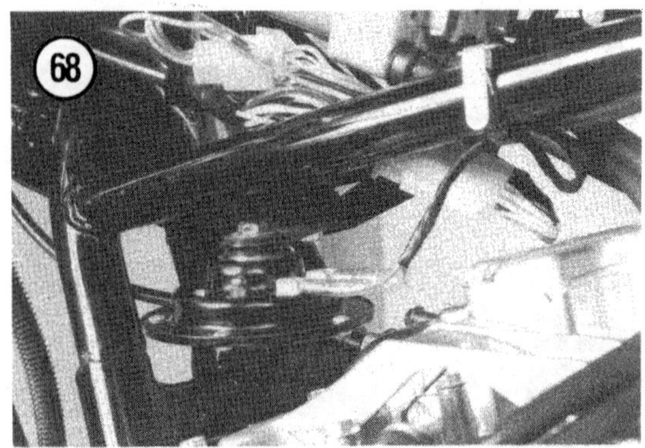

68

damaged. Tuck the spark plug leads into the upper frame to keep them clear of the engine. Blow away any dirt that may have accumulated around the spark plugs and remove the plugs. The crankshaft is easier to rotate with the spark plugs removed.

8. Remove the bolts securing the cam cover to the cylinder head. The left-front and right-rear cover bolts pass through dowel locating pins and are longer than the other cover bolts.

NOTE

To ease cam cover removal, tap around the sealing surface with a soft-faced mallet to help break it loose.

9. Torque the 12 cylinder head nuts to the value specified in **Table 4** in the order shown in **Figure 70**. Then torque both the end bolts (**Figure 71**) and the bolt between the center exhaust ports (**Figure 72**) to the specified value.

10. Remove the fasteners securing the ignition cover and remove the cover (**Figure 73**).

11. Use a 19 mm wrench to rotate the crankshaft until one camshaft lobe is positioned as shown in **Figure 74**.

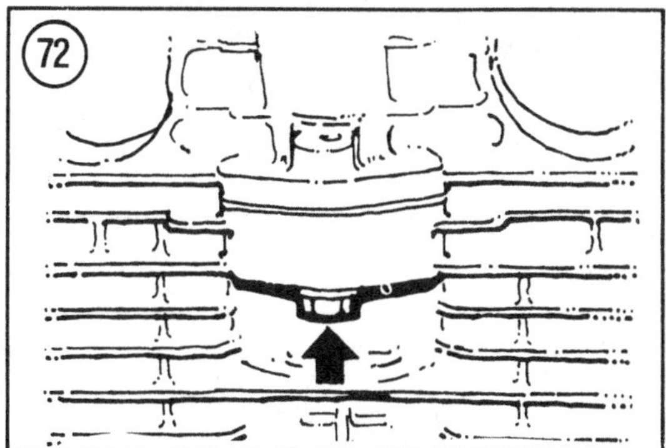

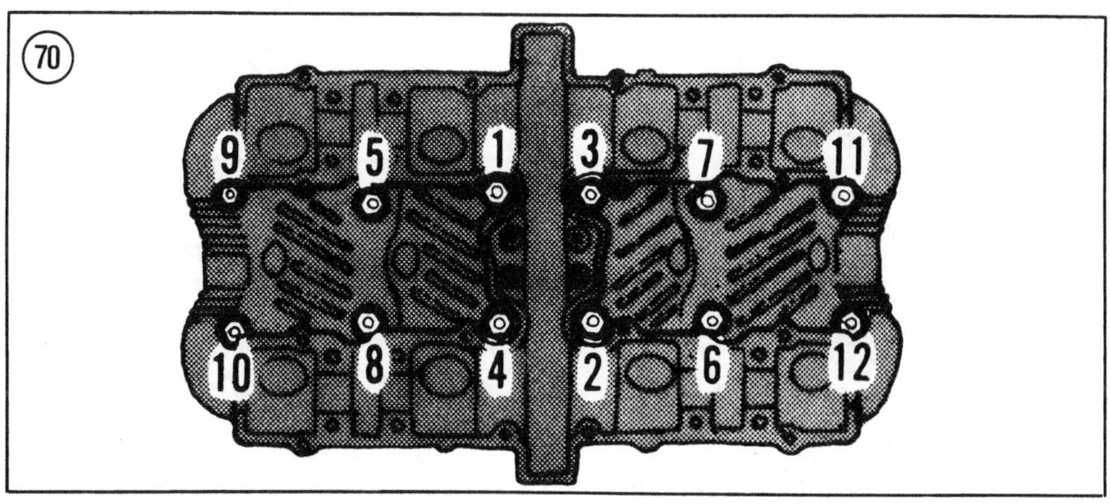

CAUTION
To rotate crankshaft, always use a wrench on the large hex portion of the advance governor as shown in ***Figure 75****. Do not attempt to rotate the crankshaft by using the small bolt that secures the advance governor or the bolt may twist off.*

12. Use a feeler gauge between the heel of the camshaft and the tappet adjuster shim as shown in **Figure 76** to measure the valve clearance. The feeler gauge blade must move smoothly between the adjustment shim and heel of the camshaft, but with noticeable resistance and no free play. The correct valve clearance for all valves (intake and exhaust) is 0.03-0.08 mm (0.001-0.003 in.).

NOTE
The Suzuki feeler gauge set (part No. 09900-20803) contains several small gauges not normally found in feeler gauge sets.

13. If the valve clearance is not as specified, write down the exact clearance for each valve tappet. Repeat Steps 11 and 12 until the clearance for all valves has been checked and each out-of-tolerance clearance recorded. To correct an out-of-tolerance condition, the adjustment shim on the top of each tappet must be replaced as described in the following steps.

14. At each valve to be adjusted, rotate the engine until the cam lobe faces away from the tappet (valve fully closed). Rotate the tappet by hand until the notch in the tappet is fully exposed and accessible (**Figure 77**).

15. Use a Suzuki tappet depressor (part No. 09916-64510) as shown in **Figure 78** to press down carefully on the tappet. Make sure that the depressor tools bears against the edge of the tappet and not on the shim (**Figure 79**).

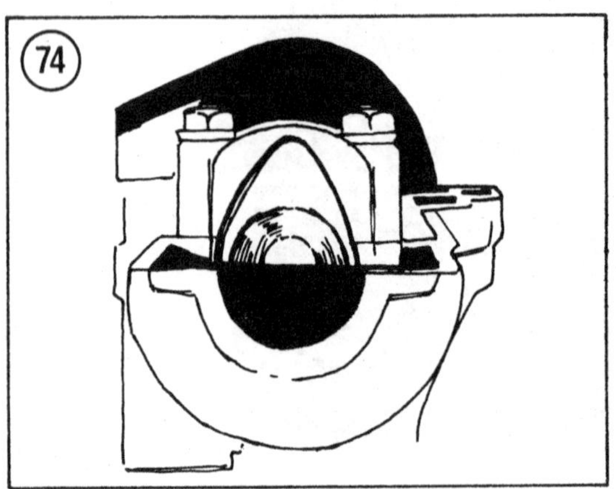
74

75

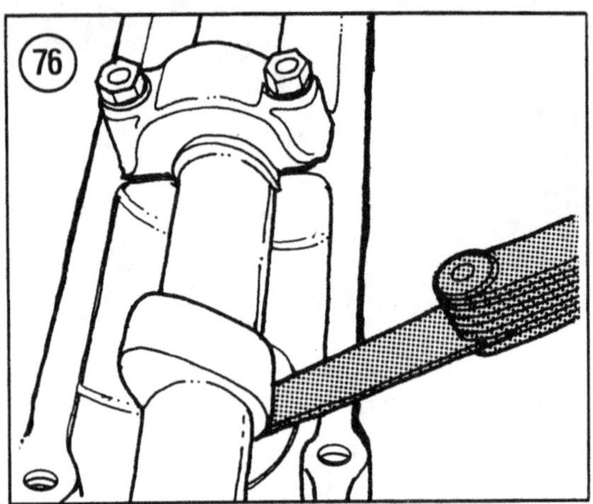
76

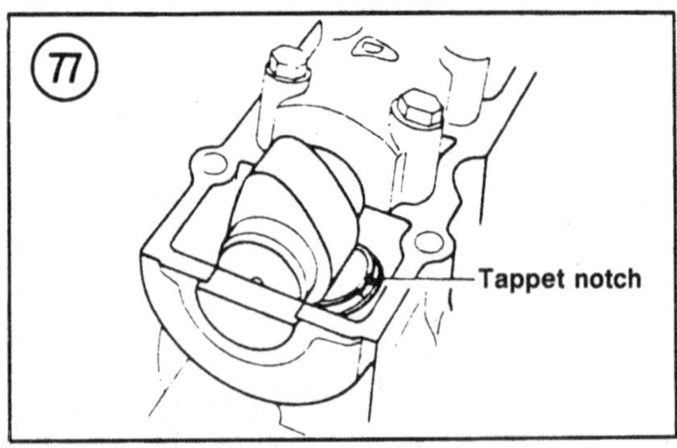

77

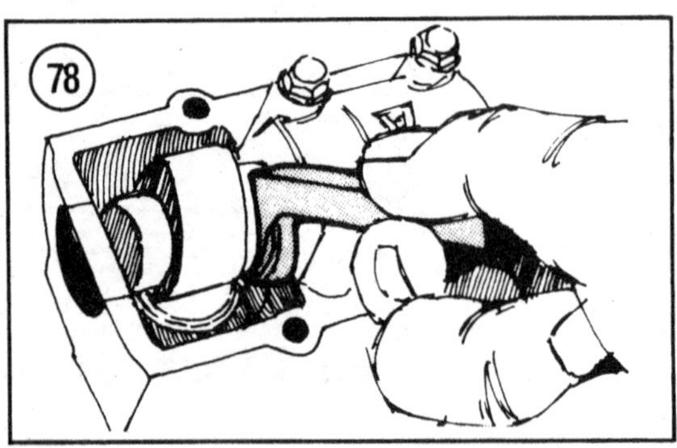
78

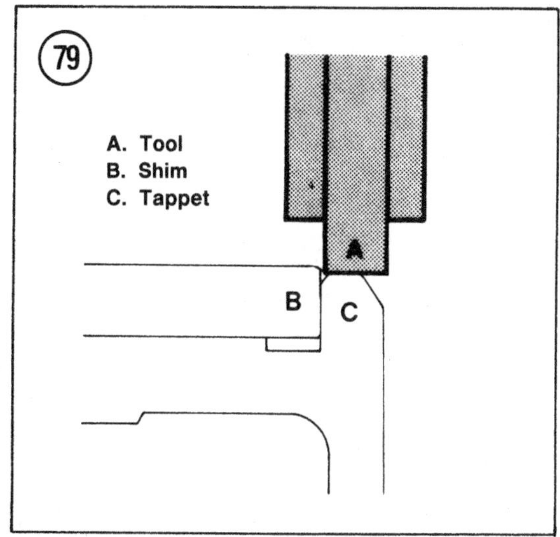

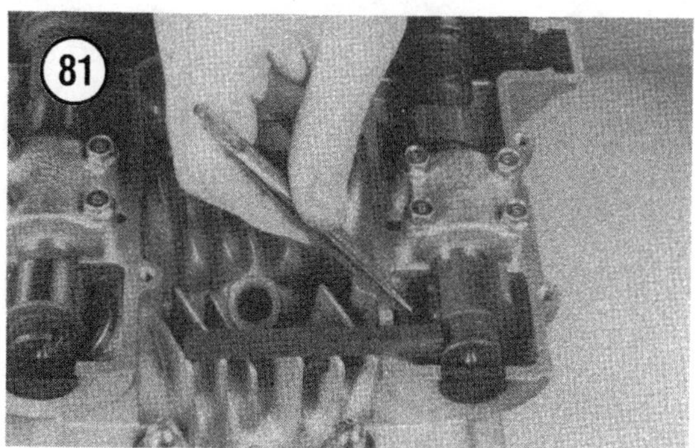

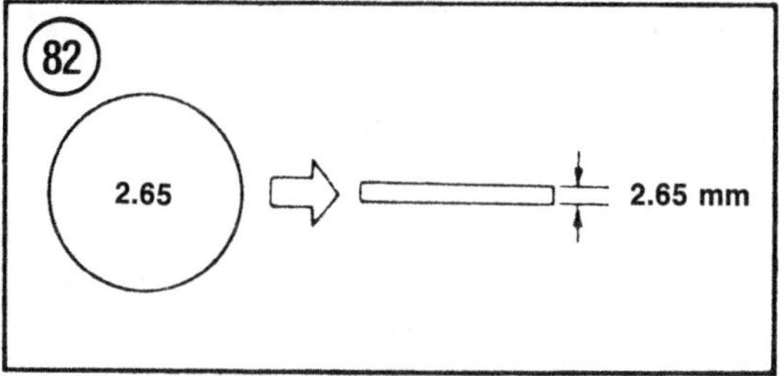

NOTE
A tappet depressor tool is also available from Rocky Cycle Co. This tool (part No. 15-0981) can be ordered from most dealers or motorcycle accessory stores.

16. Use a small screwdriver inserted in the tappet notch to pry the adjustment shim loose from the tappet (**Figure 80**); the surface tension caused by oil may make the shim difficult to remove. Use tweezers or small needlenose pliers to lift out the adjustment shim (**Figure 81**).

3

CAUTION
Never use a magnet to lift out the adjustment shims. They are made of hardened steel and are easily magnetized. A magnetized part will attract and hold metal particles which will cause excessive wear. A magnetized adjustment shim could also lift out of a tappet while the engine is running, causing serious and expensive engine damage.

17. Write down the size of each adjustment shim as it is removed. The numbers are etched on each shim (**Figure 82**).

NOTE
*If the etched numbers on the shim are not visible, it will be necessary to measure the shim thickness with a micrometer as shown in **Figure 83**.*

18. Refer to **Table 7** and calculate the required replacement shim as described in the following typical example:

Actual valve clearance: 0.10 mm.
Desired clearance (maximum): 0.08 mm.
Difference (excessive clearance): 0.02 mm.
Existing shim size: 2.45 mm.

The clearance in this example is at least 0.02 mm too large. This excessive clearance must be reduced by substituting a thicker adjustment shim. **Table 7** indicates that the next larger shim, No. 8, is 2.50 mm. This shim will reduce the clearance by 0.05 mm. The clearance will then be 0.05 mm, well within the specified clearance range.

19. Oil both sides of the replacement shim before installing the shim on the valve tappet. Install the shim with the etched numbers down against the tappet.

20. After all the adjustment shims have been replaced, rotate the crankshaft several times to make sure that the shims are properly seated in the valve tappets. Recheck the valve clearances and readjust if necessary.

21. Apply a thin film of Suzuki Bond No. 1215 or equivalent to both sides of a new cam cover gasket and install the gasket on the cam cover (**Figure 84**). Allow a few minutes for the bond to become tacky. Make sure that all 4 half-moon shaped rubber end plugs (**Figure 85**) are in place in the cylinder head.
22. Carefully position the cam cover on the cylinder head so the gasket is not disturbed. Rotate the exposed end of the tachometer drive gear (**Figure 86**) as the cam cover is installed to allow the drive gear to engage the camshaft.

CAUTION
The tachometer drive gear must engage the camshaft as the cam cover is installed or the gear will be damaged when the cover bolts are tightened.

23. Install the cam cover bolts. The 2 longer bolts are positioned in the left-front and right-rear positions. Tighten all the bolts gradually and evenly in a crisscross pattern to the torque specified in **Table 4**.
24. Install the breather cover (**Figure 67**) and connect the hose to the cover.
25. On early models, install the end covers on the cylinder head (**Figure 65**).
26. Connect the tachometer drive cable.
27. Install the ignition cover. Replace the gasket if damaged.
28. Install the spark plugs and connect the 4 spark plug leads. Make sure the caps fit securely over the spark plugs.
29. Install the fuel tank as outlined in Chapter Six and install the horn.

Valve Clearance Adjustment (TSCC Engines)

CAUTION
Valve clearance adjustments must be performed when the engine is completely cold—not run for at least 12 hours. If the engine is not completely cold, the adjustments will not be accurate and engine damage may result.

1. Remove the fuel tank as outlined in Chapter Six.
2. Spring open the clamp securing the breather hose to the breather cover (**Figure 87**) and disconnect the hose from the cover.
3. Disconnect the tachometer drive cable (**Figure 88**).
4. Remove each spark plug lead by pulling on the cap. Do not pull on the wire lead or it may be damaged. Tuck the spark plug leads into the upper frame to keep them clear of the engine. Blow away

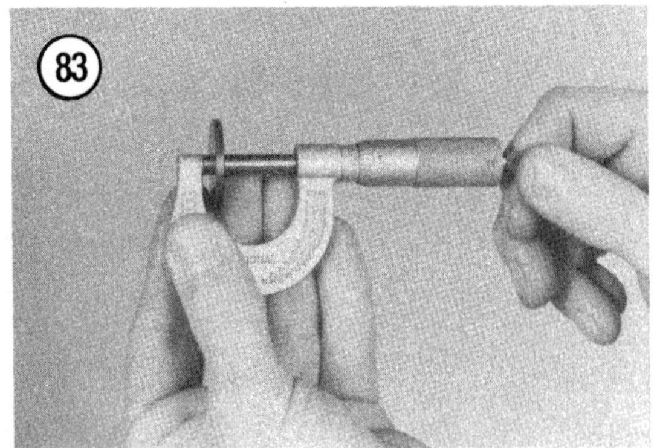
83

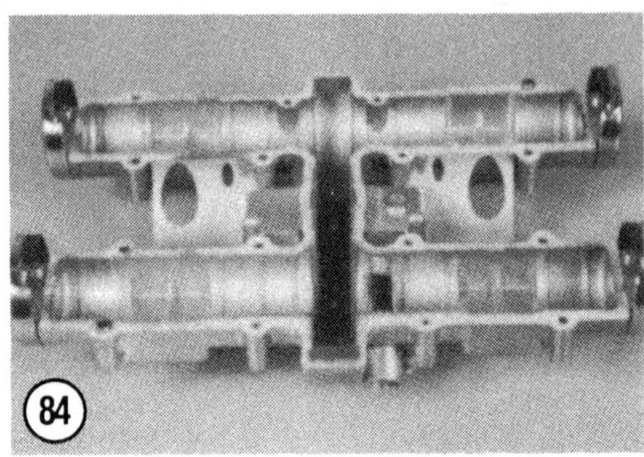
84

85

86

any dirt that may have accumulated around the spark plugs and remove the plugs. The crankshaft is easier to rotate by hand with the spark plugs removed.

5. Remove the bolts securing the cam cover and remove the cover (**Figure 89**).

NOTE

To ease cam cover removal, tap around the sealing surface with a soft-faced mallet to help break it loose.

6. Torque the 12 cylinder head nuts to the value specified in **Table 4** in the order shown in **Figure 90**. Then torque the bolt between the center exhaust ports to the specified value (**Figure 91**).

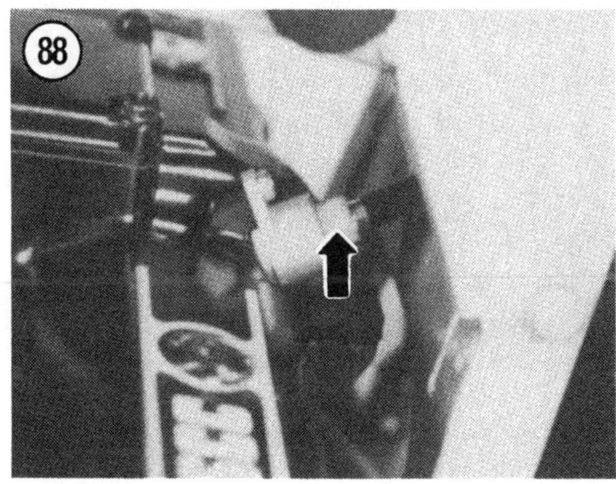

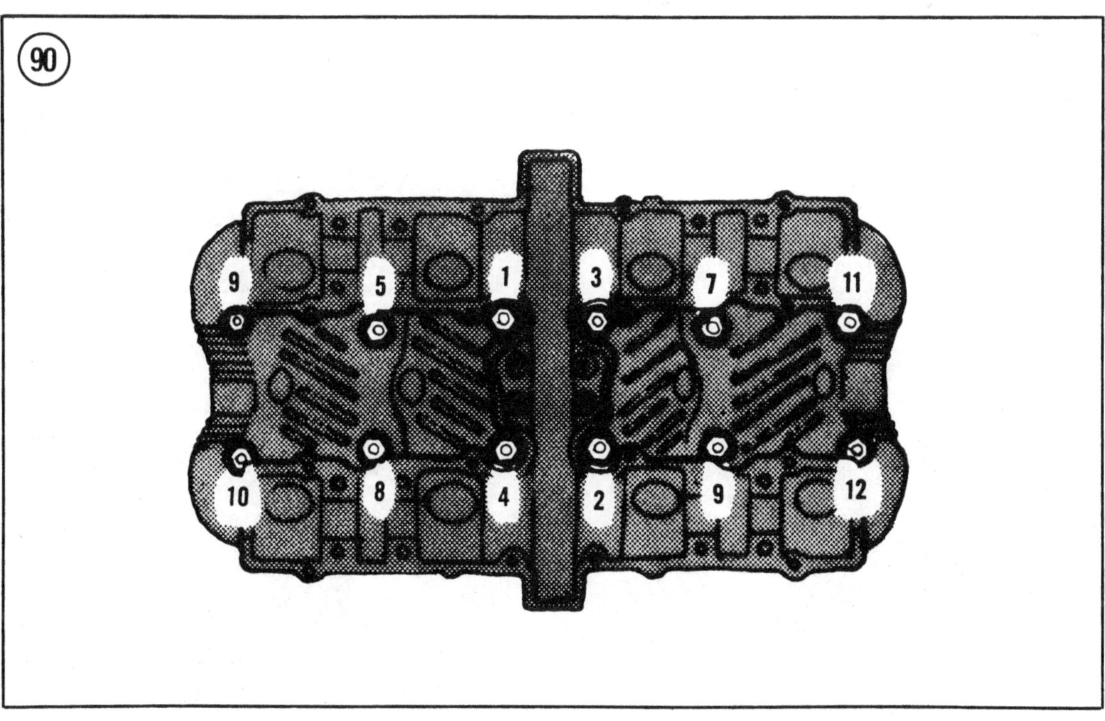

7. Remove the screws securing the ignition cover and remove the cover (**Figure 92**).
8. Use a 19 mm wrench to rotate the crankshaft until the "T" mark is aligned with the center of the left signal generator coil (**Figure 93**).
9. Observe the notches in the end of each camshaft (**Figure 94**). Refer to **Table 8** to determine which valves to adjust depending on the position of the notches. The cylinders are numbered 1 through 4 from left to right.
10. Use a feeler gauge between the valve stem and the adjuster (**Figure 95**) to determine the valve clearance. The correct valve clearance for all valves (intake and exhaust) is 0.08-0.13 mm (0.003-0.005 in.).

NOTE
The Suzuki feeler gauge set (part No. 09900-20803) contains several small gauges not normally found in feeler gauge sets.

11. If the valve clearance is not as specified, perform the following:
   a. Loosen the valve adjuster locknut with a 9 mm wrench (**Figure 96**).
   b. Place a feeler gauge blade of the correct clearance between the valve stem and adjuster and slowly rotate the adjuster until some resistance can be felt as the blade is inserted and withdrawn. The feeler gauge blade must move smoothly between the valve stem and the adjuster, but with noticeable resistance and no free play.

NOTE
The Suzuki adjuster tool (part No. 09917-14910) is recommended for use on the square shaft end of the valve adjusters. This small and inexpensive Suzuki tool is much easier to use around the confines of the cylinder head than a larger wrench.

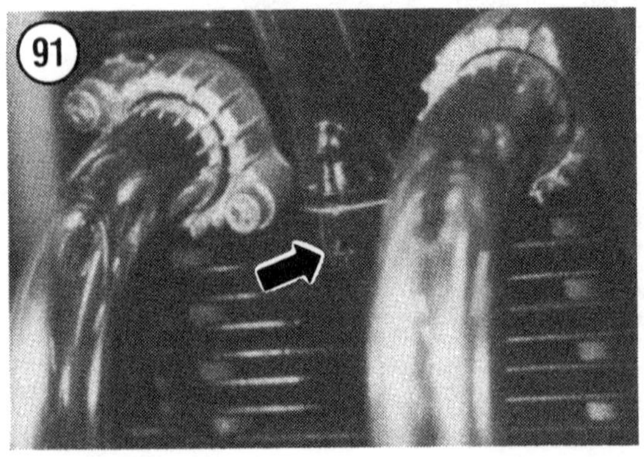
91

92

93

94

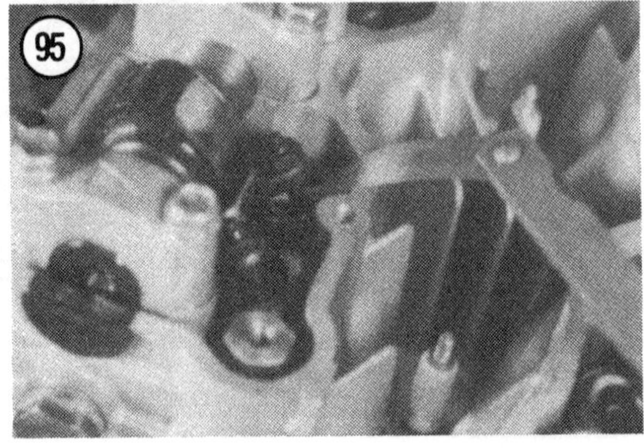
95

96

97

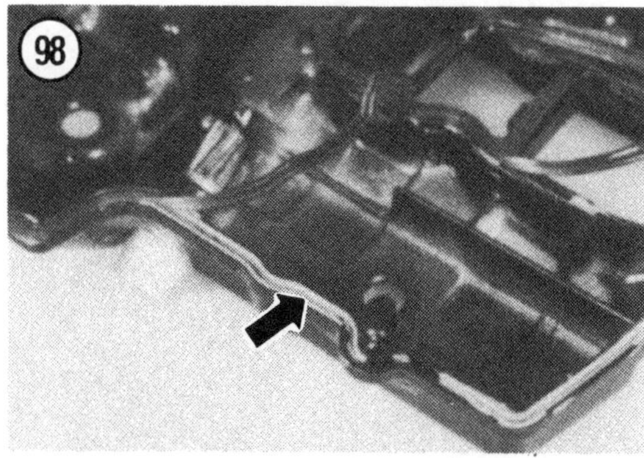
98

99

c. Hold the adjuster carefully and tighten the adjuster locknut (**Figure 97**).

d. Recheck the valve clearance. Frequently the clearance will change slightly as the locknut is tightened. Readjust if necessary. Make sure to check all valve clearances that are possible with the camshaft notches in the present position (**Table 8**).

12. Rotate the crankshaft 360° until the "T" mark is again aligned with the center of the left signal generator coil. The notches in the end of the camshaft must now point in the opposite direction from that noted in Step 9.

13. Refer to **Table 8** and check the valve clearance for the other valves. Adjust the valve clearance, if necessary, as described in Step 11.

14. After adjusting all the valve clearances, rotate the crankshaft several times and recheck all clearances. Readjust the valves as necessary. Make sure all adjuster locknuts are tight. If a torque wrench is available, tighten all locknuts to 0.9-1.1 mkg (6.5-8 ft.-lb.).

15. If installing a new gasket, apply a thin film of Suzuki Bond No. 1207B to the groove in the cam cover (**Figure 98**). Allow a few minutes for the bond to become tacky and install the new gasket into the cam cover.

16. Apply a thin film of Suzuki Bond No. 1207B or equivalent to the edge of each half-moon shaped rubber end on the cam cover gasket.

17. Check the O-rings in the top of the cam cover (**Figure 99**). Replace the O-rings if they are hardened or damaged.

18. Carefully position the cam cover on the cylinder head so the gasket is not disturbed. Rotate the exposed end of the tachometer drive gear as the cam cover is installed to allow the drive gear to engage the camshaft.

CAUTION

The tachometer drive gear must engage the camshaft as the cam cover is installed or the gear will be damaged when the cover bolts are tightened.

19. Install the cam cover bolts. Tighten all the bolts gradually and evenly in a crisscross pattern to the torque specified in **Table 4**.

20. Install the breather cover and connect the breather hose to the cover.

21. Connect the tachometer drive cable.

22. Install the spark plugs and connect the 4 spark plug leads. Make sure the caps fit securely over the spark plugs.

23. Install the fuel tank as outlined in Chapter Six.

Contact Breaker Point and Timing Adjustment (1977-1979 Models)

1. Remove the bolts securing the ignition cover and remove the cover (**Figure 100**).
2. Use a wrench on the 19 mm hex portion of the crankshaft (**Figure 101**) to rotate the crankshaft until the breaker points for cylinders No. 1 and 4 are fully open.
3. Loosen the screws securing the breaker points to the breaker plate (**Figure 102**) and set the point gap with a flat feeler gauge to 0.3-0.4 mm (0.012-0.016 in.). Tighten the screws. Recheck the point gap as it often changes when the screws are tightened. Readjust the gap if necessary.
4. Rotate the crankshaft clockwise until the "F" mark for cylinders No. 1 and 4 is aligned with the mark on the timing plate as viewed through the window in the breaker plate. See **Figure 103** (breaker plate removed for clarity). Make sure the "1-4" is visible below the "F" mark.
5. Connect a timing tester or continuity device to the electrical terminal (**Figure 104**) and a good ground on the engine. If using a continuity tester do *not* turn on the motorcycle ignition.
6. Loosen the screws securing the breaker plate (**Figure 105**) and rotate the plate until the breaker points just begin to open (no continuity on the tester). Tighten the breaker plate screws. Rotate the crankshaft a few turns and double-check the adjustment. Readjust if necessary.
7. Rotate the crankshaft clockwise until the "F" mark for cylinders No. 2 and 3 is aligned with the mark on the timing plate (**Figure 106**). Make sure the "2-3" is visible below the "F" mark.
8. Connect the continuity device leads to the point terminal shown in **Figure 107** and to ground.
9. Loosen the screws securing the half-plate (**Figure 108**) and adjust the plate until the points just begin to open (no continuity). Tighten the screws, rotate the crankshaft and double-check the adjustment. Readjust if necessary.

NOTE

This completes the breaker point adjustment and static engine timing. More precise engine timing can be achieved with a strobe-type timing light as described in the following steps.

10. Connect the timing light to cylinder No. 1 or 4 according to the light manufacturer's instructions. Either spark plug (1 or 4) will provide correct timing as both plugs spark at the same time.
11. Start and warm up the engine. Run the engine below 1,500 rpm and direct the timing light into the window on the breaker plate. The "F" mark should be correctly aligned (**Figure 103**). If the timing is not correct, loosen the breaker plate screws (**Figure 105**) and gradually move the plate until the marks are correct. Only a small amount of movement should be necessary to align the marks. Tighten the breaker plate screws.
12. Increase the engine speed above 2,500 rpm. Check that the advance timing marks align as shown in **Figure 109**. If the timing marks are not aligned, loosen the breaker plate screws and gradually move the breaker plate until the marks are aligned. Tighten the screws.

NOTE

If correct timing below 1,500 rpm and above 2,500 rpm is difficult to obtain, remove the breaker plate and make sure the advance governor weights move freely. If the advance weights do not bind and a slight variation in timing marks still exists, set the timing using the 2,500 rpm marks. This ensures the timing is perfect during the engine's normal rpm range.

13. Repeat Step 11 and Step 12 for cylinders No. 2 and 3. To adjust timing for cylinders No. 2 and 3, loosen the screws in the half-plate (**Figure 108**).
14. Install the ignition cover.

Ignition Timing (1980 and Later Models)

All 1980 and later models are equipped with a breakerless electronic ignition system. The timing is pre-set and cannot be adjusted. See Chapter Seven for ignition component test procedures if you suspect the ignition system is not operating properly.

Spark Plug Cleaning and Replacement

1. Grasp the spark plug wire by the cap and pull it off the spark plug. Never pull on the lead itself or the wire could be damaged.

3

2. If compressed air is available, blow away any dirt they may have accumulated in each spark plug well.
3. Use a spark plug socket to remove the spark plugs.
4. Inspect the spark plugs carefully. Refer to the illustrations in Chapter Two. Check for broken or cracked porcelain, excessively eroded electrodes and excessive carbon or oil fouling. If deposits are light the plugs may be cleaned in solvent or contact cleaner. A wire brush or spark plug sandblast cleaner can also be used.
5. Use a wire spark plug gauge to measure the gap between the center and side electrodes (**Figure 110**). The gauge should fit through the gap with a slight drag. If there is no drag or if the gauge will not fit, bend the side electrode with a special gapping tool (**Figure 111**).
6. Install the spark plug finger-tight, then tighten an additional 1/8-1/4 turn. If a torque wrench is available, torque the plug to 1.5-2 mkg (11-14.5 ft.-lb.).

Throttle Cable Adjustment

Throttle cable free play should be 0.5-1.0 mm (1/32-1/16 in.). If cable adjustment is necessary loosen the upper and lower locknuts securing the cable adjuster and turn the adjuster in or out until the specified free play is achieved. See **Figure 112** for machines with 2 cables and **Figure 113** for single cable models. Tighten the locknuts.

Fuel Strainer

A fuel strainer is fitted to the fuel valve. To clean the fuel strainer it is necessary to remove the fuel tank and remove the fuel valve from the tank. Refer to Chapter Six for fuel tank and fuel valve removal procedures.

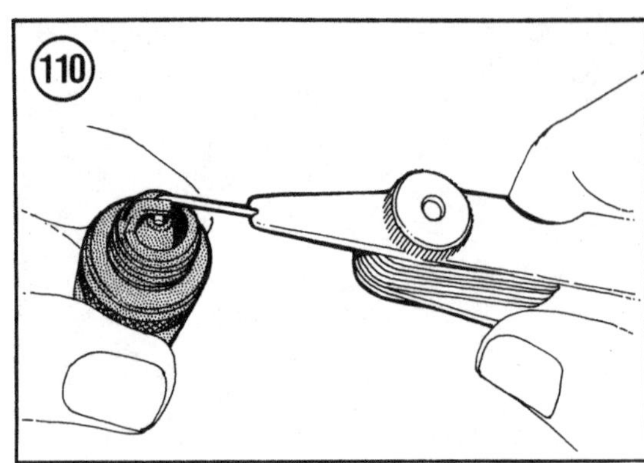

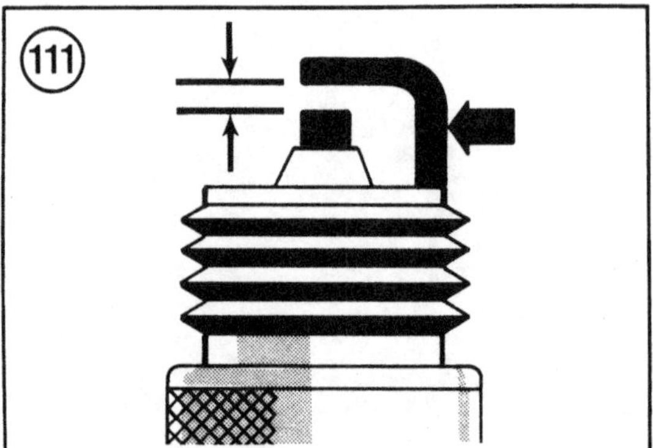

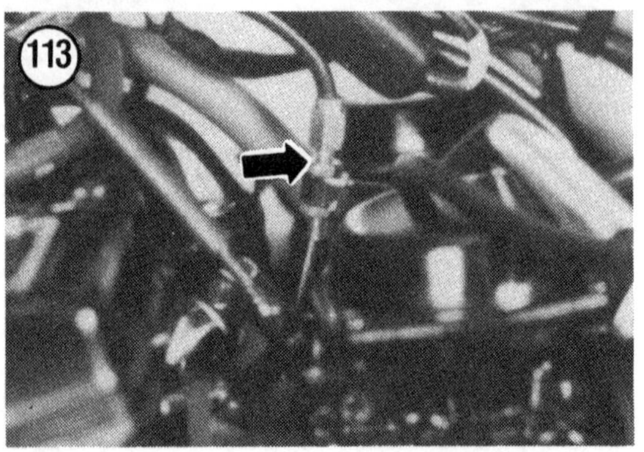

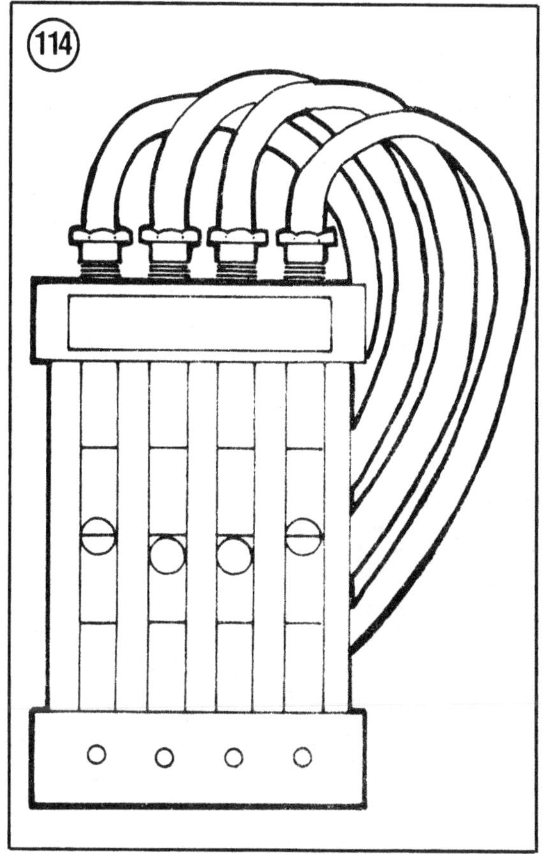

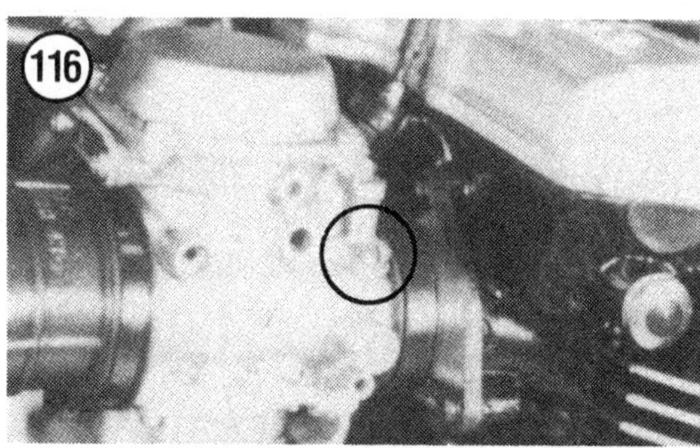

Carburetor Synchronization

Carburetor synchronization or balancing is essential for maximum performance and smooth engine operation. A special gauge, called a manometer, is required to perform the job accurately. The device shown in **Figure 114** is a typical example. Suzuki markets a similar model (part No. 00913-13121). There are other brands of gauges on the market that work equally well; check the gauge manufacturer's instructions.

NOTE
Suzuki carburetor balancer adapters are necessary for this procedure. Four adapters (part No. 09913-13140) are required for 1977-1982 models. For TSCC models, 2 adapters (part No. 09915-94511) are required.

NOTE
The following procedure describes synchronization for engines with 4 carburetors. On TSCC models with 2 carburetors, the procedure is identical; however, only 2 hoses on the gauge need be calibrated and used.

1. Before beginning the task, the gauge must be calibrated; this must be done each time the gauge is used. On 1982 and earlier models, remove one 4 mm Allen bolt from an intake manifold (**Figure 115**). On TSCC models, remove the bolt from the carburetor body (**Figure 116**).
2. Install a balancer adapter and connect the first hose of the gauge to the adapter.
3. Start the engine and adjust the throttle stop screw to maintain a steady 1,750 rpm. See **Figure 117** for 1977-1979 models and **Figure 118** for

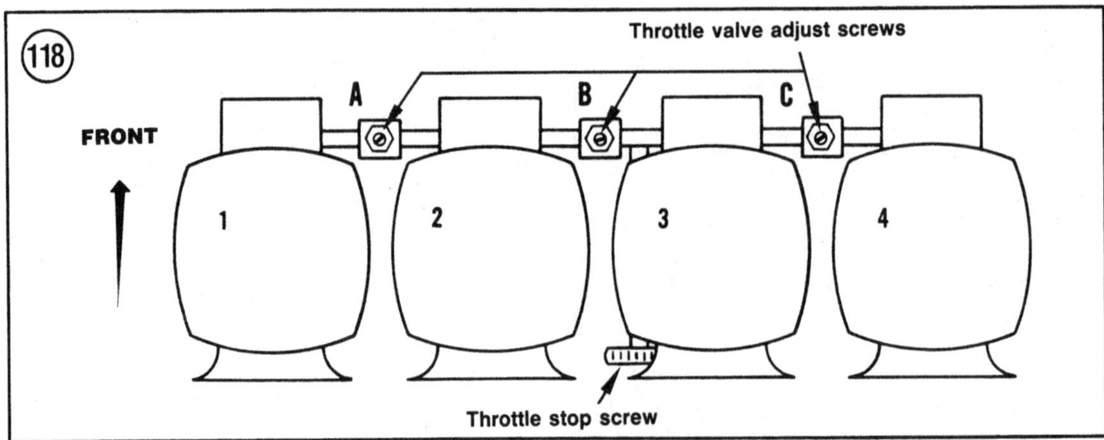

1980-1982 models. See **Figure 119** for TSCC models.

4. Turn the air adjustment screw on the gauge (for the tube connected to the engine) until the steel ball lines up with the center mark as shown in **Figure 120**. This tube is now calibrated.
5. Remove the calibrated hose and connect the other hoses, one at a time, to the same cylinder. Each time a hose is connected, adjust the respective air adjustment screw until the ball is aligned on the center mark as shown in **Figure 120**. The 4 air hoses have now been calibrated to each other.
6. Install the balance adapters in the remaining cylinders.
7. Connect all 4 hoses of the synchronization gauge to all 4 cylinders (2 on TSCC models). Start and run the engine at a steady 1,750 rpm.
8. Observe the gauge and note the following:
   a. On 1977-1979 models, balls must be aligned with each other.
   b. On 1980-1982 models, the 2 center balls must be slightly lower than the end balls as shown in **Figure 120**.
   c. On TSCC models, both gauge balls must be aligned with each other.
9. If the gauge balls are positioned as described in Step 8, the carburetors are synchronized. If further adjustment is unnecessary, proceed to Step 10. If one or more carburetors are out of sync, turn off the engine and perform the following:
   a. Remove the fuel tank as outlined in Chapter Six. Plug the tank valve-to-carburetor vacuum line with a small wooden dowel such as a golf tee or pencil. Restart the engine.

NOTE
The carburetors should contain enough gasoline to perform the adjustments

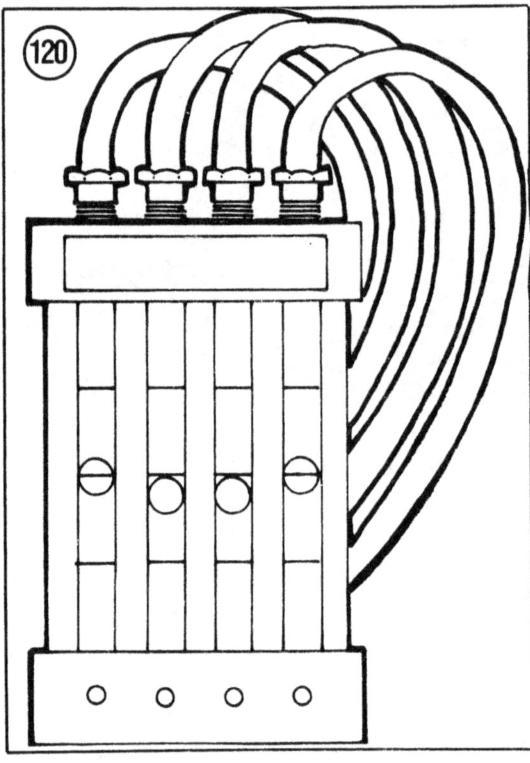

121

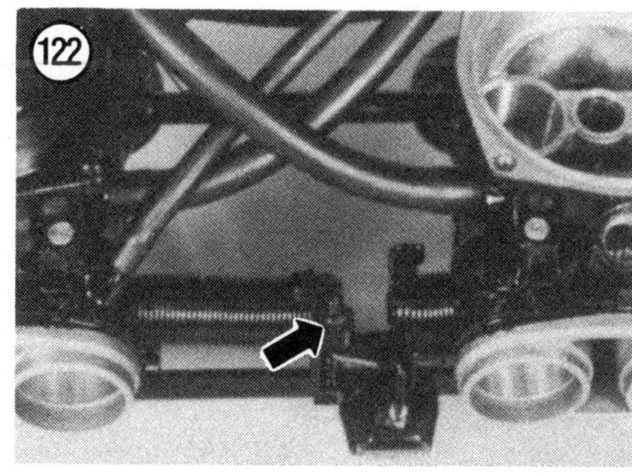

122

with the tank removed. If the engine should run out of fuel before the adjustment procedure is completed, temporarily install the fuel tank and lines. Turn the fuel valve to the "PRI" position to fill the carburetors.

b. On 1977-1979 models, remove the screws securing the cover on each carburetor that needs to be adjusted. Loosen the locknut securing the slide lifter (**Figure 121**). Turn the adjusting screw until the ball in the balancer gauge is aligned with the other cylinders. Tighten the locknut and install the cover.
c. On 1980-1982 models with CV carburetors, the No. 3 carburetor (right side inboard carburetor) is not equipped with a throttle valve adjustment screw, therefore all other carburetors must be synchronized to this carburetor (**Figure 118**). If No. 2 carburetor (left side inboard carburetor) is out of sync, loosen the locknut securing throttle valve adjustment screw B (**Figure 118**) and rotate the screw until the gauge ball is correct as shown in **Figure 120**. If either outboard carburetor is out of sync, loosen the locknut on the respective adjustment screw (A or C, **Figure 118**) and rotate the screw until the gauge balls are correct. Secure the adjustment screws with the locknuts.

NOTE
A socket on a long extension and a long, thin blade screwdriver are necessary to perform this adjustment on 1980-1982 models. The Suzuki throttle valve adjustment wrench is a set of 2 long, thin tools designed to perform this adjustment procedure. This tool can be ordered from your Suzuki dealer.

d. On TSCC models, loosen the locknut securing the balance adjustment screw (**Figure 122**) and turn the screw until both balls in the gauge are aligned. Tighten the locknut to secure the adjustment.
e. Turn off the engine.
f. Unplug the valve-to-carburetor vacuum line and install the fuel tank.

10. Remove the synchronization gauge and all the balance adapters. Install the bolts with the washers into the intake manifolds or carburetors.

CAUTION
Ensure that each bolt is fitted with a good washer or vacuum leaks will occur, resulting in poor engine performance.

11. Adjust the throttle stop screw until an engine idle speed as specified in **Table 6** is achieved.

Compression Test

During every tune-up, check the cylinder compression. Record the results and compare them at the next check. A running record will show trends in deterioration so that corrective action can be taken before a complete failure occurs.

Both a dry test and a wet test should be carried out to isolate trouble to the cylinder and piston or to the valves.

1. Warm the engine to normal operating temperature.
2. Remove all the spark plugs.
3. Connect a compression tester to one cylinder according to the manufacturer's instructions.
4. Make sure the choke is off. Hold the throttle fully open and operate the electric starter until the gauge needle ceases to rise. Record the results and repeat the process for the other cylinders.
5. When interpreting the results, look for a marked loss compared to a previous test. Cylinder compression should be as specified in **Table 9**. The maximum difference between any cylinders is 2 kg/cm^2 (28 psi). A compression reading below the specified limit for any cylinder indicates engine repair is required.
6. To determine whether the lack of compression is due to valves or piston rings, perform a second compression test after pouring approximately 15 cc (1/2 oz.) into each cylinder through the spark plug hole. If the compression reading rises significantly, the piston rings and/or cylinder bore are probably worn. If the wet compression test changes little from the dry test, the valves are probably burned or not seating correctly.

Table 1 MAINTENANCE AND LUBRICATION SCHEDULE

Every fuel stop or every month	• Check engine oil level • Check tire condition and inflation • Check battery electrolyte level • Check wheels for damage
Initial 600 miles (1,000 km)	• Check all engine, exhaust system and frame fasteners and tighten if necessary • Check and/or adjust valve clearance • Check contact breaker points and ignition timing (1977-1979 models) • Torque cylinder head nuts and bolts • Change engine oil and oil filter • Adjust engine idle speed • Adjust clutch • Check brake fluid level • Check brake pad wear • Clean, lubricate and adjust drive chain (every 600 miles) • Check and/or adjust steering stem • Adjust throttle and choke cables • Inspect tire tread condition • Perform compression check
Every 2,000 miles (3,000 km)	• Clean air filter (1983-1984 models)

(continued)

Table 1 MAINTENANCE AND LUBRICATION SCHEDULE (continued)

Every 4,000 miles (6,000 km)*	• Perform all maintenance items specified under initial 600 miles (1,000 km) plus the following: • Clean air filter element • Clean spark plugs and adjust gap • Inspect battery electrolyte level; check specific gravity • Check fork air pressure (every 6 months) • Lubricate throttle, clutch and choke cables • Lubricate clutch and brake levers • Lubricate brake pedal shaft and linkage • Lubricate sidestand pivot
Every 7,500 miles (12,000 km)	• Perform all maintenance items specified under initial 600 miles (1,000 km) and 4,000 mile (6,000 km) service plus the following: • Replace air filter element (1983-1984 models) • Replace spark plugs • Lubricate throttle grip with grease • Lubricate speedometer and tachometer cables
Every 2 years or 15,000 miles (24,000 km)	• Replace fuel line • Change brake fluid • Replace brake hoses • Lubricate steering stem bearings and swing arm bearings

* On 1977-1979 models, perform maintenance every 3,000 miles (5,000 km).

3

Table 2 RECOMMENDED FUEL AND LUBRICANTS

Fuel	Unleaded or low-lead; 85-95 octane
Engine/transmission oil	SAE 10W/40, SE rated
Fork oil	SAE 15 fork oil
Brake fluid*	Rated DOT 3 or DOT 4

* Use only glycol-based brake fluid rated DOT 3 or DOT 4. Mixing silicon- or petroleum-based fluids can cause brake component damage leading to brake system failure.

Table 3 RECOMMENDED TIRE PRESSURES

Tire	psi	kg/cm²
Front tire (normal riding)		
Solo (1977-1982)	25	1.75
Solo (1983-1984)	28	2.00
Dual (L models)	28	2.00
Dual (1983-1984)	28	2.00
Dual (all others)	25	1.75
Front tire (continuous high-speed riding)		
Solo and dual	28	2.00
Rear tire (normal riding)		
Solo (1977-1982)	28	2.00
Solo (1983-1984)	32	2.25

(continued)

Table 3 RECOMMENDED TIRE PRESSURES (continued)

Tire	psi	kg/cm²
Rear tire (normal riding) continued		
Dual (LN, LX, LZ)	32	2.25
Dual (LD models)	36	2.50
Dual (ED, ESD, EE, ESE models)	40	2.50
Dual (all others)	36	2.50
Rear tire (continuous high-speed riding)		
Solo (L models)	36	2.50
Solo (all others)	32	2.25
Dual	40	2.80

Table 4 TORQUE SPECIFICATIONS

Item	mkg	ft.-lb.
Front axle nut	3.6-5.2	26-38
Front axle pinch bolt (L models)	1.5-2.5	11-18
Caliper mounting bolts (front and rear)	2.5-4.0	18-29
Caliper housing bolts (1983-1984)	3.0-3.6	22-26
Front caliper axle bolt (1977-1982)	4.0-5.5	29-40
Front master cylinder clamp bolts	0.5-0.8	4-6
Rear master cylinder mounting bolts	1.5-2.5	11-18
Steering stem pinch bolt (except LD models)	1.5-2.5	11-18
Steering stem pinch nut (LD models)	1.2-2.0	9-15
Steering stem head nut or bolt		
1980-1982	3.6-5.2	26-38
All others	2.0-3.0	15-22
Fork cap bolts	1.5-3.0	11-22
Handlebar clamp bolts (1977-1982)	1.2-2.0	9-15
Handlebar fasteners (1983-1984)		
Set bolt (except LD)	1.5-2.5	11-18
Holder bolt (except LD models)	5.0-6.0	36-44
Holder bolt (LD models)	1.5-2.5	11-22
Holder nut (except LD models)	2.0-3.0	15-22
Holder nut (LD models)	1.0-1.5	7-11
Upper fork pinch bolt		
1977-1980	2.0-3.0	15-22
1981-1982	3.5-5.5	26-40
1983-1984	2.0-3.0	15-22
Lower fork pinch bolt		
1977-1980	2.0-3.0	15-22
1981-1984 (except LD models)	1.5-2.5	11-18
LD models	1.2-2.0	9-15
Brake disc mounting bolt	1.5-2.5	11-18
Rear sprocket nut		
1977-1982	4.0-6.0	29-43
All others	2.5-4.0	18-29
Swing arm pivot bolt		
1977-1982	5.0-8.0	36-58
LD models	5.0-8.0	36-58
All others	5.5-8.8	40-64
Shock absorber nut (1977-1982)	2.0-3.0	15-22
Rear axle nut		
1977-1982	8.5-11.5	62-83
1983-1984	5.0-8.0	36-58

(continued)

Table 4 TORQUE SPECIFICATIONS (continued)

Item	mkg	ft.-lb.
Torque link nut	2.0-3.0	15-22
Engine mounting bolts (1977-1982)		
8 mm	1.3-2.3	10-17
10 mm	2.5-4.5	18-33
Engine mounting bolts (1983-1984)		
Upper bolts	6.0-7.2	44-52
Lower bolts	6.7-8.0	49-58
Footrest mounting bolts	2.7-4.3	20-31
Exhaust pipe flange bolts		
TSCC models	0.9-1.2	6.5-8.5
All others	0.9-1.4	6.5-10.0
Exhaust pipe clamp bolts		
TSCC models	0.9-1.2	6.5-8.5
All others	0.9-1.4	6.5-10.0
Muffler mounting bolt		
TSCC models	2.2-3.5	16.0-25.5
All others	1.8-2.8	13.0-20.0

Table 5 CAPACITIES

	Fuel tank		
	Liters	U.S. gal.	Imp. gal.
1977-1978	17	4.5	3.7
E models			
1979-1981	16	4.2	3.5
1985-on			
49-state	18	4.8	3.9
California	17.5	4.2	3.5
L models			
1979-1980	13	3.4	2.9
1981-on	12	3.2	2.6
1982 M models	23	6.1	5.0
All others	16	4.2	3.5
	Engine/transmission oil		
	Liters	**U.S.qt.**	**Imp. qt.**
Without filter change			
1983-on L models	2.6	2.7	2.3
All others	2.4	2.5	2.1
With filter change			
1983-on L models	3.1	3.3	2.7
All others	2.6	2.7	2.3
After overhaul			
1983-on L models	3.3	3.5	2.9
All others	2.7	2.9	2.4
	Fork oil capacity		
	cc	**U.S. oz.**	**Imp. oz.**
E models			
1977-1980	165	5.6	5.8
1983-1984	321	10.8	11.3
1985-on	345	11.6	12.14

(continued)

Table 5 CAPACITIES (continued)

	Fork oil capacity		
	cc	U.S. oz.	Imp. oz.
ES models			
1983	321	10.8	11.3
1984	330	11.2	11.6
L models			
1979-1980	217	7.3	7.6
1981	249	8.4	8.8
1982	239	8.0	8.4
1983	288	9.7	10.1
1985	276	9.3	9.7
1986	248	8.4	8.8
1981 T model	190	6.4	6.7
1982 M model	223	7.5	7.9
All others	165	5.6	5.8

	Fork oil level*	
	mm	in.
E models		
1977-1980	204	8.0
1983-1984	125	4.9
1985-on	114	4.5
ES models		
1983	125	4.9
1984	119	4.7
L models		
1979-1980	229	9.0
1981	201	7.9
1982	144	5.7
1983	190	7.5
1985	179	7.05
1986	181	7.1
1981 T model	201	7.9
1982 M model	140	5.5
All others	204	8.0

* The maximum allowable difference between the right and left fork tubes is 1 mm (0.04 in.). Remove the spring and measure the oil level from the top of each fork leg held vertical and fully compressed.

Table 6 TUNE-UP SPECIFICATIONS

Recommended spark plugs	
1977-1982	NGK B-8ES or ND W24ES
1983-1984	NGK D9EA or ND X27ES-U
Spark plug gap	0.6-0.8 mm (0.024-0.03 in.)
Breaker point gap (1977-1979)	0.3-0.4 mm (0.012-0.016 in.)
Ignition timing (1977-1979)	
	17° BTDC below 1,550 rpm 37° BTDC above 2,500 rpm
Ignition timing (1980 and later)*	
1980-1982	15° BTDC below 1,400-1,600 rpm 40° BTDC above 2,250-2,450 rpm

(continued)

Table 6 TUNE-UP SPECIFICATIONS (continued)

1983-1984	11° BTDC below 1,550-1,750 rpm 31° BTDC above 2,900-3,100 rpm
Valve clearance	
1977-1982	0.03-0.08 mm (0.001-0.003 in.)
1983-1984	0.08-0.013 mm (0.003-0.005 in.)
Idle speed	
1977-1982	1,000-1,200 rpm
1983-1984	900-1,100 rpm
Firing order	1-2-4-3

* Timing on 1980-on models is pre-set and not adjustable.

Table 7 TAPPET SHIM SIZES (1982 AND EARLIER)

No.	Thickness (mm)	Part No.	No.	Thickness	Part No.
1	2.15	12892-45000	11	2.65	12892-45010
2	2.20	12892-45001	12	2.70	12892-45011
3	2.25	12892-45002	13	2.75	12892-45012
4	2.30	12892-45003	14	2.80	12892-45013
5	2.35	12892-45004	15	2.85	12892-45014
6	2.40	12892-45005	16	2.90	12892-45015
7	2.45	12892-45006	17	2.95	12892-45016
8	2.50	12892-45007	18	3.00	12892-45017
9	2.55	12892-45008	19	3.05	12892-45018
10	2.60	12892-45009	20	3.10	12892-45019

Table 8 VALVE ADJUSTMENT ORDER (TSCC ENGINE)

Cylinder	Valves to adjust (pairs)
Camshaft end notches point out	
No. 1	Intake and exhaust
No. 2	Exhaust
No. 3	Intake
Camshaft end notches point in	
No. 2	Intake
No. 3	Exhaust
No. 4	Intake and exhaust

Table 9 COMPRESSION PRESSURE

	Standard compression kg/cm² (psi)	Service limit kg/cm² (psi)
1977-1980	9.0-12.0 (128-171)	6.5 (92)
1981-1982	9.0-13.0 (128-185)	7.0 (100)
TSCC models	10.0-14.0 (142-199)	8.0 (114)
Maximum difference between cylinders	2.0 (28)	

CHAPTER FOUR

ENGINE

All GS550 engines are air-cooled 4-cylinder, 4-stroke models equipped with dual overhead camshafts (DOHC).

The engine in all 1982 and earlier models contains a ball and roller bearing crankshaft. The crankshaft main bearings are caged ball bearings while the connecting rods pivot on caged roller bearings.

All 1983 and later models have TSCC (Twin Swirl Combustion Chamber) engines. These engines are equipped with a one-piece forged crankshaft. The crankshaft main bearings and connecting rod bearings are automotive style plain insert bearings.

On all models, both camshafts are chain-driven from the crankshaft. The tension on the cam chain is controlled automatically by a spring-loaded slipper tensioner which bears against the rear vertical run of the chain.

The engine and transmission are lubricated from a common wet-sump oil supply. Oil is circulated throughout the engine by a clutch-driven oil pump. The oil pump on 1982 and earlier engines is a high-volume, low-pressure type. The oil pump on TSCC engines is a high-pressure type necessary to provide lubrication to plain insert type bearings. A wet-plate clutch is installed inside the right engine cover.

This chapter provides complete service and overhaul procedures for the GS550 engine. Refer to Chapter Five for transmission and clutch repair procedures.

All engine upper end repair, including camshafts, cylinder head and cylinder block, can be performed with the engine installed in the motorcycle. Engine removal is necessary to perform repair on the crankshaft, transmission, secondary shaft drive gears as well as certain components of the gearshift mechanism.

Refer to **Table 1** for all engine torque specifications. **Tables 1-15** are located at the end of the chapter.

CAMSHAFTS

Camshaft removal is essentially the same for all models. Minor differences between models are pointed out where applicable.

Removal

1. Refer to Chapter Six and remove the carburetors.
2. On earlier models, remove the screws securing the end covers and remove the covers (**Figure 1**).
3. Spring open the clamp securing the breather hose to the breather cover (**Figure 2**) and disconnect the hose from the cover.
4. On earlier models, disconnect the horn wires (**Figure 3**).
5. Disconnect the tachometer drive cable (**Figure 4**).
6. Remove each spark plug lead by pulling on the cap. Do not pull on the lead or it may be damaged. Tuck the spark plug leads into the upper frame to keep them clear of the engine. Blow away any dirt

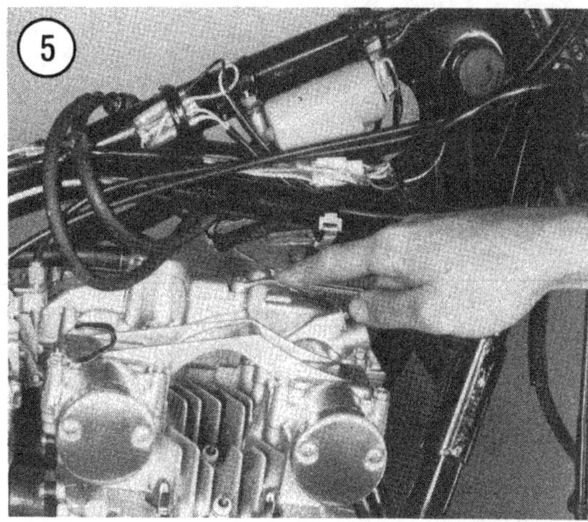

that may have accumulated around the spark plugs and remove the plugs. The crankshaft is easier to rotate with the spark plugs removed.

7. Remove the bolts securing the breather cover to the cam cover (**Figure 5**). Remove the breather cover.

8. Remove the bolts securing the cam cover to the cylinder head. On 1982 and earlier models, the left-front and right-rear cover bolts pass through dowel locating pins and are longer than the other cover bolts. On TSCC models, the cam covers are secured with 4 large-head Allen bolts (**Figure 6**).

NOTE

To ease cam cover removal, tap around the sealing surface with a soft-faced mallet to help break it loose.

9. Loosen the locknut on the cam chain tensioner and turn the slotted screw clockwise to lock the tensioner pushrod (**Figure 7**).

10. On models equipped with a chain slipper block, lift up on the cam chain to gain maximum slack and remove the slipper block (**Figure 8**).

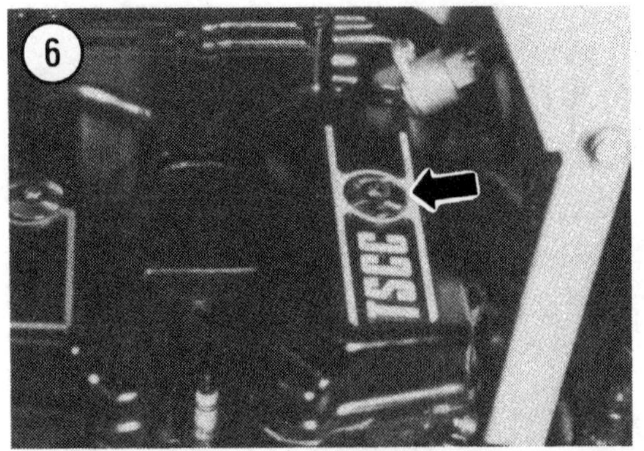

11. Remove the bolts securing the tensioner assembly to the engine and remove the assembly (**Figure 9**).

12. Stuff a clean rag in the chain opening to prevent any fasteners or debris from falling into the engine (**Figure 10**).

13. On 1977-1982 models, gradually and in a crisscross pattern loosen the bolts securing the camshaft bearing caps and remove the caps (**Figure 11**).

14. On TSCC models, perform the following:
   a. Remove the outer bearing caps (**Figure 12**).
   b. Remove the bolt securing the oil lines (**Figure 13**).
   c. Remove the bolts securing the inner bearing caps and oil line banjos (**Figure 14**). Note that the long banjo bolts are installed on the intake side. The oil lines are color-coded. A spot of yellow paint on the forward end identifies the right oil line. The left line is identified with white paint.

NOTE

*The bearing caps are marked with "A," "B," "C" and "D" (**Figure 15**) with corresponding marks on the cylinder head (**Figure 16**). The triangle enclosing each letter points forward.*

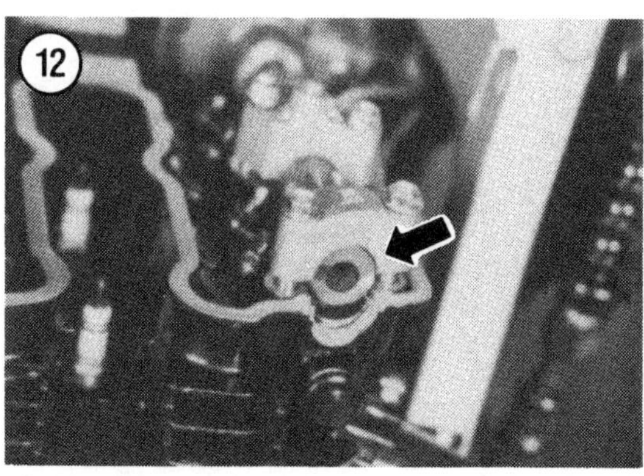

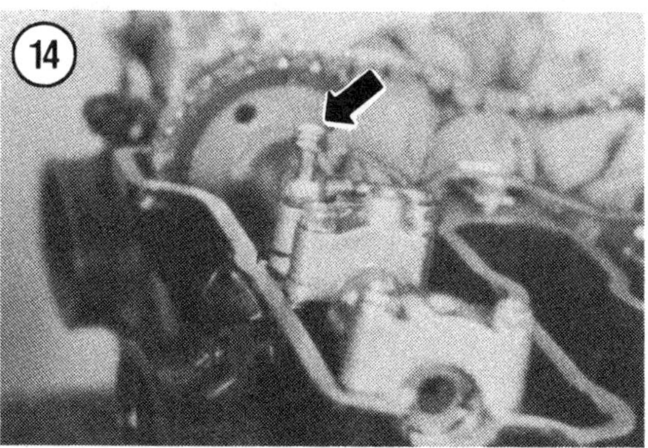

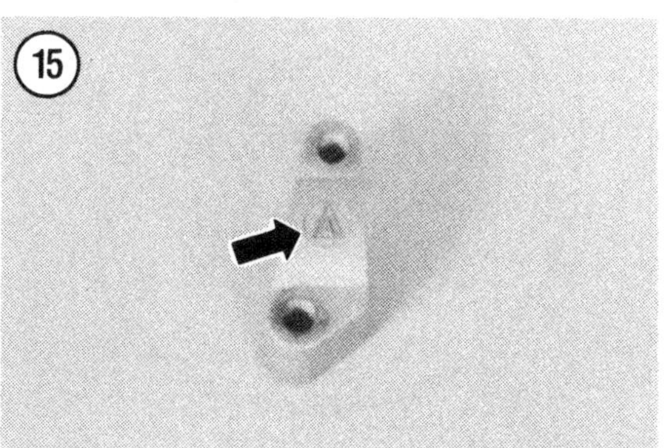

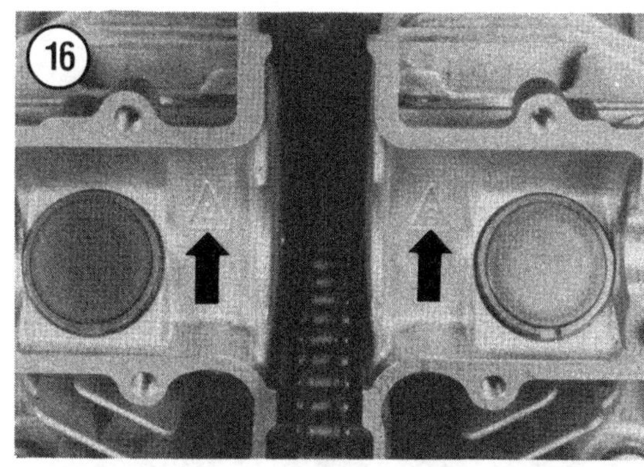

15. Lift up the cam chain and remove the intake (rear) camshaft (**Figure 17**).
16. Tie a piece of wire to the cam chain and secure it to the frame to prevent the chain from falling into the engine.

NOTE
On models equipped with a chain slipper block, the slipper block can be temporarily installed to hold the chain.

17. Disengage the cam chain and carefully lift out the exhaust camshaft (**Figure 18**).
18. Perform *Inspection*.

Inspection

1. Carefully examine both camshafts for evidence of excessive or abnormal wear on the lobes or bearing journals.
2. Inspect each cam sprocket for signs of wear. Excessive wear is unlikely except in engines with high mileage or misaligned sprockets. If sprockets are worn, they must be replaced in pairs and a new cam chain must be installed.

18

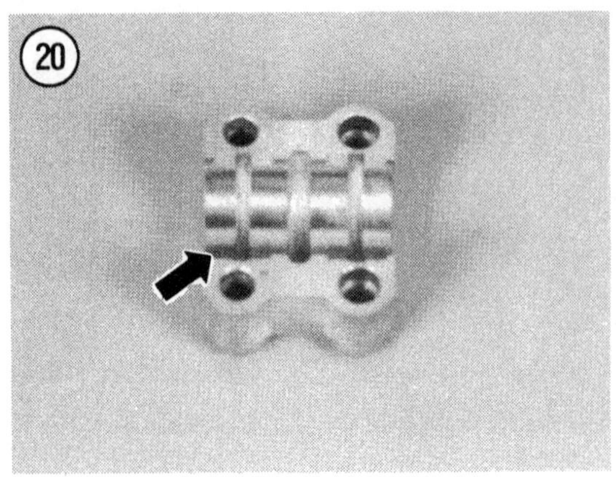

20

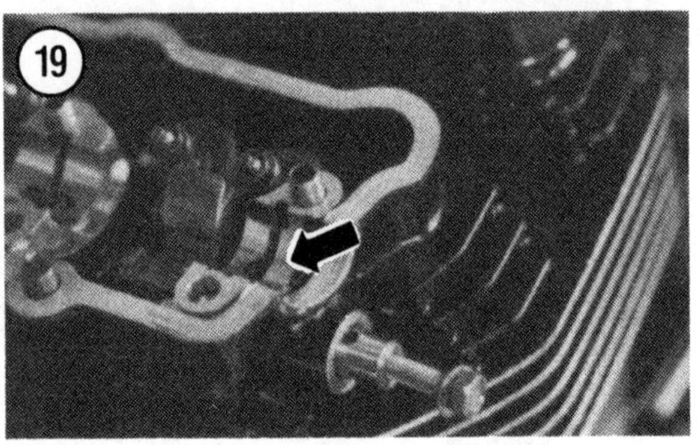

19

NOTE
*The cam chain is a one-piece unit. To replace the chain it is necessary to remove the crankshaft. Refer to **Lower End Disassembly** in this chapter.*

3. Examine the camshaft bearing surfaces on the cylinder head (**Figure 19**) and on each bearing cap (**Figure 20**). If the bearing surfaces are galled or scored in any way, the cylinder head and caps must be replaced as a set.
4. If sprockets are replaced, ensure that they are positioned correctly on the camshafts. Refer to **Figure 21** for the correct positioning of the marks in relation to the notches on the end of the camshafts.

NOTE
*Three types of fasteners are used to secure the sprockets to the camshafts. Engines up to engine No. 222865 use either 6 mm Allen bolts (**Figure 22**) or 6 mm hex head bolts with a folding lockwasher (**Figure 23**). On engines No. 222866 and later, the camshafts are secured with 7 mm hex head flange bolts (**Figure 24**).*

5. Apply a couple of drops of blue Loctite (Lock N' Seal No. 2114) to the bolts before installation.

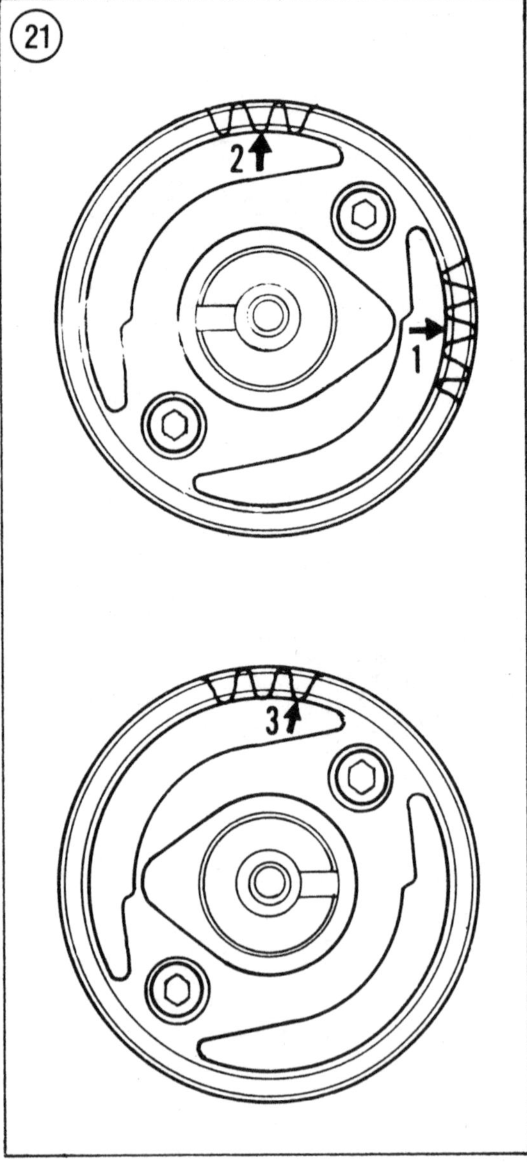

21

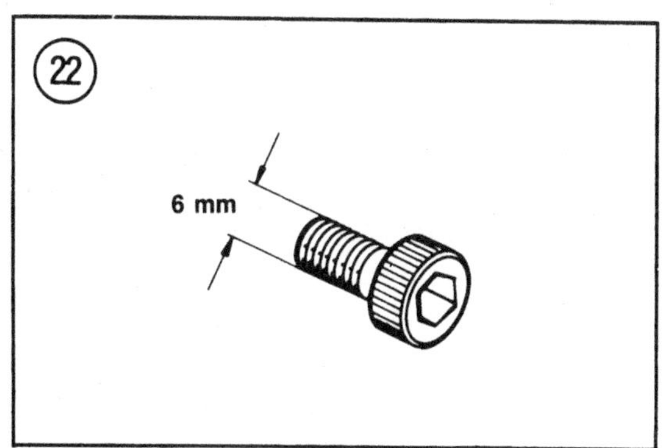

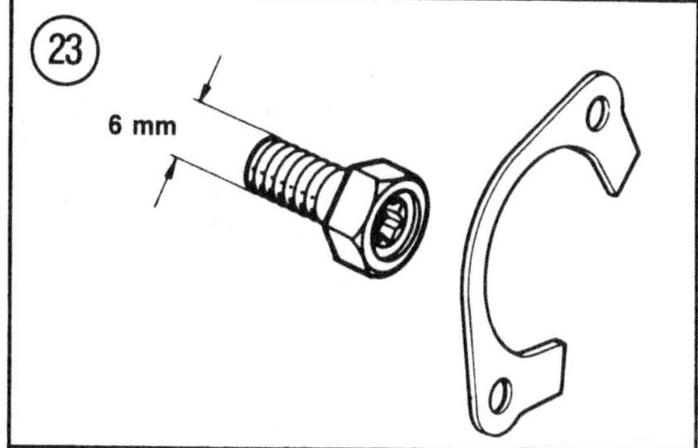

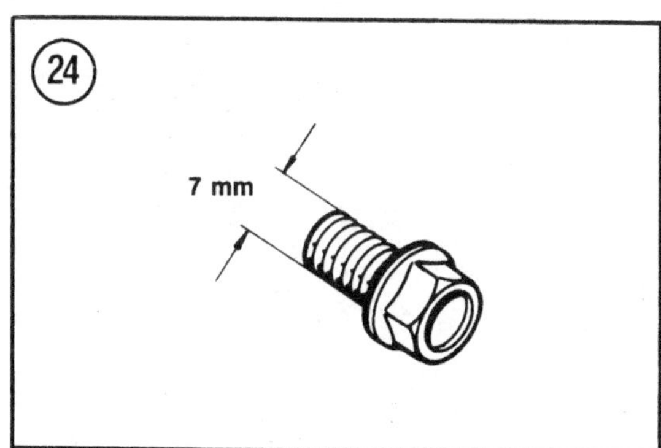

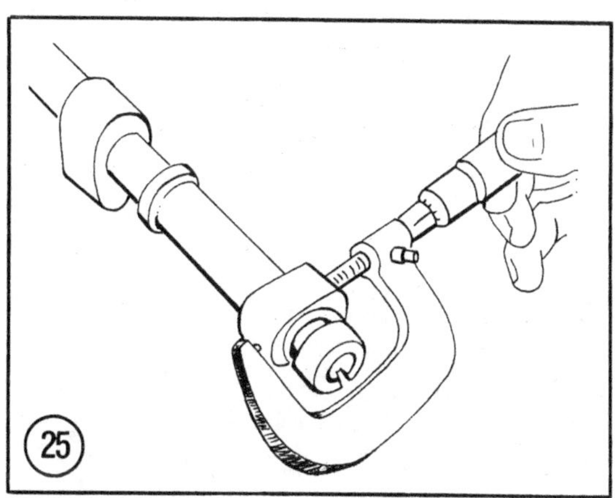

6. On camshafts with 6 mm hex head bolts, always use new folding lockwashers.

7. Torque the sprocket mounting bolts to the correct specifications as follows:

   a. 6 mm Allen bolts—0.8-1.2 mkg (6-8.5 ft.-lb.).
   b. 6 mm hex head bolts with folding locking washer—1.5-2 mkg (11-14.5 ft.-lb.).
   c. 7 mm hex head flange bolts—2.4-2.6 mkg (17.5-19 ft.-lb.).

8. Fold the lockwasher against the bolt head on models so equipped.

9. Use a micrometer to measure the height of each camshaft lobe as shown in **Figure 25**. Refer to **Table 2** or **Table 3** for wear specifications.

NOTE
*This procedure describes how to use Plastigage to measure camshaft bearing journal wear. Plastigage can be purchased from most auto supply stores and is available in several sizes. Make sure you purchase Plastigage small enough to measure the camshaft bearing clearance as specified in **Table 2** or **Table 3**.*

10. Wipe off all oil from the bearing journal and camshaft bearing surfaces and place the camshaft on the cylinder head.

11. Place a small strip of Plastigage on each cam surface (**Figure 26**).

12. Install the bearing caps. Make sure that the cast letters on the caps correspond to the cast letters on the cylinder head. Letter "A" is located on the left-front of the engine, letter "B" on the right-front, letter "C" on the left-rear and letter "D" on the right-rear. The triangle enclosing the cast letters must point forward. Tighten the bolts gradually and evenly in a crisscross pattern to 0.8-1.2 mkg (6-8.5 ft.-lb.).

NOTE
It is not necessary to install the cam chain over the camshafts to check the

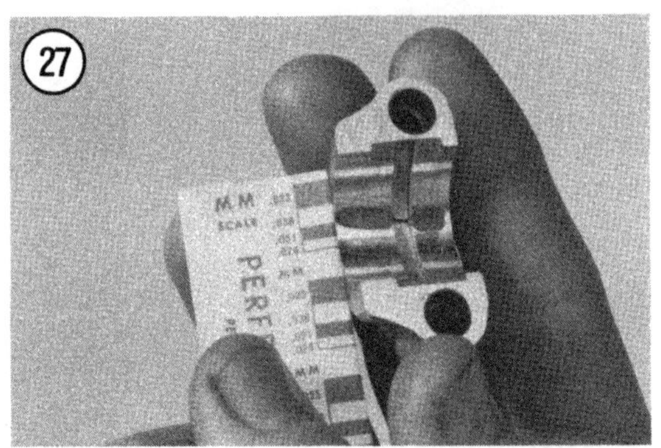
27

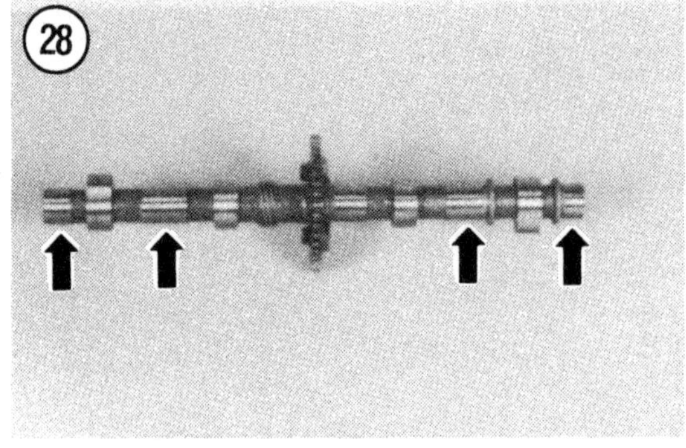
28

bearing clearance with Plastigage. Do not allow the camshaft to turn while tightening the bearing cap bolts. If the camshaft is allowed to turn, the Plastigage will be damaged and the whole procedure must be repeated.

13. Gradually and evenly remove the bolts securing the camshaft bearing caps and remove the caps. Measure the thickness of the Plastigage with the wrapper as shown in **Figure 27**. The Plastigage may adhere to the camshaft or the bearing cap; either location will provide a correct measurement. The service limit for bearing journal clearance is 0.15 mm (0.0059 in.). If the clearance exceeds the service limit, determine the defective part as follows:
   a. Measure the camshaft bearing journals with a micrometer (**Figure 28**). If the camshaft journals are not within tolerances specified in **Table 2** or **Table 3**, the camshafts must be replaced.
   b. Install the camshaft bearing caps on the cylinder head without the camshafts. Tighten the bolts gradually and evenly in a crisscross pattern to 0.8-1.2 mkg (6-8.5 ft.-lb.). Use an inside micrometer to measure the inside diameter of each bearing journal on the cylinder head. If the inside diameter exceeds the tolerances specified in **Table 2** or **Table 3**, the cylinder head and bearing caps must be replaced as a set.

14. Place each camshaft in V-blocks and use a dial indicator to measure the camshaft runout (**Figure 29**). Replace either camshaft if runout exceeds 0.1 mm (0.004 in.).

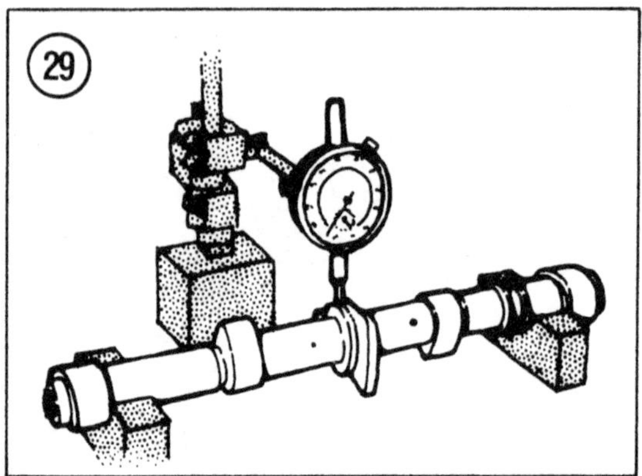
29

Installation

1. Remove the fasteners securing the ignition cover and remove the cover (**Figure 30**).
2. Use a 19 mm wrench on the large hex shoulder (**Figure 31**) to rotate the crankshaft clockwise until

30

31

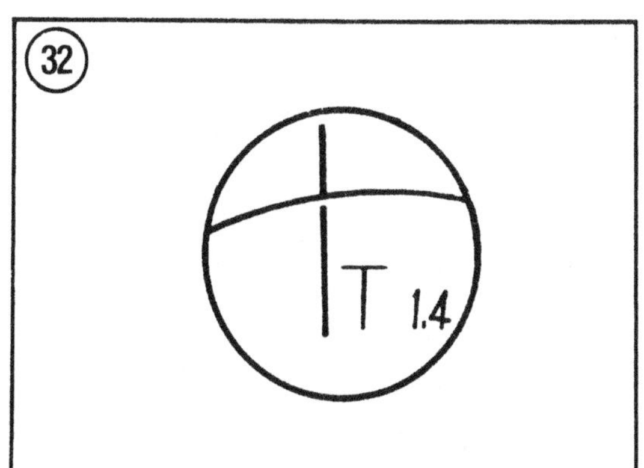

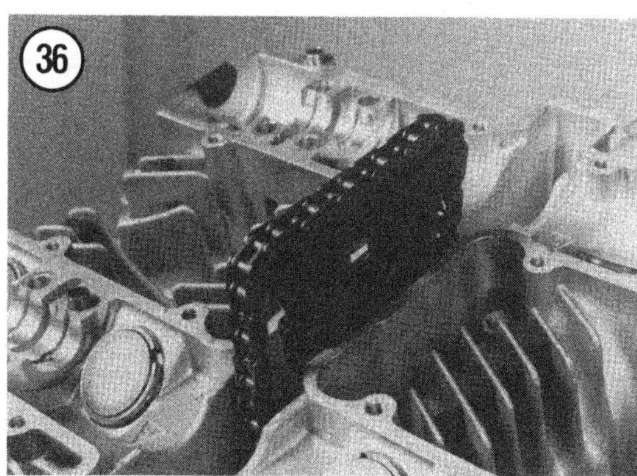

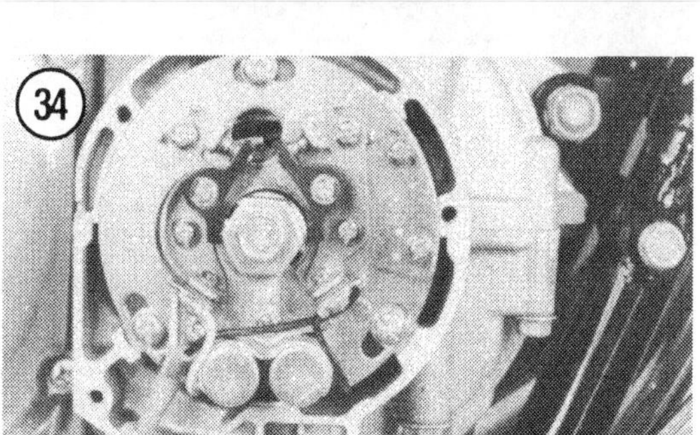

the TDC mark for cylinders No. 1-4 is correctly aligned. Observe the following:

a. On 1982 and earlier models, align TDC mark (on the left side of the "T") with the mark on the crankcase or timing plate (**Figure 32**).
b. On TSCC models, align the TDC mark (on the right side of the "T") with the center of the left signal generator coil (**Figure 33**).

NOTE
*On 1982 and earlier models, the timing mark is visible through the window in the ignition plate. See **Figure 34**. Due to the small window size and recessed location of the mark, it is recommended that the ignition plate be removed to allow a better view and a more precise alignment. Remove the screws securing the plate (**Figure 35**) and carefully remove the plate.*

3. Make sure the TDC mark is exactly aligned. Rotate the crankshaft as necessary with the 19 mm wrench to align the TDC mark.
4. Lubricate the camshaft lobes and bearing journals with molybdenum disulfide lubricant such as Bel-Ray Moly Lube. Spread the lubricant evenly without leaving any dry spots. Lubricate the bearing journals in the cylinder head with engine oil.
5. Install the cam slipper block, on models so equipped, to hold the cam chain in position (**Figure 36**).
6. Lift up the cam chain and install the exhaust camshaft in the cylinder head. On most models, the exhaust cam is marked "EX" as shown in **Figure 37**. The exhaust cam can also be identified by the tachometer drive gear (**Figure 38**). The notch in the end of the camshaft (**Figure 39**) is positioned on the *right* side of the engine.
7. Recheck that the TDC timing marks are correctly aligned as shown in **Figure 32** or **Figure**

37

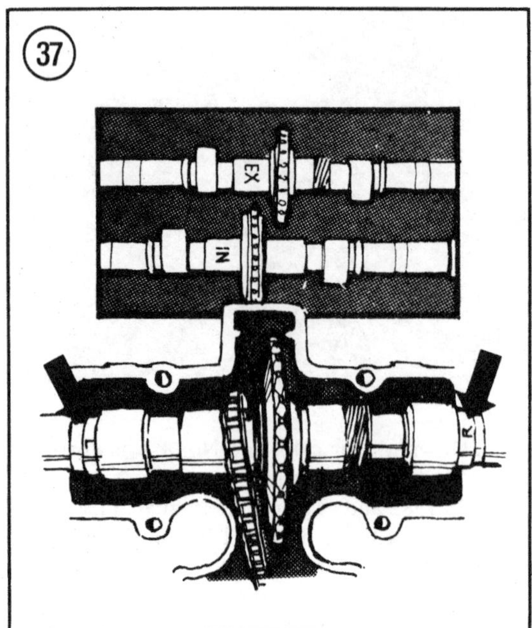

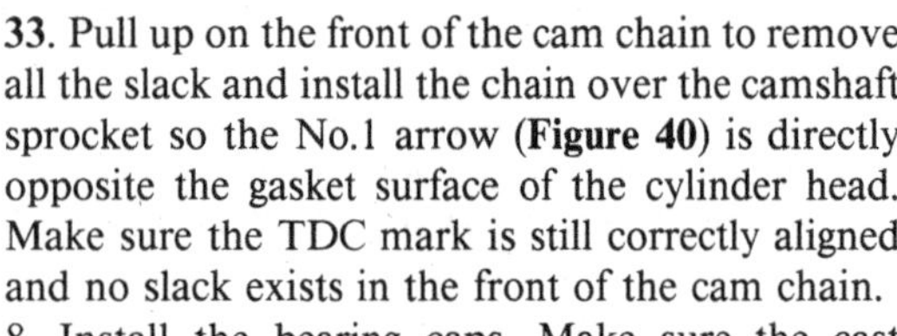
33. Pull up on the front of the cam chain to remove all the slack and install the chain over the camshaft sprocket so the No.1 arrow (**Figure 40**) is directly opposite the gasket surface of the cylinder head. Make sure the TDC mark is still correctly aligned and no slack exists in the front of the cam chain.

8. Install the bearing caps. Make sure the cast letters on the caps correspond to the cast letters on the cylinder head. Letter "A" is located on the left-front of the engine, letter "B" on the right-front, letter "C" on the left-rear and letter "D" on the right-rear. The triangle enclosing the cast letters must point forward.

9. Tighten the bearing cap bolts gradually and evenly in a crisscross pattern.

CAUTION

The bearing cap bolts are specially hardened and are identified by a "9" cast on the bolt head. Use of any other type of bolt could lead to failure and serious engine damage.

NOTE

Hold the cam chain in position on the front sprocket while tightening the bearing cap bolts. As the cap bolts are tightened, the valve spring tension against the camshaft lobes may cause the camshaft to rotate slightly causing the chain to jump off alignment by 1 or 2 sprocket teeth. If this should occur, the whole camshaft timing procedure will have to be started over from the beginning.

38

39

10. Torque the bearing cap bolts to 0.8-1.2 mkg (6-8.5 ft.-lb). Recheck the timing mark alignment and readjust if necessary. If the alignment is correct, the crankshaft can be rotated slightly to relieve the valve spring load on the camshaft and lessen the chance of the chain slipping.

11. Lubricate and install the intake camshaft through the cam chain. Make sure the notch in the end of the camshaft is on the *right* side of the cylinder head (**Figure 39**).

12. Position the cam chain on the intake cam sprocket so the specified number of chain pins are positioned between arrow 2 on the exhaust camshaft and arrow 3 on the intake camshaft as shown in **Figure 41**. The camshaft arrows on 1982 and earlier engines are 20 chain pins apart (**Figure 42**). The camshaft arrows on TSCC engines are 23 chain pins apart (**Figure 43**).

13. Install the bearing caps. Make sure the cast letters on the caps correspond to the cast letters in

the cylinder head and that the triangles enclosing the marks point forward. Tighten the bearing cap bolts gradually and evenly in a crisscross pattern to 0.8-1.2 mkg (6-8.5 ft.-lb.).

14. On TSCC models, install the oil lines between the cam bearing caps (**Figure 44**). The oil line with the yellow paint is installed on the right side (**Figure 45**). The left line is identified with white paint. The long oil line banjo bolt (with holes in the end) is installed in the intake (rear) cam bearing cap (**Figure 46**).

15. Loosen the locknut and lockscrew on the cam chain tensioner assembly. Push in on the spring-loaded plunger while rotating the large knurled nut counterclockwise (**Figure 47**). When the plunger is pushed in as far as possible, secure it with the lockscrew.

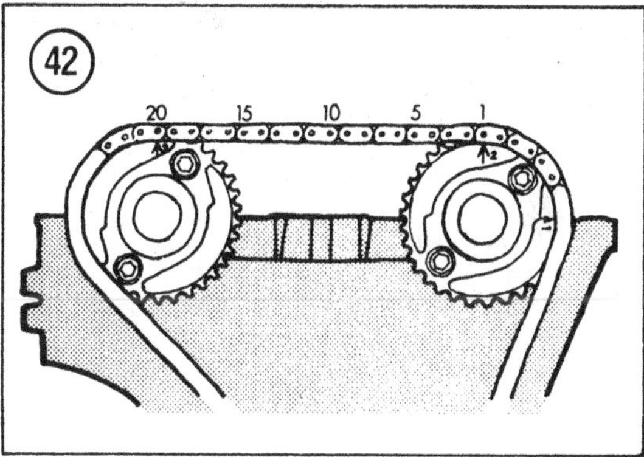

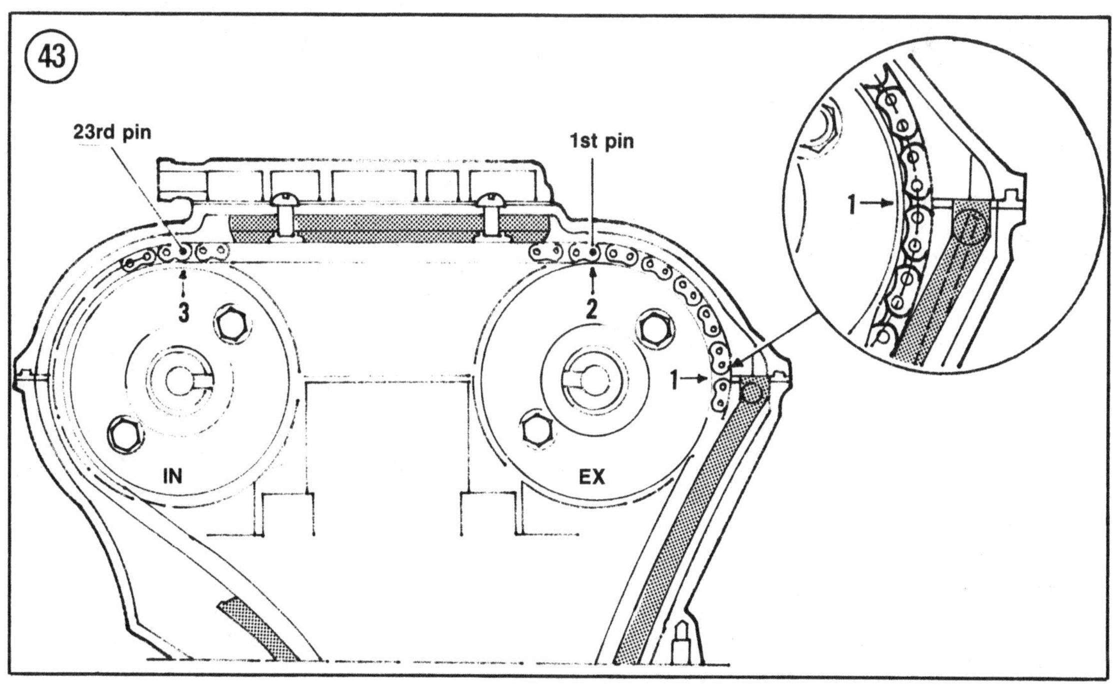

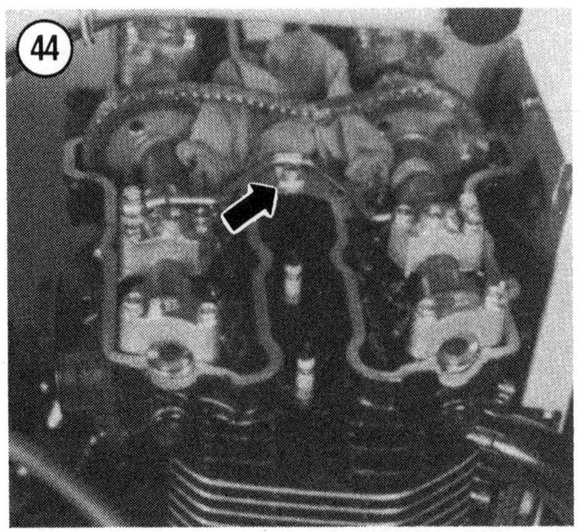

44

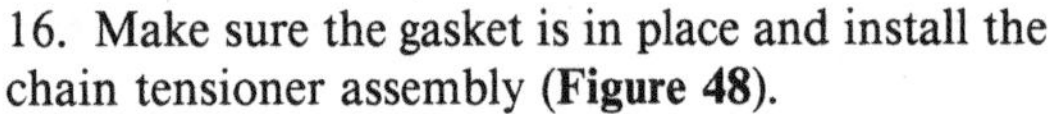

16. Make sure the gasket is in place and install the chain tensioner assembly (**Figure 48**).
17. Back out the lockscrew approximately 1/4 turn to release the spring-loaded plunger. Secure the lockscrew with the locknut (**Figure 49**).

NOTE
Do not back out the lockscrew more than 1/2 turn or the plunger may become disengaged from the tensioner body. If this should occur it will be necessary to remove the tensioner assembly to install the plunger into the tensioner body.

18. Use a 19 mm wrench on the end of the crankshaft to rotate the crankshaft several turns; make sure the camshafts and chain operate smoothly and freely. Recheck the camshaft timing in relation to the TDC marks.
19. Rotate the large knurled nut on the cam chain tensioner counterclockwise while slowly rotating the crankshaft counterclockwise. This rotation will cause the cam chain to push back against the tensioner plunger. Release the knurled nut and slowly rotate the crankshaft clockwise (normal engine rotation). The knurled nut should rotate clockwise as the plunger takes up the slack in the cam chain. If the knurled nut does not turn as described, the plunger lockscrew may be too tight or the plunger may be sticking. If necessary, refer to *Cam Chain Tensioner* in this chapter to disassemble and inspect the tensioner assembly.
20. Install the ignition plate if it was removed.
21. Perform *Valve Clearance Adjustment* as described in Chapter Three.
22. Pour a total of approximately 50 cc (2 oz.) of engine oil over each camshaft bearing and the tachometer drive gear.

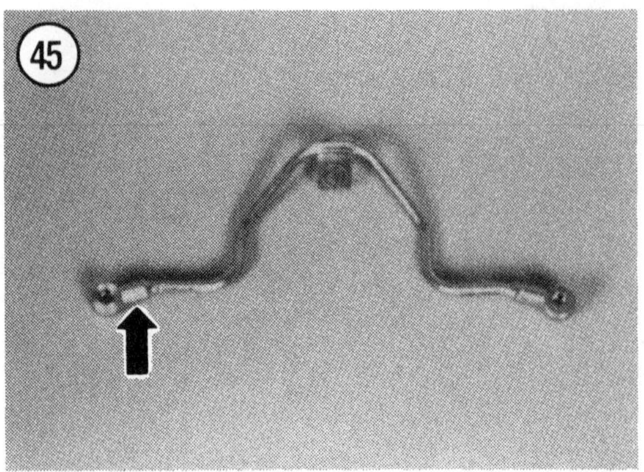

45

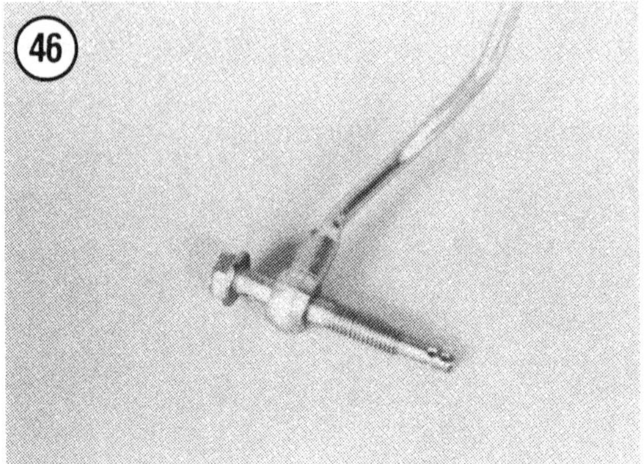

46

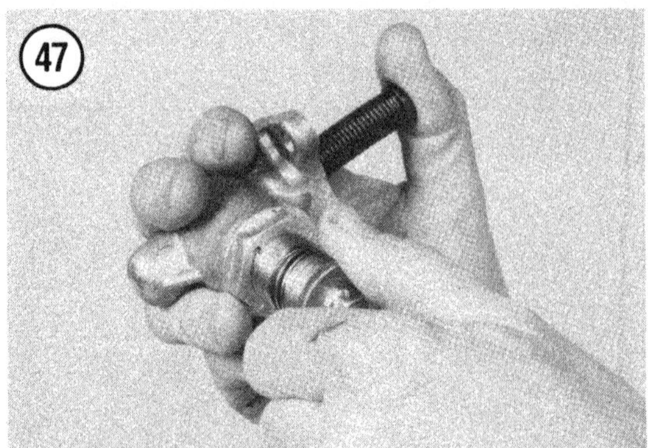

47

48

23. Install the cam cover gasket. Use a new gasket if possible. Make sure that the 4 half-moon shaped rubber end plugs (**Figure 50**) are in place. On TSCC models, check the condition of the sealing grommets in the cam cover (**Figure 51**). Replace them if they are not perfect.
24. Carefully position the cam cover on the cylinder head so the gasket is not disturbed. Rotate the exposed end of the tachometer drive gear (**Figure 52**) as the cam cover is installed so that the drive gear will engage the camshaft.

CAUTION
*The tachometer drive gear (**Figure 53**) must engage the camshaft as the cam cover is installed or the gear will be damaged when the cover bolts are tightened.*

25. Install the cam cover bolts. On 1982 and earlier models, the 2 longer bolts are positioned in the left-front and right-rear positions. Tighten all the bolts gradually and evenly in a crisscross pattern to the value specified in **Table 1**.
26. On early models, install the end covers (**Figure 1**).
27. Install the breather cover. Connect the breather hose to the breather cover and air box.
28. Connect the tachometer drive cable.
29. Connect the 4 spark plug leads. Make sure the caps fit securely over the spark plugs.
30. Install the carburetors as described in Chapter Six and install the horn, if removed.
31. On 1979 and earlier models, refer to Chapter Three and perform *Contact Breaker Point and Timing Adjustment.*

ROCKER ARMS AND ROCKER SHAFTS (TSCC MODELS)

The rocker arms and rocker arm shafts are installed in the cylinder head. Each rocker arm

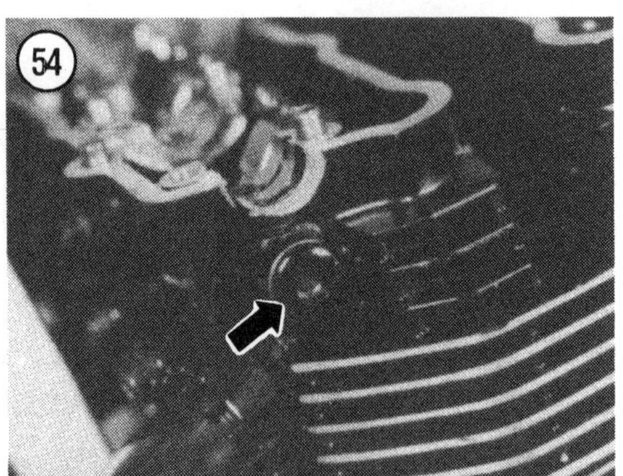

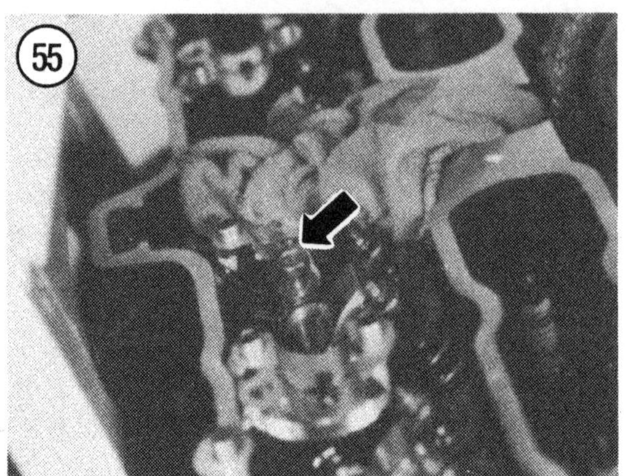

bears directly against 2 valves and is actuated by one camshaft lobe.

Removal/Installation

NOTE

It is not necessary to remove the rocker arms to remove the valves from the cylinder head.

1. Perform *Camshaft Removal* as outlined in this chapter.
2. Remove the rocker shaft end cap from the cylinder head (**Figure 54**).
3. Remove the rocker shaft stopper bolt (**Figure 55**).

CAUTION

All parts of each rocker assembly must be kept together in the proper order as they are removed. Do not mix any parts with parts from other rocker assemblies. Wear patterns have developed on these moving parts and damage or rapid and excessive wear may result if the parts are intermixed. An egg carton works well to keep the rocker components in order.

4. Screw a 6 mm bolt (bearing cap bolt) into the end of the rocker shaft and carefully slide out the rocker shaft (**Figure 56**). Collect each rocker arm and spring as the shaft is removed (**Figure 57**).
5. Perform *Inspection*.
6. Installation is the reverse of these steps. Keep the following points in mind:
   a. Use an awl or small Phillips screwdriver to locate the hole for the shaft stopper bolt as shown in **Figure 58**.

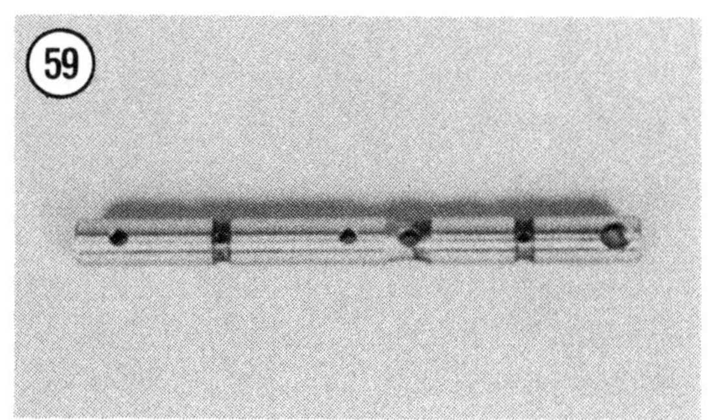

b. Make sure that the rocker arm springs are positioned on each side of the center cam shaft bearing (**Figure 57**).
c. Torque the rocker shaft stopper bolt to 0.8-1.0 mkg (6-7 ft.-lb.).
d. Make sure the gasket on each rocker shaft end cap is in good condition before installing the cap in the cylinder head.

Inspection

1. Carefully examine each rocker arm shaft (**Figure 59**) for signs of galling, scoring or excessive wear. Replace the shaft if necessary.
2. Inspect the machined surface of each rocker arm (**Figure 60**) for signs of excessive wear or damage. Replace all defective rocker arms. Make sure the oil hole is completely clear of any sludge or particles (**Figure 61**).

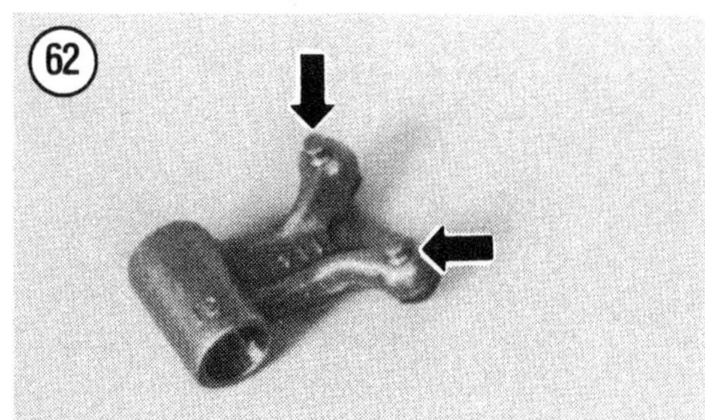

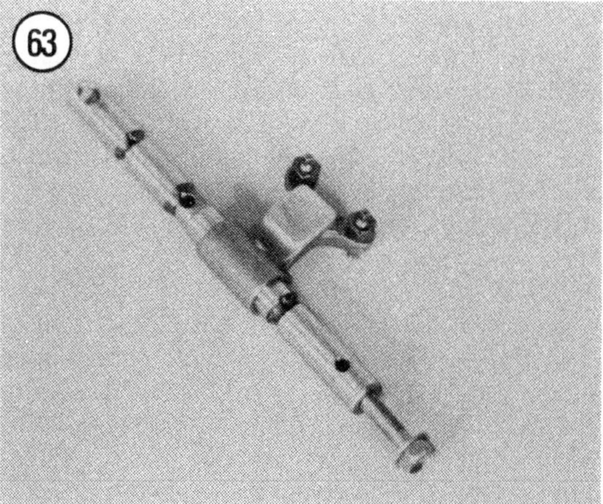

3. Carefully inspect the end of each valve adjuster where it contacts the end of the valve (**Figure 62**). Excessive or uneven wear can cause improper valve adjustment, leading to more serious damage. Valve adjuster screws can be purchased separately.
4. Slide rocker arms on each rocker shaft in the proper order. Check that the rocker arms move freely on the shaft without excessive play (**Figure 63**).
5. Use an inside micrometer to measure the inside diameter of each rocker arm. Replace any rocker arm not within the tolerances specified in **Table 4**.
6. Use a micrometer to measure the outside diameter of the rocker arm shafts at each rocker arm pivot location. Replace any rocker arm shaft not within the tolerances specified in **Table 4**.

CYLINDER HEAD

The cylinder head can be removed while the engine is in the motorcycle.

Removal

1. Perform *Camshaft Removal* as outlined in this chapter.
2. Perform *Exhaust System Removal* as outlined in Chapter Six.

3. Gently pry up on the end of the forward chain guide until the end is free from the head (**Figure 64**). Pull the chain guide straight up and out of the engine. If the engine is still installed in the frame, pull the chain guide up between the upper frame tubes to clear the lower end of the guide.
4. Remove the two 6 mm bolts from each end of the cylinder head (**Figure 65**).
5. On all 1979 and later engines (No. 141757 and higher), remove the 6 mm bolt from the front of the engine between the center exhaust ports (**Figure 66**).
6. On TSCC engines, remove the banjo bolts securing the oil lines to each side of the cylinder head (**Figure 67**). Note the metal gaskets on each side of the banjo fitting (**Figure 68**).
7. Referring to **Figure 69**, gradually and evenly remove the 12 head nuts in descending order. Numbers are cast in the head close to each head nut (**Figure 70**). A magnetic tool retriever can be used to lift the head nuts out of the center recesses.

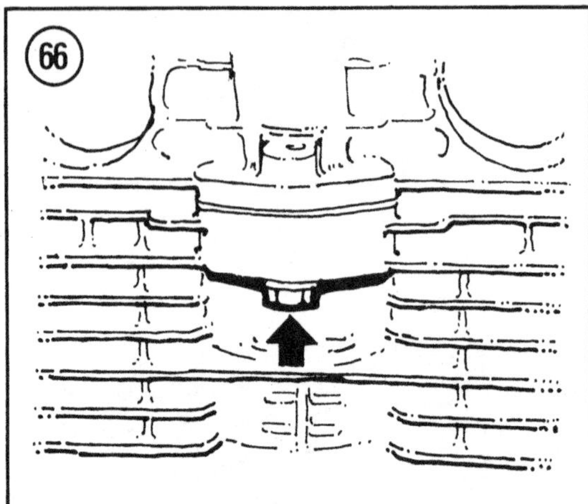

NOTE

On non-TSCC engines, two types of nuts and washers are used to secure the head. The 4 corner studs use chrome-plated acorn nuts with copper washers. The remaining 8 studs use steel washers with shouldered hex nuts. On TSCC engines, all 12 head studs use the same washers and nuts.

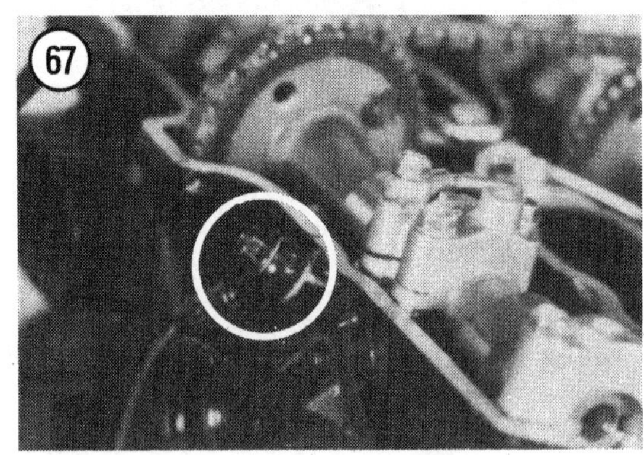

8. Tap around the base of the cylinder head with a plastic or rubber mallet to break the head loose from the cylinder and lift off the head.

CAUTION

The cooling fins on the cylinder head are fragile. Tap the cylinder head carefully to avoid damaging the fins. Never use a metal hammer.

9. Remove and discard the old head gasket. Remove the rectangular O-ring (**Figure 71**) on models so equipped.
10. Perform *Inspection*.

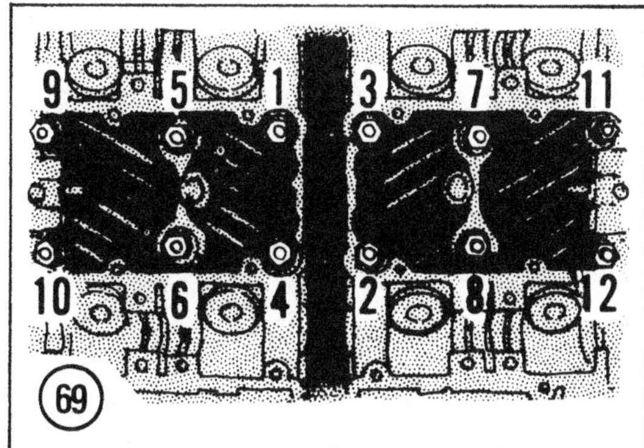

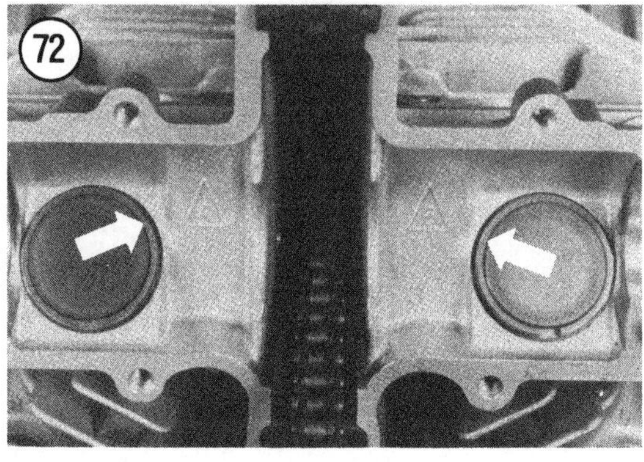

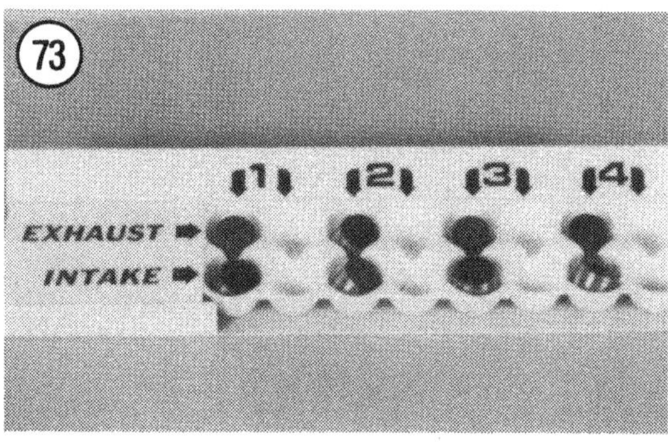

4

Inspection

1. On all except TSCC engines, remove the tappets with the adjusting shims to prevent them from falling out during cylinder head inspection (**Figure 72**). Keep the tappets and shims in an egg carton to prevent intermixing the parts (**Figure 73**).

CAUTION
Never use a magnet to lift out valve tappets or adjustment shims. They are made of hardened steel and are easily magnetized. A magnetized part will attract and hold metal particles which will cause excessive wear. A magnetized adjustment shim could also lift out of a tappet while the engine is running and cause serious and expensive damage.

CAUTION
All parts of each valve assembly must be kept together in the same order as they are removed. Do not mix any parts with parts from other valve assemblies. Wear patterns have developed on these moving parts and damage or rapid and excessive wear may result if the parts are intermixed.

2. On TSCC engines, remove the rocker arms and rocker shafts if the head is to be disassembled for repair.
3. Carefully clean all traces of gasket and sealant residue from the combustion chamber side and camshaft side of the cylinder head.
4. Without removing the valves, remove all carbon deposits from the combustion chambers with a wire brush and solvent. Stubborn deposits can be removed with a blunt scraper made of hardwood or a piece of aluminum that has been rounded and smoothed on one end as shown in **Figure 74**. Never use a hard metal scraper. Small burrs resulting from gouges in the combustion chamber will create hot spots which can cause preignition and heat erosion of the head and piston. After all carbon has been removed from the

combustion chamber and exhaust ports, clean the entire head in solvent.

NOTE

*If valve inspection and/or repair is desired, refer to **Valves** in this chapter.*

5. Carefully examine the combustion chambers and ports for cracks or damage. See **Figure 75** for 1982 and earlier engines and **Figure 76** for TSCC engines. Some types of cracks or damage can be repaired with heliarc welding. Refer such work to an authorized dealer or welding shop experienced with cylinder head repair.
6. Use a straightedge to check the gasket surface of the head in several places as shown in **Figure 77**. Replace the head if the gasket surface is warped beyond the service limit of 0.2 mm (0.008 in.).

Installation

1. Make sure that the gasket surface on the cylinder is clean and free of old gasket residue.
2. Clean all the carbon from the pistons. Wipe out each cylinder carefully to remove all debris.
3. Install a new head gasket over the studs on the cylinder. Make sure that the word "TOP," if it appears on the gasket, is up. Install a new rectagular O-ring on models so equipped (**Figure 71**).
4. Pull the cam chain up through the opening in the head and carefully lower the head down over the cylinder studs. Make sure the alignment dowels are engaged, then press the head down against the gasket.

NOTE

Stuff rags into the cam chain tunnel before attempting to install the washers over the head studs. A copper washer accidentally dropped into the chain tunnel cannot be removed with a magnetic tool retriever. Dropping a washer into the engine could easily cause a lot of extra work and aggravation.

5. On all except TSCC engines, install the chrome-plated acorn nuts on the 4 corner studs with copper washers.

NOTE

*Use a screwdriver as shown in **Figure 78** to help guide the washers over the studs.*

6. Install the remaining washers and head nuts. Remove the rags from the cam chain tunnel.
7. Tighten the head nuts gradually and evenly in the sequence shown in **Figure 69**. Torque the nuts as specified in **Table 1**.

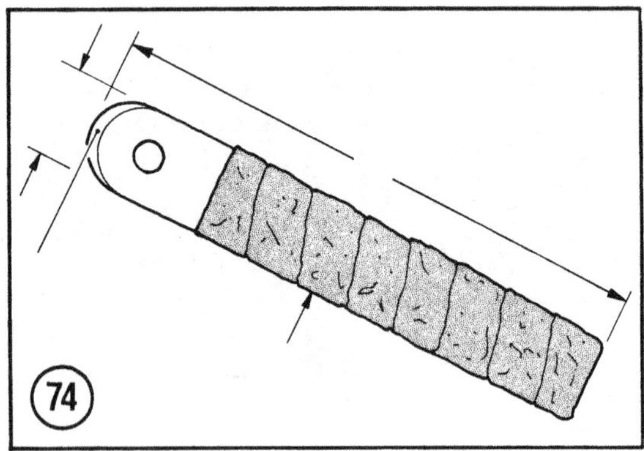

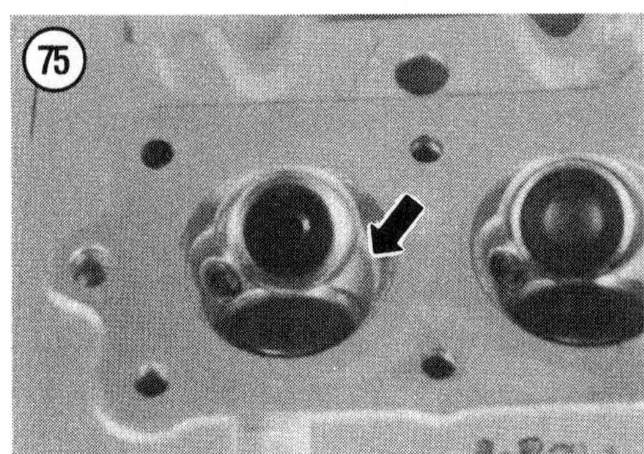

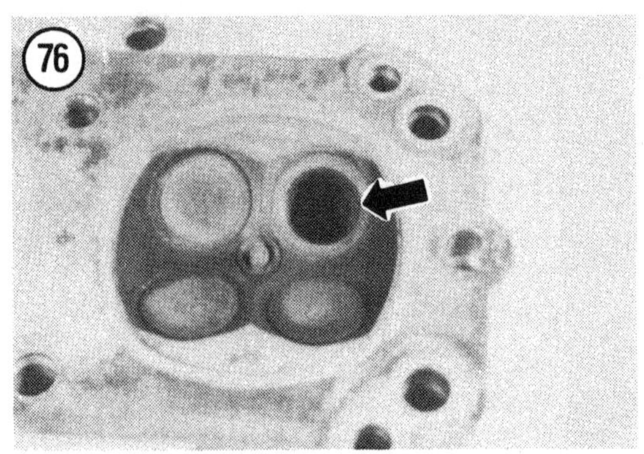

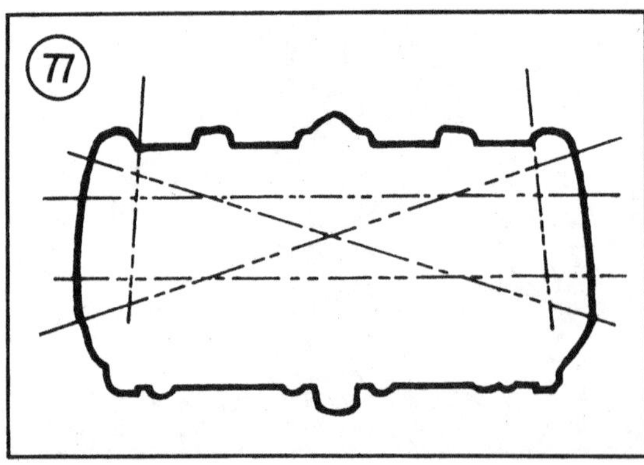

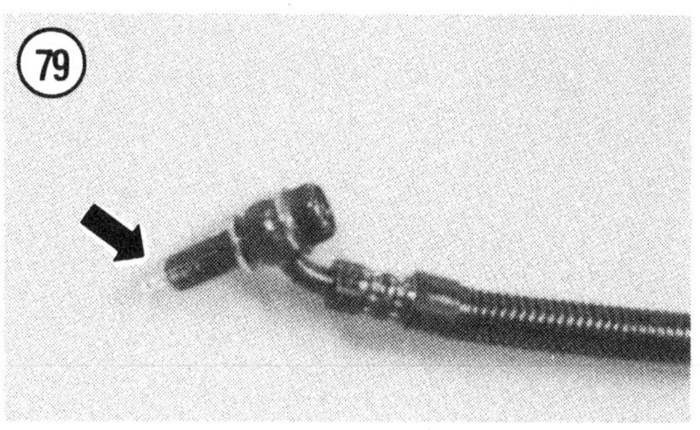

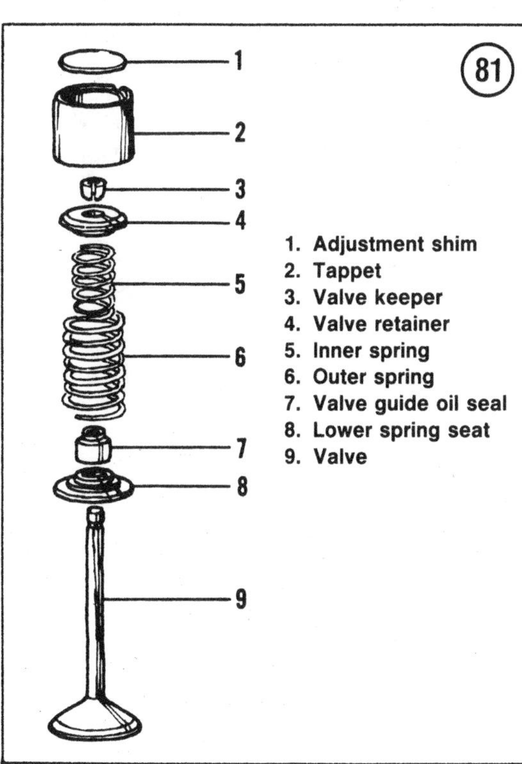

1. Adjustment shim
2. Tappet
3. Valve keeper
4. Valve retainer
5. Inner spring
6. Outer spring
7. Valve guide oil seal
8. Lower spring seat
9. Valve

8. Install the two 6 mm bolts in each end of the head and, if so equipped, the one 6 mm bolt between the center exhaust ports. See **Figure 65** and **Figure 66**. Torque the bolts to 0.9-1.1 mkg (6.5-8 ft.-lb.).
9. Install the forward chain guide. The lower end of the guide must slip into place and feel secure in the bottom of the engine. If the bottom of the guide is correctly installed, it will be necessary to slightly spring back the upper portion of the chain guide to install it in the upper cylinder head groove. Make sure that the upper end of the guide fits securely in the groove as shown in **Figure 64**.
10. On TSCC models, install the oil lines to the cylinder heads with the banjo bolts (**Figure 67**). Make sure the holes in the ends of the banjo bolts are clear of any obstructions (**Figure 79**). Install a gasket on each side of the banjo fitting and position the fittings as shown in **Figure 80**.
11. Refer to Chapter Six and install the exhaust system.
12. Perform *Camshaft Installation and Timing* as outlined in this chapter.
13. Refer to Chapter Three and perform *Valve Adjustment.*

VALVES

Valve servicing requires the use of a valve spring compressor tool to remove the valves from the head. Suitable valve spring compressors can be rented from most rental shops; however, it may be less expensive to have a dealer or other motorcycle repair shop remove the valves from the head.

Removal

Refer to **Figure 81** for this procedure.
1. Perform *Cylinder Head Removal* as outlined in this chapter.
2. Use a wire brush to thoroughly clean all the carbon deposits from the cylinder head combustion chamber.
3. Install one end of the valve spring compressor against one valve head. Place the other end of the tool squarely over the valve retainer (**Figure 82**).

CAUTION
All parts of each valve assembly must be kept together in the proper order as they are removed. Do not mix any parts with parts from other valve assemblies. Wear patterns have developed on these moving parts and damage or rapid and excessive wear may result if the parts are intermixed. Egg cartons work well to keep the valve components in order.

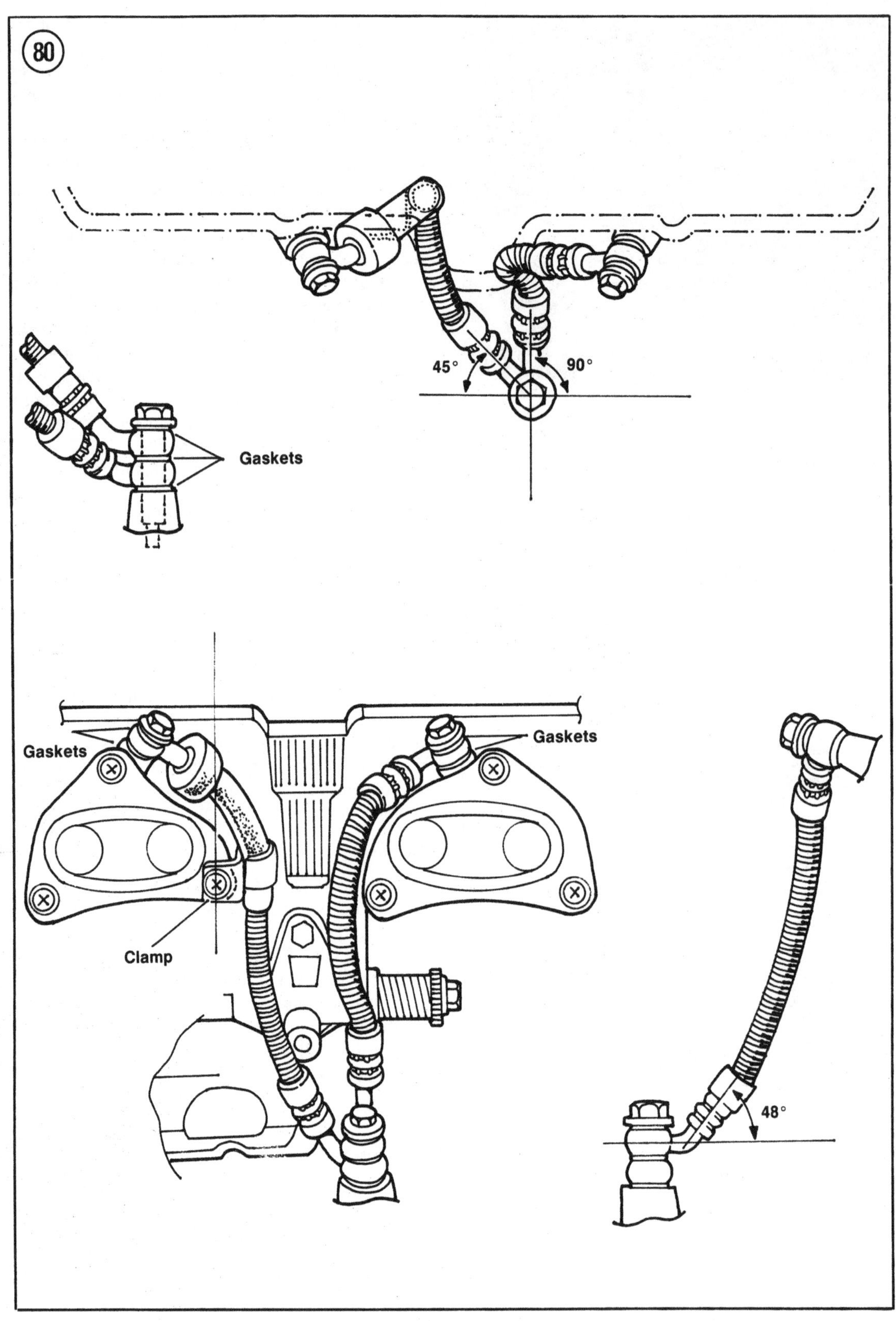
80
45°
90°
Gaskets
Gaskets
Gaskets
Clamp
48°

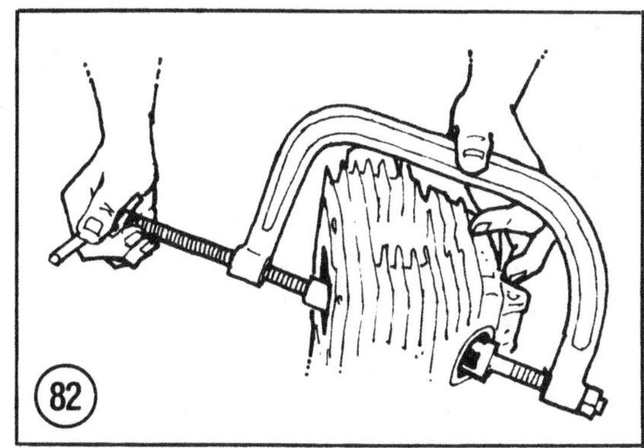

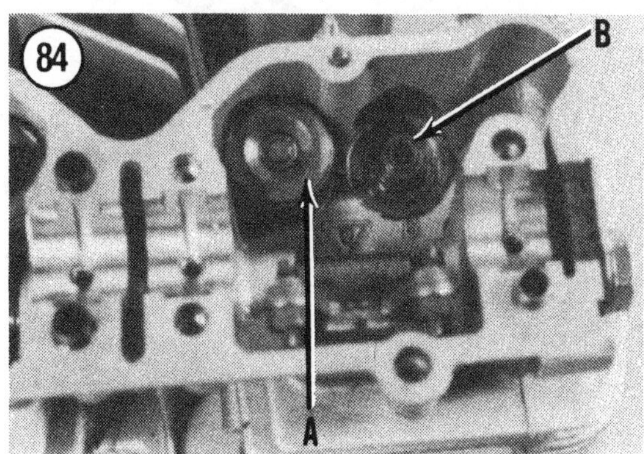

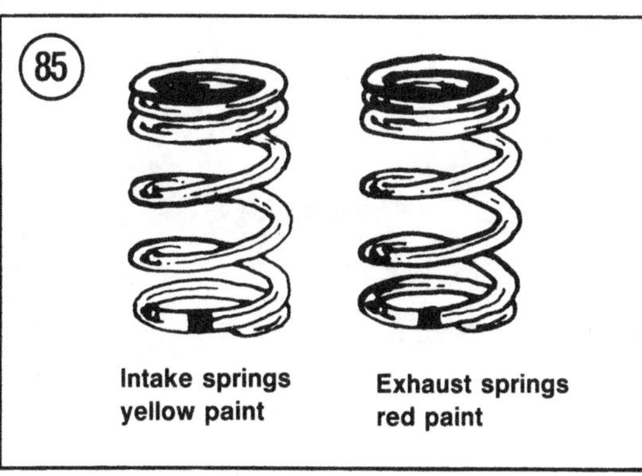

4. Tighten the valve spring compressor until the split valve keeper separates. Lift out both split keepers with needlenose pliers.
5. Gradually loosen the compressor tool and remove it from the cylinder head. Lift off the upper valve retainer. See **Figure 83** for 1982 and earlier engines, and A, **Figure 84** for TSCC engines.
6. Remove the inner and outer valve springs. Keep the springs together as they are a matched pair.

CAUTION
*The intake and exhaust valve springs are not interchangeable. Intake springs are identified by a spot of yellow paint and exhaust springs by a spot of red paint (**Figure 85**).*

7. Tip up the head and remove the valve.
8. Use needlenose pliers to remove the valve guide oil seal. See **Figure 86** for 1982 and earlier engines and B, **Figure 84** for TSCC engines. Discard the old seal as it will be destroyed when it is removed.

NOTE
Valve guide oil seals should be replaced whenever the valves are removed. Failure to replace the seals may result in excessive oil consumption.

9. Lift out the lower valve seat.
10. Repeat the procedure for the other valves.
11. Perform *Inspection.*

Inspection

1. Clean the valves with a wire brush and solvent.
2. Inspect the contact surface of each valve for burning or pitting (**Figure 87**). Replace any valve that is burned, pitted, warped or cracked. The valves are made from a specially hardened material and should not be ground or refaced.
3. Measure the valve stem with a micrometer as shown in **Figure 88**. Replace the valve if not within limits specified in **Table 5** or **Table 6**.

4

4. Remove all carbon and varnish from the valve guides with a stiff spiral wire brush.
5. Insert each valve in its guide. Hold the valve just slightly off its seat and rock it sideways in two directions as shown in **Figure 89**. If it rocks more than slightly, the guide is worn and must be replaced. If a dial indicator is available, a more accurate measurement can be made as shown in **Figure 90**. Replace any guides that exceed the valve stem-to-guide clearance specified in **Table 5** or **Table 6**. If guides must be replaced, refer the task to an authorized dealer or machine shop.
6. Use a dial indicator and V-blocks as shown in **Figure 91** to measure the valve stem deflection or runout. Replace valves if the stem deflection exceeds 0.05 mm (0.002 in.).
7. Use a dial indicator and one V-block as shown in **Figure 92** to measure the runout or deflection of the valve head. Replace valves if the head deflection exceeds 0.03 mm (0.001 in.).
8. Measure valve spring height as shown in **Figure 93**. All springs should be as specified in **Table 5** or **Table 6** with no bends or distortions. Replace defective springs in pairs.
9. Measure valve seat width (**Figure 94**). If valve seat width exceeds the dimension specified in **Table 5** or **Table 6**, the valve seat in the cylinder head must be reconditioned as described in this chapter.
10. Measure the face (margin) on each valve with a caliper (**Figure 95**). The valve face decreases as the valve seat wears. If valve face is not as specified in **Table 5** or **Table 6**, the valve must be replaced.
11. Inspect the valve seats in the cylinder head (**Figure 96**). If the seats are burned or damaged they must be reconditioned as described in this chapter. This task should be performed by an authorized dealer or local machine shop.
12. The ends of the valve stems can be refaced if necessary; however, the end of the valve must not be less than 4.0 mm (0.16 in.) for 1982 and earlier

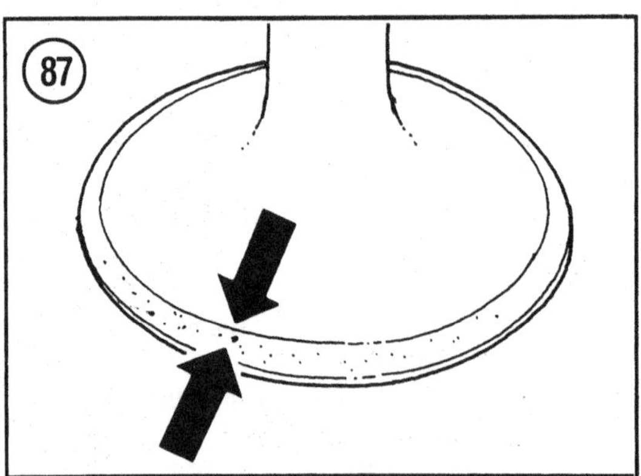

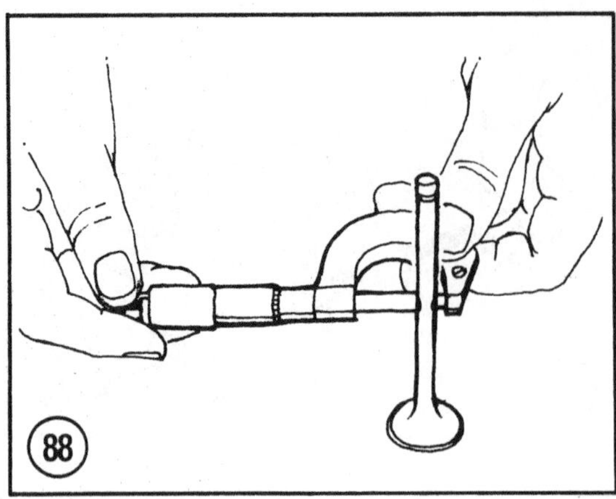

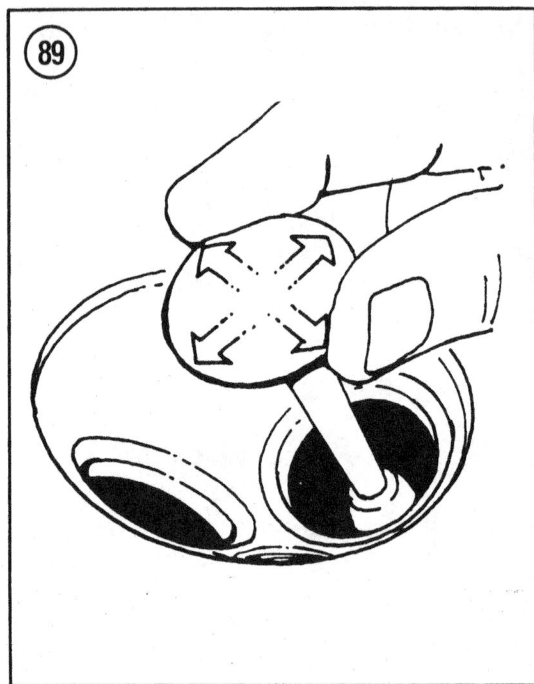

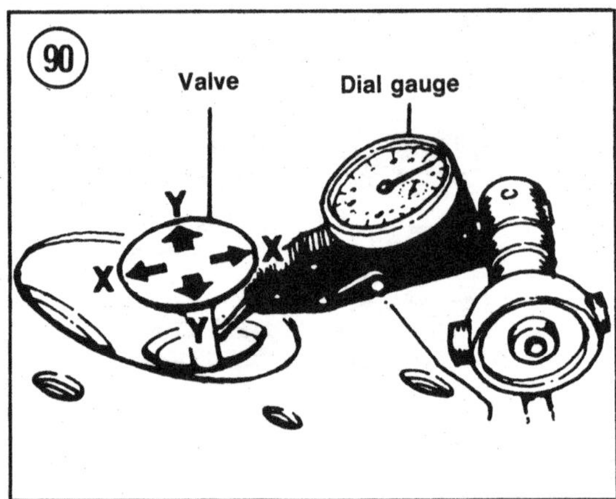

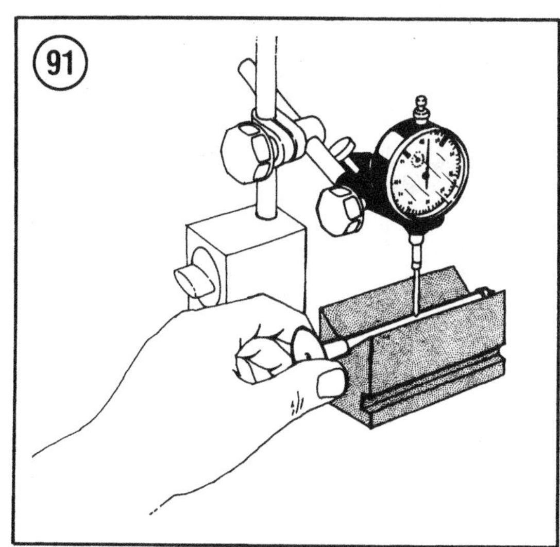

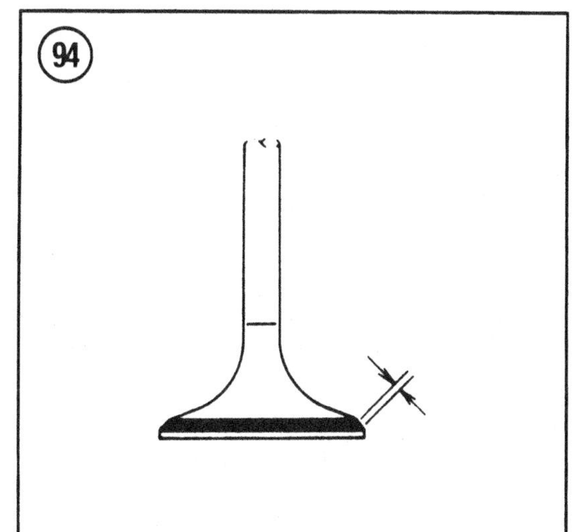

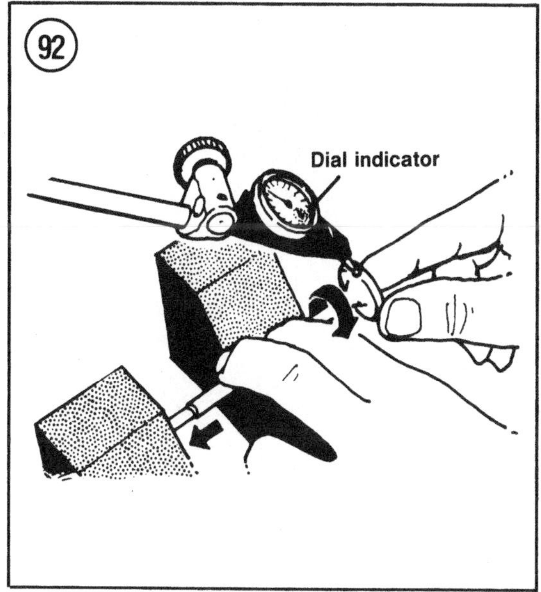
Dial indicator

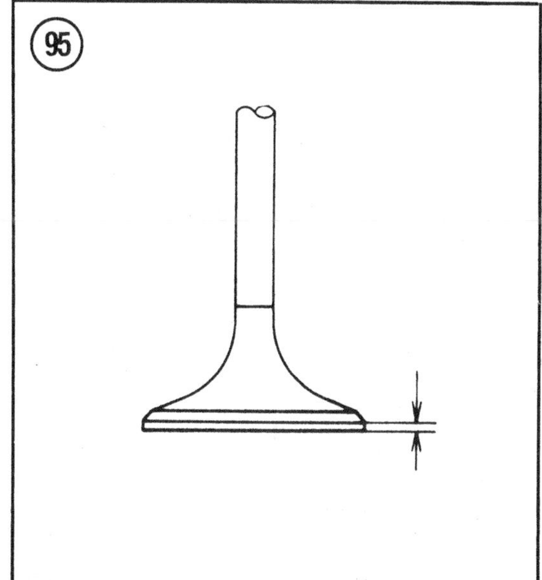

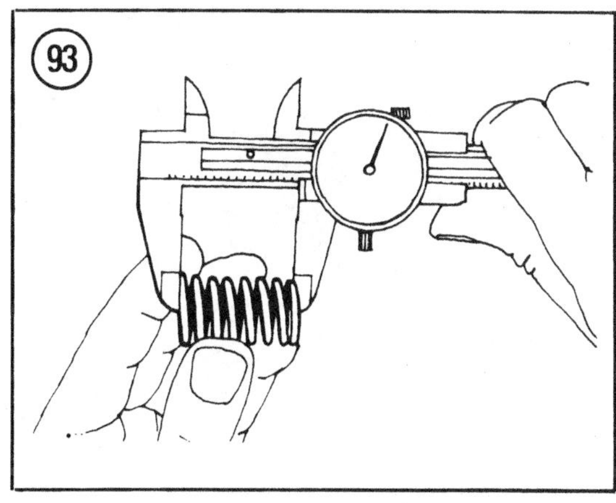

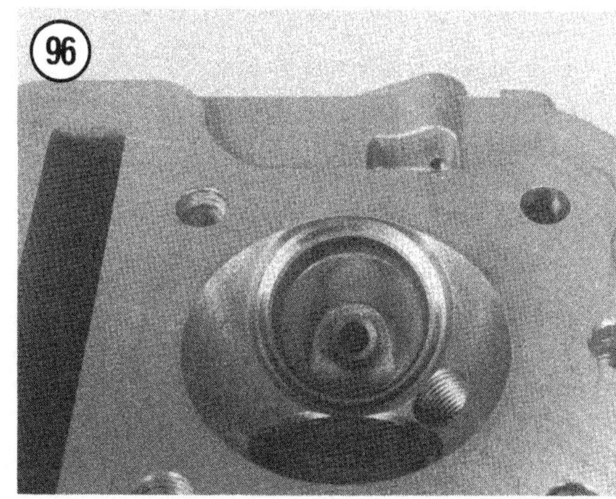

engines and 2.9 mm (0.11 in.) for TSCC engines. See **Figure 97**.

13. Inspect the upper valve retainer (**Figure 98**) for signs or damage or wear. Replace any defective valve retainers.

14. Examine the split valve keepers for damage or grooves worn in the outside of each keeper half (**Figure 99**). Replace both valve keepers as a set if either half shows signs or wear or damage.

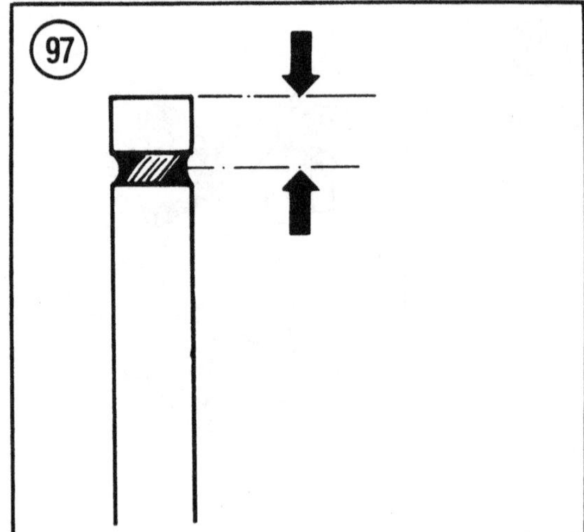

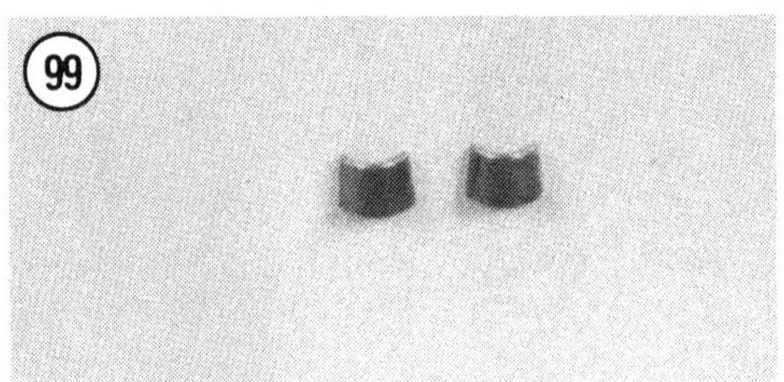

Installation

1. Install the lower spring seat over the valve guide.
2. Lubricate the lip on the new valve guide seal with engine oil. Use a 10 mm socket (7 or 8 mm for TSCC engines) as a seal installing tool and position the seal over the end of the valve guide. Gently tap the seal into place. Make sure the seal is seated squarely over the valve guide and is locked into place. See **Figure 100** and **Figure 101**.
3. Install the inner and outer valve springs. Note that the coils are closer together on the bottom end (toward cylinder head) of the springs (**Figure 102**). Make sure the springs are installed correctly.
4. Lubricate the valve stems with Bel-Ray Moly Lube or equivalent and install the valves in the head.
5. Place the upper spring retainer over the valve springs. Install the spring compressor tool and tighten the compressor until the end of the valve is exposed enough to install the split keepers.
6. Apply a small amount of grease to each keeper half and stick the keeper to a small screwdriver to aid installation. Install the split keepers on the valve stem and back off the spring compressor until the split keepers secure the valve mechanism.
7. Remove the valve spring compressor. Use a soft drift or a soft-faced hammer and tap the end of each valve to make sure the keepers are properly seated.
8. Perform *Cylinder Head Installation.*

Valve Seat and Seal Inspection

1. Use a caliper and measure the width of the seat on the valve (**Figure 103**). If the seat width is not within the tolerance specified in **Table 5** or **Table 6**, the valve seat in the cylinder head must be reconditioned.
2. The most accurate method for checking the seal of the valve is to use Prussian Blue or machinist's dye, available from auto part stores or machine shops. To check the valve seal with Prussian Blue or machinist's dye, perform the following:
   a. Thoroughly clean the valve and valve seat with solvent or detergent.

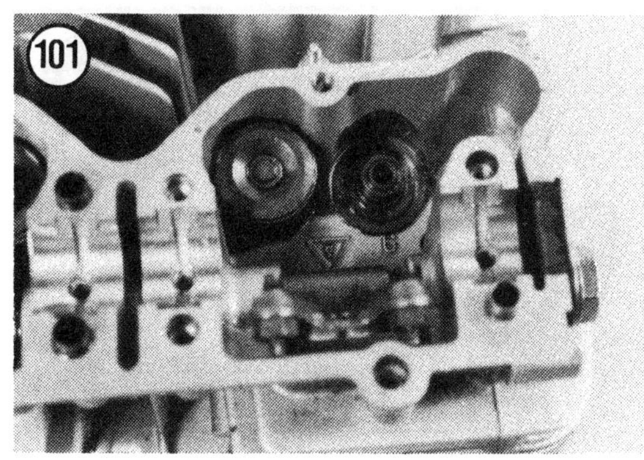

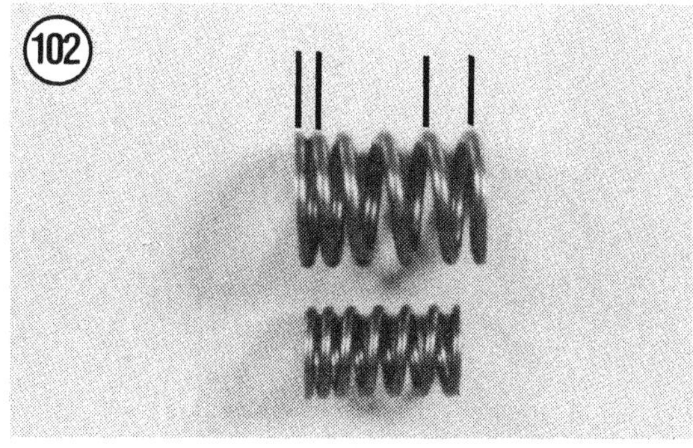

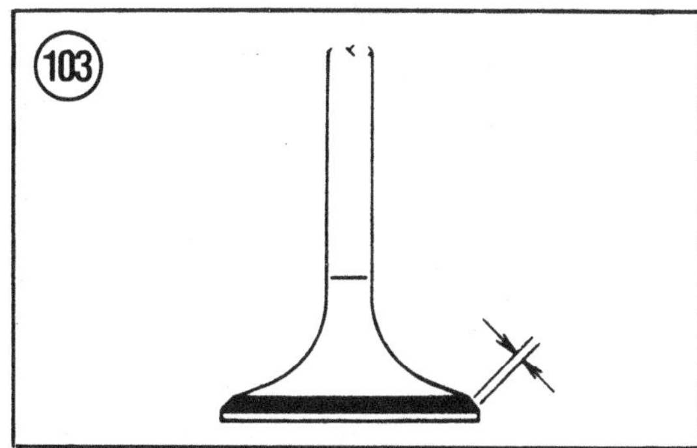

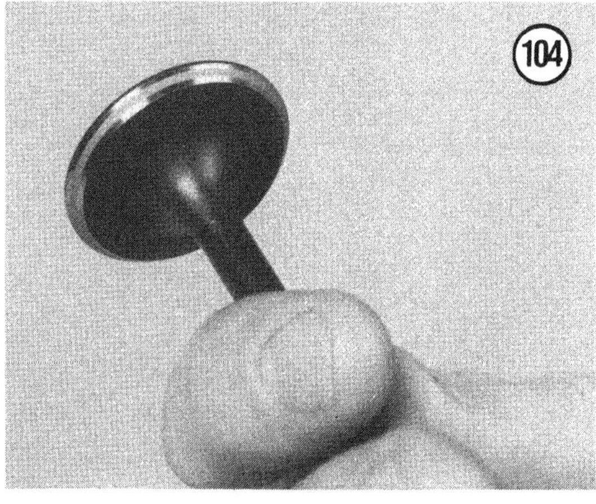

b. Spread a thin layer of Prussian Blue or machinist's dye evenly on the valve face (**Figure 104**).
c. Moisten the end of a suction cup valve tool (**Figure 105**) and attach it to the valve. Insert the valve into the guide.
d. Tap the valve up and down in the head. Do *not* rotate the valve or a false indication will result.
e. Remove the valve and examine the impression left by the Prussian Blue or dye. If the impression left in the dye (on the valve or in the head) is not even and continuous and the valve seat width (**Figure 103**) is not within specified tolerance (**Table 5** or **Table 6**), the seat in the cylinder head must be reconditioned as described in this chapter.

3. Closely examine the valve seat in the cylinder head. It should be smooth and even with a polished seating surface.
4. Install the valves as described in this chapter.

Valve Guide Replacement

Inspect the valves to determine the condition of the valve guides. The valve guides must be replaced if there is excessive stem-to-guide clearance or valve tipping. Guide replacement requires special tools as well as considerable expertise. If guide replacement is required, refer the task to an authorized dealer or machine shop.

Valve Seat Reconditioning

Special valve cutter tools and considerable expertise are required to properly recondition the valve seats in the cylinder head. You can save money by removing the cylinder head and taking just the head to a dealer or machine shop. The following procedure is provided in the event that you are not near a dealer and the local machine shop is not familiar with the cutting process used on GS550 engines.

The cutting technique is slightly different between 1982 and earlier engines and TSCC engines.

1982 and earlier engines

Refer to **Figure 106** for this procedure.

1. Use a 45 degree cutter and descale and clean the valve seat with one or two turns.
2. Measure the width of the valve seat as shown in **Figure 103**. The seat should be 1.0-1.2 mm (0.039-0.047 in.). If the seat is burned or pitted, additional turns with the 45 degree cutter are required.

4

NOTE
Measure the valve seat contact area in the cylinder head after each cut to make sure the contact area is correct and to prevent removing too much material.

3. If the seat contact area is too low on the valve or too narrow (**Figure 107**), a 75 degree cutter must be used to raise and widen the contact area.
4. If the seat contact area is too high on the valve or too wide (**Figure 108**), a 15 degree cutter must be used to lower and narrow the contact area.
5. Recheck the seat width and recut the seat with the 45 degree cutter if necessary.
6. Check that the finished valve seat has a smooth and velvety surface. Do *not* lap the finished seat. The final seating of the valve will take place when the engine is first run.
7. Thoroughly clean all valve components and the cylinder head in solvent or detergent and hot water. Install the valves and fill the ports with solvent to check for leaks. If any leaks are present, the valve seats must be inspected for foreign material or burrs that can prevent a proper seal.

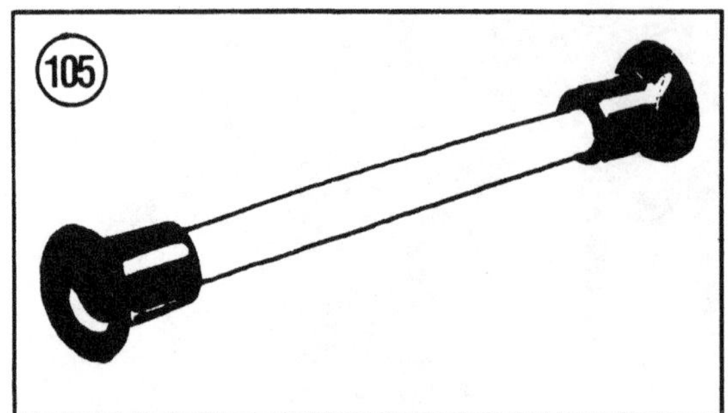
105

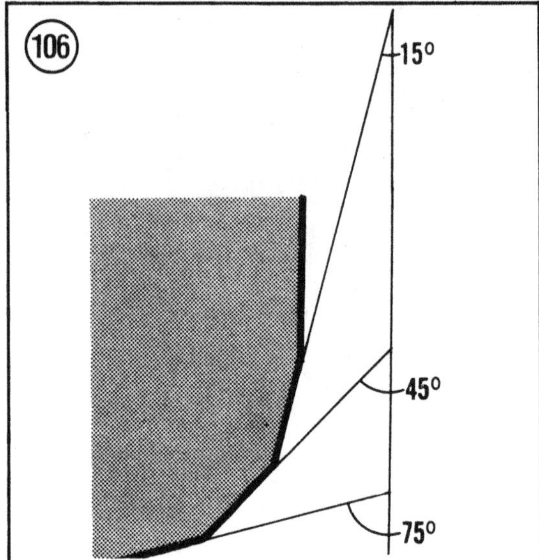

106

TSCC engines

Refer to **Figure 109** for this procedure.
1. Use a 45 degree cutter and descale and clean the valve seat with one or two turns.
2. Measure the width of the valve seat as shown in **Figure 103**. The seat should be 0.9-1.1 mm (0.035-0.043 in.). If the seat is burned or pitted, additional turns with the 45 degree cutter are required.

NOTE
Measure the valve seat contact area in the cylinder head after each cut to make sure the contact area is correct and to prevent removing too much material.

3. If the seat contact area is too low on the valve or too narrow (**Figure 107**), a 45 degree cutter must be used to raise and widen the contact area.
4. If the seat contact area is too high on the valve or too wide (**Figure 108**), a 15 degree cutter must be used to lower and narrow the contact area.
5. Recheck the seat width and recut the seat with the 45 degree cutter if necessary.
6. Check that the finished valve seat has a smooth and velvety surface. Do *not* lap the finished seat. The final seating of the valve will take place when the engine is first run.
7. Thoroughly clean all valve components and the cylinder head in solvent or detergent and hot water. Install the valves and fill the ports with solvent to check for leaks. If any leaks are present,

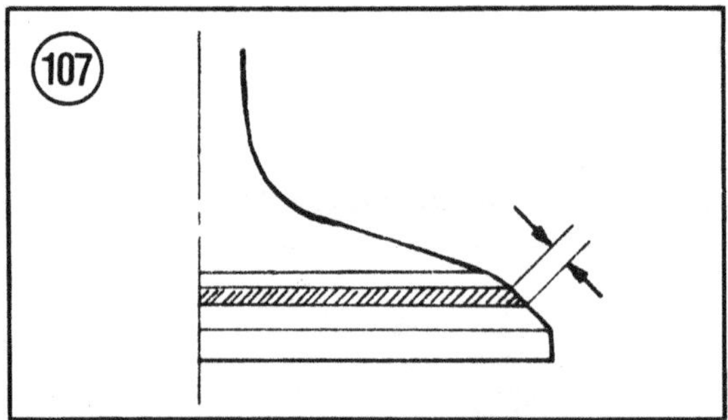
107

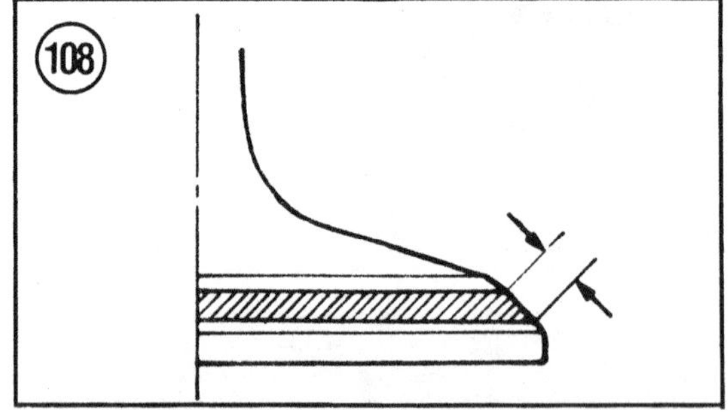
108

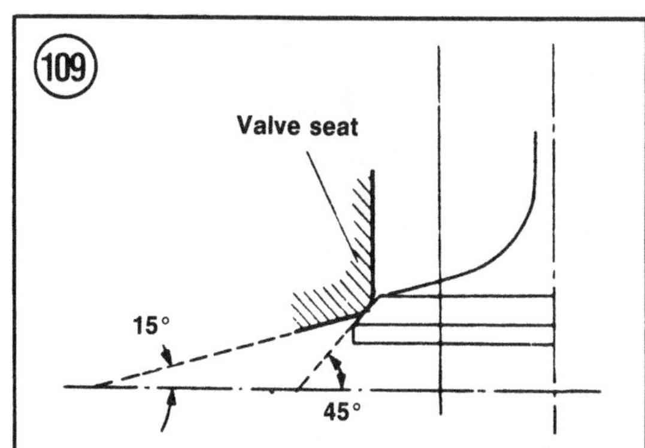

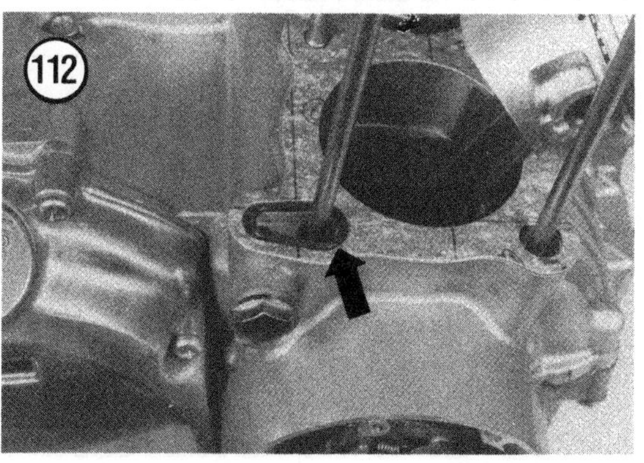

the valve seats must be inspected for foreign material or burrs that can prevent a proper seal.

CYLINDER BLOCK AND PISTONS

Cylinder block and piston repair work can be performed with the engine installed in the motorcycle.

Removal

1. Remove the cylinder head as described in this chapter.
2. Tap around the base of the cylinder with a rubber mallet or plastic hammer to break the cylinder loose from the crankcase.

CAUTION
The cooling fins on the cylinder block are fragile. Tap the cylinder block carefully to avoid fin damage. Never use a metal hammer.

3. Gently lift up and remove the cylinder block from the engine (**Figure 110**). Note that the arrows on all the pistons point forward (**Figure 111**).
4. Remove and discard the cylinder base gasket. On 1982 and earlier engines, remove the oval-shaped O-rings (**Figure 112**).
5. Stuff clean rags into the crankcase openings around each connecting rod to prevent dirt and piston pin snap rings from falling into the engine.
6. Use a small screwdriver or awl and carefully pry out the snap ring through the notch in the piston (**Figure 113**). Partially cover the opening in the piston with your thumb to prevent the snap ring from flying out. Discard the old snap ring.
7. Use a wooden dowel or socket extension to push out the piston pin (**Figure 114**). Remove the pin and lift off the piston. On some engines the piston pin may be difficult to remove. Do not attempt to drive out the pin or connecting rod damage may result. If the piston pin cannot be

pushed or gently tapped out, use a piston pin extractor tool. Refer to **Figure 115** for an example of a locally made type. If such a tool is not available, have a dealer remove the piston pin. It is a quick and inexpensive job with the right tools and will prevent expensive engine damage.

8. Mark the inside of the piston with a felt pen or scribe to identify its location. Repeat the removal procedure for the other pistons.

NOTE

*If the engine is to be completely disassembled, you may want to leave one piston installed. An installed piston can be used with a piston holding fixture to prevent the crankshaft from turning. This may be required if the magneto rotor or ignition advance governor must be removed. Refer to **Lower End Disassembly**.*

9. Perform *Cylinder Block Inspection* and *Piston and Ring Inspection*.

Cylinder Block Inspection

The following procedure requires the use of highly specialized and expensive measuring equipment. If such equipment is not available, have a dealer or machine shop perform the following measurements.

1. Use an inside micrometer or cylinder bore gauge to measure the cylinder bore (**Figure 116**). Measure the bore at 3 locations as shown in **Figure 117** and in 2 positions, 90° apart. Compare the measurements with the specifications in **Table 7** or **Table 8** and rebore the cylinder if necessary.
2. Examine the cylinder bore; the cylinder should be rebored if the surface is scored or abraded. Pistons are available in oversize increases of 0.5 mm and 1.0 mm. Purchase the oversize pistons before having the cylinder bored. The pistons must first be measured and the cylinder bored to match them in order to maintain the specified piston-to-cylinder clearance. All pistons should be replaced as a set.

Piston and Ring Inspection

1. Measure the pistons at the point shown in **Figure 118**. If any piston is not within the tolerance specified in **Table 7** or **Table 8**, replace all pistons as a set.
2. Use a bore gauge or a snap gauge and micrometer to measure the piston pin bore in each piston (**Figure 119**). Use a micrometer to measure each piston pin at the center and at each end. Subtract the piston pin dimension from the inside

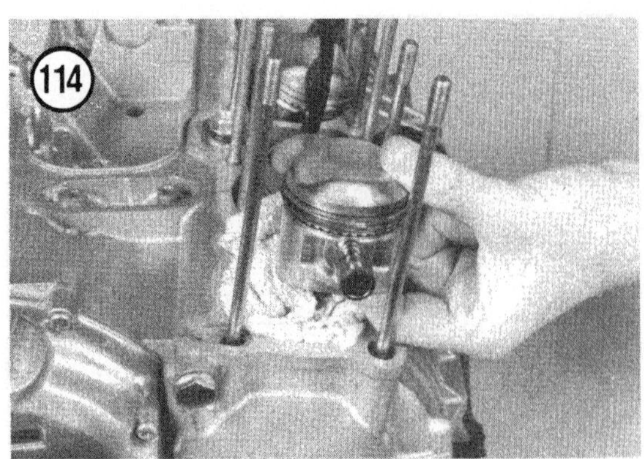

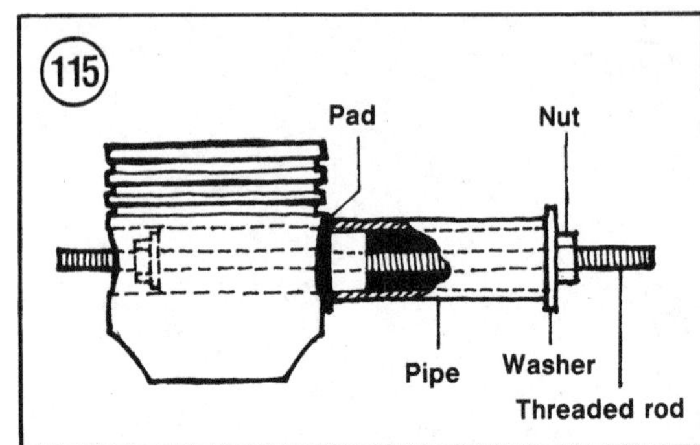

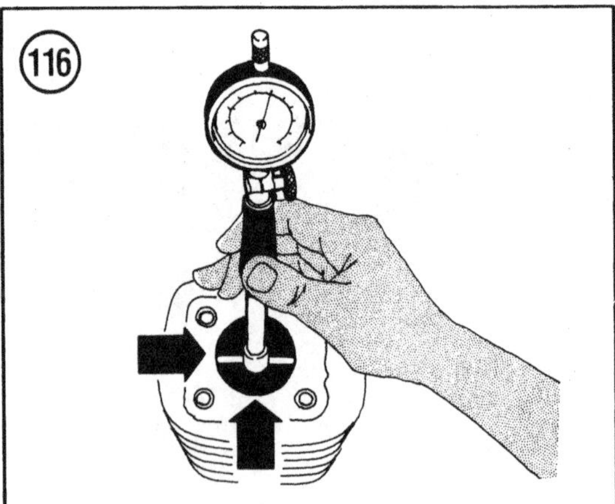

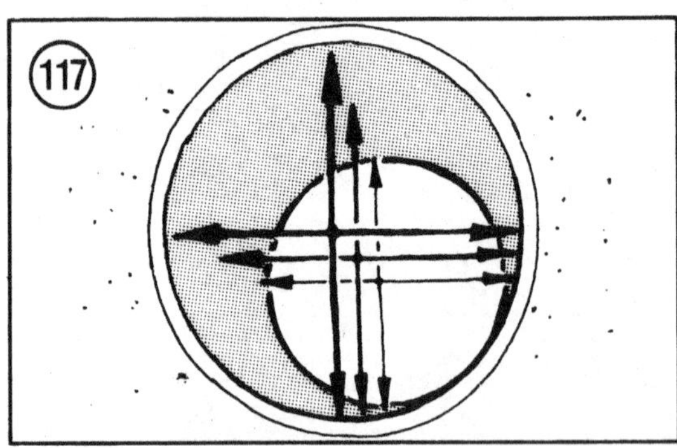

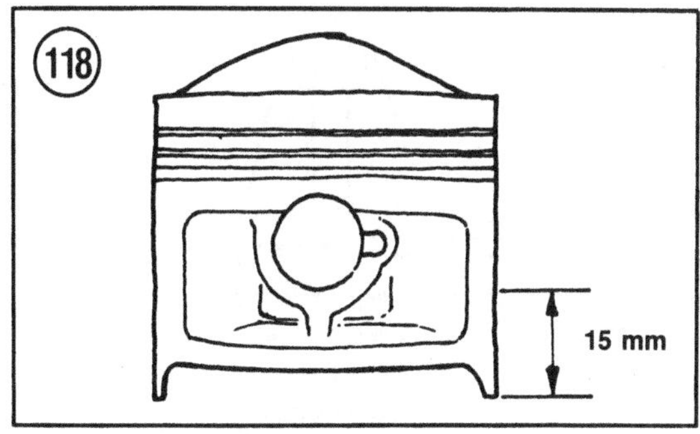

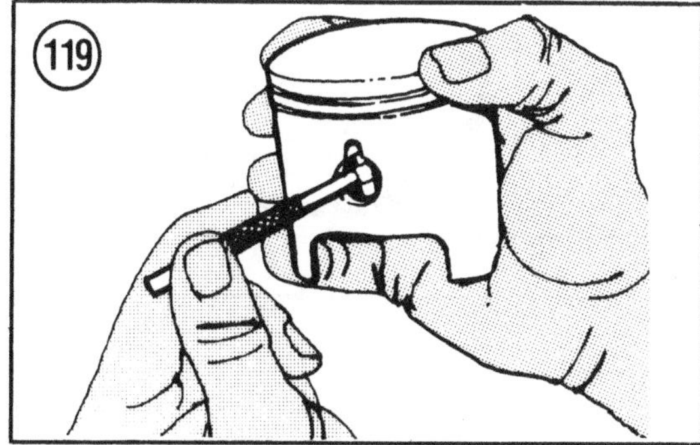

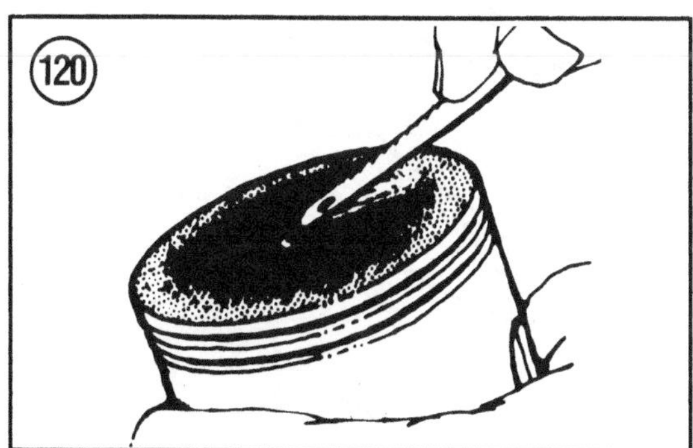

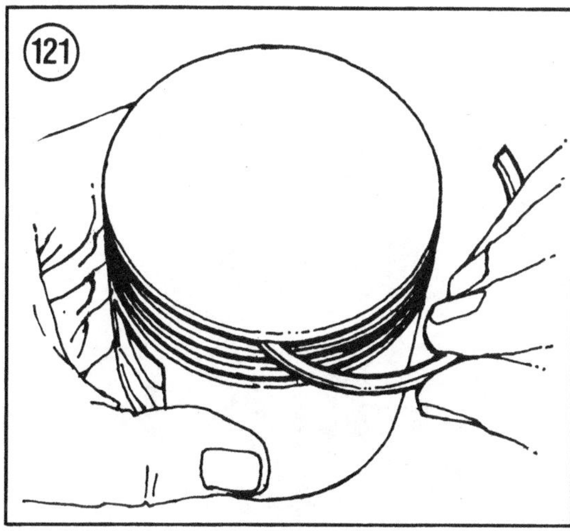

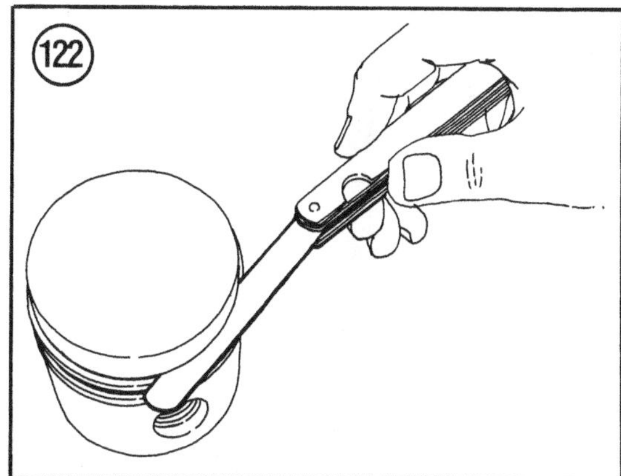

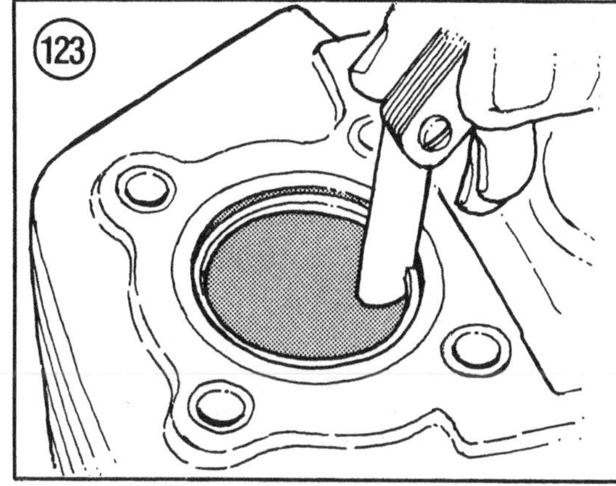

piston pin bore dimension to obtain the piston pin-to-pin bore clearance. If the bore clearance dimension exceeds the service limit of 0.12 mm (0.0047 in.), replace the piston and pin as a set.

3. Clean the top of the pistons with a soft metal scaper to remove carbon (**Figure 120**). Use a piece of old piston ring to clean the ring grooves (**Figure 121**). Thoroughly clean the pistons in solvent or detergent and hot water.

4. Use a feeler gauge to check the side clearance of the rings in the piston grooves (**Figure 121**). If the clearance is greater than that specified in **Table 9**, measure the ring thickness and the groove width to determine which part is worn. All parts worn beyond their respective service limits must be replaced. Ring thickness and groove width specifications are listed in **Table 9**.

5. Place the 2 top piston rings, one at a time, into the cylinder bore and measure the ring end gap (**Figure 123**). Use the piston to push the ring squarely into the cylinder bore approximately 25 mm (1 in.). This measurement is required for new rings as well as old ones. Compare the actual ring gap to **Table 9** and replace the old rings if their gap

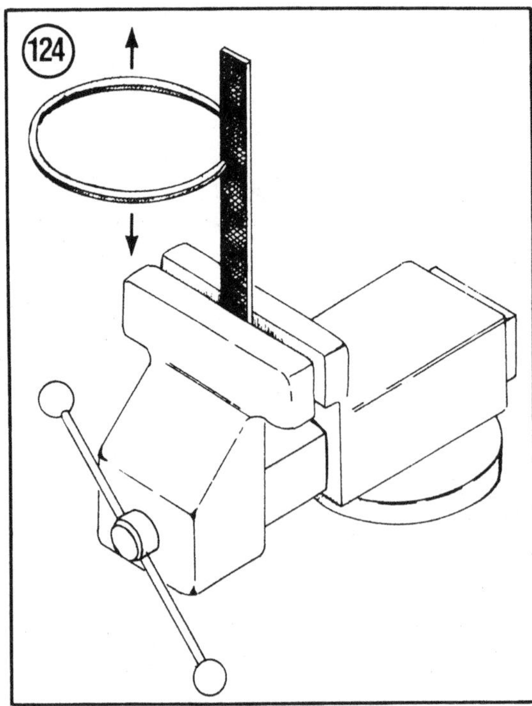

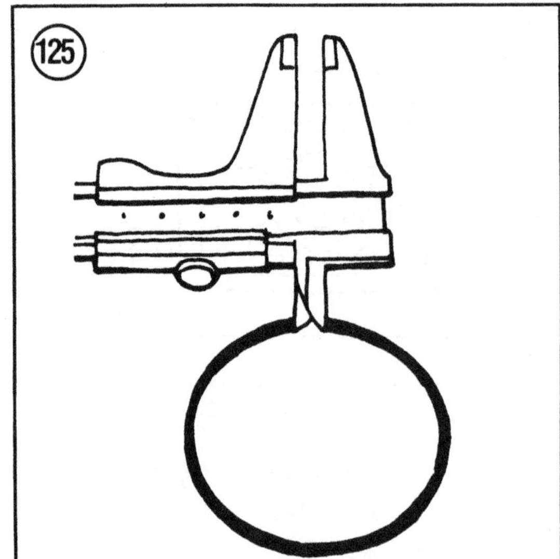

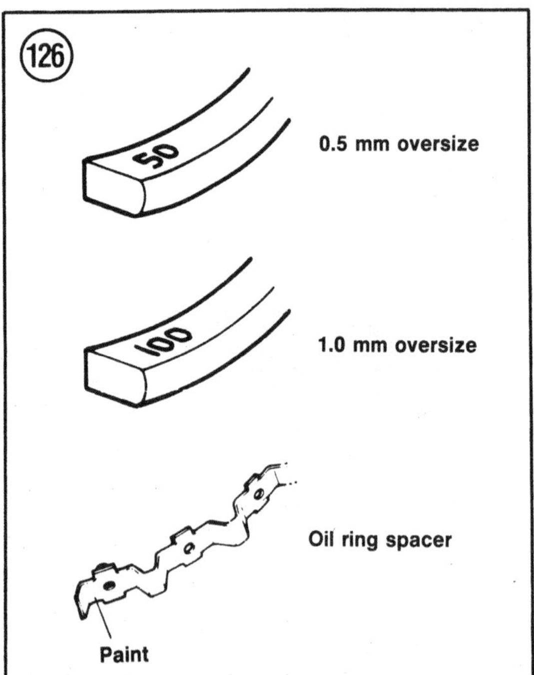

is greater than the specified service limit. For new rings it is more likely that the gap will be less than minimum. If such is the case, clamp a fine file in a vise and carefully file the ring ends as shown in **Figure 124**.

6. Measure the free-state ring gap as shown in **Figure 125**. If the free-state ring gap is less than specified, the ring does not have sufficient spring tension to seat well and must be replaced.

7. Existing rings that are oversize can be identified in the following ways:

   a. The top 2 rings are stamped with code numbers next to the letter on the ring end (**Figure 126**). A 0.5 mm oversized ring is stamped with the number "50" while a 1.0 mm oversize ring is stamped with the number "100."
   b. Oil ring spacers are identified by color codes painted on the ends. A standard size spacer has a red paint spot. A 0.5 mm oversized spacer is painted blue while a 1.0 mm oversize spacer is painted yellow.
   c. Oversized oil ring side rails must be measured with a caliper to determine their size in relation to standard size side rails.

8. Carefully examine each piston around the area of the skirt, pin and ring grooves for signs of cracks, stress or metal fatigue (**Figure 127**). Replace all the pistons as a set if any signs of abnormal wear are present on any piston.

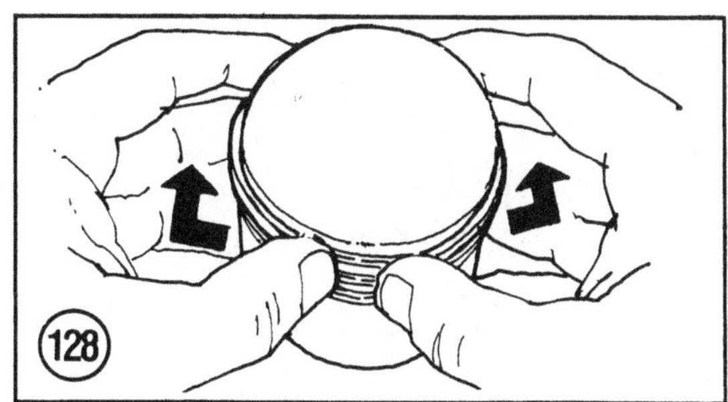

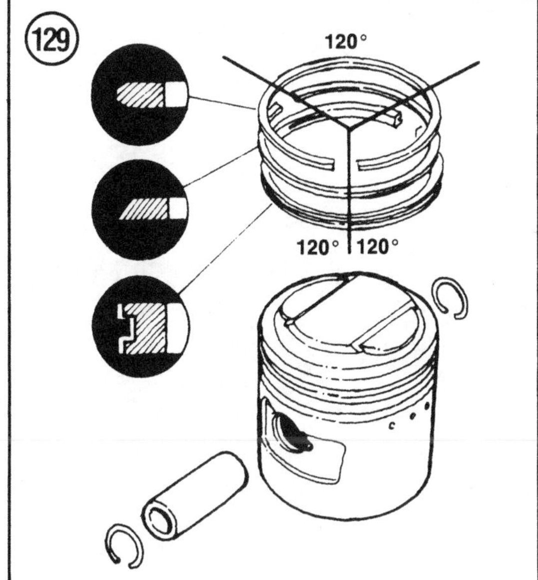

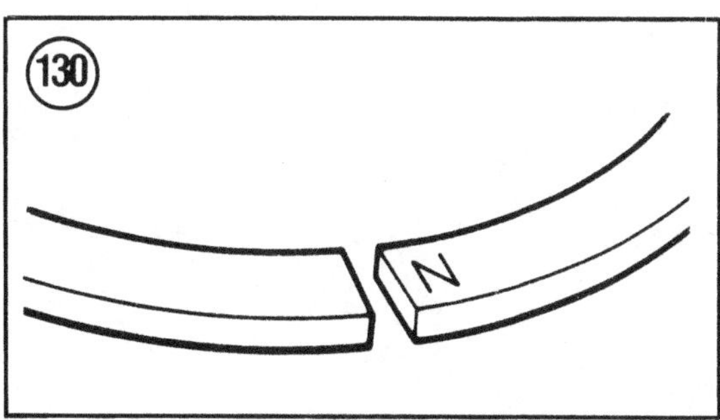

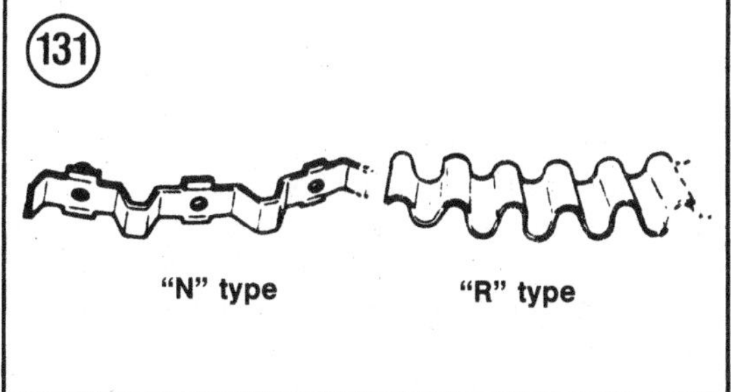

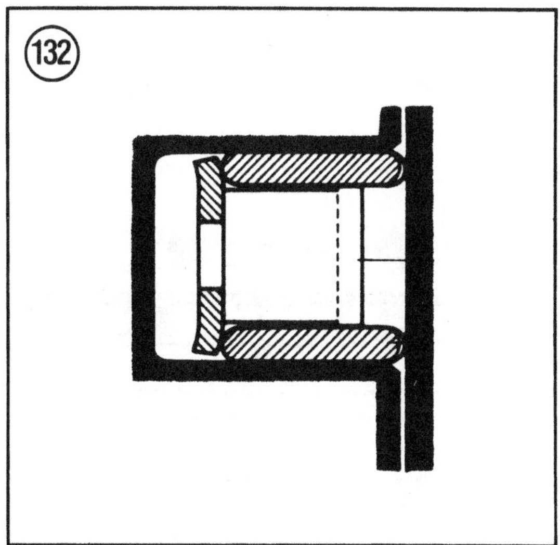

Installation

1. Carefully spread the piston rings with your thumbs as shown in **Figure 128** and install the rings in the appropriate grooves (**Figure 129**). The 2 top rings are stamped with either an "R" or "N" as shown in **Figure 130**. The identifying letters on the ring ends always face toward the top of the piston. The shape of the top and 2nd ring differ as shown in **Figure 129**. The top ring is chrome-plated and brighter than the 2nd ring.
2. Two types of oil ring spacers are used (**Figure 131**). The "R" type spacer must be installed with "R" type upper rings and "N" type spacer with "N" type upper rings. The side rails on the oil rings are not marked and can be used with either type of oil ring spacer.
3. Install the oil ring spacer first. The 2 side rails can then be installed. There is no top or bottom orientation for the side rails. Make sure the side rails fit around the spacer as shown in **Figure 132**. Some clearance may be present between the ends of the oil ring spacer (**Figure 133**). Do *not* allow the ends of the oil spacer to overlap.
4. Install one new snap ring into the piston pin groove.

CAUTION

If possible, always use new snap rings to secure the piston pin. An old snap ring could work out and cause serious and expensive engine damage.

5. Lubricate the piston, piston pin and connecting rod with assembly oil or engine oil and install the piston on the connecting rod (**Figure 134**). Make sure the arrow on the piston points forward, toward the front of the engine.

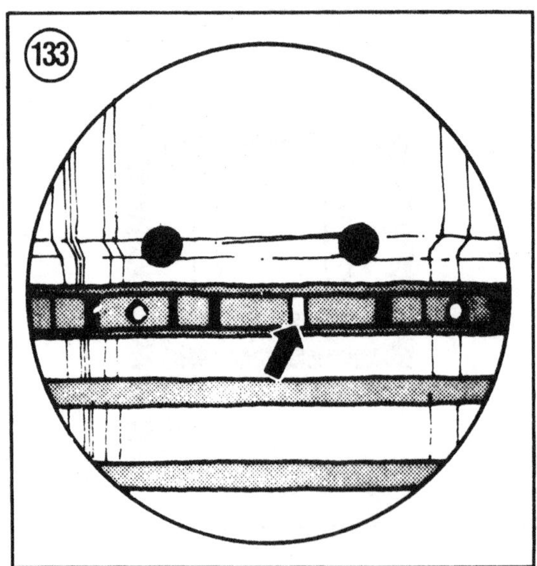

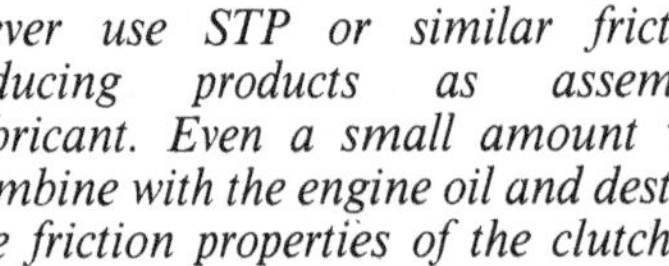

CAUTION
Never use STP or similar friction reducing products as assembly lubricant. Even a small amount will combine with the engine oil and destroy the friction properties of the clutch. If this should occur, the entire engine's lubrication system must be flushed and new clutch plates installed.

CAUTION
If it is necessary to tap the piston pin into the connecting rod, do so with a soft-faced hammer. Make sure you support the piston to prevent the lateral shock from being transmitted to the lower connecting rod bearing.

6. Partially hold a new snap ring in position with your thumb and install the snap ring into the piston groove (**Figure 135**). Make sure the snap ring locks into the groove. Rotate the snap ring so that a solid portion of the snap ring is opposite the notch in the piston (**Figure 136**).

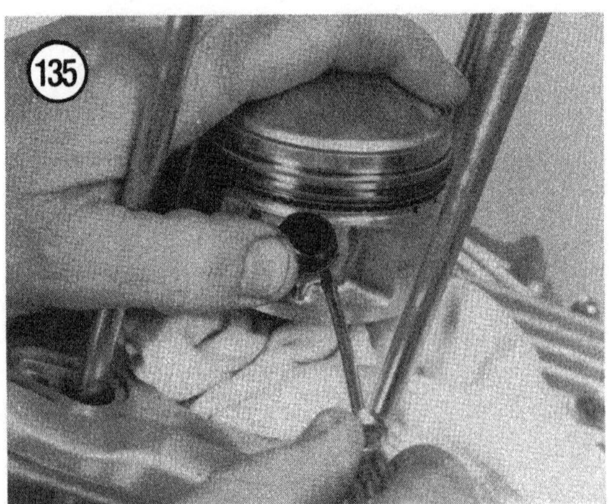

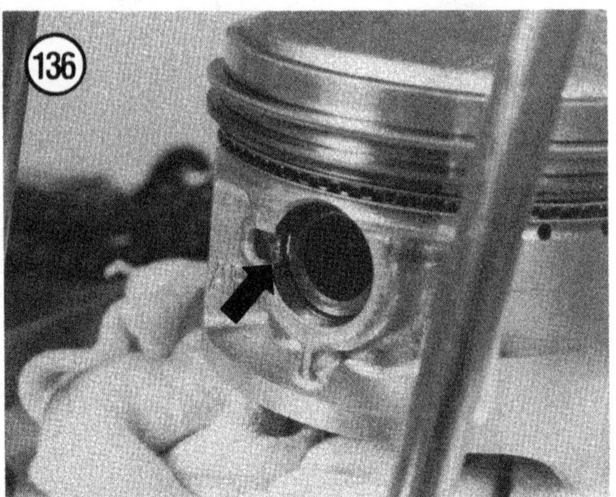

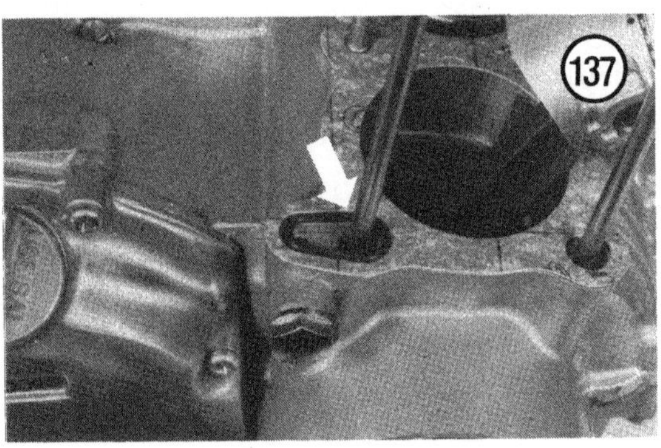

7. Make sure the engine base and the bottom of the cylinder block are clean and free of old gasket residue. Install a new base gasket on the crankcase. On 1982 and earlier engines, install new oval-shaped O-rings as shown in **Figure 137**.

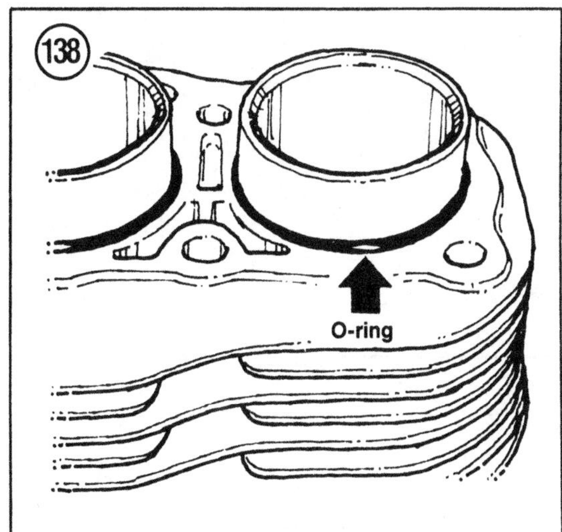

8. Remove the old O-rings from the base of each cylinder liner and replace with new ones (**Figure 138**).
9. Stagger the rings on each piston so that the end gaps are approximately 120° from each other (**Figure 129**).
10. Install a piston holding fixture under one or both inboard pistons (**Figure 139**) to hold the pistons in position while installing the cylinder block. Carefully rotate the crankshaft until the pistons are firmly against the holding fixture.

NOTE
*A simple homemade holding fixture can be made of wood. Refer to **Figure 140**.*

11. Oil each piston and cylinder bore with assembly oil or engine oil. Feed the cam chain up through the chain tunnel and start the cylinder block down over the studs (**Figure 141**). Compress the rings on the 2 inboard pistons with your fingers or a ring compressor and carefully slide the cylinder block over the pistons until the cylinder block contacts the 2 outboard pistons.

NOTE
*A large hose clamp (**Figure 142**) makes an effective and inexpensive ring compressor.*

12. Using your fingers or a ring compressor, carefully compress the outboard piston rings while pushing down on the cylinder block until all 3 rings on each piston are fully installed into the cylinder bores.
13. Remove the ring compressors and piston holding fixture. Push the cylinder block down completely against the gasket.

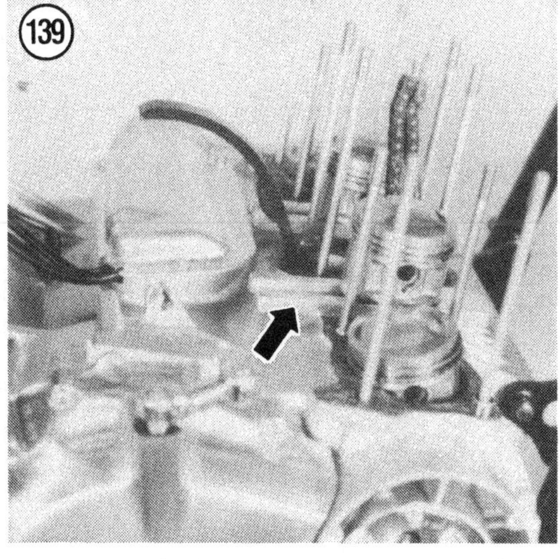

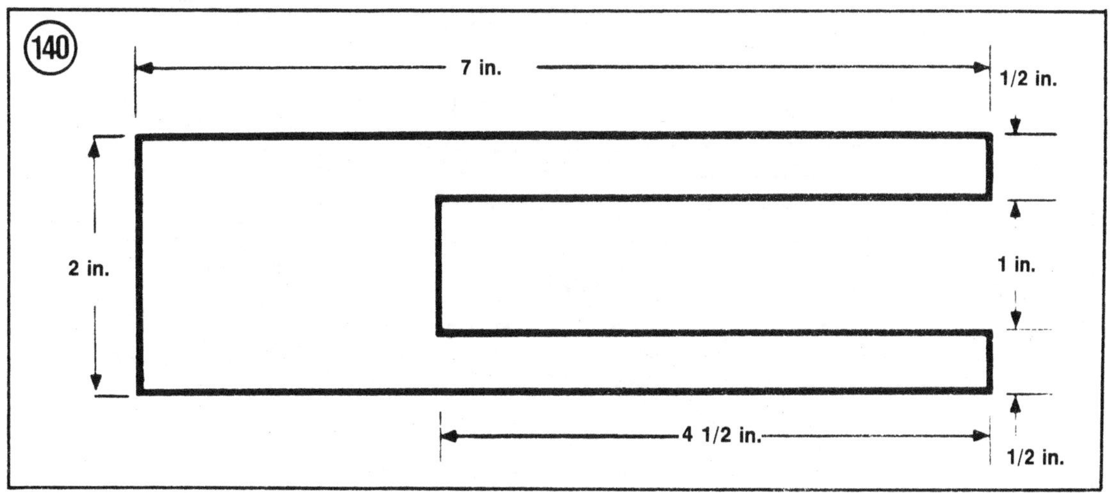

4

14. Install the cylinder head as described in this chapter.

ENGINE REMOVAL AND INSTALLATION

The engine must be removed from the frame to perform repair on the crankshaft, transmission and most of the gearshifting mechanism. It is easier to first remove the cylinder head and cylinder block; head and block removal will greatly reduce the weight of the engine, making it much more manageable.

NOTE

The following procedure contains several steps that are only necessary if complete engine disassembly is desired. Certain parts are more easily removed while the engine is still in the frame. Perform the entire procedure if disassembly is desired.

1. Thoroughly clean the motorcycle at a coin-operated car wash or with detergent and a hose. Make sure the engine and all nuts and bolts are as clean as possible. A clean motorcycle is not only more pleasant to work on, it helps prevent contamination of vital moving parts.
2. Remove any accessories such as a fairing or safety bars that may interfere with engine removal.
3. Place the motorcycle on the centerstand and place a drain pan under the engine. Use a socket to remove the oil drain plug (**Figure 143**). Allow several minutes for the oil to drain completely.
4. Move the drain pan under the oil filter housing and remove the acorn nuts securing the oil filter cover (**Figure 144**). Remove the cover and the oil filter.

141

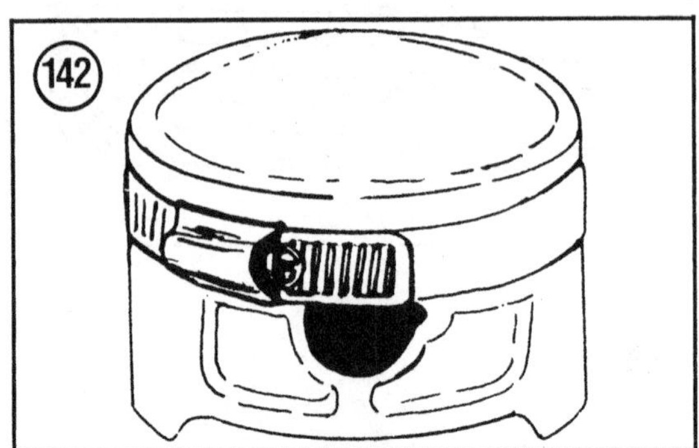
142

144

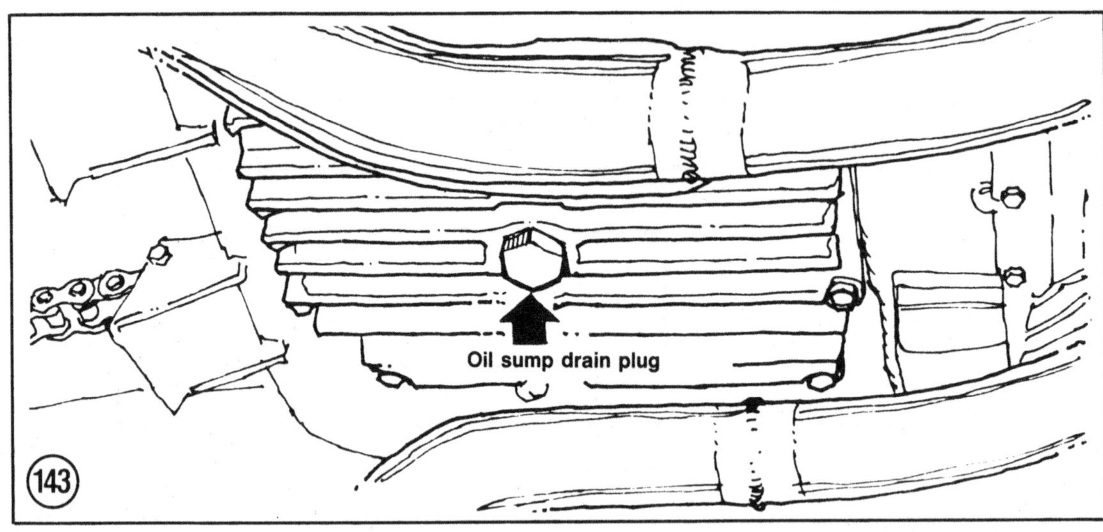

143

NOTE
Use an 8 mm Allen wrench to remove the socket head mounting bolts on models so equipped.

5. Remove the pinch bolt securing the footbrake pedal (**Figure 145**). Disengage the return spring and slide the pedal off the shaft. Note that the punch mark on the shaft is aligned with the split opening on the brake pedal (**Figure 146**).

NOTE
When removing the brake pedal and gearshift lever, it may be necessary to slightly pry open the split opening in the pedal or lever with a screwdriver to ease removal.

6. Remove the bolts securing the right footrest (**Figure 147**) and remove the footrest. Do not lose the two rubber bushings used with each bolt.
7. Remove the seat and remove the bolts securing the fuel tank to the frame (**Figure 148**).
8. Disconnect the fuel line and vacuum line from the fuel tank valve (**Figure 149**).
9. On models with a fuel gauge, disconnect the black/white and yellow/black fuel gauge wires near the left or right rear corner of the fuel tank (**Figure 150**).

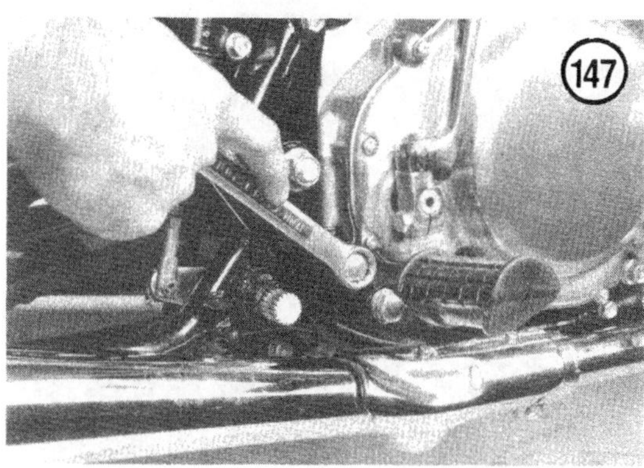

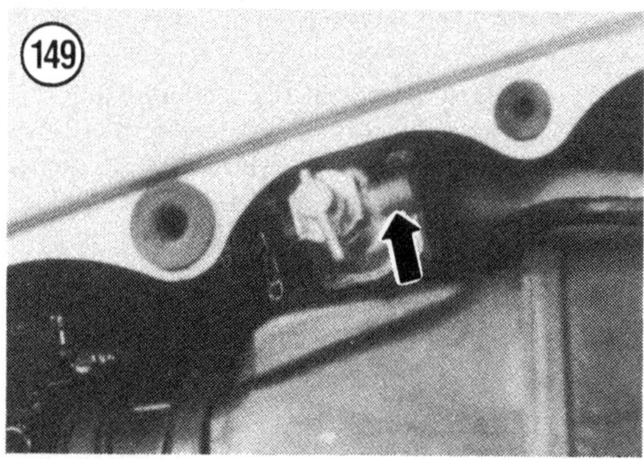

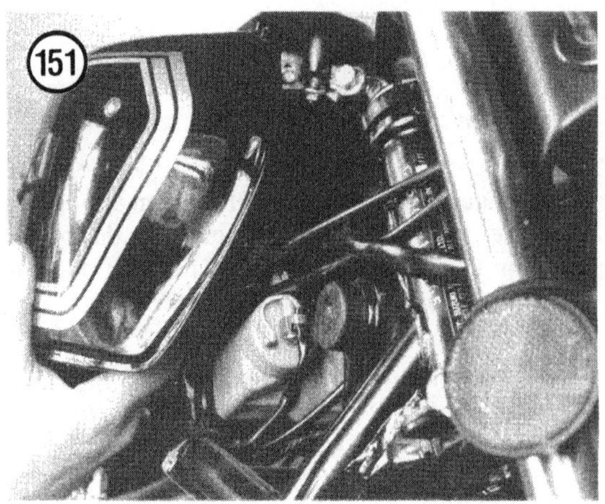

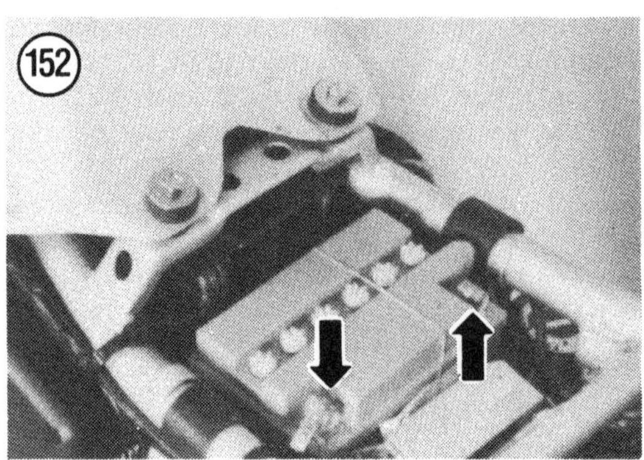

10. Lift up on the rear of the tank and slide the tank back enough to disengage the front rubber mounting pads (**Figure 151**). Make sure the rubber washers on the mounting bolts are not lost.

11. On TSCC models with an oil cooler, remove the oil cooler or disconnect the oil lines from the crankcase as described under *Oil Cooler* in this chapter.

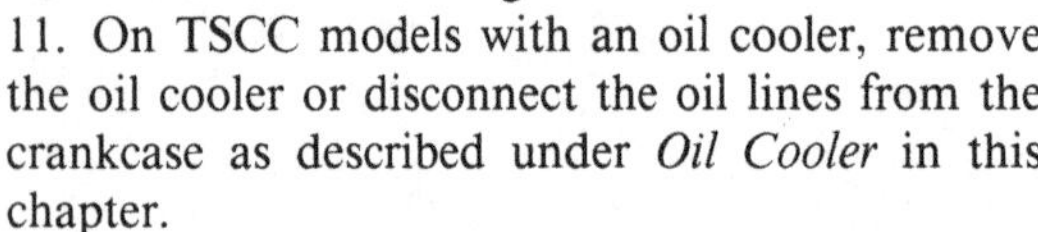

12. Refer to Chapter Six and remove the carburetors and exhaust system.

13. Disconnect the battery leads, negative first, then positive (**Figure 152**).

14. Remove the side covers and disconnect the following wires:
  a. On 1982 and earlier models, white/green, white/blue and yellow alternator wires (**Figure 153**).
  b. On TSCC models, 3 yellow alternator wires (**Figure 154**).
  c. Starter motor lead wire (**Figure 155**).
  d. On 1979 and earlier models, black and white breaker point wires (**Figure 156**).
  e. On 1980-1982 models, signal generator connector—brown, black/white and green/white wires (A, **Figure 157**).

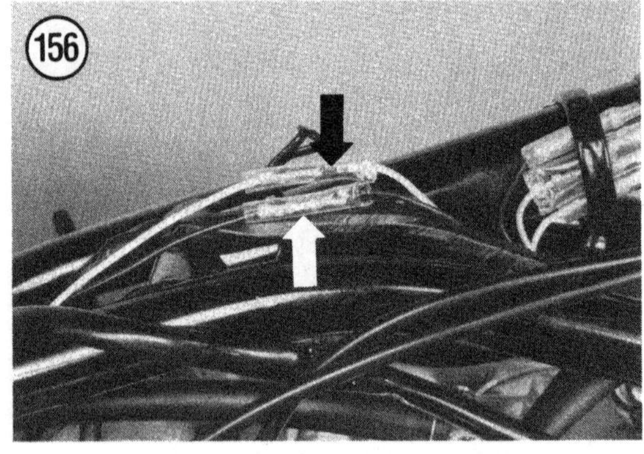

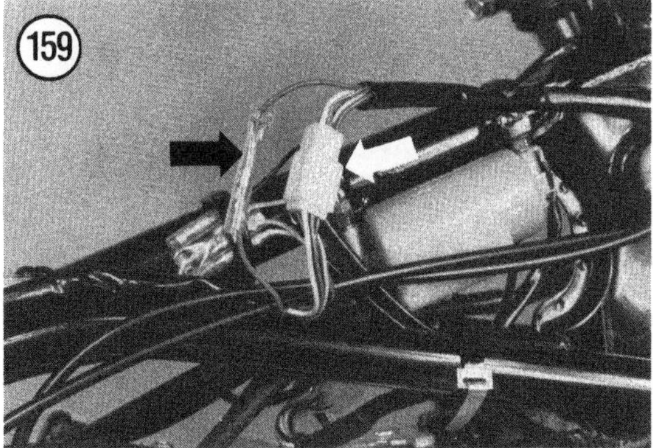

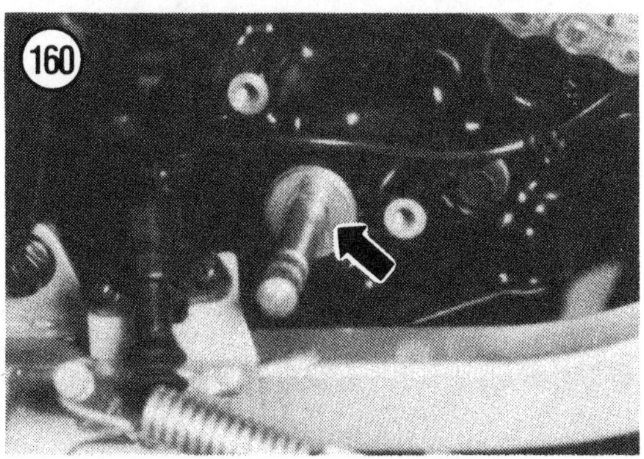

f. On TSCC models, signal generator connector—brown, black/white and green/white wires.
g. On 1982 and earlier models, green/yellow oil pressure sensor wire (B, **Figure 157**).
h. On TSCC models, oil pressure sensor wire and side stand switch connector (**Figure 158**).
i. Blue neutral indicator wire and gear position indicator connector (**Figure 159**).

NOTE

If complete engine disassembly is desired, perform Steps 15 through 22. If engine removal without further disassembly is desired, proceed to Step 23.

15. Remove the camshafts, cylinder head, cylinder block and pistons as outlined in this chapter.
16. Remove the engine sprocket as outlined in this chapter.
17. Remove the clip and washer securing the gearshift shaft (**Figure 160**).
18. Bend back the locking tabs securing the seal retainer bolts (**Figure 161**) and remove the retainer.
19. Remove the screws securing the gearshift indicator switch and remove the switch (**Figure 162**). Note how switch wiring is routed around the crankcase.

20. Remove the O-ring and spring-loaded plunger from the end of the gearshifting cam (**Figure 163**).
21. Refer to Chapter Five and remove the clutch and external gearshift components.
22. Remove the alternator cover and ignition advance governor as outlined in this chapter.
23. If the camshafts or cylinder head have not been removed, unscrew the tachometer cable from the cylinder head (**Figure 164**).

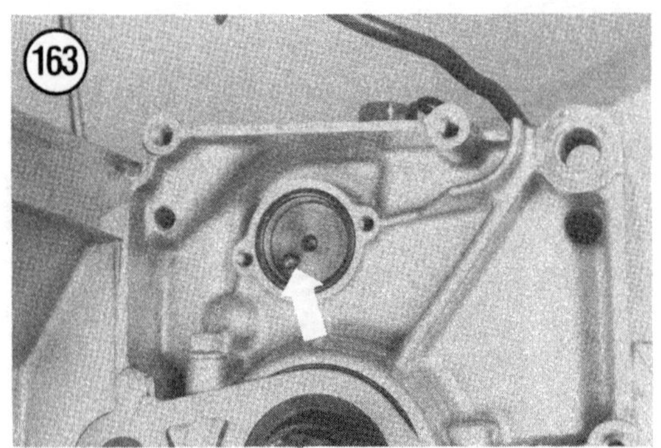

NOTE
If the engine is to be removed with the head in place, you must remove the breather cover from the top of the cam cover as described under ***Camshaft Removal*** *in this chapter.*

NOTE
Carefully check that the engine is free of all cables, wires, hoses and accessories that may interfere with engine removal.

24. Place a jack or block under the engine to support the engine weight while removing the mounting bolts. Slight variations exist in the bolt locations among different models. Refer to **Figure 165** for a typical example of mounting bolt locations. Remove the engine mounting bolts and note the following items:
   a. Note the location of any spacers and each different length mounting bolt.
   b. The lower mounting bolts are secured by nut plates (**Figure 166**).
   c. Carefully lift the engine out from the right side of the motorcycle.
25. Installation is the reverse of these steps. Keep the following points in mind:
   a. Install all long engine mounting bolts from the left side.
   b. Refer to **Figure 167** for bushing and spacer locations on TSCC engines.
   c. Install the oil cooler, sprocket cover and alternator cover as outlined in this chapter.
   d. Refer to Chapter Five to install the clutch and gearshift components.
   e. Refer to Chapter Six and install the carburetors and exhaust system.
   f. Torque all engine fasteners to the values specified in **Table 1**.
26. Refer to Chapter Three and perform the following:
   a. Install the oil filter and add engine oil.
   b. Adjust the clutch.
   c. Adjust the drive chain.

167

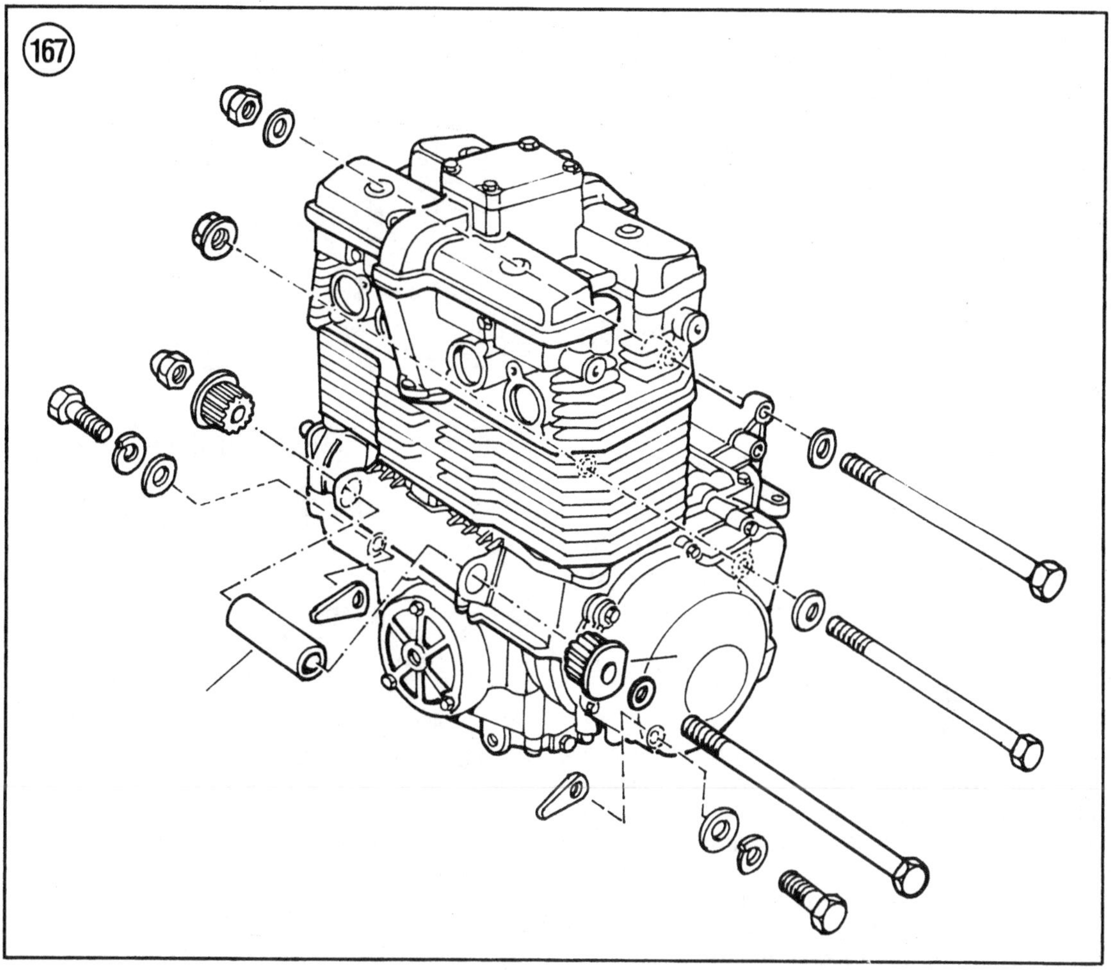

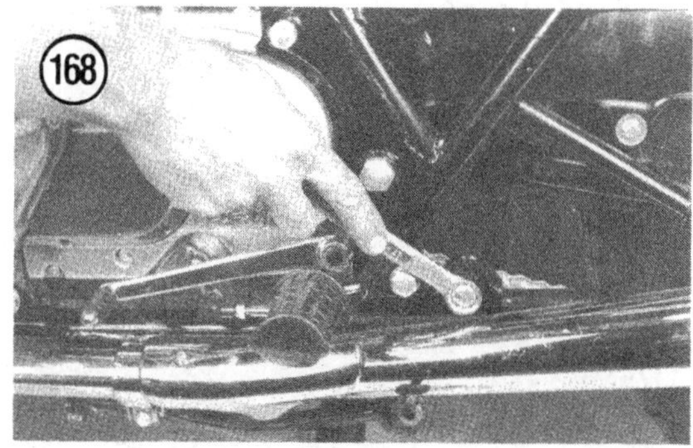

168

169

ENGINE SPROCKET

Removal/Installation

1. Remove the bolts securing the left footrest (**Figure 168**) and remove the footrest. Do not lose the rubber bushings with each bolt.
2. On TSCC E and ES models, remove the pinch bolt securing the gearshift lever (**Figure 169**). The bolt must be removed completely, not just loosened. Slide off the shift lever.
3. On all other models with gearshift linkage, perform the following:
   a. Remove the circlip securing the gearshift lever (**Figure 170**).
   b. Remove the pinch bolt securing the shifting arm to the gearshift shaft (**Figure 171**).

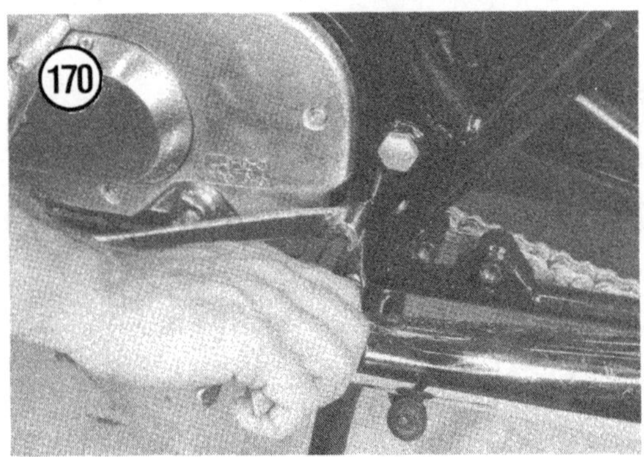

c. Remove the gearshift lever and shifting arm complete with shifting linkage.

4. Remove the fasteners securing the sprocket cover (**Figure 172**) and swing the cover clear of the engine. If the cover must be completely removed, disconnect the clutch cable from the actuating mechanism (**Figure 173**).

5. Use a chisel or screwdriver to bend back the fold on the locking washer (**Figure 174**).

6. Temporarily install the gearshift lever and the brake pedal. Shift the transmission into gear and hold the rear brake on. Remove the engine sprocket nut and lockwasher. Note that the recess in the nut is positioned toward the sprocket (**Figure 175**).

7. Remove the drive chain from the sprocket and slide the sprocket off the transmission drive shaft. It may be necessary to loosen the drive chain to provide enough slack to remove the sprocket. Refer to *Drive Chain Adjustment and Lubrication* in Chapter Three.

8. Installation is the reverse of these steps. Keep the following points in mind:

a. Make sure the spacer is installed over the transmission drive shaft.

b. Slip the drive chain over the sprocket and install the sprocket over the drive shaft. Install the locking washer and the nut. Make sure the recess in the nut is positioned in, toward the engine.

NOTE
*It may be necessary to loosen the drive chain adjusters to provide enough slack to install the chain over the sprocket. Refer to **Drive Chain Adjustment and Lubrication** in Chapter Three.*

c. Temporarily install the shift lever and shift the transmission into gear. Hold on the rear brake and torque the sprocket nut as specified

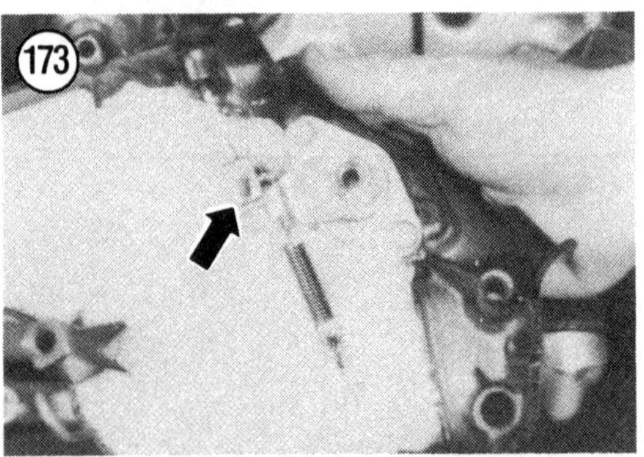

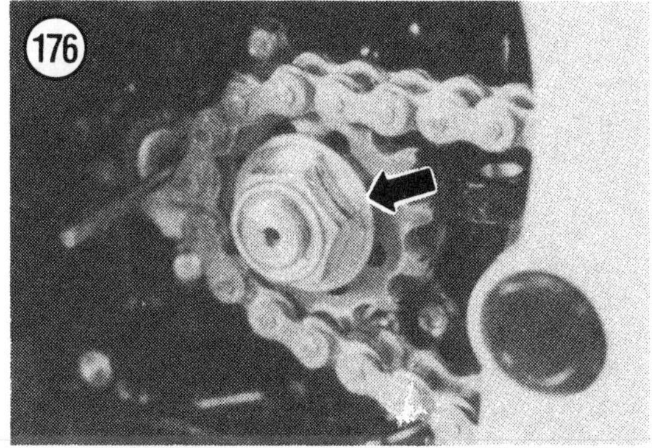

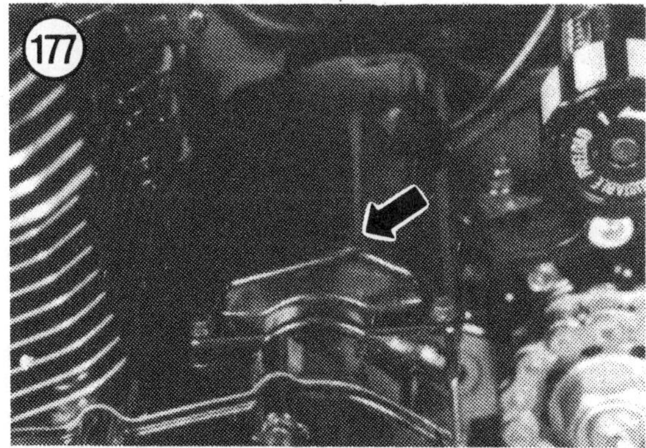

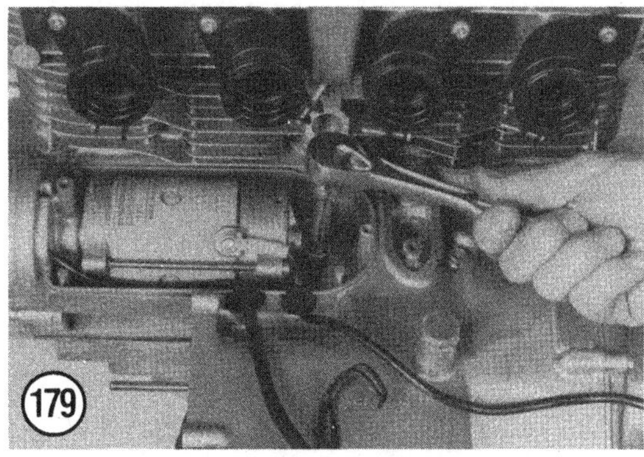

in **Table 1**. Fold over the locking washer to secure the nut (**Figure 176**).

d. Install the sprocket cover and tighten the fasteners evenly and securely (**Figure 174**).

e. Install the gearshift lever and linkage.

ALTERNATOR COVER AND STARTER CLUTCH

Removal

The alternator cover and starter clutch mechanism can be removed with the engine installed in the frame.

NOTE

It is not necessary to remove the alternator rotor/starter clutch assembly to remove the crankshaft or to disassemble the engine. Starter clutch removal is only required if the crankshaft or the alternator rotor/starter clutch must be replaced.

1. Remove the side covers and disconnect the alternator wires—three yellow wires on TSCC models and one white/blue, one white/green and one yellow wire for all other models.
2. Remove the screws securing the starter motor cover and remove the cover (**Figure 177**).
3. Pull back the rubber boot and remove the lead from the starter motor (**Figure 178**). Remove the bolts securing the starter motor (**Figure 179**). Lift the motor up slightly and slide it out.
4. Remove the fasteners securing the alternator cover (**Figure 180**). Note the location of the different length fasteners. Carefully remove the alternator cover and the old gasket (**Figure 181**). Have a few rags handy as some oil may run out when the cover is removed. Note how the

alternator wires are routed in the cover and through the crankcase.

CAUTION
Do not pry the alternator cover loose with a screwdriver or similar tool or damage may result to the cover or the crankcase. The cover is held tight by the magnetic attraction of the alternator rotor. A strong pull is required to overcome the magnetic field.

5. On 1982 and earlier models, perform the following:
   a. Remove the thrust washer from the idler gear shaft (**Figure 182**). If the washer is not on the shaft, it may be stuck to the inside of the alternator cover.
   b. Hold the idler gear in place and withdraw the idler gear shaft enough to disengage the shaft end from the engine (**Figure 183**). Remove the idler gear, shaft and 2nd thrust washer. The washer may be stuck to the back of the idler gear or the engine.
6. On TSCC models, hold the idler gear in place and withdraw the idler gear shaft enough to disengage the shaft end from the engine (**Figure 184**). Remove the idler gear and shaft.
7. If alternator rotor/starter clutch assembly removal is desired, a slide hammer with a special attachment is necessary. The Suzuki part number for the slide hammer is 09930-30102 and the part number for the attachment is 09930-30180. If these tools are not available, have an authorized dealer perform the task. If the tools are available, perform Steps 8-11.

CAUTION
Do not attempt to remove the alternator rotor without the proper tools or expensive damage to the engine or the alternator rotor may result.

8. If the engine is installed and the cylinder block has not been removed, shift the transmission into

gear and step on the rear brake to keep the engine from turning while loosening the alternator rotor bolt. If the bolt cannot be loosened in this manner, it will be necessary to use an impact tool or the special Suzuki holding tool (part No. 09930-44911).

9. If the cylinder block has been removed, install a piston holding fixture under a piston as shown in **Figure 185** to keep the crankshaft from turning.

10. Remove the bolt securing the alternator rotor/starter clutch assembly (**Figure 186**).

11. Thread the slide hammer attachment tool into the end of the rotor/starter clutch assembly. Operate the slide hammer until the rotor is free and remove the assembly from the crankshaft.

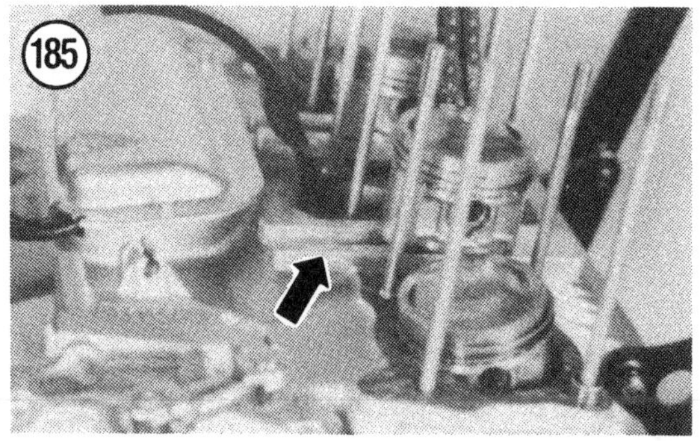

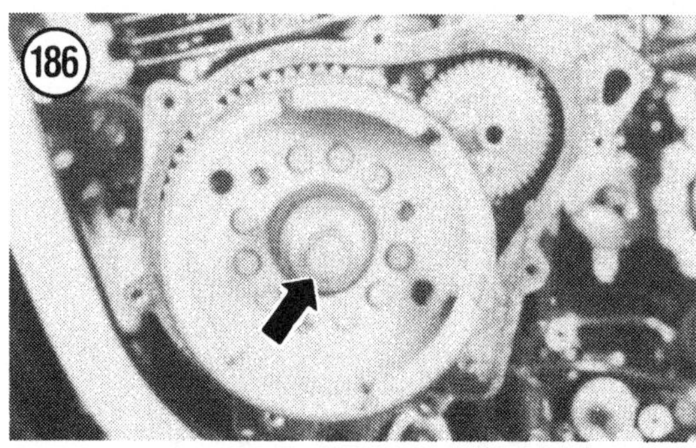

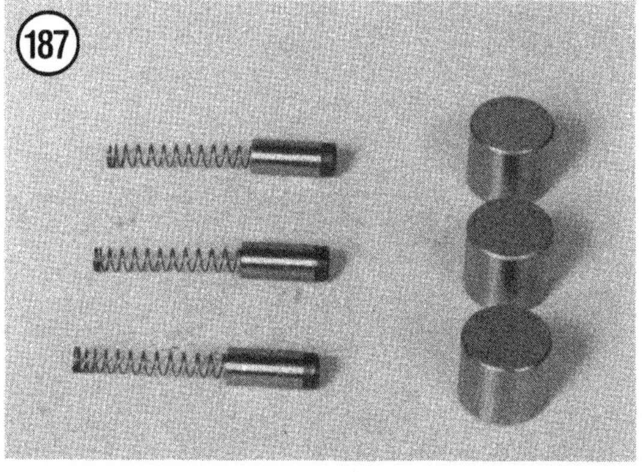

NOTE

*The starter clutch assembly contains 3 rollers and 3 spring-loaded plungers (**Figure 187**). Take care that no parts are lost as some rollers usually fall out when the clutch is removed. Roller installation is described during the starter clutch installation procedure.*

12. Refer to **Figure 188** and remove the large starter gear from the crankshaft.

13. On 1982 and earlier engines, slide off the 2 roller bearings and the brass thrust washer. Note that the chamfer on the thrust washer faces toward the engine (**Figure 189**).

4

Installation

If the alternator rotor/starter clutch was not removed, start this procedure at Step 4.

1. On 1982 and earlier engines, install the brass thrust washer and 2 roller bearings as shown in **Figure 188**. Make sure the chamfer on the thrust washer faces toward the engine.

2. Install the large starter gear and starter clutch assembly. If any rollers fell out when the starter clutch assembly was removed, refer to **Figure 188** and perform the following:

   a. Place the assembly on a clean surface and install a spring and plunger (push piece). Hold the plunger in position with a small wire or drill bit inserted through the hole in the assembly body (**Figure 190**).
   b. Slide a roller into place and carefully withdraw the wire or drill bit so the spring tension holds the roller in place (**Figure 191**). Repeat for other rollers, if necessary.

CAUTION

Carefully examine the magnets in the alternator rotor. Remove all foreign objects, metal filings, washers, etc. that may have been picked up by the magnets. A small washer or nut stuck to the magnets could cause serious damage to the alternator stator assembly.

3. Wipe the tapered end of the crankshaft clean with lacquer thinner or contact spray. Install the starter clutch/rotor assembly on the crankshaft. Keep the crankshaft from turning as described during the removal procedure. Apply a few drops of red Loctite (Stud N' Bearing Mount No. 2214) to the alternator rotor bolt and install the bolt (**Figure 186**). Torque the bolt as specified in **Table 1**.

4. On 1982 and earlier engines, apply a small amount of grease to one idler gear shaft thrust

188

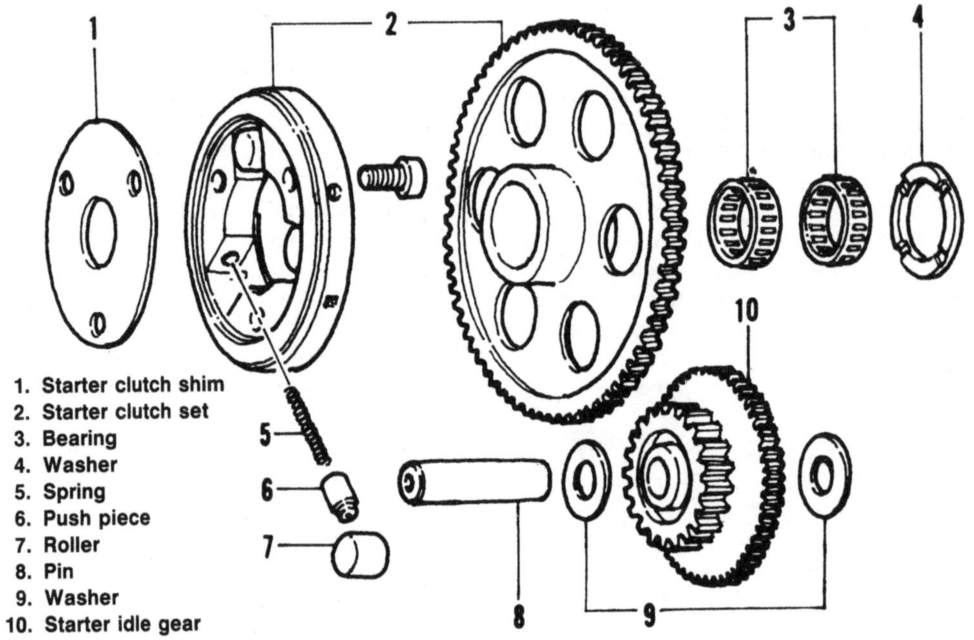

1. Starter clutch shim
2. Starter clutch set
3. Bearing
4. Washer
5. Spring
6. Push piece
7. Roller
8. Pin
9. Washer
10. Starter idle gear

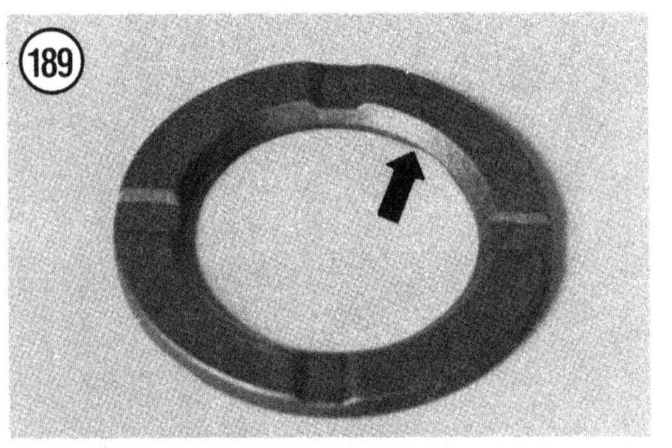

washer and stick the washer in place as shown in **Figure 192**.

5. On all engines, hold the starter idler gear in place and install the idler gear shaft (**Figure 184**).
6. On 1982 and earlier engines, install the outer thrust washer on the idler gear shaft (**Figure 182**).
7. Make sure the alternator wires are correctly routed in the alternator cover and the grommet is installed in the notch as shown in **Figure 193**.
8. Install a new cover gasket and route the alternator wires into the crankcase opening. Hold the gasket in place and install the alternator cover (**Figure 194**).
9. Install the starter motor (**Figure 195**). Apply a couple of drops of blue Loctite (Lock N' Seal No. 2114) to the bolts securing the starter motor and install the bolts. Connect the starter lead wire to the starter motor (**Figure 196**).
10. Install the starter motor cover and secure the cover with the screws.
11. Connect the alternator wires and install the side covers.

IGNITION ADVANCE GOVERNOR ASSEMBLY

Removal/Installation

1. Remove the screws securing the ignition cover and remove the cover (**Figure 197**).
2. On 1982 and earlier models, perform the following:
   a. Remove the screws securing the breaker point plate or signal generator (A, **Figure 198**). Remove the point plate or signal generator.
   b. Remove the bolt securing the ignition advance governor mechanism (B, **Figure 198**). Note how the drive pin on the end of the crankshaft engages the slot in the advance mechanism (**Figure 199**).
3. On TSCC models, remove the Allen bolt securing the rotor/advance governor unit and remove the unit (**Figure 200**).

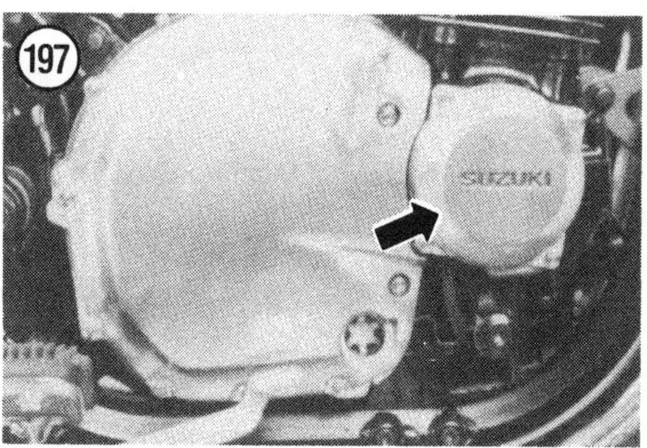

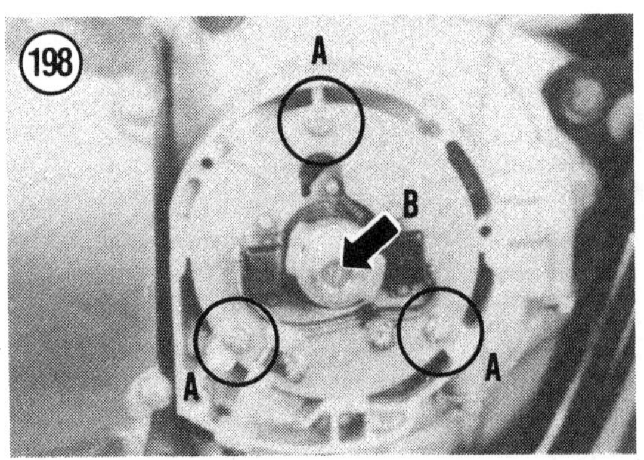

4. If the ignition advance governor mechanism was disassembled, perform the following:
   a. Position the advance mechanism so that the "F 1-4" marks are at the 12 o'clock position.
   b. Slide the signal generator rotor (or breaker point cam) over the advance mechanism so the rotor lug is 90° to the left of the "F 1-4" marks (A, **Figure 201**).
   c. Carefully spread the spring-loaded advance weights and engage the tabs of each weight into the notches (B, **Figure 201**).
5. Install the ignition advance governor on the crankshaft. Make sure the notch in the governor is aligned with the dowel in the end of the crankshaft as shown in **Figure 199**. Torque the governor retaining bolt as specified in **Table 1**.

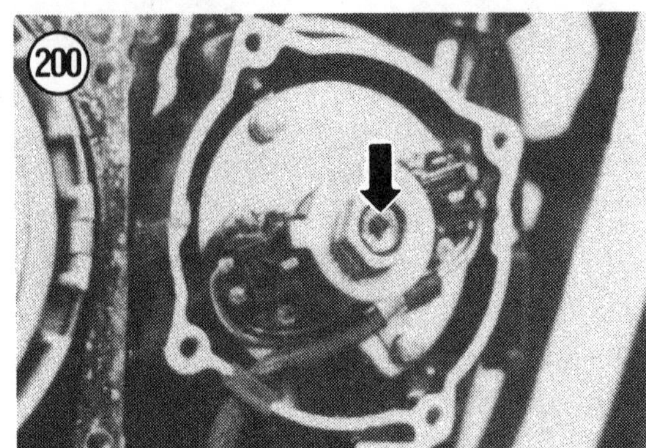

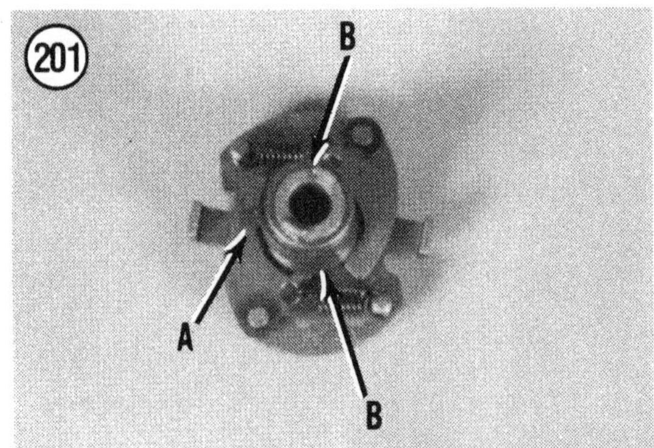

OIL COOLER (TSCC MODELS)

Removal/Installation

1. Drain the engine oil as outlined in Chapter Three.
2. Place a drain plan beneath the engine and remove the union bolts securing the oil lines to the crankcase (**Figure 202**). Note the copper gaskets on each side of the oil line fittings.
3. If oil line removal is desired, hold the cooler with a wrench and remove the oil line fitting from the cooler (**Figure 203**).

CAUTION
Do not attempt to remove the oil line fitting from the oil cooler without using a separate wrench to hold the oil cooler. The cooler is aluminum and easily damaged.

4. Remove the bolts securing the oil line clamps to the frame.
5. Remove the bolts and rubber cushions from the upper and lower oil cooler mounts and remove the oil cooler. See **Figure 204** and **Figure 205**.

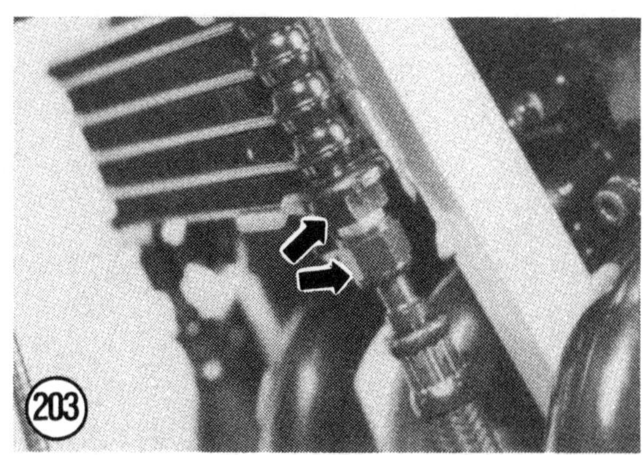
203

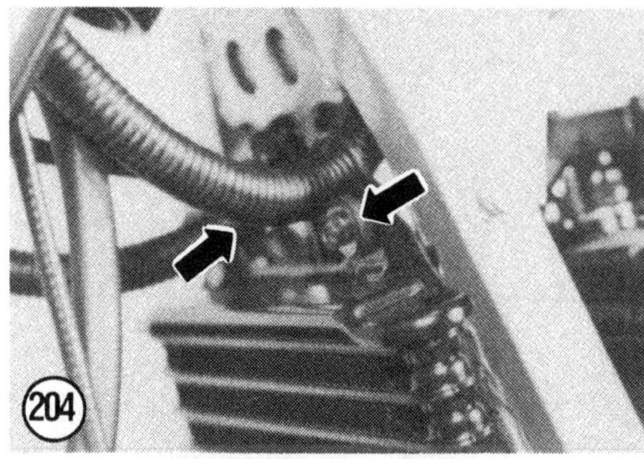
204

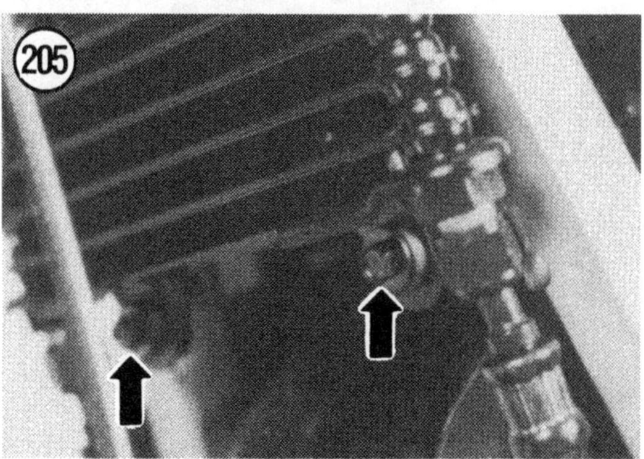
205

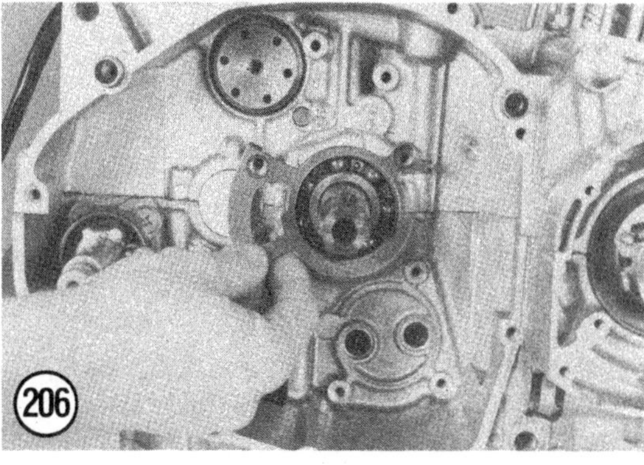
206

6. Installation is the reverse of these steps. Keep the following points in mind:
   a. Use a copper gasket on each side of the lower end of the oil lines.
   b. Tighten the oil line union bolts and fitting bolts as specified in **Table 1**.

ENGINE LOWER END (1982 AND EARLIER MODELS)

It is necessary to split the crankcase to gain access to the crankshaft, connecting rods, transmission and inner gearshift components.

The following procedures represent a complete step-by-step process that should be followed if an engine is to be completely reconditioned. However, if you are replacing a known failed part, the disassembly need only be carried out until the failed part is accessible. Further disassembly is unnecessary as long as you know that the remaining components are in good condition and that they were not affected by the failed part.

Disassembly

1. Perform the complete engine removal procedure as outlined in this chapter. Several preliminary disassembly steps are performed during engine removal.
2. Remove the following items, if not previously removed:
   a. Cylinder head, cylinder block and pistons.
   b. Alternator cover and ignition advance governor assembly.
   c. Clutch and external gearshift mechanism (Chapter Five).
3. Remove the screws securing the bearing retainer (**Figure 206**).
4. Refer to **Figure 207** and remove the bolt securing the upper crankcase.

NOTE
Before removing the crankcase bolts, cut a cardboard template the approximate size and shape of the engine. Punch holes in the template for each bolt location. Place the bolts in the template holes as they are removed. This will greatly speed up assembly time.

5. Turn the engine over to gain access to the bottom crankcase bolts.

NOTE
Have plenty of rags handy. Approximately 1/2 pint of oil is trapped in the engine and will run out when the engine is turned over.

4

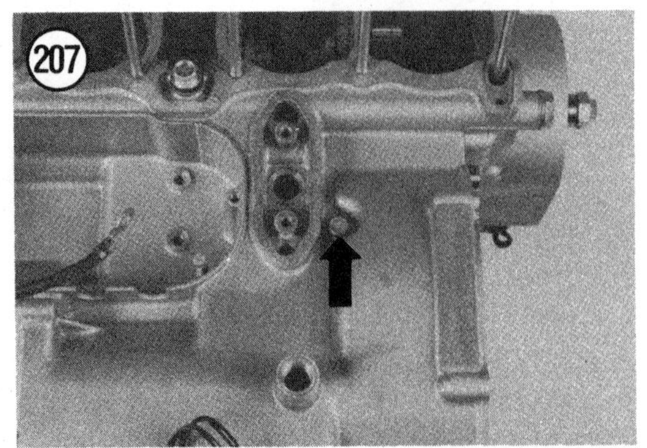

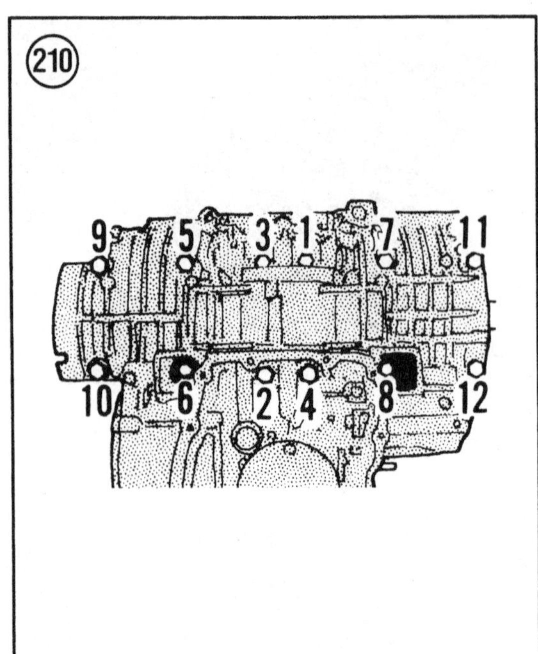
9
5
3
1
7
11
10
6
2
4
8
12

6. Gradually and evenly loosen the bolts securing the oil sump (**Figure 208**). Note the position of the ignition wire clips. Remove the bolts and remove the oil sump. It may be necessary to tap around the edge of the sealing surface with a plastic or rubber mallet to help break the sump loose from the crankcase.
7. Remove the screws securing the oil pickup screen (**Figure 209**) and remove the screen.
8. Refer to **Figure 209** and remove the O-ring from the oil passage.
9. Gradually loosen then remove the bolts securing the lower crankcase. Refer to **Figure 210** and remove the 8 mm bolts in descending order according to the numbers cast in the crankcase.

NOTE
*Five bolts are deeply recessed in the crankcase as shown in **Figure 211**.*

10. Make sure the upper and lower bolts located by the transmission drive shaft are removed (**Figure 212**). These fasteners are usually hidden under dirt and grease.
11. Gently tap around the bottom crankcase half with a rubber or plastic mallet to break it loose, then lift off the crankcase half.

CAUTION
Never attempt to pry the crankcase halves apart with a screwdriver or similar tool. Serious damage will result to the crankcase sealing surfaces. The crankcase halves are a matched set and are very expensive. Damage to one crankcase half requires replacing the entire set.

12. At this point of disassembly, major service can be performed on the crankshaft, transmission and gearshift components. Carefully lift out the crankshaft assembly, if desired, and place it on a clean rag.
13. If transmission or gearshift repairs are desired, refer to Chapter Five.
14. Remove and discard the oil passage O-ring (**Figure 213**).
15. Use solvent to thoroughly clean all dirt, oil and sludge deposits from both crankcase halves.

4

Inspection

Except for preliminary checks, crankshaft service and inspection should be entrusted to a dealer or machine shop experienced in multi-cylinder crankshaft service. The crankshaft is pressed together and requires a large hydraulic press to separate and assemble it. The crankshaft must be diassembled to replace any connecting rod or main bearing (except the outer bearings). Considerable expertise is also required to correctly align and true the crankshaft. In most cases, if the crankshaft or connecting rods are damaged, a new crankshaft unit will have to be installed.

Refer to **Table 10** for crankshaft specifications.

NOTE
Some parts of the following procedure require the use of specialized and expensive measuring equipment. If such equipment is not available, have a dealer or machine shop perform the measurements.

1. Carefully examine the condition of all the crankshaft bearings. Slide back the outer races as shown in **Figure 214** and carefully check all the rollers for cracks or other signs of excessive wear or damage. If you are in doubt as to the condition of any bearings, have them examined by a dealer or machine shop.
2. Measure the big end side clearance of each connecting rod with a feeler gauge as shown in **Figure 215**. If the side clearance of any connecting rod exceeds 1.0 mm (0.0039 in.), refer the crankshaft to a dealer or machine shop for repair.

215

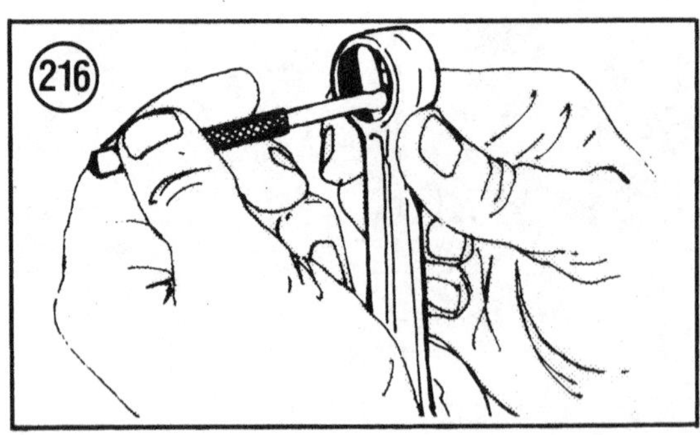

216

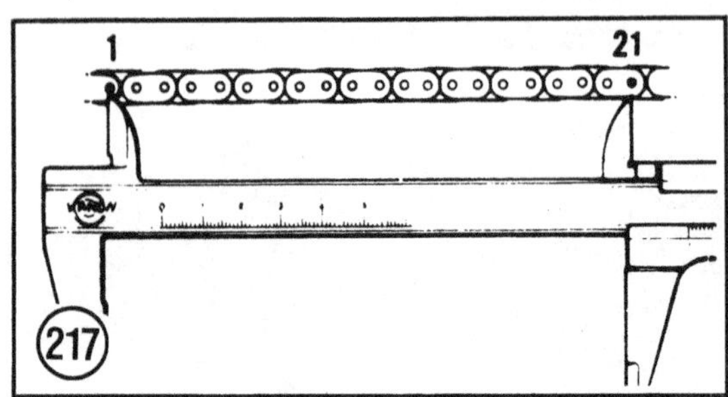

217

218

3. Use a bore gauge or inside micrometer to measure the piston pin bore in each connecting rod (**Figure 216**). If the pin bore inside diameter exceeds 16.040 mm (0.6315 in.), the connecting rod must be replaced.
4. Place the crankshaft on 2 V-blocks, one at each end, and position a dial indicator against one of the center main bearings. Rotate the crankshaft to measure the amount of runout or deflection. If the runout exceeds 0.10 mm (0.004 in.), the crankshaft must be replaced.
5. Place the crankshaft on 2 V-blocks, one at each end, and position a dial indicator against the piston end of each connecting rod. Fully extend the connecting rod (top dead center position) and move the connecting rod as much as possible from side to side. Read the dial indicator to measure the wear between the crankpin and big end bearing (connecting rod deflection). If the indicated deflection exceeds 3.0 mm (0.12 in.), replace the crankshaft assembly or have the crankshaft disassembled and replace the worn parts.
6. Stretch the cam chain tight and measure across 21 pins with a caliper as shown in **Figure 217**. Replace the chain if the 21 pin length exceeds 157.8 mm (6.213 in.).

Assembly

CAUTION
Never use STP or similar friction reducing products as assembly lubricant. Even a small amount will combine with the engine oil and destroy the friction properties of the clutch. If this should occur, the engine's lubrication system must be completely flushed and new clutch plates installed.

CAUTION
During all phases of engine assembly, frequently rotate the crankshaft and other moving parts. If any binding or stiffness is present, find out why and correct the problem before continuing the assembly. An engine that feels rough or tight when rotated by hand will not "wear in." Such an engine will likely cause expensive damage to itself if run.

CAUTION
Use a thread locking compound such as blue Loctite (Lock N' Seal No. 2114) on all internal fasteners during engine assembly. A small bolt or screw working loose inside the engine could have disastrous and expensive consequences.

219

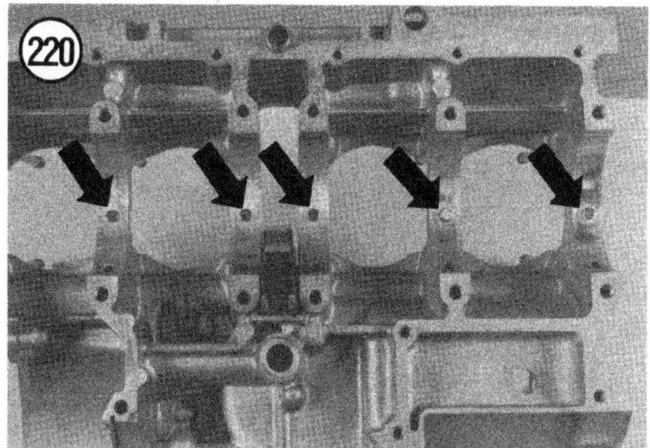
220

221

222

223

1. Make sure all engine parts are clean and all fasteners are in good condition. Replace all bolts, nuts and screws with damaged heads or threads.
2. Carefully remove all traces of old sealant residue from the sealing surfaces on both crankcase halves. Use a wooden scraper or similar device to clean off the old sealant. Never use a metal scraper or the sealing surfaces can be damaged. Wipe the surfaces clean with solvent or lacquer thinner.
3. Make sure that the bearing retainer C-ring is properly positioned in the crankcase (**Figure 218**).

NOTE
On engines undergoing a complete rebuild, it is recommended that a new cam chain be installed.

4. Route the cam chain into the chain tunnel and carefully place the crankshaft into the upper crankcase half. Make sure that the groove on the outer bearing engages the C-ring in the crankcase.
5. The other 5 crankshaft bearing races have machined holes (**Figure 219**) that must engage alignment dowels installed in the crankcase (**Figure 220**). With the crankshaft in place in the crankcase, slowly rotate each bearing race until the hole in the race can be felt engaging the alignment dowel. When the bearing races are properly positioned, small punch marks on each bearing race (**Figure 221**) will be nearly perpendicular to the crankcase sealing surface.
6. Rotate the outer bearing race until the locating pin is properly positioned in the notch as shown in **Figure 222**.
7. If transmission or internal gearshift components were removed for repair, install the transmission and gearshift components. Refer to Chapter Five. Make sure the locating pins on all the transmission bearings are properly fitted into the crankcase notches (**Figure 223**).
8. Install a new O-ring in the crankcase oil passage (**Figure 213**).
9. Check that the gasket surfaces on both crankcase halves are clean and free of moisture, oil and old sealant.

10. Carefully apply a thin layer of a non-hardening sealant to the sealing surfaces on the lower crankcase half. Use Suzuki Bond No. 1215 or equivalent. Do not use a silicone sealant.

CAUTION
*Apply crankcase sealant with care. All surfaces must be covered or oil leaks may occur. Do **not** allow any sealant to contact any of the bearing surfaces. Use only a thin layer of sealant or the excess may squeeze into the crankshaft or transmission bearing areas.*

11. Carefully install the lower crankcase half over the upper half. Gently tap the crankcase halves together with a rubber mallet or block of wood. The dowel pins should align and both sealing surfaces should fit together. If the lower crankcase half does not fit down fully, stop and investigate the interference.

CAUTION
The crankcase halves should fit together without force. If they do not fit together fully, do not attempt to pull them together with the crankcase bolts or the crankcases will be damaged. Remove the lower half and investigate the cause of the interference. The upper and lower crankcases are a matched set and are very expensive. Do not risk damage by trying to force the cases together.

12. Install all the lower crankcase bolts finger-tight. Tighten the crankcase bolts in 2 steps to make sure they are properly torqued. Tighten all the 8 mm bolts in the order designated in **Figure 224**. Tighten each 6 mm bolt a little at a time to 0.6 mkg (4.5 ft.-lb.), then tighten the 8 mm bolts (in designated order) to 1 mkg (7 ft.-lb.). Torque each 6 mm bolt to the final value of 1 mkg (7 ft.-lb.) and each 8 mm bolt to 2 mkg (14.5 ft.-lb.).

13. Turn the engine over. Refer to **Figure 225** and install the 6 mm bolt securing the upper crankcase. Torque the bolt to 1 mkg (7 ft.-lb.).

14. Make sure the crankcase fasteners near the transmission drive shaft are installed (**Figure 226**).

15. Install the bearing and seal retainers as shown in **Figure 227** and **Figure 228**. Apply a small amount of blue Loctite (Lock N' Seal No. 2114) to the retainer screws before installing them.

16. Install the oil pump pick-up screen (**Figure 229**). Use a small amount of blue Loctite on the screws securing the screen. Install a new O-ring in the oil passage.

17. Make sure the sealing surfaces on the oil sump and crankcase are clean and free of old gasket residue. Use a new gasket and install the oil sump. Gradually and evenly tighten all the oil sump bolts

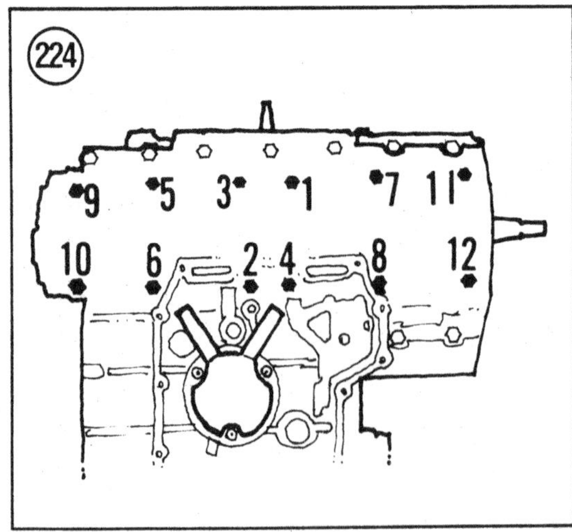

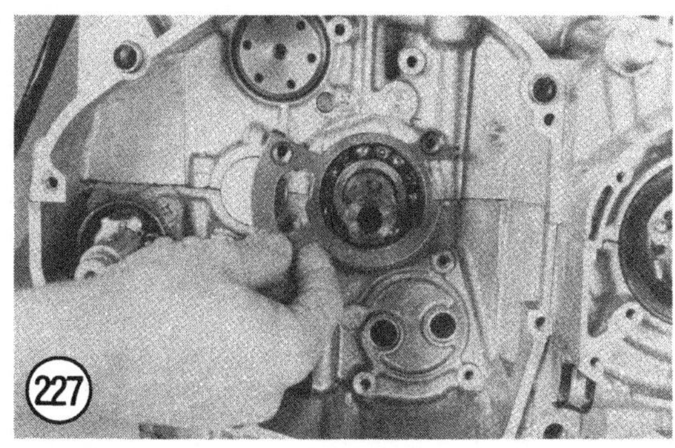

227

228

229

230

in a crisscross pattern. Torque the bolts to 1 mkg (7 ft.-lb.).

18. Install the following items:
   a. Cylinder head, cylinder block and pistons.
   b. Alternator cover and ignition advance governor assembly.
   c. Clutch and external gearshift mechanism (Chapter Five).

19. Install the engine in the frame as described in this chapter.

ENGINE LOWER END (TSCC MODELS)

It is necessary to split the crankcase to gain access to the crankshaft, connecting rods, transmission and inner gearshift components.

The following procedures represent a complete step-by-step process that should be followed if an engine is to be completely reconditioned. However, if you are replacing a known failed part, the disassembly need only be carried out until the failed part is accessible. Further disassembly is unnecessary as long as you know that the remaining components are in good condition and that they were not affected by the failed part.

Disassembly

1. Perform the complete engine removal procedure as outlined in this chapter. Several preliminary disassembly steps are performed during engine removal.
2. Remove the following items, if not previously removed:
   a. Cylinder head, cylinder block and pistons.
   b. Alternator cover, ignition advance governor assembly and oil pump.
   c. Clutch and external gearshift mechanism (Chapter Five).
3. Remove the screws securing the bearing retainer (**Figure 230**).

NOTE

Do not mix the bearing retainer screws with the screws removed from the gearshift cam guide and pawl lifter. The bearing retainer screws are 16 mm long, while the gearshift component screws are 12 mm long.

4. Remove the bolts securing the upper crankcase. Refer to **Figure 231**.

NOTE

Before removing the crankcase bolts, cut a cardboard template the approximate size and shape of the engine. Punch holes in the template for each bolt location. Place the bolts in the template holes as they are removed. This will greatly speed up assembly time.

5. Turn the engine over to gain access to the bottom crankcase bolts.

NOTE
Have plenty of rags handy. Approximately 1/2 pint of oil is trapped in the engine and will run out when the engine is turned over.

6. Gradually and evenly loosen the bolts securing the oil sump (**Figure 232**). Remove the bolts and remove the oil sump. It may be necessary to tap around the edge of the sealing surface with a plastic or rubber mallet to help break the sump loose from the crankcase.
7. Remove the screws securing the oil pickup screen (**Figure 233**) and remove the screen. Note the arrow and "FRONT" mark are positioned toward the front of the engine.
8. Remove the 6 mm bolts and 8 mm bolts securing the lower crankcase. Remove the twelve 8 mm crankcase bolts in descending order as shown in **Figure 234**. Make sure the 8 mm bolts in the sump area are removed. The two center 8 mm Allen bolts can be reached through the oil filter sump (**Figure 235**). Use a cardboard template as previously described to keep all the bolts in order as they are removed.

NOTE
If using an Allen wrench fitted to a socket, it is usually necessary to fit the Allen wrench into the bolt through the filter opening and then install a socket extension down through the crankcase opening. Most sockets are too large to pass through the crankcase bolt holes.

9. Gently tap around the bottom crankcase half with a rubber or plastic mallet to break it loose, then lift off the crankcase half.

CAUTION
Never attempt to pry the crankcase halves apart with a screwdriver or similar tool. Serious damage will result to the crankcase sealing surfaces. The crankcase halves are a matched set and are very expensive. Damage to one crankcase half requires replacing the entire set.

10. At this point of disassembly, major service can be performed on the crankshaft, connecting rods, transmission, shaft drive gears and gearshift components. All crankshaft and connecting rod insert bearings can be removed and replaced and all major inspections can be performed. If transmission, shaft drive and gearshift repairs are necessary, refer to Chapter Five.
11. Remove and discard the oil passage O-ring (**Figure 236**). Remove the small flat washer and unscrew the oil control jet from the oil passage (**Figure 237** and **Figure 238**).
12. To remove the connecting rods, remove the nuts securing each connecting rod to the crankshaft

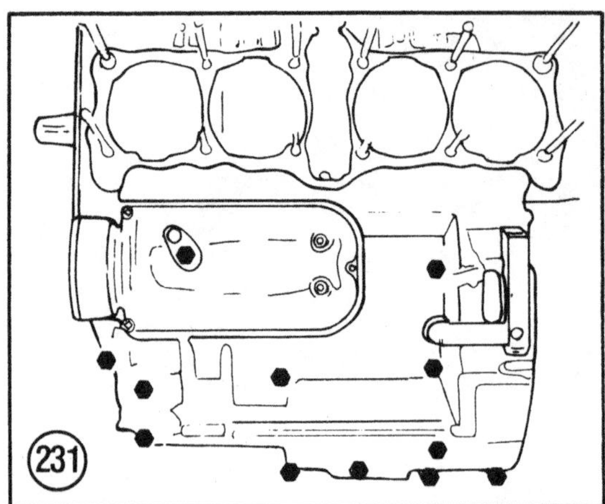

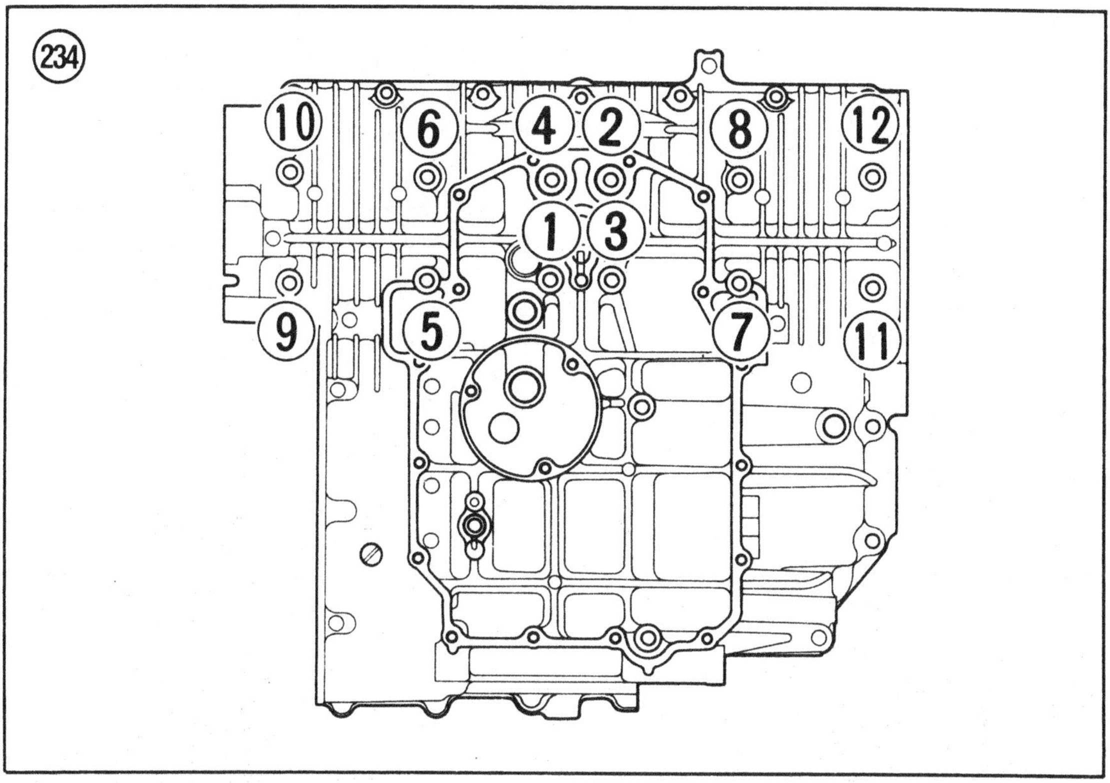

234
10
6
4
2
8
12
1
3
9
5
7
11

235

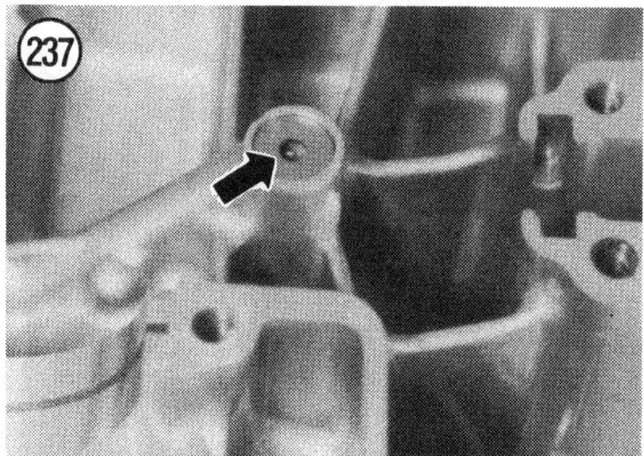
237

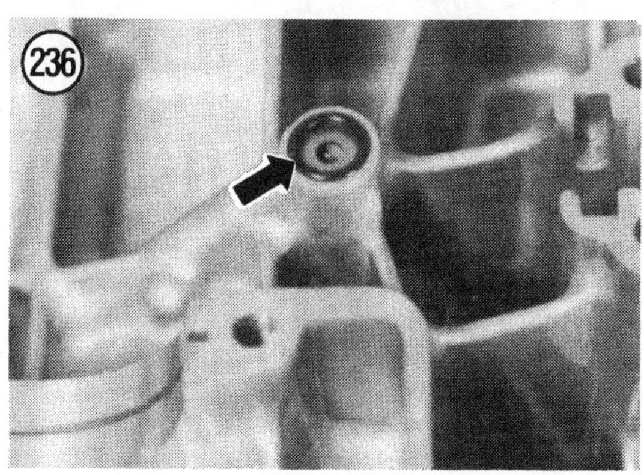
236

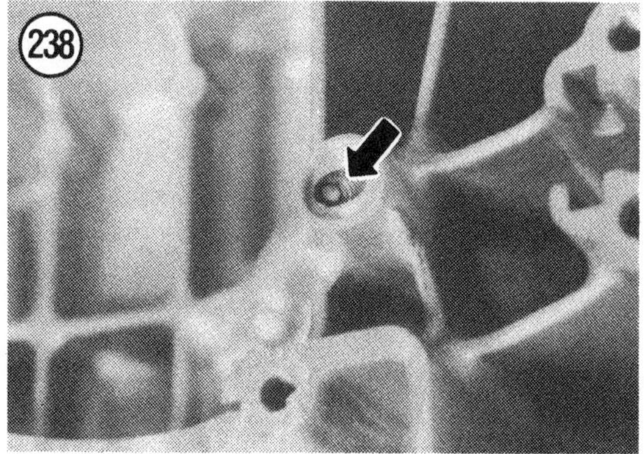
238

(**Figure 239**). Carefully lift off each bearing cap and remove each rod assembly.

CAUTION
Use a felt tip pen or scribe and carefully mark the location of each connecting rod and rod cap as well as the position of the bearing inserts if they are to be reused. Do not mark on the bearing surface; mark on the exterior of the connecting rod and bearing cap. All parts must be installed in the exact position and location from which they were removed as wear patterns have developed on all parts. If the parts are intermixed with others, rapid and excessive wear may result.

CAUTION
Do not attempt to remove the bolts from the connecting rods. The bolts are factory-fit and aligned with each bearing cap. If the bolts are disturbed, the bearing cap alignment will be disturbed.

13. If desired, carefully lift out the crankshaft assembly. Place the crankshaft on clean rags.

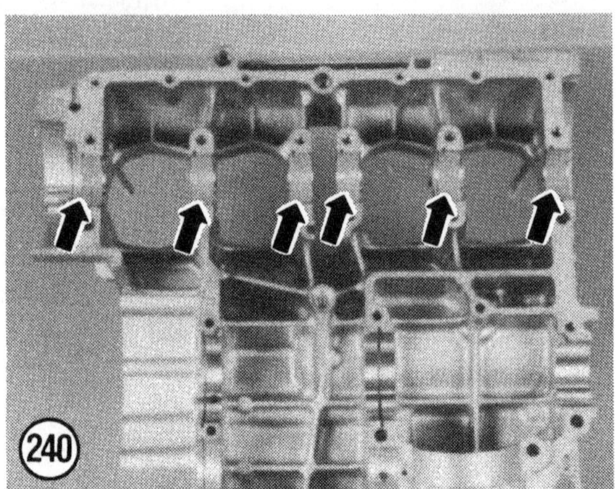

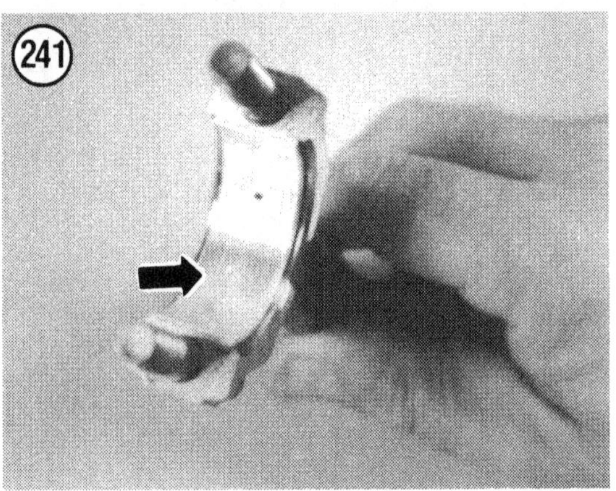

Crankshaft and Connecting Rod Inspection

NOTE
*Some steps in the following procedure require the use of highly specialized and expensive measuring equipment. If such equipment is not available, have a dealer or machine shop perform the measurements. Refer to **Table 11** and **Table 12** for connecting rod and crankshaft specifications.*

1. Carefully examine the main bearing inserts in both halves of the crankcase (**Figure 240**). Examine all the connecting rod bearing inserts (**Figure 241**). The inserts should be replaced if there are any signs of bluish tint (burned), flaking, abrasion or scoring. If the bearing inserts are good they may be reused, provided the bearing clearance is within tolerance. Refer to the appropriate bearing clearance inspection procedure in this chapter. If any insert is questionable, replace the entire set.
2. Use a bore gauge or inside micrometer to measure the piston pin bore in each connecting rod (**Figure 242**). Use a micrometer to measure the diameter of each piston pin (**Figure 243**). If the clearance exceeds 0.080 mm (0.0031 in.), replace the out-of-tolerance connecting rod and piston pin as a set.
3. Use a feeler gauge to measure the side clearance between each connecting rod and the crankshaft (**Figure 244**). If the clearance exceeds 0.3 mm (0.012 in.), the connecting rod or crankshaft must be replaced. Perform the following to determine which component is worn:
   a. Use a micrometer to measure the width of the big end of the connecting rod (**Figure 245**). If

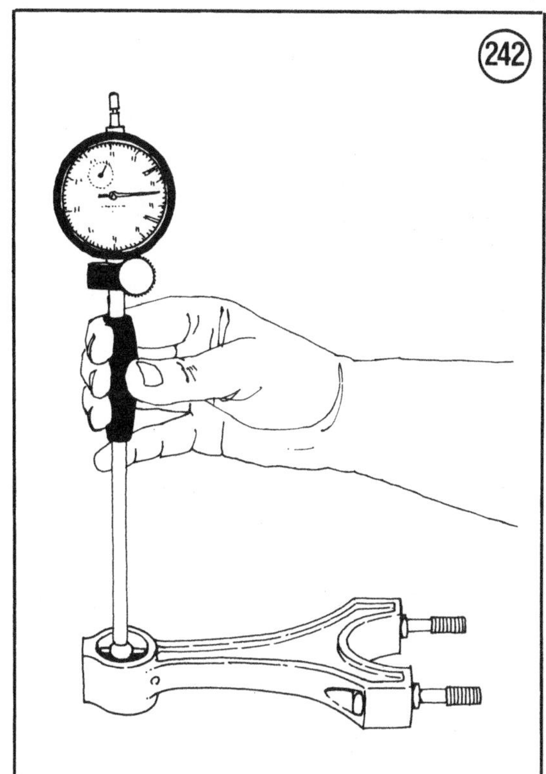

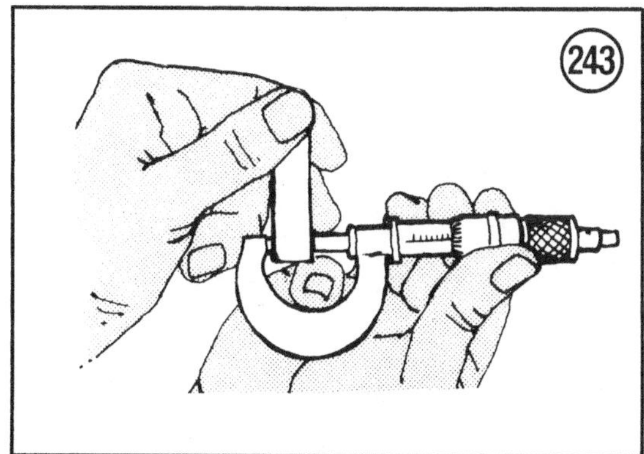

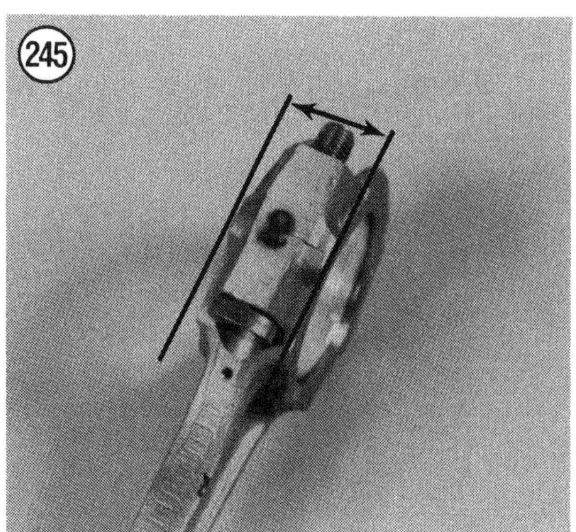

the big end width is not as specified in **Table 11**, replace the connecting rod.

b. Use an inside micrometer to measure the inside width of the crank pin journal (**Figure 246**). If the journal width is not as specified in **Table 11**, replace the crankshaft.

4. Place the crankshaft on 2 V-blocks, one at each end, and position a dial indicator against one of the center main bearing journals. Rotate the crankshaft to measure the amount of runout or deflection. If the runout exceeds 0.05 mm (0.002 in.), the crankshaft must be replaced.

5. Temporarily install the crankshaft in the crankcase and push the crankshaft to the alternator side as far as possible (**Figure 247**). Use a feeler gauge to measure the side thrust (end play) clearance between the crankshaft and the thrust bearing on the alternator side of the engine (**Figure 248**). Standard clearance is 0.045-0.100 mm (0.0018-0.0039 in.). If the clearance is not as specified, one or both thrust bearings must be replaced. Refer to *Crankshaft Thrust Bearing Selection.*

6. Use a micrometer to measure accurately the diameter of each main bearing journal (**Figure 249**) and crank pin journal (**Figure 250**). All main and crank pin journals must be within the specifications in **Table 11** and **Table 12**, or the crankshaft must be replaced. Write down all measurements. The measurements can be used to determine the required bearing inserts, if new inserts are to be installed.

Connecting Rod Bearing Clearance Inspection

To accurately measure the bearing clearance it is necessary to use Plastigage. A strip of Plastigage is

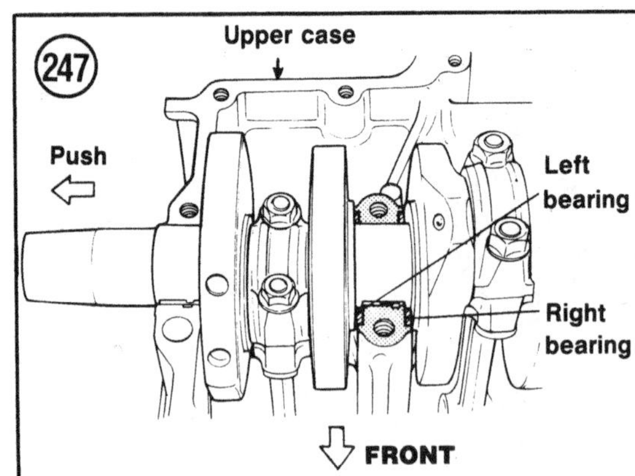

installed between the bearing surface and the crankshaft and is compressed when the bearing cap is tightened to the proper torque. The thickness of the compressed Plastigage is then measured with the Plastigage wrapper. This method, when properly performed, results in an accurate measurement of the true bearing clearance.

1. Remove the nuts securing the connecting rod bearing cap and carefully remove the bearing cap and connecting rod (**Figure 251**).

CAUTION
Use a felt tip pen or scribe and carefully mark the location of each connecting rod and rod cap as well as the position of the bearing inserts if they are to be reused. Do not mark on the bearing surface; mark on the exterior of the connecting rod and bearing cap. All parts must be installed in the exact position and location from which they were removed as wear patterns have developed on all parts. If the parts are intermixed with others, rapid and excessive wear may result.

CAUTION
Do not attempt to remove the bolts from the connecting rods. The bolts are factory-fit and aligned with each bearing cap. If the bolts are disturbed, the bearing cap alignment will be disturbed.

2. Clean the connecting rod bearing surface as well as the crank pin journal with solvent or spray contact cleaner.

3. Place a strip of green Plastigage on the top or bottom (TDC or BDC) of the crank pin journal. Make sure the strip does not cover the oil hole in the journal. Use a strip as long as the journal so the clearance can be checked at both ends of the bearing.

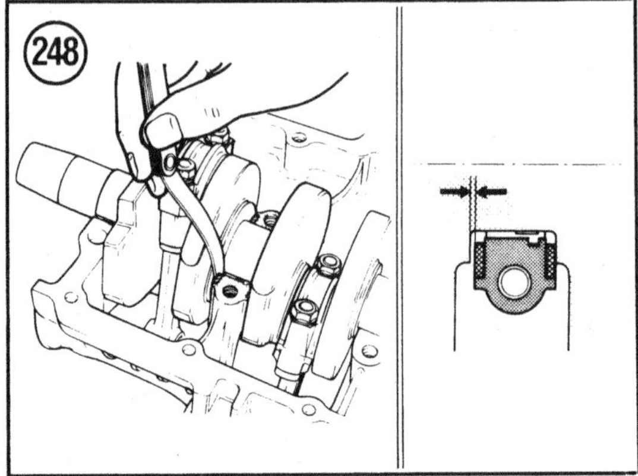

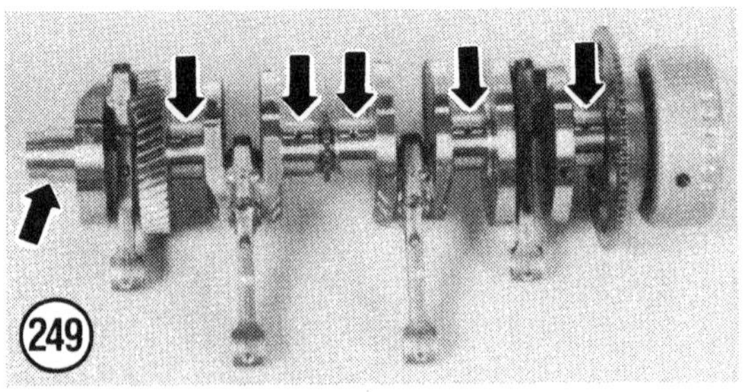

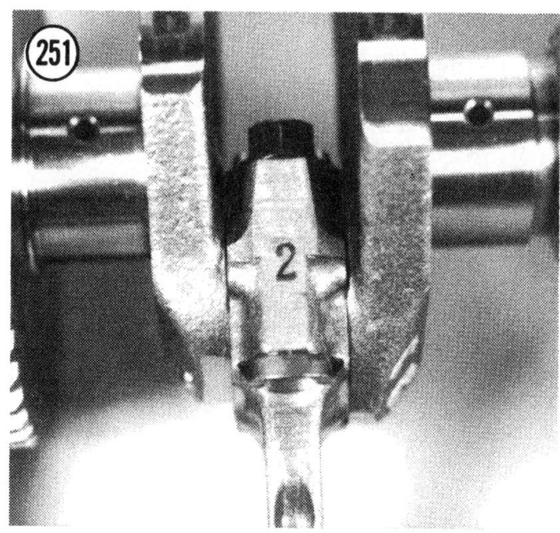

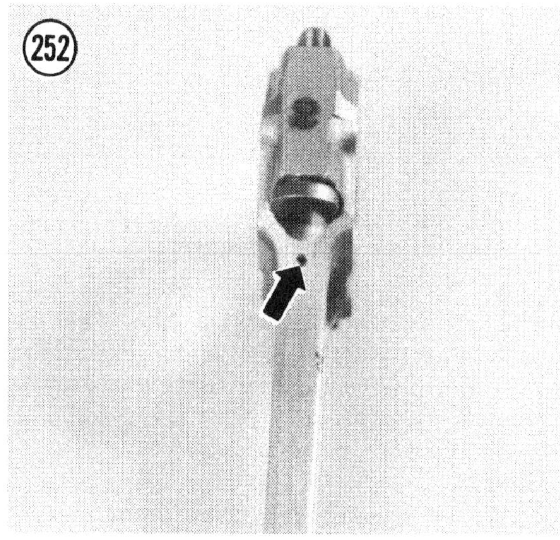

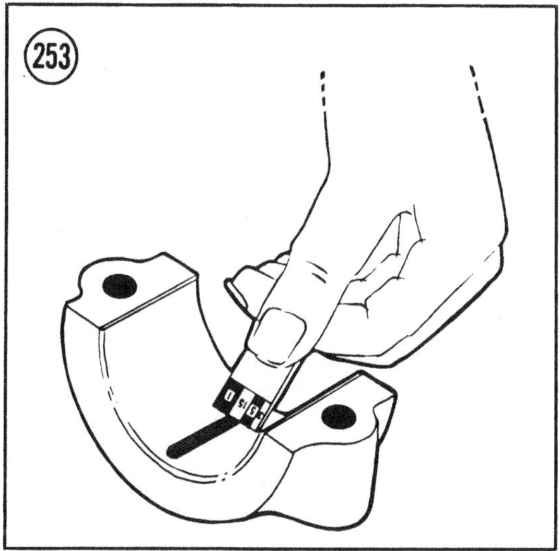

NOTE
Plastigage is available in different colors, corresponding to the range of measurement possible. Green Plastigage should be used for this procedure.

4. Carefully install the connecting rod and bearing cap on the crank pin journal. Make sure the connecting rod is installed with the oil hole (**Figure 252**) toward the rear of the engine.

NOTE
Do not allow the crankshaft to turn or the Plastigage strip will be ruined. The connecting rod must then be removed and a new strip of Plastigage installed.

5. Tighten the bearing cap nuts in 2 steps to make sure they are properly torqued. Tighten each bearing cap nut a little at a time to 1.6-2.2 mkg (11.5-16 ft.-lb.) then torque each nut to the final value of 3.3-3.7 mkg (24-27 ft.-lb.).
6. Carefully remove the nuts securing the bearing cap and remove the cap and connecting rod.
7. Use the Plastigage wrapper to measure the clearance at both ends of the Plastigage strip as shown in **Figure 253**. If the clearance exceeds the service limit of 0.080 mm (0.0031 in.), the bearing inserts must be replaced. If the indicated clearance varies more than 0.025 mm (0.001 in.) on each end of the Plastigage strip, the crank pin journal is tapered excessively. The crankshaft must be reground or replaced.

NOTE
The Plastigage may adhere to the bearing cap, connecting rod or crank pin journal. Any of these positions will provide an accurate indication of bearing clearance.

8. If the bearing inserts must be replaced, proceed to *Connecting Rod Bearing Insert Selection and Installation.* If the bearing clearance is within tolerance and the bearing inserts appear serviceable, install the connecting rods and bearing caps as outlined in *Assembly.*

Crankshaft Main Bearing Clearance Inspection

To accurately measure the bearing clearance it is necessary to use Plastigage. A strip of Plastigage is installed between the bearing insert and the crankshaft and is compressed when both crankcase halves are bolted together and the bolts are tightened to the proper torque. The thickness of the compressed Plastigage is then measured with the

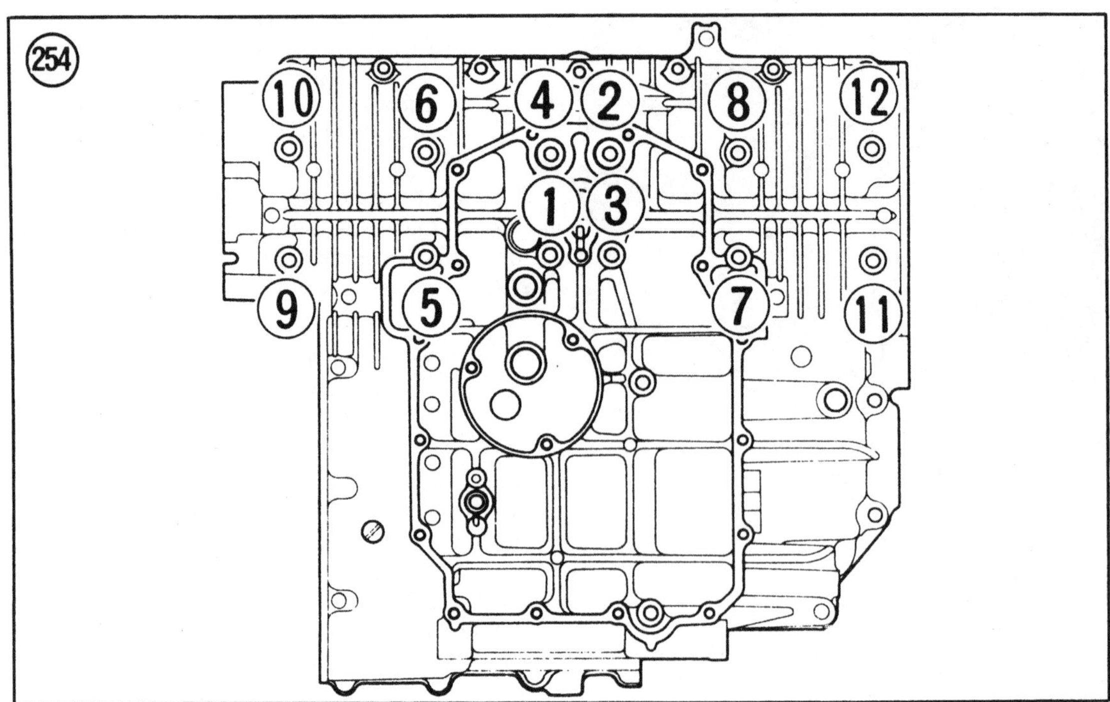

Plastigage wrapper. This method, when properly performed, results in an accurate measurement of the bearing clearance.

1. Remove the crankshaft as described under *Disassembly*. Do not remove the bearing inserts at this time.
2. Use solvent or spray contact cleaner to clean the main bearing journals on the crankshaft and the main bearing inserts in both crankcase halves.
3. Clean all the sealant residue from the sealing surfaces of both crankcase halves.

CAUTION
Make sure all sealant residue is removed from the crankcase sealing surfaces. Left-over sealant residue may not allow the crankcase halves to bolt together completely. The Plastigage may then not be completely compressed between the bearing surfaces, resulting in an incorrect bearing clearance measurement.

4. Place the upper crankcase half on a work bench and carefully install the crankshaft in the upper crankcase half.

CAUTION
Make sure the crankshaft is installed correctly or inaccurate bearing clearance measurements will result. When the engine is viewed from the inside with the crankshaft at the top, the alternator end of the crankshaft must be on the right end.

5. Place a strip of green Plastigage on each crankshaft main bearing journal. Make sure the strip does not cover the oil hole in the journal. Use a strip as long as the journal so the clearance can be checked at both ends of the bearing.

NOTE
Plastigage is available in different colors, corresponding to the range of measurement possible. Green Plastigage should be used in this procedure.

6. Carefully install the lower crankcase half over the upper half. Install all the crankcase bolts finger-tight.

NOTE
Do not allow the crankshaft to turn or the Plastigage strips will be ruined. The lower crankcase must then be removed and new strips of Plastigage installed on all the main bearing journals.

7. Tighten the crankcase bolts in 2 steps to make sure they are properly torqued. Tighten the 8 mm crankcase bolts in the order designated in **Figure 254**. Tighten each 8 mm bolt a little at a time (in designated order) to 1.3 mkg (9.5 ft.-lb.). Torque each 8 mm bolt to the final value of 2-2.4 mkg (14.5-17.5 ft.-lb.).

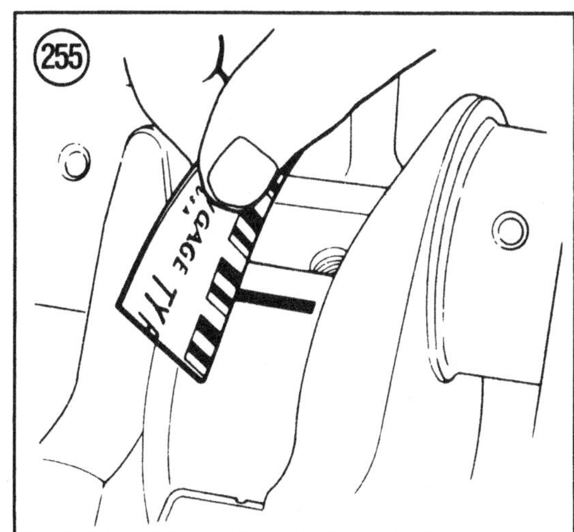

255

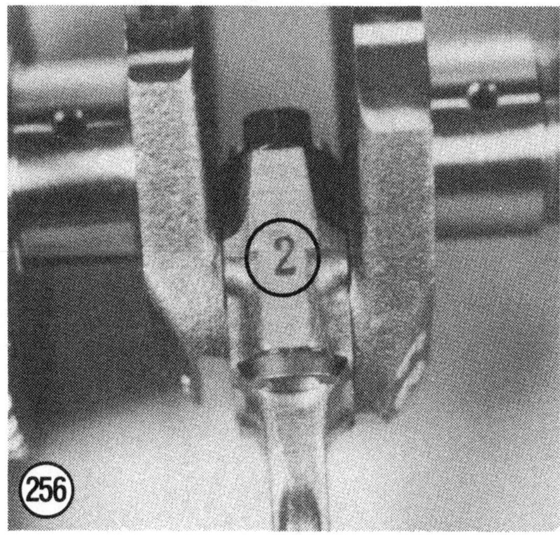

256

8. Remove the bolts securing the crankcase halves and carefully lift off the lower crankcase half.
9. Use the Plastigage wrapper to measure the clearance at both ends of the Plastigage strip as shown in **Figure 255**. If the clearance indicated by the Plastigage exceeds the service limit of 0.080 mm (0.0031 in.), the bearing inserts must be replaced. If the indicated clearance varies more than 0.025 mm (0.001 in.) on each end of the Plastigage strip, the main bearing journal is tapered excessively. The crankshaft must be reground or replaced.

NOTE
The Plastigage may adhere to the bearing insert or the crankshaft journal. Either location will provide an accurate indication of bearing clearance.

10. If the bearing inserts must be replaced, proceed to *Crankshaft Main Bearing Insert Selection and Installation*. If the bearing clearance is within tolerance and the bearing inserts appear serviceable, install the crankshaft as outlined in *Assembly*.

Crankshaft Thrust Bearing Selection

1. Perform *Crankshaft and Connecting Rod Inspection* to determine if the crankshaft side thrust (end play) is within tolerance. If the crankshaft side thrust is out of tolerance, one or both thrust bearings must be replaced.
2. Remove the right-hand thrust bearing. Measure the bearing thickness with a micrometer. Standard thickness is 2.425-2.450 mm (0.0955-0.965 in.). If the bearing is worn out of tolerance, replace it and again measure the crankshaft side clearance. If crankshaft end play is still out of tolerance with a new right-hand bearing, a new left-hand bearing must be installed.
3. Remove the left-hand thrust bearing and measure the side thrust *without* the bearing as shown in **Figure 248**. New left-hand thrust bearings are color-coded according to size. Refer to **Table 13** and select a left-hand thrust bearing that will create the standard thrust clearance of 0.045-0.100 mm (0.0018-0.0039 in.).

NOTE
The right-hand thrust bearing is the same as the green left-hand bearing.

4. Recheck side thrust after the new bearings have been installed.

Connecting Rod Bearing Selection and Installation

Refer to **Table 14** for this procedure.

1. Perform *Crankshaft and Connecting Rod Inspection* to determine if crank pin journals and connecting rods are serviceable.
2. Perform *Connecting Rod Bearing Clearance Inspection* to determine if the bearing clearance is within tolerances specified in **Table 14**. If bearing clearance is not as specified, the bearing inserts must be replaced as a set.
3. Each connecting rod is etched with a code number "1" or "2" as shown in **Figure 256**.
4. Each crank pin journal on the crankshaft is identified with a code number "1," "2" or "3" as shown in **Figure 257**.

NOTE
Do not confuse the crank pin code numbers "1," "2" and "3" with the letters

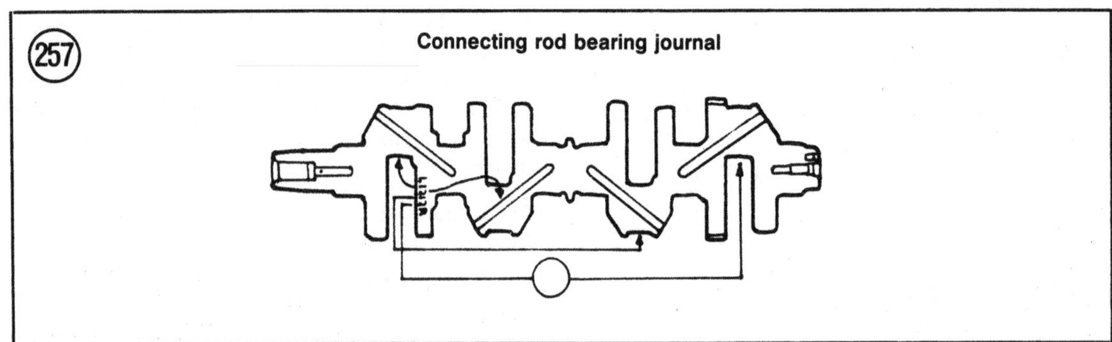

*"A," "B" or "C" on the crankshaft. The **letter** codes are used to select crankshaft **main** bearing inserts.*

5. Each bearing insert is color-coded on the edge of the bearing (**Figure 258**).
6. Bearing selection is determined by the connecting rod code and crank pin code as shown in **Table 14**. If the crank pin dimensions are within the tolerances stated for each number code, the bearings can be simply selected by color-code. For example; the 2nd crank pin shown in **Figure 257** is stamped "2." It was determined with a micrometer, during inspection, that this crank pin measured 31.989 mm (1.2594 in.). This is within the tolerances stated in **Table 14** for a number "2" crank pin. The connecting rod used on this crank pin is etched "2" as shown in **Figure 256**. The required bearing insert for a "2" connecting rod and a "2" crank pin journal is color-coded brown as specified in **Table 14**.
7. If any crank pin measurements taken during inspection do not fall within the tolerance range for the stamped numbered code, the serviceability of the crankshaft must be carefully examined. If the crank pin journal in question is not tapered, out-of-round or scored, the crankshaft may still be used; however, the bearing selection will have to be made based on the measured diameter of the crank pin and not by the stamped number code. Suzuki recommends the crankshaft be replaced whenever a crank pin journal dimension is beyond the specified range of the stamped code number.
8. To install new connecting rod bearing inserts, perform the following:
   a. Use a small screwdriver or awl and carefully pry out each old insert by the tab as shown in **Figure 259**.

CAUTION
Do not touch the bearing surface of new inserts. The bearing surfaces are easily contaminated and damaged by dirt, grit and skin acids.

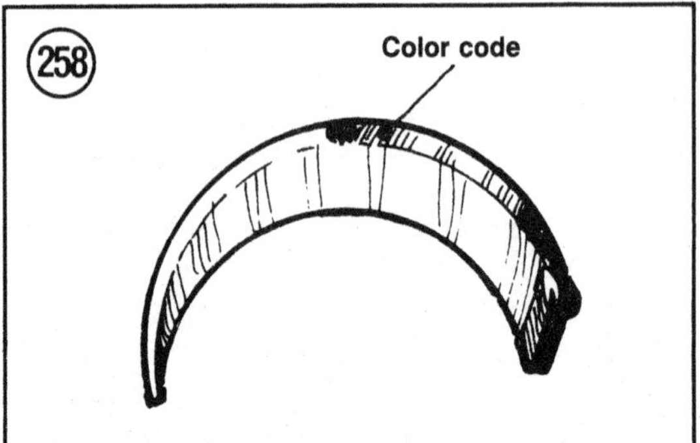

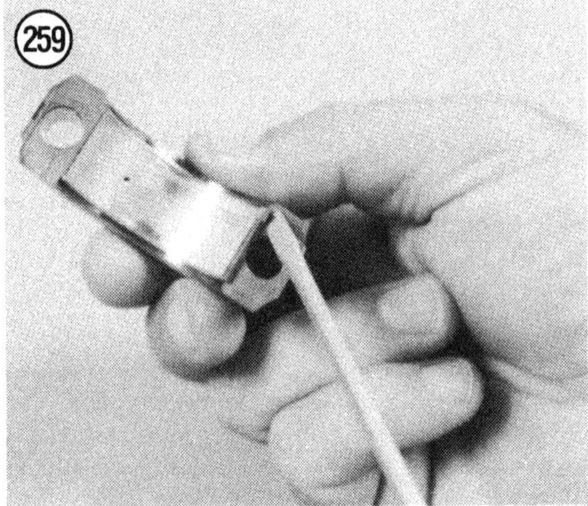

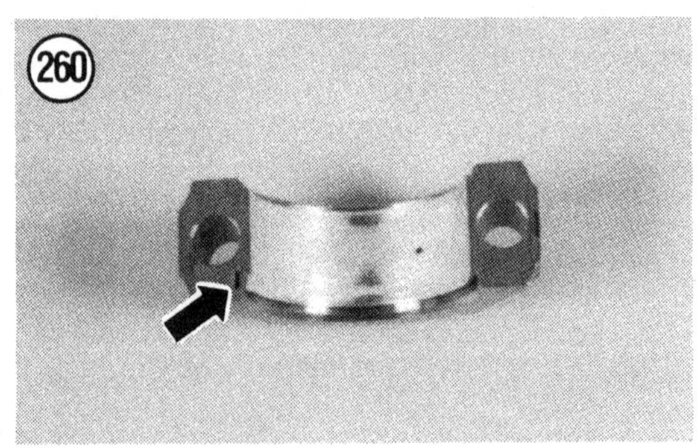

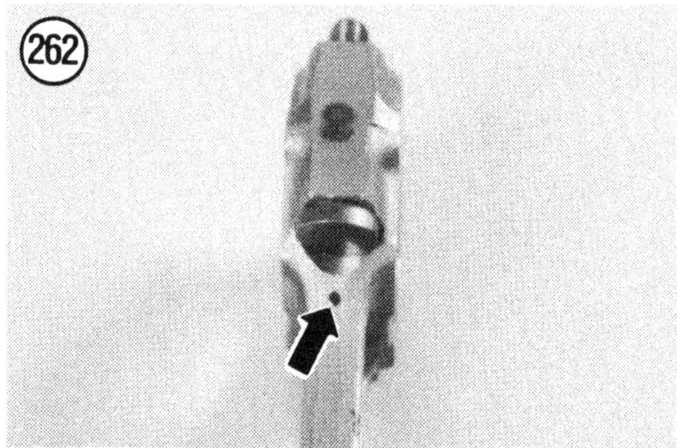

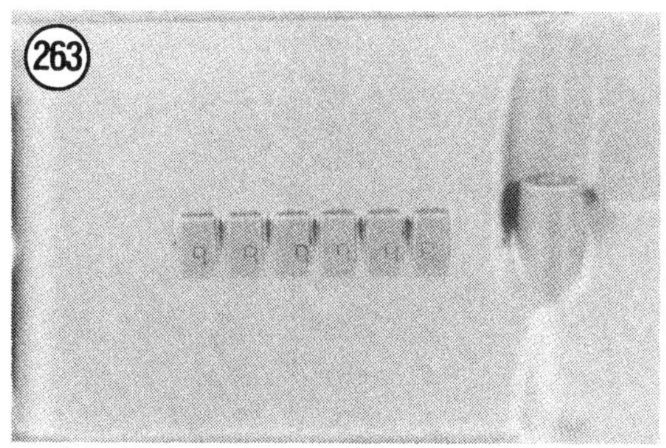

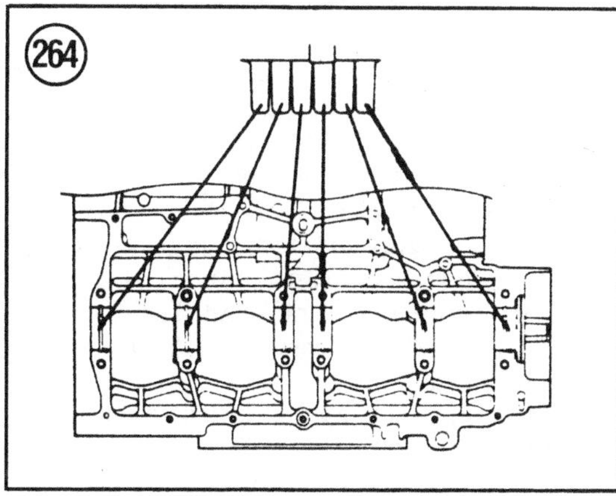

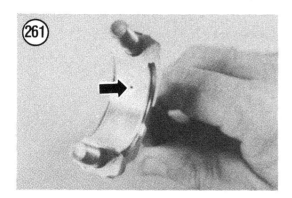

b. Make sure the inner surfaces of each connecting rod and bearing cap are perfectly clean. Engage the tab on the insert with the notch in the connecting rod or bearing cap and carefully press the other end of the insert into place. Make sure the tabs are correctly positioned in the notches as shown in **Figure 260**.

CAUTION

*The oil hole in the bearing insert (**Figure 261**) must be aligned with the oil hole in the connecting rod (**Figure 262**).*

NOTE

Both connecting rod bearing inserts are equipped with oil holes, therefore the inserts are interchangeable; they can be installed in either the connecting rod or the bearing cap. The bearing cap is not fitted with an oil hole.

c. Make sure each insert is flush with the edge of the connecting rod or bearing cap.

9. Install the connecting rods as outlined in *Assembly*.

Crankshaft Main Bearing Insert Selection and Installation

Refer to **Table 15** for this procedure.

1. Perform *Crankshaft and Connecting Rod Inspection* to determine if the crankshaft main bearing journals are serviceable.
2. Perform *Crankshaft Main Bearing Clearance Inspection* to determine if the bearing clearances are within tolerances specified in **Table 15**. If bearing clearances are not as specified, the bearing inserts must be replaced as a set.
3. Each crankcase main bearing is identified by a letter code "A" or "B" stamped on panels at the rear of the upper crankcase half as shown in **Figure 263**. These stamped letter codes correspond to each crankcase bearing in the order shown in **Figure 264**.
4. Each main bearing journal on the crankshaft is identified by a code letter "A," "B" or "C" stamped on the crankshaft counterweight as shown in **Figure 265**.

NOTE

*Do not confuse the main bearing code letters "A," "B" and "C" with the numbers "1," "2" or "3" on the crankshaft counterweights. The **number** codes are only used to select **connecting rod** bearing inserts.*

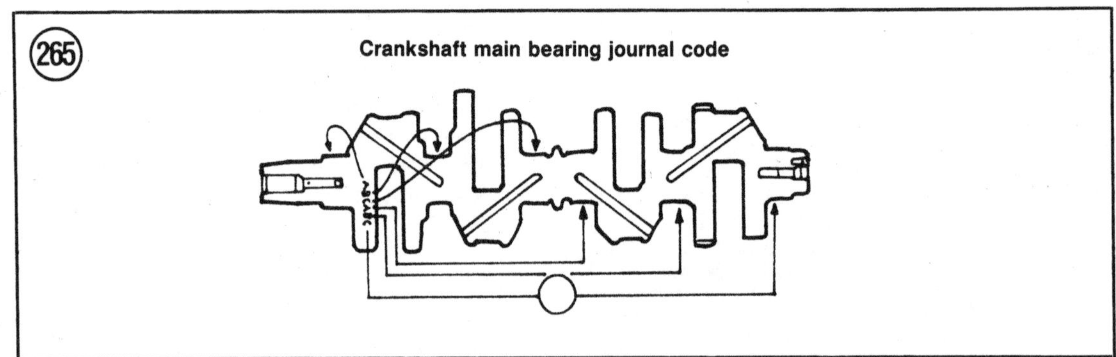

265

5. Each bearing insert is color-coded on the edge of the bearing (**Figure 266**).
6. Bearing selection is determined by the crankcase code and the crankshaft counterweight code as shown in **Table 15**. If the crankshaft main bearing dimensions are within the tolerances stated for each letter code, the bearings can be simply selected by color-code. For example; the main bearing journal shown in **Figure 265** is stamped "A." It was determined with a micrometer, during inspection, that this journal measured 31.994 mm (1.2596 in.). This is within the tolerances stated in **Table 15** for a letter "A" main bearing journal. The crankcase code for this main bearing is stamped "B" as shown in **Figure 263**. The required bearing insert for a "B" crankcase bearing and a "A" crankshaft main bearing journal is color-coded black as specified in **Table 15**.
7. If any main bearing journal measurements taken during inspection do not fall within the tolerance range for the stamped letter codes, the serviceability of the crankshaft must be carefully examined. If the main bearing journal in question is not tapered, out-of-round or scored, the crankshaft may still be used; however, the bearing selection will have to be made based on the measured diameter of the bearing journal and not by the stamped letter code. Suzuki recommends the crankshaft be replaced whenever a main bearing journal dimension is beyond the specified range of the stamped code letter.
8. To install new main bearing inserts, perform the following:
   a. Use a small screwdriver or awl and carefully remove each old insert by prying up on the locating tab (**Figure 267**).

CAUTION
Do not touch the bearing surface of new inserts. The bearing surfaces are easily contaminated and damaged by dirt, grit and skin acids.

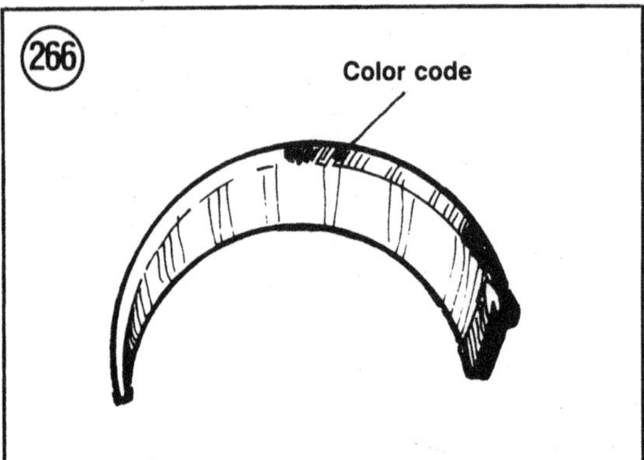

266

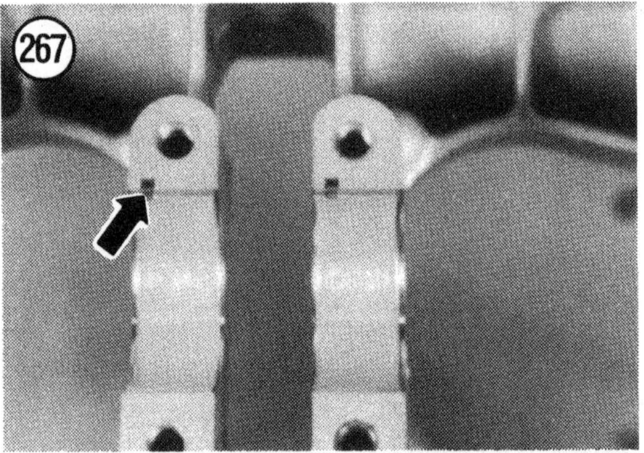
267

   b. Make sure the inner bearing surfaces of both crankcase halves are perfectly clean. Engage the tab on the insert with the notch in the crankcase and carefully press the other end of the insert into place.
   c. Refer to **Figure 268**. Install grooved bearings in all lower crankcase locations and in the center of the upper crankcase. The remainder of the upper crankcase bearings are non-grooved.
   d. Make sure each insert is flush with the edge of the crankcase.
9. Install the crankshaft as outlined in *Assembly*.

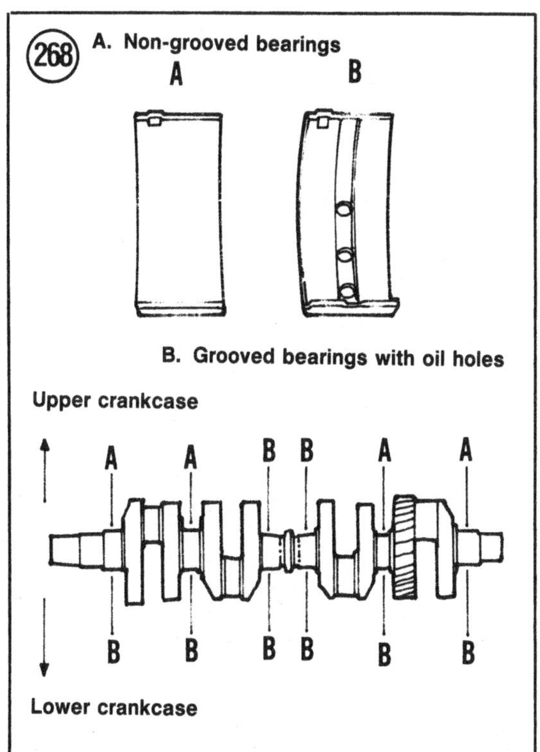

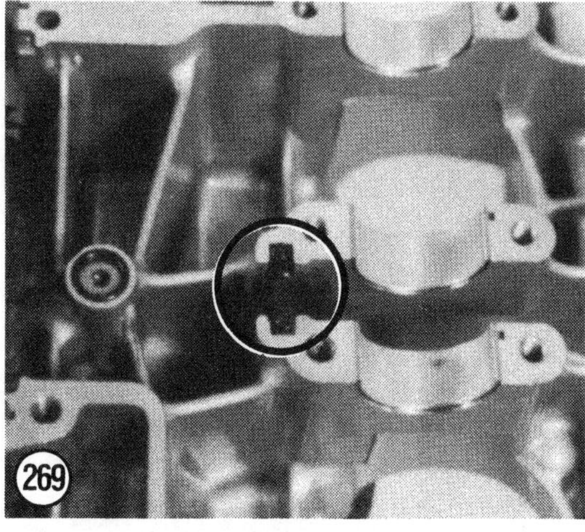

Assembly

CAUTION
Never use STP or similar friction reducing products as assembly lubricant. Even a small amount of these products will combine with the engine oil and destroy the friction properties of the clutch. If this should occur, the engine's lubrication system must be completely flushed and new clutch plates installed.

CAUTION
During all phases of engine assemby, frequently rotate the crankshaft and other moving parts. If any binding or stiffness is present, find out why and correct the problem before continuing the assembly. An engine that feels rough or tight when rotated by hand will not "wear in." Such an engine will likely cause expensive damage to itself if run.

CAUTION
Use a thread locking compound such as blue Loctite (Lock N' Seal No. 2114) on all internal fasteners during engine assembly. A small bolt or screw working loose inside the engine could have disastrous and expensive consequences.

1. Make sure all engine parts are clean and all fasteners are in good condition. Replace all bolts, nuts and screws with damaged heads or threads.
2. Carefully remove all traces of old sealant residue from the sealing surfaces on both crankcase halves. Use a wooden scraper or similar device to clean off the old sealant. Never use a metal scraper or the sealing surfaces can be damaged. Wipe the surfaces clean with solvent or lacquer thinner (not paint thinner).
3. If the crankshaft was removed, perform the following:
   a. Slide the rear cam chain tensioner into place. Make sure the ends of the tensioner completely engage the notches in the crankcase.
   b. Install the 2 rubber cushions over the ends of the chain tensioner (**Figure 269**). The small tips of the cushions must point toward the inside of the engine.
   c. Apply a thin film of molybdenum disulfide lubricant such as Bel-Ray Moly Lube on the bearing inserts in both crankcase halves as well as on the main bearing journals on the crankshaft.
   d. Stretch the cam chain tight and measure the length between 21 chain pins with a caliper as shown in **Figure 270**. Replace the cam chain if the length between 21 pins exceeds 128.9 mm (5.07 in.).
   e. Install the cam chain over the crankshaft.

NOTE
On engines undergoing a complete rebuild, it is recommended that a new cam chain be installed.

4

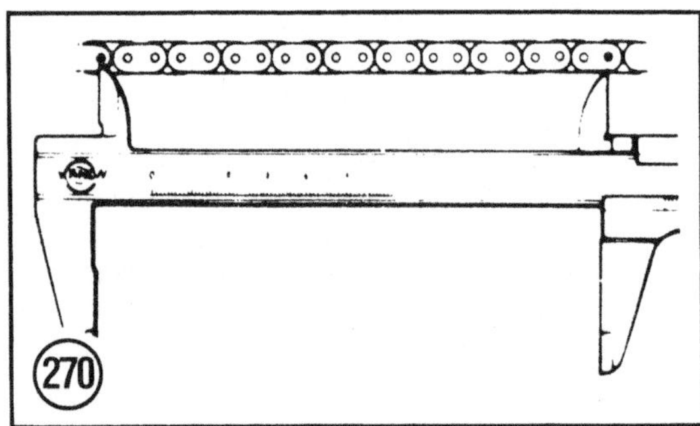

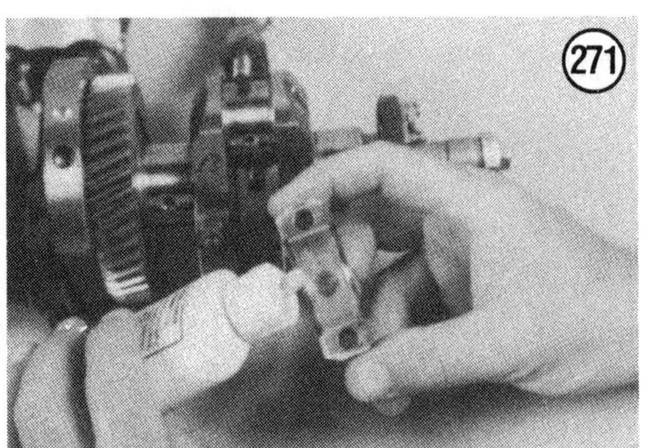

f. Route the cam chain into the chain tunnel and carefully install the crankshaft into the upper crankcase half.

4. If the connecting rods were removed from the crankshaft, perform the following:

a. Apply engine assembly oil or Bel-Ray Moly Lube to both halves of each connecting rod bearing insert (**Figure 271**).

b. Carefully install each connecting rod over the correct crank pin journal with the oil hole (**Figure 272**) toward the *rear* of the engine. Install the bearing cap over the connecting rod bolts with the etched numbers on the connecting rods together as shown in **Figure 273**.

CAUTION

*Make sure all connecting rod components are installed exactly as removed. Intermixing connecting rod components may cause serious and excessive engine wear. If the connecting rods are not installed with the oil holes (**Figure 272**) toward the rear of the engine, expensive engine damage will result.*

c. Install all connecting rod nuts finger-tight. Tighten each nut a little at a time to a torque value of 1.6-2.2 mkg (11.5-16 ft.-lb.). Gradually and evenly torque the nuts to a final torque value of 3.3-3.7 mkg (24-27 ft.-lb.).

5. If transmission or internal gearshift components were removed for repair, install them at this time. Refer to Chapter Five for installation procedures. Make sure the locating pins on the transmission bearings are properly fitted into the crankcase notches.

6. Install the oil control jet and flat washer (**Figure 274** and **Figure 275**).

7. Install a new O-ring in the crankcase oil passage (**Figure 276**).

8. Make sure the crankcase sealing surfaces are clean and free of oil, moisture and old sealant

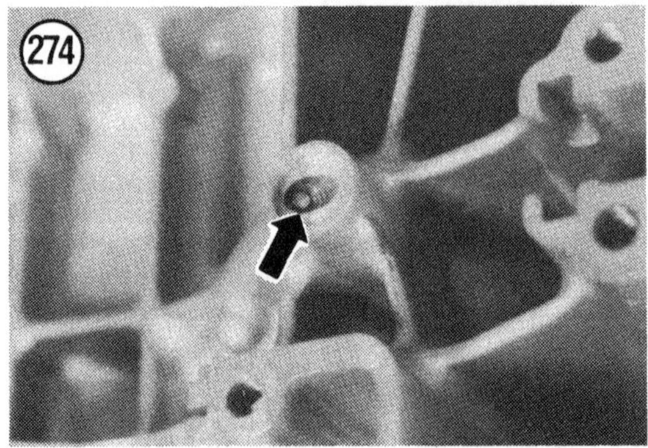

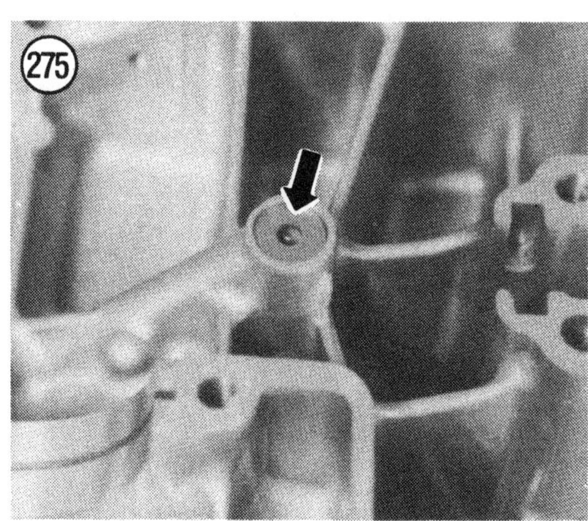

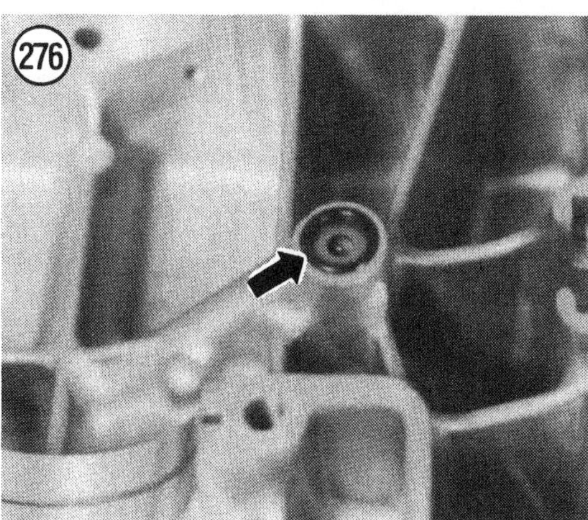

residue. Carefully apply a thin layer of Suzuki Bond No. 1215 (or equivalent) to the sealing surfaces on the lower crankcase half. Do *not* use a silicone sealant.

CAUTION
*Apply crankcase sealant with care. All surfaces must be covered or oil leaks may occur. Do **not** allow any sealant to contact any of the bearing surfaces. Use only a thin layer of sealant or the excess may squeeze into the crankshaft or transmission bearing areas.*

9. Carefully install the lower crankcase half over the upper half. Gently tap the crankcase halves together with a rubber mallet or block of wood. The dowel pins should align and both sealing surfaces should fit together. If the lower crankcase half does not fit down fully, stop and investigate the interference.

CAUTION
The crankcase halves should fit together without force. If they do not fit together fully, do not attempt to pull them together with the crankcase bolts or the crankcases will be damaged. Remove the bottom half and investigate the cause of the interference. The upper and lower crankcases are a matched set and are very expensive. Do not risk damage by trying to force the cases together.

10. Install all the crankcase bolts finger-tight.
11. Tighten the crankcase bolts in 2 steps to make sure they are properly torqued. Tighten the 8 mm crankcase bolts in the order designated in **Figure 277**. Tighten each 6 mm bolt a little at a time to 0.6 mkg (4.5 ft.-lb.), then tighten each 8 mm bolt a little at a time (in designated order) to 1.3 mkg (9.5 ft.-lb.). Torque each 6 mm bolt to a final value 1.3 mkg (9.5 ft.-lb.) and each 8 mm bolt to a final value of 2.4 mkg (17.5 ft.-lb.).
12. Turn the engine over. Refer to **Figure 278** and install the bolts securing the upper crankcase. Tighten the upper crankcase in the same manner and to the same torque values as the lower crankcase bolts.
13. Install the bearing retainer as shown in **Figure 279**. Apply a small amount of blue Loctite (Lock N' Seal No. 2114) to the retainer screws before installing them.

NOTE
Do not mix the bearing and seal retainer screws with the screws removed from the gearshift cam guide and gearshift pawl retainer. The bearing retainer screws are 16 mm long, while the 4 gearshift screws are 12 mm long.

14. Install a new O-ring in the oil passage (A, **Figure 280**). Install the oil pump pick-up screen with the arrow and "FRONT" mark positioned toward the front of the engine (B, **Figure 280**). Use a small amount of blue Loctite on the screws securing the screen.
15. Make sure the sealing surfaces on the oil sump and crankcase are clean and free of old gasket residue. Use a new gasket and install the oil sump (**Figure 281**). Gradually and evenly tighten all the oil sump bolts in a crisscross pattern. Torque the bolts to 1.2-1.6 mkg (8.5-11.5 ft.-lb.).
16. Install the following items:
   a. Cylinder head, cylinder block and pistons.
   b. Alternator cover, ignition advance governor assembly and oil pump.
   c. Clutch and external gearshift mechanism (Chapter Five).

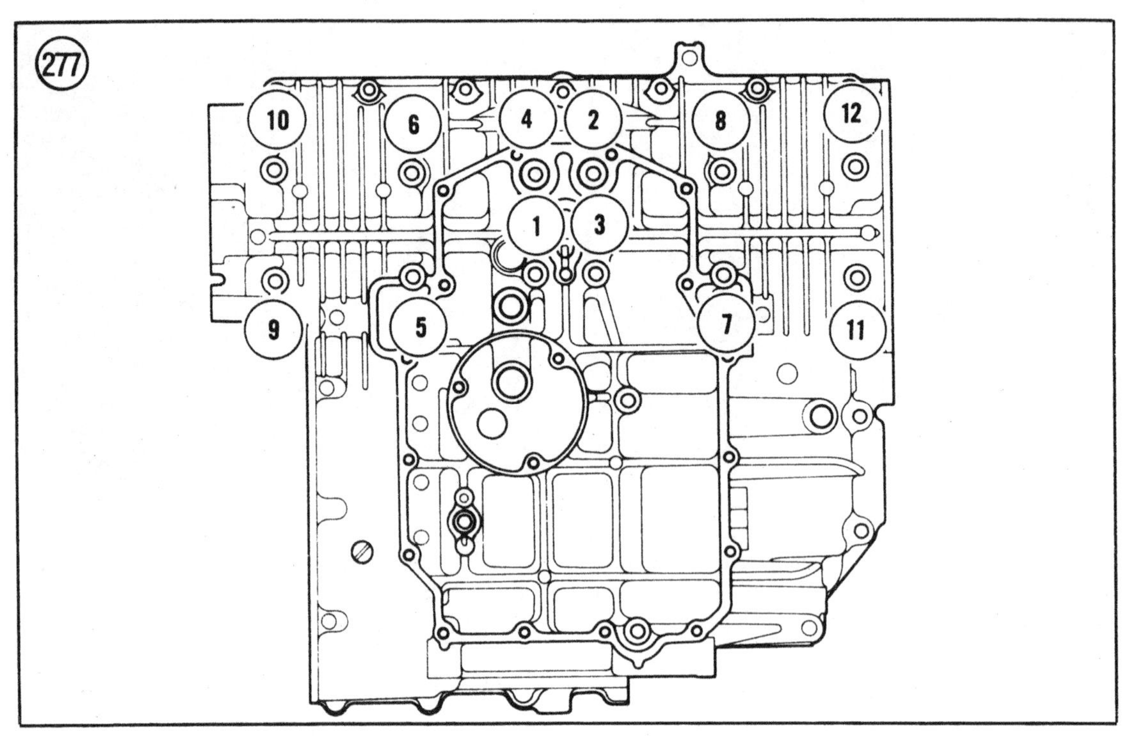
277
10
6
4
2
8
12
1
3
9
5
7
11

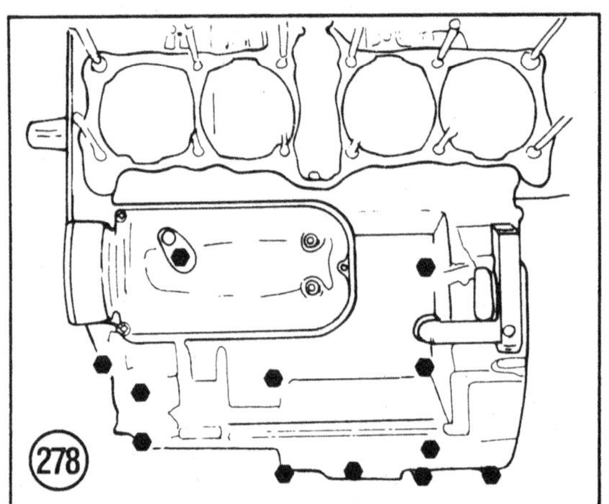
278

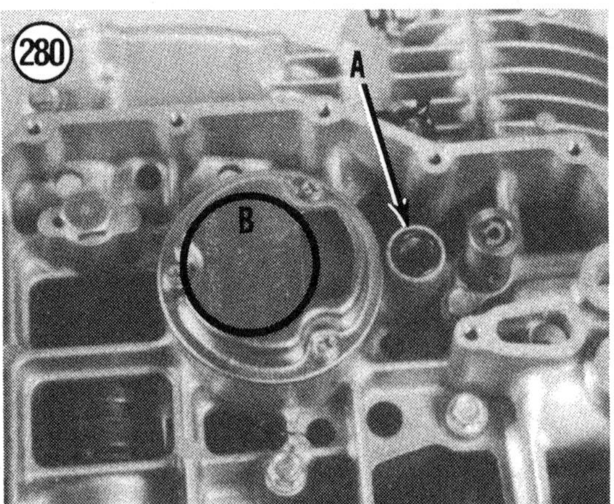
280
A
B

279

281

282

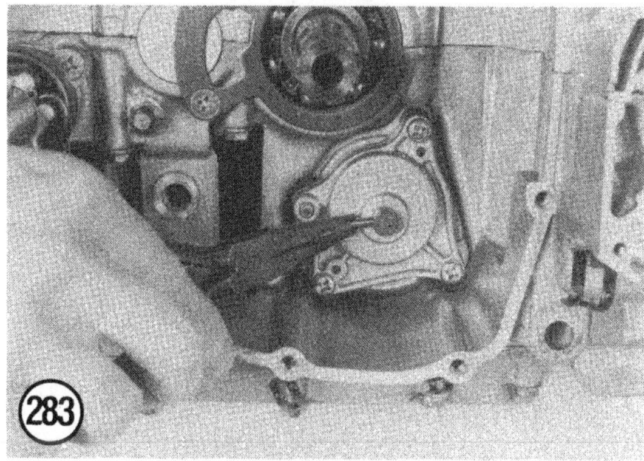
283

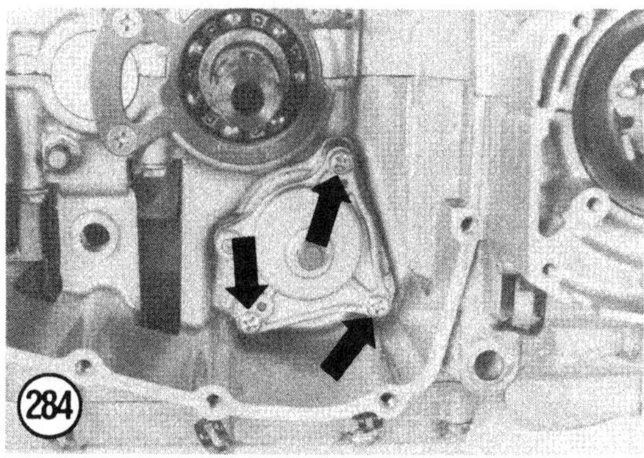
284

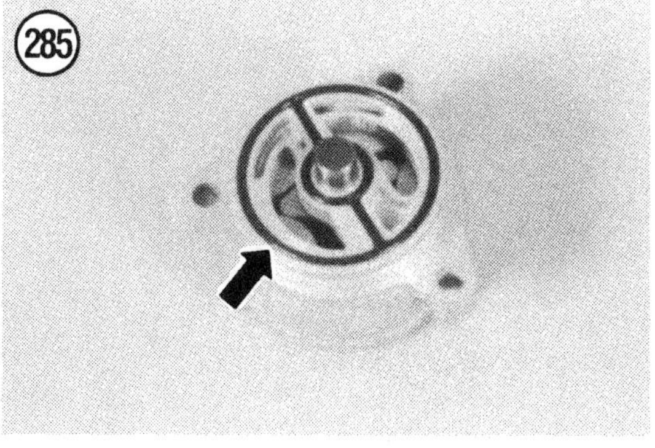
285

OIL PUMP

The engines on 1982 and earlier models have a high-volume, low-pressure oil pump. Normal oil pressure is greater than 0.1 kg/cm² (1.42 psi) and less than 0.5 kg/cm² (7.11 psi) at 3,000 rpm.

All TSCC engines are fitted with a high-pressure oil pump. Normal oil pressure is greater than 2.5 kg/cm² (36 psi) and less than 5.5 kg/cm² (78 psi) at 3,000 rpm.

The oil pump is not repairable. On 1977-1982 models, it should be carefully cleaned, inspected and (if necessary) replaced if the engine is undergoing a complete rebuild. On TSCC models, the pump cannot be disassembled for inspection.

If abnormal oil pressure is suspected, have the pressure checked by a dealer; a special gauge is required.

Removal/Installation

1. Remove the clutch as described in Chapter Five.
2. Remove the snap ring securing the pump drive gear (**Figure 282**) and remove the gear.
3. Remove the gear drive pin and thrust washer (**Figure 283**) from the pump shaft.
4. Remove the screws securing the oil pump and remove the pump (**Figure 284**).
5. On TSCC engines, remove the O-ring seal from the pump body (**Figure 285**). The seal may be stuck to the crankcase or the pump body.
6. On 1982 and earlier engines, remove the 2 O-rings from the oil pump passages (**Figure 286**).
7. Installation is the reverse of these steps. Keep the following points in mind:
   a. Use grease to hold the O-rings in place on the pump body (**Figure 285**) or in the passages in the crankcase.
   b. Apply a small amount of blue Loctite (Lock N' Seal No. 2114) to the screws securing the pump.
   c. On all models, make sure the thrust washer is installed between the pump body and the drive gear (**Figure 287**).
   d. Install the drive pin in the pump shaft and carefully position the drive gear over the pin (**Figure 283**).

Disassembly/Inspection/Assembly (1977-1982)

The following procedure is provided to determine the overall condition of the oil pump. The pump is not repairable and must be replaced if any tolerance is greater than specified.

4

CAUTION

On TSCC engines, the screw securing the pump halves is secured with super thread lock (such as Loctite). Suzuki recommends not attempting to disassemble the pump or damage may occur. Individual pump parts are not available. The complete unit must be replaced if the pump is worn or defective.

1. On 1982 and earlier models, remove the screw (if so equipped) securing the pump body (**Figure 288**).
2. Gently tap the pins (**Figure 289**) out enough until the pump body can be separated.
3. Push the shaft back through the pump body. Disassemble the pump inner and outer rotors from the pump body (**Figure 290**).
4. Clean the pump components in solvent. Carefully examine all component parts for signs of wear or damage. The pump must be replaced if any signs of damage are present.
5. Check for wear around the drive pin and inner rotor as shown in **Figure 291**.
6. Install the pump rotors into the pump body (**Figure 292**). Use a feeler gauge to measure the clearance between the inner and outer rotors (**Figure 293**). The clearance limit is 0.2 mm (0.008 in.).
7. Measure the outer rotor clearance as shown in **Figure 294**. The clearance limit is 0.25 mm (0.0098 in.).
8. Use a straightedge with a feeler gauge to measure the pump side clearance (**Figure 295**). The clearance must not exceed 0.15 mm (0.0059 in.).
9. When reassembling the pump, use blue Loctite (Lock N' Seal No. 2114) on the screws securing the pump assemby.

CAM CHAIN TENSIONER

Removal/Installation

NOTE

If the engine is still installed in the motorcycle, you must remove the carburetors to reach the tensioner assembly. Refer to Chapter Six for carburetor removal.

1. Loosen the locknut securing the lockscrew and tighten the lockscrew to hold the tensioner plunger (**Figure 296**).
2. Remove the bolts securing the tensioner assembly to the cylinder block and remove the tensioner assembly (**Figure 297**).

286

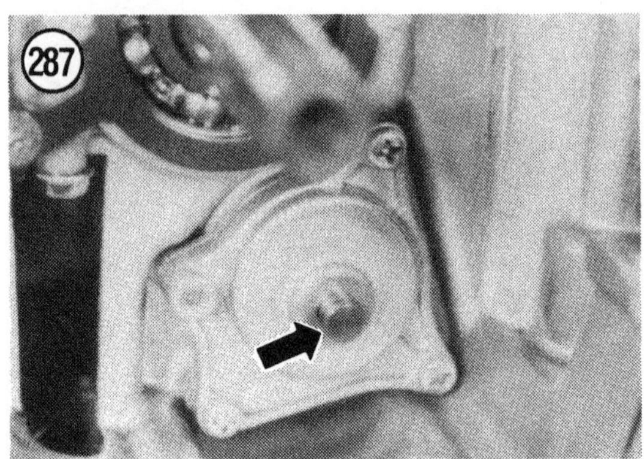
287

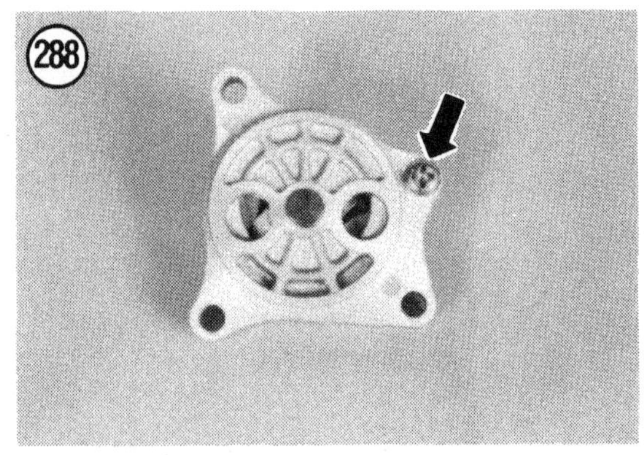
288

289

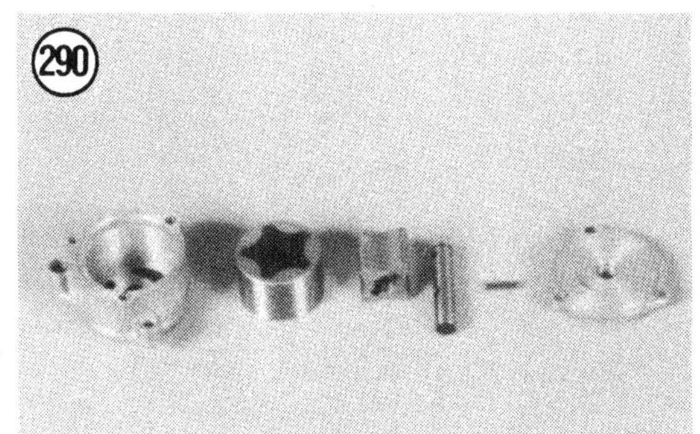
290

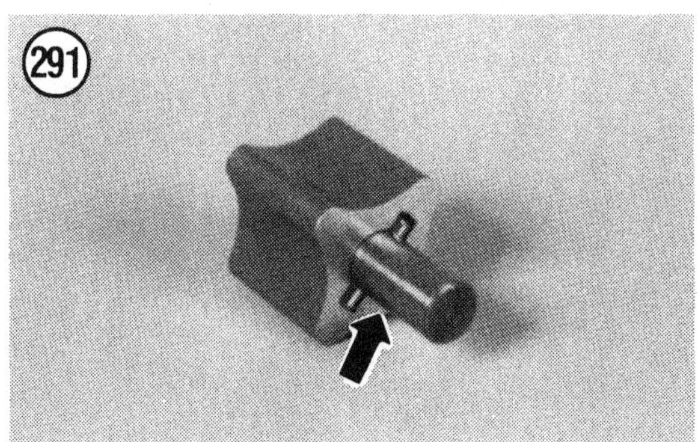
291

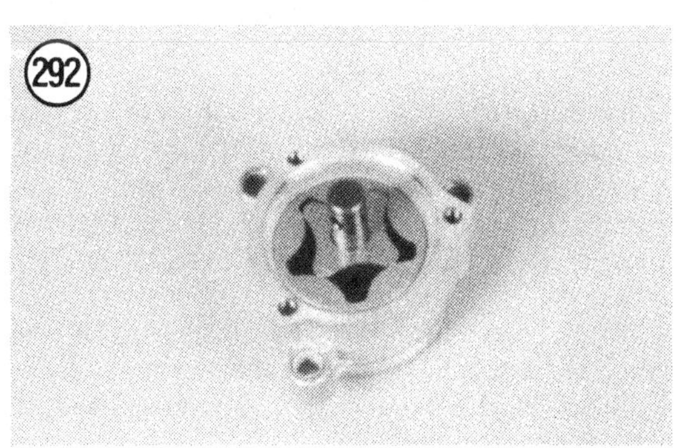
292

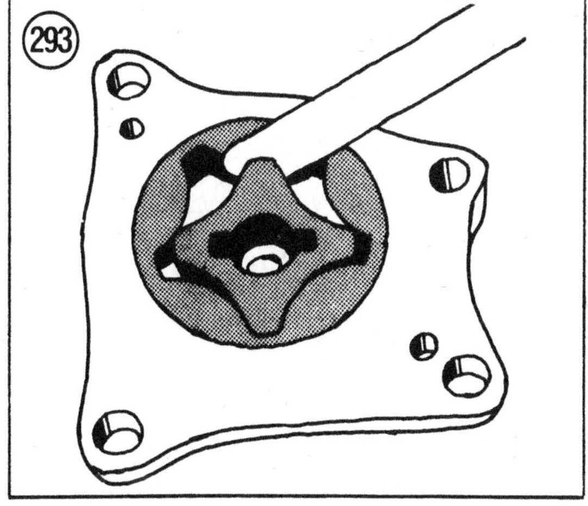
293

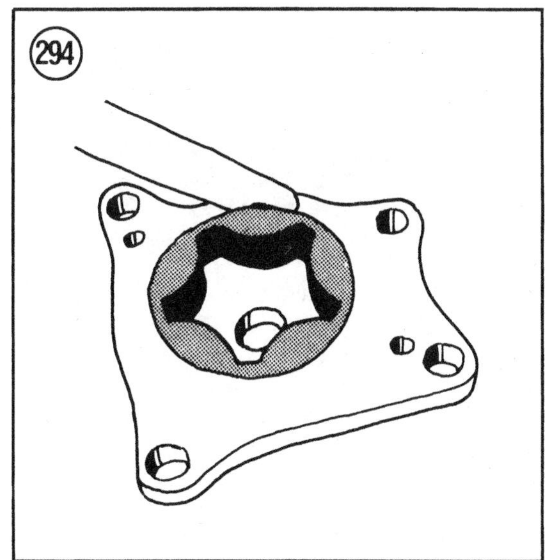
294

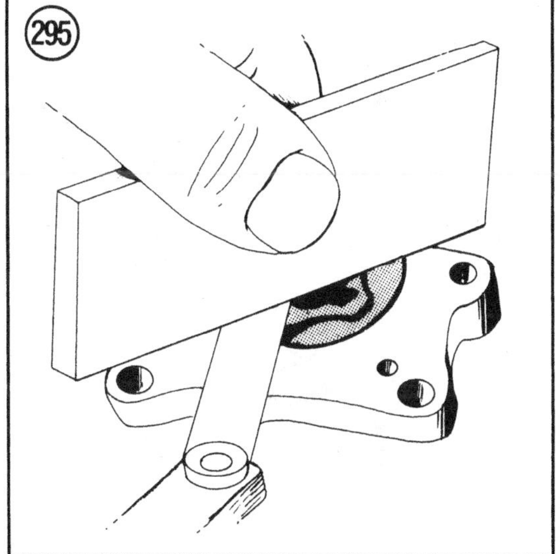
295

296

297

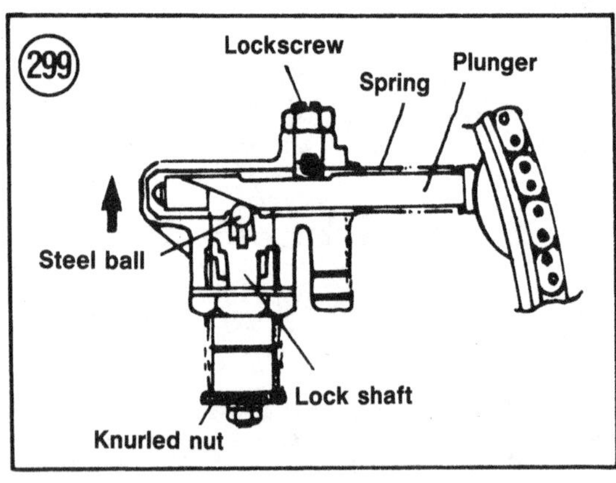

3. Loosen the locknut and lockscrew on the tensioner assembly. Push in on the spring-loaded plunger while rotating the large knurled nut counterclockwise (**Figure 298**). When the plunger is pushed in as far as possible, secure it with the lockscrew.

4. Make sure the gasket is installed on the tensioner assembly and place the assembly on the cylinder block. Torque the mounting bolts to 0.6-0.8 mkg (4.5-6 ft.-lb.).

5. Loosen the locknut securing the lockscrew and back off the lockscrew 1/4 turn to allow the spring-loaded plunger to move in against the internal chain tensioner. Tighten the locknut to secure the lockscrew.

NOTE

Do not back the lockscrew out more than 1/2 turn or the spring-loaded plunger may become disengaged from the tensioner body. If this happens, you must remove the tensioner assembly and reinstall the plunger into the tensioner body.

Disassembly/Assembly

Refer to **Figure 299** for this procedure.

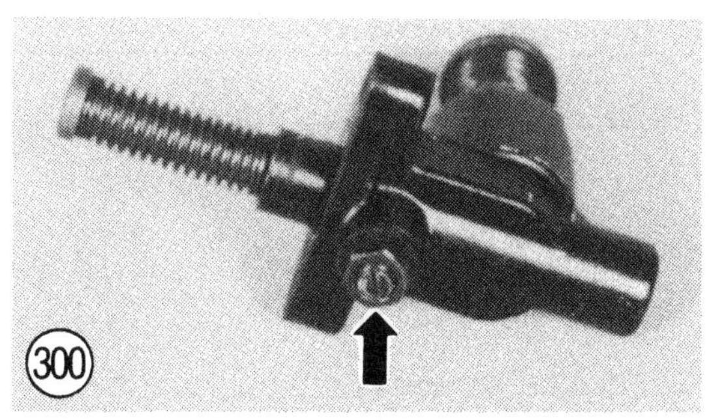

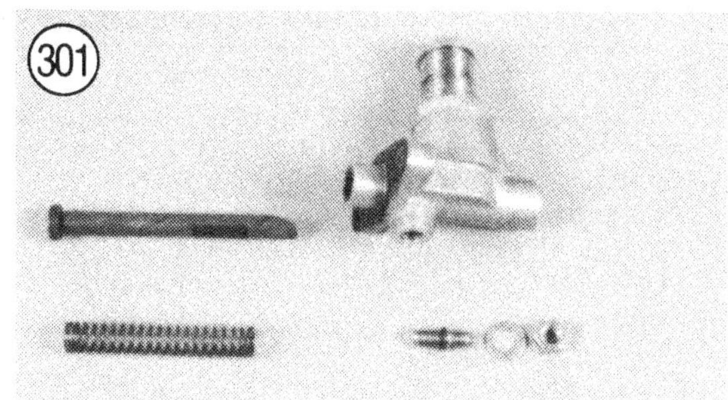

1. Loosen the locknut securing the lockscrew and remove the lockscrew from the tensioner body (**Figure 300**).

2. Remove the plunger, spring and O-ring.

3. Clean the parts in solvent and inspect the plunger and tensioner body for damage or excessive wear (**Figure 301**). Replace the worn parts as necessary.

4. Install a new O-ring on the lockscrew. Oil the O-ring and lockscrew and install the lockscrew a few turns into the tensioner body.

5. Apply molybdenum lubricant such as Bel-Ray Moly Lube to the plunger. Install the spring and plunger in the tensioner body. Make sure the flat spot on the plunger aligns with the lockscrew. Move the plunger in and out several times to make sure that it moves freely without sticking or binding.

6. Fully compress the plunger and secure the plunger in the compressed position with the lockscrew.

Table 1 ENGINE TORQUE SPECIFICATIONS

Item	mkg	ft.-lb.
Camshaft cover bolt		
1977-1982	0.7-1.1	5.0-8.0
1983-1984	1.3-1.5	9.5-11.0
Ignition advance governor	1.8-2.3	13.0-16.5
Cylinder head nut	2.3-2.8	16.5-20.0
Cylinder head bolt	0.7-1.1	5.0-8.0
Camshaft bearing cap bolts	0.8-1.2	6.0-8.5
Camshaft sprocket bolt		
1977-1979 (6 mm hex)	1.5-2.0	11.0-14.5
1977-1979 (6 mm Allen)	0.8-1.2	6.0-8.5
1980-1984 (7 mm hex)	2.4-2.6	17.5-19.0
Cam chain tensioner bolts	0.6-0.8	4.5-6.0
Cam chain adjuster locknut		
1977-1982	1.0-1.2	7.0-8.5
1983-1984	0.9-1.4	6.5-10.0
Alternator rotor bolt		
1977-1982	6.0-7.0	43.5-50.5
1983-1984	14.0-16.0	101.5-115.5
Starter clutch bolts		
1977-1982	1.5-2.0	11.0-14.5
1983-1984	2.3-2.8	16.5-20.0
Crankcase bolts (1977-1982)		
6 mm	0.6-1.0	4.5-7.0
8 mm	1.8-2.2	13.0-16.0
Starter motor bolts	0.4-0.7	3.0-5.0
Oil sump bolts		
1977-1982	1.0	7.0
1983-1984	1.2-1.6	8.5-11.5

(continued)

Table 1 ENGINE TORQUE SPECIFICATIONS (continued)

Item	mkg	ft.-lb.
Oil filter cover nuts	0.6-0.8	4.5-6.0
Oil line banjo bolts (TSCC models)	0.8-1.2	6.0-8.5
Oil cooler (TSCC models)		
Oil line fittings	1.5-1.8	11.0-13.0
Union bolts	2.5-3.0	18.0-21.5
Clutch sleeve hub nut		
1977-1982	4.0-6.0	29.0-43.5
1983-1984	5.0-7.0	36.0-50.5
Clutch spring bolt		
1977-1982	0.6-1.0	4.5-7.0
1983-1984	1.1-1.3	8.0-9.5
Drive sprocket nut		
1977-1982	5.0-7.0	36.0-50.5
1983-1984	10.0-15.0	72.5-108.5
Neutral cam stopper bolt	1.8-2.8	13.5-20.0
Exhaust pipe flange bolt		
1977-1982	0.9-1.4	6.5-10.0
1983-1984	2.0-2.5	14.5-18.0
Engine mount bolts (1977-1982)		
8 mm	1.3-2.3	9.5-16.5
10 mm	2.5-4.5	18.0-32.5
Engine mount bolts (1983-1984)		
Lower (front and rear)	6.0-7.2	43.5-52.0
Upper (front and rear)	6.7-8.0	48.5-58.0
Spark plugs	1.5-2.0	11.0-14.0
Gearshift lever bolt	0.6-1.0	4.5-7.0

Table 2 CAMSHAFT SPECIFICATIONS (1977-1982 MODELS)

Item	Standard	Service limit
Cam lobe height		
Intake	35.485-35.515 mm (1.3970-1.3982 in.)	35.190 mm (1.3854 in.)
Exhaust	35.285-35.315 mm (1.3892-1.3904 in.)	34.990 mm (1.3776 in.)
Camshaft deflection	—	0.10 mm (0.004 in.)
Camshaft journal diameter	21.959-21.980 mm (0.8645-0.8654 in.)	
Camshaft journal clearance (ET, LT models)	0.032-0.066 mm (0.0013-0.0026 in.)	0.150 mm (0.0059 in.)
Camshaft journal clearance (all other models)	0.020-0.054 mm (0.0008-0.0021 in.)	0.150 mm (0.0059 in.)
Camshaft bearing cap inside diameter (ET, LT models)	22.012-22.025 (0.8666-0.8671 in.)	
Camshaft bearing cap inside diameter (all other models)	22.000-22.013 (0.8661-0.8667 in.)	

Table 3 CAMSHAFT SPECIFICATIONS (TSCC ENGINES)

Item	Standard	Service limit
Cam lobe height		
Intake	34.940-34.980 mm (1.3756-1.3772 in.)	34.640 mm (1.3638 in.)
Exhaust	34.360-34.400 mm (1.3528-1.3543 in.)	34.060 mm (1.3409 in.)
Camshaft deflection	—	0.10 mm (0.004 in.)
Camshaft journal clearance (center journals)	0.050-0.084 mm (0.0020-0.0033 in.)	0.150 mm (0.0059 in.)
Camshaft journal clearance (other journals)	0.032-0.066 mm (0.0013-0.0026 in.)	0.150 mm (0.0059 in.)
Camshaft journal diameter	21.959-21.980 mm (0.8645-0.8654 in.)	
Camshaft bearing cap inside diameter (center journals)	22.039-22.043 (0.8673-0.8678 in.)	
Camshaft bearing cap inside diameter (other journals)	22.012-22.025 (0.8666-0.8671 in.)	

Table 4 ROCKER ARM AND ROCKER SHAFT SPECIFICATIONS (TSCC MODELS)

Rocker arm inside diameter	12.000-12.018 mm (0.4724-0.4731 in.)
Rocker shaft diameter	11.973-11.984 mm (0.4714-0.4718 in.)

Table 5 VALVE SPECIFICATIONS (1977-1982 MODELS)

Item	Standard	Service limit
Valve face (margin)	—	0.5 mm (0.02 in.)
Valve stem deflection	—	0.05 mm (0.002 in.)
Vale head deflection	—	0.03 mm (0.001 in.)
Valve stem-to-guide clearance intake and exhaust	—	0.35 mm (0.014 in.)
Valve stem diameter (ET, LT models)		
Intake	6.960-6.975 mm (0.2740-0.2746 in.)	
Exhaust	6.945-6.960 mm (0.2734-0.2740 in.)	
Valve stem diameter (all other models)		
Intake	6.965-6.980 mm (0.2742-0.2748 in.)	
Exhaust	6.955-6.970 mm (0.2738-0.2744 in.)	
Valve seat width (TX, LX, LZ, MZ models)	0.9-1.1 mm (0.035-0.043 in.)	
Valve seat width (all other models)	1.0-1.2 mm (0.039-0.047 in.)	
Valve spring free length		
Inner	—	33.9 mm (1.33 in.)
Outer		41.3 mm (1.63 in.)

4

Table 6 VALVE SPECIFICATIONS (TSCC MODELS)

Item	Standard	Service limit
Valve face (margin)	—	0.5 mm (0.02 in.)
Valve stem deflection	—	0.05 mm (0.002 in.)
Valve head deflection	—	0.03 mm (0.001 in.)
Valve stem-to-guide clearance		
Intake and exhaust	—	0.35 mm (0.014 in.)
Valve stem diameter		
Intake	4.960-4.975 mm (0.1953-0.1959 in.)	
Exhaust	4.945-4.960 mm (0.1947-0.1953 in.)	
Valve seat width	0.9-1.1 mm (0.035-0.043 in.)	
Valve spring free length		
Inner	—	31.6 mm (1.24 in.)
Outer		35.1 mm (1.38 in.)

Table 7 PISTON AND CYLINDER SPECIFICATIONS (1977-1982 MODELS)

Item	Standard	Limit
Piston pin bore	16.002-16.008 mm (0.6300-0.6302 in.)	16.030 mm (0.6311 in.)
Piston pin diameter	15.995-16.000 mm (0.6297-0.6300 in.)	15.980 mm (0.6291 in.)
Piston diameter (TX, LX, LZ, MZ models)	55.950-55.965 mm (2.2028-2.2033 in.)	55.880 mm (2.1999 in.)
Piston diameter (all other models)	55.945-55.960 mm (2.2026-2.2031 in.)	55.880 mm (2.1999 in.)
Piston measuring point	15 mm (0.6 in.) from piston skirt end	
Cylinder inner diameter	56.000-56.015 mm (2.2047-2.2053 in.)	56.085 mm (2.2080 in.)
Piston-to-cylinder clearance (TX, LX, LZ, MZ models)	0.045-0.055 mm (0.0018-0.0022 in.)	0.120 mm (0.0047 in.)
Piston-to-cylinder clearance (all other models)	0.050-0.060 mm (0.0020-0.0024 in.)	0.120 mm (0.0047 in.)
Cylinder distortion (warpage)	—	0.6 mm (0.010 in.)

Table 8 PISTON AND CYLINDER SPECIFICATIONS (TSCC MODELS)

Item	Standard	Limit
Piston pin bore	16.002-16.008 mm (0.6300-0.6302 in.)	16.030 mm (0.6311 in.)
Piston pin diameter	15.995-16.000 mm (0.6297-0.6300 in.)	15.980 mm (0.6291 in.)
Piston diameter	59.965-59.980 mm (2.3608-2.3614 in.)	59.880 mm (2.3575 in.)

(continued)

Table 8 PISTON AND CYLINDER SPECIFICATIONS (TSCC MODELS) (continued)

Item	Standard	Limit
Piston measuring point	15 mm (0.6 in.) from piston skirt end	
Cylinder inner diameter	60.000-60.015 mm (2.3622-2.3628 in.)	60.100 mm (2.3661 in.)
Piston-to-cylinder clearance	0.030-0.040 mm (0.0012-0.0016 in.)	0.120 mm (0.0047 in.)
Cylinder distortion (warpage)	—	0.2 mm (0.008 in.)

Table 9 PISTON RING SPECIFICATIONS

Item	Standard	Limit
Ring-to-groove clearance		
Top ring	—	0.18 mm (0.007 in.)
Middle ring		0.15 mm (0.006 in.)
Ring thickness		
Top ring (TSCC models)	1.175-1.190 mm (0.0384-0.0390 in.)	
Top ring (all others)	1.175-1.190 mm (0.0463-0.0469 in.)	
Middle ring	1.170-1.190 mm (0.0461-0.0469 in.)	
Ring groove width		
Top ring (TSCC models)	1.010-1.030 mm (0.0390-0.0410 in.)	
Top ring (all others)	1.210-1.230 mm (0.0476-0.0484 in.)	
Middle ring	1.210-1.230 mm (0.0476-0.0484 in.)	
Oil ring	2.510-2.530 mm (0.0988-0.0996 in.)	
Ring end gap		
Top and middle rings	0.10-0.30 mm (0.004-0.012 in.)	0.7 mm (0.03 in.)
Ring free end gap ("N" and "T" type rings)		
TSCC models (top)	Approx. 8.0 mm (0.31 in.)	6.4 mm (0.25 in.)
TSCC models (middle)	Approx. 8.5 mm (0.33 in.)	6.8 mm (0.27 in.)
All other models (top and middle)	Approx. 6.5 mm (0.26 in.)	5.2 mm (0.20 in.)

Table 10 CRANKSHAFT SPECIFICATIONS (1977-1982 MODELS)

	Standard	Limit
Crankshaft runout (1981-1982)	—	0.10 mm (0.004 in.)
Crankshaft runout (1977-1980)	—	0.05 mm (0.002 in.)
Connecting rod small end inside diameter	16.006-16.014 mm (0.6302-0.6305 in.)	16.040 mm (0.6315 in.)
Connecting rod deflection	—	3.0 mm (0.12 in.)
Connecting rod big end side clearance	0.10-0.65 mm (0.004-0.026 in.)	1.00 mm (0.039 in.)

Table 11 CONNECTING ROD SPECIFICATIONS (TSCC ENGINES)

	Standard	Limit
Small end inside diameter	16.010-16.018 mm (0.6303-0.6306 in.)	16.040 mm (0.6315 in.)
Piston pin outside diameter	15.995-16.000 mm (0.6297-0.6300 in.)	15.980 mm (0.6291 in.)
Big end width	19.95-20.00 mm (0.785-0.787 in.)	—
Big end side clearance	0.10-0.20 mm (0.004-0.008 in.)	0.30 mm (0.012 in.)
Big end bearing clearance	0.024-0.048 mm (0.0009-0.0019 in.)	0.080 mm (0.0031 in.)
Crankshaft crank pin (rod journal) width	20.10-20.15 mm (0.791-0.793 in.)	—
Crankshaft crank pin (rod journal) outside diameter	31.976-32.000 mm (1.2589-1.2598 in.)	—

Table 12 CRANKSHAFT SPECIFICATIONS (TSCC ENGINES)

	Standard	Limit
Crankshaft runout	—	0.05 mm (0.0020 in.)
Crankshaft thrust bearing clearance	0.045-1.00 mm (0.0018-0.0039 in.)	—
Crankshaft thrust bearing thickness		
Right side	2.425-2.500 mm (0.0955-0.0965 in.)	—
Left side*	2.350-2.500 mm (0.0925-0.0984 in.)	—
Crankshaft main bearing clearance	0.020-0.044 mm (0.0008-0.0017 in.)	0.080 mm (0.0031 in.)
Crank pin (rod journal) outside diameter	31.976-32.000 mm (1.2589-1.2598 in.)	—
Crankshaft main bearing journal outside diameter	31.976-32.000 mm (1.2589-1.2598 in.)	—

* The left-side thrust bearing dimension covers a range of six possible bearing sizes. The correct bearing size required must be found with the crankshaft installed in the crankcase. Refer to Chapter Four.

Table 13 CRANKSHAFT THRUST BEARING SELECTION (TSCC ENGINES)

Clearance without left thrust bearing	Left bearing required (color/part No.); bearing size
2.420-2.445 mm (0.0953-0.0963 in.)	Red/12228-43411 2.350-2.375 mm (0.0925-0.0935 in.)
2.445-2.470 mm (0.0963-0.0972 in.)	Black/12228-43412 2.375-2.400 mm (0.0935-0.0945 in.)

(continued)

Table 13 CRANKSHAFT THRUST BEARING SELECTION (TSCC ENGINES) (continued)

Clearance without left thrust bearing	Left bearing required (color/part No.); bearing size
2.470-2.495 mm (0.0972-0.0982 in.)	Blue/12228-43413 2.400-2.425 mm (0.0945-0.0955 in.)
2.495-2.520 mm (0.0982-0.0992 in.)	Green/12228-43414* 2.425-2.450 mm (0.0955-0.0965 in.)
2.520-2.545 mm (0.0992-0.1002 in.)	Yellow/12228-43415 2.450-2.475 mm (0.0965-0.0974 in.)
2.545-2.575 mm (0.1002-0.1014 in.)	White/12228-43416 2.475-2.500 mm (0.0974-0.0984 in.)
Thrust bearing clearance	0.045-0.100 mm (0.0018-0.0039 in.)

* Right-side thrust bearing is the same as green left-side bearing (part No. 12228-43414).

4

Table 14 CONNECTING ROD BEARING SELECTION (TSCC ENGINES)

		Crank pin code and dimension		
		Code 1 31.992-32.000 mm (1.2595-1.2598 in.)	Code 2 31.984-31.992 mm (1.2592-1.2595 in.)	Code 3 31.976-31.984 mm (1.2589-1.2592 in.)
Connecting rod code and dimension				
Code 1	35.000-35.008 mm (1.3780-1.3783 in.)	Green	Black	Brown
Code 2	35.008-35.016 mm (1.3783-1.3786 in.)	Black	Brown	Yellow

Color/Suzuki part No.	Bearing thickness
Green/12164-43400-010	1.484-1.488 mm (0.0584-0.0586 in.)
Black/12164-43400-020	1.488-1.492 mm (0.0586-0.0587 in.)
Brown/12164-43400-030	1.492-1.496 mm (0.0587-0.0589 in.)
Yellow/12164-43400-040	1.496-1.500 mm (0.0589-0.0591 in.)

Table 15 CRANKSHAFT MAIN BEARING SELECTION (TSCC ENGINES)

		Crankshaft main bearing journal code and dimension		
		Code A 31.992-32.000 mm (1.2595-1.2598 in.)	Code B 31.984-31.992 mm (1.2592-1.2595 in.)	Code C 31.976-31.984 mm (1.2589-1.2592 in.)
Crankcase journal code and dimension				
Code A	35.000-35.008 mm (1.3780-1.3783 in.)	Green	Black	Brown
Code B	35.008-35.016 mm (1.3783-1.3786 in.)	Black	Brown	Yellow

Non-grooved crankcase bearing color code/thickness Color/Suzuki part No.	Bearing thickness
Green/12229-43410-010	1.486-1.490 mm (0.0585-0.0587 in.)
Black/12229-43410-020	1.490-1.494 mm (0.0587-0.0588 in.)
Brown/12229-43410-030	1.494-1.498 mm (0.0588-0.0590 in.)
Yellow/12229-43410-040	1.498-1.502 mm (0.0590-0.0591 in.)

Grooved crankcase bearing color code/thickness Color/Suzuki part No.	Bearing thickness
Green/12229-43400-010	1.486-1.490 mm (0.0585-0.0587 in.)
Black/12229-43400-020	1.490-1.494 mm (0.0587-0.0588 in.)
Brown/12229-43400-030	1.494-1.498 mm (0.0588-0.0590 in.)
Yellow/12229-43400-040	1.498-1.502 mm (0.0590-0.0591 in.)

CHAPTER FIVE

CLUTCH AND TRANSMISSION

This chapter provides replacement and overhaul procedures for the clutch, transmission and gearshift mechanism.

All clutch components and some gearshift components can be removed with the engine installed in the motorcycle. To remove the transmission and internal components of the gearshift mechanism, you must remove and disassemble the engine. Refer to Chapter Four for engine removal and disassembly procedures.

Tables 1-4 are at the end of the chapter.

CLUTCH

Cable Replacement

1. Remove the fuel tank as outlined in Chapter Six.
2. Pull up the rubber boot and loosen the locknut securing the cable adjuster (**Figure 1**). Screw in the adjuster to provide maximum cable slack.
3. Pull back the rubber boot and loosen the large knurled locknut securing the cable adjuster on the clutch lever (**Figure 2**). Screw in the cable adjuster and disengage the cable end from the lever.
4. Remove the pinch bolt securing the gearshift arm or gearshift lever (**Figure 3**). The bolt must be removed completely, not just loosened. On ED and ESD models, remove the gearshift lever and proceed to Step 7.
5. On all but TSCC models, remove the bolts securing the left footrest and remove the footrest (**Figure 4**).
6. Use snap ring pliers to remove the snap ring securing the shift lever to the pivot (**Figure 5**). Slide off the shift lever with the shift linkage.

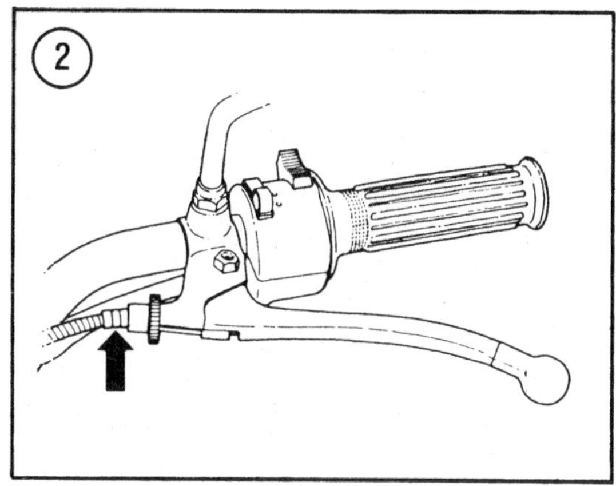

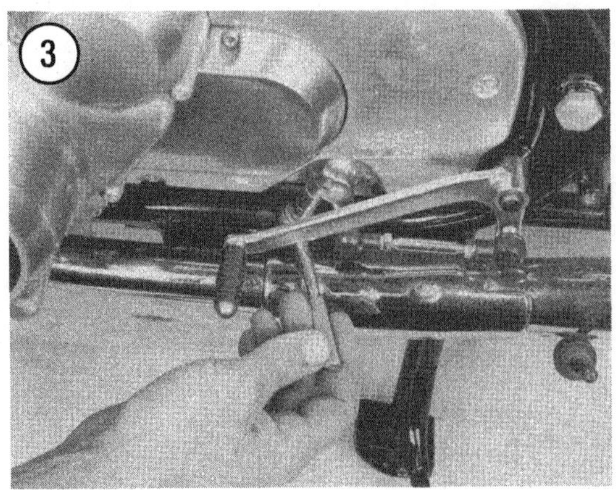

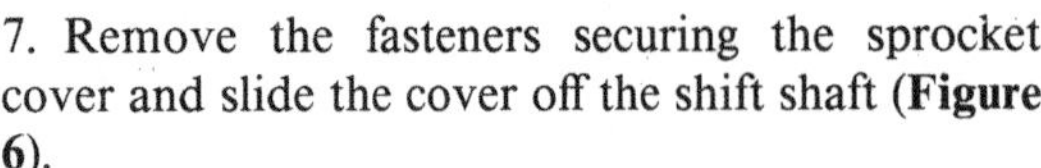

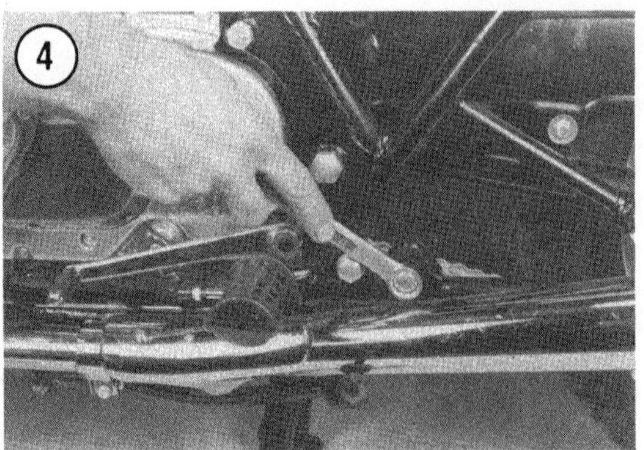

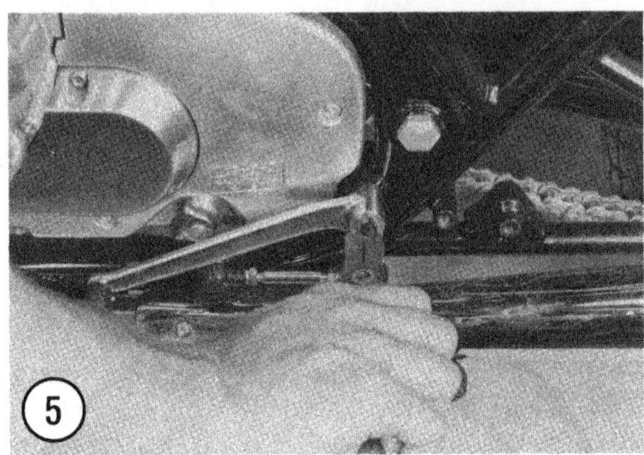

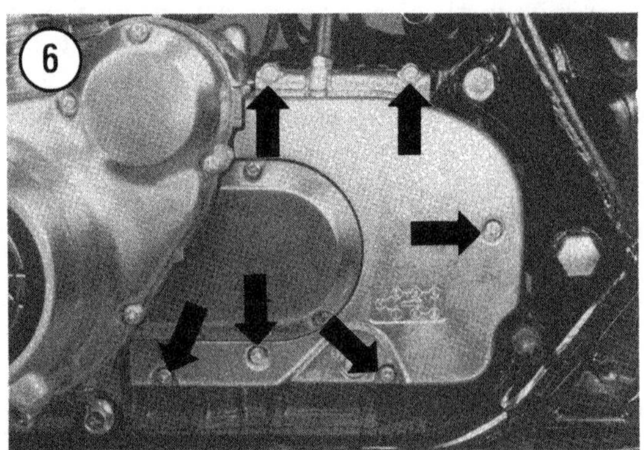

7. Remove the fasteners securing the sprocket cover and slide the cover off the shift shaft (**Figure 6**).
8. Disconnect the return spring from the clutch arm (**Figure 7**).
9. Slip the cable out of the slot in the clutch arm. Disengage the brass cable retainer from the cable end.
10. Route the new cable alongside the old cable. Loosen or remove all the straps securing the cable to the motorcycle frame.
11. Remove the adjuster screw from the sprocket cover.
12. Disengage the cable from the motorcycle frame.
13. Cable installation is the reverse of these steps. Keep the following points in mind:
    a. Make sure the new cable is routed exactly like the old cable and is properly secured with cable straps.
    b. Screw in the handlebar cable adjuster completely and secure the adjuster with the knurled locknut.
    c. Refer to Chapter Three and perform the clutch adjustment procedure.

Clutch Removal/Installation

Special preparation should be made before performing a complete clutch removal. A special holding tool or an impact wrench (air or electric) is necessary to remove the nut securing the clutch sleeve hub.

Refer to **Figure 8** for a typical clutch mechanism.

1. If the engine has not been removed from the motorcycle, perform the following:
    a. Remove the oil filler cap and remove the oil drain plug from the engine (**Figure 9**). Allow several minutes for the oil to drain completely.

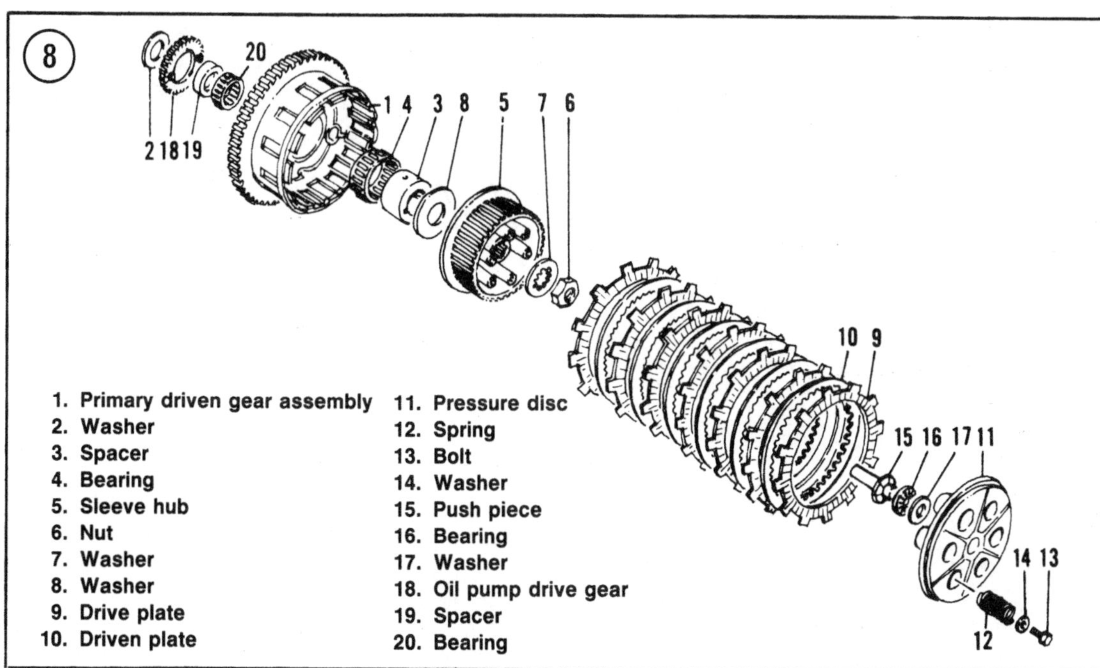

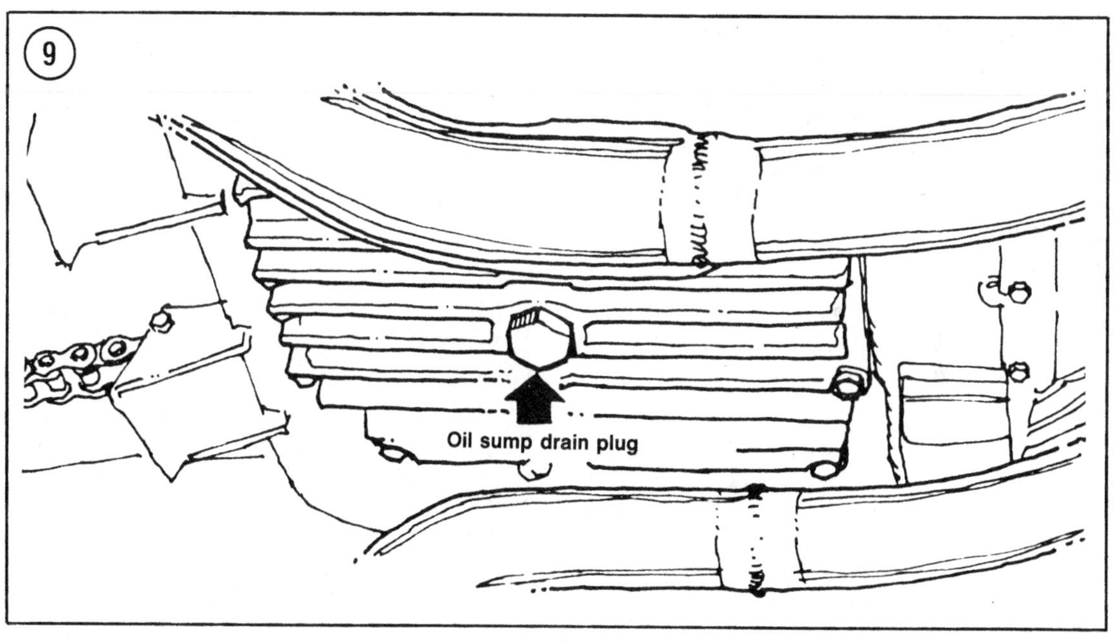

b. On models equipped with a kickstarter, remove the bolt securing the kickstarter lever (**Figure 10**) and remove the lever.

2. Remove the fasteners securing the right engine cover. See **Figure 11** for TSCC models and **Figure 12** for earlier models. On TSCC models, the 2 center bolts are fitted with gaskets. Note the location of the different length fasteners as they are removed. Gently tap around the edge of the cover with a soft-faced mallet to help break the cover loose from the engine and remove the cover. Have a few rags ready as some oil is bound to run out.

CAUTION

Do not attempt to pry the cover loose with a screwdriver or similar object or the sealing surface on the cover and/or the engine will be damaged.

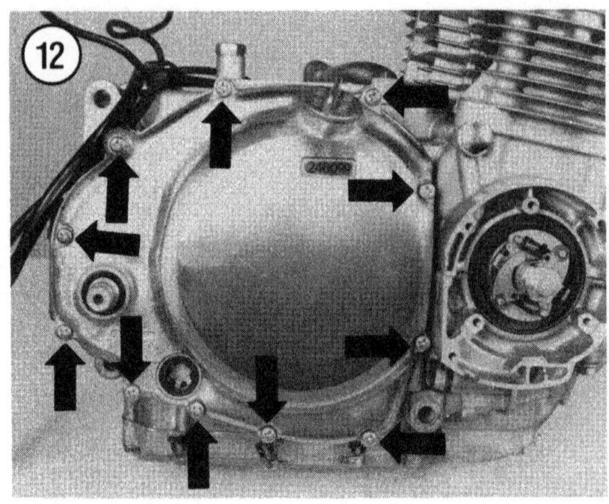

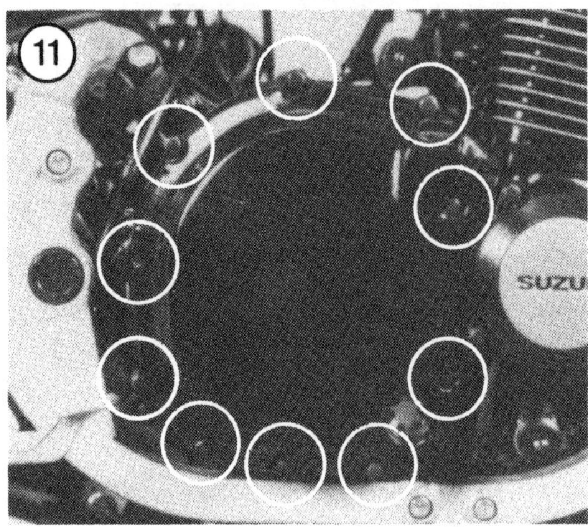

NOTE
On some models it may be necessary to hold down the brake pedal to provide clearance while removing the cover.

3. Working in a crisscross pattern, gradually and evenly loosen the 6 bolts securing the pressure plate. Remove the bolts with the washers and springs (**Figure 13**).
4. Lift out the pressure plate (**Figure 14**). Remove the release bearing assembly if it was not removed with the pressure plate (**Figure 15**).
5. Pull out and remove the clutch pushrod (**Figure 16**).
6. Remove the clutch drive and driven plates (**Figure 17**). Note the alternating pattern of drive and driven plates. If only plate replacement or inspection is desired, further disassembly is unnecessary; proceed to Step 15. If complete clutch disassembly is desired, continue this procedure.
7. Use a chisel or screwdriver and fold back the tab on the sleeve nut locking washer (**Figure 18**).

NOTE

*To remove the sleeve hub nut, it is necessary to use a special holding tool or an impact wrench (air or electric). A simple tool can be made by welding a rod to a steel driven plate as shown in **Figure 19**. A universal holding tool (part No. 09920-53710) is available*

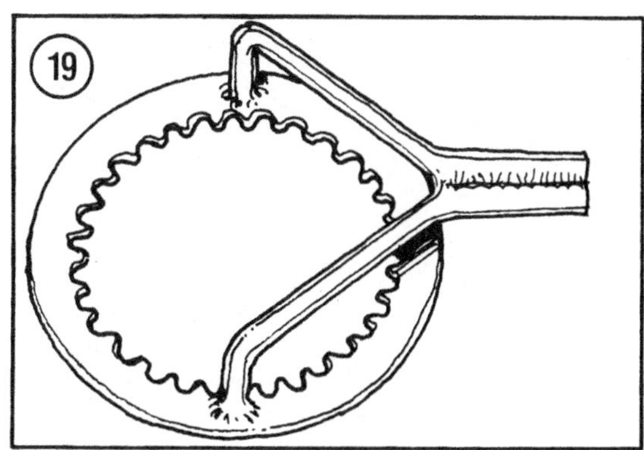

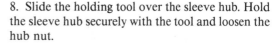

from Suzuki; the tool is expensive. The "Grabbit" from Joe Bolger Products, Inc., Barre, MA 01005 can also be used.

8. Slide the holding tool over the sleeve hub. Hold the sleeve hub securely with the tool and loosen the hub nut.

CAUTION

*While holding the sleeve hub nut with the holding tool, make sure that no part of the tool bears against the clutch housing/primary driven gear assembly or the clutch housing may be damaged. On kickstarter models, the kickstarter shaft can be used to hold the tool in place (**Figure 20**).*

9. Remove the sleeve hub nut and folding lockwasher.

10. Lift out the sleeve hub (**Figure 21**) and the large washer behind the hub (**Figure 22**). Note the following:

a. On 1982 and earlier models, the washer has 2 large machined grooves facing in toward the engine.

b. On TSCC models, the beveled edge of the washer faces out.

NOTE
On TSCC models, the innermost driven plate is secured to the sleeve hub with a stopper ring (piano wire clip). Do not remove the stopper ring unless the plate must be replaced. Removal of the stopper ring is described under ***Inspection****.*

11. Install a 6 mm (1982 and earlier) or 4 mm (TSCC) bolt or screw into the large clutch spacer as shown in **Figure 23**. Pull on the screw and remove the large spacer (**Figure 24**).
12. Hold the clutch housing in place and carefully remove the large bearing as shown in **Figure 25**.
13. Slide the clutch housing/primary driven gear assembly off center and disengage the driven gear assembly from the crankshaft drive gear. Lift out and remove the clutch housing assembly (**Figure**

26). On 1982 and earlier models, perform the following:

a. Remove the oil pump drive gear (**Figure 27**).
b. Remove the small bearing and spacer (**Figure 28**).

14. Remove the large washer next to the transmission bearing (**Figure 29**). On TSCC models, remove the small thrust washer behind the large washer.
15. Perform *Inspection.*
16. Installation is the reverse of these steps. Keep the following points in mind:

a. On 1982 and earlier models, make sure the notches in the clutch housing (**Figure 30**)

5

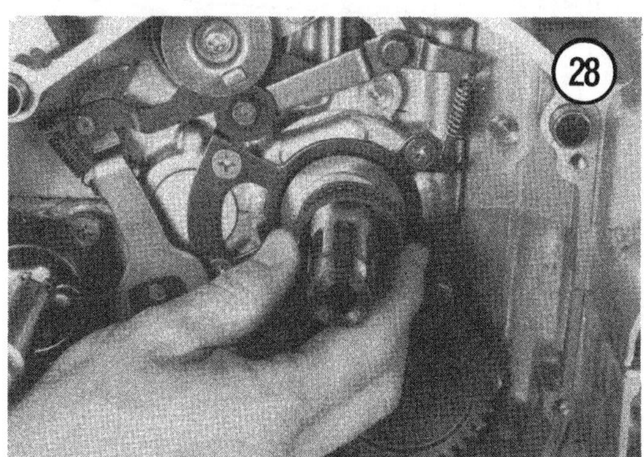

engage the drive dogs on the oil pump drive gear (**Figure 31**).

b. On TSCC models, install the small thrust washer next to the transmission bearing.

c. Install the large washer between the clutch housing and sleeve hub. On TSCC models, the beveled edge must face out. On 1982 and earlier models, the grooves on the washer (**Figure 32**) face in toward the engine.

d. Hold the sleeve hub with the holding tool (**Figure 33** shows a "Grabbit" in use) and torque the sleeve hub nut as specified in **Table 1**.

e. Fold over the locking tab to secure the hub nut.

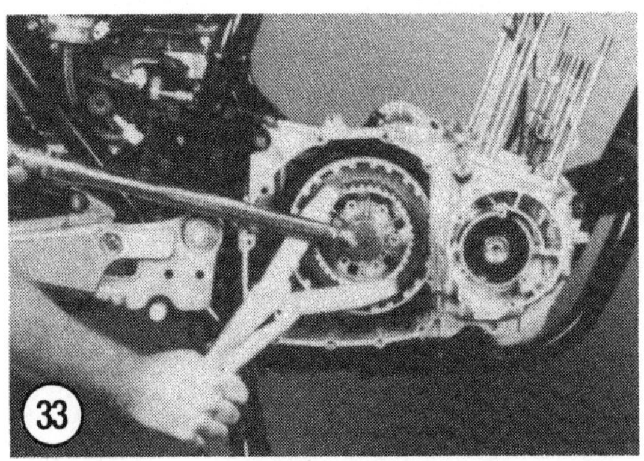

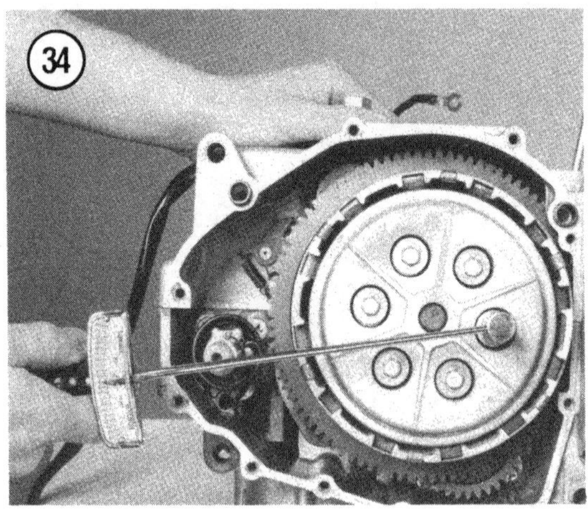

f. Install a clutch drive plate first, then install the remaining plates alternately.
g. Install the clutch pushrod, then install the pressure plate.
h. Install the bolts securing the pressure plate. Torque the bolts evenly in a crisscross pattern to the value specified in **Table 1** (**Figure 34**).

CAUTION
If it is necessary to replace a pressure plate retaining bolt, always use the exact Suzuki replacement bolt. They are specially hardened for that application. Using an incorrect bolt may cause clutch failure and subsequent expensive engine damage.

i. Install a new gasket. Make sure the gasket is properly positioned over the dowel locating pins on the engine.
j. On TSCC engines, install new gaskets under the 2 center clutch cover bolts (**Figure 35**).

17. Install the right engine cover.
18. Add engine oil and perform *Clutch Adjustment* in Chapter Three.

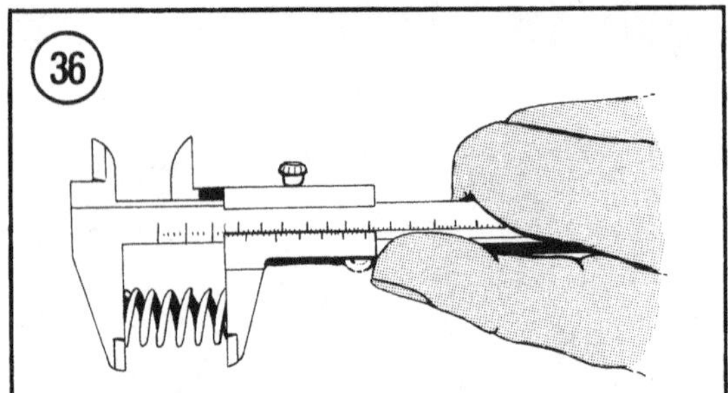

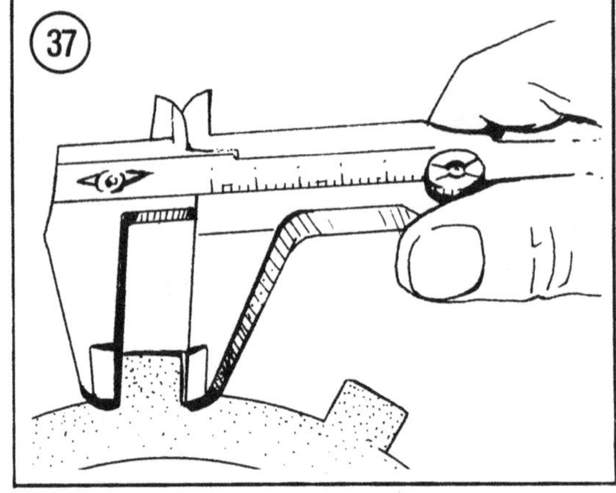

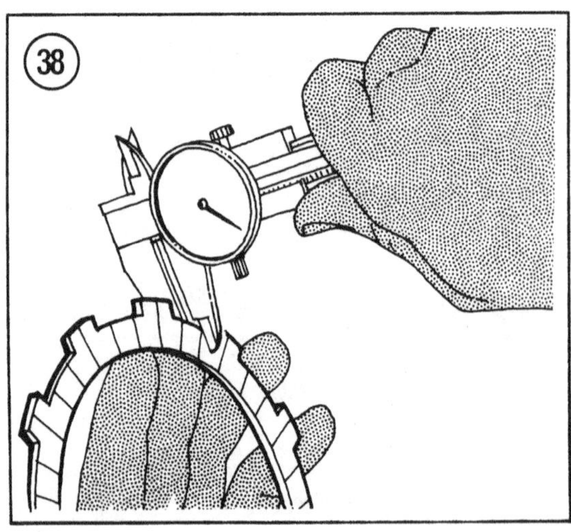

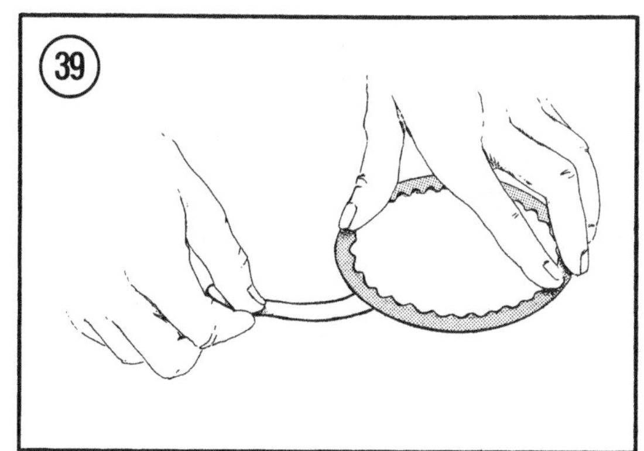

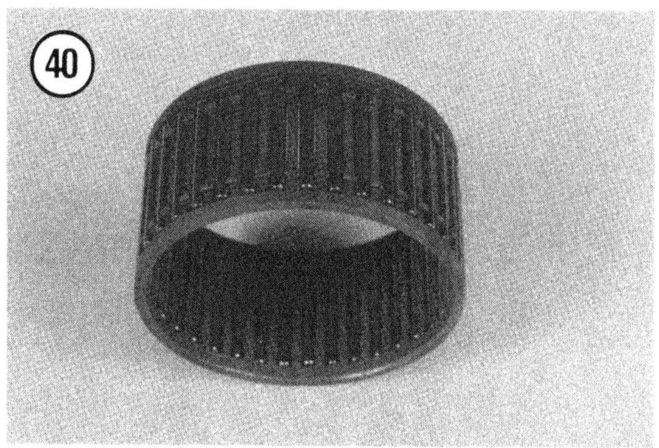

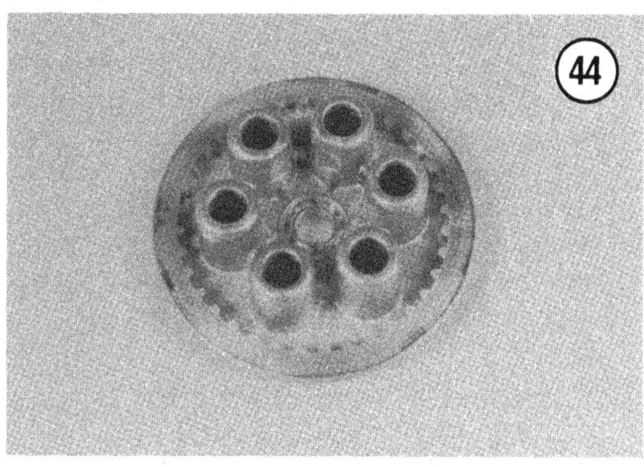

Inspection

Refer to **Table 2** for clutch specifications. If any one of the clutch springs or clutch plates does not meet specifications, you should replace them all as a set to maintain peak clutch performance.

1. Measure the free length of the clutch springs as shown in **Figure 36**. Replace any springs that are not within the limits specified in **Table 2**.
2. Measure the drive plate claw width as shown in **Figure 37**. Replace any drive plates worn beyond the service limits specified in **Table 2**.
3. Measure the thickness of the clutch drive plates as shown in **Figure 38**. Replace any plates worn beyond the specified service limits.
4. Measure each driven plate for distortion with a feeler gauge on a piece of plate glass as shown in **Figure 39**. Replace any plate that is warped beyond the limits specified in **Table 2**.
5. Carefully examine the large and small bearings (**Figure 40** and **Figure 41**). Replace the bearings if worn or damaged.
6. Check the condition of the clutch housing (**Figure 42**). Deep grooves on the housing edges caused by the drive plates will prevent proper clutch operation. Replace the clutch housing if deep grooves are present.
7. Examine the clutch release bearing assembly (**Figure 43**). Replace worn or damaged components.
8. Check the pressure plate (**Figure 44**) for signs of excessive wear or damage. Replace if defective.

9. Inspect all the grooves in the sleeve hub (**Figure 45**) for damage or abnormal wear. On TSCC models, it is not necessary to routinely remove the driven plate, wave washer and washer seat from the sleeve hub. These items should only be removed if component replacement is required. If removal is desired, perform the following:
   a. Pry out the stopper ring (piano wire clip) from the sleeve hub (**Figure 46**).
   b. Remove the driven plate, wave washer and washer seat.
   c. When installing the components always use a new piano wire clip. Make sure the clip ends are properly secured in the sleeve hub (**Figure 47**). Make sure the clip is completely installed in the sleeve hub groove (**Figure 46**).

10. Examine the teeth and drive dogs on the oil pump drive gear (**Figure 48**). Replace the gear if worn or damaged.

GEARSHIFT MECHANISM (1982 AND EARLIER MODELS)

Gearshift repair work, except for the shifting cam and shift forks, can be carried out with the engine in the motorcycle. To remove the shifting cam and shift forks, it is necessary to remove the engine and separate the crankcase halves as described in Chapter Four.

Removal/Installation

Refer to **Figure 49** for this procedure.

1. Perform *Clutch Removal* as outlined in this chapter.
2. If the engine has not been removed from the frame, perform the following:
   a. Remove the gearshift arm and shift lever.
   b. Remove the sprocket cover.

NOTE
If the engine is not being disassembled, stuff a clean rag into the crankcase openings to prevent any parts from falling into the lower crankcase.

3. Remove the retaining clip and washer securing the gearshift shaft (**Figure 50**). The retaining clip may be hidden under dirt and grease.
4. Remove the shouldered bolt securing the No. 1 cam stopper (**Figure 51**). Disconnect the spring and remove the cam stopper (**Figure 52**).
5. Disengage the spring-loaded shifting pawl on the gearshift shaft and remove the shaft from the engine as shown in **Figure 53**.
6. Use a hammer-driven impact tool, if necessary, and remove the machine screw securing the drive

45

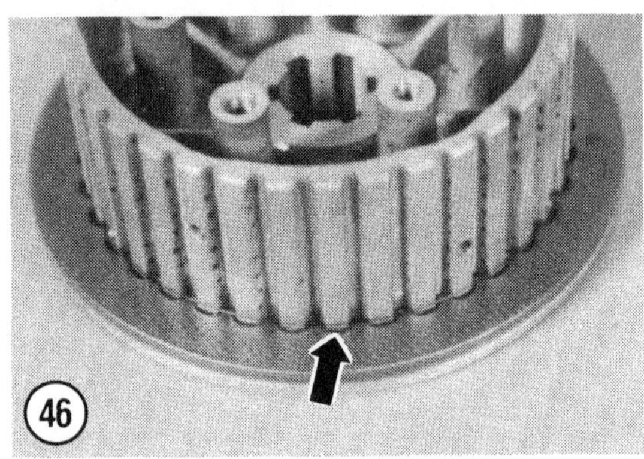
46

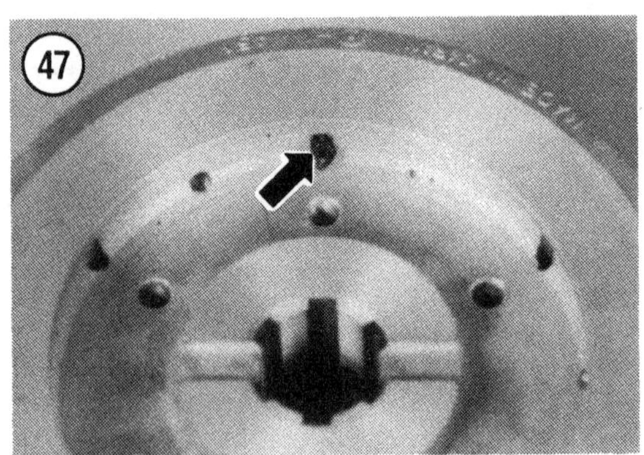
47

48

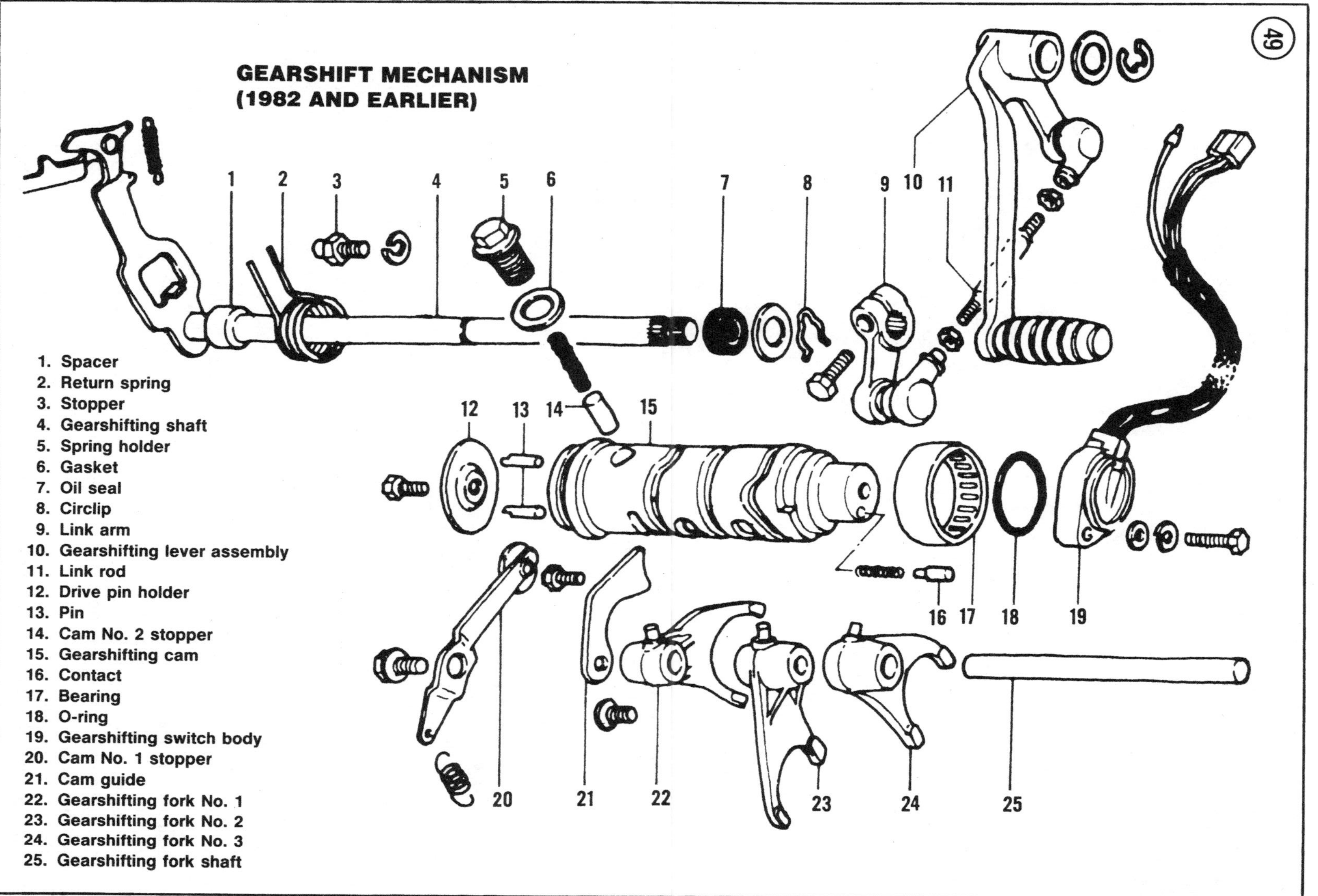
49
GEARSHIFT MECHANISM
(1982 AND EARLIER)
1. Spacer
2. Return spring
3. Stopper
4. Gearshifting shaft
5. Spring holder
6. Gasket
7. Oil seal
8. Circlip
9. Link arm
10. Gearshifting lever assembly
11. Link rod
12. Drive pin holder
13. Pin
14. Cam No. 2 stopper
15. Gearshifting cam
16. Contact
17. Bearing
18. O-ring
19. Gearshifting switch body
20. Cam No. 1 stopper
21. Cam guide
22. Gearshifting fork No. 1
23. Gearshifting fork No. 2
24. Gearshifting fork No. 3
25. Gearshifting fork shaft

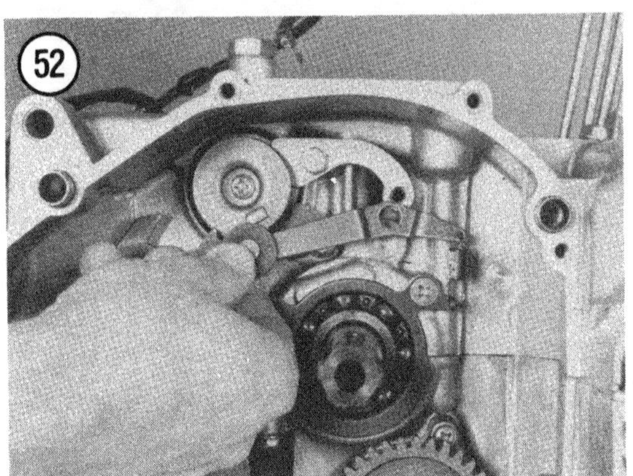

pin retainer (**Figure 54**). Carefully remove the retainer.

7. Carefully remove the six drive pins from the end of the shifting cam (**Figure 55**). Note that one pin has a machined flat spot.
8. Remove the bolt securing the cam guide and remove the guide (**Figure 56**).

NOTE

Further disassembly is not required unless it is necessary to remove the gearshifting cam and shift forks. If shifting cam and shift fork removal is desired, it is necessary to remove the engine and separate the crankcase halves. Refer to Chapter Four for engine removal and disassembly procedures. If further disassembly is not required, proceed to Step 14.

9. Remove the spring-loaded No. 2 cam stopper holder, spring and cam stopper from the top of the engine (**Figure 57**). This spring-loaded cam stopper assembly is the neutral detent mechanism.
10. Remove the transmission gearsets as outlined in this chapter.
11. Use a hammer-driven impact tool to remove the screw securing the shift fork shaft (**Figure 58**).
12. Slide out the shift fork shaft and remove the shifting forks (**Figure 59**). Carefully note the position of each fork. The forks are not interchangeable and must be installed exactly as removed.
13. Remove the gearshifting switch plunger from the end of the shifting cam if not previously removed (**Figure 60**).
14. Carefully slide out and remove the shifting cam (**Figure 61**).
15. Perform *Inspection.*
16. Installation is the reverse of these steps. Keep the following points in mind:

CAUTION

Use blue Loctite (Loctite 242) or equivalent on all the fasteners securing the gearshift components. A loose fastener adrift in the engine could cause serious and expensive damage.

a. Install the shifting cam, shift fork shaft and shift forks. Ensure that the forks are in the exact order and position as removed (**Figure 62**). Position the forks so that the pins will engage the slots in the shifting cam.
b. Apply blue Loctite to the shift fork shaft locking screw and install the screw to secure the shaft (**Figure 58**).
c. Install the transmission gear sets as outlined in this chapter. Refer to Chapter Four and assemble the crankcase halves.
d. Rotate the countershaft and the drive shaft by hand to determine if the gears are in neutral. Each shaft will rotate independently when in

53

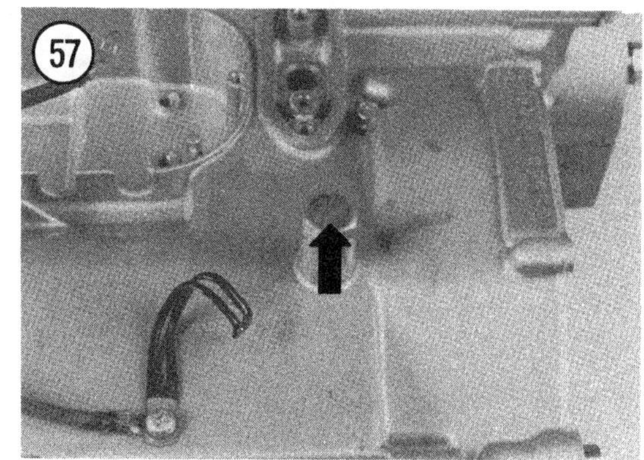
57

54

58

55

59

56

60

neutral. If not in neutral, rotate the countershaft by the clutch end and slowly rotate the shifting cam until neutral position is located. Install the No. 2 cam stopper, spring and stopper holder to hold the shifting cam in the neutral position (**Figure 57**). Torque the stopper holder to 1.8-2.8 mkg (13-20 ft.-lb.).

e. Apply blue Loctite to the bolt securing the cam guide and install the cam guide (**Figure 56**).
f. Install the 6 drive pins. Make sure the pin with the machined flat is positioned as shown in **Figure 63**.
g. Apply blue Loctite to the screw securing the drive pin retainer and install the retainer. Make sure the cut-away portion of the retainer is positioned over the machined drive pin as shown in **Figure 64**.
h. Install the gearshift shaft and the No. 1 cam stopper as shown in **Figure 65** and **Figure 66**.

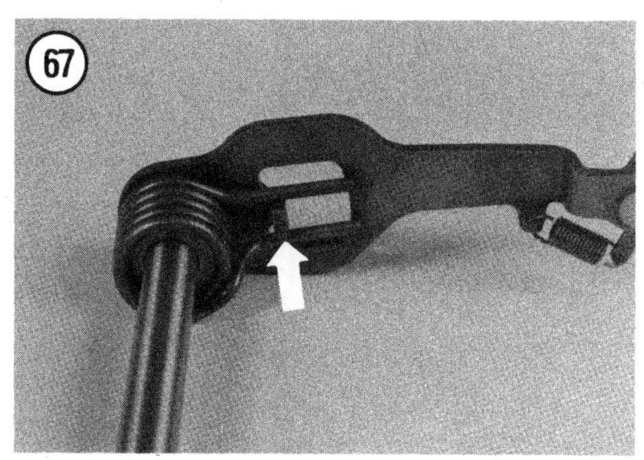

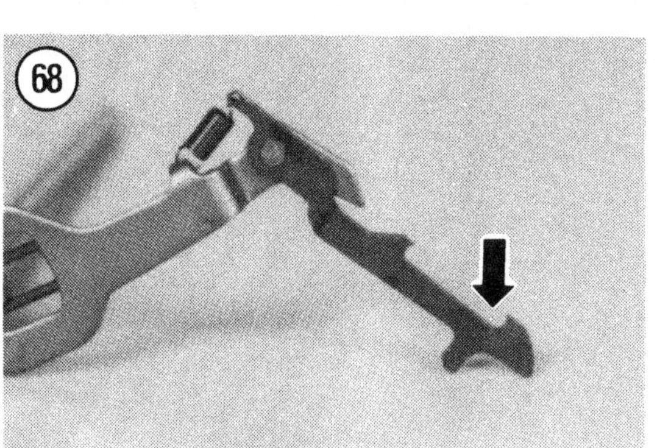

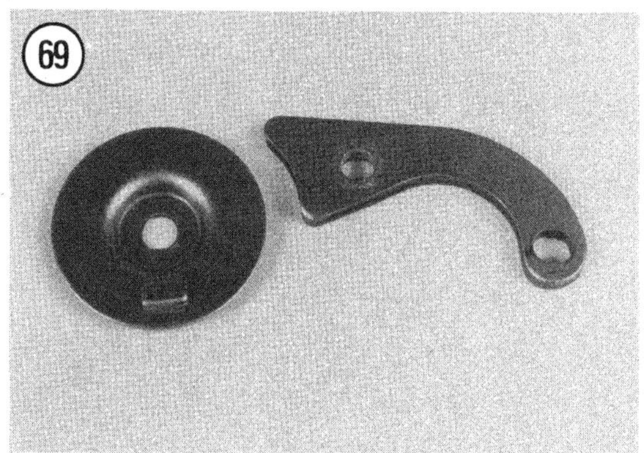

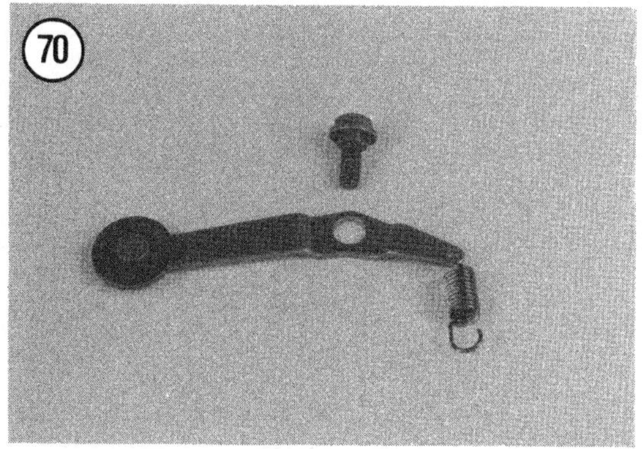

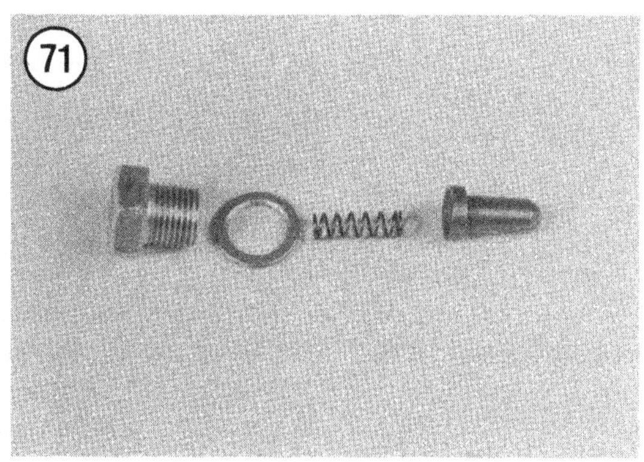

Make sure the cam stopper pivots freely on the shouldered bolt and the spring tension holds the cam stopper against the drive pins.

CAUTION

Temporarily install the gearshift lever on the shift shaft. Rotate the clutch end of the transmission countershaft by hand and upshift and downshift the transmission through each gear. Make sure that each gear engages and the shift mechanism works freely without binding or sticking. Stop and correct any problems before continuing engine assembly.

i. Install the engine as outlined in Chapter Four and install the clutch as outlined in this chapter.

Inspection

1. Clean all gearshift components thoroughly in clean solvent.
2. Examine the gearshift shaft for signs of damage or excessive wear. Roll the shaft on a smooth, flat surface and check for bends or distortion. Make sure the shaft spring is centered on the shaft as shown in **Figure 67**. Examine the spring-loaded shifting pawl for damage or wear (**Figure 68**).
3. Carefully examine the cam guide and drive pin retainer for signs of damage or wear (**Figure 69**) and replace if necessary.
4. Check the No. 1 cam stopper and shouldered bolt for wear or damage (**Figure 70**) and replace if necessary.
5. Refer to **Figure 71** and examine the No. 2 cam stopper (neutral detent) components for wear or damage. Replace the components if necessary.
6. Carefully examine the grooves in the shifting cam for wear or roughness (**Figure 72**). Replace the shifting cam if the grooves are less than perfect. A

5

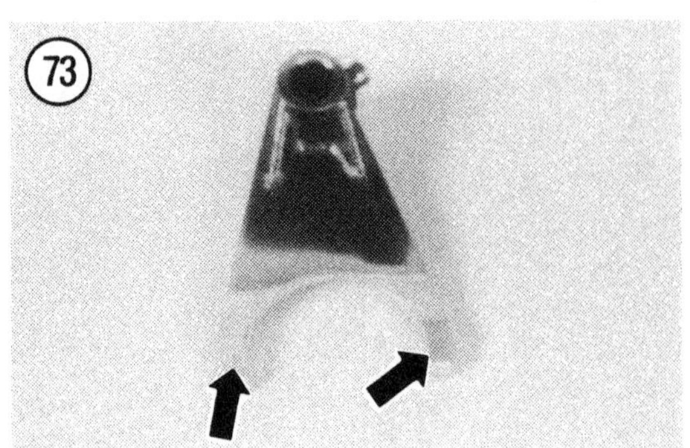

defective shifting cam can cause the transmission to shift hard or jump out of gear.

7. Inspect the wear surface of all three shift forks for damage or excessive wear (**Figure 73**). Measure the thickness of the shift forks with a micrometer or calipers as shown in **Figure 74**. Refer to **Table 3** for fork dimensions.

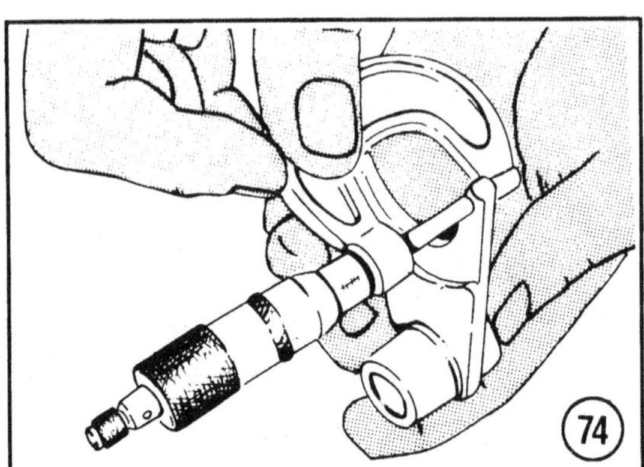

CAUTION
It is recommended that marginal shift forks be replaced. Worn forks can cause missed shifts and slipping out of gear which can lead to more serious and expensive damage.

8. Install each shift fork in its respective gear. Use a feeler gauge to measure the clearance between the fork and the gear as shown in **Figure 75**. Refer to **Table 3** for fork clearance specifications.

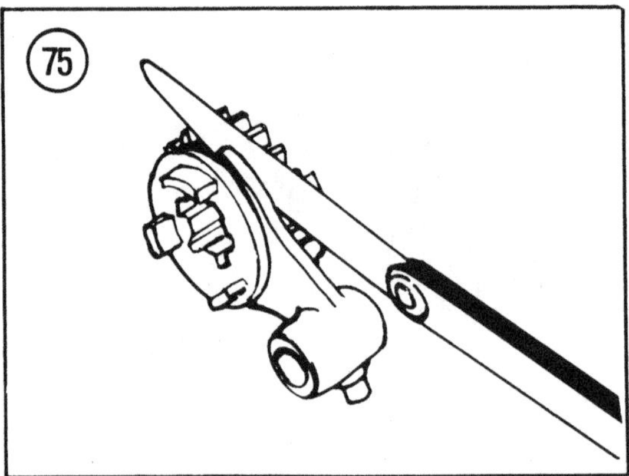

NOTE
*If the width of a shift fork is within tolerance but the shift fork-to-groove clearance is excessive, use calipers to measure the gear groove width. If the groove width exceeds the tolerance specified in **Table 3**, replace the gear.*

9. Slide the shift forks on the fork shafts and make sure the forks slide freely, but without excessive play (**Figure 76**).

10. Inspect the shifting cam bearing in the crankcase for damaged or worn rollers (**Figure 77**).

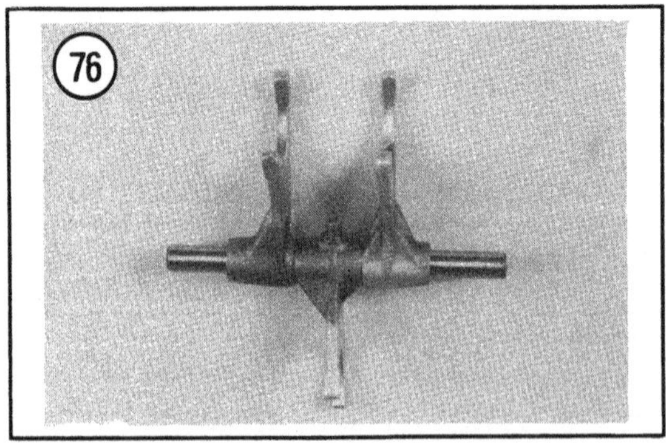

CAUTION
The shifting cam bearing is a press fit in the crankcase. Do not attempt to remove the bearing for inspection or the bearing will be damaged. If bearing replacement is necessary, refer the task to a dealer or qualified specialist.

GEARSHIFT MECHANISM (TSCC MODELS)

Gearshift repair work, except for the shifting cam and shift forks, can be carried out with the

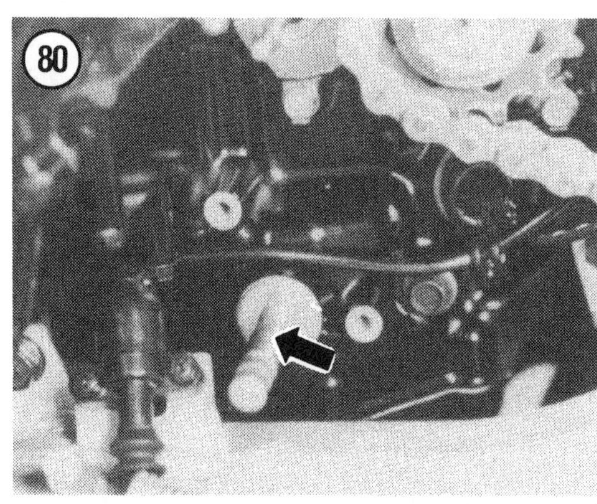

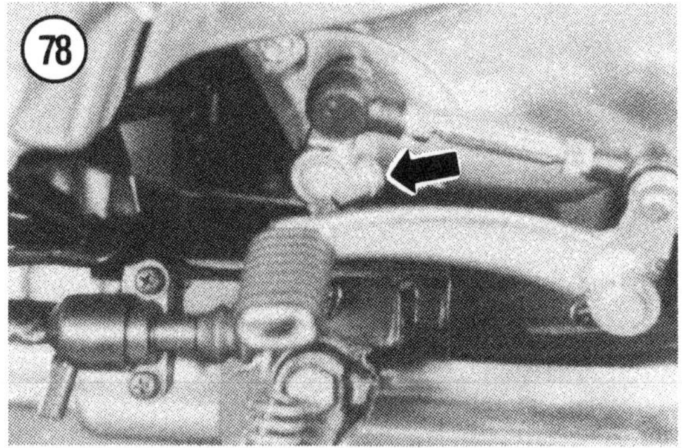

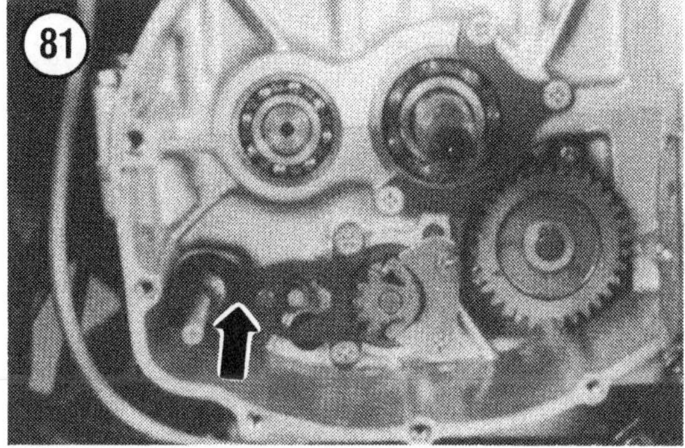

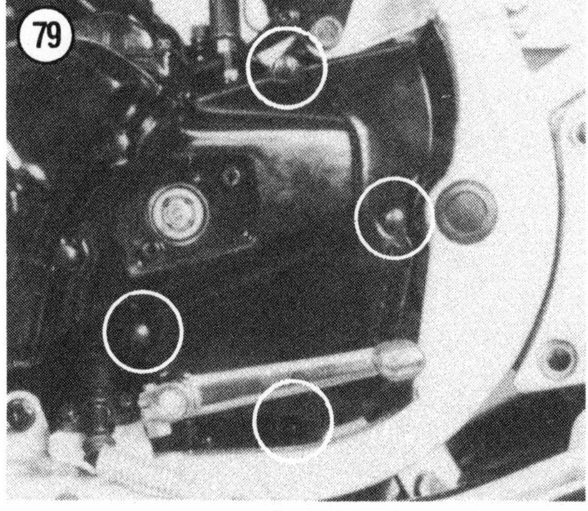

engine in the motorcycle. To remove the shifting cam and shift forks, it is necessary to remove the engine and separate the crankcase halves as described in Chapter Four.

Removal/Installation

1. Perform *Clutch Removal* as outlined in this chapter.
2. Remove the pinch bolt securing the gearshift arm or gearshift lever (**Figure 78**). The bolt must be removed completely, not just loosened. On LD models, remove the snap ring and remove the gearshifting linkage.
3. Remove the bolts securing the sprocket cover and remove the cover (**Figure 79**).
4. Remove the retaining clip and washer securing the gearshift shaft (**Figure 80**).
5. Slide the gearshift shaft out of the crankcase (**Figure 81**).
6. Remove the screws securing the gear shifting cam guide and pawl lifter (**Figure 82**) and remove the components.

CAUTION
If the engine is being disassembled, do not mix the cam guide and pawl lifter screws with the screws from the seal retainer behind the clutch. The cam guide and pawl lifter screws are 12 mm long. The bearing retainer screws are 16 mm long.

7. Carefully grasp and compress the spring-loaded pawl holder assembly (**Figure 83**) and remove the assembly from the engine. Store the pawl holder

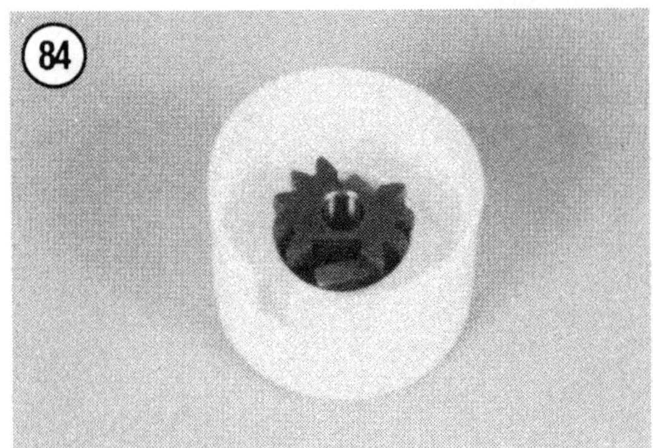

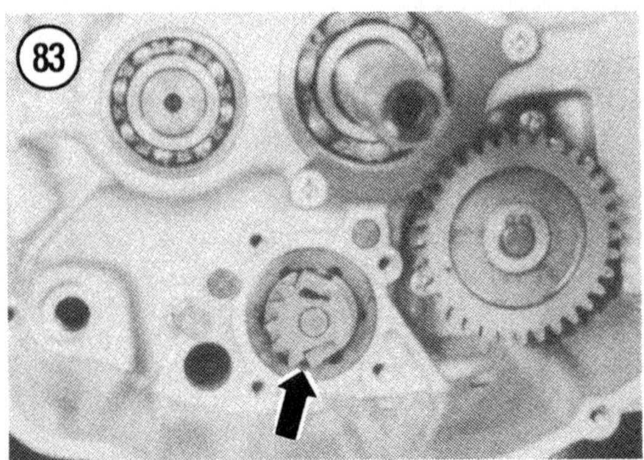

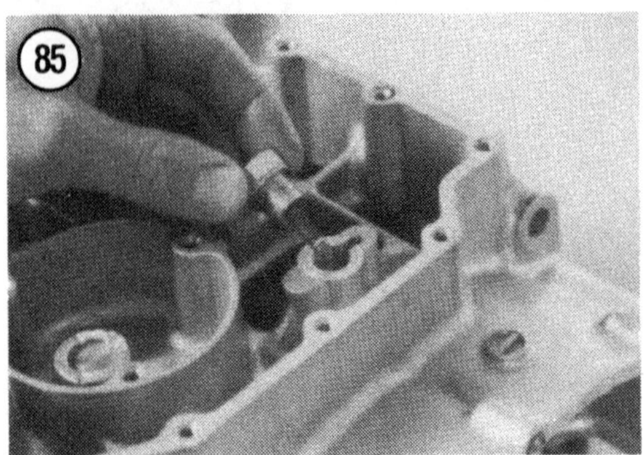

assembly in a spray paint can top to keep all the components together as shown in **Figure 84**.

NOTE
Further disassembly is not required unless it is necessary to remove the gearshifting cam and shift forks. If shifting cam and shift fork removal is desired, it is necessary to remove the engine and separate the crankcase halves. Refer to Chapter Four for engine removal and disassembly procedures. Make sure that the transmission and secondary driven gear assembly remain in the upper crankcase half. If further disassembly is not required, proceed to Step 12.

8. Remove the spring-loaded cam stopper holder and spring (**Figure 85**). Tip up the crankcase and allow the cam stopper to fall out. This spring-loaded cam stopper assembly (**Figure 86**) is the neutral detent mechanism.
9. Disengage the spring end securing the gear position cam stopper (**Figure 87**). Remove the circlip and slide the cam stopper off the shaft.
10. Slide out the shift fork shaft and remove the shift forks. Carefully note the position and location of each shift fork. The forks are not

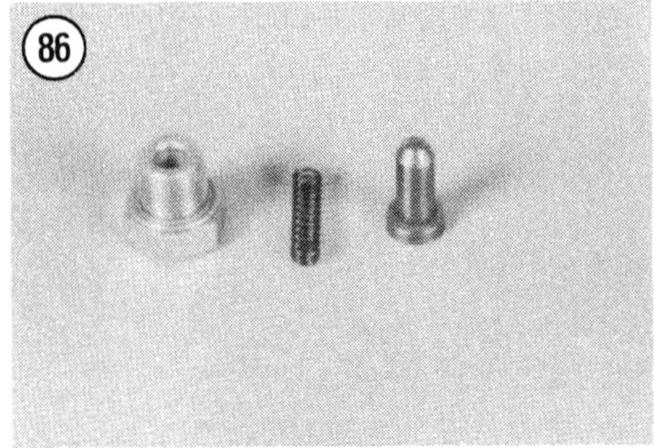

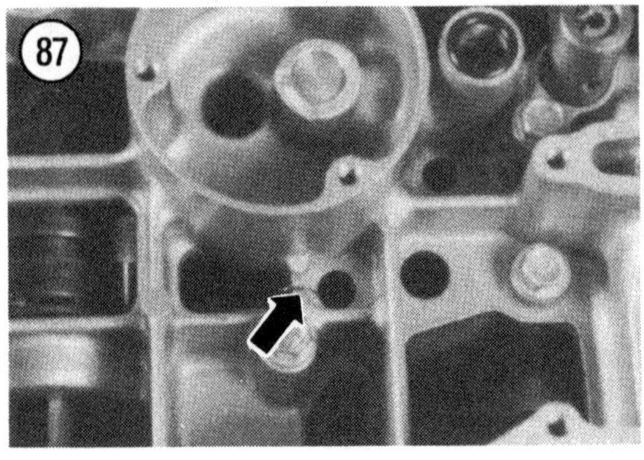

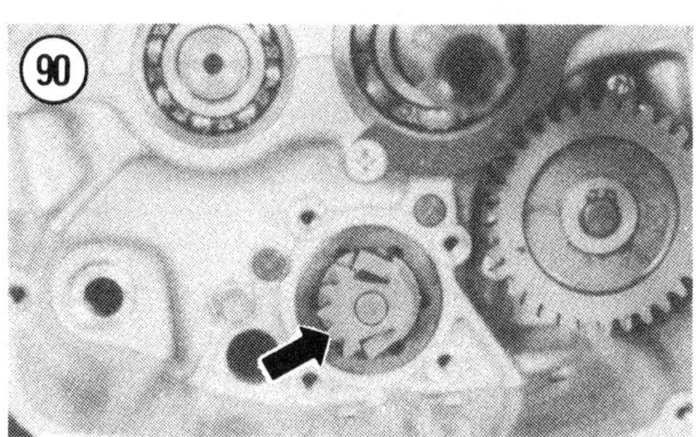

interchangeable and must be installed exactly as removed.

11. Carefully slide out and remove the shifting cam (**Figure 88**). Take care not to drop the thin thrust washer from the end of the shifting cam (**Figure 89**).
12. Perform *Inspection*.
13. Installation is the reverse of these steps. Keep the following points in mind:
    a. Make sure the shift forks are installed in the exact order and position as removed. Position the forks so that the pins will engage the slots in the shifting cam.
    b. Make sure the gear position cam stopper is positioned on the shaft so that the wheel of the cam stopper is installed in the groove in the shifting cam.
    c. Turn the crankcase over and secure the cam stopper spring to the crankcase.
    d. Install the neutral detent cam stopper, spring and stopper holder. Torque the stopper holder to 1.8-2.8 mkg (13-20 ft.-lb.). Rotate the shifting cam until the neutral detent holds the cam in the neutral position.

CAUTION
Use blue Loctite (Loctite 242) or equivalent on all the fasteners securing the gearshift components. A loose fastener adrift in the engine could cause serious and expensive damage.

    e. Refer to Chapter Four and complete the engine assembly.
    f. Install the pawl holder assembly (**Figure 90**) with the 5 teeth pointing toward the rear of the engine.
    g. Apply blue Loctite to the cam guide and pawl lifter screws and install the cam guide and pawl lifter (**Figure 91**).
    h. Install the gearshift shaft so the teeth are centered with the teeth on the pawl holder as shown in **Figure 92**. Make sure the shaft spring

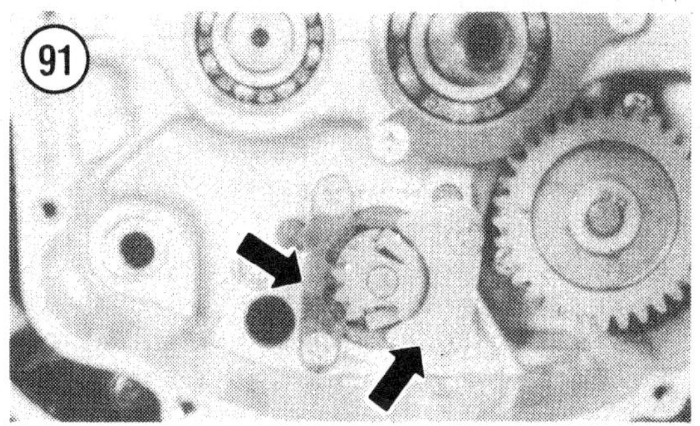

5

93

is centered over the pin in the crankcase as shown in **Figure 93**.

CAUTION
Temporarily install the gearshift lever on the shift shaft. Rotate the clutch end of the transmission countershaft by hand and upshift and downshift the transmission through each gear. Make sure that each gear engages and the shift mechanism works freely without binding or sticking. Stop and correct any problems before continuing engine assembly.

i. Install the engine as outlined in Chapter Four and install the clutch as outlined in this chapter.

Inspection

1. Clean all gearshift components thoroughly in clean solvent.
2. Examine the gearshift shaft for signs of damage or excessive wear (**Figure 94**). Roll the shaft on a smooth, flat surface and check for bends or distortion. Make sure the shaft spring is centered on the shaft as shown in **Figure 95**.
3. Carefully inspect the pawl lifter (**Figure 96**) and cam guide (**Figure 97**) for signs of wear. Replace both components if worn.
4. Disassemble the pawl holder and inspect the rollers, springs and pawls for wear or damage (**Figure 98**). Assemble the pawl holder assembly with the rounded ends of the pawl rollers in the grooves as shown in **Figure 99**. The grooves in the pawls are offset. When the pawls are correctly installed, the rear edge of the pawls are flush with the rear edge of the pawl holder as shown in **Figure 100**.

NOTE
When reassembling pawl holder components, use a piece of tape to hold

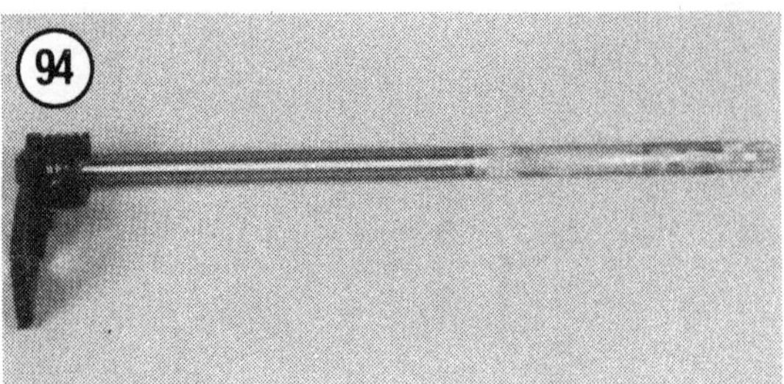
94

95

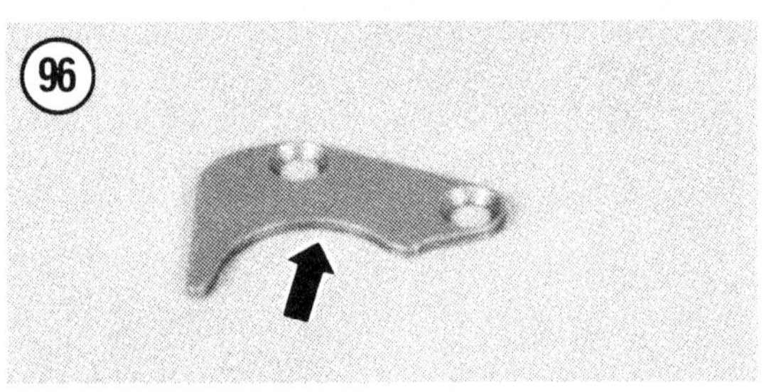
96

one of the spring-loaded pawls in position while installing the second pawl.

5. Refer to **Figure 101** and examine the neutral detent cam stopper components for wear or damage. Replace the components if necessary.
6. Carefully examine the grooves in the shifting cam for wear or roughness (**Figure 102**). Replace the shifting cam if the grooves show any wear. A defective shifting cam can cause the transmission to shift hard or jump out of gear.
7. Carefully examine the gear position cam stopper (**Figure 103**). Replace the cam stopper if signs of wear or damage are present.
8. Inspect the wear surface of all shift forks for damage or excessive wear (**Figure 104**). Measure the thickness of the shift forks with a micrometer or calipers as shown in **Figure 105**. The standard dimension for the forks is 5.30-5.40 mm (0.209-0.213 in.).

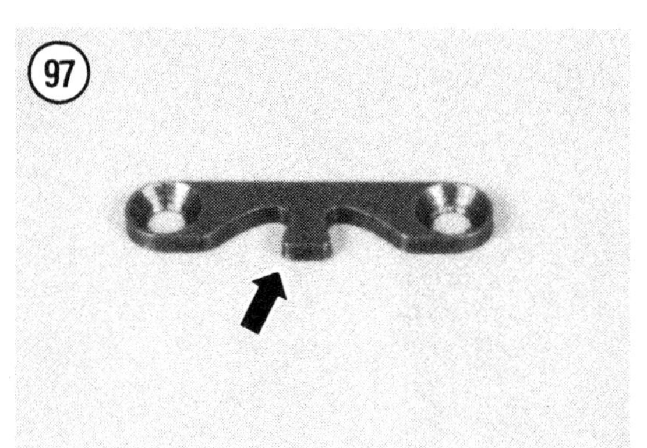
97

98

99

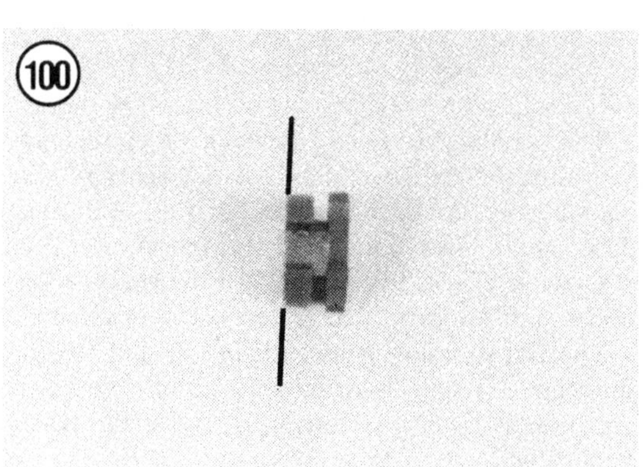
100

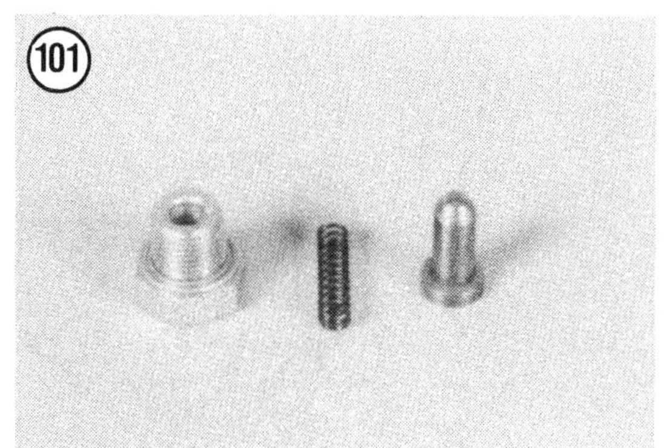
101

102

103

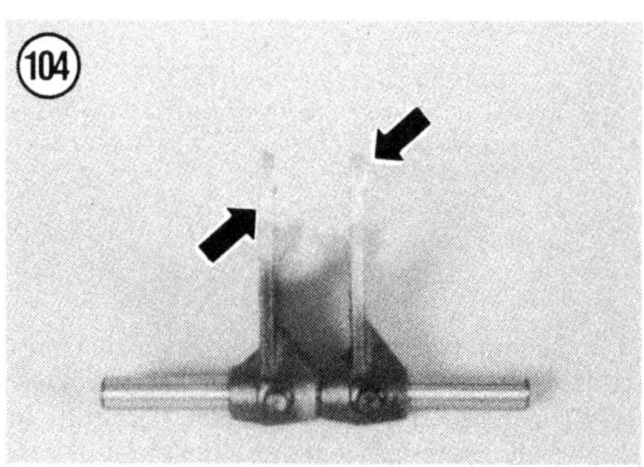
104

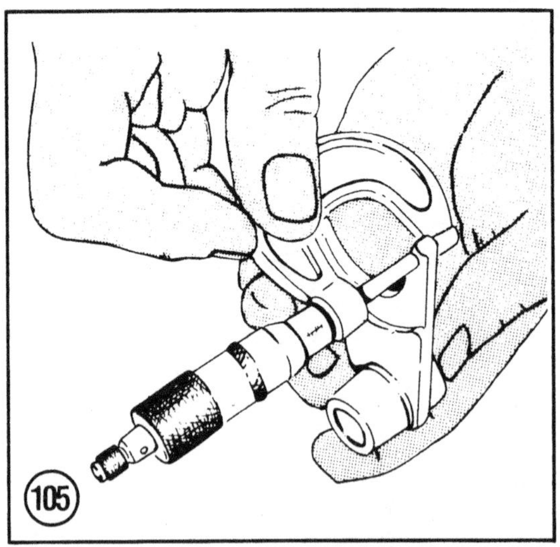

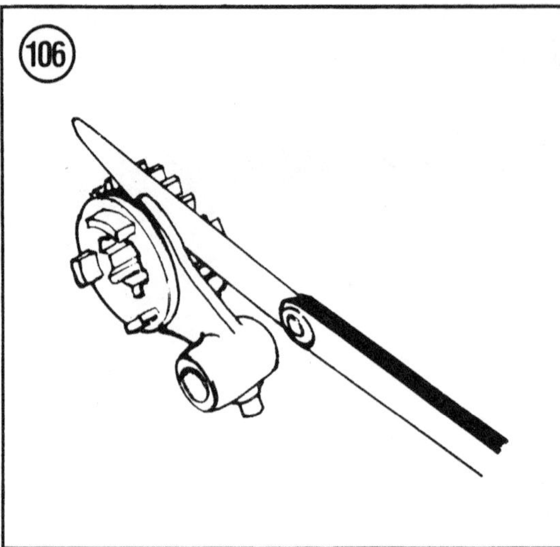

CAUTION
It is recommended that marginal shift forks be replaced. Worn forks can cause missed shifts and slipping out of gear which can lead to more serious and expensive damage.

9. Install each shift fork in its respective gear. Use a feeler gauge to measure the clearance between the fork and the gear as shown in **Figure 106**. Refer to **Table 3** for fork clearance specifications.

NOTE
If the width of a shift fork is within tolerance but the shift fork-to-groove clearance is excessive, use calipers to measure the gear groove width. If the groove width exceeds the tolerance specified in ***Table 3****, replace the gear.*

10. Slide the shift forks on the fork shaft and make sure the forks slide freely, but without excessive play (**Figure 107**).
11. Inspect both shifting cam bearing in the crankcase for damaged or worn rollers (**Figure 108**).

CAUTION
The shifting cam bearing is a press fit in the crankcase. Do not attempt to remove the bearing for inspection or the bearing will be damaged. If bearing replacement is necessary, refer the task to a dealer or qualified specialist.

TRANSMISSION

To perform transmission service the engine must be removed and the crankcase halves separated. Refer to Chapter Four. It is not necessary to remove the crankshaft to remove the transmission.

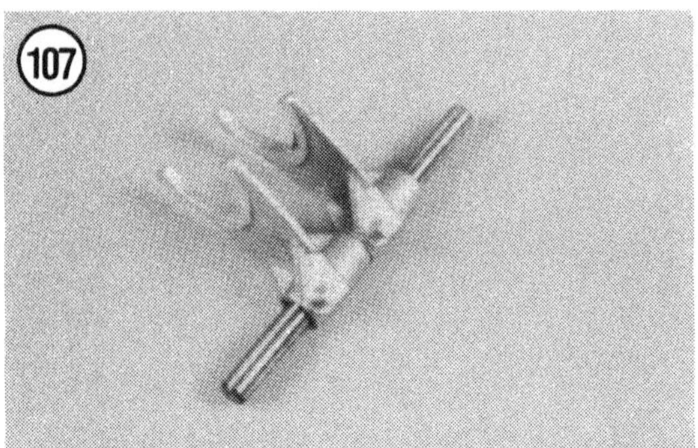

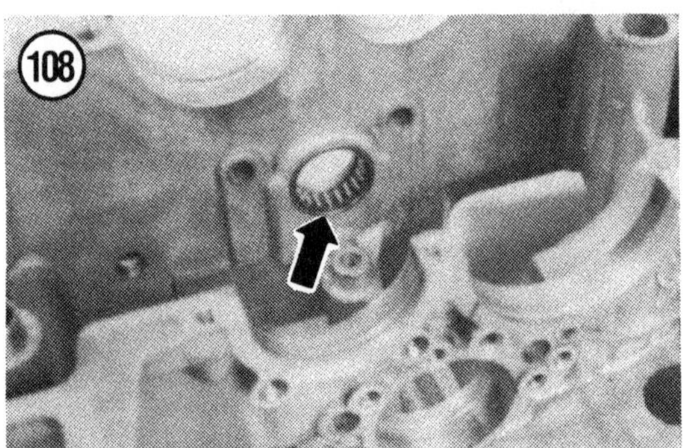

The countershaft (also known as the input shaft) is connected to the clutch. All the gears on the countershaft are identified as "drive" gears. The drive shaft (also known as the output shaft) is connected to the drive chain. All the gears on the drive shaft are identified as "driven" gears.

The transmission is essentially the same for all models. Minor changes in TSCC model gear sets are noted in the following procedures, where applicable.

Removal/Installation

1. Remove the engine and separate the crankcase halves as outlined in Chapter Four.
2. Before removing gear sets carefully note the position of the bearing locating pins, oil seals, seal retainers and shift forks. Carefully lift out the countershaft gear set (**Figure 109**) then the drive shaft gear set (**Figure 110**). Place each gear set on a clean rag.
3. Perform *Inspection.* If any gears or bearings must be replaced, refer to the gear set disassembly procedure in this chapter.

NOTE

If gear replacement is required due to damage, excessive wear or worn engagement dogs, it is recommended that the mating gears and the corresponding gearshift forks also be replaced.

4. Installation is the reverse of these steps. Keep the following points in mind:
   a. Make sure the drive shaft bearing is installed with the seal side facing out.
   b. Make sure the bearing and seal retainer C-rings are properly positioned in each side of the crankcase.
   c. Make sure the indentation on the countershaft end bearing engages the dowel in the crankcase (**Figure 111**).
   d. Position the locating pins on the countershaft and drive shaft bearings in the crankcase notches as shown in **Figure 112** and **Figure 113**.
   e. Make sure the gear set seals are correctly positioned. Assemble the engine as outlined in Chapter Four.

Inspection

1. Clean and carefully inspect all gears for burrs, chips, or roughness on the teeth.

2. Closely examine all bearings for wear, missing rollers or cracks (**Figure 114**).
3. Carefully check all the gear engagement dogs. See **Figure 115** for inside dogs and **Figure 116** for outside dogs. Both gears in a dog set must be replaced if the engagement dogs are damaged or rounded on the corners. Worn or rounded engagement dogs will cause the transmission to fail to shift or to jump out of gear.

CAUTION
If both gears in a dog set are not replaced at the same time, the newly replaced gear will be damaged.

Gear Set Disassembly/Assembly

Gear set disassembly is simple and straightforward. All gears slide on the shafts; however, some gears are retained by circlips and 2-piece lockwashers. If possible, never work on more than one gearset at a time to avoid mixing the gear set components. Always have a clean work area with enough space to lay out the components in the exact order they were removed. If possible, use an egg carton to help keep all the gears, washers and circlips in the correct order and proper position as shown in **Figure 117**.

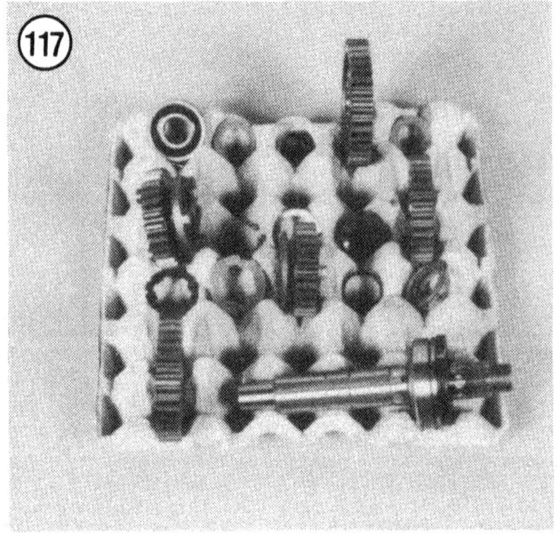

When repairing the transmission refer to **Figure 118** and keep the following points in mind.
1. If the large bearings are to be replaced, carefully pry them from the shaft (**Figure 119**). Gently tap the new bearings in place with the groove for the locating C-ring toward the outside.
2. To remove the 2-piece lockwasher between the 3rd and 4th driven gears, turn the lockwashers (**Figure 120**) slightly until the No. 1 lockwasher (outer lockwasher) can be removed from the shaft (**Figure 121**). Remove both lockwashers and remove the gear.
3. On TSCC models, note the bushings installed in the 2nd driven and 5th drive gears. The shoulder of each bushing bears against the circlip.

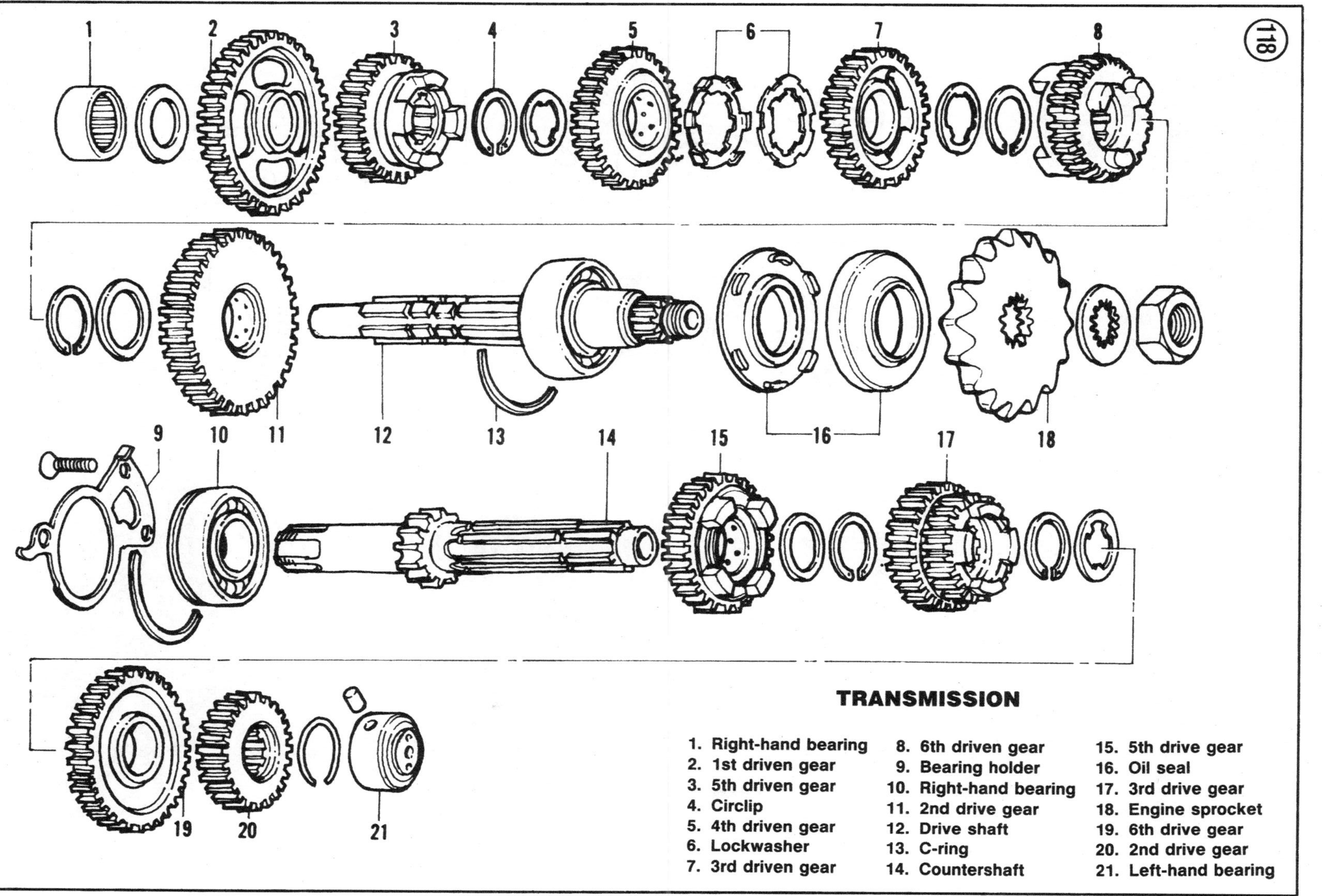
118
1
2
3
4
5
6
7
8
9
10
11
12
13
14
15
16
17
18
19
20
21
TRANSMISSION
1. Right-hand bearing
2. 1st driven gear
3. 5th driven gear
4. Circlip
5. 4th driven gear
6. Lockwasher
7. 3rd driven gear
8. 6th driven gear
9. Bearing holder
10. Right-hand bearing
11. 2nd drive gear
12. Drive shaft
13. C-ring
14. Countershaft
15. 5th drive gear
16. Oil seal
17. 3rd drive gear
18. Engine sprocket
19. 6th drive gear
20. 2nd drive gear
21. Left-hand bearing

4. Assembly is the reverse of the disassembly steps. Keep the following points in mind:

CAUTION
To prevent possible transmission damage always use new circlips to secure the gears during assembly. Never open a circlip more than necessary to slide on the shaft. Ensure that the circlip is fully locked into the groove in the shaft and the rounded edge of the circlip butts against the washer or gear as shown in ***Figure 122****.*

a. Apply a light film of molybdenum disulfide lubricant such as Bel-Ray Moly Lube to the shaft before installing the gears.
b. On TSCC models, when assembling the countershaft, measure the clearance between the 2nd and 6th drive gears as shown in **Figure 123**. Correct clearance is 0.1-0.3 mm (0.004-0.012 in.). If the clearance is incorrect, refer to **Table 4** and select the required shim to achieve the proper clearance.
c. On TSCC models, the bushings in the 2nd driven and 5th drive gears are installed with the shoulder against the circlip.

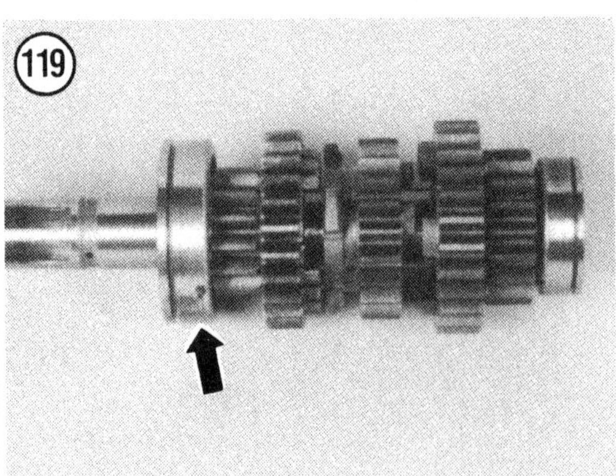

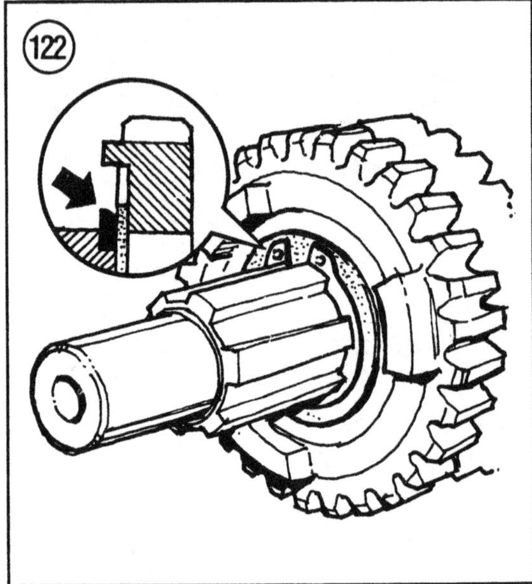

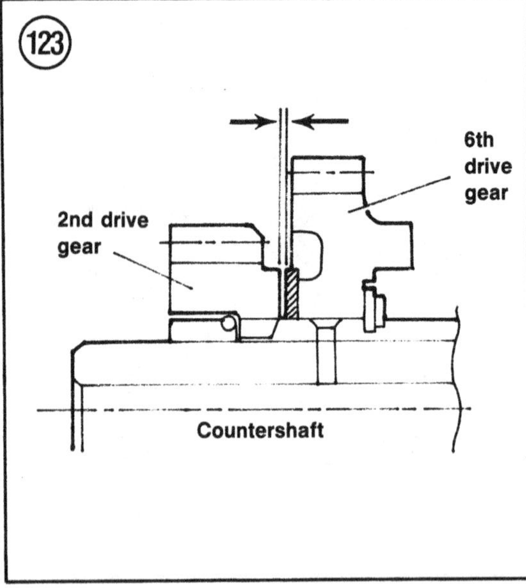

d. On the drive shaft, install the 2-piece lockwasher as shown in **Figure 121**. Turn the No. 2 lockwasher to fit into the shaft groove. Install the No. 1 lockwasher so the ears on the washer engage the notches in the No. 2 lockwasher as shown in **Figure 120**.
e. Make sure all the circlips are fully locked into the grooves in the shaft. Make sure the rounded edge of the circlip butts against the gear as shown in **Figure 122**.
f. Install a new O-ring on the sprocket end of the drive shaft (**Figure 124**).
g. Lubricate the lips of new inner and outer shaft seals with grease and install both seals over the shaft.

KICKSTARTER ASSEMBLY (1979 AND EARLIER MODELS)

To remove the entire kickstarter assembly it is necessary to remove and disassemble the engine. The kickstarter return spring can be replaced with the engine installed in the motorcycle.

Removal/Installation

Refer to **Figure 125** for this procedure.

1. If only the return spring must be replaced, refer to *Clutch Removal* in this chapter and perform Step 1 and Step 2 to gain access to the return spring.
2. Use snap ring pliers to remove the snap ring securing the return spring guide (**Figure 126**).
3. Pull out and remove the spring guide as shown in **Figure 127**.
4. Use pliers and disengage the return spring from the kickstarter shaft (**Figure 128**). Note that the spring is positioned in the hole closer to the inside. Unhook the spring end from the crankcase and remove the spring.
5. Use snap ring pliers to remove the snap ring securing the kickstarter shaft (**Figure 129**).
6. Remove the screws securing the shaft holder and remove the holder (**Figure 130**).
7. Slide the shaft assembly out of the drive gear as shown in **Figure 131** and remove the shaft assembly. Lift out the drive gear.

5

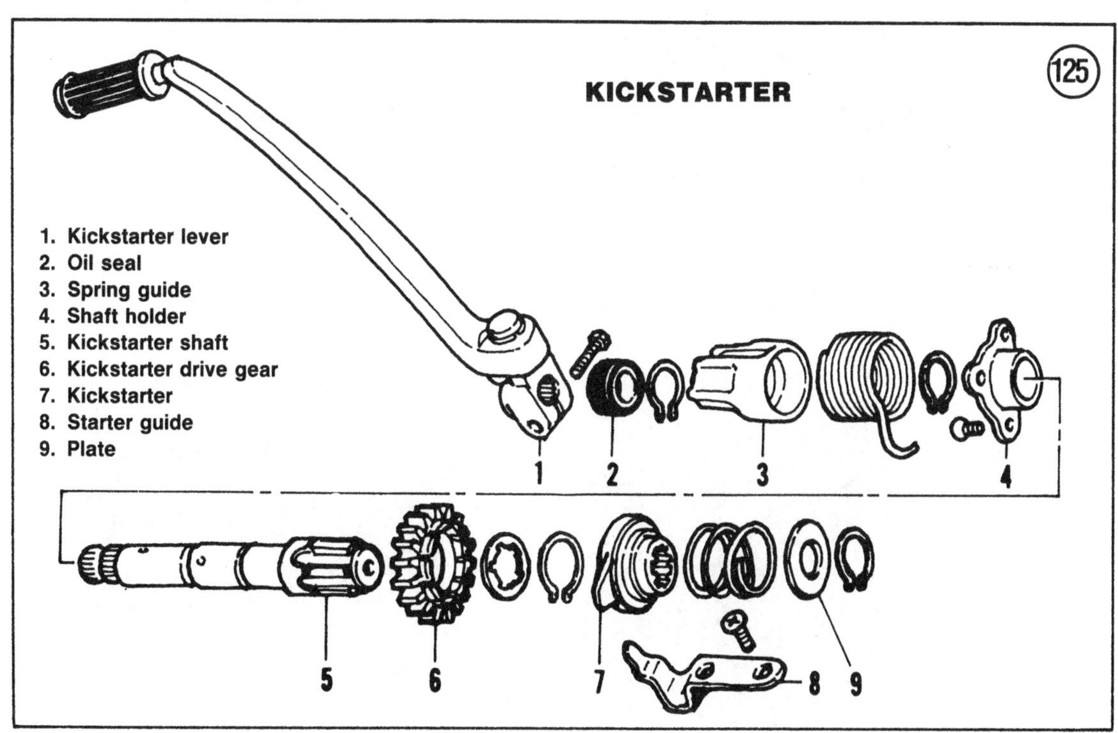

8. If further disassembly of the kickstarter components is required, remove the snap ring from the end of the shaft (**Figure 132**).

9. Perform *Inspection.*

10. Installation is the reverse of these steps. Keep the following points in mind:

a. If the kickstarter shaft was disassembled, make sure that the punch marks on the shaft and kickstarter component are aligned as shown in **Figure 133**.
b. Use blue Loctite (Lock N' Seal No. 2114) or equivalent on the screws securing the shaft holder.
c. Make sure the snap ring securing the shaft is fully installed into the shaft groove (**Figure 129**).
d. Before installing the shaft return spring, rotate the shaft fully clockwise against the starter guide to preset the shaft position.
e. Make sure the return spring end is hooked in the crankcase, then rotate the spring counterclockwise until the free end can be installed in the shaft hole.
f. Install the spring guide and secure it with the snap ring (**Figure 134**).

128

129

126

127

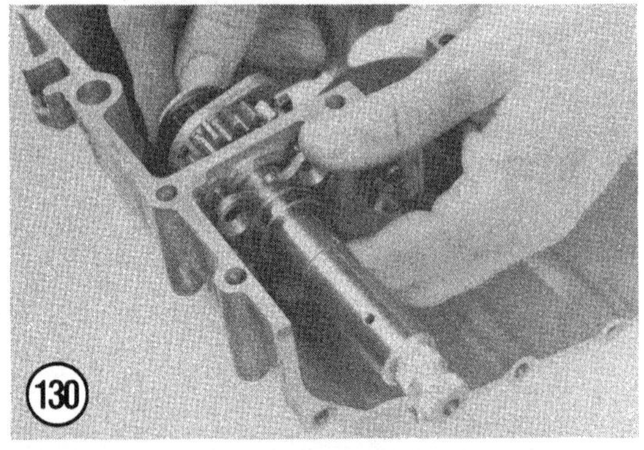

130

131

Inspection

NOTE
Replace any kickstarter components in marginal condition. A part failure at a later date when the engine is assembled will cause a great deal of labor to repair.

1. Carefully examine the starter drive gear for damaged teeth and excessive wear (**Figure 135**). Replace the gear if damaged or worn in any way.

2. Check the return spring for signs of cracking or metal fatigue. Replace the spring if not perfect.

3. Examine the shaft for twisted splines or other signs of damage.

4. Inspect the starter guide and replace if any signs of wear are present.

Tables are on the following page.

Table 1 TORQUE SPECIFICATIONS

Item	mkg	ft.-lb.
Clutch sleeve hub nut		
1977-1982	4.0-6.0	29-43
1983-1984	5.0-7.0	36-51
Clutch spring bolts		
1977-1982	0.6-1.0	5-7
1983-1984	1.1-1.3	8-10
Neutral cam stopper bolt	1.8-2.8	13-20
Gearshift lever bolt	0.6-1.0	5-7
Clutch release arm bolt	0.6-0.8	5-6

Table 2 CLUTCH SPECIFICATIONS

Item	Standard	Limit
Clutch cable free play	2-3 mm (1/16-1/8 in.)	
Clutch spring free length	—	36.5 mm (1.44 in.)
Drive plate thickness		
1977-1982	2.9-3.1 mm (0.11-0.12 in.)	2.6 mm (0.10 in.)
1983-1984	3.05-3.20 mm (0.12-0.13 in.)	2.75 mm (0.11 in.)
Drive plate claw width	11.8-12.0 mm (0.46-0.47 in.)	11.0 mm (0.43 in.)
Driven plate thickness		
1977-1982	1.54-1.66 mm (0.058-0.062 in.)	
1983-1984		
No.1	1.54-1.66 mm (0.058-0.062 in.)	
No.2	1.94-2.06 mm (0.076-0.081 in.)	
Driven plate distortion	—	0.10 mm (0.004 in.)

Table 3 GEAR AND SHIFT FORK SPECIFICATIONS

Item	Standard	Limit
Shift fork thickness	5.30-5.40 mm (0.209-0.211 in.)	
Shift fork groove width	5.50-5.60 mm (0.217-0.220 in.)	
Shift fork-to-groove clearance	0.10-0.30 mm (0.004-0.012 in.)	0.50 mm (0.020 in.)

Table 4 COUNTERSHAFT SHIM SELECTION (TSCC MODELS)

Shim thickness	Suzuki part No.
0.5 mm (0.019 in.)	09181-25036
0.6 mm (0.023 in.)	09181-25037
0.7 mm (0.027 in.)	09181-25038
0.8 mm (0.031 in.)	09181-25039

NOTE: If you own a 1985 or later model, first check the Supplement at the back of the book for any new service information.

CHAPTER SIX

FUEL AND EXHAUST SYSTEMS

6

For correct operation, a gasoline engine must be supplied with fuel and air mixed in proper proportions by weight. A rich mixture is one in which there is an excess of fuel. A lean mixture is one which contains an insufficient amount of fuel. It is the function of the carburetors to supply the correct fuel-air mixture to the engine under all operating conditions.

This chapter includes removal and maintenance of the fuel tank, carburetors and exhaust system. Air cleaner service is outlined in Chapter Three.

Table 1 is at the end of the chapter.

FUEL TANK AND FUEL VALVE

Fuel Tank Removal/Installation

1. Remove the seat.
2. Disconnect the fuel line and vacuum line from the fuel valve (**Figure 1**).
3. On models equipped with a fuel gauge, disconnect the black/white and yellow/black fuel gauge wires under the left side of the fuel tank.
4. Remove the bolts securing the rear of the tank. See **Figure 2** for early models and **Figure 3** for TSCC models.
5. Lift up on the rear of the tank and slide the tank back enough to disengage the front rubber mounting pads (**Figure 4**). Make sure the rubber washers on the mounting bolts are not lost (**Figure 5**).
6. Installation is the reverse of these steps. Lightly lubricate the tank mounting pads with rubber lubricant or WD-40 to aid tank installation. Make sure the fuel gauge wires are correctly connected.

Fuel Valve Removal/Installation

1. Remove the fuel tank.
2. Turn the valve to the PRI (prime) position and drain the fuel into a suitable container.

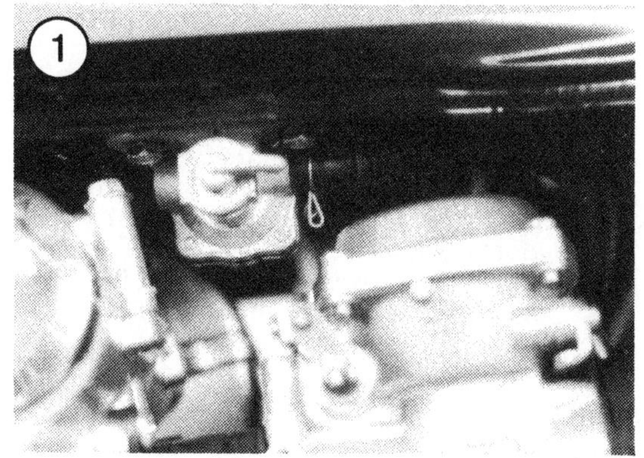

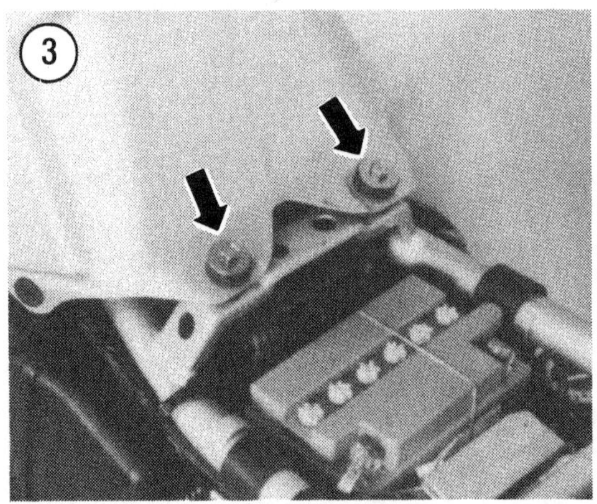

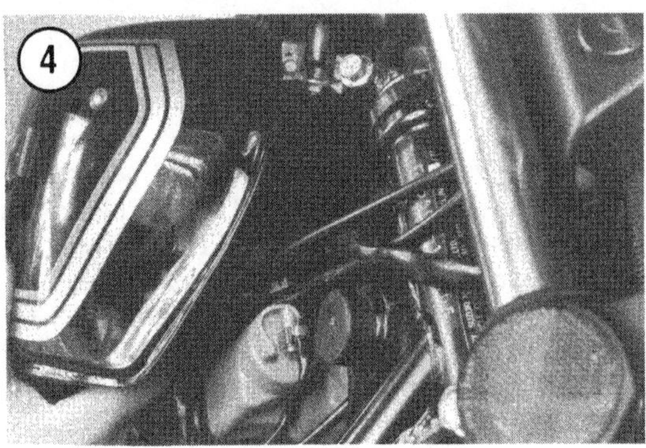

3. Remove the bolts securing the valve to the tank and remove the valve (**Figure 6**). Take care not to damage the fuel strainer.
4. Rinse the strainer (**Figure 7**) in clean gasoline to remove any dirt and contaminants. Carefully examine the strainer. If the strainer is damaged, the fuel valve must be replaced.
5. Installation is the reverse of these steps. Ensure that the sealing O-ring is in good condition and properly positioned before the valve is secured to the tank.

CARBURETORS

All models are equipped with Mikuni carburetors. Three different type of carburetors are installed on the various models:

a. 1977-1979 models: 4 VM22SS carburetors.
b. 1980-1982 models: 4 BS32SS constant velocity (CV) carburetors.
c. 1983 and later models: 2 BSW30SS constant velocity (CV) carburetors.

Removal for all types of carburetors is basically the same. Minor differences are pointed out where necessary. Separate disassembly procedures are provided for each type of carburetor.

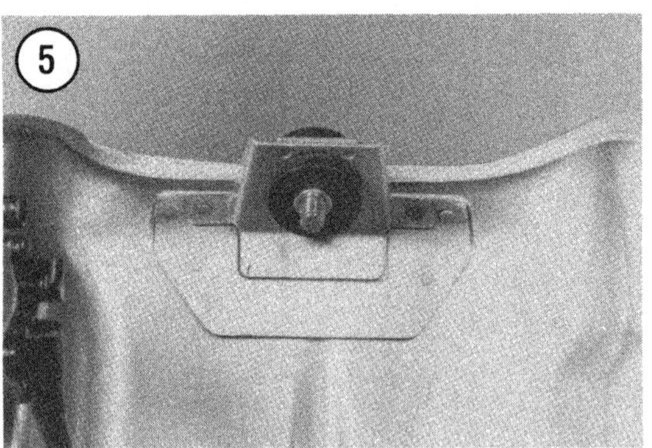

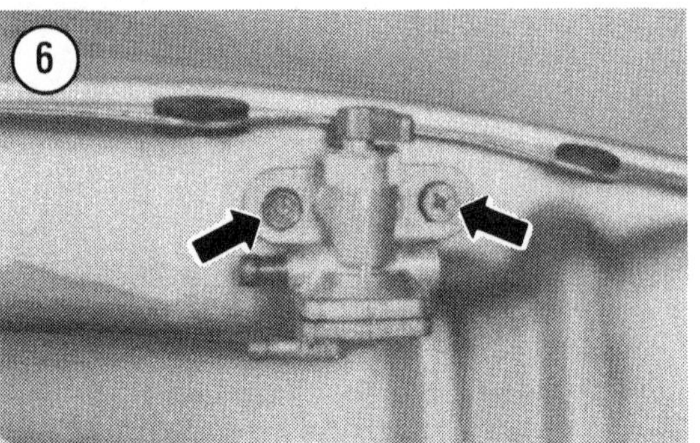

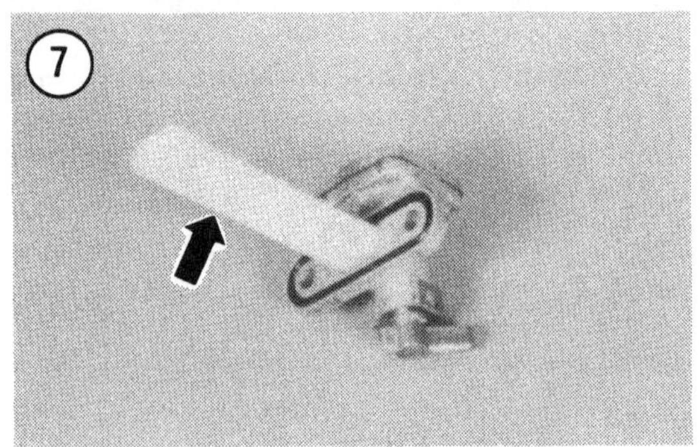

NOTE
The carburetors on all U.S. models are engineered to meet stringent EPA (Environmental Protection Agency) regulations. The carburetors are flow tested and preset at the factory for maximum performance and efficiency within EPA regulations. Altering carburetor jet needle and air screw preset adjustments is forbidden by law. Failure to comply with E.P.A. regulations may result in heavy fines.

Removal/Installation

1. Remove the fuel tank as described in this chapter.

8

9

10

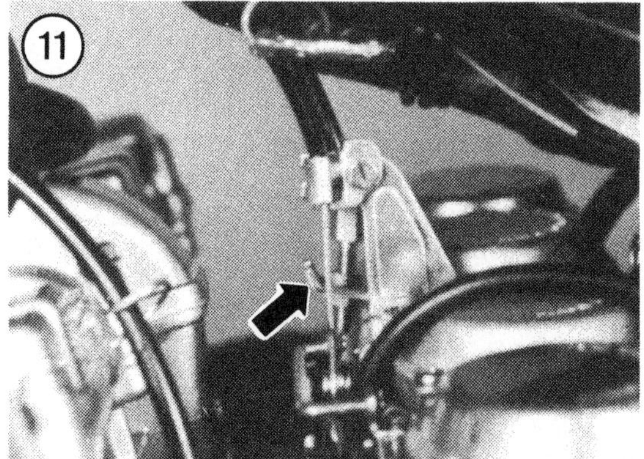
11

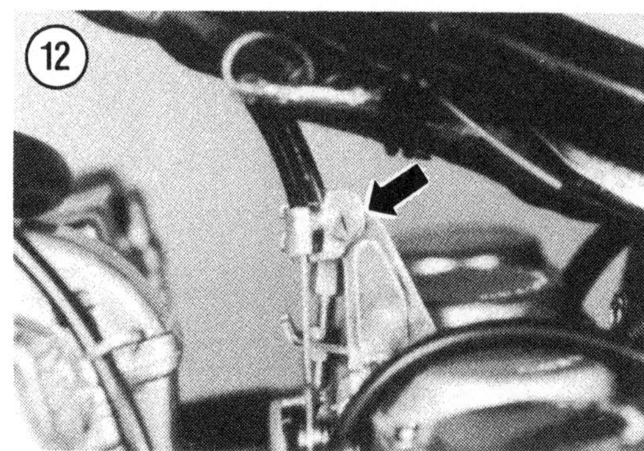
12

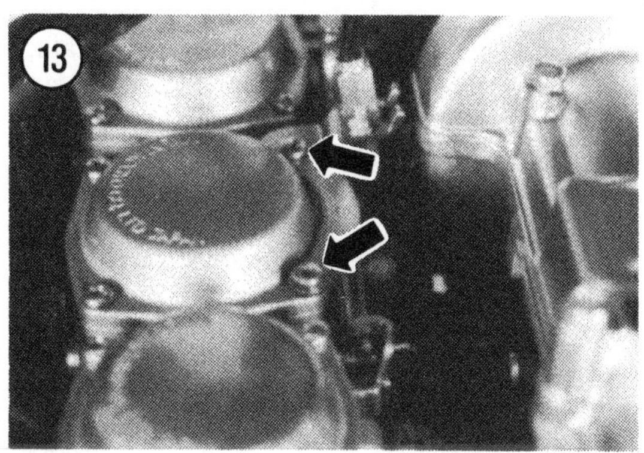
13

2. Remove the bolts (**Figure 8** and **Figure 9**) securing the air box.
3. Loosen the locknuts securing the throttle cable(s) to the mounting bracket(s). See **Figure 10** for models with 2 throttle cables and **Figure 11** for models with one cable. Slide the outer cable end out of the mounting bracket and disconnect the inner cable end from the throttle lever.

NOTE
It may be easier to disconnect the throttle cable from the throttle lever when the carburetors are removed from the mounting flanges.

4. On models equipped with a choke cable, perform the following to disconnect the choke cable:
   a. On 1981 models, remove the bolt securing the choke cable to the carburetor bracket (**Figure 12**).
   b. On 1982 models, remove the screws securing the cable bracket to the carburetor (**Figure 13**). Disengage the choke cable end from the actuating lever.
   c. On TSCC models, unscrew the choke plunger from each carburetor (**Figure 14**).

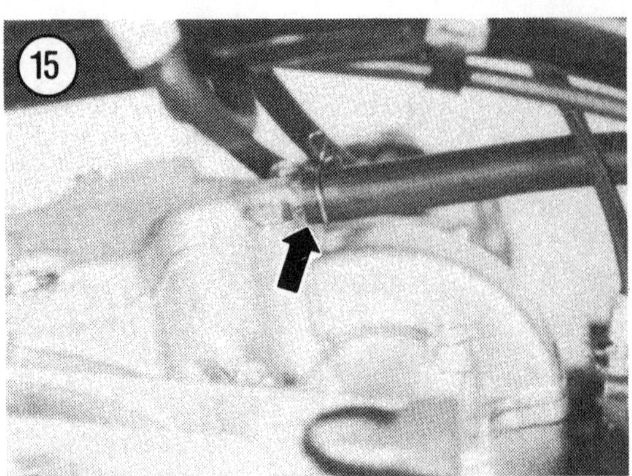

5. Spring open the clamps securing the breather hose to the engine and air box (**Figure 15**) and remove the breather hose.
6. Loosen the clamp screws securing the carburetors to the engine flanges and the air box (**Figure 16**).
7. Pull the carburetors and air box toward the rear of the motorcycle as far as possible and pull the carburetors out of the engine flanges. Move the carburetors forward out of the air box. Lower the carburetors enough to clear the wires and the upper frame tube and remove the carburetors from the left side of the motorcycle. Note how the all the carburetor vent tubes are routed.
8. Installation is the reverse of these steps. Keep the following points in mind:
   a. Connect the throttle cable(s) to the throttle shaft on the carburetors before installing the carburetors into the engine flanges. Carefully install the air box flanges over the carburetor throats.

   NOTE
   Lightly lubricate the carburetor mounting flanges with WD-40 or equivalent to ease carburetor installation.

   b. Secure the air box to the frame then tighten the clamp screws securing the front and rear of each carburetor to the mounting flanges. Refer to **Figure 17** and **Figure 18**.
   c. On 1981-1982 models equipped with choke cables, connect the cable end to the carburetor actuating lever. For 1981 models, secure the cable to the bracket as shown in **Figure 12**. For 1982 models, secure the cable bracket to the carburetor as shown in **Figure 13**. Loosen the locknut securing the cable adjuster and rotate the adjuster until 0.5-1.0 mm (1/32-1/16 in.) of cable free play is obtained. Tighten the locknut to secure the adjuster.
   d. On TSCC models, install the choke plungers into each carburetor (**Figure 14**).
   e. Adjust the throttle cable adjuster for 0.5-1.0 mm (1/32-1/16 in.) of cable free play and secure the adjuster with the locknuts.
   f. Route the large carburetor vent hoses over the top of the air box and secure the ends of the hoses under the air box clip as shown in **Figure 19**.

CAUTION
Ensure that the carburetor vent hoses are properly routed and are not pinched shut when the fuel tank and seat are installed. A pinched vent hose will drastically affect engine performance.

Disassembly/Assembly (VM22SS Carburetors)

Refer to **Figure 20** for this procedure.

1. Remove the screws securing the covers on each carburetor and remove the covers (**Figure 21**).
2. Remove the bolt securing each throttle slide lifter (**Figure 22**).
3. Loosen the screws securing the choke lifter to each carburetor (**Figure 23**).
4. Remove the screw securing the choke lever to No. 1 carburetor (**Figure 24**). Note the location of the plastic and spring steel washers. Slide the choke shaft out of the carburetors. Remove the choke lifters from each carburetor.
5. Remove the screw securing the shaft locking plate and remove the plate as shown in **Figure 25**.
6. Remove the bolt securing the throttle control to the throttle shaft (**Figure 26**).
7. Gently pry out the rubber plug from the end carburetor (**Figure 27**).
8. Use a socket extension to push the throttle shaft out of the carburetors (**Figure 28**).

16

21

17

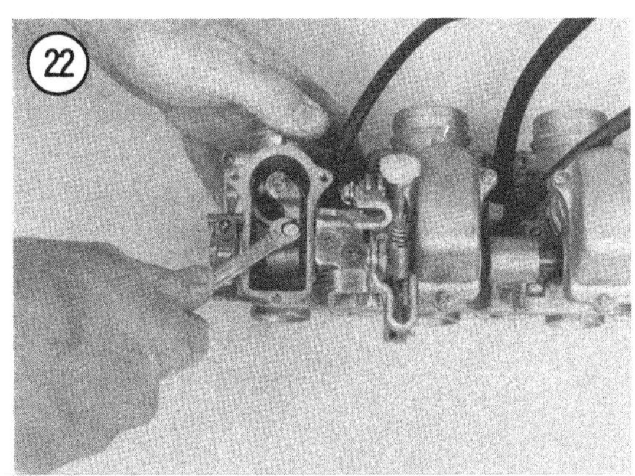
22

18

23

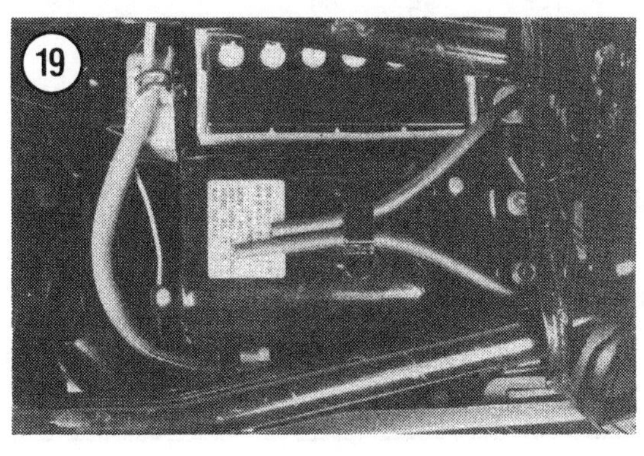
19

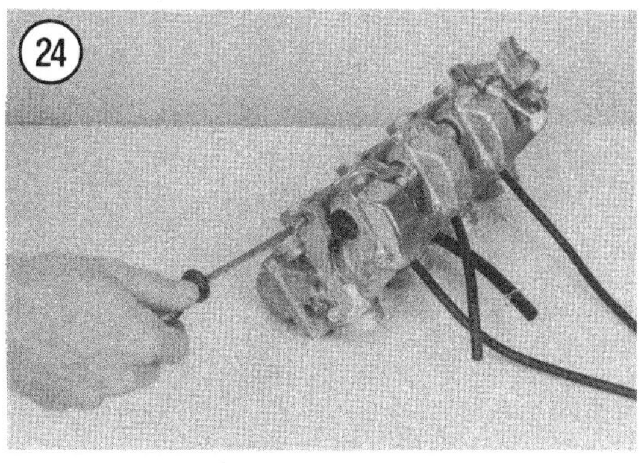
24

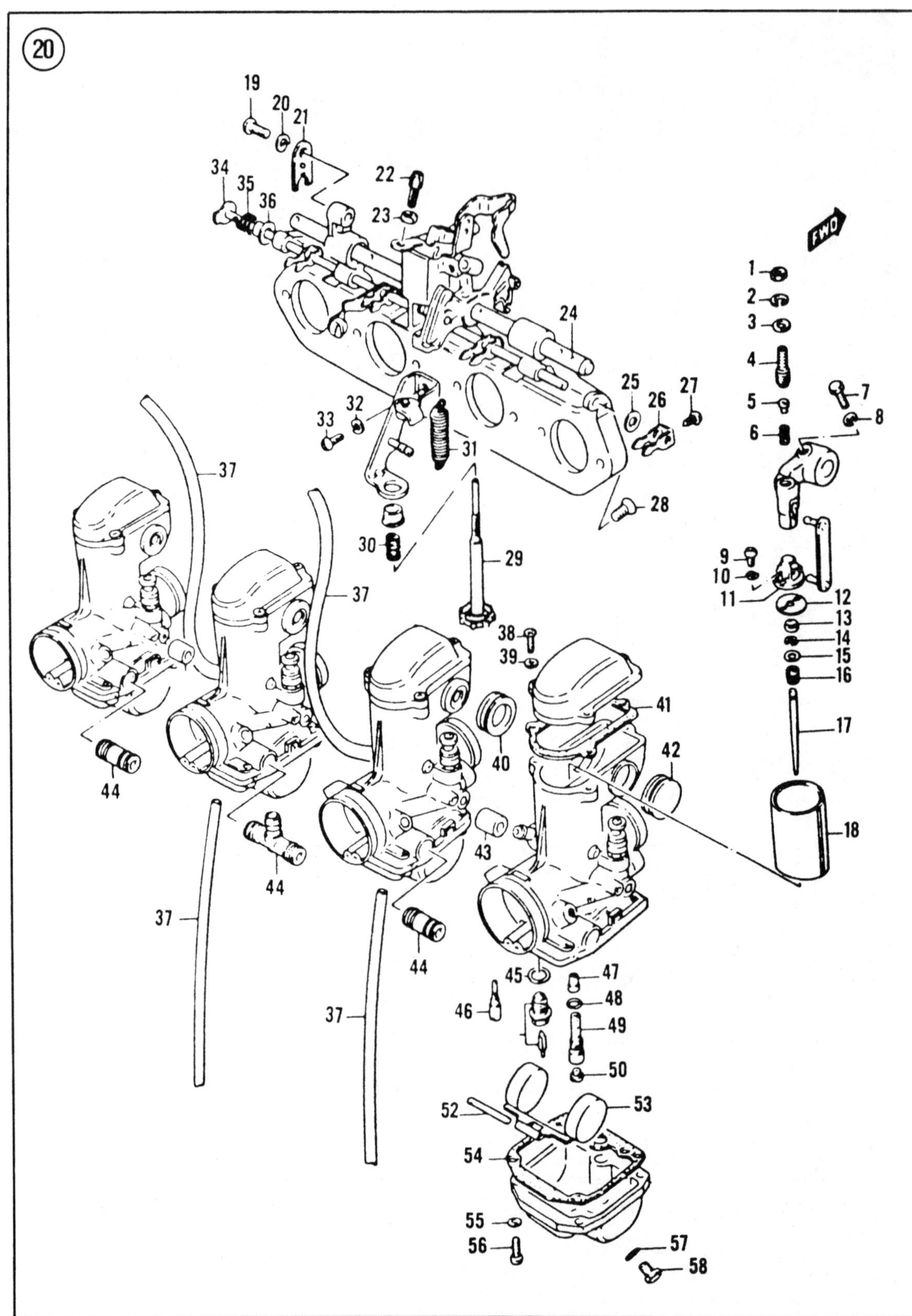
20
FWD
1
2
3
4
5
6
7
8
9
10
11
12
13
14
15
16
17
18
19
20
21
22
23
24
25
26
27
28
29
30
31
32
33
34
35
36
37
37
37
37
38
39
40
41
42
43
44
44
44
45
46
47
48
49
50
52
53
54
55
56
57
58

CARBURETOR (1977-1979 MODELS)

1. Nut
2. Lockwasher
3. Washer
4. Adjuster
5. Pin
6. Spring
7. Bolt
8. Lockwasher
9. Screw
10. Lockwasher
11. Bracket
12. Plate
13. Ring
14. Needle clip
15. Washer
16. Spring
17. Jet needle
18. Throttle valve
19. Screw
20. Lockwasher
21. Plate
22. Cable adjuster
23. Locknut
24. Throttle shaft
25. Washer
26. Choke lever
27. Set screw
28. Screw
29. Throttle stop screw (idle speed adjuster)
30. Spring
31. Throttle return spring
32. Lockwasher
33. Screw
34. Choke shaft
35. Spring
36. Washer
37. Hose
38. Screw
39. Lockwasher
40. Seal
41. Cover gasket
42. Cap
43. Hose
44. Nipple
45. Gasket
46. Pilot jet
47. Needle jet
48. O-ring
49. Breather pipe
50. Main jet
51. Float needle valve assembly
52. Float pin
53. Float
54. Gasket
55. Lockwasher
56. Screw
57. O-ring
58. Screw

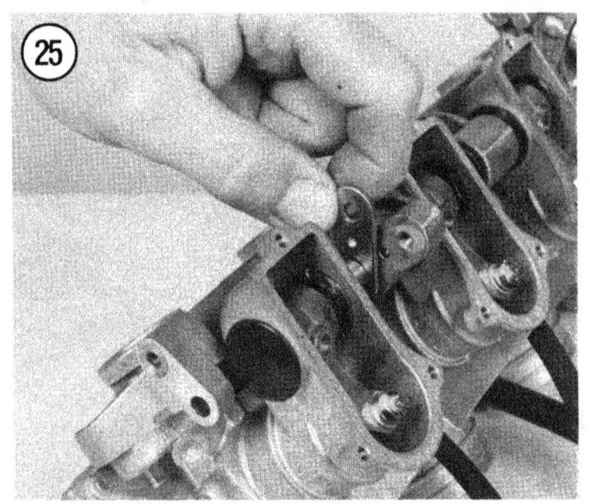
25

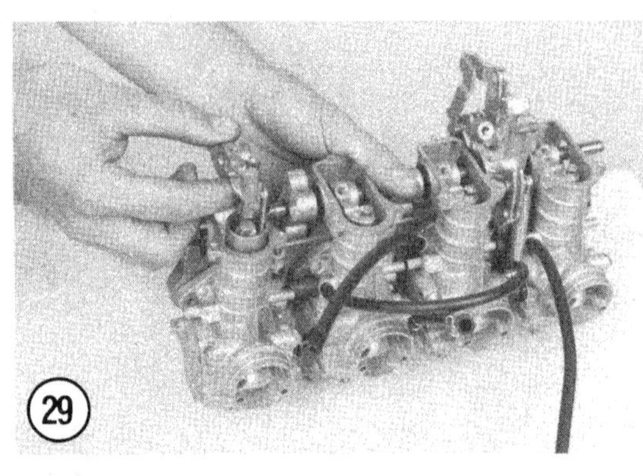
29

26

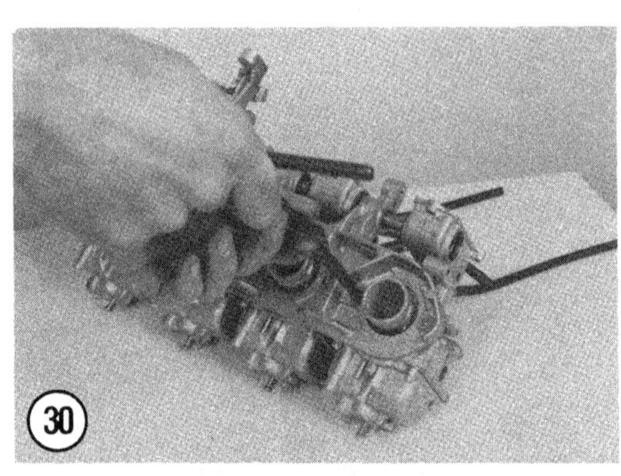
30

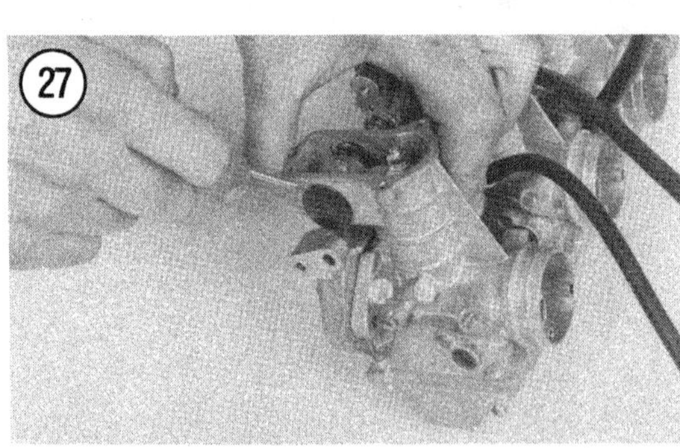
27

31

28

32

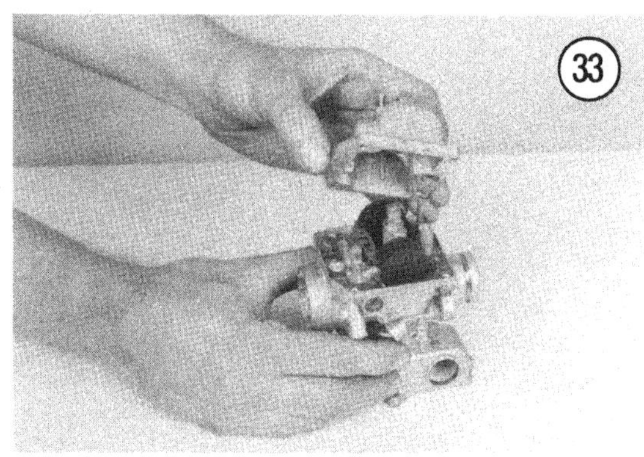

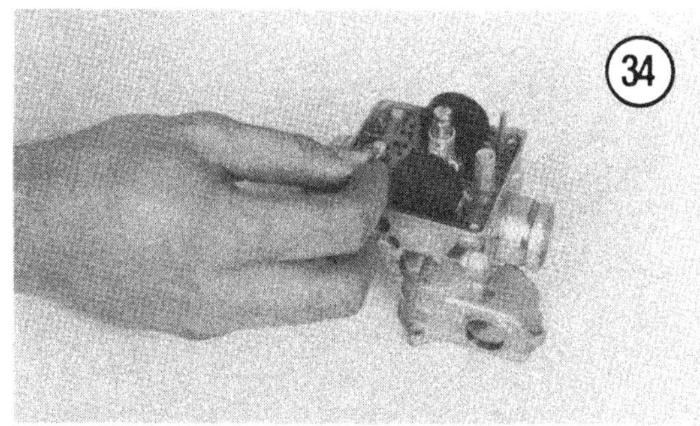

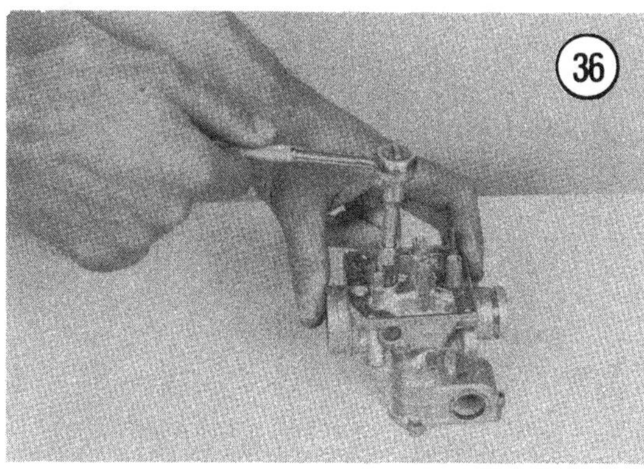

9. Lift up on the slide lifter and remove the throttle slide (**Figure 29**).
10. Remove the screws securing the carburetor to the mounting plate (**Figure 30**). Carefully separate the carburetors, taking care not to damage the nipples and hoses connecting the carburetors.
11. Remove the pilot air screw (**Figure 31**).
12. Refer to **Figure 32** and remove the choke plunger assembly and the throttle shaft seal.
13. Remove the screws securing the float chamber and lift off the chamber (**Figure 33**).
14. Remove the float hinge pin (**Figure 34**) and lift out the float assembly.
15. Remove the pilot jet and main jet (**Figure 35**).
16. Remove the needle valve assembly as shown in **Figure 36**.

CAUTION
*Do not disturb the small jet with the colored paint seal (**Figure 37**). This jet is pre-set at the factory and cannot be recalibrated in the field. If disturbed the carburetor adjustment can be severely affected.*

17. Assembly is the reverse of these steps. Keep the following points in mind:
   a. Lightly grease the throttle shaft before installation.
   b. Apply a small amount of blue Loctite (Lock N' Seal No. 2114) to the bolts securing the throttle shaft and screws securing the choke lifters.
   c. Use a caliper or homemade gauge to set the float level to 26 mm (1.02 in.) as shown in

Figure 38 without the float chamber gasket. Reduce the measurement by 1 mm if the gasket is still installed. Bend the tang on the float arm until the specified float level is achieved.

d. *Gently* turn in the pilot air screw as far as it will go, then back out approximately 2 turns for a preliminary setting.

CAUTION

Do not overtighten the pilot air screw or the tip will be scored or grooved. The slightest screw damage will affect carburetor performance.

Disassemby/Assembly (BS32SS Carburetors)

Refer to **Figure 39** for this procedure.

1. If it is necessary to separate all 4 carburetors for cleaning or repair, perform the following:
   a. Loosen the set screws securing the choke links to the choke shaft (**Figure 40**). Make sure the set screws are loosened enough for the screw points to clear the indentations in the choke shaft.
   b. Pull out the choke shaft and remove the choke links from each carburetor.
   c. Remove the screws securing the upper and lower brackets (**Figure 41** and **Figure 42**).
   d. Carefully separate the carburetors. Note how the throttle linkage is fitted. Make sure the fuel hoses connecting each carburetor are not damaged.
2. Remove the 4 screws securing the diaphragm cover and remove the cover (**Figure 43**). Lift out the diaphragm spring (**Figure 44**).

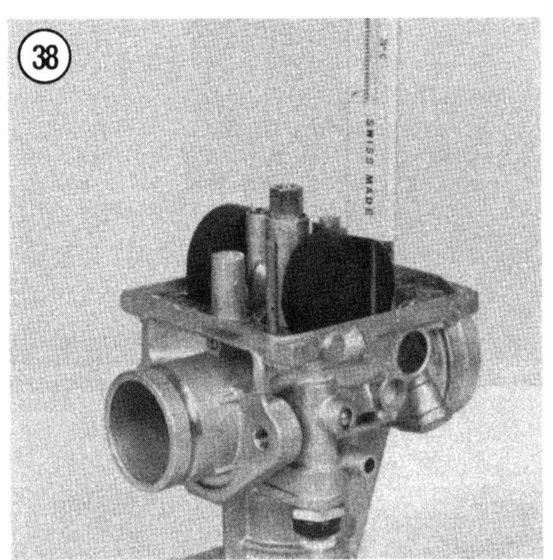

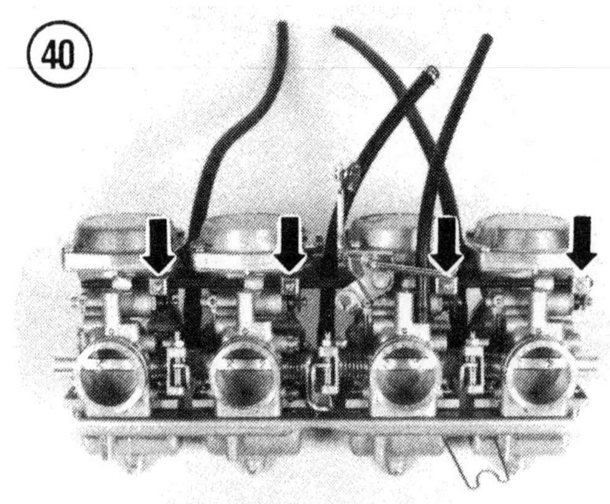

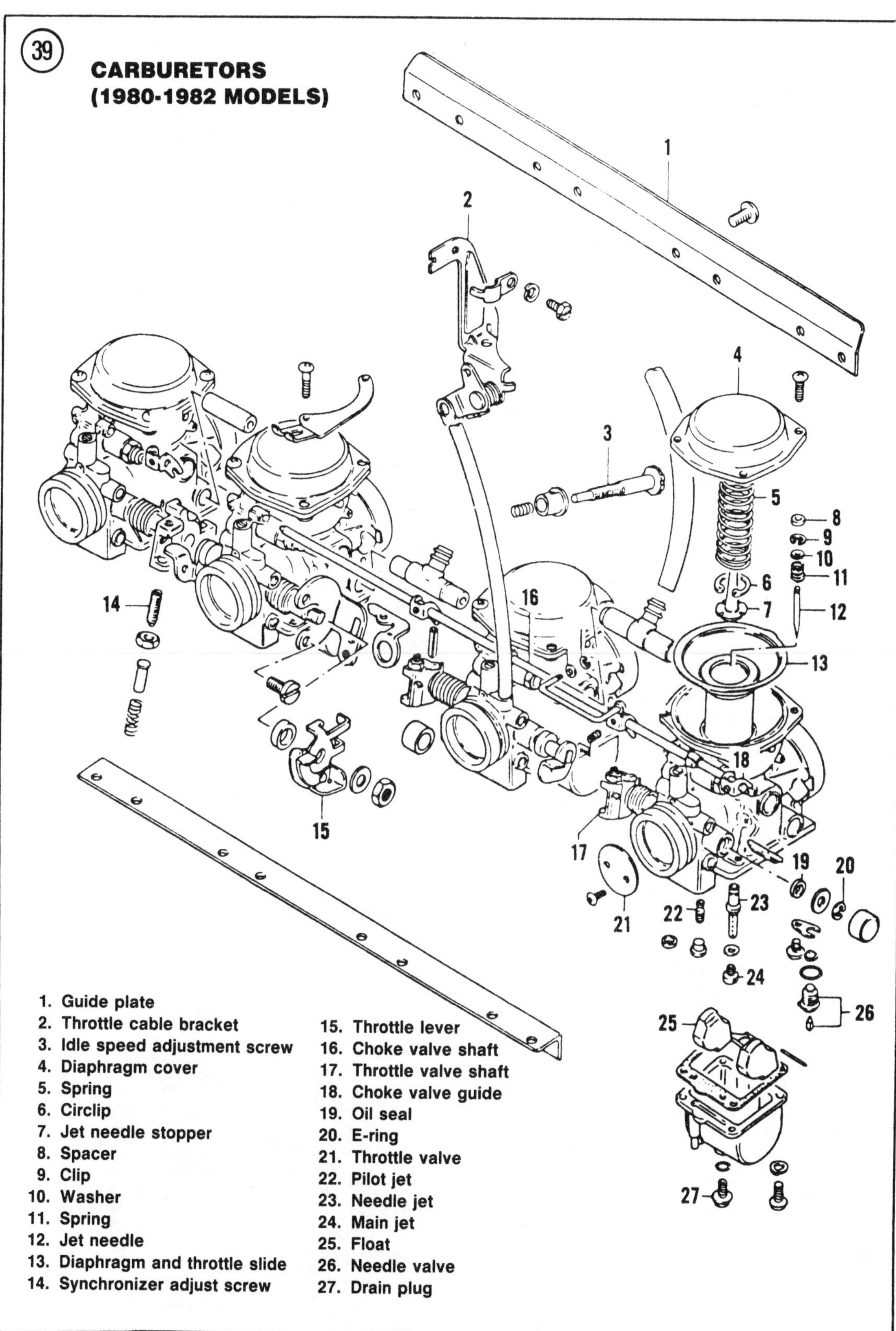
39
CARBURETORS
(1980-1982 MODELS)
1
2
3
4
5
6
7
8
9
10
11
12
13
14
15
16
17
18
19
20
21
22
23
24
25
26
27
1. Guide plate
2. Throttle cable bracket
3. Idle speed adjustment screw
4. Diaphragm cover
5. Spring
6. Circlip
7. Jet needle stopper
8. Spacer
9. Clip
10. Washer
11. Spring
12. Jet needle
13. Diaphragm and throttle slide
14. Synchronizer adjust screw
15. Throttle lever
16. Choke valve shaft
17. Throttle valve shaft
18. Choke valve guide
19. Oil seal
20. E-ring
21. Throttle valve
22. Pilot jet
23. Needle jet
24. Main jet
25. Float
26. Needle valve
27. Drain plug

6

3. Carefully lift out the diaphragm assembly (**Figure 45**).
4. Remove the 4 screws securing the float chamber and remove the chamber (**Figure 46**).
5. Carefully remove the main jet and washer (**Figure 47**).
6. Slide the needle jet out of the carburetor body. Note the O-ring on the needle jet.
7. Push out the hinge pin securing the float assembly and lift out the float (**Figure 48**).
8. Use a socket to remove the needle valve assembly.
9. Perform *Cleaning and Inspection.*
10. Assembly is the reverse of these steps. Keep the following points in mind:
   a. Install the needle jet so that the groove engages the locating pin as shown in **Figure 49**.
   b. When installing the diaphragm assembly, make sure the locating tab on the diaphragm is positioned in the locating notch (**Figure 50**).
   c. Apply a small amount of blue Loctite (Lock N' Seal No. 2114) to the set screws securing the choke links.
   d. Use a caliper and set the float level to 21.4-23.4 mm (0.84-0.92 in.) as shown in **Figure 51** without the float chamber gasket. Reduce the measurement approximately 1 mm if the gasket is still installed. If the float level is not as specified, carefully bend the tang on the float arm until the correct level is achieved.

Disassemby/Assembly (BSW30SS Carburetors)

Refer to **Figure 52** for this procedure.
1. If it is necessary to separate the carburetors for cleaning or repair, perform the following:
   a. Remove the screws securing the upper and lower brackets (**Figure 53** and **Figure 54**).
   b. Carefully separate the carburetors. Note how the throttle linkage is fitted. Make sure the hoses connecting each carburetor are not damaged.
2. Remove the screws securing the diaphragm cover and remove the cover (**Figure 55**).
3. Carefully lift out the diaphragm assembly with both throttle slides as shown in **Figure 56**. Separate the throttle slides from the diaphragm (**Figure 57**). If jet needle replacement is desired, carefully remove the jet needle holder and slide the needle and washers out of the throttle slide (**Figure 58**).
4. Remove the screws securing the float chamber and remove the chamber (**Figure 59**).
5. Unscrew and remove both pilot jets (**Figure 60**).

44

45

46

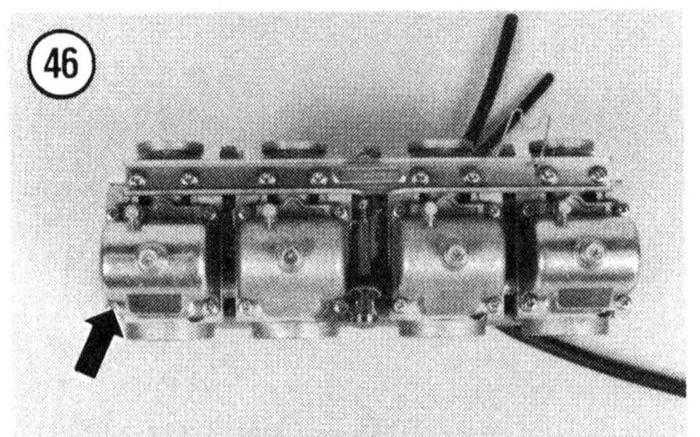

47

48

53

49

54

50

55

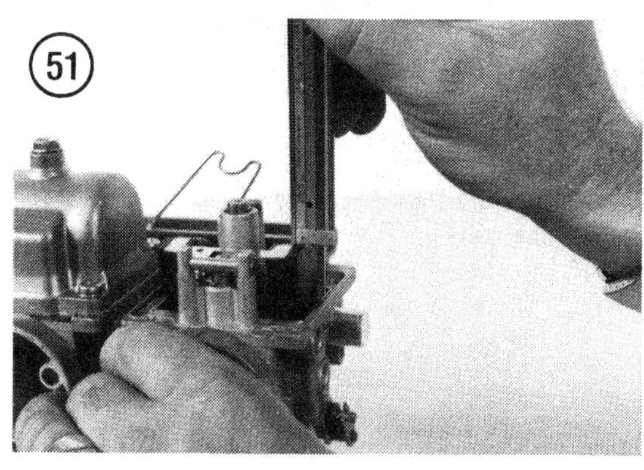
51

56

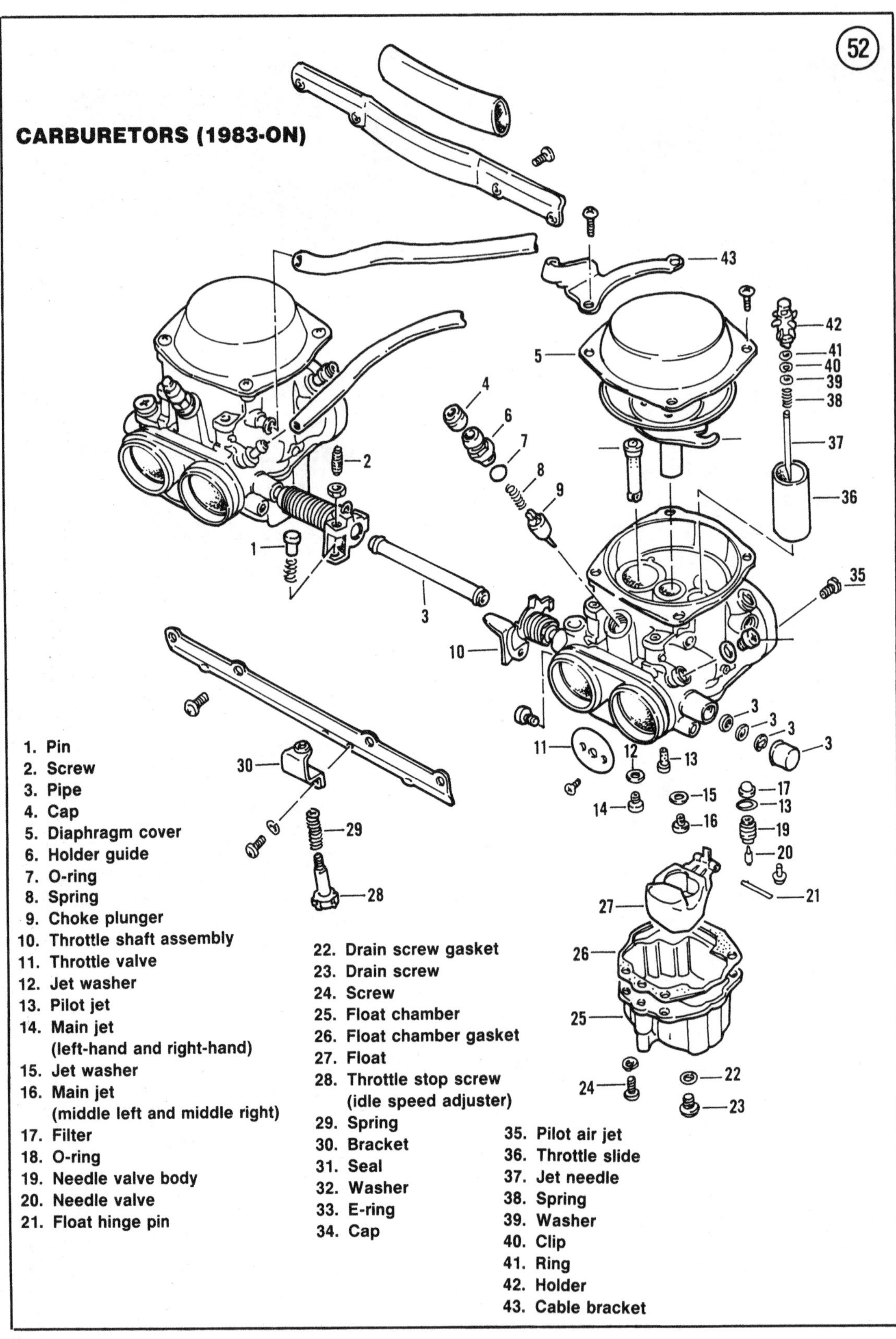
52
CARBURETORS (1983-ON)
1. Pin
2. Screw
3. Pipe
4. Cap
5. Diaphragm cover
6. Holder guide
7. O-ring
8. Spring
9. Choke plunger
10. Throttle shaft assembly
11. Throttle valve
12. Jet washer
13. Pilot jet
14. Main jet (left-hand and right-hand)
15. Jet washer
16. Main jet (middle left and middle right)
17. Filter
18. O-ring
19. Needle valve body
20. Needle valve
21. Float hinge pin
22. Drain screw gasket
23. Drain screw
24. Screw
25. Float chamber
26. Float chamber gasket
27. Float
28. Throttle stop screw (idle speed adjuster)
29. Spring
30. Bracket
31. Seal
32. Washer
33. E-ring
34. Cap
35. Pilot air jet
36. Throttle slide
37. Jet needle
38. Spring
39. Washer
40. Clip
41. Ring
42. Holder
43. Cable bracket

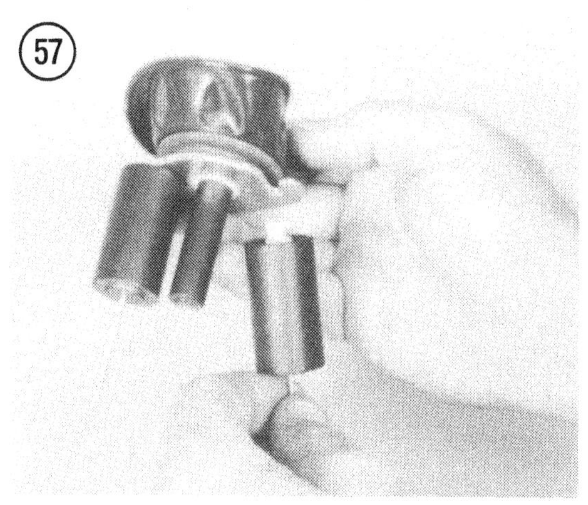

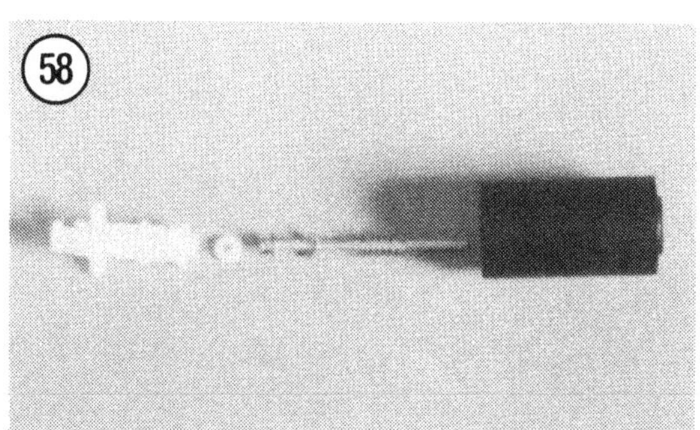

6. Slide out the hinge pin securing the float assembly and lift out the float (**Figure 61**).
7. Carefully lift out the needle valve as shown in **Figure 62**.
8. Remove the screw securing the needle valve body (**Figure 63**).
9. Carefully lift out the needle valve body as shown in **Figure 64**. Take care not to damage the O-ring and strainer on the needle valve body.
10. Remove both main jets and washers. See **Figure 65** and **Figure 66**.
11. Slide the needle jets out of the carburetor body (**Figure 67**). It may be necessary to push them out with a small punch or screwdriver. Take care not to damage the parts.
12. If throttle valve removal is desired, note that numbers on each throttle valve are on the bottom side of the carburetor (**Figure 68**).
13. Perform *Cleaning and Inspection.*
14. Assembly is the reverse of these steps. Keep the following points in mind:
   a. Make sure the screen on the end of the needle valve body is clean and not damaged (**Figure 69**). Replace the O-ring if it is damaged.
   b. Apply a small amount of blue Loctite (Lock N' Seal No. 2114) to the screw securing the

6

63

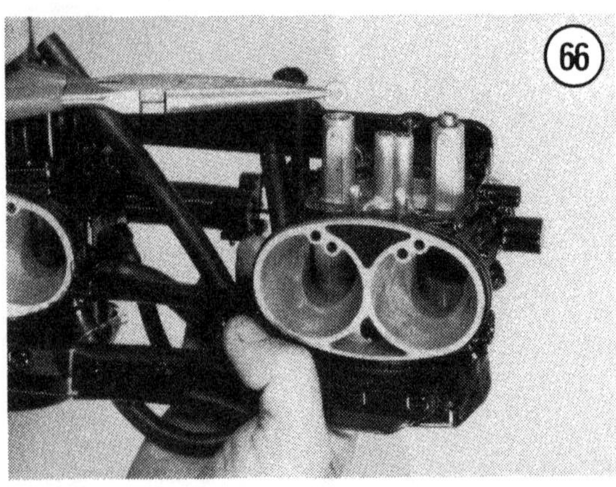

66

64

67

65

68

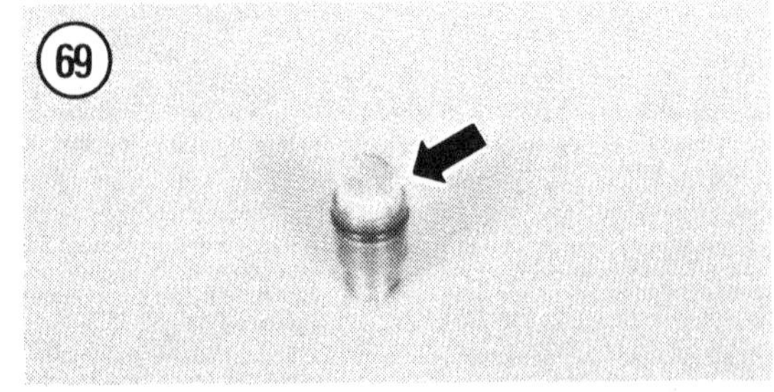

69

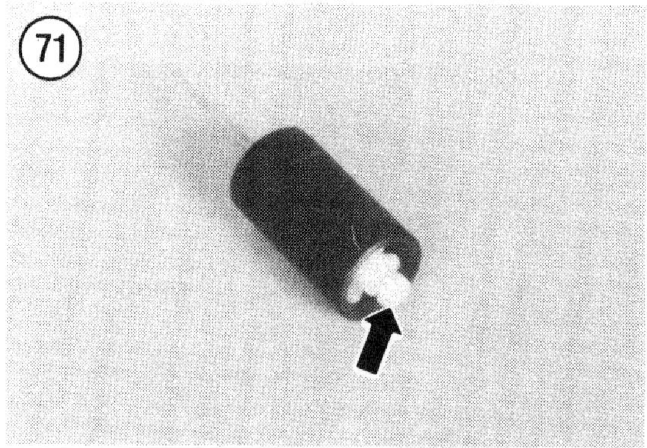

needle valve body (**Figure 70**). If the throttle valves were removed, apply blue Loctite to the screws securing the throttle valves (**Figure 68**).

c. Make sure the needle jet components are arranged as shown in **Figure 58** and the jet needle holder is firmly in place in the throttle slide (**Figure 71**).

d. When installing the diaphragm assembly, make sure the locating tab on the diaphragm is positioned in the locating notch (**Figure 72**).

e. Use a caliper to set the float level to 19.5-21.5 mm (0.77-0.85 in.) as shown in **Figure 73** without the float chamber gasket. Reduce the measurement approximately 1 mm if the gasket is still installed. If the float level is not as specified, carefully bend the tang on the float arm until the correct level is achieved.

6

Cleaning and Inspection

1. Soak all of the metal components in carburetor cleaning solution or solvent. Carburetor cleaning solution is available from most automotive parts and supply stores in a small resealable tank with a dip basket. The solution will last for several carburetor rebuilds if the container is tightly sealed after each use.

CAUTION

Do not put non-metallic parts such as floats, gaskets and O-rings in the carburetor cleaning solution. The solution will destroy most non-metallic parts.

2. Check the slides and slide bores for wear. Generally, many thousands of miles of use are necessary before this sort of wear is apparent.
3. Blow out the jets with compressed air.

CAUTION

Do not use wire or sharp instruments to clean any carburetor parts. Small orifices in carburetor components are easily burred and distorted, causing improper carburetor operation.

4. Inspect all the O-rings for damage, deterioration or distortion and replace any that are less than perfect.
5. Examine the cone on the needle valve and replace the valve and seat if scored or pitted.
6. Inspect the rubber seating surface on the choke plunger. Replace the plunger if the seat is deeply grooved or damaged.
7. Carefully examine the diaphragm assembly for holes or tears. If the diaphragm is damaged in any way the entire assembly must be replaced.

EXHAUST SYSTEM

The exhaust system consists of four exhaust pipes (head pipes) and 2 mufflers. The center exhaust pipes are connected by a crossover pipe. Obvious physical differences exist between the exhaust systems of various models; however, removal and installation procedures are the same for all machines.

Removal

1. Loosen the clamp bolts securing the inner exhaust pipes to the mufflers.
2. Loosen the bolts on each side that secure the muffler to the frame (**Figure 74**). Do not remove the bolts at this time.
3. Remove the bolts securing each exhaust pipe flange to the engine (**Figure 75**). Note that on some models, the flanges are asymmetrical (they can be installed in only one direction). Slide the flanges down the exhaust pipes as far as possible.
4. Support the weight of the exhaust system and remove the rear mounting bolts completely. Spread the mufflers apart slightly while pulling the whole exhaust system forward enough to disengage the exhaust pipes from the engine (**Figure 76**).
5. Move the entire exhaust system forward until it clears the motorcycle and remove the exhaust system. Separate the inboard pipes from the mufflers, if desired.

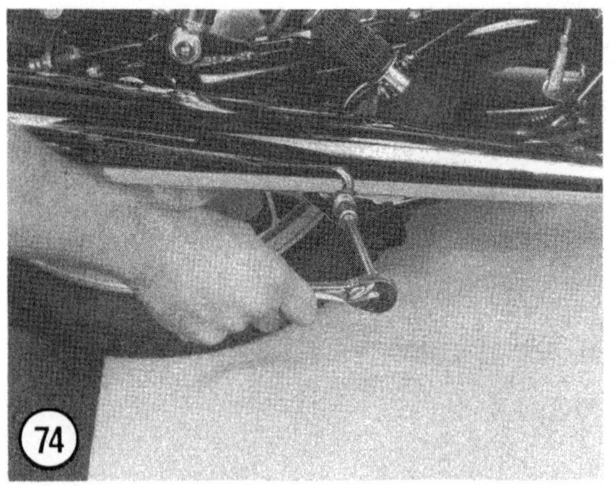

74

75

Installation

1. Slide the exhaust pipes into the cylinder ports and install the rear muffler mounting bolts to secure the rear of the exhaust system. Leave the bolts loose at this time so the exhaust system can be shifted around as it is secured.
2. Hold the exhaust pipes into the cylinder ports and install the bolts to secure the exhaust pipe flanges. Tighten the bolts finger-tight at this time.

CAUTION
On some models, the exhaust pipe flanges are asymmetrical and can be installed in only one direction. If the flanges are not positioned properly, the bolt holes will not align correctly and damage to the threads in the cylinder head may result.

3. Tighten the bolts securing the mufflers to the frame. Torque the bolts as specified in **Table 1**.
4. Make sure all the exhaust pipe flanges are correctly positioned and the exhaust pipes are correctly aligned. Tighten the flange bolts and the inboard pipe clamp bolts to torque values specified in **Table 1**.

76

Table 1 EXHAUST SYSTEM TORQUE SPECIFICATIONS

Item	mkg	ft.-lb.
Exhaust pipe flange bolts		
TSCC models	0.9-1.2	6.5-8.5
All others	0.9-1.4	6.5-10.0
Exhaust pipe clamp bolts		
TSCC models	0.9-1.2	6.5-8.5
All others	0.9-1.4	6.5-10.0
Muffler mounting bolt		
TSCC models	2.2-3.5	16.0-25.5
All others	1.8-2.8	13.0-20.0

CHAPTER SEVEN

ELECTRICAL SYSTEM

Complete wiring diagrams are included at the end of the book. **Table 1** and **Table 2** are at the end of the chapter.

CHARGING SYSTEM

The charging system consists of the battery, alternator, rectifier and regulator. See **Figure 1** for 1979 and earlier models and **Figure 2** for 1980 and later models.

The alternator generates an alternating current (AC) which the rectifier converts to direct current (DC). The regulator controls the voltage going to the battery and the load (lights, ignition, etc.) at a constant voltage regardless of the variations in engine speed and load.

On 1979 and earlier models, the rectifier and regulator are separate components. A charging system malfunction can be isolated to one or the other components. On 1980 and later models, the rectifier and regulator are combined in one unit. If either function of the unit fails, the entire unit must be replaced.

Whenever a charging system trouble is suspected, make sure the battery is fully charged and in good condition before beginning any tests. Make sure all connections are clean and tight. See *Battery* in this chapter.

NOTE

On some GS models the regulator/rectifier is grounded with a black/white wire that attaches to the rubber mounted battery box. If this ground circuit fails, the results will be no charging system output. To ensure that the regulator/rectifier is properly grounded, cut the eyelet off the wire, solder a length of wire to the cut wire and ground the regulator/rectifier directly to the negative battery terminal.

Charging System Output Test (1979 and Earlier Models)

The alternator provides a 3-phase output. Two phases are routed to the rectifier at all times. The third phase is routed to the rectifier only when lights are on. To test all phases of the alternator output, a "no load" condition must be created.

1. On U.S. and Canadian models, remove the screw securing the light switch cap and remove the cap (**Figure 3**). Switch off the lights.

2. Remove or raise the seat and remove the right-hand side cover.

3. Pull the alternator wires out of the large rubber boot and disconnect the yellow wire from the regulator (**Figure 4**).

4. Connect the white/green wire from the alternator to the white/red wire from the rectifier. This bypasses the light switch and connects all 3 phases of alternator output to the rectifier.

5. Turn off all lights. Start and warm up the engine. Connect a voltmeter positive lead to the red wire from the rectifier. Connect the voltmeter negative lead to a good ground on the motorcycle. Bring the engine speed up to 5,000 rpm and hold at that point. If the voltmeter indicates 16.5 volts DC or more, the alternator and rectifier are good; proceed to the next step to check the regulator. If the voltmeter indication is less than 16.5 volts DC, the alternator or rectifier is defective. Refer to

①

CHARGING SYSTEM (1979 AND EARLIER)

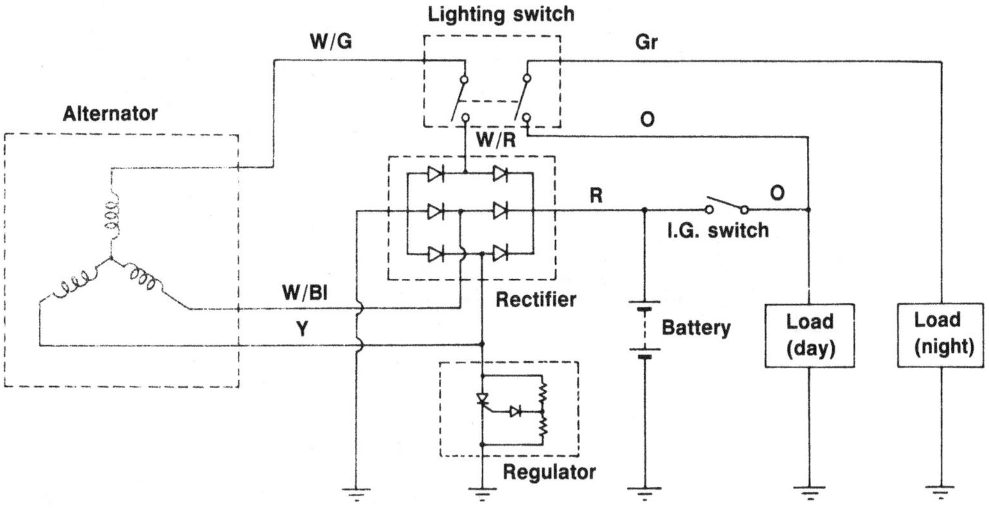

Lighting switch
W/G
Gr
Alternator
O
W/R
R
O
I.G. switch
W/Bl
Rectifier
Y
Battery
Load (day)
Load (night)
Regulator

Y=Yellow
O=Orange
R=Red
Gr=Gray
W/G=White with green tracer
W/Bl=White with blue tracer

②

CHARGING SYSTEM (1980-ON)

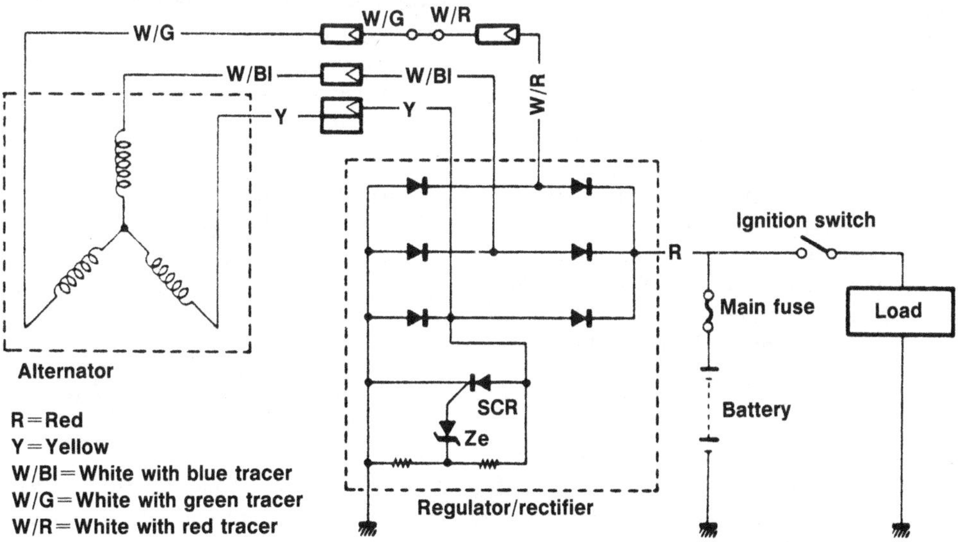

W/G
W/G
W/R
W/Bl
W/Bl
Y
Y
W/R
Ignition switch
R
Main fuse
Load
Alternator
SCR
Ze
Battery
Regulator/rectifier

R=Red
Y=Yellow
W/Bl=White with blue tracer
W/G=White with green tracer
W/R=White with red tracer

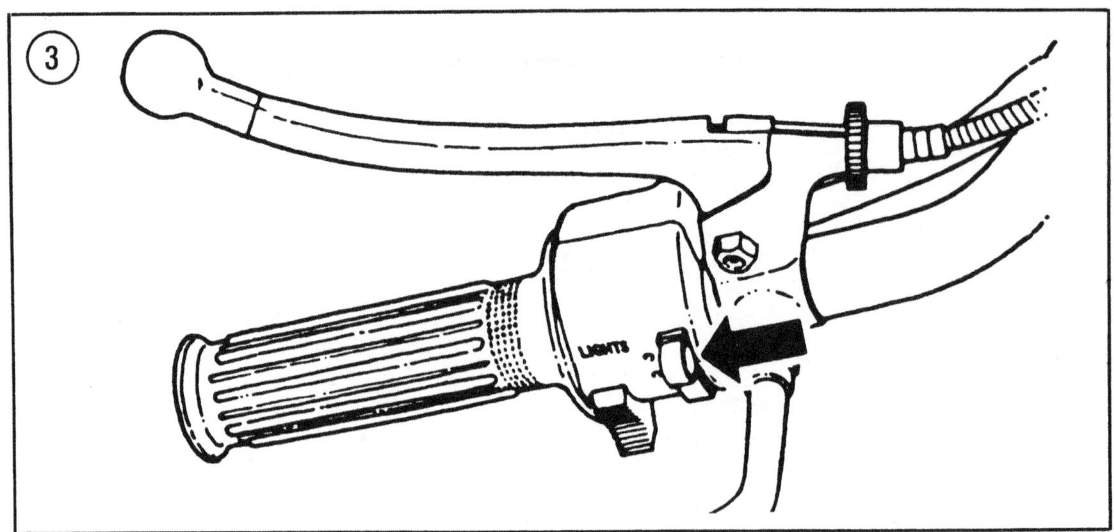

Rectifier Test. If the rectifier tests good, the alternator is defective.

6. Shut off the engine and reconnect the wiring in the normal manner. Make sure the light switch is still OFF.
7. Connect the voltmeter between the positive lead of the battery and a good ground on the frame. Start the engine and run it at 5,000 rpm. If the voltmeter indicates 14-15.5 volts DC, the regulator is good. If the voltage is less than 14 or more than 15.5, the regulator is defective.
8. Install the headlight switch cap, seat and side cover.

Charging System Output Test (1980 and Later Models)

1. Remove the side covers or seat to gain access to the battery.
2. Connect the positive lead of a voltmeter to the red (+) lead on the battery. Connect the negative lead of the voltmeter to the negative terminal on the battery or a good ground on the frame.
3. Start the engine and switch the headlight to high beam. Run the engine up to 5,000 rpm. The voltmeter should indicate 14-15.5 volts DC (13.5-15.5 on TSCC models). If the reading is as specified, all charging system components are operating correctly; remove the voltmeter and install the side covers or seat.
4. If the voltmeter indicates more than 15.5 volts DC, replace the regulator/rectifier.
5. If the voltmeter indicates less than 14 volts DC (13.5 on TSCC models), the regulator/rectifier or the alternator may be defective. Perform the *No-Load Alternator Test* to determine if the alternator is operating correctly. If the no-load test

is satisfactory, replace the regulator/rectifier to correct the low voltage condition.
6. Install the side covers or seat.

No-Load Alternator Test (1980 and Later Models)

1. Remove the seat and side covers to gain access to the alternator wires and disconnect the wires.

NOTE
On 1980-1982 models, the alternator wires are white/blue, white/green and yellow. On TSCC models, all three alternator wires are yellow.

2. Refer to **Figure 5** and connect the leads of an AC voltmeter between the alternator leads. Switch the headlamp to high beam and with each test connection run the engine at 5,000 rpm. The AC voltmeter should indicate 80 volts AC (75 on TSCC models) or more for each test connection.

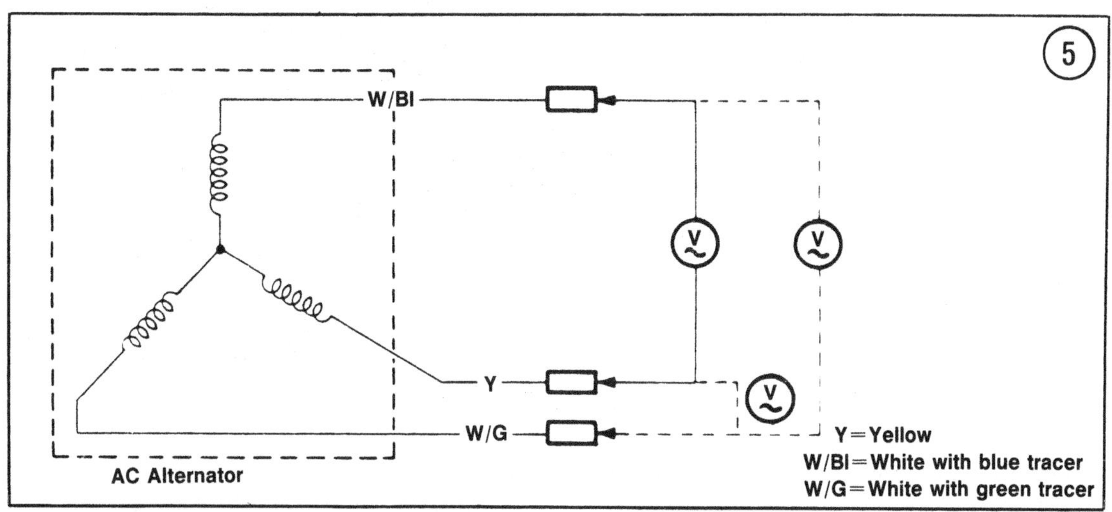

Less than specified voltage on any test connection indicates a faulty alternator.

3. Reconnect the alternator leads. Install the side covers or seat.

Rectifier Test (1979 and Earlier Models)

The 6 diodes in the rectifier are the electrical equivalent of one-way valves; they permit current to flow in a forward direction and prevent it from flowing in the reverse direction—if they are functioning correctly.

CAUTION

Use a VOM (as described in Chapter One) for this test. Do not use a megger instrument or other continuity device as the voltage will destroy otherwise good diodes.

CAUTION

Do not run the engine with the rectifier lead disconnected or the regulator and/or the alternator will be damaged.

1. Disconnect all the leads from the rectifier (**Figure 6**).
2. Set the VOM to the lowest ohm scale and touch the tester's negative lead to the ground terminal (black/white). Touch the positive lead first to the yellow wire, then the white/red, then the white/blue. In each case continuity must be indicated. If there is no continuity on any lead, the rectifier is defective and must be replaced. If all leads check good, proceed to the next step.
3. Switch the tester leads—positive lead to ground (black/white) and negative lead to the yellow, white/red, then white/blue wires. There should be *no* continuity with any of the connections. If continuity exists on any connection, the rectifier is defective and must be replaced. If all leads check good, proceed to the next step.
4. Repeat Steps 2 and 3 to check the other 3 diodes. Use the red wire as the ground terminal, first with the negative lead on the red wire, then the positive lead on the red wire. Replace the rectifier if any diode does not check correctly.

Alternator Stator Removal/Installation

1. Drain the engine oil as outlined in Chapter Three.
2. Remove the bolts securing the starter motor cover and remove the cover.
3. Remove the seat or side covers and disconnect the alternator wires.
4. Loosen the fasteners securing the alternator cover (**Figure 7**).
5. Remove the fasteners, cover and gasket. Note the location of the different length fasteners. Keep

7

a few rags handy, as some oil is bound to run out when the cover is removed. Note how the alternator wires are routed through the cover and crankcase.

CAUTION

Do not pry the cover loose with a screwdriver or the cover or the crankcase sealing surfaces will be damaged. The cover is held tight by the magnetic attraction of the alternator rotor. A strong pull is required to overcome the magnetic field.

7

6. Remove the screws securing the stator assembly and wire retaining clips to the alternator case and remove the stator assembly (**Figure 8**). Note how the wiring is routed.
7. Installation is the reverse of these steps. Keep the following points in mind:
   a. Make sure the alternator wires are correctly routed in the alternator cover and the grommet is installed in the notch (**Figure 9**).
   b. Install a new cover gasket and route the alternator wires into the crankcase opening. Hold the gasket in place and install the alternator cover.
   c. Connect the alternator wires and install the starter motor cover.

8

Alternator Rotor Removal/Installation

The alternator rotor is a permanent magnet. Rotor removal is usually only necessary if the crankshaft must be replaced or the motorcycle has been damaged in an accident. A special puller is required for rotor removal as outlined in Chapter Four.

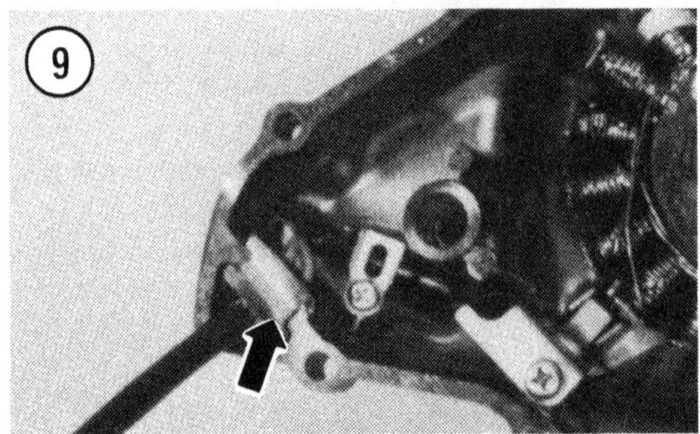

9

Rectifier Removal/Installation (1979 and Earlier Models)

1. Remove the right-hand side cover.
2. Remove the screws securing the rectifier unit (**Figure 6**). Disconnect the wires and remove the unit.
3. Installation is the reverse of these steps. Make sure the wires are connected securely.

Regulator Removal/Installation (1979 and Earlier Models)

1. Remove the left-hand side cover and raise the seat.
2. Remove the screws securing the regulator unit (**Figure 10**). Disconnect the wires and remove the unit.

10

3. Installation is the reverse of these steps. Make sure the wires are connected securely.

Regulator/Rectifier Removal/Installation (1980 and Later Models)

1. Remove the left-hand side cover on 1980-1982 models. On TSCC models, remove the seat.
2. Remove the screws securing the regulator/rectifier unit. See **Figure 11** for 1980-1982 models and **Figure 12** for TSCC models. Disconnect the wires and remove the unit.
3. Installation is the reverse of these steps. Make sure the wires are connected securely.

STARTING SYSTEM

The starting system consists of a starter motor and starting relay (solenoid). Refer to **Figure 13** for a schematic of the starting system.

Before checking for a suspected trouble in the starting system, make sure all the connections are clean and tight. Make certain that the battery is in good condition, with correct electrolyte level and fully charged.

If the system is functioning correctly, the relay will make a single audible click when the starter button is pressed and the starter motor will begin to turn at once. See **Figure 14** for relay location on 1982 and earlier models. See **Figure 15** for TSCC models.

If the relay makes no sound, the motor does not turn and the battery is fully charged, an open

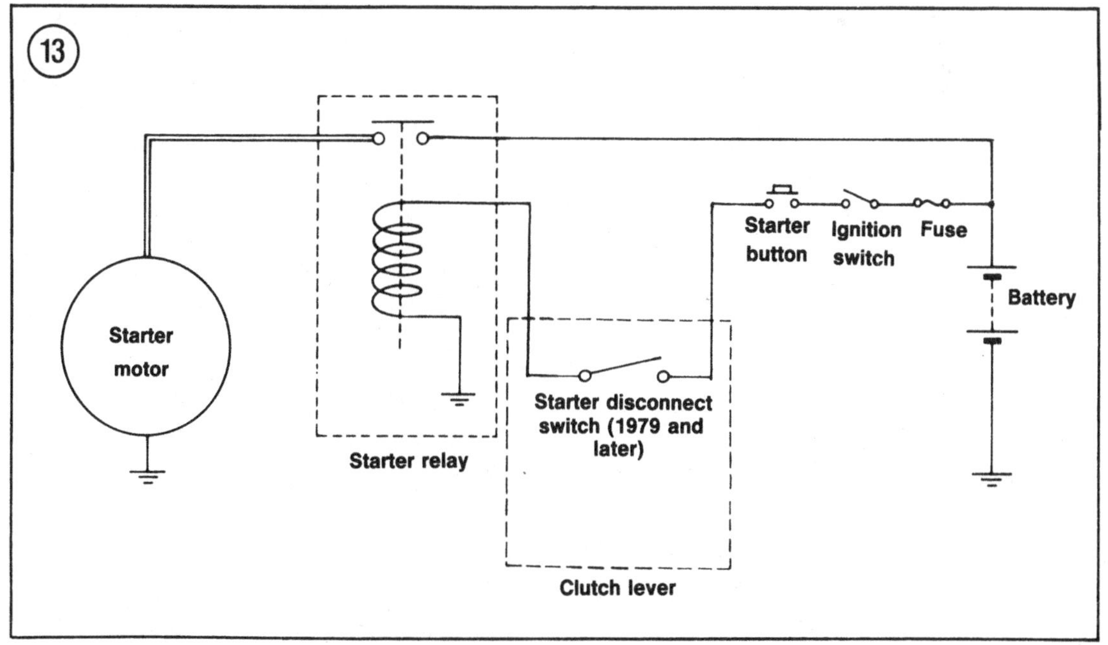

circuit in the relay coil is likely; the relay must be replaced.

If the relay chatters when the button is pressed and the motor does not turn, there may be a bad ground connection, the relay contacts may be faulty or the motor may have an internal open circuit. In such a case, the problem should be referred to a dealer or electrical specialist for thorough testing.

Starter Relay Removal/Installation

1. Remove the carburetors as described in Chapter Six.
2. Disconnect the battery and starter motor lead wires from the relay. See **Figure 14** for 1982 and earlier models. See **Figure 15** for TSCC models.
3. Remove the screws securing the relay and remove the relay.
4. Installation is the reverse of these steps. Ensure that the mounting screws and electrical connections are tight.

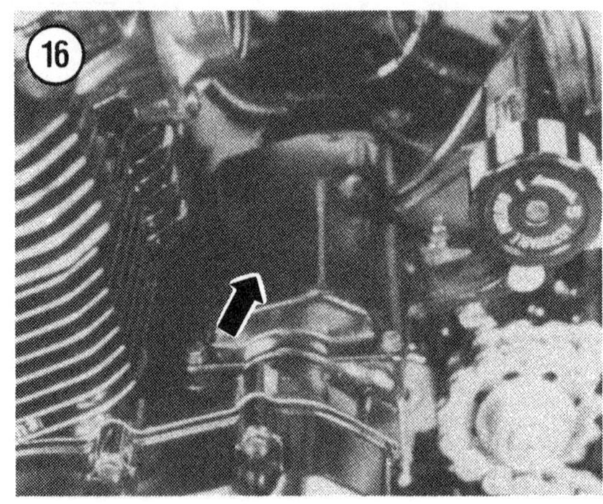

Starter Motor Removal/Installation

1. Refer to Chapter Six and perform *Carburetor Removal.*
2. Remove the cam chain tensioner assembly as outlined in Chapter Four.
3. Remove the bolts securing the starter motor cover and remove the cover (**Figure 16**).
4. Remove the lead wire from the starter motor (**Figure 17**).

5. Remove the bolts securing the starter motor and slide out the motor (**Figure 18**).

6. Installation is the reverse of these steps. Before installing the cover, make sure the wires are correctly routed in the crankcase grooves (**Figure 19**).

BATTERY

Removal/Cleaning/Installation

1. Remove the seat and the left-hand side cover.

2. Disconnect the ground wire (-) then the positive wire (+) from the battery. See **Figure 20** for 1982 and earlier models and **Figure 21** for TSCC models.

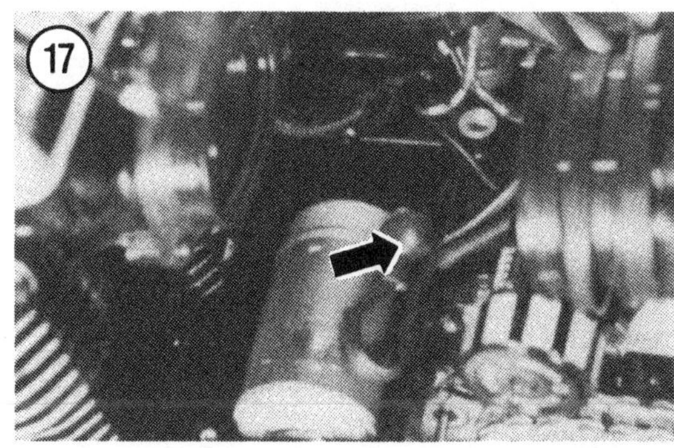

3. Remove the hose from the battery vent.

4. Remove the rubber strap securing the battery and carefully lift the battery out of the motorcycle.

5. Clean the top of the battery with a solution of baking soda and water. Scrub off any stubborn deposits with a brush and rinse the battery with clear water. Dry the battery thoroughly.

CAUTION
Keep the cleaning solution out of the battery cells or the electrolyte will be severely weakened.

6. Clean the battery leads and terminals with a wire brush or sandpaper.

7. Inspect the battery case for cracks. If any cracks are found the battery must be replaced as soon as possible. The condition of the battery will deteriorate rapidly and leaking electrolyte will damage painted, plated and polished surfaces as well as electrical insulation.

8. Coat the terminals with petroleum jelly or a battery corrosion preventative.

9. Check electrolyte level and top off, if necessary, with distilled water.

CAUTION
Never add battery acid (electrolyte) to a battery in service or the battery will be damaged.

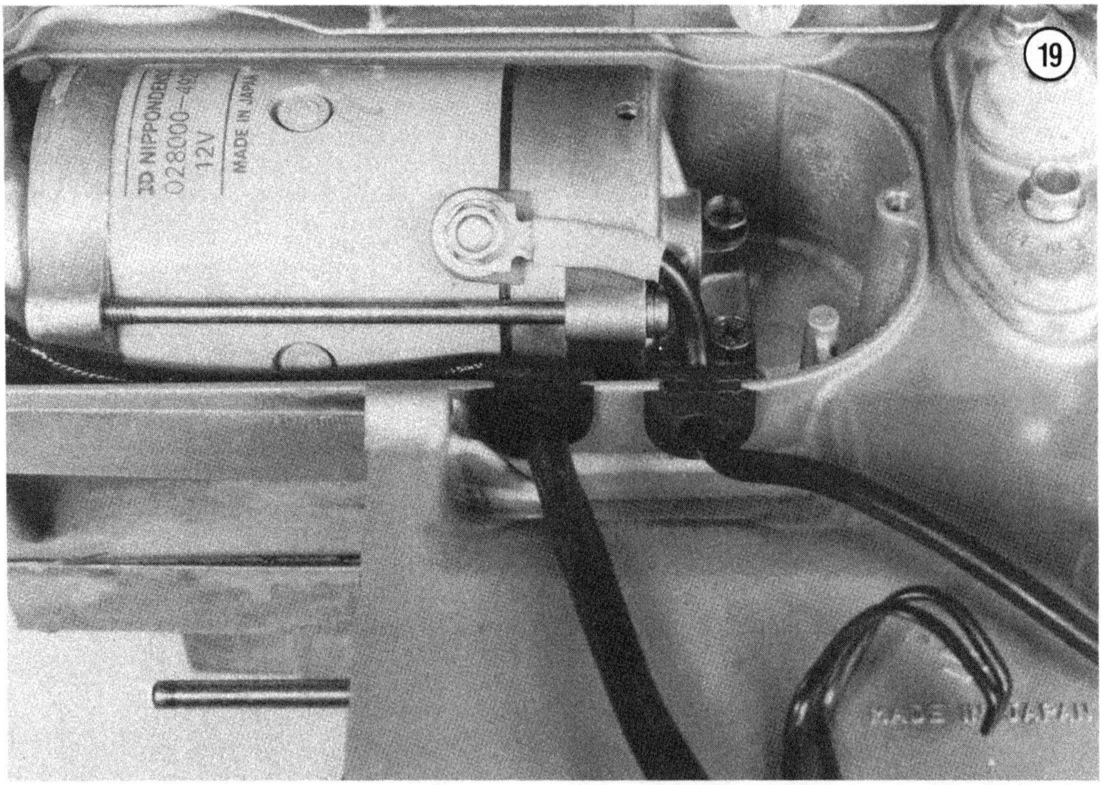

19

20

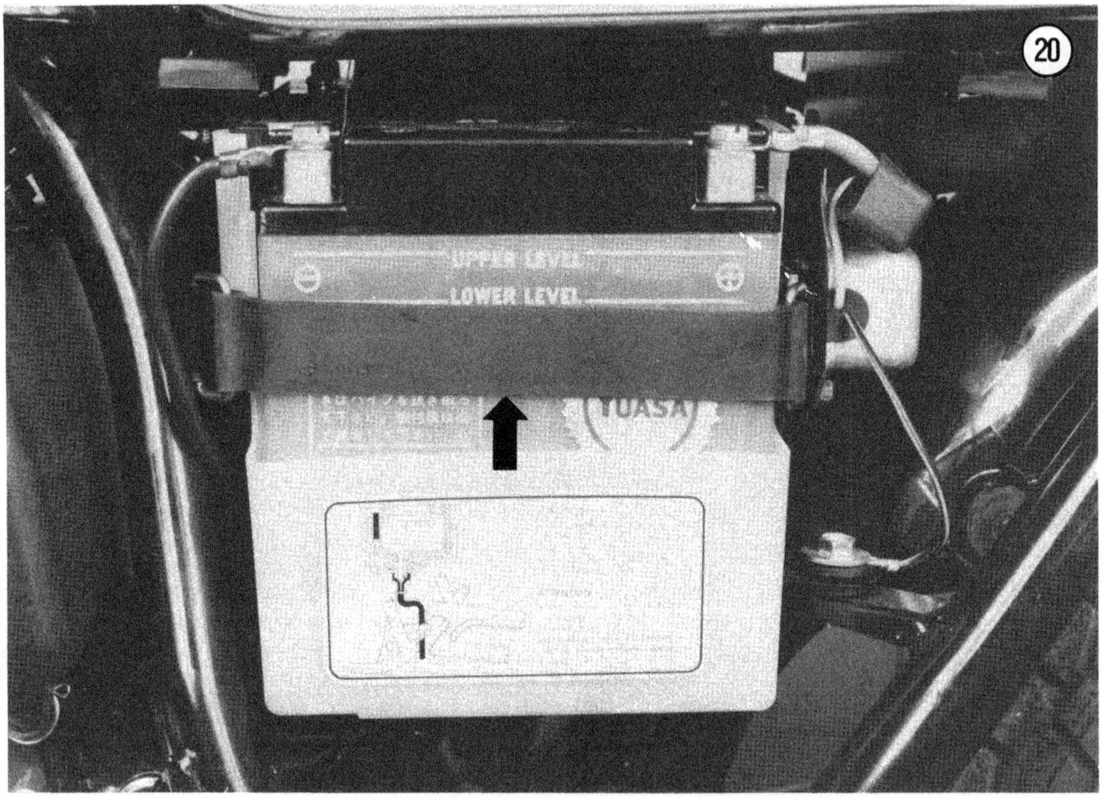

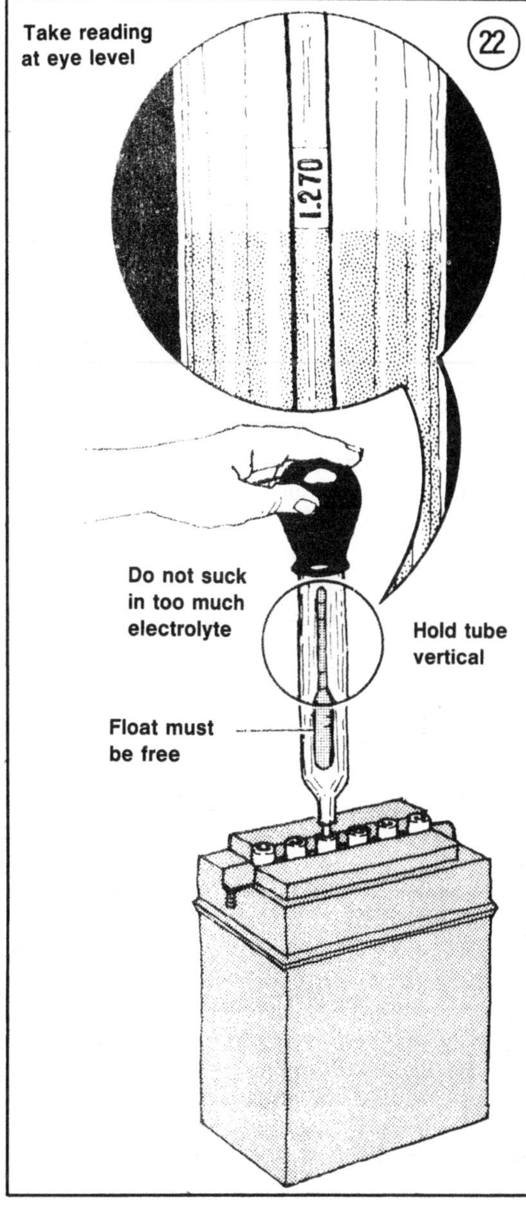

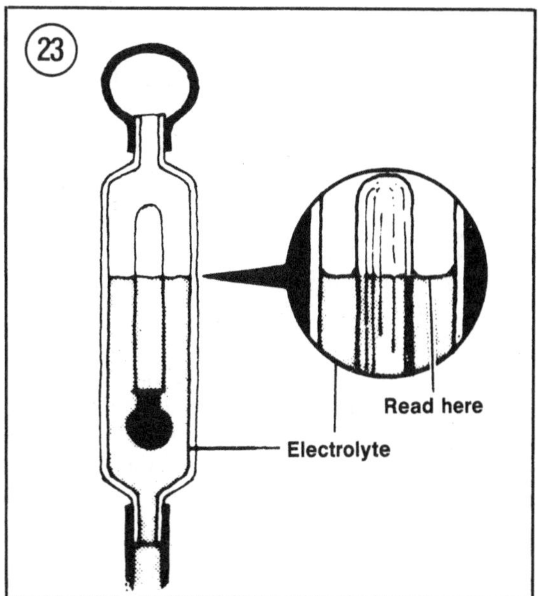

10. Install the battery and connect the leads, positive first, then ground. Make sure the battery cables are connected securely and the vent tube is attached.

Testing

Hydrometer testing is the best way to check battery condition. Use a hydrometer with numbered graduations from 1.100 to 1.300 rather than one with color-coded bands. To use the hydrometer, squeeze the rubber ball, insert the tip in the battery cell and release the ball. Draw in enough electrolyte to float the weighted float inside the hydrometer (**Figure 22**). Note the number in line with the surface of the electrolyte (**Figure 23**); this is the specific gravity for this cell. Return the electrolyte to the cell from which it came.

The specific gravity of the electrolyte in each battery cell is an excellent indication of that cell's condition. Refer to **Table 1** for specific gravities in relation to an approximate state of the charge.

Specific gravity varies with temperature. If you are not using a temperature-compensated hydrometer, for each 10° that the electrolyte temperature exceeds 80° F, add 0.004 to the reading indicated on the hydrometer. Subtract 0.004 from the reading for each 10° below 80° F.

Charging

CAUTION
Always disconnect both battery cables before connecting charging equipment or you may damage the charger or motorcycle electrical system.

7

1. The battery can be charged while installed in the motorcycle; however, it is much safer to remove the battery. Charge only in a well ventilated area.

WARNING

Keep all smoking materials and open flame away from the battery during charging. Highly explosive hydrogen gas is formed during charging. Never arc the terminals to check the condition of the charge; the resulting spark could ignite the hydrogen gas.

2. Connect the charger positive-to-positive and negative-to-negative as shown in **Figure 24**.
3. Remove the caps from each cell and check the electrolyte level. Correct the level, if necessary, by adding only distilled water. Leave the caps off during charging.

CAUTION

Never add battery acid (electroltye) to a battery in service or the battery will be damaged.

4. If the charger output is variable, select a low rate (1.5-3 amps), turn on the charger and allow the battery to charge as long as possible. If it is severely discharged, as long as 8 hours may be required to charge it completely.
5. When charging is complete, check the battery with the hydrometer. If the specific gravity level is satisfactory, wait an hour and test it again. If the specific gravity is still correct, the battery is fully charged and in good condition. If the specific gravity drops between the tests, it is likely that one or more cells are sulfated and the battery should be replaced as soon as possible.

IGNITION SYSTEM

Two types of ignition systems are installed on GS550 models. All 1979 and earlier models are fitted with a breaker point system (**Figure 25**). All 1980 and later models are fitted with a Kokusan transistorized (breakerless) ignition system (**Figure 26**).

The breaker point system consists of 2 coils with condensers, 2 contact breaker point sets and 4 spark plugs. The transistorized system also has ignition coils and spark plugs; however, the breaker points and condensers are replaced by a signal generator and an igniter unit. The signal generator is driven by the engine crankshaft and generates pulses which are routed to the igniter unit. The igniter unit amplifies the pulses and triggers the output of the ignition coils.

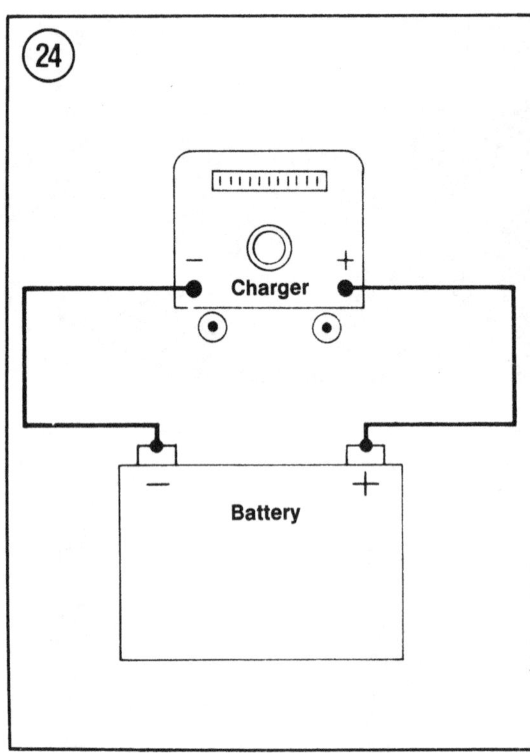

Periodic adjustment of breaker points and timing on 1979 and earlier models is outlined under *Engine Tune-Up* in Chapter Three.

Ignition timing on the transistorized system is pre-set and non-adjustable, so the ignition system requires no periodic maintenance.

Ignition Coil Test

The easiest test for a suspected coil is to replace it with a coil that is known to be good. For example, if 2 of the cylinders are operating correctly, exchange the ignition coils and see if the symptoms move to the other 2 cylinders.

Ignition Coil Removal/Installation

1. Remove the fuel tank as outlined in Chapter Six.
2. Disconnect the primary leads from the coils (**Figure 27**).
3. Disconnect the high-tension leads (spark plug leads) from the spark plugs. Grasp the spark plug caps, not the wires, to pull them off.
4. Remove the bolts securing the coils to the coil mounts (**Figure 28**) and remove the coils.
5. Installation is the reverse of these steps. Make sure the primary wires are connected correctly and the spark plug leads are routed to the correct cylinders. See **Figure 29** and **Figure 30**.

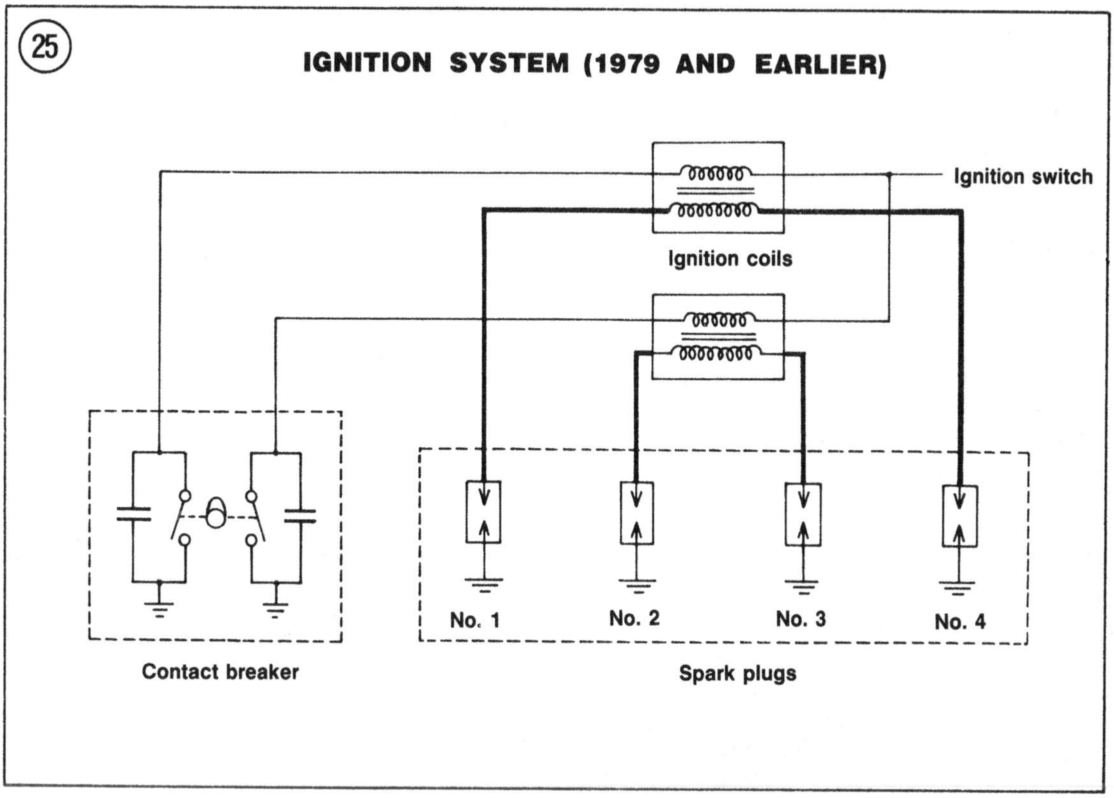
25
IGNITION SYSTEM (1979 AND EARLIER)
Ignition switch
Ignition coils
No. 1
No. 2
No. 3
No. 4
Contact breaker
Spark plugs

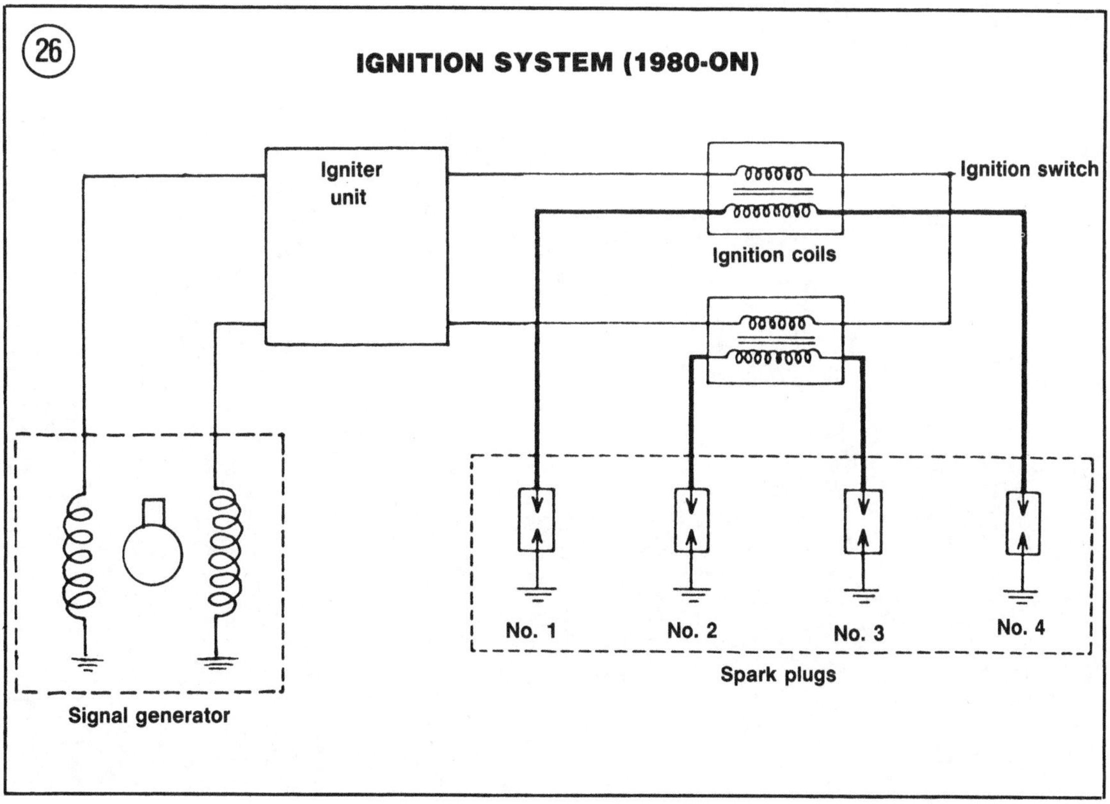
26
IGNITION SYSTEM (1980-ON)
Igniter unit
Ignition switch
Ignition coils
No. 1
No. 2
No. 3
No. 4
Spark plugs
Signal generator

Signal Generator Test

Refer to **Figure 31** for this procedure.

1. Remove the side covers to gain access to the signal generator wires.
2. Pull back the rubber boot to expose the signal generator wires and disconnect the connector. See **Figure 32** for 1980-1982 models and **Figure 33** for TSCC models.
3. On the signal generator side of the connector, connect an accurate ohmmeter between the brown wire and ground (black/white), then between the green/white wire and ground. See **Figure 34**. On 1980-1982 models, the ohmmeter must indicate 60-80 ohms for each connection. On TSCC models, the ohmmeter must indicate 250-500 ohms for each connection. If the ohmmeter reading is not correct, the signal generator unit is defective.
4. Reconnect the wires and install the side covers.

Igniter Unit Test

Refer to **Figure 35** for this test.

1. Carefully remove spark plug leads from No. 3 and No. 4 spark plugs. Remove the spark plugs and reconnect the spark plug leads. Lay both spark plugs against the cylinder head so that each plug is grounded on the head.
2. Remove the side covers and disconnect the signal generator wire connectors. See **Figure 32** for

27

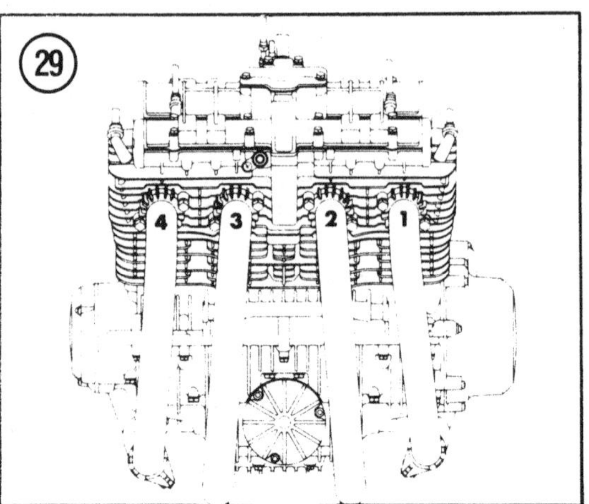

29

28

30

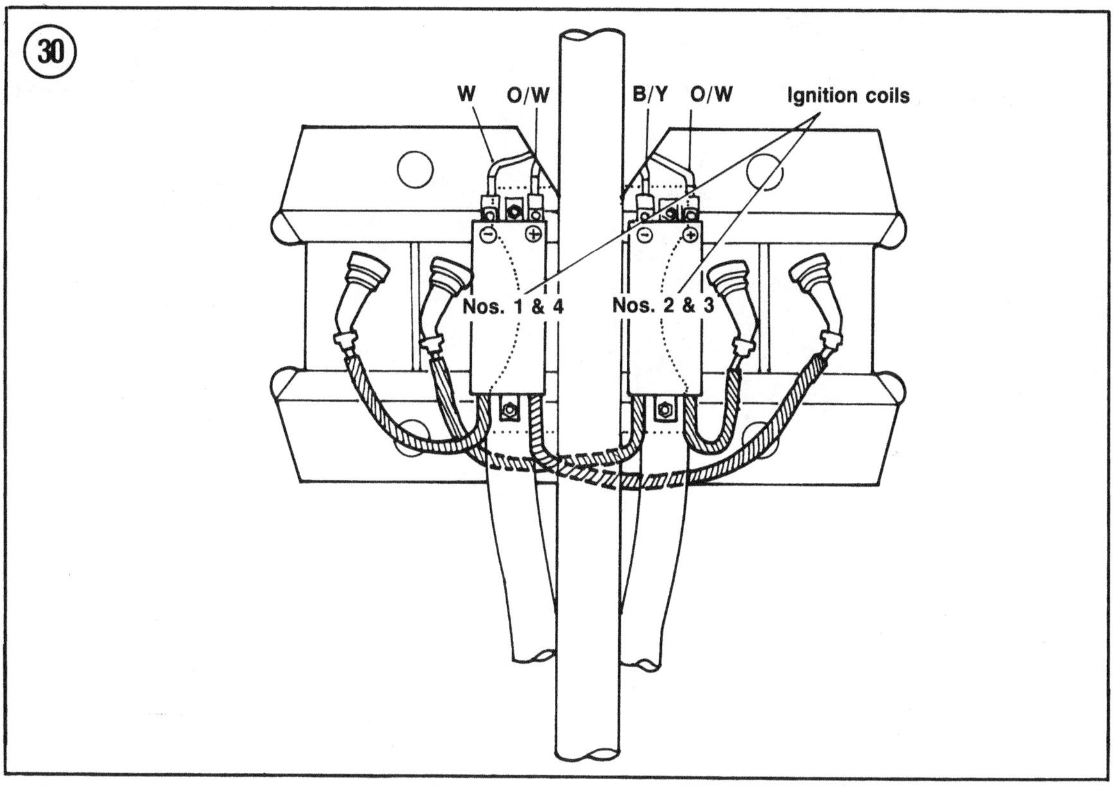

W
O/W
B/Y
O/W
Ignition coils
Nos. 1 & 4
Nos. 2 & 3

31

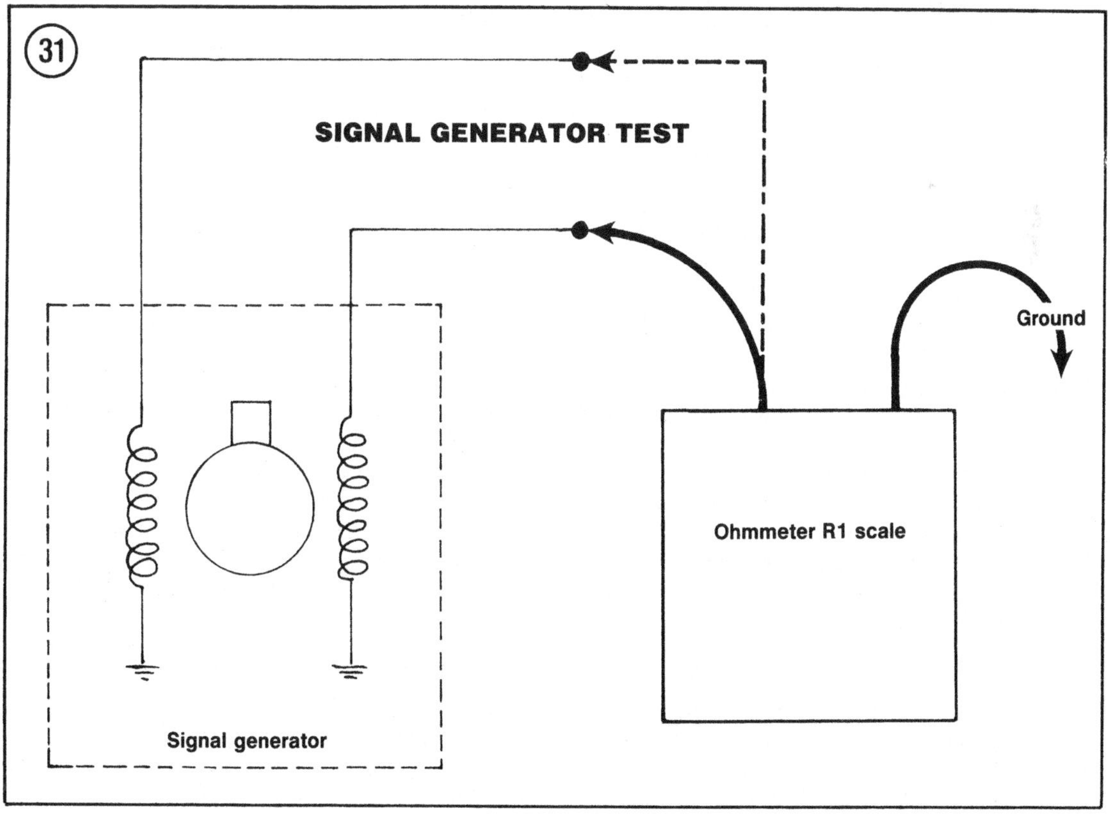

SIGNAL GENERATOR TEST
Ground
Ohmmeter R1 scale
Signal generator

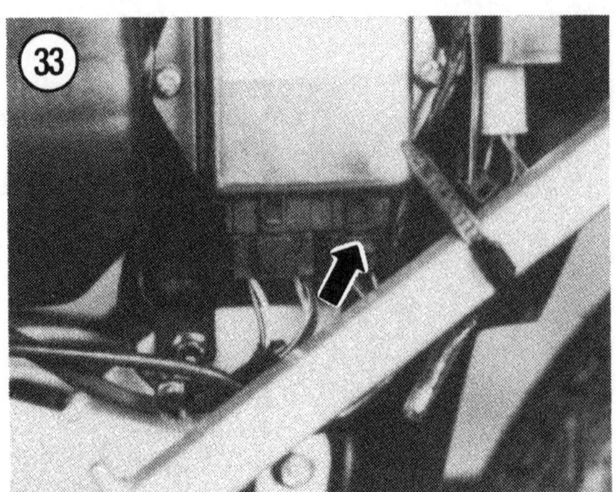

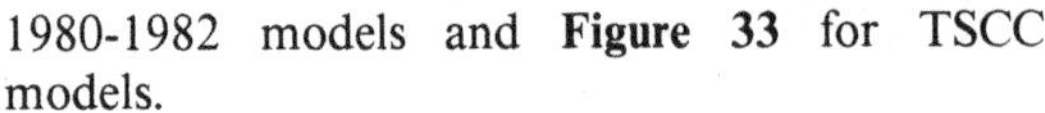

1980-1982 models and **Figure 33** for TSCC models.

3. Turn *on* the motorcycle ignition.

NOTE
This test utilizes the 1-1/2 volt battery in the ohmmeter to simulate the pulse from the signal generator. A 1-1/2 volt power source such as a dry cell battery can also be used for this test.

CAUTION
Make sure the correct polarity is observed for this test or the igniter unit will be destroyed. The negative lead connects to the black/white wire on the igniter unit side of the connector and the positive lead connects to the green/white or brown wire on the igniter unit side of the connector. On TSCC models, extra care must be taken as the wire colors on the igniter side of the connector cannot be seen. Keep the signal generator connector close by to ensure the proper connections are made. Refer to ***Figure 36*** *for LD models.*

4. Set the ohmmeter to the lowest ohm scale and connect the negative lead to the black/white lead *on the igniter unit side of the connector.*
5. Connect the ohmmeter positive (+) lead to either the green/white or brown wire on the *igniter unit side* of the connector. This simulates the pulse from one-half of the signal generator. As the positive lead is connected to the igniter unit connector, one spark plug should fire. When the positive lead is connected to the other wire in the igniter unit connector, the other spark plug should fire. If both spark plugs are properly grounded and one or both fail to fire, replace the igniter unit.
6. Install both spark plugs. Reconnect the igniter unit wires and install the side covers.

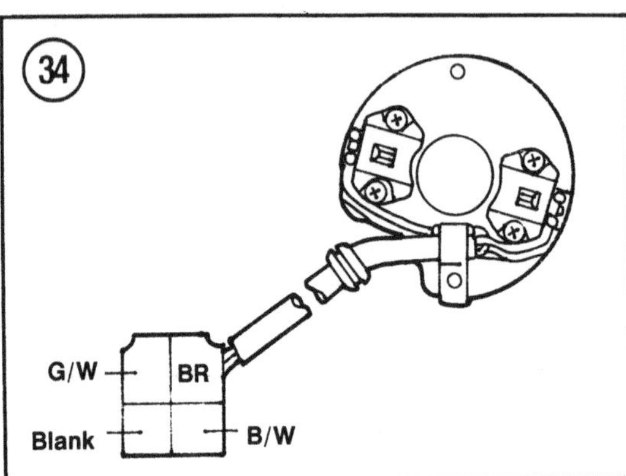

Signal Generator Removal/Installation

1. Remove the fasteners securing the ignition cover and remove the cover (**Figure 37**). Take care not to damage the cover gasket.
2. Remove the side covers and disconnect the signal generator wire connectors. See **Figure 32** for 1980-1982 models and **Figure 33** for TSCC models.
3. Remove the screws securing the signal generator unit and remove the unit. See **Figure 38** for 1980-1982 models and **Figure 39** for TSCC models. Note how the wiring is routed along the engine sump.
4. Installation is the reverse of these steps. Make sure the signal generator wires are tightly connected and the wiring is routed correctly in the retaining clips (**Figure 40**).

Igniter Unit Removal/Installation

1. Remove the side covers.
2. Disconnect the signal generator/igniter unit connector. See **Figure 32** for 1980-1982 models and **Figure 33** for TSCC models.

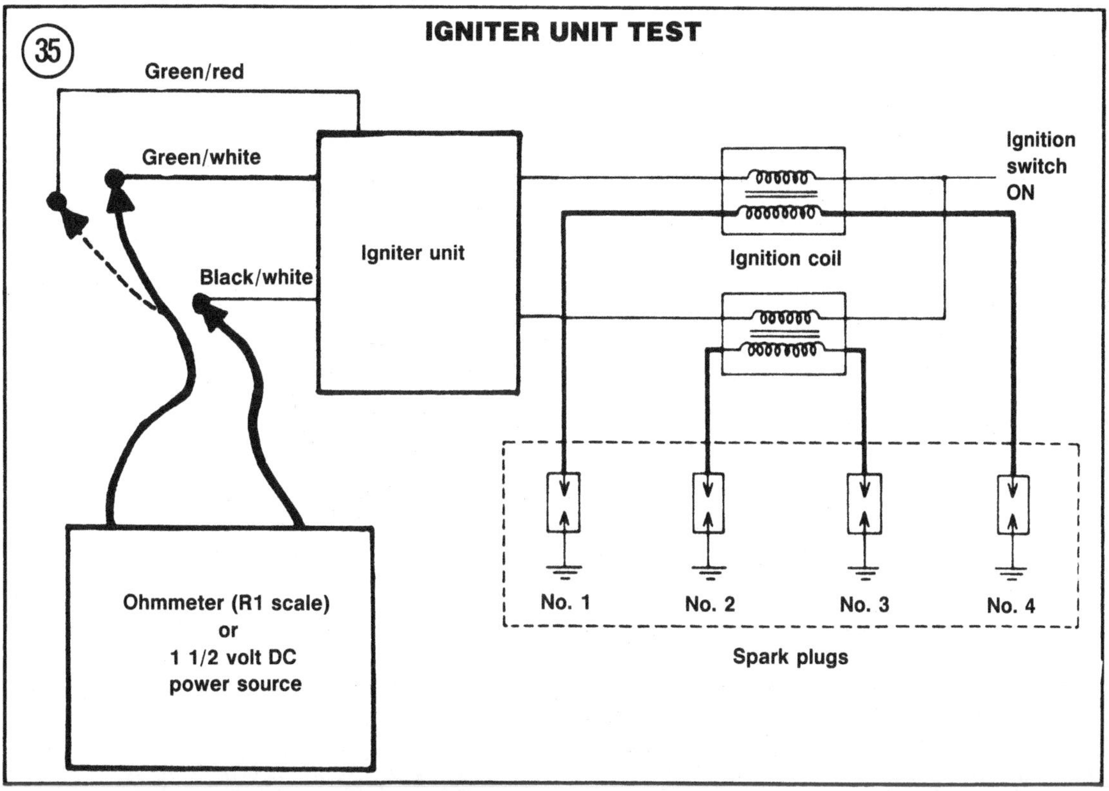

35
IGNITER UNIT TEST
Green/red
Green/white
Black/white
Igniter unit
Ignition switch ON
Ignition coil
Ohmmeter (R1 scale) or 1 1/2 volt DC power source
No. 1
No. 2
No. 3
No. 4
Spark plugs

36
IGNITER

38

37
SUZUKI

39

7

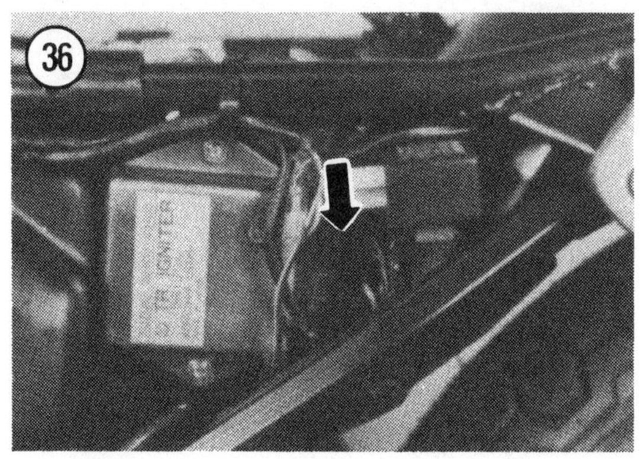

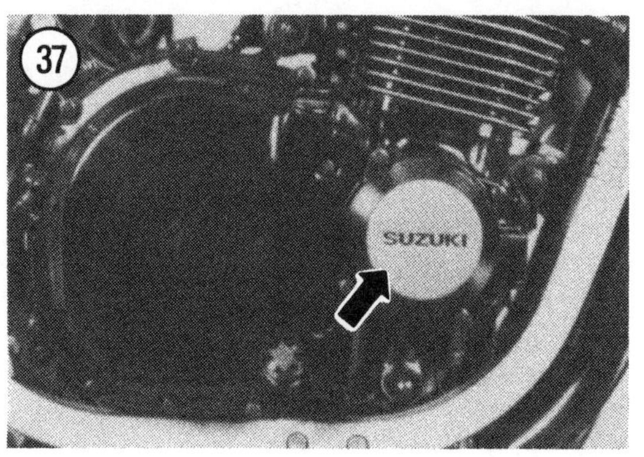

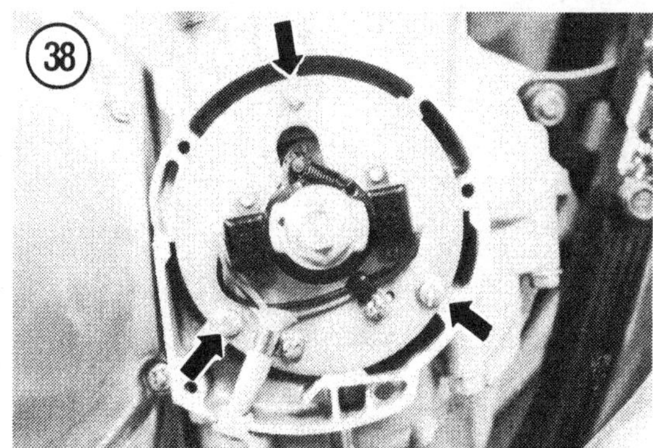

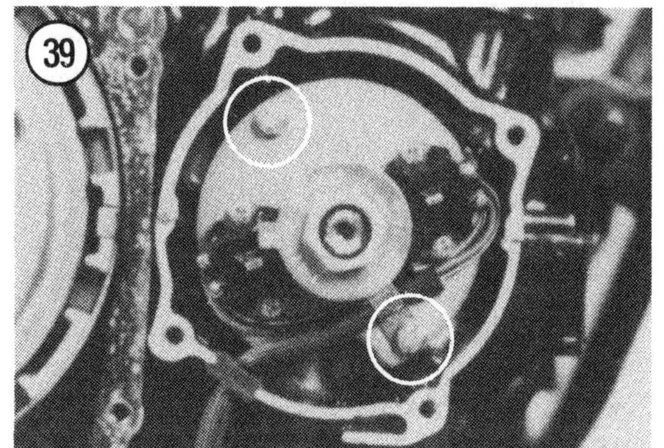

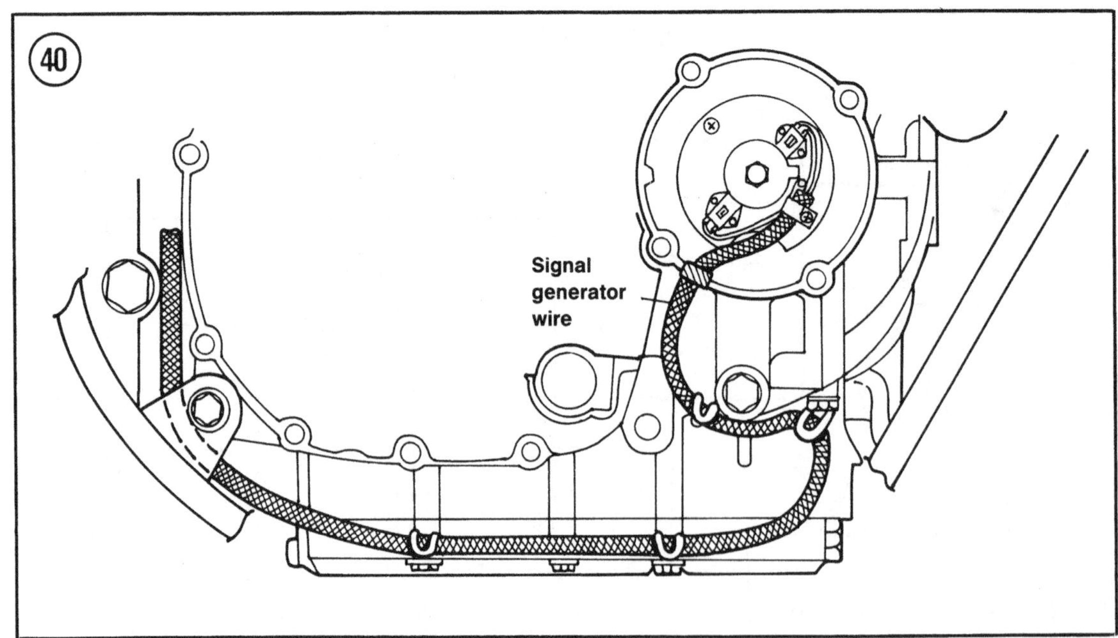

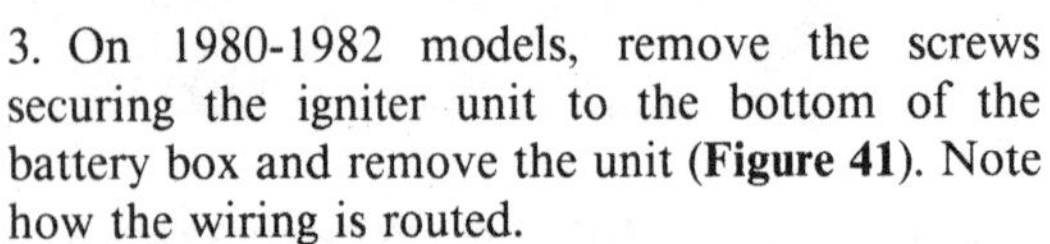
3. On 1980-1982 models, remove the screws securing the igniter unit to the bottom of the battery box and remove the unit (**Figure 41**). Note how the wiring is routed.

4. On TSCC models, remove the screws securing the unit to the frame and remove the unit (**Figure 42**).

5. Installation is the reverse of these steps. Make sure the wires are tightly connected and the wiring is routed as noted during removal.

LIGHTING SYSTEM

The lighting system consists of the headlamp (with 2 filaments for high-beam and low-beam operation), the taillamp, stoplamp, directional signals, warning lamps and indicator lamps. **Table 2** lists replacement bulbs for all lighting system applications.

Headlamp Bulb Replacement

The headlight unit on 1980 LT models and all 1981 and later models is a halogen type bulb (**Figure 43**). Earlier models are fitted with a single sealed-beam headlamp unit. Headlights which have just burned out can be very hot.

CAUTION
Use a clean rag when removing and installing a halogen bulb to avoid getting oils from your skin on the bulb. Oil will cause hot spots which lead to early bulb failure.

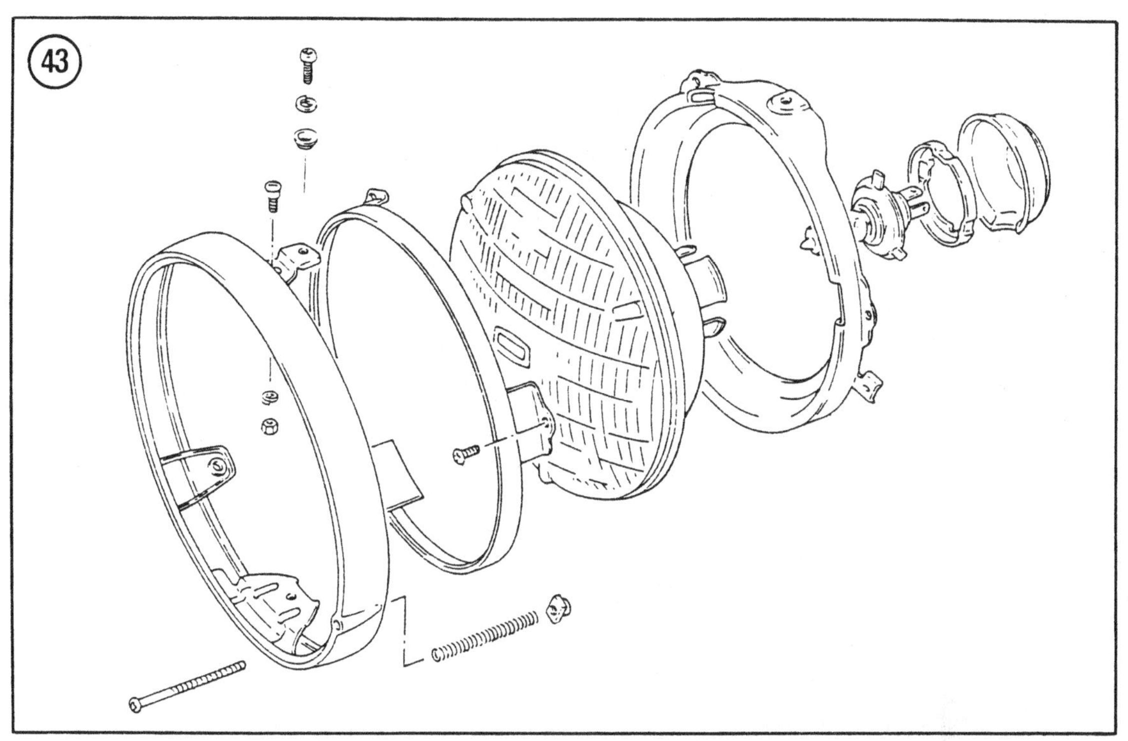

1. On models equipped with fairings, perform the following:
   a. Refer to Chapter Nine and remove the fairing.
   b. Remove the bolts securing the headlamp unit and remove the unit from the mounting brackets (**Figure 44**).
2. On round headlamp models, remove the screws securing the headlamp rim to the lamp housing and carefully remove the rim (**Figure 45**).
3. Unplug the connector from the rear of the headlamp (**Figure 46**).
4. On sealed beam models, remove the clips securing the lamp unit to the rim and remove the lamp (**Figure 47**).

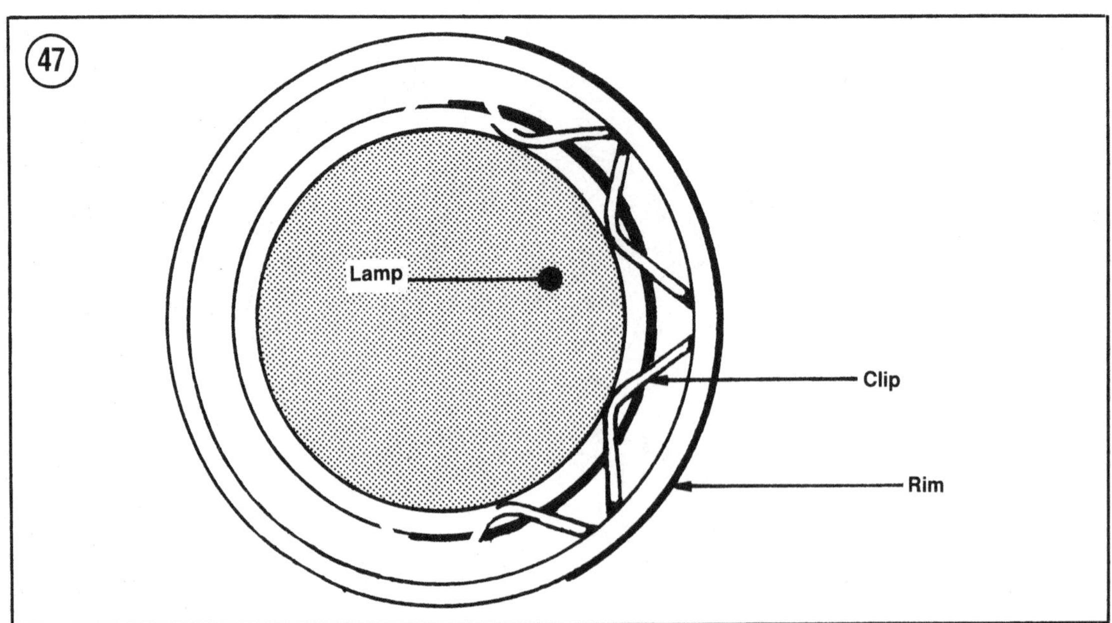

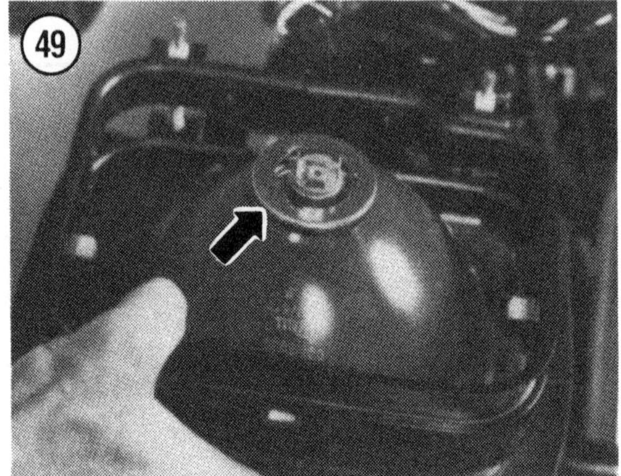

5. On halogen bulb models, perform the following:
   a. Remove the rubber boot (**Figure 48**).
   b. Carefully turn and remove the bulb retaining ring (**Figure 49**).
   c. Carefully lift out the halogen bulb. Do not touch the glass on the bulb during installation (**Figure 50**).
6. Installation is the reverse of these steps. Adjust the headlamp as described in this chapter.

Headlamp Adjustment

Adjust the headlamp beam horizontally and vertically according to the motor vehicle regulations in your area.

1. On round headlamp models:
   a. To adjust the beam horizontally, rotate the adjusting screw (**Figure 51**).

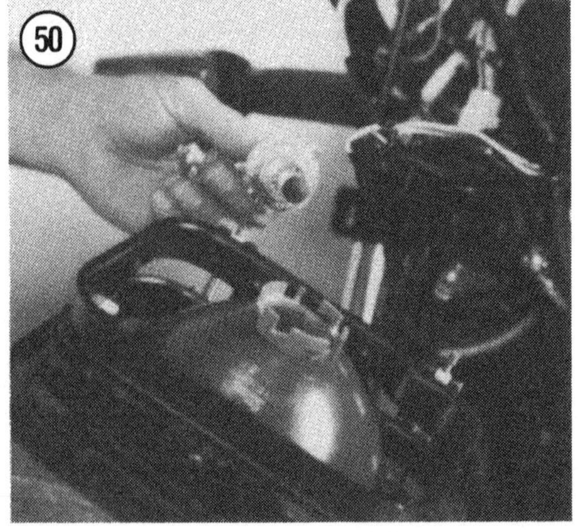

51

55

52

56

53

54

b. To adjust the beam vertically, loosen the headlamp mounting bolts on both sides and move the headlamp body up or down as required (**Figure 52**). Tighten the mounting bolts.

2. On square headlamp models:
   a. To adjust the beam horizontally, rotate the knobs on the adjusting screws as required (**Figure 53**).
   b. To adjust the beam vertically, loosen the headlamp mounting screws on both sides and move the headlamp up or down as required (**Figure 54**). Tighten the mounting screws.

Turn Signal Relay Removal/Installation

1. Remove the left-hand side cover.
2. Slide the relay out of the frame clip. See **Figure 55** or **Figure 56**.
3. Disconnect the wires from the relay and remove the relay.
4. Installation is the reverse of these steps.

57

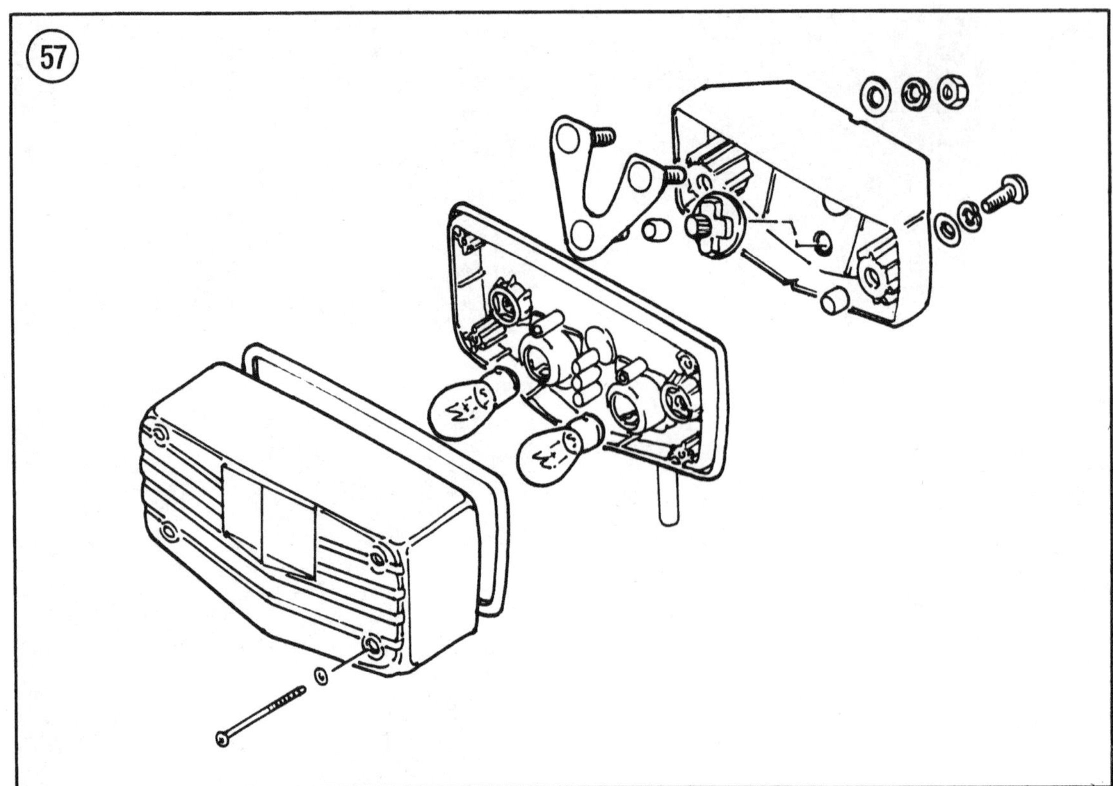

Taillamp, Stoplamp, and License Plate Bulb Replacement

Refer to **Figure 57** for this procedure.

A single large bulb functions as a taillamp and stoplamp while a smaller bulb functions as the license plate illumination lamp.

To replace a defective bulb, remove the screws securing the lens and remove the lens. Replace the bulb and install the lens. Make sure the gasket behind the lens is properly positioned. Do not overtighten the lens screws or the lens may crack.

Directional Lamp Bulb Replacement

Refer to **Figure 58** for this procedure.

To replace any of the 4 directional signal lamps, remove the screws securing the lens and remove the lens. Make sure the gasket behind the lens is properly positioned and install the lens. Do not overtighten the lens screws or the lens may crack.

Front Stoplamp Switch Removal/Installation

The front stoplamp switch is actuated by the front brake lever.

1. Remove the 2 screws securing the switch cover to the brake lever assembly (**Figure 59**).
2. Carefully lift off the switch housing. Do not lose the spring-loaded switch contact in the switch body. Replace the brass switch contact if worn.
3. Installation is the reverse of these steps. Make sure the small spring is installed beneath the brass contact (**Figure 60**). The holes in the switch cover are slightly elongated to allow for adjustment.

Rear Stoplamp Switch Removal/Installation/Adjustment

Refer to **Figure 61** for 1982 and earlier models and **Figure 62** for TSCC models.

1. Disconnect the return spring from the switch plunger.
2. Pull back the rubber boot and disconnect the switch wires.
3. Remove the locknut securing the switch to the frame and remove the switch.
4. Installation is the reverse of these steps. Adjust the switch locknuts so that the stoplamp comes on when the brake pedal is pressed approximately 12 mm (1/2 in.).

INSTRUMENTS

All models are fitted with an instrument cluster which includes a tachometer, speedometer, gear position indicator lights and warning lights.

58

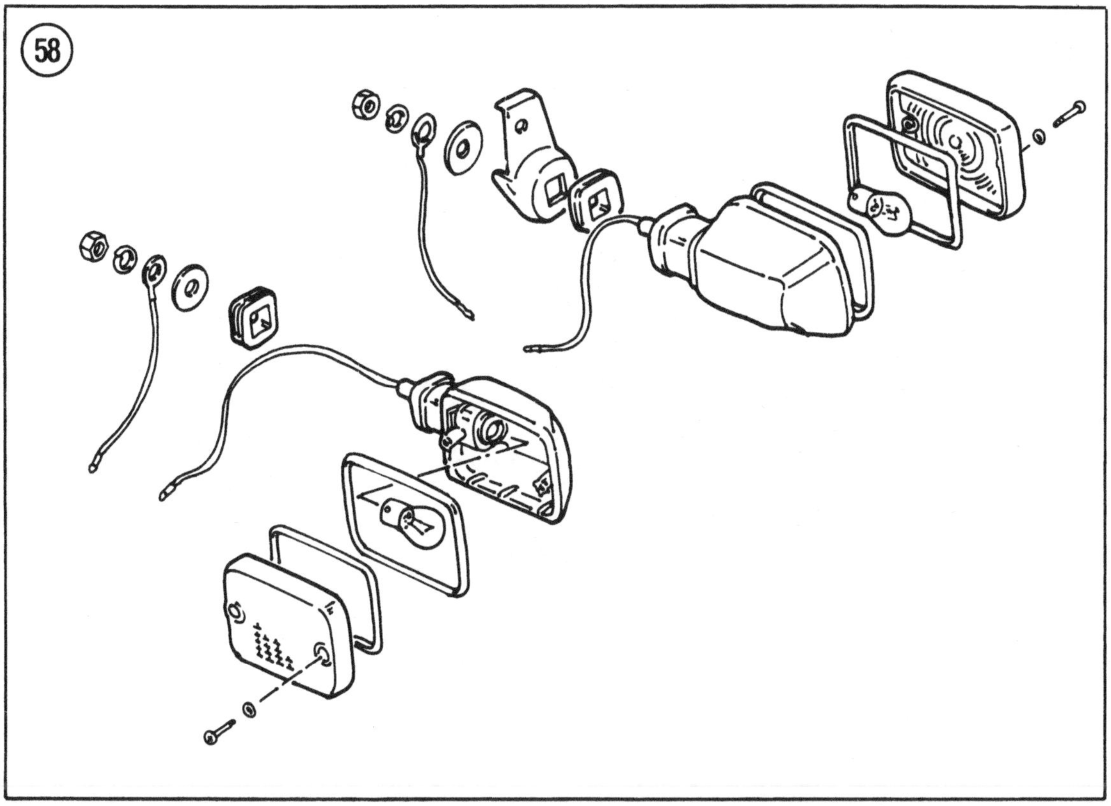

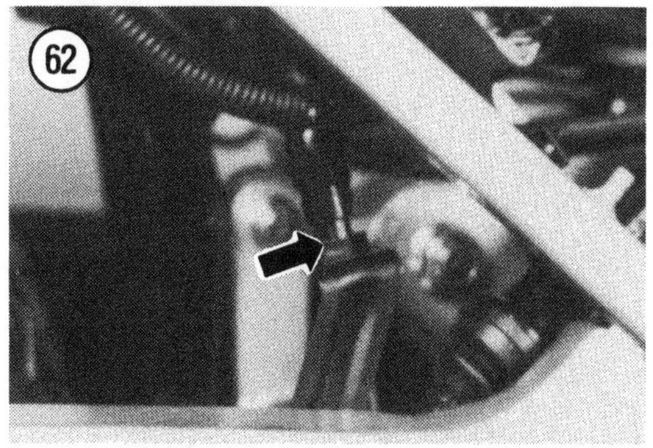

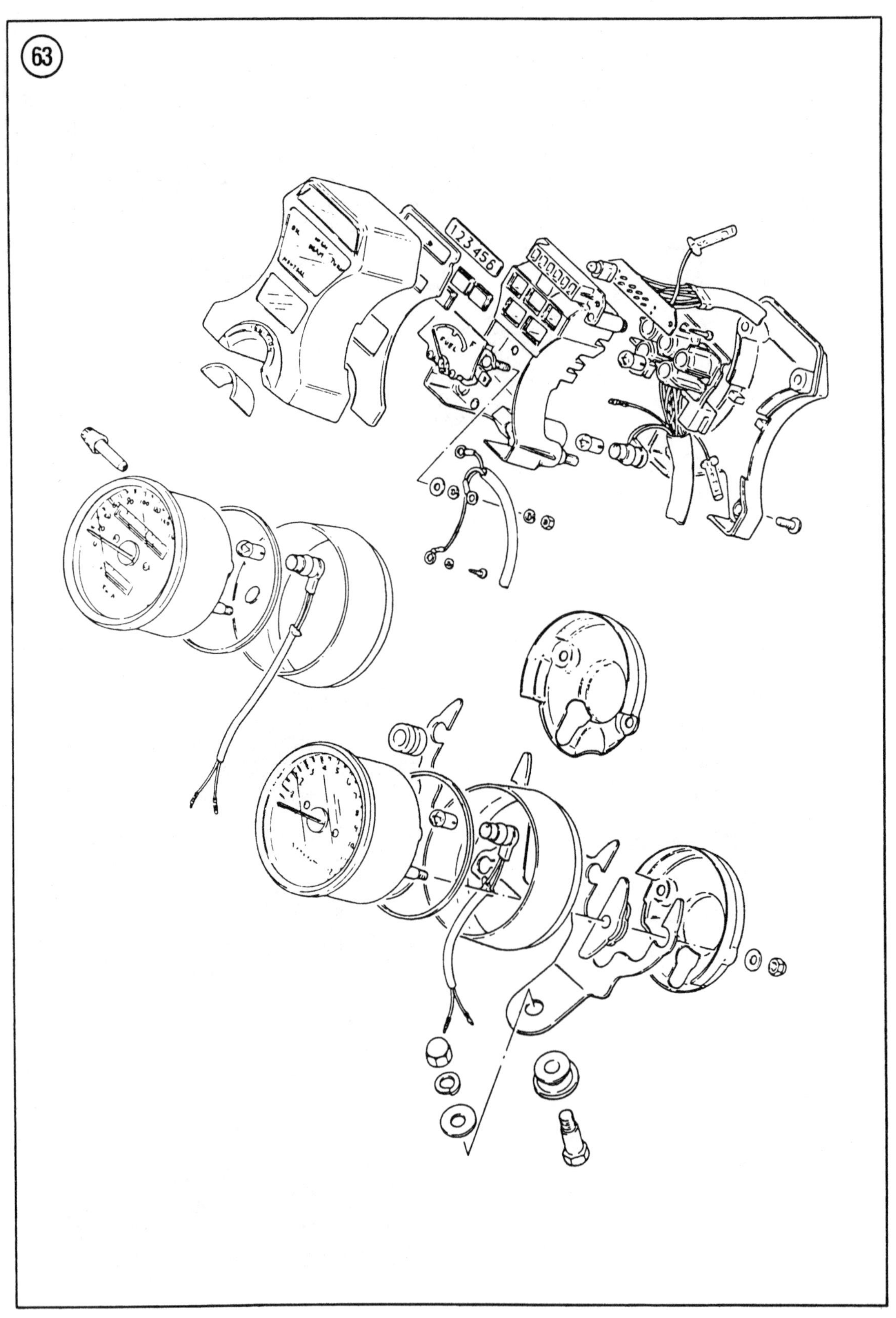
63
123456
FUEL

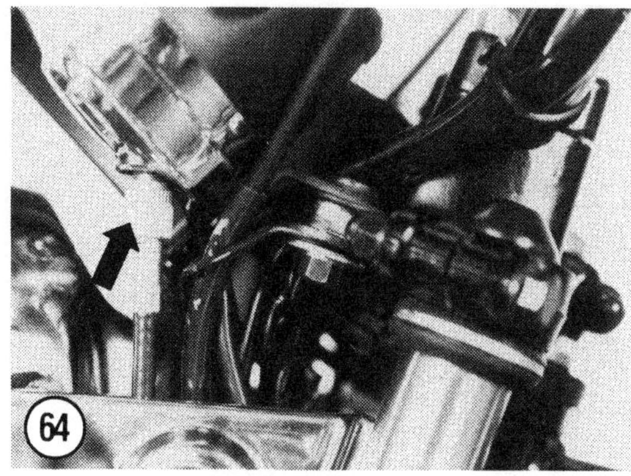

Instrument Cluster
Removal/Installation
(Except Fairing Equipped Models)

Refer to **Figure 63** for this procedure.

1. Refer to Chapter Six and remove the fuel tank to protect the tank from possible damage.
2. Remove the headlamp as described in this chapter.
3. Disconnect the instrument assembly wiring connectors located inside the headlamp housing.
4. Disconnect the speedometer and tachometer cables (**Figure 64**).
5. Remove the bolts securing the instrument cluster to the mounting bracket (**Figure 65**). Carefully note the location of the rubber washers, grommets and cable straps. Remove the instrument cluster.
6. Installation is the reverse of these steps. Make sure all wiring connectors and cables are properly connected.

Instrument Cluster
Disassembly/Assembly
(Except Fairing Equipped Models)

Refer to **Figure 63** for this procedure.

1. Remove the instrument cluster as described in this chapter.
2. Remove the screws securing the rear cover on the center instrument cluster and remove the cover.
3. Remove the nuts securing the mounting bracket to the instrument cluster and remove the bracket.

NOTE
*Refer to **Figure 66** and perform continuity tests to isolate a defective indicator bulb or wiring fault.*

4. To replace indicator bulbs in the instrument cluster, carefully pull the rubber bulb holder out of the panel.
5. To replace the fuel gauge, remove the nuts securing the gauge to the instrument panel and carefully lift out the gauge.
6. To gain access to an indicator bulb in the tachometer or speedometer it is necessary to remove the nuts securing the instrument to the mounting bracket and remove the instrument from the housing.

7

Instrument Cluster
Removal/Installation
(Fairing Equipped Models)

Refer to **Figure 67** for this procedure.

1. Remove the fairing as outlined in Chapter Nine.
2. Remove the headlamp unit as described in this chapter.

NOTE
*If only instrument bulb replacement is desired, it is not necessary to remove the headlamp unit or the instrument cluster. Refer to **Instrument Cluster Disassembly**.*

3. Disconnect the tachometer and speedometer cables (**Figure 68**).
4. Disconnect the wiring connectors from the instrument cluster (**Figure 69**).
5. Remove the bolts securing the instrument cluster to steering stem and remove the cluster (**Figure 70**).
6. Installation is the reverse of these step. Make sure all wiring connectors and properly connected.

Instrument Cluster
Disassembly/Assembly
(Fairing Equipped Models)

Refer to **Figure 67** for this procedure.

NOTE
If only bulb replacement is desired, it is not necessary to remove the instrument cluster.

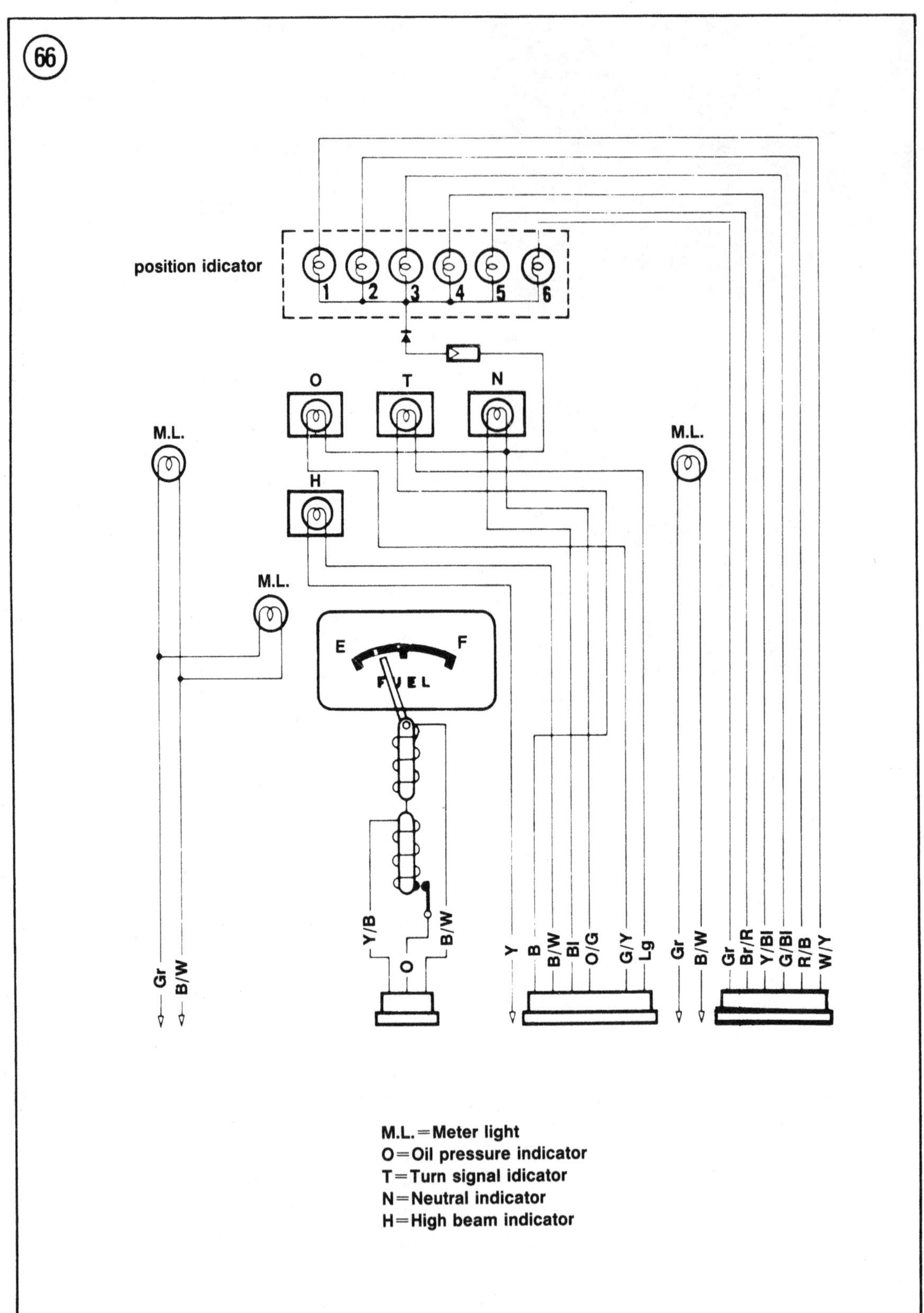
66
position idicator
1
2
3
4
5
6
O
T
N
M.L.
M.L.
H
M.L.
E
F
FUEL
Y/B
O
B/W
Gr
B/W
Y
B
B/W
Bl
O/G
G/Y
Lg
Gr
B/W
Gr
Br/R
Y/Bl
G/Bl
R/B
W/Y
M.L.=Meter light
O=Oil pressure indicator
T=Turn signal indicator
N=Neutral indicator
H=High beam indicator

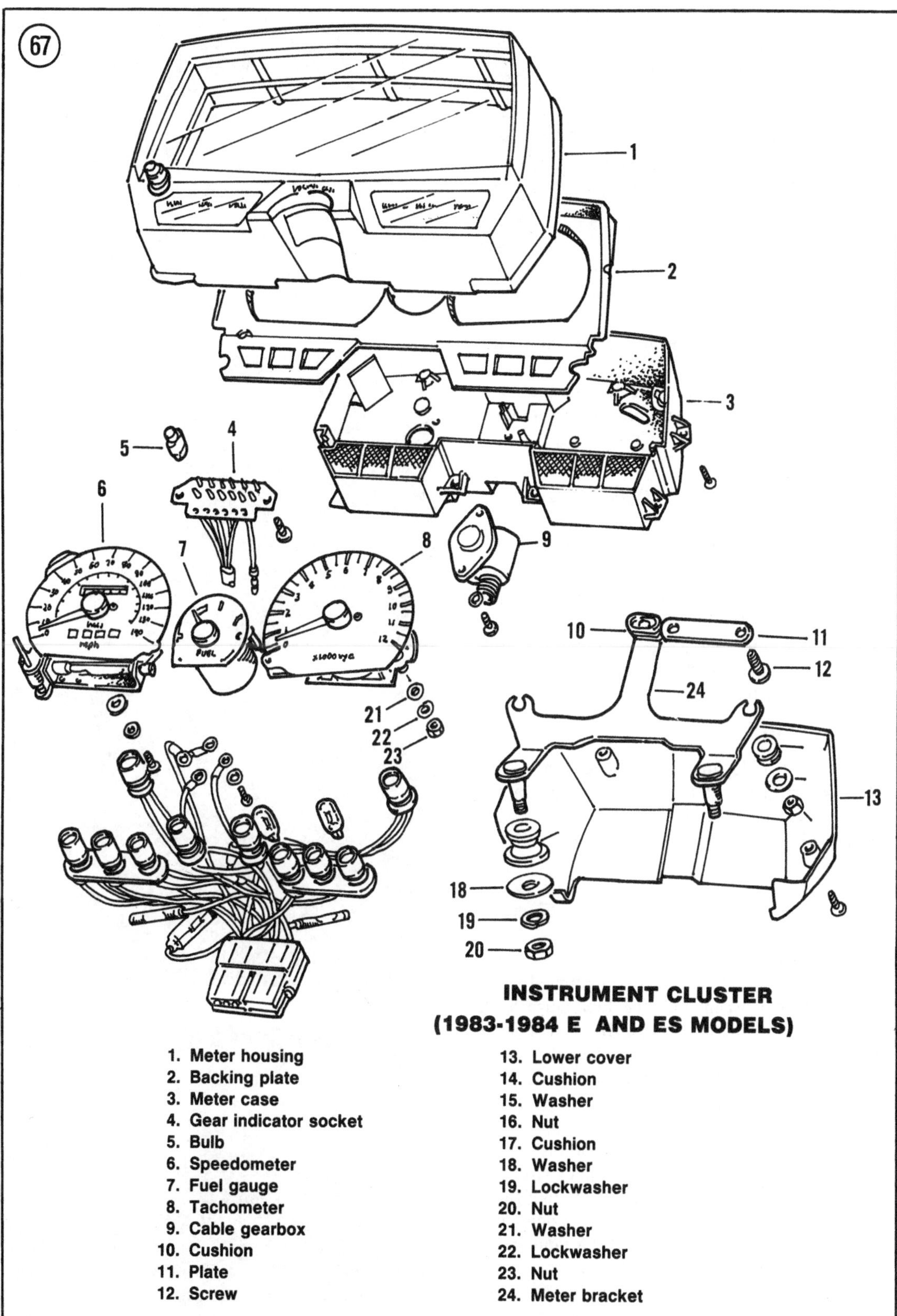

INSTRUMENT CLUSTER (1983-1984 E AND ES MODELS)

1. Meter housing
2. Backing plate
3. Meter case
4. Gear indicator socket
5. Bulb
6. Speedometer
7. Fuel gauge
8. Tachometer
9. Cable gearbox
10. Cushion
11. Plate
12. Screw
13. Lower cover
14. Cushion
15. Washer
16. Nut
17. Cushion
18. Washer
19. Lockwasher
20. Nut
21. Washer
22. Lockwasher
23. Nut
24. Meter bracket

7

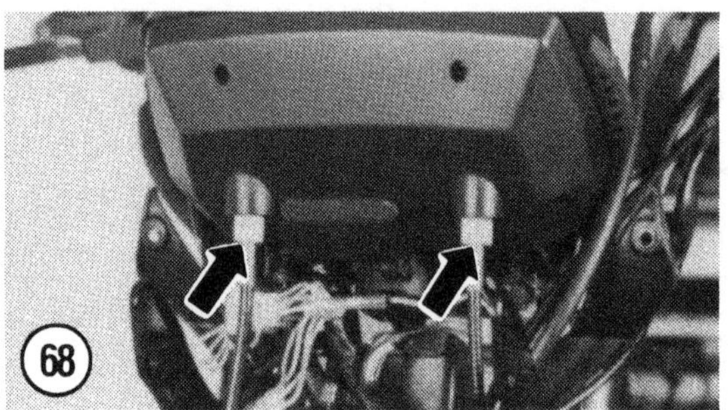

1. Remove the instrument cluster as described in this chapter.
2. Remove the screws securing the rear cover and remove the cover (**Figure 71**).
3. Remove the nuts securing the mounting bracket to the instrument cluster and remove the bracket (**Figure 72**).

NOTE
*Refer to **Figure 73** or **Figure 74** and perform continuity tests to isolate a defective indicator bulb or wiring fault.*

4. To replace indicator bulbs in the instrument cluster, carefully pull the rubber bulb holder out of the panel (**Figure 75**).
5. To replace the fuel gauge, remove the nuts securing the gauge to the instrument panel and carefully lift out the gauge.

Fuel Gauge Test

Perform the following test to determine if the fuel tank sending unit or the fuel gauge in the instrument cluster is defective.

Refer to **Figure 76** for this procedure.

1. Remove the side covers.
2. Disconnect the fuel tank sending unit wires near the edge of the air box and fuel tank. See **Figure 77** or **Figure 78**.
3. Turn *on* the motorcycle ignition.
4. Use a jumper wire such as a straightened paper clip and short between both the fuel gauge leads (not the tank sending unit leads). If the fuel gauge needle fails to move, the gauge unit or the wiring harness is defective. If the fuel gauge needle does move, the tank sending unit or the wiring harness is defective.
5. To determine if the fuel gauge or the wiring harness is defective, use the jumper wire and ground the yellow/black fuel lead. If the fuel gauge needle does not move, the gauge unit is defective. Extreme needle movement indicates a fault in the wiring or the connectors.
6. To determine if the tank sending unit or the wiring harness is defective, use an accurate

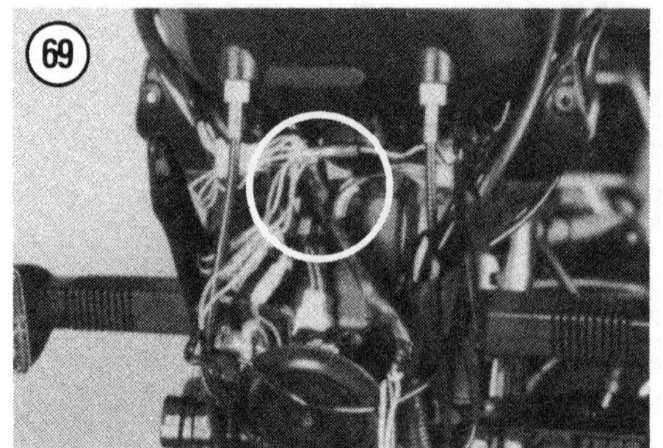

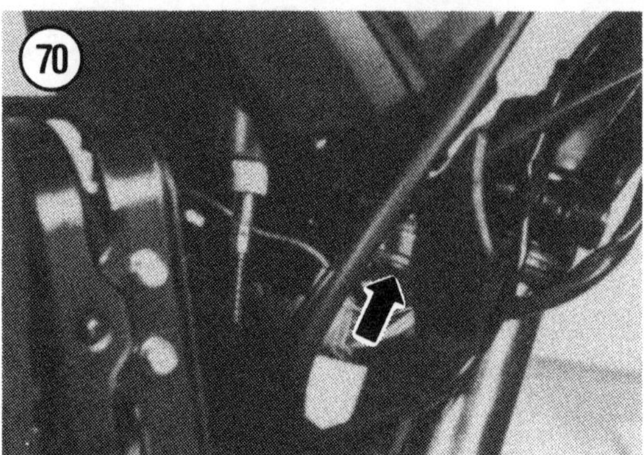

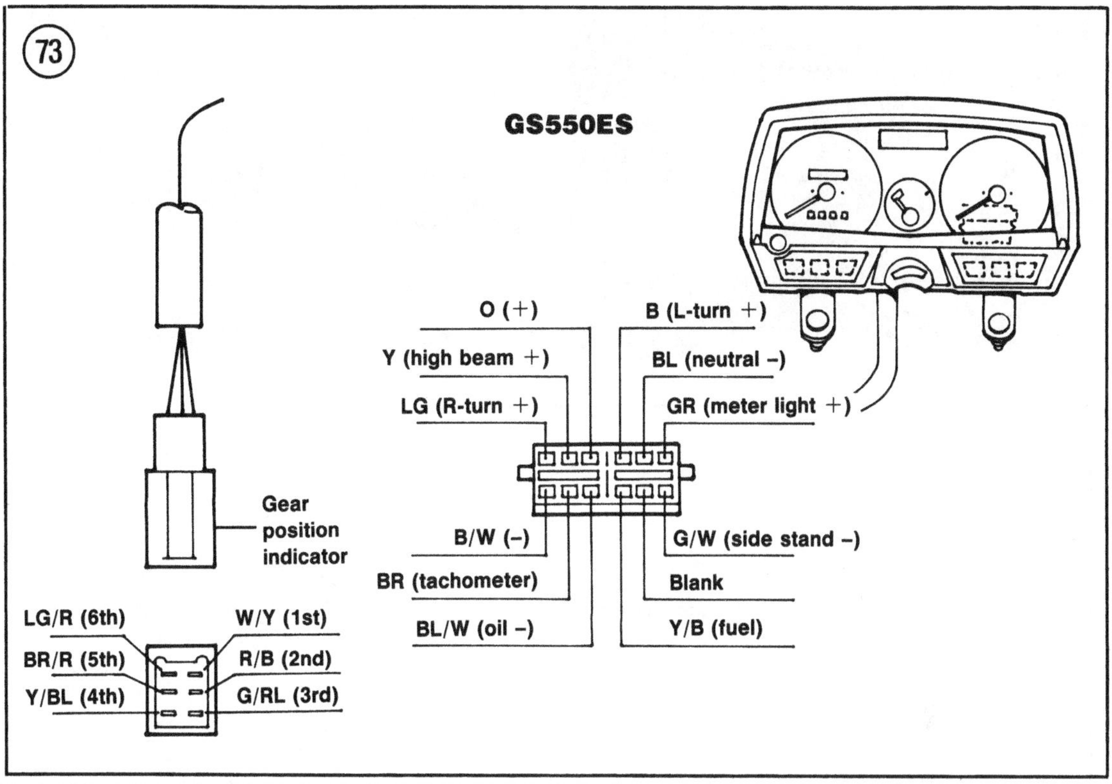

73

GS550ES

O (+)
Y (high beam +)
LG (R-turn +)
B (L-turn +)
BL (neutral –)
GR (meter light +)
B/W (–)
BR (tachometer)
BL/W (oil –)
G/W (side stand –)
Blank
Y/B (fuel)

Gear position indicator

LG/R (6th)
BR/R (5th)
Y/BL (4th)
W/Y (1st)
R/B (2nd)
G/RL (3rd)

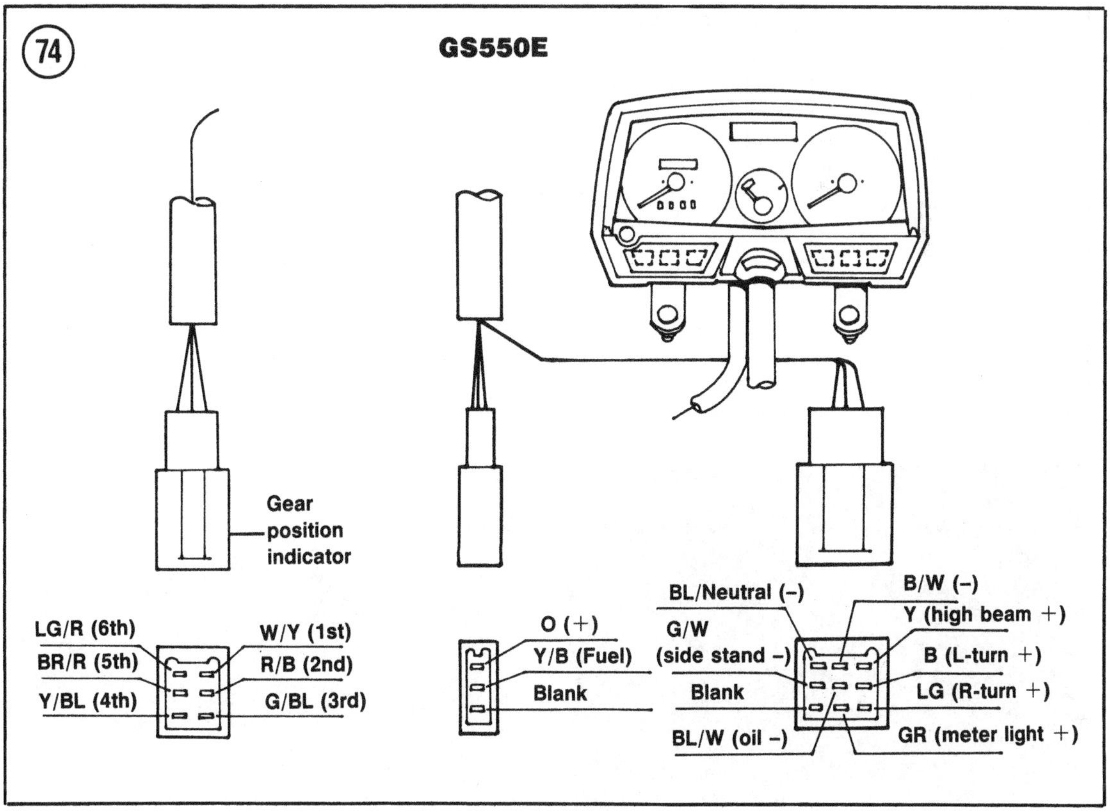

74

GS550E

Gear position indicator

LG/R (6th)
BR/R (5th)
Y/BL (4th)
W/Y (1st)
R/B (2nd)
G/BL (3rd)

O (+)
Y/B (Fuel)
Blank

BL/Neutral (–)
G/W
(side stand –)
Blank
BL/W (oil –)
B/W (–)
Y (high beam +)
B (L-turn +)
LG (R-turn +)
GR (meter light +)

7

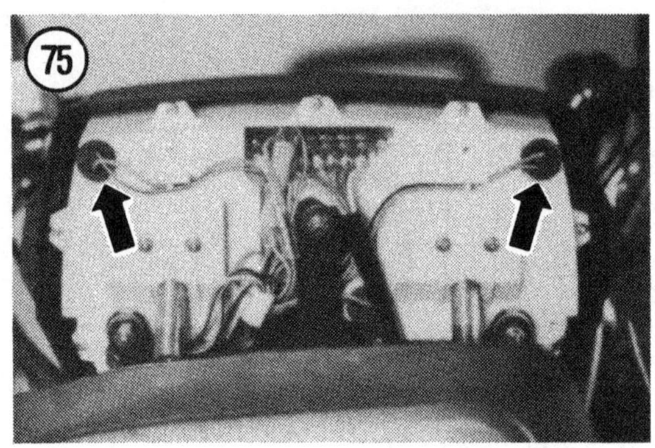

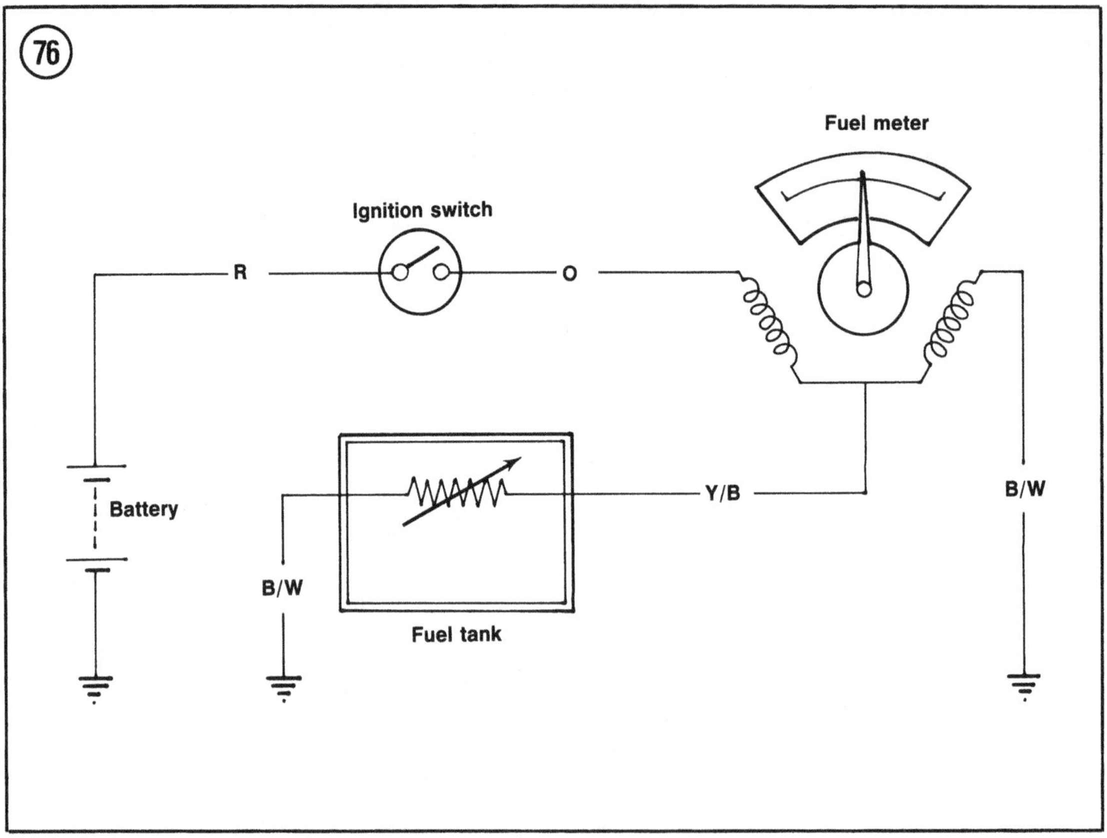

76

Fuel meter

Ignition switch

R

O

Battery

Y/B

B/W

B/W

Fuel tank

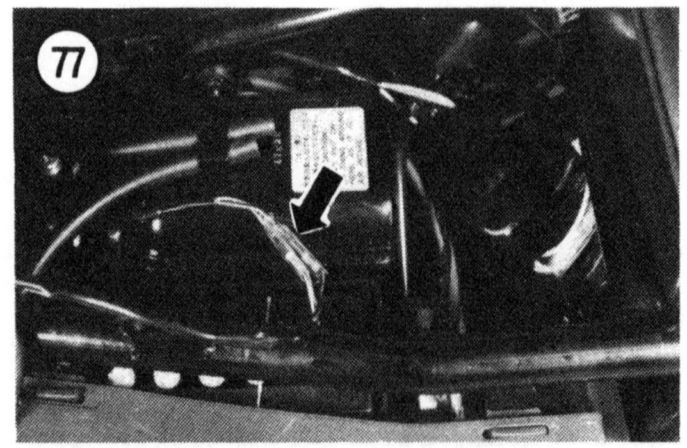

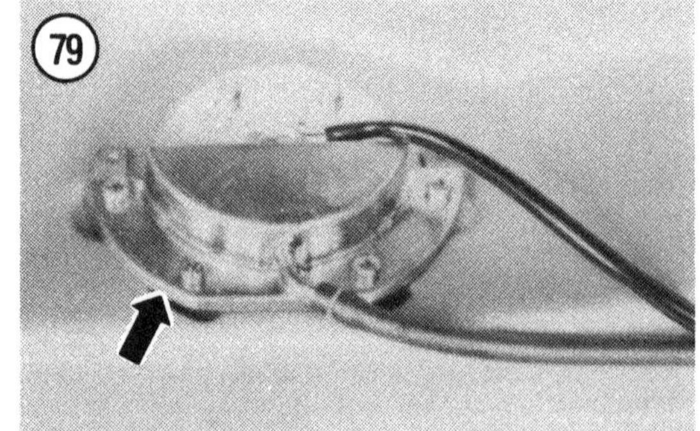

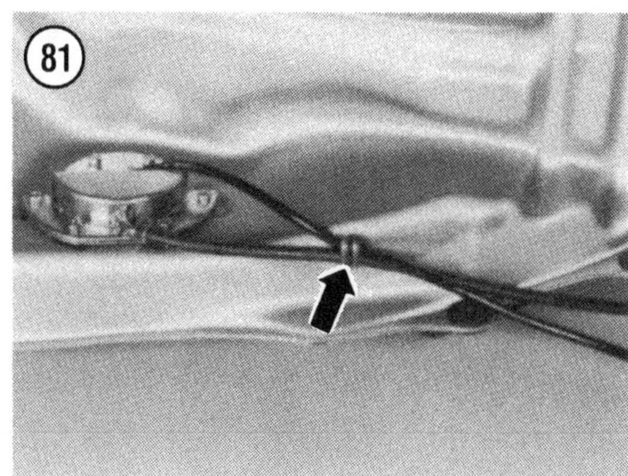

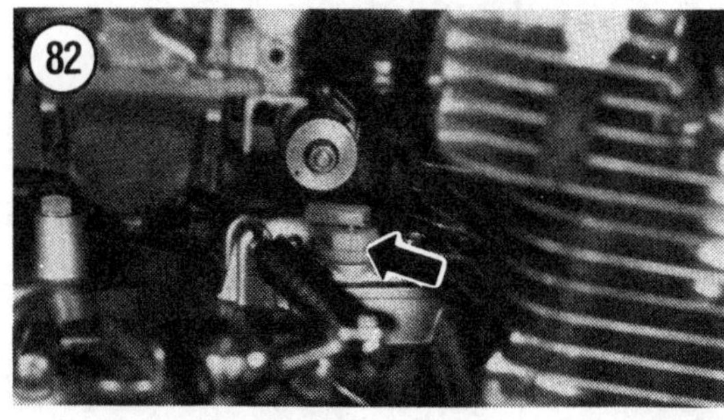

ohmmeter and measure the resistance between the tank sending unit leads. A large unstable resistance reading indicates a defective sending unit. A normal resistance of approximately 1-120 ohms (depending on the level of fuel in the tank) means the fault lies in the wiring or connectors. A reading of approximately 100-120 ohms is for an empty tank.

Fuel Gauge Unit Removal/Installation

The fuel gauge unit is housed in the instrument cluster. To replace the gauge unit, remove and disassemble the instrument cluster as described in this chapter.

Fuel Tank Sending Unit Removal/Installation

1. Refer to Chapter Six and remove and drain the fuel tank.
2. Turn the fuel tank over and carefully drain any remaining gasoline into a suitable container.
3. Remove the screws securing the half-moon shaped fuel drain plate and gasket (**Figure 79**).
4. Remove the bolts securing the sending unit to the fuel tank (**Figure 80**). Carefully remove the sending unit.
5. Installation is the reverse of these steps. Make sure the sending unit gasket is in good condition and properly positioned before installing the sending unit. Secure the hose from the fuel drain plate and the sending unit wires as shown in **Figure 81**.

Oil Pressure Sending Unit Removal/Installation (1982 and Earlier Models)

1. Disconnect the wire from the sending unit (**Figure 82**).
2. Remove the bolts securing the sending unit and remove the unit.
3. Installation is the reverse of these steps. Make sure the gasket is in good condition and installed properly.

Oil Pressure Sending Unit Removal/Installation (TSCC Models)

1. On LD models, remove the screws securing the sending unit cover and remove the cover (**Figure 83**).
2. Loosen the screw securing the wire to the sending unit and remove the wire. See **Figure 84** for LD models and **Figure 85** for E and ES models.
3. Use a socket to remove carefully the sending unit.

84

4. Installation is the reverse of these steps. Apply a light film of Suzuki Bond No. 1215 or equivalent to the threads of the oil pressure sending unit to prevent oil leakage. Torque the sending unit to 1.3-1.7 mkg (9.5-12.5 ft.-lb.).

Side Stand Switch Removal/Installation (TSCC Models)

All TSCC models are equipped with a side stand warning circuit to indicate when the side stand is down.

1. Remove the screws securing the switch to the frame. See **Figure 86** for E and ES models and **Figure 87** for LD models.
2. Disconnect the wiring connector and remove the switch.
3. Installation is the reverse of these steps.

FUSES

All 1978 and earlier models are fitted with a single main fuse (**Figure 88**). Later models are fitted with a fuse panel. See **Figure 89** for 1979-1982 models and **Figure 90** for 1983 and later models.

Remove the right-hand side cover to gain access to the main fuse panel. If any fuse blows, find out the reason for the failure before replacing it. Usually the trouble is a short circuit in the wiring. This may be caused by worn-through insulation or a disconnected wire shorting to ground.

CAUTION
Never substitute tinfoil or wire for a fuse. Never use a higher amperage fuse than specified. An overload could result in a fire and the loss of the motorcycle.

85

86

87

HORN

Removal/Installation

1. Disconnect the wires from the horn. See **Figure 91** for a typical horn installation. On fairing equipped models, remove the fairing to gain access to the horn (**Figure 92**).
2. Remove the nut securing the horn to the mounting bracket and remove the horn.
3. Installation is the reverse of these steps. Make sure the rubber bushing is properly located on the horn bracket.

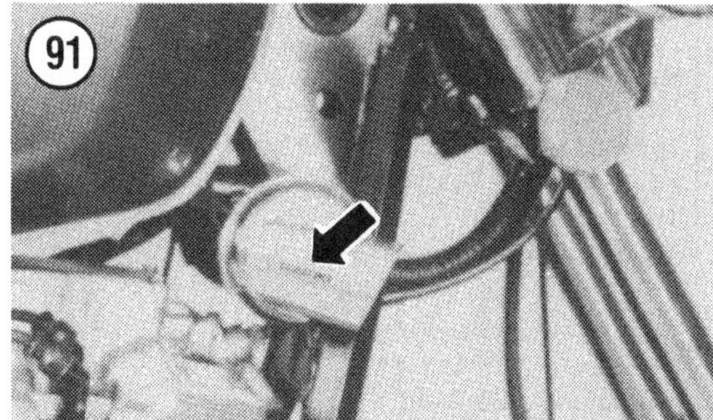

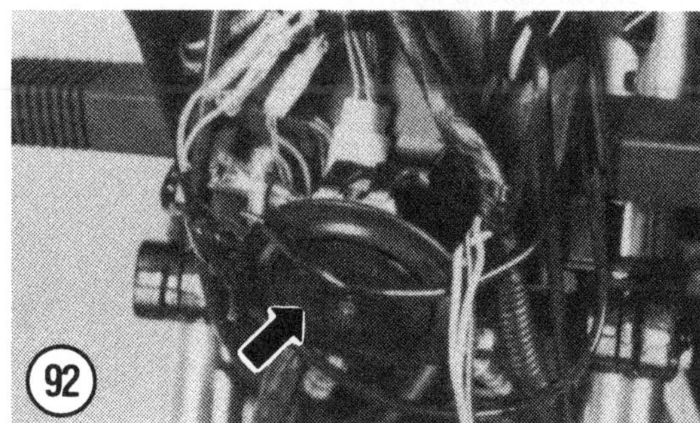

7

Tables are on the following page.

Table 1 STATE OF CHARGE

Specific gravity	State of charge
1.110 - 1.130	Discharged
1.140 - 1.160	Almost discharged
1.170 - 1.190	One-quarter charged
1.200 - 1.220	One-half charged
1.230 - 1.250	Three-quarters charged
1.260 - 1.280	Fully charged

Table 2 REPLACEMENT BULBS

Bulbs	Rating (watts)
Headlamp	
High beam	60
Low beam	55
Taillight/brake light	8/23
Turn signal light	23
Speedometer indicator light	3.4
Tachometer indicator light	3.4
Turn signal indicator light	3.4
High beam indicator light	3.4
Neutral indicator light	3.4
Oil pressure indicator light	3.4
Sidestand check light	3.4
Gear position indicator light	1.4
Fuel gauge light	3.4

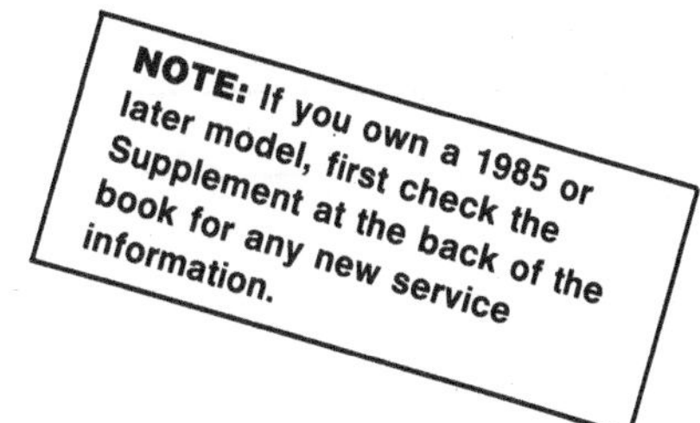
NOTE: If you own a 1985 or later model, first check the Supplement at the back of the book for any new service information.

CHAPTER EIGHT

FRONT SUSPENSION AND STEERING

This chapter includes repair and service procedures for the front wheel, steering components and forks. Front brake repair is outlined in Chapter Ten.

Table 1 and **Table 2** are at the end of the chapter.

FRONT WHEEL

Removal/Installation

1. Place the motorcycle on the centerstad and support the engine so that the front wheel is clear of the ground (**Figure 1**).
2. Unscrew and disconnect the speedometer cable (**Figure 2**).
3. Remove the cotter pin securing the axle nut (**Figure 3**) and loosen the nut. On models with leading axle type forks, loosen the pinch bolt securing the axle (**Figure 4**).
4. On models equipped with dual front disc brakes, remove the bolts securing the right or left brake caliper (**Figure 5**). Carefully remove the caliper.

CAUTION
Suspend the caliper with a heavy cord or wire. Do not allow the caliper to hang by the brake hose or the hose may be damaged.

NOTE
Do not actuate the front brake with a caliper or the front wheel removed or the brake pads will be pushed out of the caliper body. If this should occur, refer to Chapter Ten and compress the pad and piston back into the caliper body.

5. On models with straight leg type front forks, remove the nuts securing the axle holder (**Figure 6**) and remove the holder.
6. Slide out the axle and carefully note the position and location of the spacers to aid reassembly.
7. Carefully disengage the speedometer drive and remove the front wheel.
8. Installation is the reverse of these steps. Keep the following points in mind:
   a. Assemble the axle and wheel components as shown in **Figure 7** or **Figure 8**.
   b. Lift the front wheel into place and install the axle from the left side. Make sure the

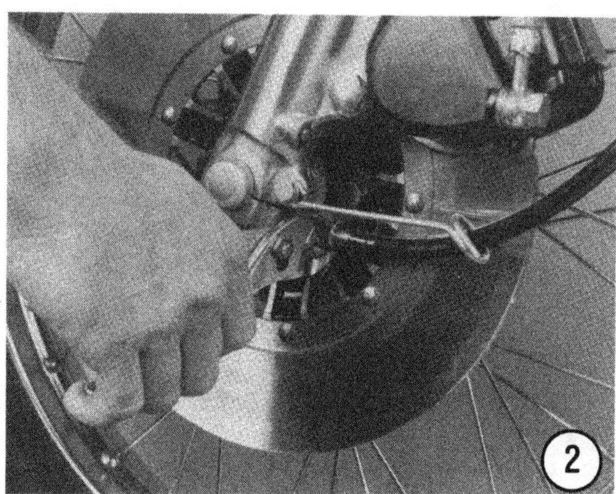
2

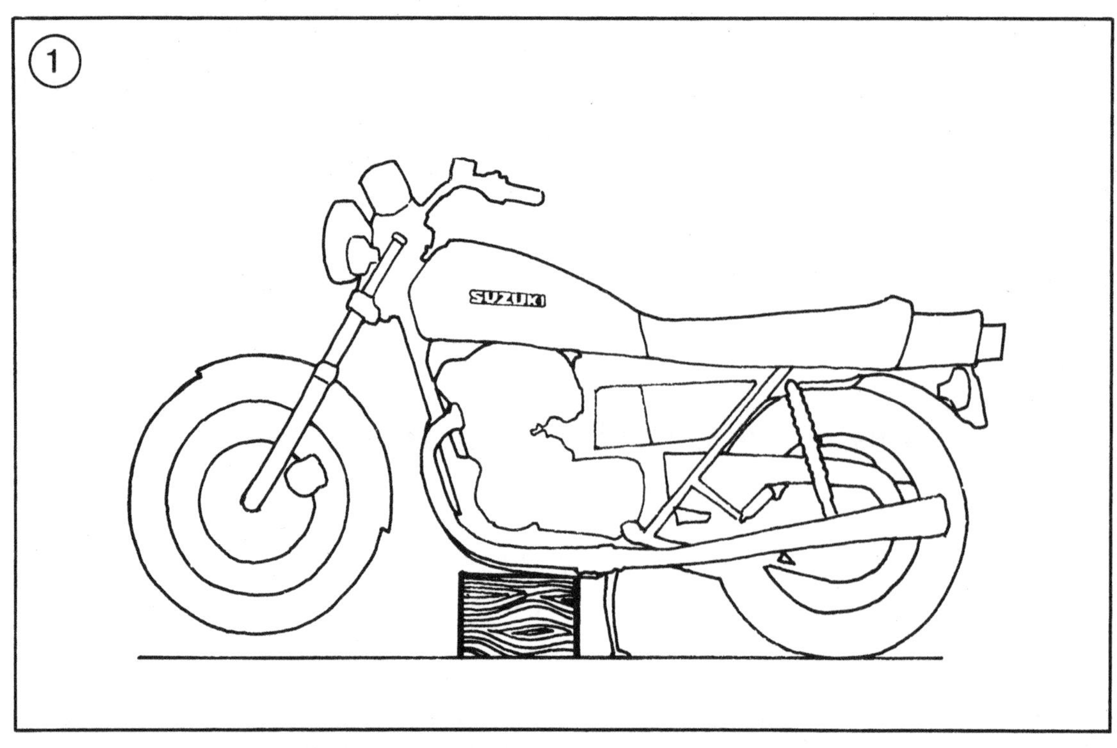
1
SUZUKI

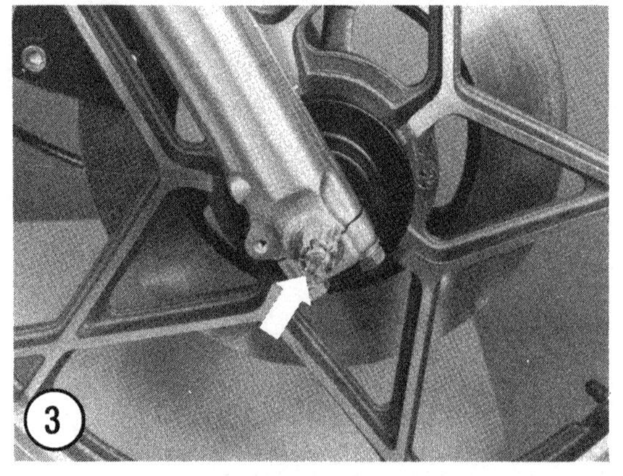
3

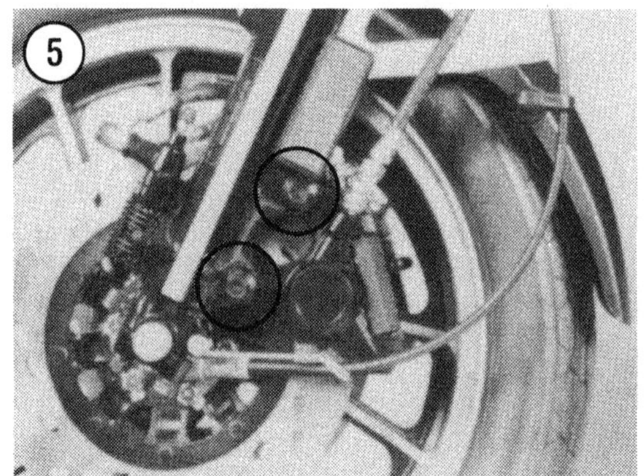
5

4

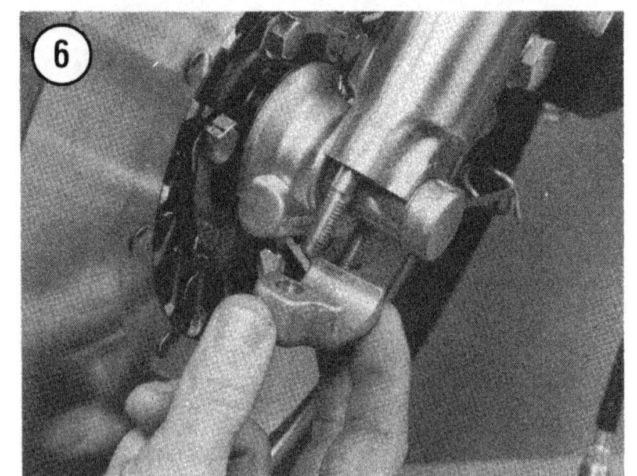
6

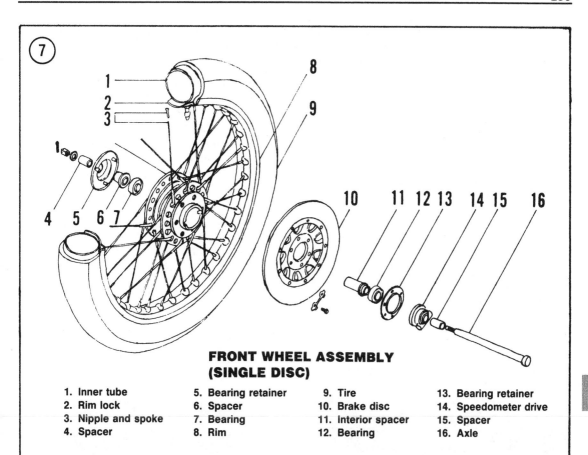

(7)

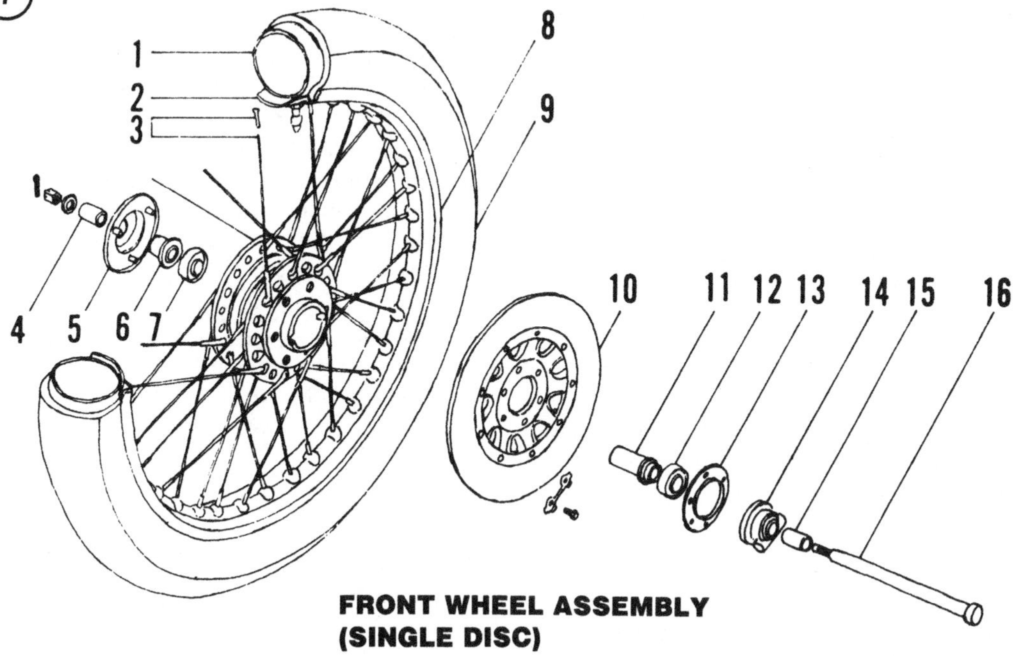

FRONT WHEEL ASSEMBLY (SINGLE DISC)

1. Inner tube
2. Rim lock
3. Nipple and spoke
4. Spacer
5. Bearing retainer
6. Spacer
7. Bearing
8. Rim
9. Tire
10. Brake disc
11. Interior spacer
12. Bearing
13. Bearing retainer
14. Speedometer drive
15. Spacer
16. Axle

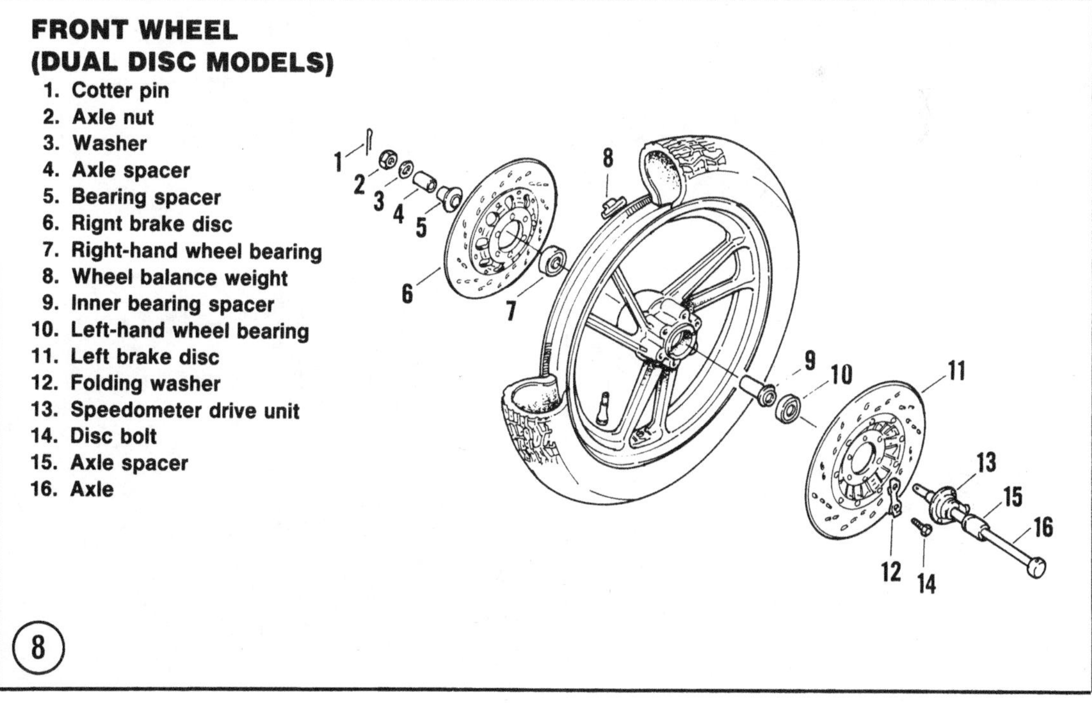

FRONT WHEEL (DUAL DISC MODELS)

1. Cotter pin
2. Axle nut
3. Washer
4. Axle spacer
5. Bearing spacer
6. Rignt brake disc
7. Right-hand wheel bearing
8. Wheel balance weight
9. Inner bearing spacer
10. Left-hand wheel bearing
11. Left brake disc
12. Folding washer
13. Speedometer drive unit
14. Disc bolt
15. Axle spacer
16. Axle

(8)

speedometer drive unit is installed with the ears aligned with the slots in the hub (**Figure 9**). Position the speedometer drive so that the "UP" embossed on the unit is on top as shown in **Figure 10**. Install the axle nut finger-tight.

c. Tighten the axle nut, axle pinch bolt and brake caliper mounting bolts to torque values specified in **Table 1**.

CAUTION

Insert a screwdriver shaft or drift through the hole in the axle shaft head to prevent the axle from turning while tightening the axle nut. If the axle turns, the speedometer drive unit may be damaged.

d. Spin the front wheel several times to make sure the wheel spins freely and the brake pads do not drag.

Disassembly

Refer to **Figure 7** or **Figure 8** for this procedure.

1. If brake disc removal is desired, straighten the locking tabs on the disc mounting bolts (**Figure 11**). Remove the bolts and remove the brake disc.

NOTE

On models fitted with dual disc brakes, each disc is stamped "L" or "R" for the right or left sides.

2. Remove the bearing cover on models so equipped. Tap the bearings out of the hub with a long aluminum or brass drift. Remove the left bearing first. Collect the inner spacer as the bearings are removed.

CAUTION

Do not routinely remove the wheel bearings for inspection or lubrication. The bearings are usually overstressed and/or damaged when removed, therefore it is recommended that used bearings not be re-installed in the wheel hubs.

Inspection

1. Inspect the brake components as described in Chapter Ten.

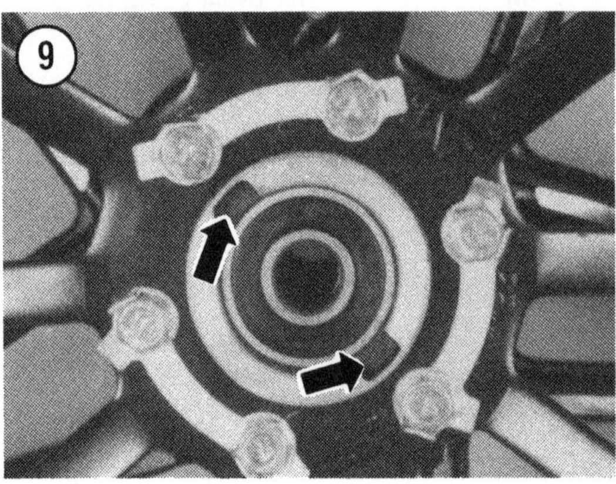

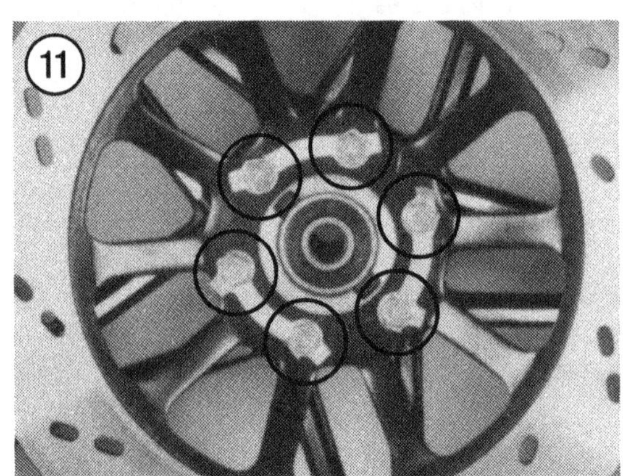

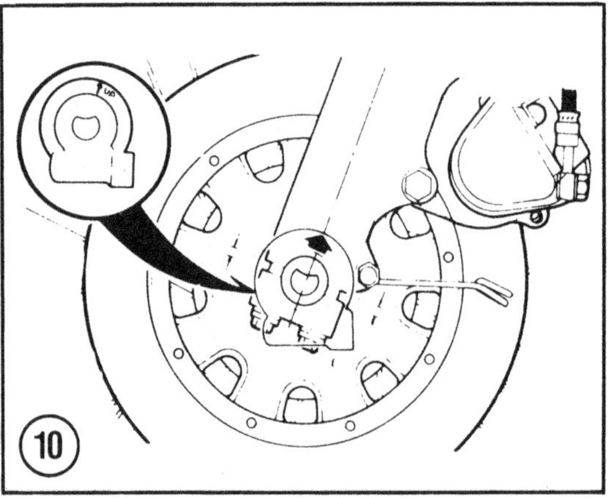

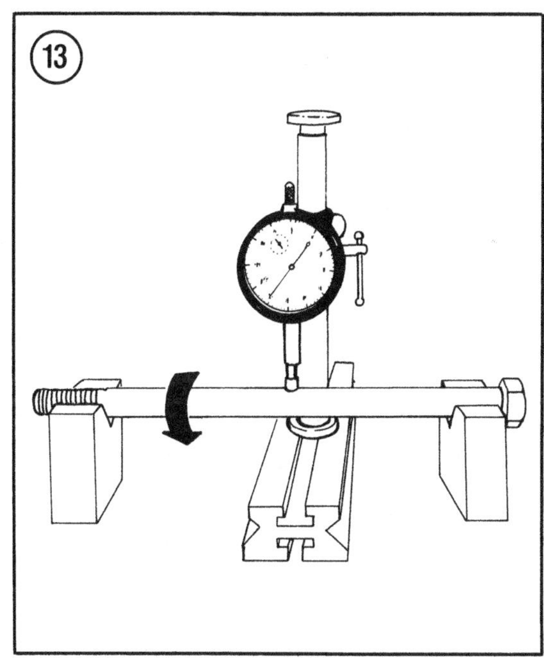

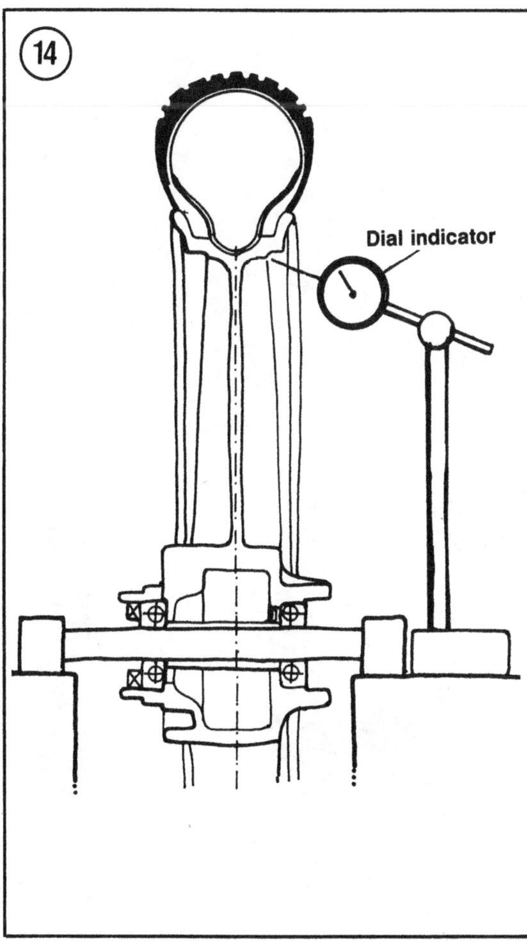

2. Clean the inside and outside of the hub as well as the spacers and axle with solvent.
3. Turn each bearing carefully by hand and check it for smoothness and excessive play (**Figure 12**). The bearings should turn quietly and smoothly with no more than a just perceptible amount of axial play. Replace both bearings as a set if either is unserviceable.
4. Inspect the axle for runout as shown in **Figure 13**. If the runout exceeds 0.25 mm (0.010 in.) the axle must be replaced. Do *not* attempt to straighten a bent axle.
5. Measure the axial and radial runout of the wheel with a dial indicator as shown in **Figure 14**. Maximum runout in either direction is 2.0 mm (0.08 in.).

NOTE

*If a dial indicator is not available, a simple gauge can be improvised as shown in **Figure 15**.*

6. If the runout on a spoke wheel is excessive, refer to *Spoke Wheels* in this chapter and attempt to true the wheel. If the runout on an alloy wheel is excessive, check the wheel bearings and/or replace the wheel. The stock Suzuki alloy wheel cannot be serviced; it must be replaced.

8

Assembly

Refer to **Figure 7** or **Figure 8** for this procedure.
1. Lubricate the inside of each wheel bearing with a good grade of wheel bearing grease. Apply a light film of grease to the outer edge of both wheel bearings.
2. Install the left bearing in the hub with the sealed portion facing out as shown in **Figure 16**. Using a bearing driver or a socket that is only fractionally smaller in diameter than the outer bearing race, carefully tap the bearing into place until the outer race of the bearing is flush with the edge of the wheel hub. Using a proper tool is essential so that the force required to drive the bearing into the hub is applied only to the outer race of the bearing.

CAUTION

If the proper tools for bearing installation are not available, have the task performed by a dealer. Do not risk damage to an expensive wheel hub by using improper tools or techniques.

3. Install the interior spacer through the inside of the hub. The shoulder on the spacer rests against the left side wheel bearing.
4. Carefully install the right bearing in the same manner as the left bearing.

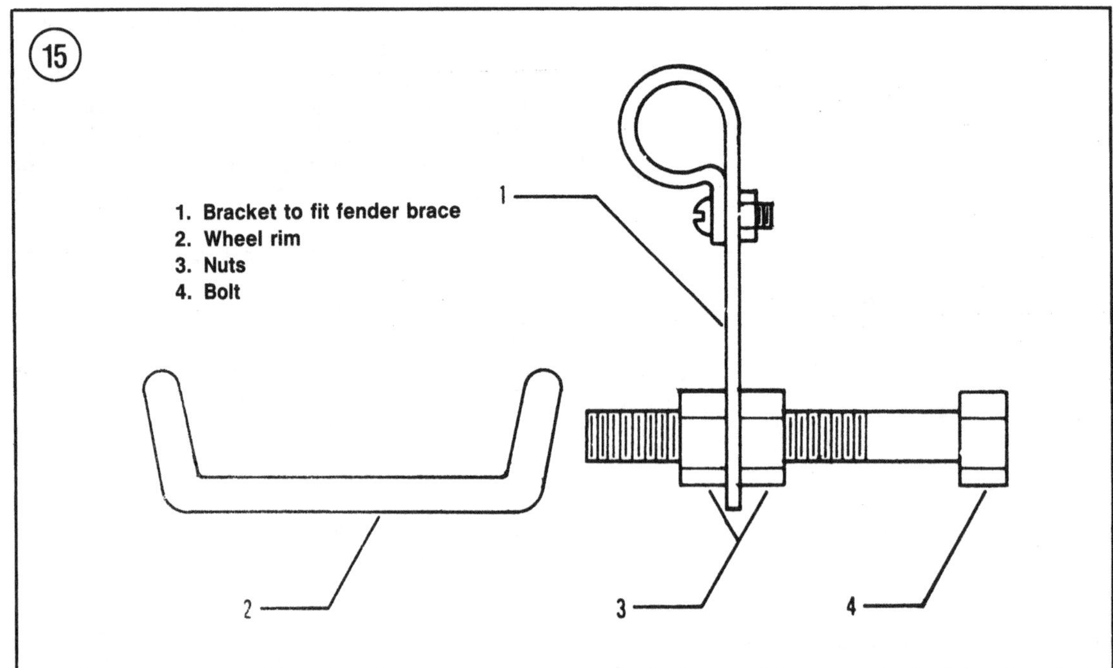

5. Install the brake disc, if removed, and tighten the bolts as specified in **Table 1**. Bend over the locking tabs to secure the bolts (**Figure 11**).

WHEEL BALANCING

An unbalanced wheel can adversely affect the handling of the motorcycle and make the machine very uncomfortable to ride.

Wheels are relatively easy to balance without special equipment. Most dealers or motorcycle accessory shops carry an assortment of balance weights. Weights for spoke wheels can be crimped on the spokes as shown in **Figure 17**. Alloy wheels will accept standard automotive type weights or adhesive weights designed for automobile mag wheels. Buy a couple of each weight available. If the weights are unused they can usually be returned.

Many dealers now have high-speed spin balancing services available. This type of balancing is very fast and accurate. Have your wheels balanced by the high-speed spin method if such services are available.

Before attempting to balance a wheel, make sure the wheel bearings are in good condition and properly lubricated. If the front wheel is to be balanced while still installed on the motorcycle, make sure the brake pads do not drag. A brake that drags will prevent the wheel from turning freely, resulting in an inaccurate wheel balance. The rear wheel must be removed before it can be balanced.

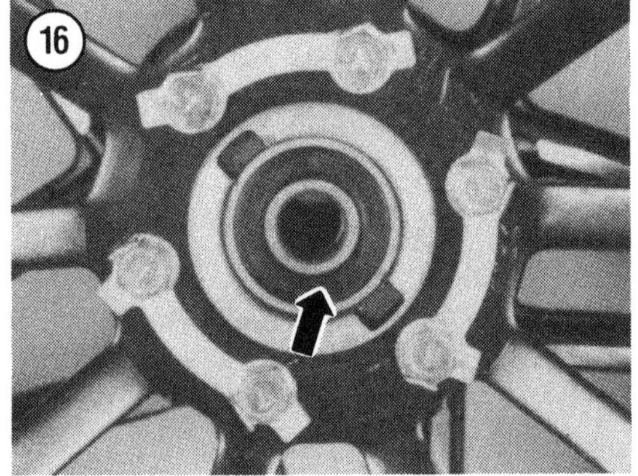

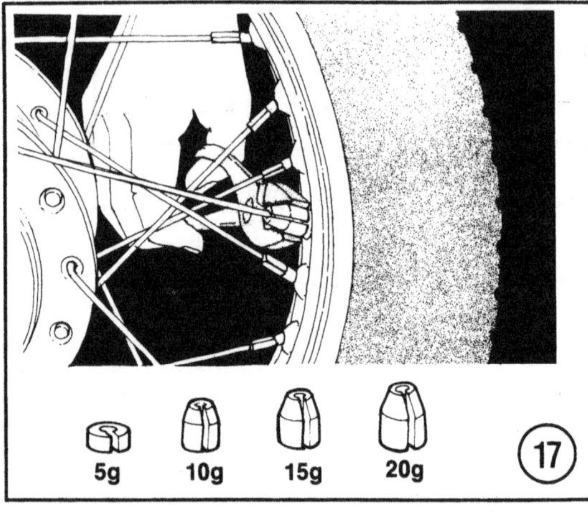

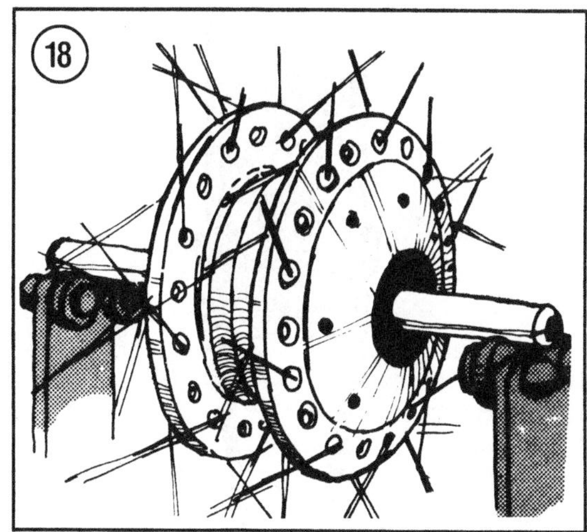

18

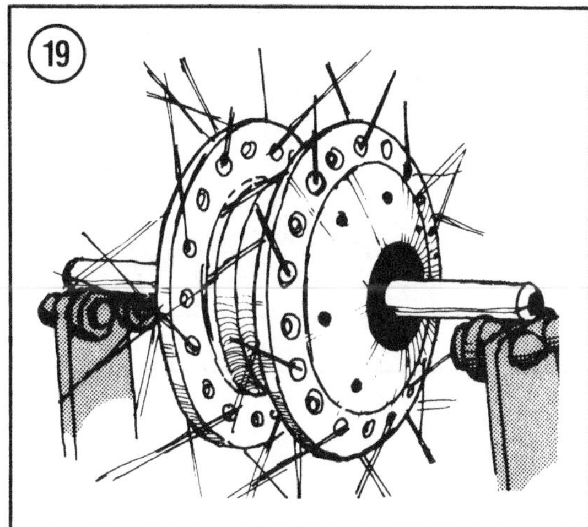

19

1. Rotate the wheel slowly and allow it to come to rest by itself. Make a chalk mark on the tire at the 6 o'clock position and rotate the wheel as before, several times, noting the position of the chalk mark each time the wheel comes to rest. If the wheel stops at different positions each time, the wheel is balanced.

NOTE

To balance the rear wheel, remove it as outlined in Chapter Nine and support the wheel in a stand as shown in ***Figure 18****.*

2. If the chalk mark stops at the same position—6 o'clock—each time, add weight to the 12 o'clock position until the chalk mark stops at a different position each time.
3. Install the wheel, if removed, and road test the motorcycle on a smooth, straight road. Repeat the balance procedure if necessary.

SPOKE WHEELS

Spokes should be routinely checked for tightness. The "tuning fork" method for checking spoke tightness is simple and works well. Tap each spoke with a spoke wrench or the shank of a screwdriver and listen to the tone. A correctly tightened spoke will emit a clear, ringing tone, while a loose spoke will sound flat. All of the spokes in a correctly tightened wheel will emit tones of similar pitch, but not necessarily the same precise tone.

Bent, broken or stripped spokes should be replaced as soon as they are detected, as they can destroy an expensive hub.

NOTE

Most professional motorcycle mechanics use and recommend the Rowe Products spoke wrench. It will not round off the square edges of the spoke nipples and it fits virtually all sizes of spokes.

Runout Adjustment (Truing)

1. To measure the runout of the rim, support the wheel in a stand as shown in **Figure 19** or support the motorcycle so that the wheel being checked is free of the ground.
2. Install a dial indicator (**Figure 14**) or locally fabricated runout indicator (**Figure 15**). Adjust the position of the bolt until it just clears the rim.
3. Rotate the rim and note whether the clearance between the rim and the indicator increases or decreases. Mark the tire with chalk or crayon at areas where the clearance is large or small. Maximum runout on the edge and/or the face of the rim is 2.0 mm (0.08 in.).
4. To pull or "true" the rim, tighten spokes which are located on the same side of the hub and loosen spokes which are located on the opposite side of the hub (**Figure 20**). In most cases, only a slight amount of adjustment is necessary. After adjustment, rotate the rim and make sure that another area of the rim has not been pulled out of true. Continue adjusting and checking until runout does not exceed 2.0 mm (0.08 in.). Be patient and thorough, adjusting the position of the rim a small amount at a time.

NOTE

If rims cannot trued within 2.0 mm (0.08 in.) of edge or face runout, the rim is damaged and must be replaced. Unless you are experienced in wheel lacing, this task is best left to a dealer or motorcycle shop experienced in wheel repair.

8

5. Always tighten spokes gradually and evenly in a crisscross pattern, first on one side of the hub, then the other. Turn spokes approximately 1/4-1/2 turn at a time. Do not overtighten, or the wheel will be pulled out of true.
6. After tightening spokes, always check the runout to make sure that the rim has not been pulled out of true.

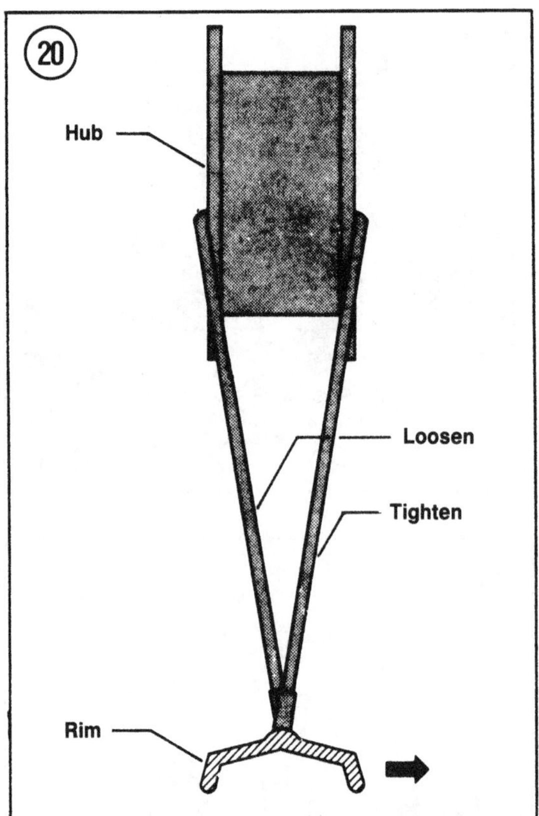

Spoke Replacement

A stripped or broken spoke can usually be replaced with the tire still installed on the wheel, providing the spoke nipple is in good condition. If the nipple is damaged or more than 2 or 3 spokes need replacing, the tire must first be removed. If several spokes need replacing, the rim is also probably damaged. Unless you are skilled in wheel lacing and rim replacement, this task is best left to a dealer or motorcycle shop skilled in wheel repair.

To replace one or 2 damaged spokes with the tire still mounted, perform the following procedure.

1. Inflate the tire to at least 30 psi to help hold the spoke nipple in the rim.
2. Unscrew the nipple from the damaged or broken spoke. If the old spoke is not broken, press the nipple into the rim far enough to free the end of the damaged spoke. Take care not to push the nipple back into the rim and remove the old spoke.

21

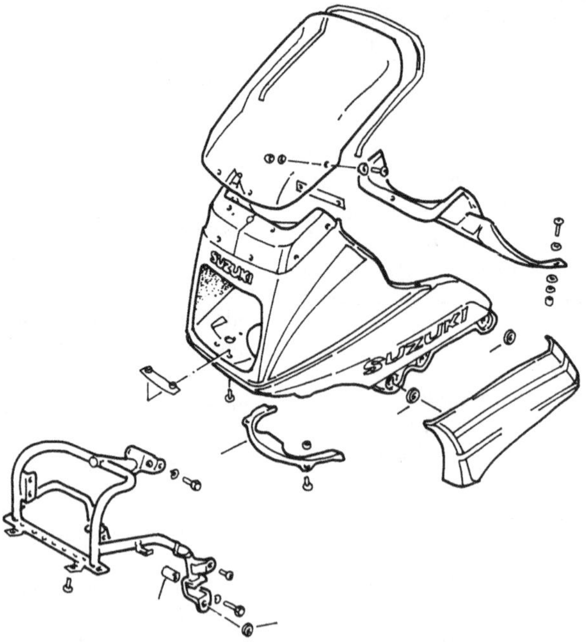

22

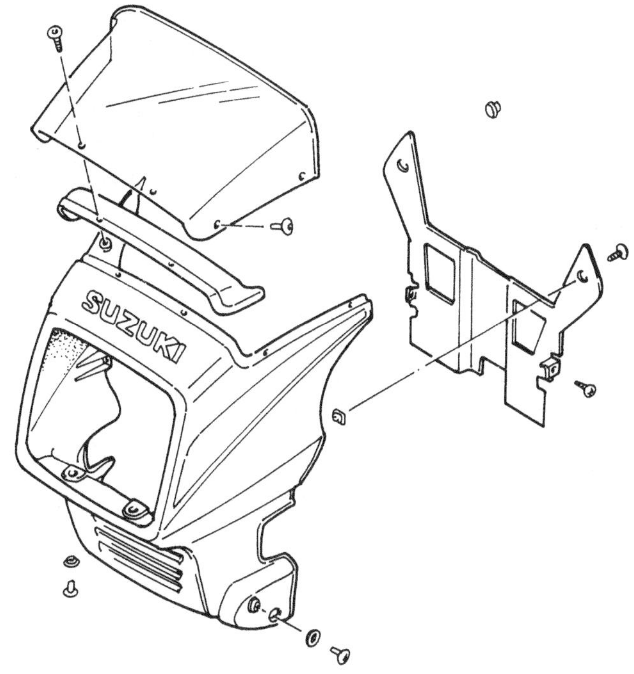

SUZUKI

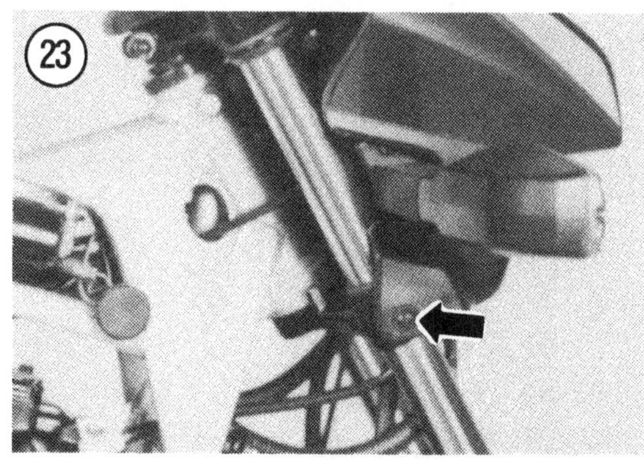

23

24

3. Trim the threaded end of the new spoke so that it is about 2 or 3 threads shorter than the old spoke. This permits the new spoke to stretch without the risk of puncturing the inner tube.
4. Install the new spoke into the hub and gently bow it so it can be inserted into the nipple.
5. Tighten the spoke nipple until the tone of the new spoke is similar to the other spokes in the wheel.
6. The tightness of the new spoke must be checked frequently. The spoke will stretch and must be retightened several times before it takes a final set. Make the first check after 30 minutes to one hour of riding.

FAIRING REMOVAL/INSTALLATION (TSCC MODELS)

Refer to **Figure 21** or **Figure 22** for this procedure.

1. On ES models, remove the lower fairing covers from each side. Unbolt and remove both front turn signals.
2. Remove the screws securing the side of the fairing (**Figure 23**).
3. Remove the screws securing the front of the fairing (**Figure 24**) and carefully slide the fairing off the motorcycle.

4. Installation is the reverse of these steps. Keep the following points in mind:
   a. Make sure the handlebar wires and cables are carefully routed between the fairing and instrument cluster (**Figure 25**).
   b. Do not tighten the mounting screws until the fairing is fully in place and all wires and cables are clear.
   c. On ES models, install the turn signals and lower fairing covers.

FRONT FORK

Three basic types of front fork are installed on GS550 models. Each fork is very similar and operates in essentially the same manner. On 1980 and later models, the fork is fitted with Teflon coated "DU" rings to decrease internal friction. Some TSCC models are equipped with an anti-dive fork that has special valve assemblies connected to the brake system. Repair procedures for each type are basically the same; differences will be pointed out where necessary.

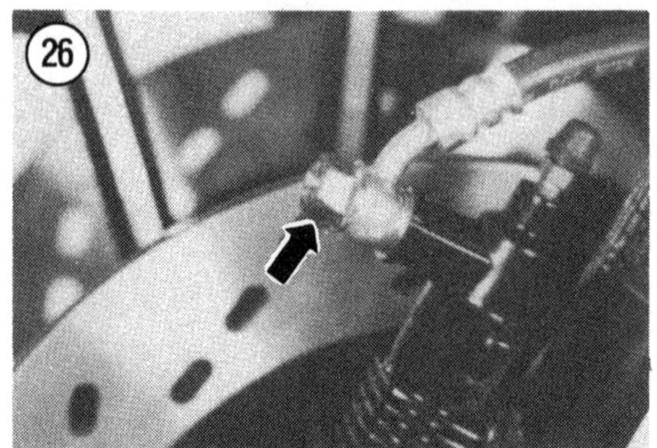

Removal

1. Remove the front wheel as described in this chapter.
2. On models equipped with an anti-dive fork, remove the banjo bolt securing the brake hose to the anti-dive valve assembly (**Figure 26**). Have a container ready to catch any dripping brake fluid.

CAUTION
Do not allow any brake fluid to drip on painted parts or the paint will be damaged.

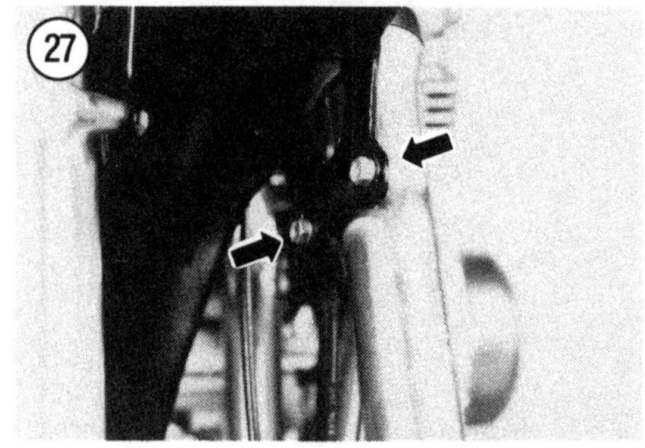

3. On models equipped with dual front brakes, remove the bolts securing the remaining brake caliper and remove the caliper. Support the caliper from the handlebars with a piece of wire or Bungee cord. Do not allow the caliper to hang by the hose.
4. If so equipped, remove the brake hose clamp from the fender mount. Remove the 4 fender bolts and remove the front fender (**Figure 27**).
5. If the fork is being removed for disassembly, perform the following:
   a. On models equipped with fork air valves, remove the rubber fork cap (**Figure 28**) or the screw cap from the air valves (A, **Figure 29**) and gently bleed off the fork air pressure.

NOTE
Failure to bleed off the fork air pressure gently usually results in a quick squirt of fork oil.

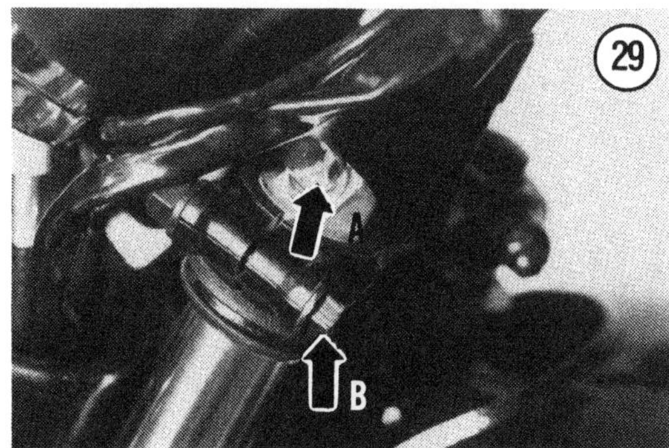

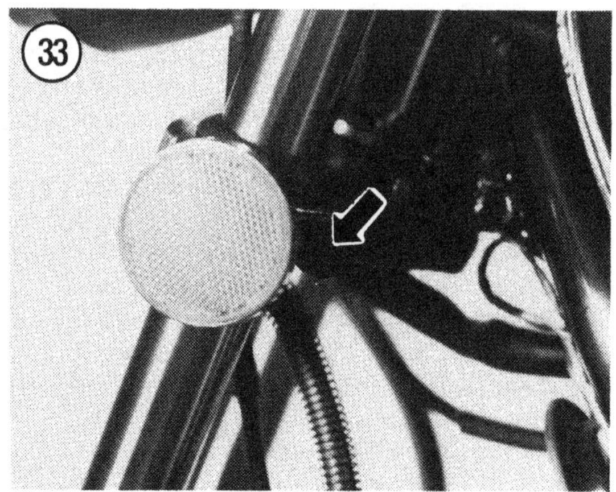

b. Remove the drain screw (**Figure 30**) and drain the oil from each fork leg. Allow several minutes for the forks to drain completely.

6. Loosen the upper pinch bolt securing each fork leg (B, **Figure 29**).

7. If the forks are to be disassembled, on models equipped with screw type fork cap bolts (**Figure 31**), loosen the cap bolts at this time.

8. Loosen the lower pinch bolts securing each fork leg (**Figure 32**).

NOTE
*All L models are fitted with 2 pinch bolts on each side of the lower steering stem as shown in **Figure 32**. All other models are fitted with single bolts in the lower steering stem (**Figure 33**).*

9. Pull down and remove both fork legs.

NOTE
The fork legs often fit very snugly in the upper and lower steering brackets. If the forks legs are difficult to remove, install the axle in each fork leg, one at a time, and use the axle as a handle to help pull down and remove the fork leg.

Installation

1. Wipe out the fork tube bores in the upper and lower steering stem brackets with a clean rag.

2. Carefully install both fork legs into the steering stem brackets. Keep the following points in mind:
   a. On models with screw-type fork cap bolts, position the top edge of each fork tube (not the cap bolt) flush with the upper surface of the steering stem upper bracket (**Figure 34**).
   b. On all other models, install the fork tube so that the engraved line on the inside of the tube is aligned with the top edge of the steering stem upper bracket (**Figure 35**).

8

3. Install the front fender and secure with the 4 bolts. Secure the brake hose clamp to the fender mount as shown in **Figure 36**, if so equipped.
4. Torque the fork pinch bolts and fork cap bolts as specified in **Table 1**.
5. Install the front wheel as outlined in this chapter.
6. Install the front brake calipers and torque the caliper mounting bolts as specified in **Table 1**.
7. On models with anti-dive forks, install the brake hose to the anti-dive valve assembly. Torque the banjo bolt as specified in **Table 1**. Refer to Chapter Ten and bleed the brakes.
8. Refer to Chapter Three and pressurize the front forks.

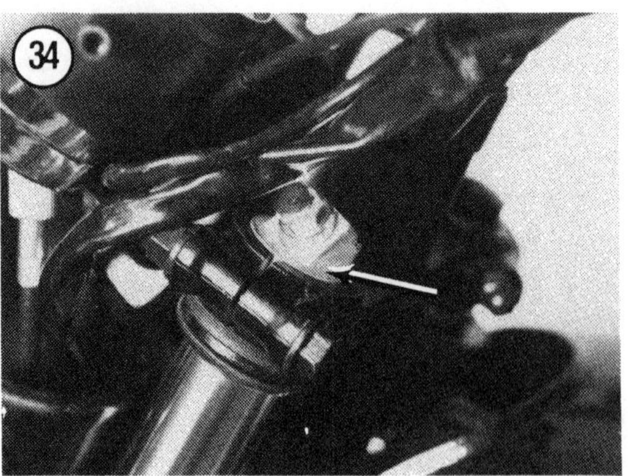

34

35

36

Disassembly/Assembly

Refer to **Figure 37** or **Figure 38** for this procedure.

On 1980 and later models, each fork inner tube contains 2 Teflon coated metal "DU" rings. These "DU" rings decrease the internal friction between the inner fork tube and the outer slider unit, allowing the forks to operate more smoothly. The Teflon surface of these "DU" rings is often damaged when the inner fork tubes are removed, therefore Suzuki recommends replacing these rings each time the forks are disassembled.

NOTE
On models fitted with anti-dive forks, Suzuki specifies that the anti-dive modulator valve assembly is a non-repairable item. Should the anti-dive mechanism fail to operate properly, the modulator valve must be replaced. Refer any suspected modulator valve failure to your dealer.

Preparation should be made prior to starting the disassembly as an impact tool (air or electric) or a special holding tool is necessary to remove the Allen retaining bolt in the bottom of each fork leg. The Allen bolt is secured with a thread locking compound (such as Loctite) and is often difficult to remove because the damper rod will turn inside the fork tube. If an impact tool is not available, remove the Allen bolts with an Allen wrench and the special Suzuki holding tool Attachment "D" (Suzuki part No. 09940-34561). The special holding tool is used inside the fork tube to hold the damper rod. Attachment "D" can be used with the Suzuki handle (Suzuki part No. 09940-34520) or with one or two long 3/8 in. drive socket extensions equaling approximately 18 inches.

1. Remove the front forks as outlined in this chapter.
2. If an impact tool is to be used to remove the Allen retaining bolt in the bottom of the fork tube, leave the fork cap bolt or spring stopper and fork springs installed until the Allen bolt is removed. The internal spring pressure against the damper rod assembly helps hold it in place as the Allen bolt is removed. Extend the fork tubes and hold them extended against the pressure of the rebound spring while removing the Allen bolt with the impact tool (**Figure 39**).

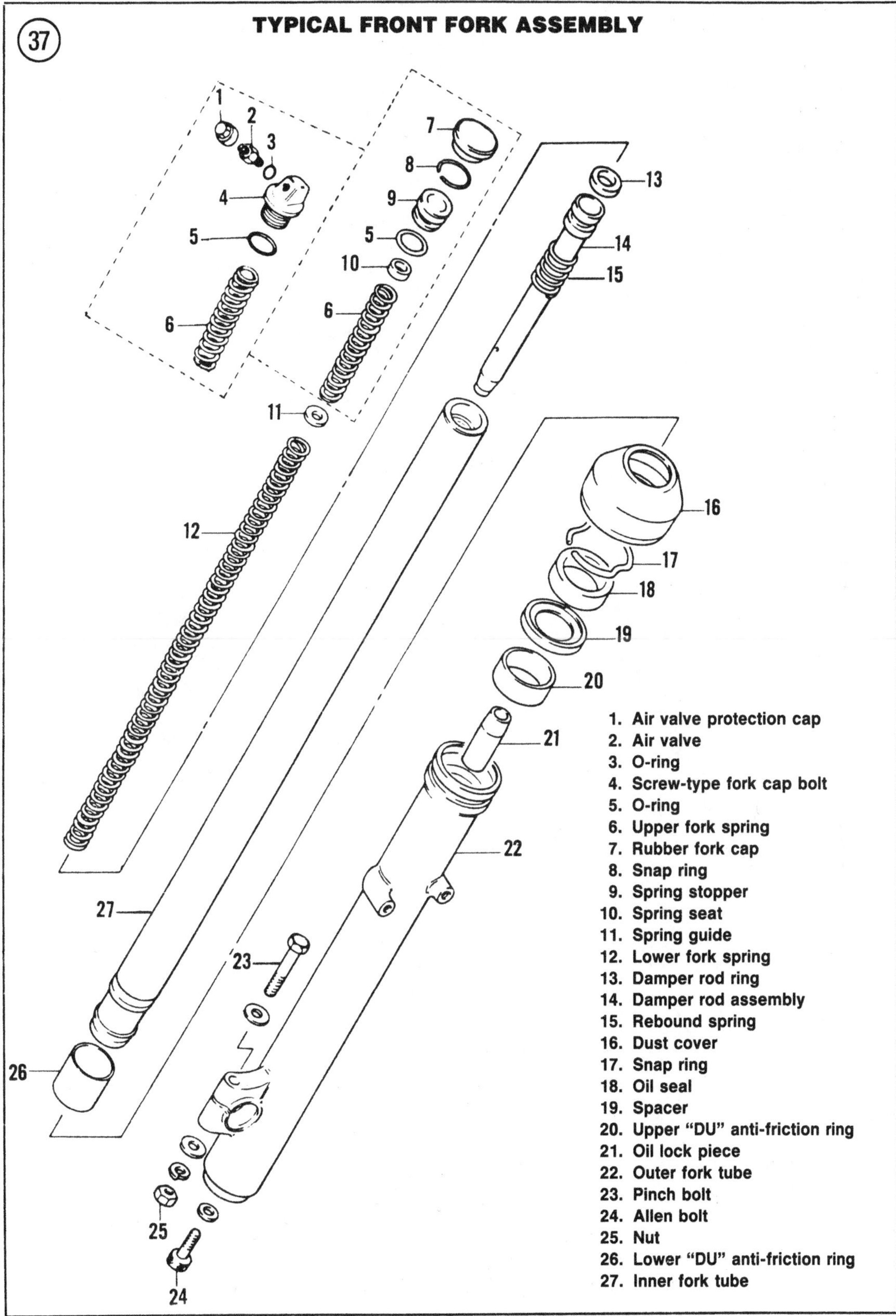
37
TYPICAL FRONT FORK ASSEMBLY
1
2
3
4
5
6
7
8
9
5
10
6
11
12
13
14
15
16
17
18
19
20
21
22
23
24
25
26
27
1. Air valve protection cap
2. Air valve
3. O-ring
4. Screw-type fork cap bolt
5. O-ring
6. Upper fork spring
7. Rubber fork cap
8. Snap ring
9. Spring stopper
10. Spring seat
11. Spring guide
12. Lower fork spring
13. Damper rod ring
14. Damper rod assembly
15. Rebound spring
16. Dust cover
17. Snap ring
18. Oil seal
19. Spacer
20. Upper "DU" anti-friction ring
21. Oil lock piece
22. Outer fork tube
23. Pinch bolt
24. Allen bolt
25. Nut
26. Lower "DU" anti-friction ring
27. Inner fork tube

38

1. Air valve protection cap
2. Air valve
3. O-ring
4. Screw-type fork cap bolt
5. O-ring
6. Fork spring
7. Damper rod ring
8. Rebound spring
9. Damper rod assembly
10. Inner fork tube
11. Lower "DU" anti-friction ring
12. Dust seal
13. Snap ring
14. Washer
15. Oil seal
16. Washer
17. Lower "DU" anti-friction ring
18. Anti-dive valve washer, top and bottom
19. Anti-dive valve washer, middle
20. Oil lock piece
21. Outer fork tube
22. Gasket
23. Drain screw
24. Lockwasher
25. Allen bolt
26. Nut
27. Lockwasher
28. Flat washer
29. Axle holder
30. Anti-dive modulator valve
31. O-ring
32. Modulator bolt
33. Modulator plunger assembly
34. Bleed valve cap
35. Bleed valve
36. Plunger assembly bolt

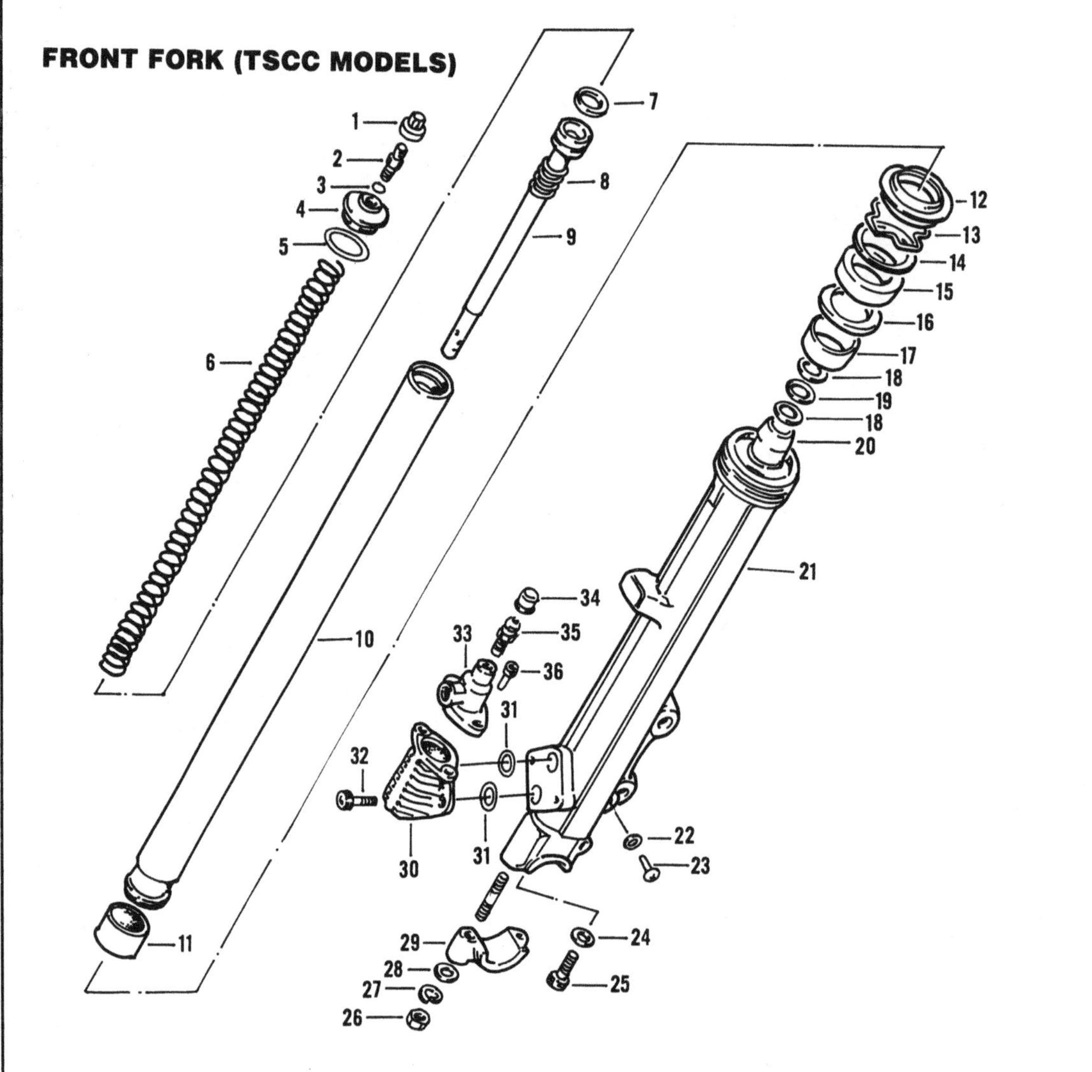

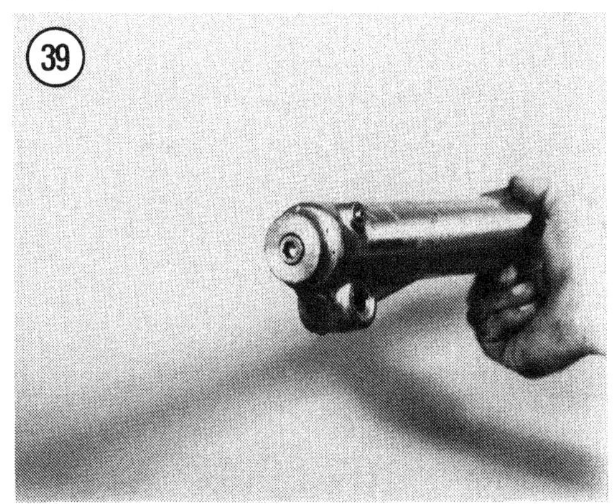
39

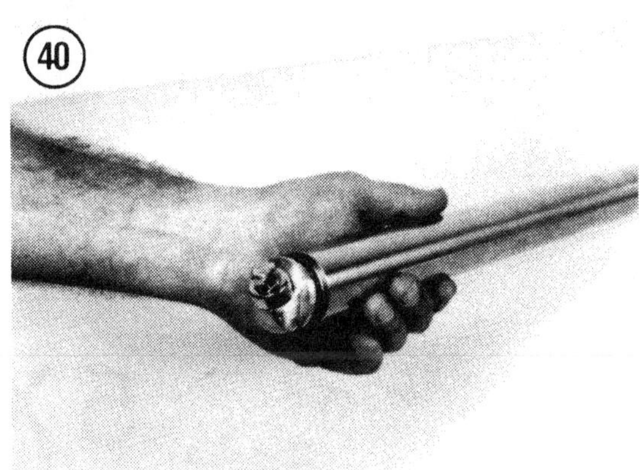
40

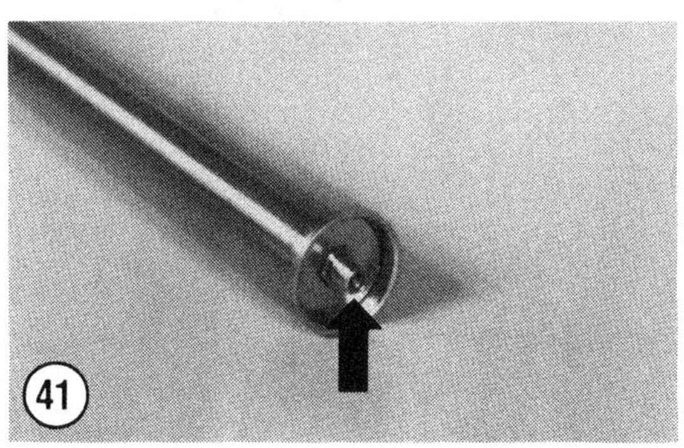
41

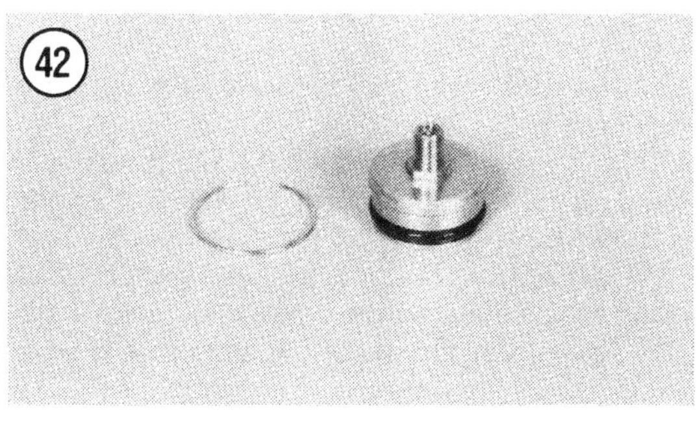
42

43

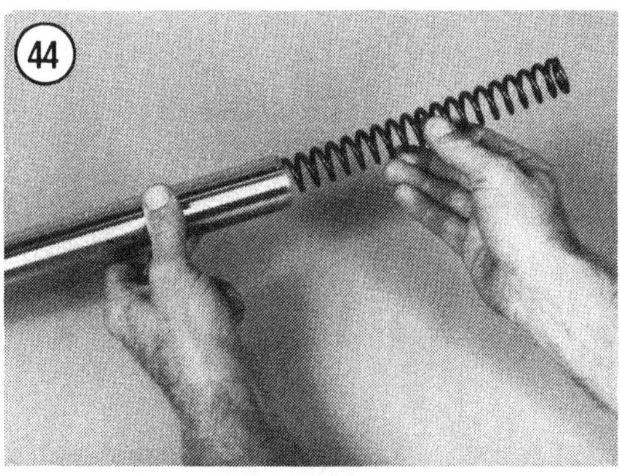
44

NOTE
On anti-dive models, it is not necessary to remove the anti-dive modulator valve assembly to disassemble the forks.

3. Remove the screw type fork cap bolt (**Figure 40**) from the inner tube on models so equipped.
4. On all other models, carefully remove the snap ring securing the spring stopper (**Figure 41**). Remove the spring stopper with the O-ring (**Figure 42**).
5. Remove the short upper spring and the spring guide (**Figure 43**) if so equipped.
6. Remove the long fork spring (**Figure 44**). Have a few rags handy as the spring will be quite oily.
7. Tip up the fork tube and completely drain the remaining fork oil. Stroke the fork several times over a drain pan to pump out any remaining oil. Stand the fork tube in the drain pan and allow the tube to drain for several minutes.
8. If the Allen retaining bolts were not removed with an impact tool, use Suzuki tool Attachment "D" (Suzuki part No. 09940-34561) and socket extensions to hold the damper rod from turning. Remove the Allen bolt from the bottom of the fork outer tube (**Figure 39**).
9. On 1977-1979 models, slide the inner tube out of the lower fork leg (**Figure 45**).

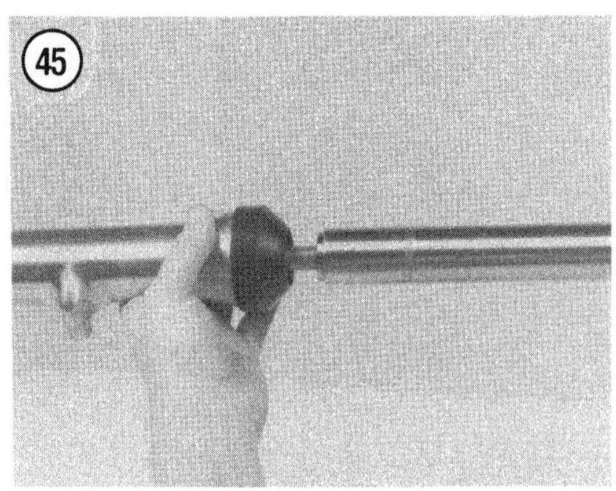

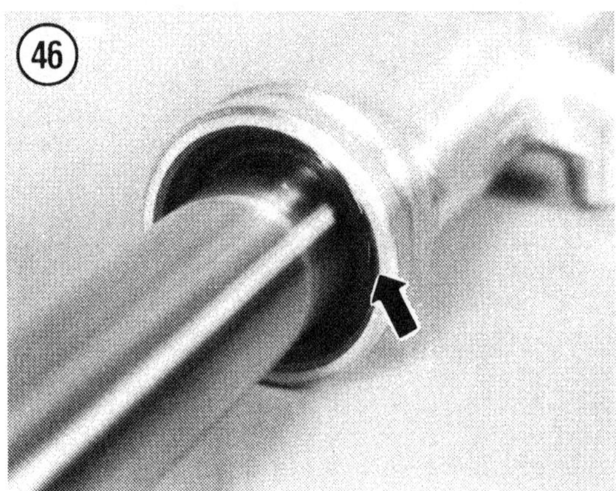

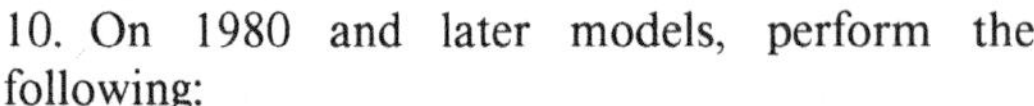

10. On 1980 and later models, perform the following:
   a. Remove the outer dust cover to gain access to the snap ring securing the fork oil seal. Use snap ring pliers with strong tips to remove the snap ring (**Figure 46**).
   b. Pad the jaws of a vise with wooden blocks or soft aluminum plates. Place the fork leg in the vise and clamp the vise securely on the brake caliper mounting lugs as shown in **Figure 47**.
   c. Use several quick slide-hammer motions to remove the inner tube from the outer tube. The seal, seal washer and upper "DU" ring are removed with the inner tube (**Figure 48**).

11. Remove the oil lock piece from the end of the damper rod (**Figure 49**). See **Figure 50** for anti-dive models.

NOTE
The oil lock piece (and anti-dive valve washers on models so equipped) may be loose in the bottom of the outer fork tube. Make sure the pieces are not lost. Anti-dive washer arrangement is described during fork assembly.

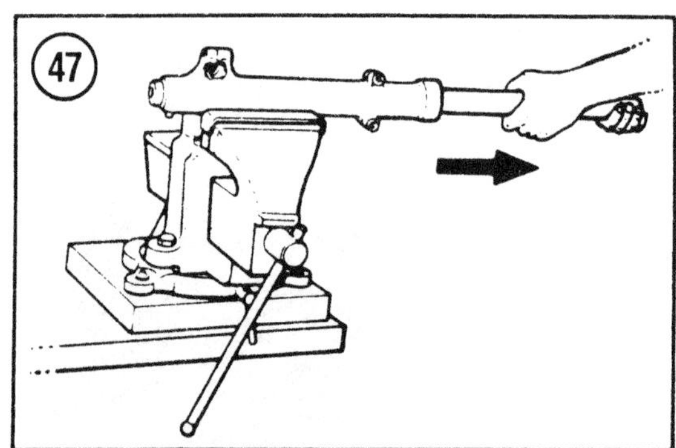

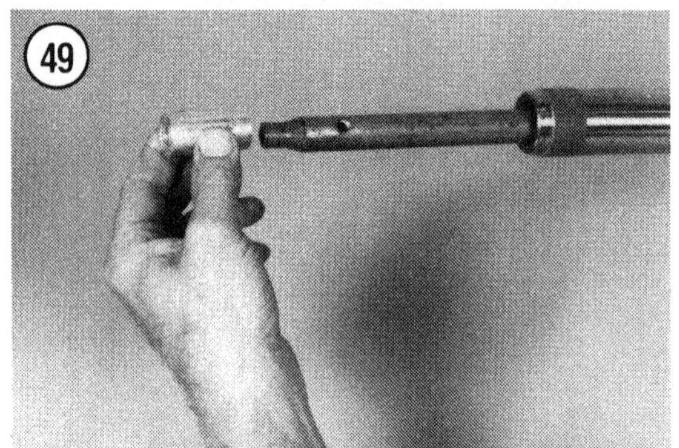

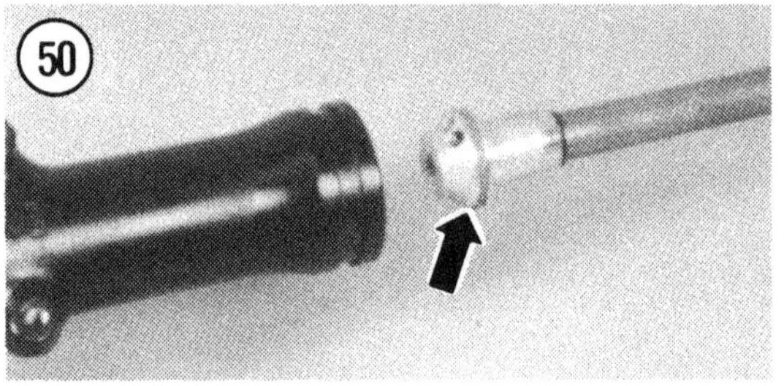

12. On anti-dive models, remove the flat and wave valve washers (**Figure 51**).

13. Tip up the inner tube and slide out the damper rod assembly complete with the rebound spring (**Figure 52**).

14. On 1980 and later models, use a screwdriver blade to carefully spread open and remove the "DU" ring from the end of the inner tube (**Figure 53**).

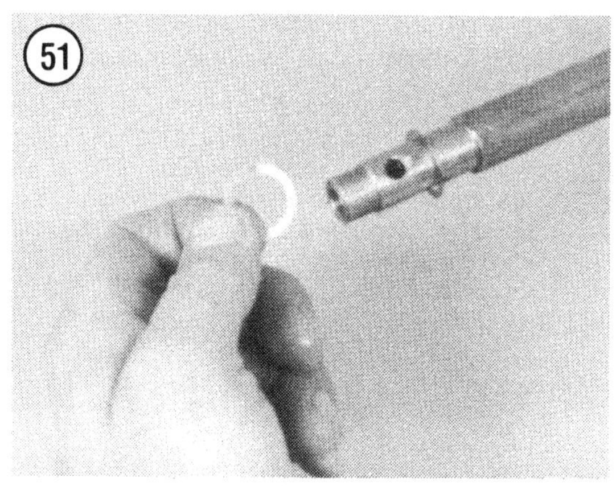

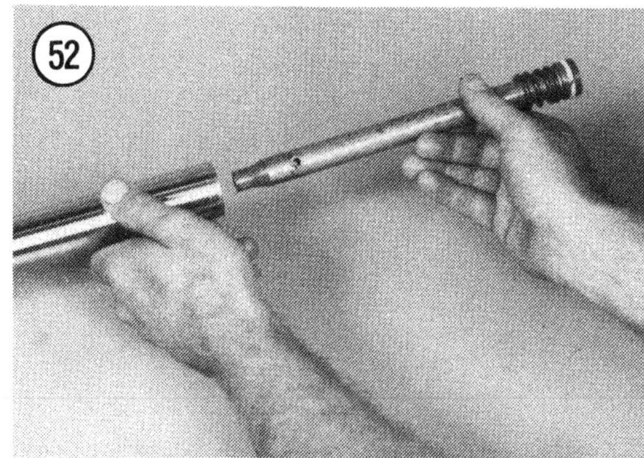

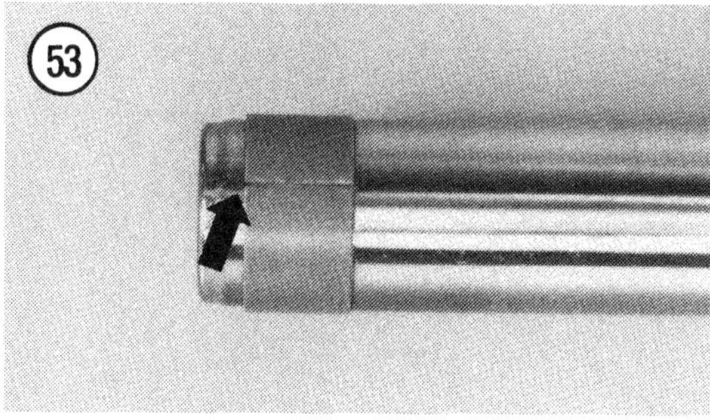

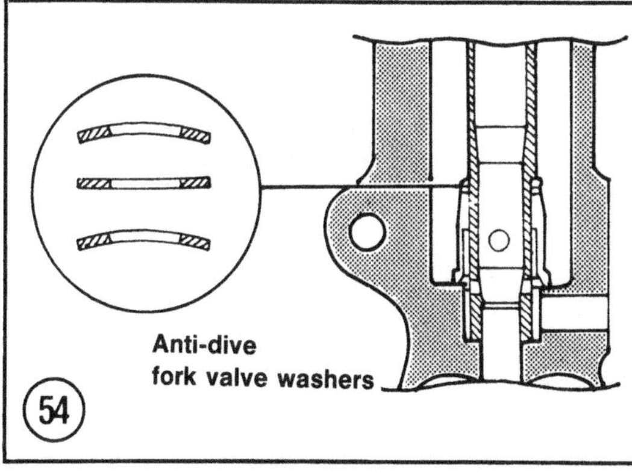

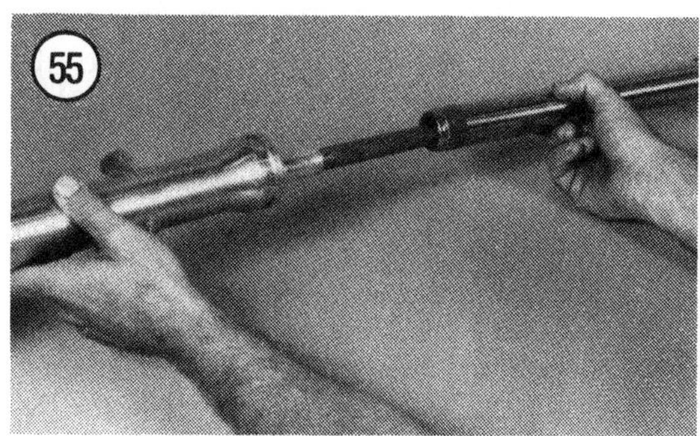

15. Perform *Inspection and Seal Replacement.*
16. Assembly is the reverse of these steps. Keep the following points in mind:
   a. Make sure all fork components are clean and dry. Wipe out the seal bore in the outer fork tube.
   b. On 1980 and later models, carefully install a new "DU" ring on the end of the inner tube (**Figure 53**). Take care not to damage the Teflon surface of the "DU" ring.
   c. Apply a light film of grease to the outer edge and lips of each new fork seal.
   d. Slide the lower "DU" ring, seal washer and oil seal on the inner fork tube in the order shown in **Figure 48**.
   e. Lightly oil the inner and outer tubes and damper rod assembly with clean fork oil before assembling the parts.
   f. Make sure the rebound (top-out) spring is installed on the damper rod and install the damper rod assembly into the inner fork tube (**Figure 52**).

NOTE
Temporarily install the fork springs and the fork cap bolt or spring stopper. The tension of the fork springs will keep the damper rod extended through the end of the fork tube and ease the assembly process.

   g. On anti-dive models, install the flat and wave valve washers on the damper rod in the order shown in **Figure 54**.
   h. Slide the oil lock piece over the end of the damper rod assembly as shown in **Figure 49**.
   i. Carefully install the inner tube with the damper rod assembly into the outer tube as shown in **Figure 55**.
   j. Clean the threads of the Allen retaining bolt thoroughly with solvent or spray contact cleaner. Make sure the washer is fitted to the Allen bolt and apply Suzuki Bond No. 1215 or equivalent to the first few threads next to the

washer. Apply a couple of drops of blue Loctite (Lock N' Seal No. 2114) to the remaining threads on the bolt. Install the bolt and tighten using the impact tool or Suzuki holding tool. Torque the bolt to 1.5-2.5 mkg (11-18 ft.-lb.).

k. On 1980 and later models, slide the upper "DU" ring, seal washer and seal into the outer fork tube. Use a piece of pipe over the inner tube or a seal installation tool to carefully tap the oil seal into place. Make sure that the seal is fully seated into the outer fork tube. Secure the seal with the snap ring (**Figure 46**). Make sure the snap ring is locked into the groove in the fork tube. Install the dust cover over the top of the outer fork tube.

NOTE
If Suzuki special tools are available, use the oil seal installation tool (part No. 09940-50111).

17. Remove the fork cap bolt or spring stopper and fork springs. Refer to **Table 2** and add the specified amount and type of fork oil to each fork tube. Use a graduate or a baby bottle (**Figure 56**) to make sure the oil amount is correct for each fork tube.

18. The fork oil level can also be measured from the top of the fork tube. Use an accurate ruler or the Suzuki oil level gauge (part No. 09943-74110) to make sure the oil level is as specified in **Table 2**. The oil level must be measured with the forks completely compressed and without springs.

NOTE
*An oil level measuring device can be made locally as shown in **Figure 57**. Fill the fork with a few cc's more than the required amount of oil. Position the hose clamp on the top edge of the fork tube and draw out the excess oil. Oil is sucked out until the level reaches the small diameter hole. A precise oil level can be achieved with this simple device.*

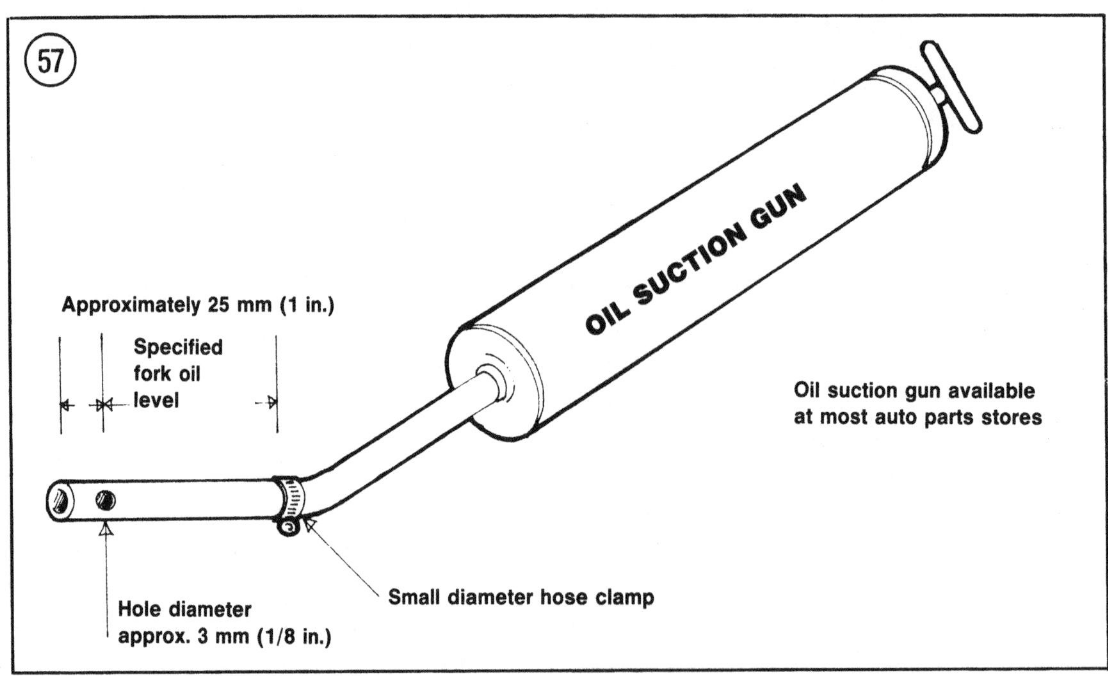

19. Install the fork springs and spring guide. Make sure the closer coils on the long spring are pointed up.
20. Make sure the O-ring on the fork cap bolt or spring stopper is in good condition (**Figure 58**). On models equipped with a spring stopper, install the stopper and secure it with the snap ring as shown in **Figure 59**. On models equipped with a screw type fork cap bolt, install the cap bolt finger-tight.

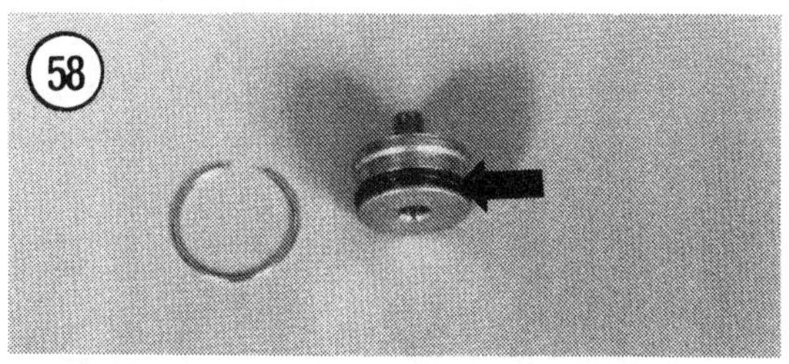

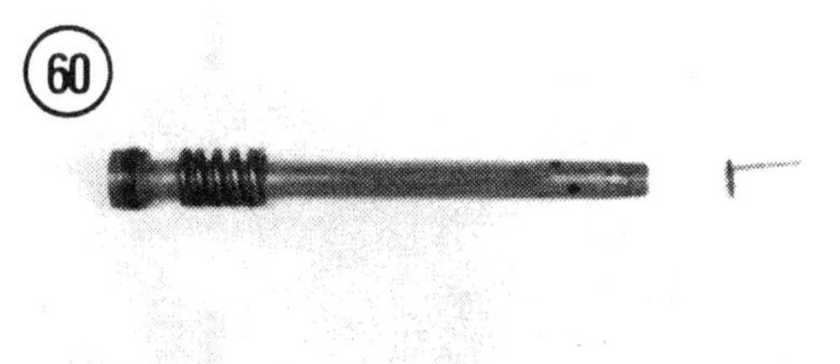

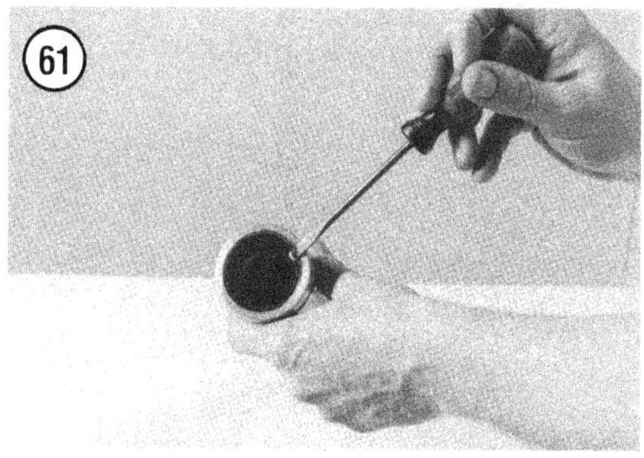

The cap bolt can be tightened after the forks have been installed on the motorcycle.

Inspection and Seal Replacement

1. Thoroughly clean all parts in solvent and dry them completely. Lightly oil and assemble the inner and outer fork tubes, then slide the tubes together. Check for looseness, noise or binding. Replace any defective parts.
2. Carefully examine the area of the inner fork tube that passes through the fork seal. Any scratches or roughness on the tube in this area will damage the oil seal. If the inner fork tube is scratched or pitted it should be replaced.
3. Inspect the damper rod assembly for damage or roughness (**Figure 60**). Check for signs of galling, deep scores or excessive wear. Replace the parts as necessary. Make sure all the oil passages are clean and free of any sludge or oil residue.
4. Inspect the dust cover on each fork tube for holes or abrasive damage. A damaged cover will allow dirt and moisture to pack up next the fork seal. Packed-in dirt can scratch the surface of the fork tubes as well as damage the fork seal. Install new dust covers if any damage exists.
5. Accurately measure the fork springs. If any spring is shorter than the length specified in **Table 2**, replace the springs as a set.
6. On 1980 and later models, lightly grease the lips of a new fork seal and slide the seal over the fork tube with the open side of the seal toward the bottom of the fork tube (**Figure 48**).
7. On 1977-1979 models, to replace the oil seal, perform the following:
   a. Carefully pry out the snap ring securing the seal (**Figure 61**).
   b. Pad the edge of the fork tube with a rag or piece of soft aluminum and pry out the old fork seal.
   c. Wipe out the seal bore. Lightly grease the outer edge of the new seal and install the seal open end down. Drive the seal into place with a suitably sized socket or seal driver.
   d. Secure the seal with the snap ring.

ANTI-DIVE MODULAR VALVE REMOVAL/INSTALLATION (TSCC MODELS)

Refer to **Figure 38** for this procedure.

The anti-dive modular valve and the modulator plunger assembly are not repairable. If you suspect the anti-dive mechanism is not working, take the bike to your dealer. A defective part must be replaced.

8

Often a "spongy" feeling anti-dive operation can be cured by a complete and thorough bleeding of the brake system. Refer to Chapter Ten and bleed the brakes and anti-dive components in the proper order.

1. If the fork leg has not been removed, perform the following:
   a. Remove the fork cap bolt (**Figure 62**).
   b. Place a drain pan under the fork leg and remove the drain screw (**Figure 63**). Drain the fork leg.
2. Remove the banjo bolt securing the brake line to the modulator valve (A, **Figure 64**). Have a container ready to catch any brake fluid.
3. Remove the Allen bolts securing the modulator valve assembly to the fork leg and remove the valve assembly (B, **Figure 64**).
4. If the modulator valve or modulator plunger must be replaced, remove the Allen bolts holding them together.
5. Installation is the reverse of these steps. Keep the following points in mind:
   a. Make sure the O-rings on the modulator valve are in good condition and install the modulator valve (**Figure 65**).
   b. Make sure a gasket is installed on each side of the banjo bolt and install the brake line. Torque the banjo bolt as specified in **Table 1**.
   c. Refer to Chapter Three and fill the fork tube with fork oil.
   d. Refer to Chapter Ten and thoroughly bleed the brake system.

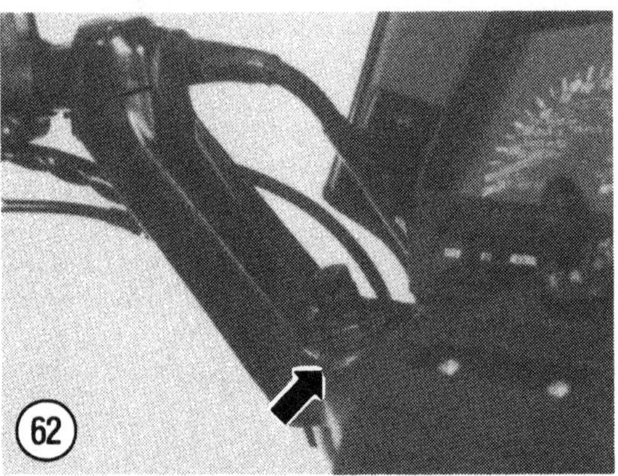

62

63

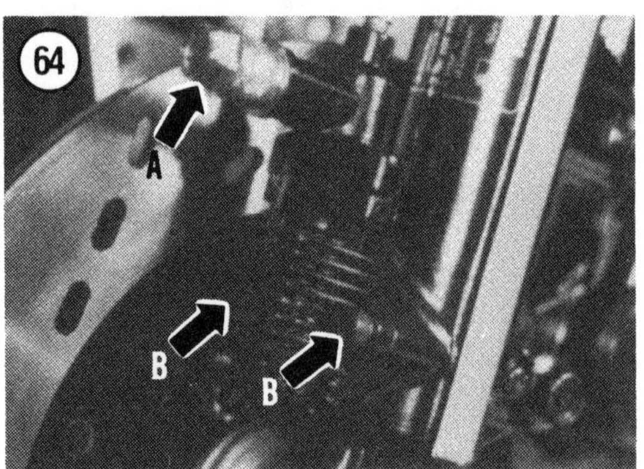

64

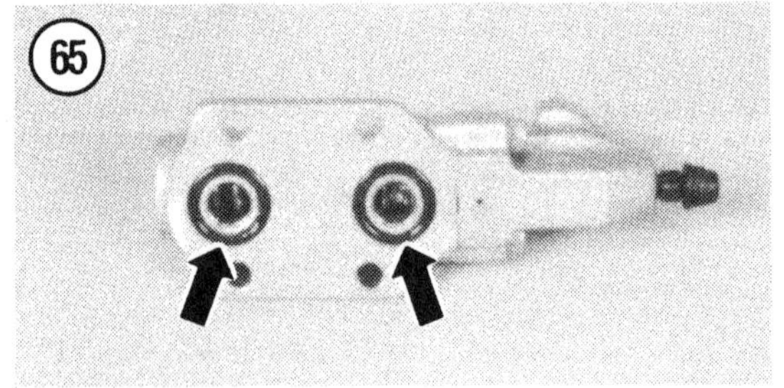

65

STEERING HEAD

Three types of steering head assemblies are used on GS550 models. All are very similar. Minor differences exist on certain models in the type of bearings and component arrangement.

All 1980 and later models are equipped with tapered roller bearings in both upper and lower bearing races. Earlier models use 18 loose bearing balls in both bearings.

The steering head should be disassembled periodically and the bearings packed with new grease. Use a good heavy grade of grease such as wheel bearing grease when lubricating the bearings.

Disassembly/Lubrication/Assembly

Refer to **Figure 66**, **Figure 67** or **Figure 68** for this procedure.

1. Remove the front forks as outlined in this chapter.
2. Remove the fuel tank as outlined in Chapter Six to avoid possible damage to the tank.

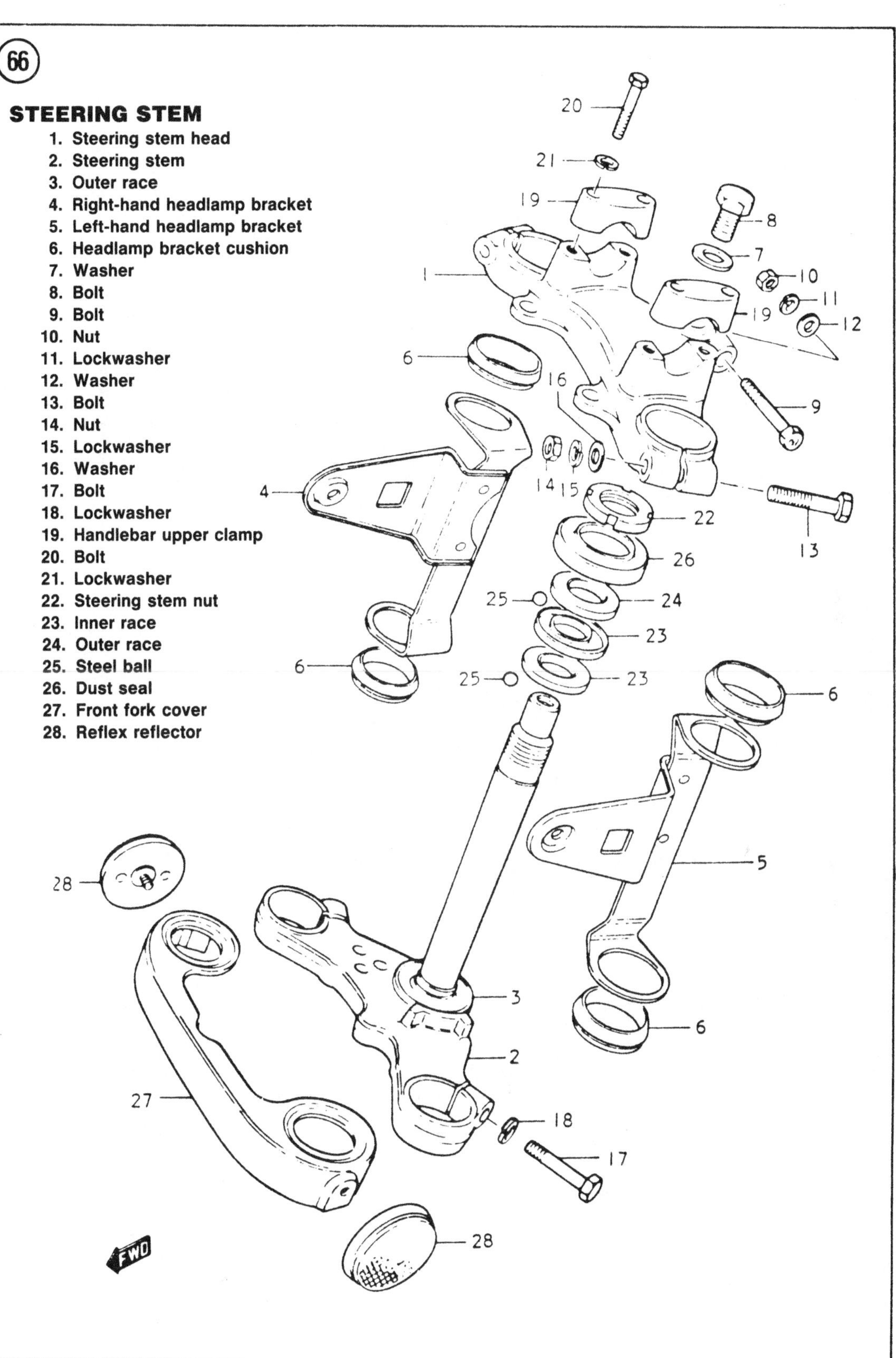
66
STEERING STEM
1. Steering stem head
2. Steering stem
3. Outer race
4. Right-hand headlamp bracket
5. Left-hand headlamp bracket
6. Headlamp bracket cushion
7. Washer
8. Bolt
9. Bolt
10. Nut
11. Lockwasher
12. Washer
13. Bolt
14. Nut
15. Lockwasher
16. Washer
17. Bolt
18. Lockwasher
19. Handlebar upper clamp
20. Bolt
21. Lockwasher
22. Steering stem nut
23. Inner race
24. Outer race
25. Steel ball
26. Dust seal
27. Front fork cover
28. Reflex reflector
FWD

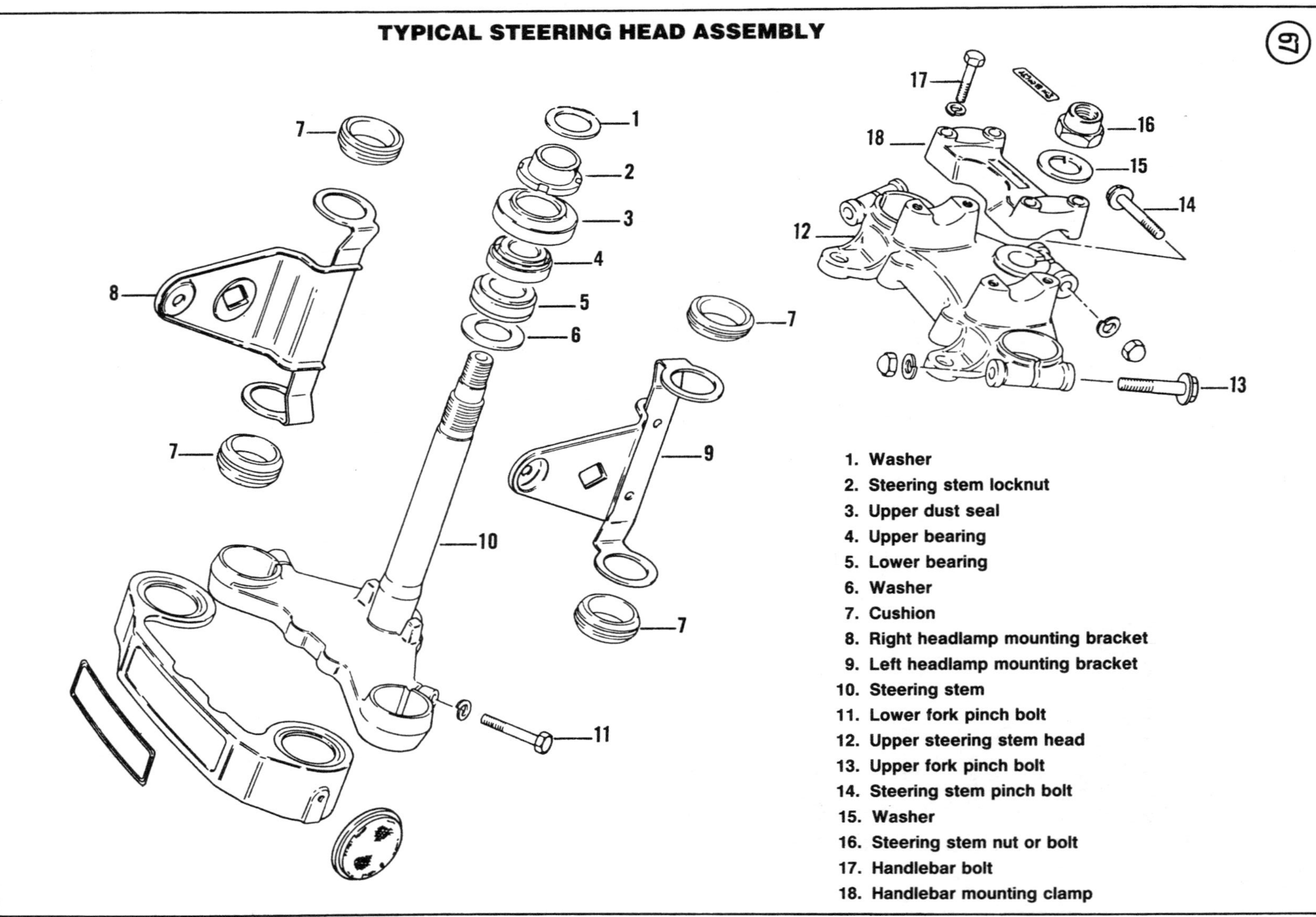
67
TYPICAL STEERING HEAD ASSEMBLY
1. Washer
2. Steering stem locknut
3. Upper dust seal
4. Upper bearing
5. Lower bearing
6. Washer
7. Cushion
8. Right headlamp mounting bracket
9. Left headlamp mounting bracket
10. Steering stem
11. Lower fork pinch bolt
12. Upper steering stem head
13. Upper fork pinch bolt
14. Steering stem pinch bolt
15. Washer
16. Steering stem nut or bolt
17. Handlebar bolt
18. Handlebar mounting clamp

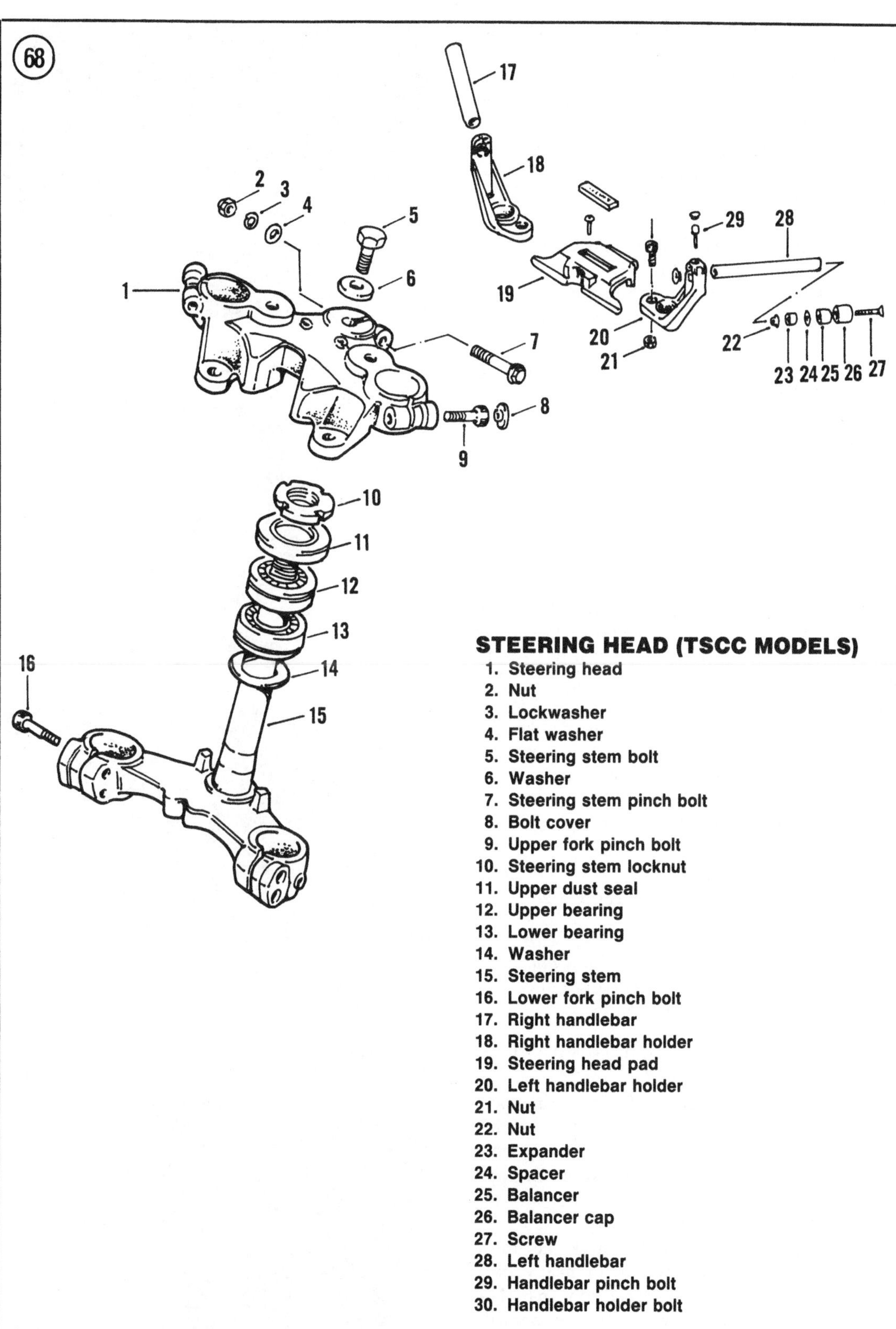

STEERING HEAD (TSCC MODELS)

1. Steering head
2. Nut
3. Lockwasher
4. Flat washer
5. Steering stem bolt
6. Washer
7. Steering stem pinch bolt
8. Bolt cover
9. Upper fork pinch bolt
10. Steering stem locknut
11. Upper dust seal
12. Upper bearing
13. Lower bearing
14. Washer
15. Steering stem
16. Lower fork pinch bolt
17. Right handlebar
18. Right handlebar holder
19. Steering head pad
20. Left handlebar holder
21. Nut
22. Nut
23. Expander
24. Spacer
25. Balancer
26. Balancer cap
27. Screw
28. Left handlebar
29. Handlebar pinch bolt
30. Handlebar holder bolt

3. On models equipped with a fairing, perform the following:
   a. Remove the fairing as described in this
   b. Remove the fuel tank to gain access to the headlight wiring connector.
   c. Remove the headlight assembly and the fairing mounting bracket.
4. On 1981 models, remove the bolt securing the choke cable to the carburetor bracket (**Figure 69**). Loosen the locknut securing the choke cable and remove the cable (**Figure 70**).
5. On TSCC models, remove the screws securing the steering head cover and remove the cover (**Figure 71**).
6. Loosen the pinch bolt securing the large steering stem nut or bolt (**Figure 72**).
7. Perform *Instrument Cluster Removal* as outlined in Chapter Seven.
8. Remove the large steering stem nut or bolt (**Figure 73**).
9. Lift up on the handlebars and lift off the upper steering stem head.
10. Remove the steering stem locknut and lift off the dust cover. Use a locally made tool as shown in **Figure 74** or Suzuki special tool part No. 09940-14910 to remove the locknut. If care is taken, a hammer and punch may also be used to tap off the nut.
11. Lift out the upper roller bearing.
12. The entire steering stem can now be partially withdrawn from the frame. On 1977-1979 models, place a container under the steering head to catch any bearing balls that may fall out. To lubricate the bearings, further disassembly is unnecessary.

NOTE

To completely remove the steering stem it is necessary to remove the brake hose manifold, disconnect cable and wire retainers, directional light wiring and all other components secured to the lower steering stem bracket.

13. Assembly is the reverse of disassembly. Keep the following points in mind:
   a. On 1977-1979 models, pack the bearing races with heavy duty grease and install 18 bearing balls in each race. Tighten the steering stem nut fully to seat the balls in the races. Back off the nut just enough for smooth steering movement without any free play.
   b. On 1980 and later models, pack the upper and lower roller bearings with heavy duty grease. Use the Suzuki special tool (part No. 09940-14940) or equivalent to temporarily torque the steering stem locknut to 4-5 mkg

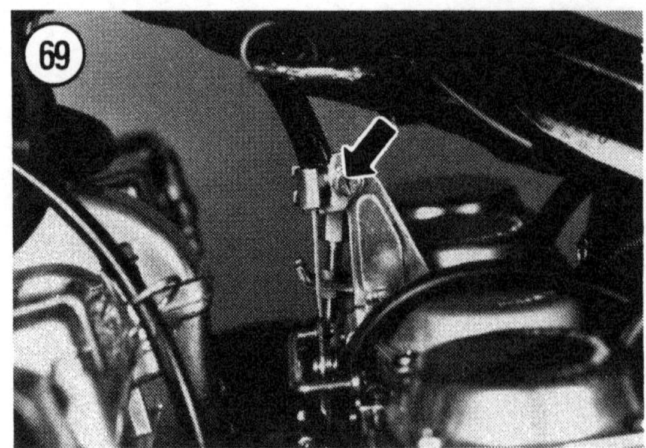

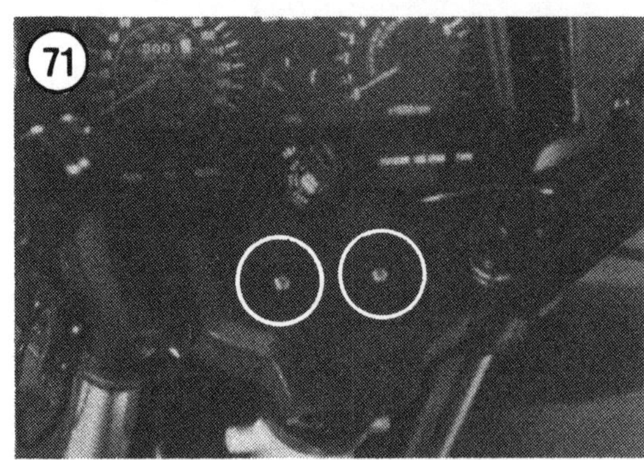

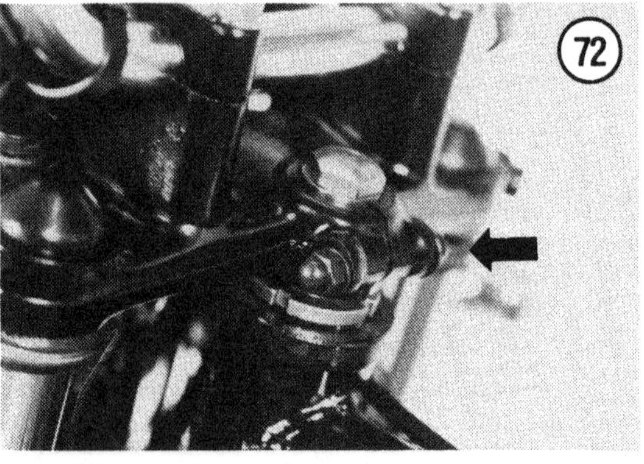

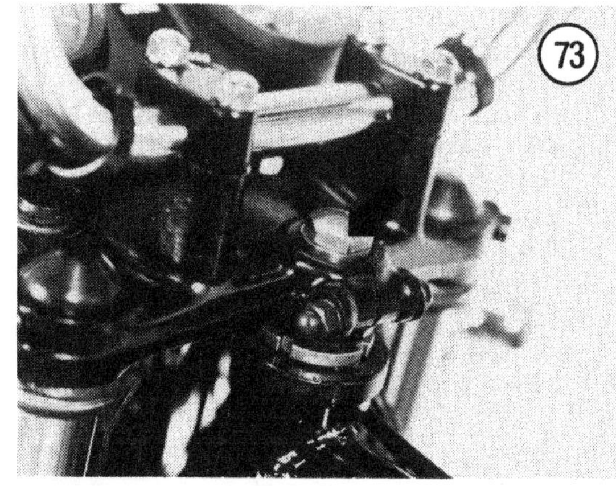
73

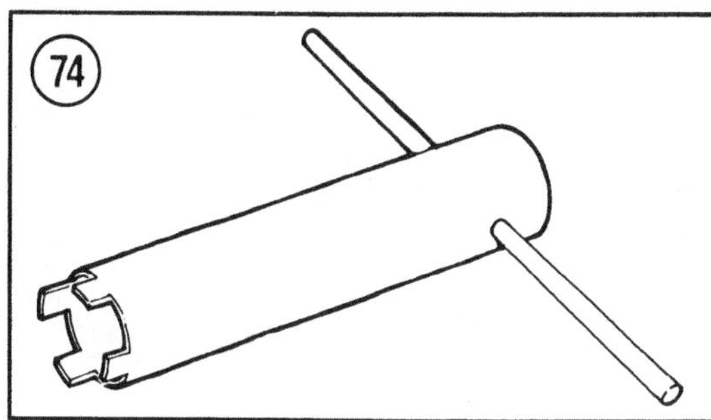
74

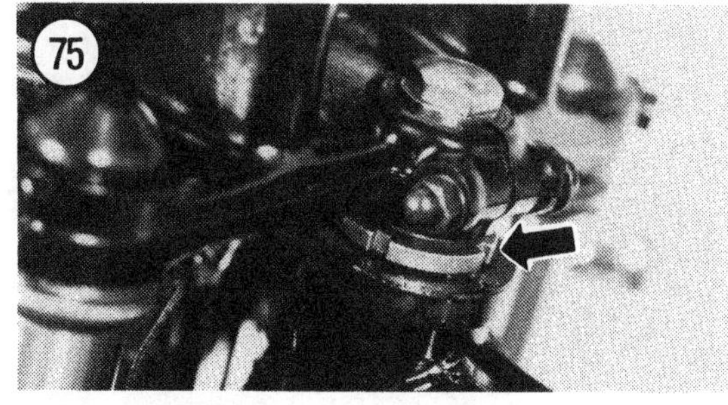
75

(29-36 ft.-lb.) to seat the roller bearings. Turn the steering stem lock-to-lock 5 or 6 times to make sure the movement is smooth without excessive play. Back off the steering stem locknut approximately 1/4-1/2 turn. Make sure the steering is still smooth, but without any play.

c. Install the steering stem nut and torque as specified in **Table 1**. Check that the steering stem moves easily and smoothly from side to side and no vertical play is present. Readjust the steering stem locknut if necessary.
d. Torque the steering stem pinch bolt to 1.5-2.5 mkg (11-18 ft.-lb.).
e. If the lower steering bracket was removed, install all wire and cable retainers and the brake hose manifold. Bleed the brakes as outlined in Chapter Ten if any brake hoses were opened.

Inspection

1. Clean the bearing races and bearings with solvent.
2. Check the frame welds around the steering head for crack and fractures. If any are found, have them repaired by a competent frame shop or welding service.
3. Check the bearings for pitting, scratches or signs of corrosion. If they are less than perfect, replace them as a set.
4. Check the races for pitting, galling and corrosion. If any of these conditions exist, replace the races. See the applicable bearing replacement procedure.

NOTE
Several special tools and considerable expertise are required to replace the steering head bearing races. It is recommended that this task be referred to an authorized dealer who is equipped with the necessary tools.

5. Check the steering stem for cracks, damage or wear.

Steering Head Adjustment

1. Place the motorcycle on the center stand and place a block under the engine so the front wheel is clear of the ground. Grasp each fork leg at the lower end and attempt to move the front end back and forth. If any fore and aft movement of the front end is detected, the steering stem locknut will have to be adjusted.
2. Loosen the pinch bolt securing the steering stem head nut or bolt (**Figure 72**). Loosen the head nut (**Figure 73**).
3. Use the Suzuki spanner wrench (part No. 09940-10122) to adjust the steering stem locknut (**Figure 75**) until all play is removed from the steering head, yet the front end turns freely from side to side under its own weight. If the Suzuki spanner is not available the steering locknut can be gently tapped with a hammer and a punch or screwdriver. Take care not to damage the locknut.
4. Torque the steering stem head bolt or nut to the value specified in **Table 1**.

Handlebar Removal/Installation (1977-1982)

1. If the handlebars are to be replaced, it is necessary to remove the clutch lever, front master

cylinder and throttle grip. Refer to Chapter Ten to remove the front master cylinder.

2. Remove the bolts securing the handlebar clamps (**Figure 76**) and remove the handlebars.

3. Install the handlebar with the dot and handlebar clamps positioned as shown in **Figure 77**. Torque the clamp bolts to 1.2-2.0 mkg (8.5-14.5 ft.-lb.).

4. Install the clutch lever, front master cylinder and throttle grip if removed.

Handlebar Removal/Installation (TSCC Models)

1. Remove the screws securing the steering head cover and remove the cover (**Figure 71**).

2. On all but L models, carefully pry out the plastic cover and remove the pinch bolt securing each handlebar to the handlebar holder (**Figure 78**). Slide each handlebar out the holder.

NOTE
On L models, the handlebar and holder are one-piece units.

3. On all but L models, if handlebar holder removal is desired, perform the following:

a. Remove the fork cap bolts.
b. Remove the bolts securing each handlebar holder to the steering head (**Figure 79**).

4. Installation is the reverse of these steps. Keep the following points in mind:

a. Install the handlebar into the holder so the groove is aligned with the pinch bolt (**Figure 80**).
b. On L models, make sure the wires are routed up the handlebar as shown in **Figure 81**.
c. Torque the handlebar components as specified in **Table 1**.

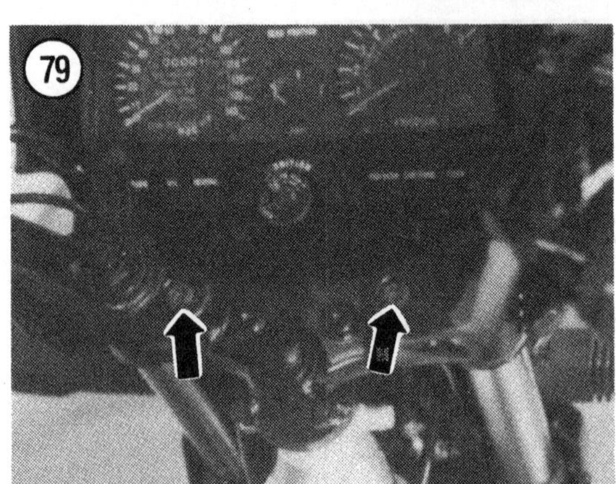

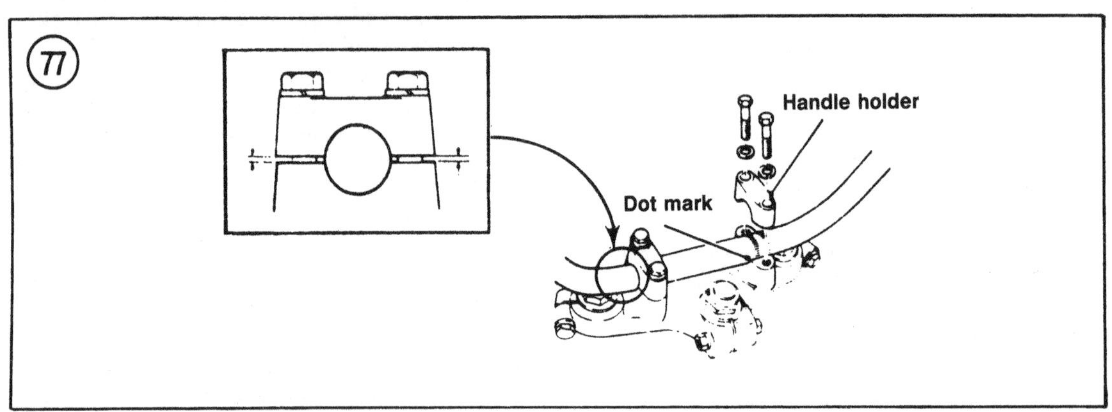

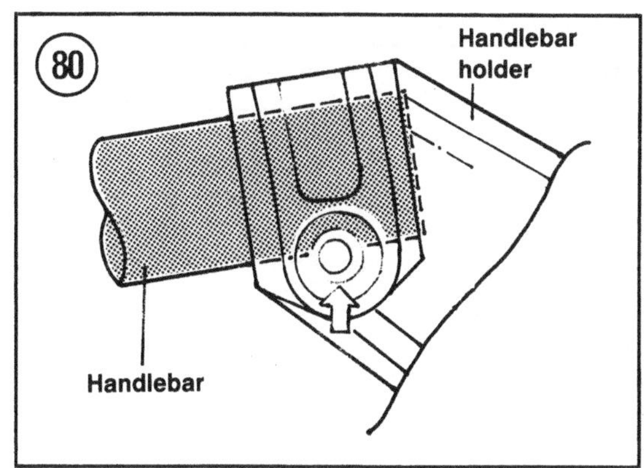

Table 1 FRONT SUSPENSION TORQUE SPECIFICATIONS

Item	mkg	ft.-lb.
Front axle nut	3.6-5.2	26-38
Front axle pinch bolt (L models)	1.5-2.5	11-18
Front caliper mounting bolt	2.5-4.0	18-29
Front caliper axle bolt (1977-1982)	4.0-5.5	29-40
Upper fork pinch bolt		
1977-1980; 1983-1984	2.0-3.0	15-22
1981-1982	3.5-5.5	26-40
Lower fork pinch bolt		
1977-1980	2.0-3.0	15-22
1981-1984 (except LD models)	1.5-2.5	11-18
LD models	1.2-2.0	9-15
Fork damper rod bolt		
1983-1984 (except LD models)	2.0-2.6	15-19
All others	1.5-2.5	11-18
Steering stem pinch bolt (except LD models)	1.5-2.5	11-18
Steering stem pinch bolt (LD models)	1.2-2.0	9-15
Steering stem head nut or bolt		
1980 and 1982	3.6-5.2	26-38
All others	2.0-3.0	15-22
Handlebar clamp bolts (1977-1982)	1.2-2.0	9-15
Handlebar fasteners (1983-1984)		
Set bolt (except LD)	1.5-2.5	11-18
Holder bolt (except LD)	5.0-6.0	36-44
Holder bolt (LD models)	1.5-2.5	11-18
Holder nut (except LD)	2.0-3.0	15-22
Holder nut (LD models)	1.0-1.5	7-11
Fork cap bolts	1.5-3.0	11-22
Brake disc mounting bolt	1.5-2.5	11-18

Table 2 FRONT FORK SPECIFICATIONS

Fork oil capacity	cc	U.S. oz.	Imp. oz.
B, C, EC, N, E, ET	165	5.6	5.8
LN, LT	217	7.3	7.6
TX	190	6.4	6.7
LX	249	8.4	8.8
LZ	239	8.0	8.4
MZ	223	7.5	7.9
LD	288	9.7	10.1
ED, ESD, EE	321	10.8	11.3
ESE	330	11.2	11.6
Fork oil level*	**mm**	**in.**	
B, C, EC, N, EN, ET	204	8.0	
LN, LT	229	9.0	
TX	201	7.9	
LX	208	8.2	
TX	201	7.9	
LZ	144	5.7	
MZ	140	5.5	
LD	190	7.5	
ED, ESD	125	4.9	
ESE	119	4.7	
Fork spring length Model		**Service limit**	
ET, LT models			
Upper		93.0 mm (3.66 in.)	
Lower		393.0 mm (15.47 in.)	
TX models			
Upper		92.9 mm (3.65 in.)	
Lower		396.4 mm (15.61 in.)	
LX models			
Upper		159.1 mm (6.26 in.)	
Lower		448.7 mm (17.67 in.)	
LZ models		528.0 mm (20.79 in.)	
MZ models		494.0 mm (19.45 in.)	
ESD, ESE models		490.0 mm (19.3 in.)	
LD models		513.0 mm (20.2 in.)	

* The maximum allowable difference in oil level between the right and left fork tubes is 1 mm (0.04 in.). Measure oil level from the top of the fork leg with the fork leg held vertical, spring removed and fork leg fully compressed.

CHAPTER NINE

REAR SUSPENSION

This chapter includes repair and replacement procedures for the rear wheel and rear suspension components. Refer to Chapter Eight for wheel balancing procedures. All rear brake repair is outlined in Chapter Ten.

Table 1 is at the end of the chapter.

REAR WHEEL

Removal/Installation

Refer to **Figure 1** for a typical rear wheel for 1977-1982 models. Refer to **Figure 2** for a typical TSCC model rear wheel.

1. Place the motorcycle on the centerstand. If desired, the exhaust system can be removed as outlined in Chapter Six to provide better access to the rear wheel components.
2. On models so equipped, remove the adjuster support bolts from each side (**Figure 3**).
3. Loosen the chain adjuster bolts. On 1977-1982 models, refer to **Figure 4** and first loosen the locknuts securing the adjuster bolts. On TSCC models back out the adjuster bolts 2-3 turns (**Figure 5**).
4. Remove the cotter pin securing the rear axle nut and loosen the axle nut (**Figure 6**).
5. Remove the bolts securing the chain guard and remove the guard (**Figure 7**).
6. On models with drum brakes, perform the following:
   a. Remove the adjuster nut from the brake rod and disengage the rod from the brake lever (**Figure 8**). Take care not to lose the pivot pin (**Figure 9**).
   b. Remove the snap clip or cotter pin securing the torque link bolt (**Figure 10**). Remove the torque link bolt and disconnect the torque link from the brake backing plate (**Figure 11**).
7. On disc brake models, perform the following:
   a. Refer to **Figure 12** and remove the bolts securing the torque link and brake caliper. Lift the caliper off the mounting bracket.

CAUTION
Support the caliper from the frame with a piece of wire or Bungee cord. Do not allow the caliper to suspend from the brake hose or the hose may be damaged.

8. On models with loose chain adjusters, pull the rear wheel back as far as possible and swing the chain adjusters down (**Figure 13**).
9. Push the rear wheel as far forward as possible to gain maximum chain slack.
10. Remove the axle nut and slide out the rear axle.
11. Disengage the drive chain from the rear sprocket. Tilt the top of the wheel slightly to the left and roll the rear wheel out of the frame (**Figure 14**).
12. Installation is the reverse of these steps. Keep the following points in mind:
   a. Turn the chain adjuster bolts equally on both sides until the chain deflection is 20-30 mm

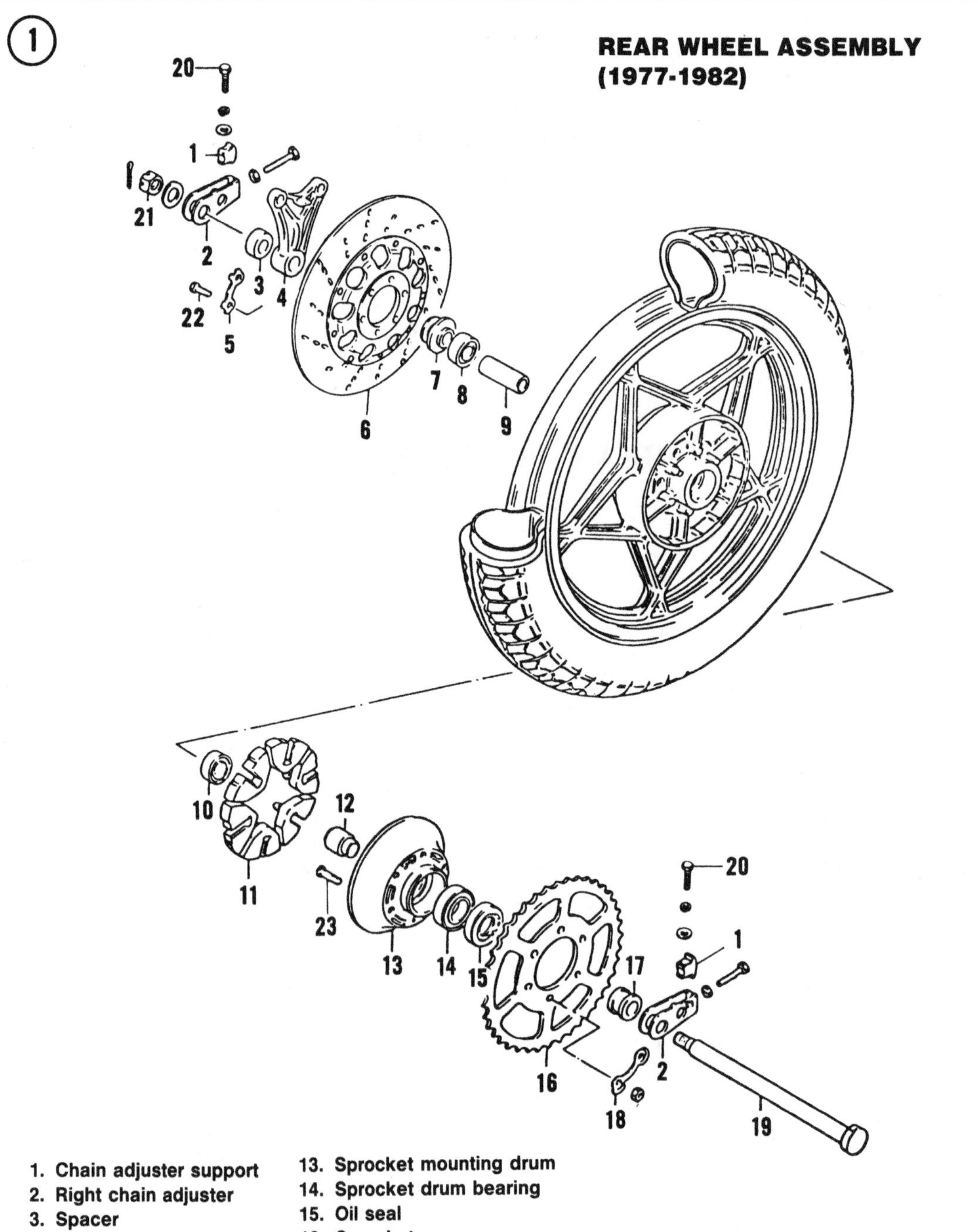

1. Chain adjuster support
2. Right chain adjuster
3. Spacer
4. Caliper mounting bracket
5. Folding lockwasher
6. Brake disc
7. Bearing spacer
8. Right wheel bearing
9. Center spacer
10. Left wheel bearing
11. Hub cushion
12. Bearing holder
13. Sprocket mounting drum
14. Sprocket drum bearing
15. Oil seal
16. Sprocket
17. Spacer
18. Folding lockwasher
19. Axle
20. Adjuster support bolt
21. Axle nut
22. Disc bolt
23. Sprocket bolt

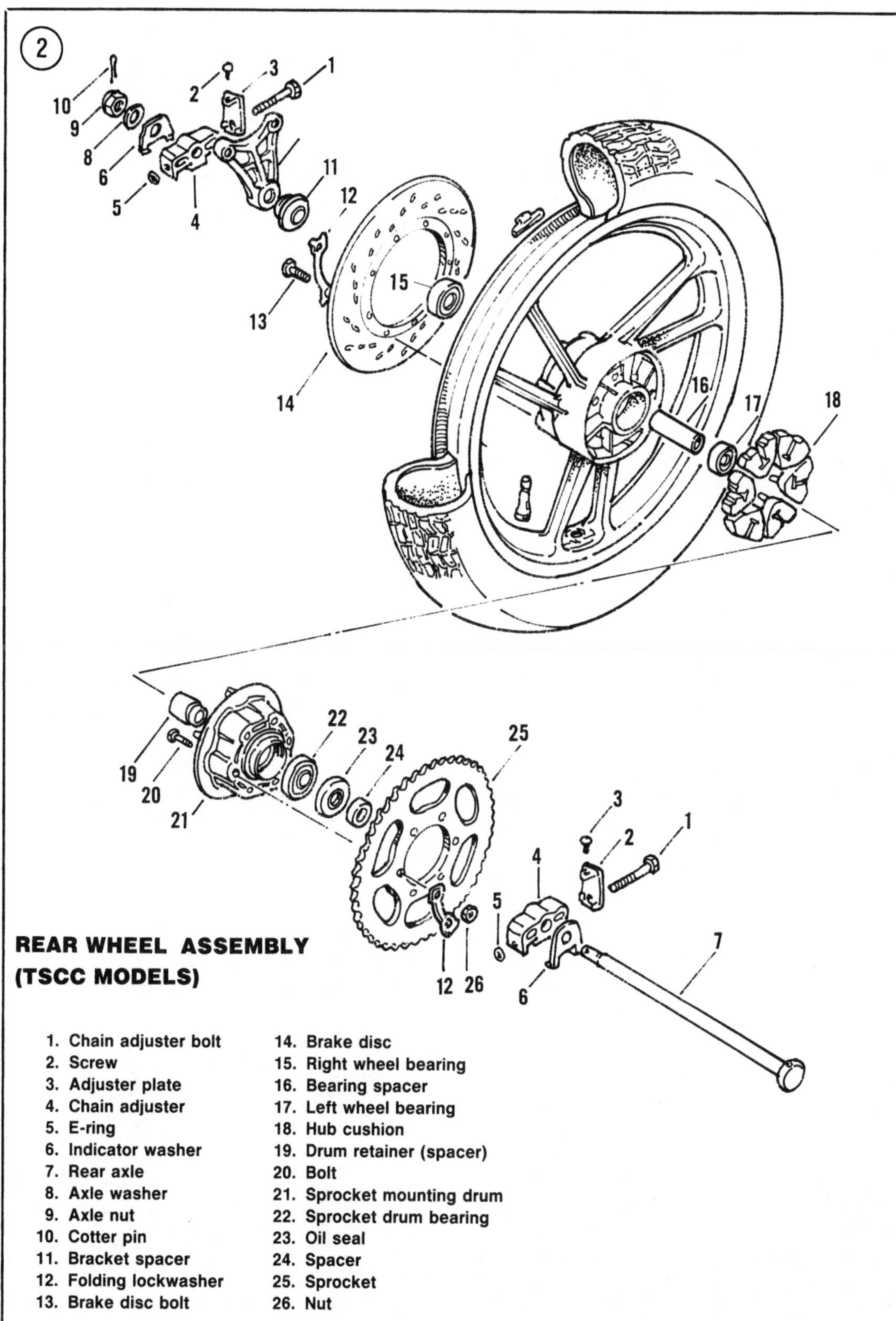

REAR WHEEL ASSEMBLY (TSCC MODELS)

1. Chain adjuster bolt
2. Screw
3. Adjuster plate
4. Chain adjuster
5. E-ring
6. Indicator washer
7. Rear axle
8. Axle washer
9. Axle nut
10. Cotter pin
11. Bracket spacer
12. Folding lockwasher
13. Brake disc bolt
14. Brake disc
15. Right wheel bearing
16. Bearing spacer
17. Left wheel bearing
18. Hub cushion
19. Drum retainer (spacer)
20. Bolt
21. Sprocket mounting drum
22. Sprocket drum bearing
23. Oil seal
24. Spacer
25. Sprocket
26. Nut

3

4

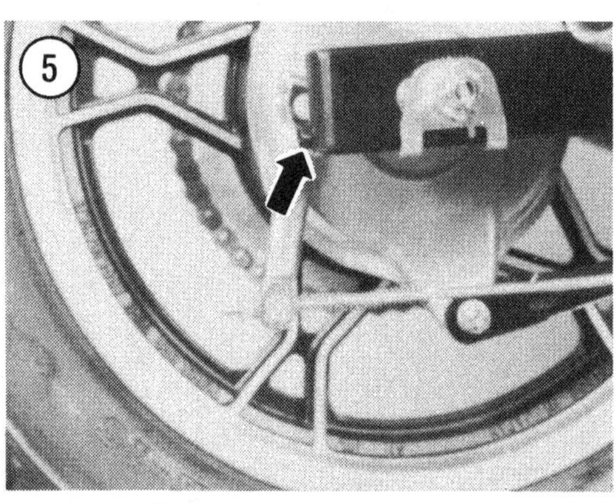
5

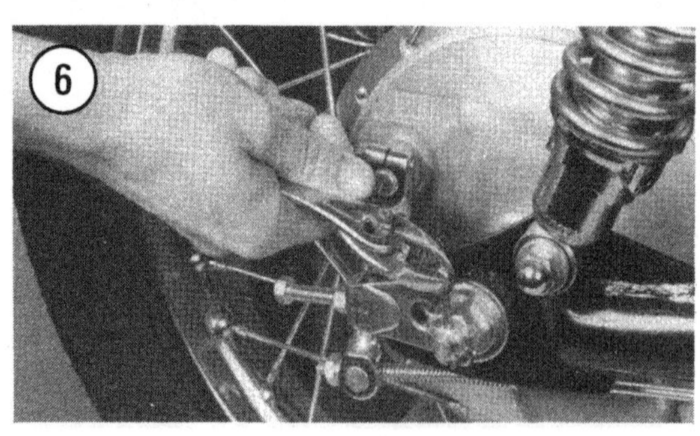
6

7

8

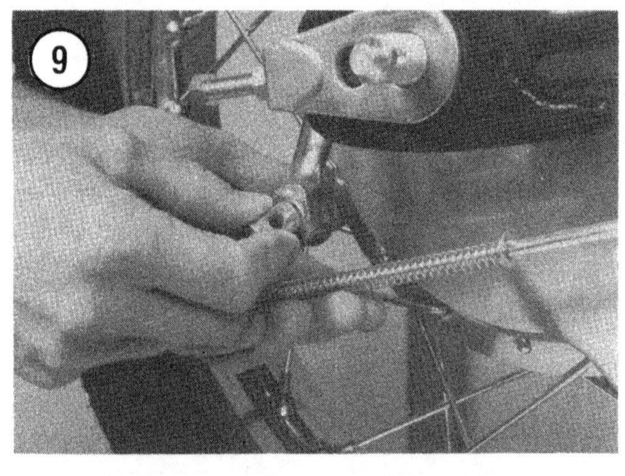
9

10

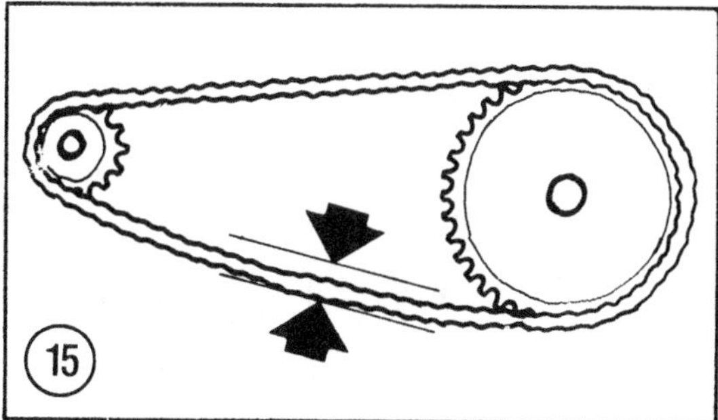

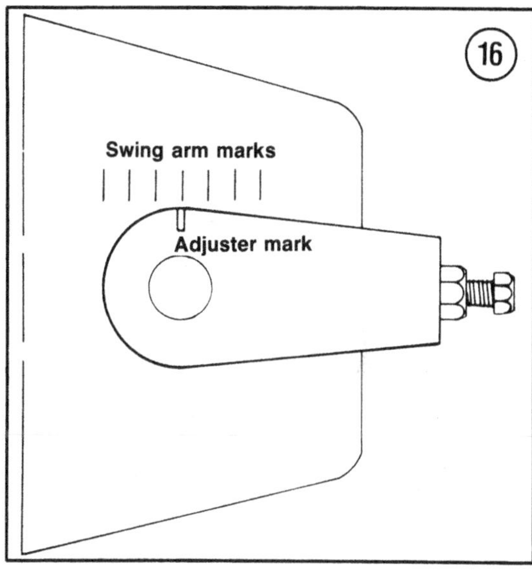

(3/4-1 3/16 in.) as shown in **Figure 15**. Make sure the index marks on the adjusters are aligned equally on both sides (**Figure 16**). Tighten the locknuts to secure the adjuster bolts on models so equipped.

b. Torque the axle nut, caliper mounting bolts, torque link nut and adjuster support bolts as specified in **Table 1**. Put a Phillips screwdriver shaft through the head of the axle to keep the axle from turning while tightening the axle nut.
c. Secure the rear axle nut and torque link nut with new cotter pins.
d. On drum brake models, adjust the rear brake adjuster nut to provide the following brake pedal free play: 20-30 mm (3/4-1 1/4 in.) on 1977-1982 models; 5-15 mm (1/4-9/16 in.) on TSCC L models.

Disassembly/Assembly

Refer to **Figure 17**, **Figure 1** or **Figure 2** for this procedure.

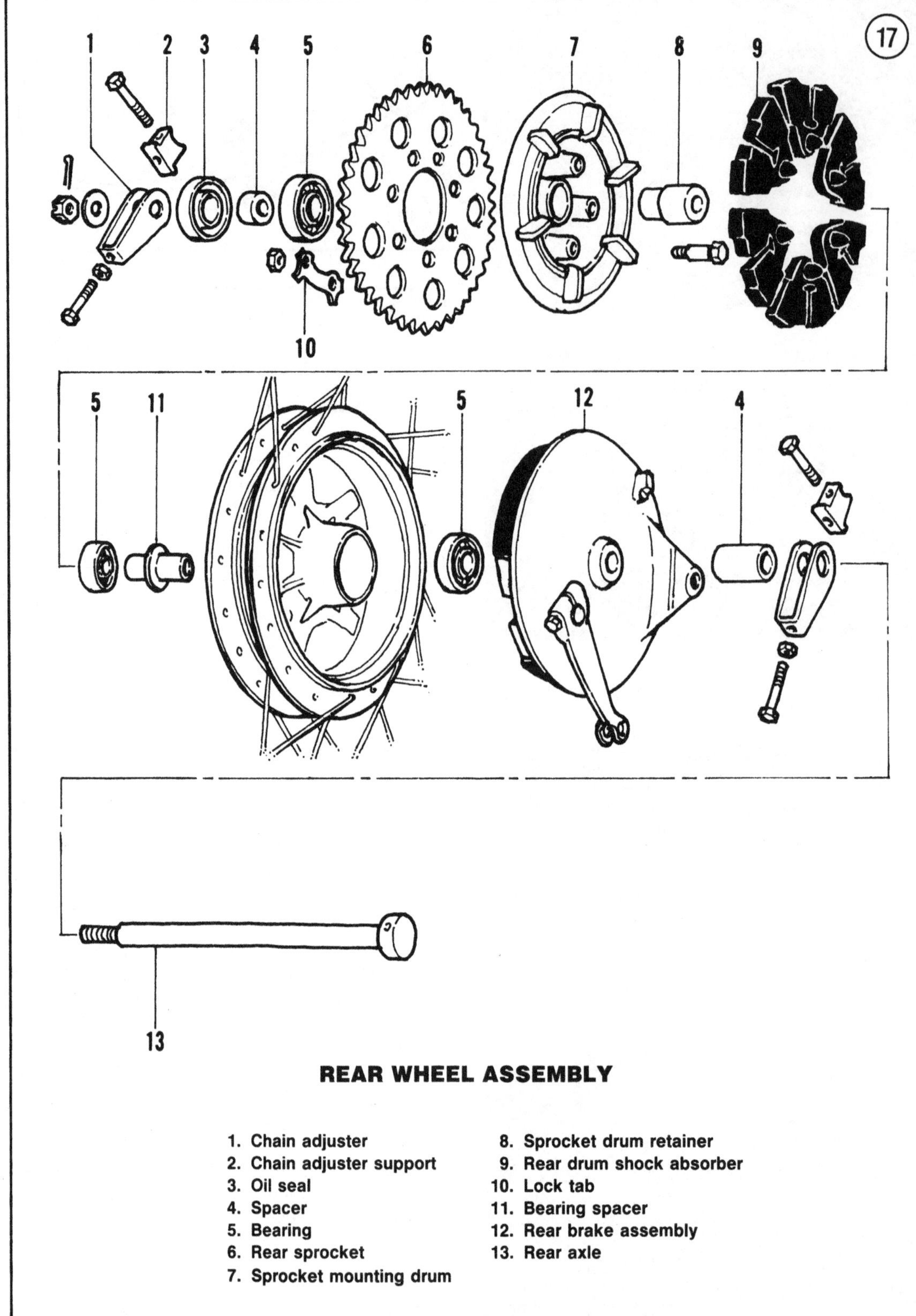

REAR WHEEL ASSEMBLY

1. Chain adjuster
2. Chain adjuster support
3. Oil seal
4. Spacer
5. Bearing
6. Rear sprocket
7. Sprocket mounting drum
8. Sprocket drum retainer
9. Rear drum shock absorber
10. Lock tab
11. Bearing spacer
12. Rear brake assembly
13. Rear axle

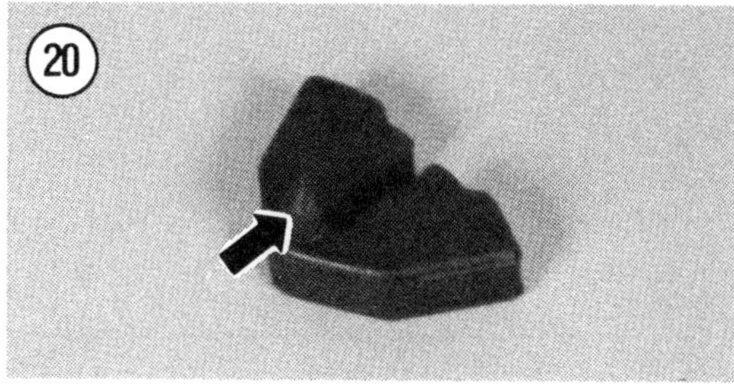

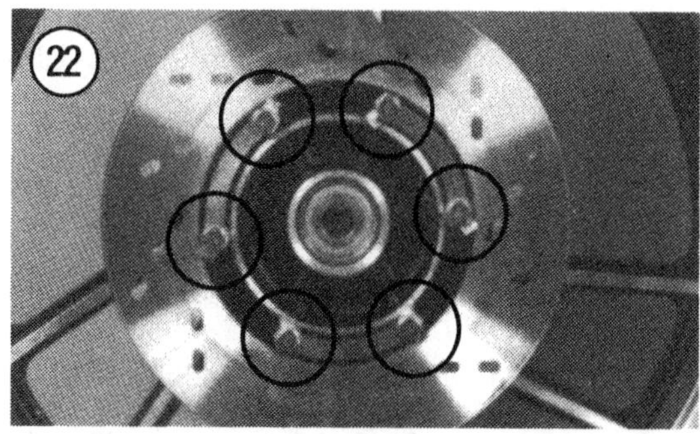

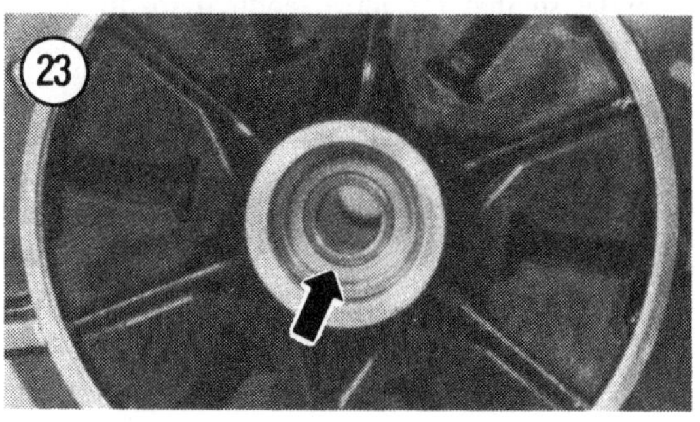

1. Remove the rear wheel. Remove the axle and collect both right and left side spacers.
2. Lift out the sprocket mounting drum and remove the drum retainer (bearing holder) as shown in **Figure 18**.
3. If rubber drive cushion replacement is desired, carefully pry up and remove each cushion (**Figure 19**). Lightly lubricate the tip of each new hub cushion (**Figure 20**) with rubber lubricant or liquid detergent. Carefully install the hub cushions so the tip on each cushion fully locks into the hole in the hub.
4. To remove the sprocket, fold back the locking tabs securing the sprocket nuts (**Figure 21**). Remove the bolts and lift off the sprocket.
5. To remove the brake disc, fold back the locking tabs securing the disc mounting bolts (**Figure 22**). Remove the bolts and remove the disc.
6. Assembly is the reverse of these steps. Keep the following points in mind:
   a. Inspect the brake disc or drum as outlined in Chapter Ten.
   b. Torque the sprocket and disc mounting bolts as specified in **Table 1**.
   c. Carefully bend over the locking tabs securing the sprocket nuts and disc bolts.

Inspection/Bearing Replacement

1. Rotate the wheel bearings by hand (**Figure 23**) check for excessive play or roughness. If roughness

9

is apparent, carefully drive the bearings out of the hub from the inside with a drift. Remove the right side bearing first.

CAUTION
Do not remove the bearings for routine inspection. They are usually damaged when removed. Remove the bearings only when replacement is required.

2. Install new bearings in the hub using a bearing driver or a socket only slightly smaller than the outside diameter of the bearing race. This is essential so that the force required to drive the bearing into the hub is applied only to the outer race. Install the right side bearing first.

NOTE
The right and left bearings are not interchangeable. The outside of the left-hand bearing is fitted with a metal seal while the outside of the right-hand bearing is fitted with a rubber type seal. Make sure the bearings are correctly installed.

3. Use a large screwdriver or tire tool to replace the seal in the sprocket mounting drum as shown in **Figure 24**. Pad the edge of the sprocket mounting drum with a rag to prevent damage to the drum. Lightly grease the edge of the new seal and tap it into place with the closed side out (**Figure 25**).
4. Check the rear sprocket for side wear and signs of undercutting as shown in **Figure 26**. If the sprocket is worn as shown, both sprockets and the chain should be replaced.

CAUTION
Always replace both sprockets as a set if either is worn excessively or when installing a new drive chain. Never run a new chain on old sprockets or an old chain on new sprockets. Rapid and uneven wear will result and seriously damage the new components.

5. Check the axle for straightness as shown in **Figure 27**. If the axle is bent more than 0.25 mm (0.010 in.), it must be replaced. Never try to straighten a bent axle.
6. Measure the axial and radial runout of the wheel with a dial indicator as shown in **Figure 28**. The maximum runout in either direction is 2.0 mm (0.08 in.). If the runout exceeds the maximum, check the wheel bearings and/or replace the wheel. The stock Suzuki alloy wheels cannot be serviced, except for balancing. If the wheel is damaged, it must be replaced.

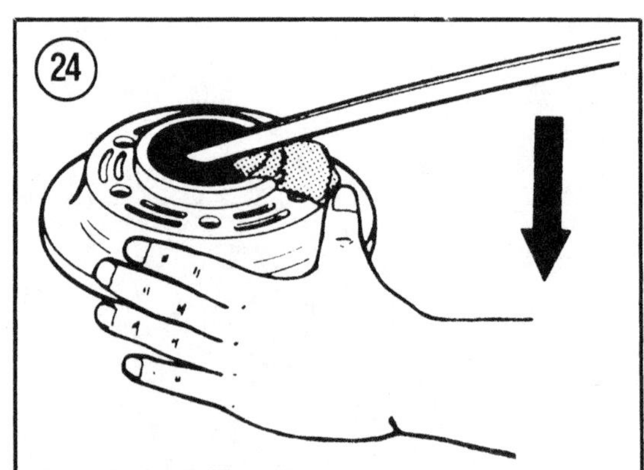

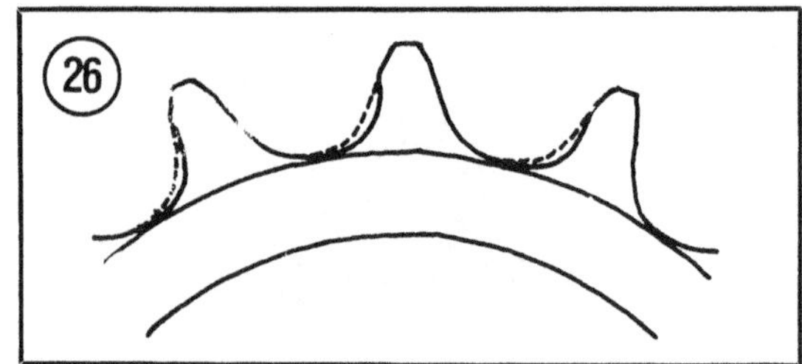

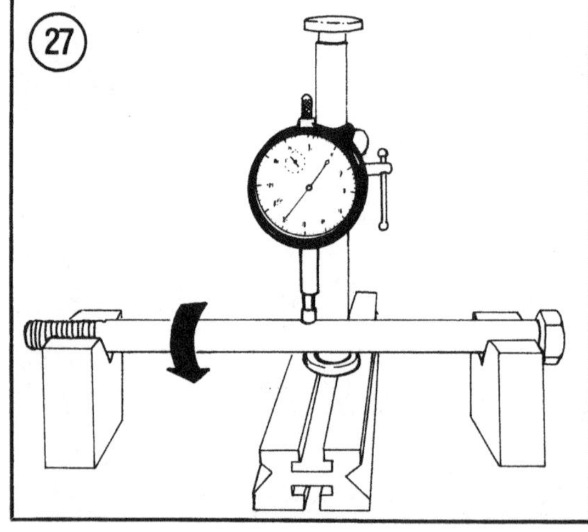

REAR SUSPENSION (TWIN-SHOCK)

Rear Suspension Unit Removal/Installation

The rear suspension units (shock absorber/spring assemblies) are non-repairable items. If the units fail to dampen adequately, replace them as a set.

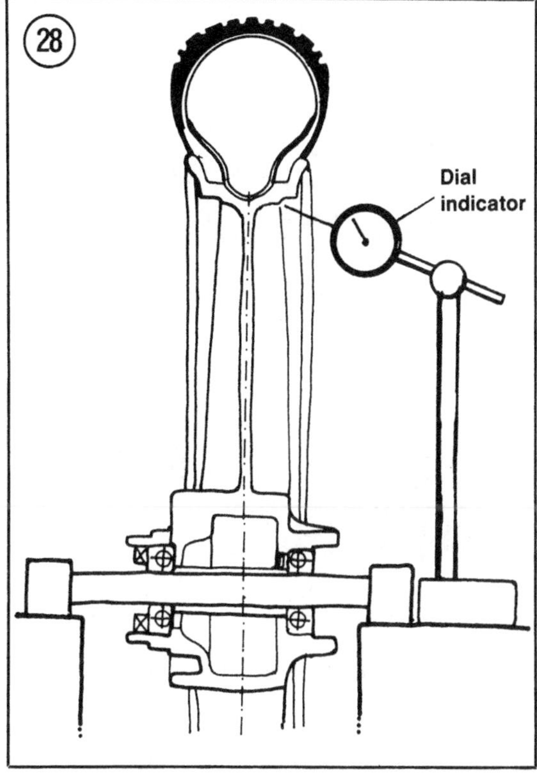

1. Place the motorcycle on the centerstand and set the spring pre-load adjuster to the softest setting.
2. Remove the lower and upper nuts and washers securing one suspension unit (**Figure 29** and **Figure 30**).
3. Slide the suspension unit off the upper mounting stud then raise the rear wheel enough to allow the lower mount to clear the muffler. Remove the suspension unit.

NOTE
Removal and installation of one unit at a time makes the task easier. The unit that remains in place will maintain the correct relationship of the swing arm to the frame.

4. Installation is the reverse of these steps. Torque the fasteners to 2-3 mkg (14.5-21.5 ft.-lb.).

CAUTION
Do not overtorque the mounting fasteners or the bushings may seize.

Inspection

1. Clamp the lower eye of the shock absorber in a vise fitted with jaw protectors. With assistance, compress the spring and remove the spring keeper from the top of the unit. Remove the spring.
2. Visually check the shaft for bending. If bending is apparent, the unit is unserviceable and must be replaced.
3. Check around the shaft for oil. If oil is present (more than a light film), the shock absorber seal is defective and the unit must be replaced.
4. Grasp the upper mounting eye and repeatedly compress and extend the damper rod to check for

9

damping resistance. Resistance during extension of the rod should be noticeably greater than during the compression stroke. Check the resistance in all damping settings. The resistance in both directions should be smooth throughout the stroke. If the shock absorber fails on any of these points, it is unsatisfactory and should be replaced.

5. Before reassembling the spring and shock absorber, accurately measure the free length of the spring and write it down (**Figure 31**). If the free length difference between the springs is greater than 3-4 mm (1/8-3/16 in.), the springs should be replaced as a set.

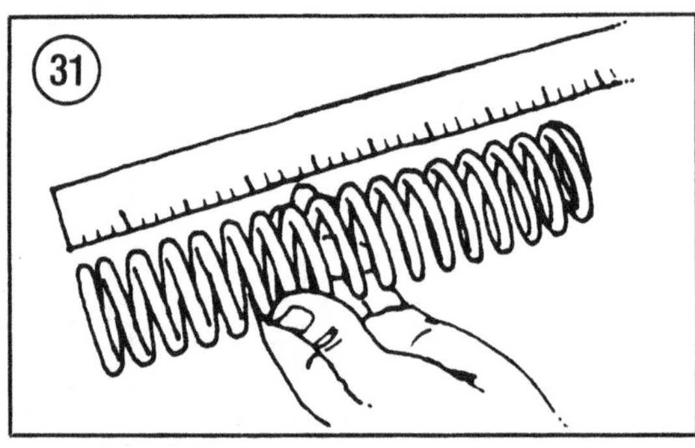

Swing Arm Removal/Installation

The swing arm is supported by caged roller bearings on each side. The bearings should be lubricated periodically to provide maximum service life.

The condition of the bearings can greatly affect handling performance. Worn bearings will produce wheel hop and pulling to one side under acceleration and pulling to the other side during braking. If the condition of the bearings is doubtful, remove the rear wheel and torque the swing arm pivot bolt as specified in **Table 1**. Grasp the swing arm and attempt to move it from side-to-side in a horizontal arc. If more than a just perceptible movement is felt, the bearings are worn and must be replaced.

If bearings must be replaced, remove the swing arm and have a dealer perform the task. Special tools should be used to remove and install the bearings to prevent possible damage to the swing arm or the new bearings.

Refer to **Figure 32** for this procedure.

1. Remove the rear wheel and the suspension units as outlined in this chapter.
2. On models with a rear disc brake, remove the rear brake caliper and remove the brake hose from under the swing arm clips and the torque link mount.
3. Remove the nut securing the swing arm pivot bolt (**Figure 33**) and remove the bolt. Remove the swing arm assembly from the frame.

CAUTION

It may be necessary to tap the pivot bolt out of the frame with a drift. Remove the bolt with care to prevent damage to the swing arm bearings and the pivot bolt.

4. Remove the dust cover and washer from each side of the swing arm (**Figure 34**).
5. Remove the inner bearing race (spacer) as shown in **Figure 35**.
6. Check the condition of the needle bearings (**Figure 36**). If the bearings are worn, galled or feel rough they must be replaced. Refer bearing replacement to a dealer.

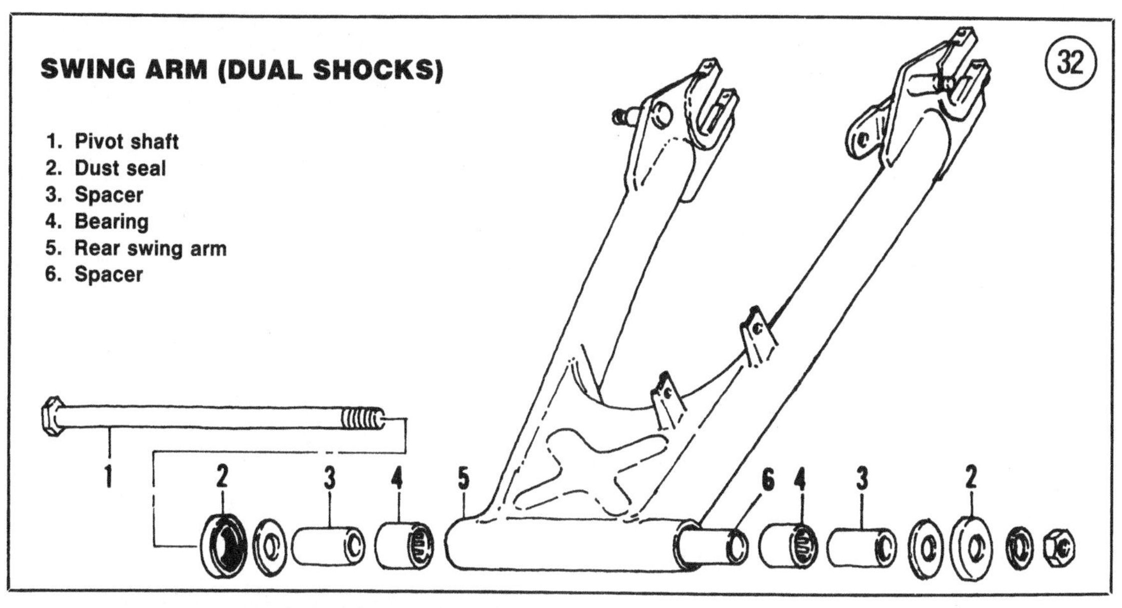
SWING ARM (DUAL SHOCKS)
32
1. Pivot shaft
2. Dust seal
3. Spacer
4. Bearing
5. Rear swing arm
6. Spacer
1
2
3
4
5
6 4
3
2

33
2400cc

34

35

9

7. Installation is the reverse of these steps. Keep the following points in mind:
   a. Lubricate both swing arm bearings with heavy grease such as boat trailer wheel bearing grease.
   b. Lightly grease the pivot bolt and install it from the right side.
   c. On disc brake models, route the brake hose carefully under the retaining clips and torque link mount on the swing arm.
   d. Torque the rear suspension components and the brake banjo hose (if removed) to values specified in **Table 1**.
   e. Use new cotter pins to secure the torque link nuts and rear axle nut.
   f. Install the rear wheel as outlined in this chapter.

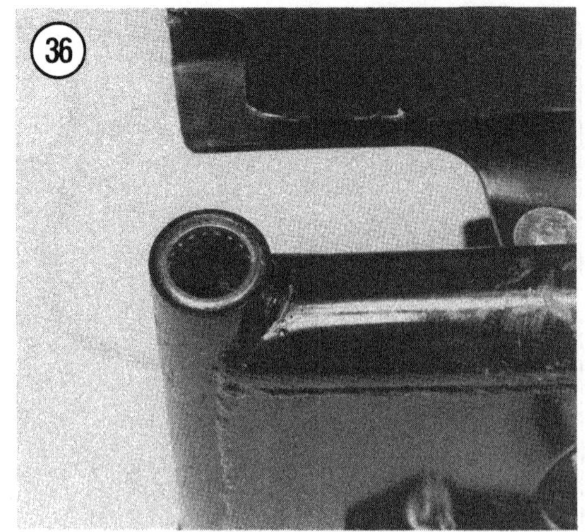

(37)

SWING ARM (SINGLE SHOCK)

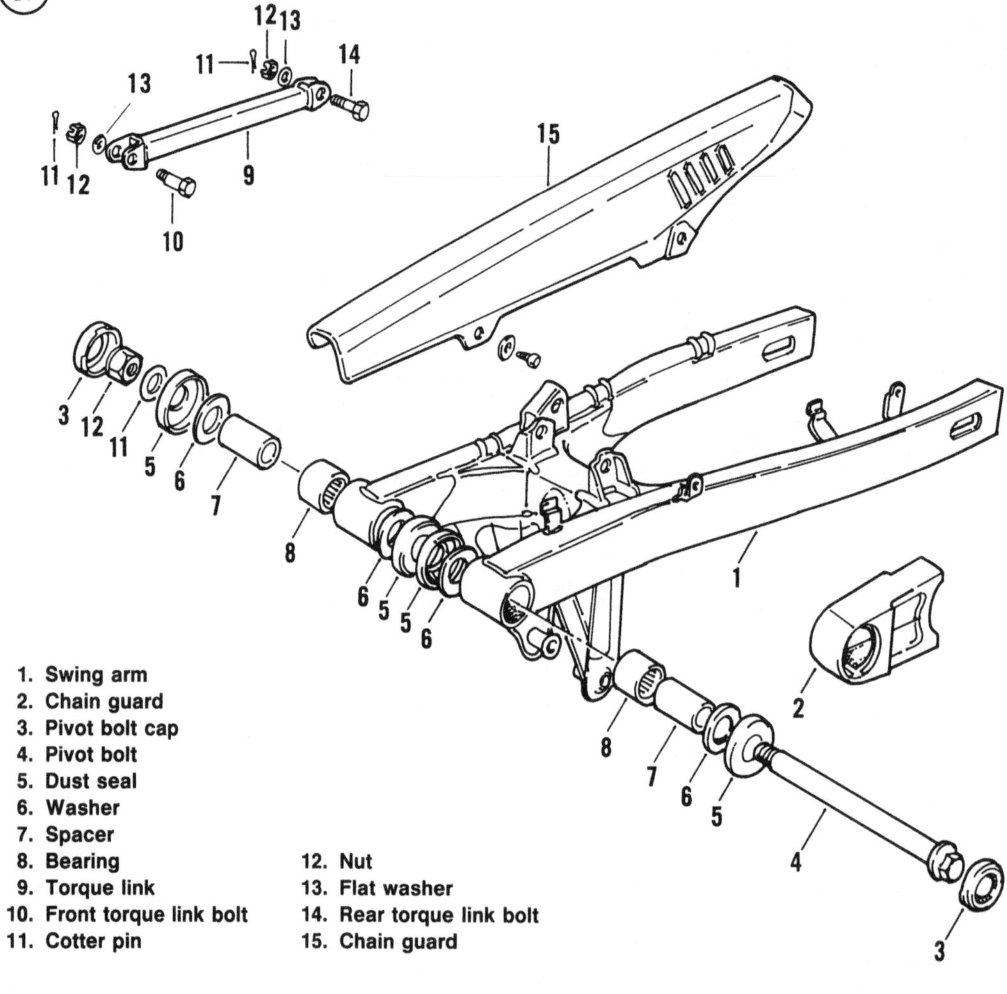

1. Swing arm
2. Chain guard
3. Pivot bolt cap
4. Pivot bolt
5. Dust seal
6. Washer
7. Spacer
8. Bearing
9. Torque link
10. Front torque link bolt
11. Cotter pin
12. Nut
13. Flat washer
14. Rear torque link bolt
15. Chain guard

REAR SUSPENSION (SINGLE SHOCK)

The Suzuki Full-Floater rear suspension consists of a single spring/shock absorber unit, a rocker arm type cushion lever, and a swing arm. To provide proper operation of the suspension as well as maximum service life, the pivot joints on all components should be disassembled, inspected and lubricated any time rear suspension repair is performed.

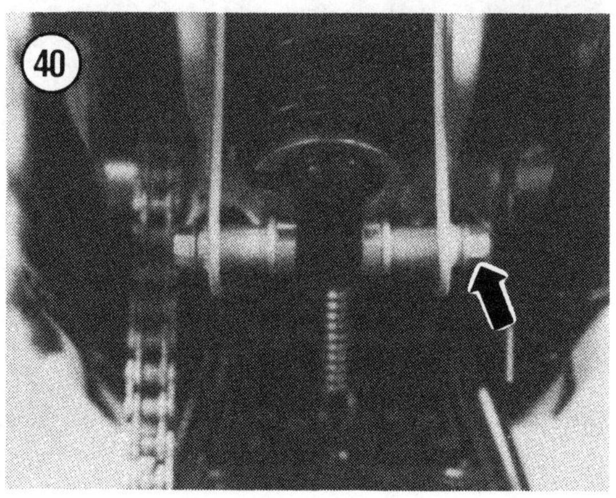

The spring/shock absorber unit is equipped with a remote hydraulic pre-load adjuster. The spring/shock absorber unit is equipped with pivots at each end and is mounted between the swing arm and the forward portion of the cushion lever. The center of the cushion lever pivots in needle bearings in the upper part of the motorcycle frame, while the rear portion of the lever is connected to the swing arm.

The Full Floater suspension allows the rear wheel to move easily over small bumps for a comfortable ride, but provides progressively more compression damping as the rear wheel moves toward the limits of the suspension travel.

This chapter outlines procedures to remove, disassemble, lubricate and repair the components of the rear suspension.

Swing Arm Bearing Condition Check

Refer to **Figure 37** for this procedure.

The swing arm is supported by caged roller bearings on each side. The lower end of the shock absorber is connected to the swing arm.

The condition of the swing arm bearings can greatly affect the handling of the motorcycle. Worn bearings will cause wheel hop, pulling to one side under acceleration and pulling to the other side during braking; a generally ill handling machine under most riding conditions. To check the condition of the swing arm bearings, perform the following steps.

1. Remove the rear wheel as outlined in this chapter.
2. Remove the plastic cover on each side of the swing arm pivot points (**Figure 38**). Tighten the swing arm pivot bolt (**Figure 39**) to the torque specified in **Table 1**.
3. Remove the bolts securing the rear fender and remove the fender.
4. Remove the bolt securing the bottom end of the shock absorber to the swing arm (**Figure 40**). Take care not to lose the collars on each side of the shock mount.
5. Remove the bolt securing the cushion lever rod to the swing arm (**Figure 41**). Take care not to lose the dust seal and washer from each end of the cushion lever rod. The swing arm is now free to move under its own weight.
6. Grasp the swing arm and attempt to move it from side-to-side in a horizontal arc. If more than a just perceptible movement is felt, the bearings are worn and must be replaced.

7. Connect the shock absorber and cushion lever rod to the swing arm. Tighten the bolts to the torque value specified in **Table 1**.
8. Install the rear fender and rear wheel.

Swing Arm Removal/Installation

Refer to **Figure 37** for this procedure.

1. Remove the banjo bolt securing the brake line to the rear caliper (**Figure 42**). Have a container ready to catch any dripping brake fluid.

CAUTION
Do not allow brake fluid to contact any painted surfaces or the paint will be damaged.

2. Remove the bolt securing the forward end of the torque link (**Figure 43**).
3. Remove the rear wheel as outlined in this chapter. Remove the torque link while removing the rear brake caliper.
4. Remove the bolts securing the rear fender and remove the fender.
5. Remove the bolt securing the bottom end of the shock absorber to the swing arm (**Figure 40**). Take care not to lose the collars on each side of the shock mount.
6. Remove the bolt securing the cushion lever rod to the swing arm (**Figure 41**). Take care not to lose the dust seal and washer from each end of the cushion lever rod.
7. Remove the plastic cover on each side of the swing arm pivot points (**Figure 38**). Remove the nut securing the pivot bolt (**Figure 39**), but do not remove the pivot bolt at this time.
8. Remove the brake hose from the clips on the swing arm. Support the weight of the swing arm and carefully tap the pivot bolt out of the frame. Remove the swing arm while sliding the brake hose through the torque link mount (**Figure 44**).
9. Inspect and lubricate the swing arm bearings as described in this chapter.
10. Installation is the reverse of these steps. Keep the following points in mind:
    a. Make sure the swing arm components are correctly positioned as shown in **Figure 37**.
    b. Route the drive chain over the chain side of the swing arm and slide the swing arm into the frame. Lightly grease the pivot bolt and install it from the left side.
    c. Connect the lower end of the shock absorber and the cushion lever rod to the swing arm.
    d. Torque all rear suspension components as specified in **Table 1**.

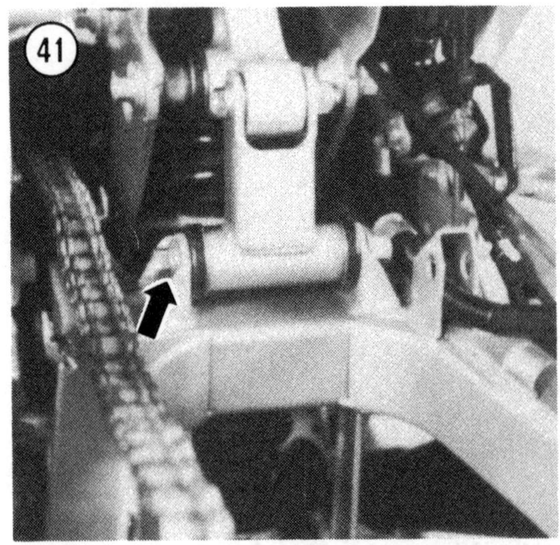
41

42

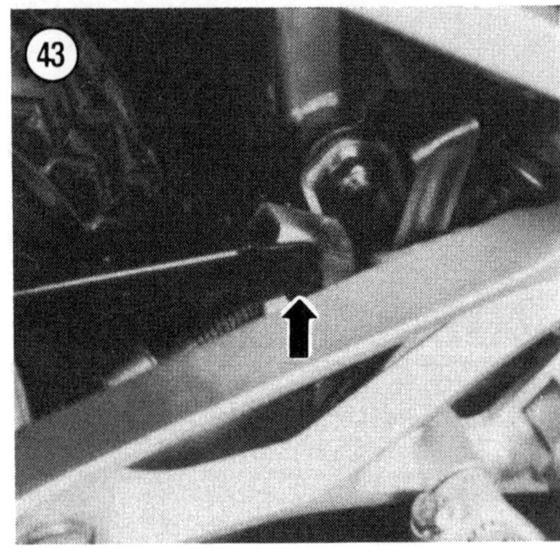
43

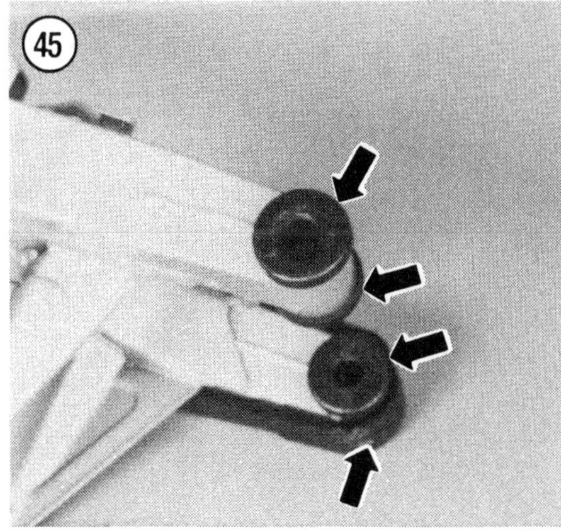

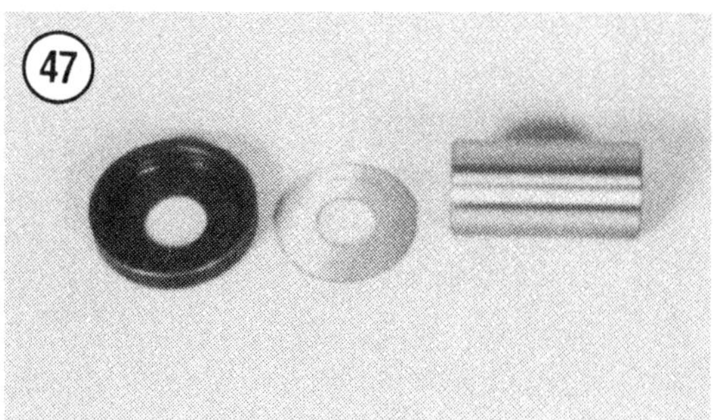

Swing Arm Bearing Inspection, Lubrication and Replacement

CAUTION
Do not attempt to remove the bearings just for inspection as they are usually destroyed when removed.

1. Remove the inner and outer dust seals and inner bearing races (spacers) from each side of the swing arm (**Figure 45**).
2. Clean the spacers and bearings in solvent if possible. If solvent is not available, wipe the bearings and spacers with a clean rag.
3. Examine the inner needle bearings in each side of the swing arm (**Figure 46**). If the bearings appear worn or damaged in any way they must be replaced.
4. Carefully inspect the outer dust seal, washer and inner bearing race (**Figure 47**) for signs of wear or damage. Carefully examine the dust seal lips for damage (**Figure 48**). A damaged seal will allow dirt and moisture into the swing arm bearings.
5. Install the spacers into the needle bearings. Check that the spacers turn freely without noise, tight spots or excessive looseness.
6. Remove the chain adjuster assemblies from each side of the swing arm (**Figure 49**). Replace chain adjusters if damaged or worn.
7. If any swing arm component (dust seal, washer or bearing) is damaged or worn, it is recommended that the components be replaced by a dealer or machine shop.

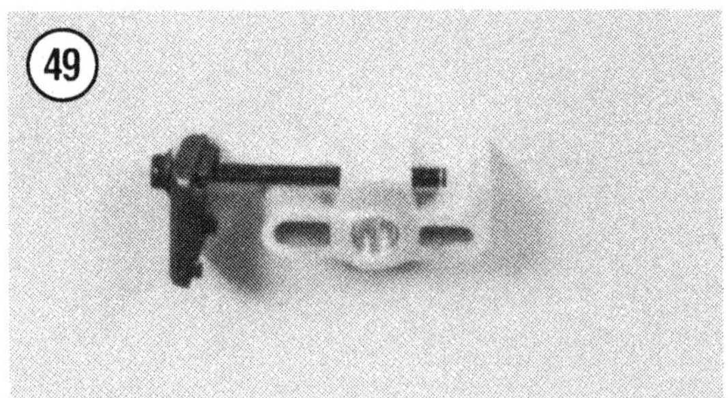

CAUTION
Special tools and/or a hydraulic press are often needed to remove the old bearings, especially if they are excessively worn or damaged by rust and corrosion. Do not attempt to drive out the old components or install the new components with a hammer and punch or damage to the swing arm and new components will surely result. Refer the task to a dealer. It is a simple and quick job with the right tools.

8. Remove and replace the drive chain buffer (**Figure 50**) if excessively worn or damaged.
9. Lubricate the swing arm bearings and spacers with a heavy waterproof grease such as boat trailer wheel bearing grease.
10. Assemble the spacers, washers, dust seals and chain buffer on the swing arm (**Figure 51**).
11. Check the pivot bolt for straightness with V-blocks and a dial indicator as shown in **Figure 52**. If the runout of the pivot bolt exceeds 0.3 mm (0.019 in.), it must be replaced. If V-blocks and a dial indicator are not available, have this task performed by a dealer.

Shock Absorber Removal/Installation

The spring/shock absorber unit is an oil damped shock absorber fitted with an external spring and a remote pre-load adjuster (**Figure 53**).
1. Remove the swing arm as outlined in this chapter.
2. Remove the screws securing the remote pre-load adjuster to the frame (**Figure 54**).
3. Remove the bolt securing the top of the shock absorber to the cushion lever (**Figure 55**). Slide the shock off the cushion lever.
4. Remove the bolts securing the engine mounting bracket to the frame (**Figure 56**) and remove the bracket.
5. While removing the shock absorber, route the remote pre-load adjuster across the top of the engine and back through the space behind the engine mounting bracket.

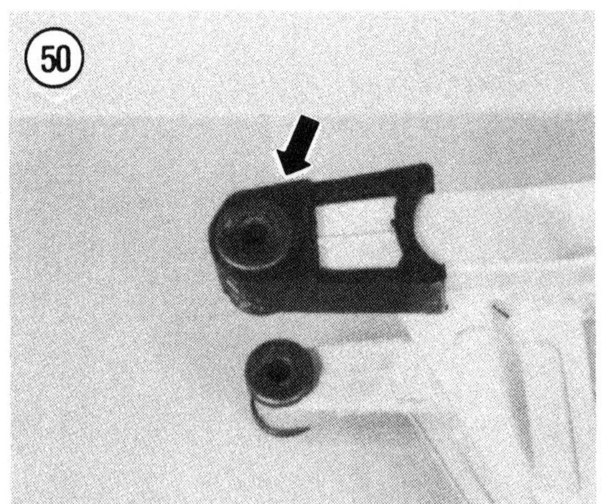

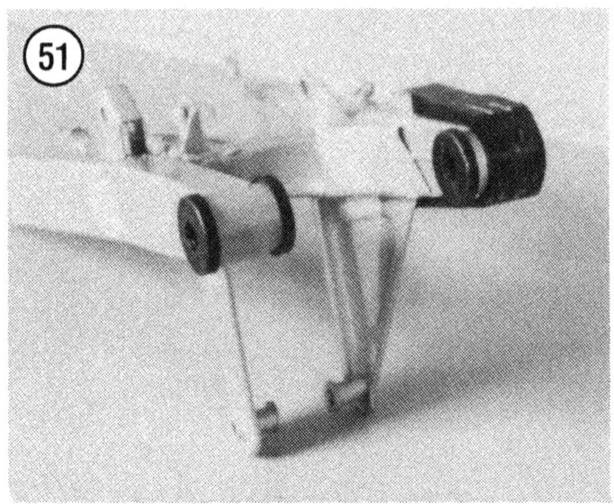

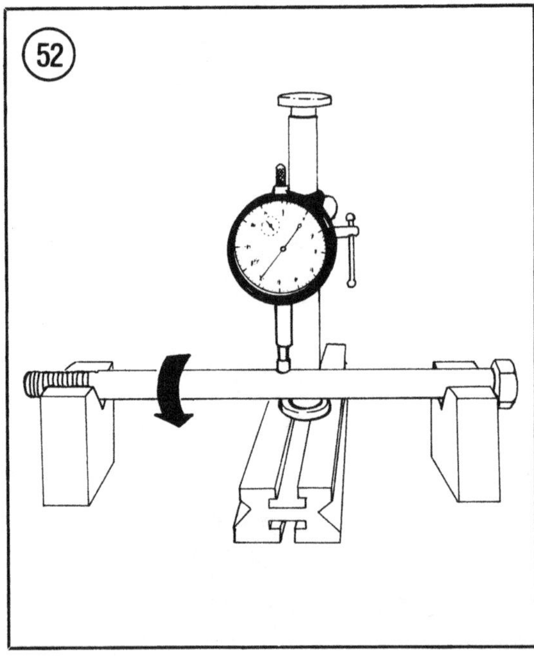

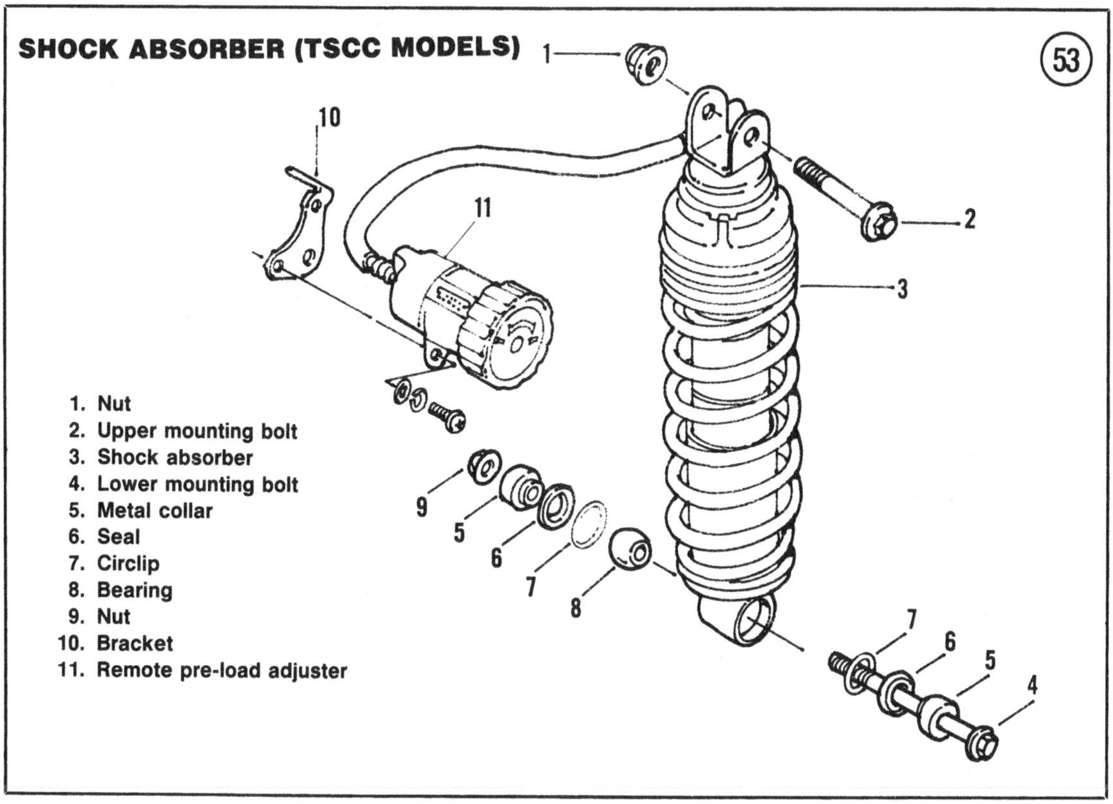

SHOCK ABSORBER (TSCC MODELS) (53)

1. Nut
2. Upper mounting bolt
3. Shock absorber
4. Lower mounting bolt
5. Metal collar
6. Seal
7. Circlip
8. Bearing
9. Nut
10. Bracket
11. Remote pre-load adjuster

54

56

55

6. Inspect and lubricate the pivot joint as described in this chapter.
7. Installation is the reverse of these steps. Keep the following points in mind:
   a. Install the shock absorber mounting bolts and tighten as specified in **Table 1**.
   b. Route and secure the remote pre-load adjuster to the frame as shown in **Figure 54**. Install the engine mounting bracket (**Figure 56**).
   c. Torque the engine mounting bolt and suspension bolts as specified in **Table 1**.

d. Install the swing arm as outlined in this chapter.

Pivot Joint Inspection and Lubrication

Refer to **Figure 53** for this procedure.

CAUTION
Do not attempt to remove the hose from the shock absorber or the remote pre-load adjuster. The shock absorber is not repairable.

1. Remove the metal collars from the lower pivot joint (**Figure 57**).
2. Carefully lift out the seal from each side of the pivot joint (**Figure 58**).
3. Examine the pivot joint bearing (**Figure 59**). Check the bearing for signs of wear or excessive play caused by dirt or corrosion. The bearing should pivot freely without tight spots.
4. If the bearing is worn or damaged, it must be replaced. Perform the following steps:
   a. Remove the wire snap rings securing the bearing and tap the old bearing out with a socket slightly smaller than the opening in the shock absorber.
   b. Lightly grease the outside of the new bearing and gently tap the new bearing into the shock absorber. Secure the bearing with the wire snap rings.
5. Lubricate the bearing with moly grease or heavy waterproof grease such as boat trailer wheel bearing grease.
6. Install the seals over each side of the bearings with the seal lips positioned toward the outside (**Figure 58**).
7. Grease the inner lips of the seals and install the metal collars into the shock absorber (**Figure 60**).
8. Roll back the rubber boot on the end of shock absorber and check for signs of oil leakage (**Figure 61**). Oil leakage indicates the shock absorber seals are worn or damaged and the shock absorber must be replaced.

Shock Absorber Inspection

1. Back off the remote pre-load adjuster to position I (softest).
2. Clamp the lower eye of the shock absorber in a vise fitted with jaw protectors. With assistance, use 2 bars or large screwdrivers to compress the spring enough to remove the spring guide (**Figure 62**) from the top of the unit. Remove the spring.

NOTE
Aftermarket spring compressors may also be suitable for spring removal. If the proper tools are not available, have a dealer remove the spring.

3. Visually check the damper rod for bending. If any bends or scatches on the damper rod are apparent, the unit is unserviceable and must be replaced.
4. Grasp the upper mount and repeatedly compress and extend the damper rod to check for damping resistance. Resistance during extension of the rod should be noticeably greater than during

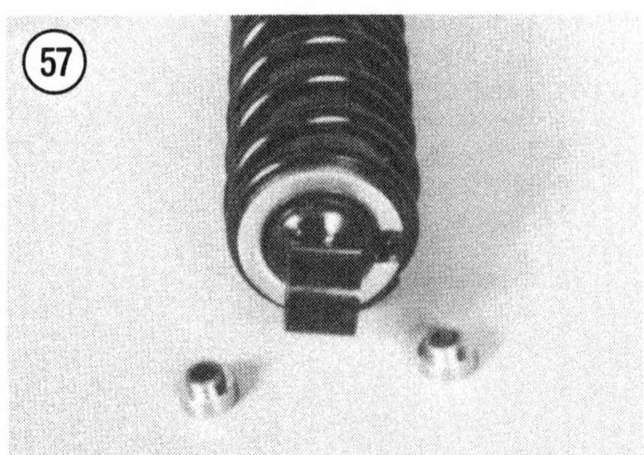
57

58

59

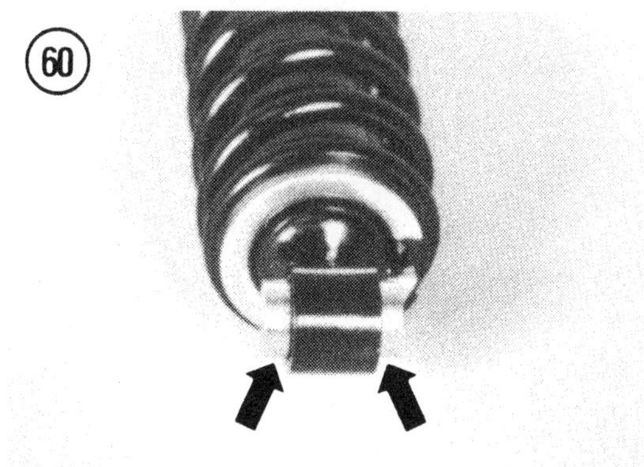

the compression stroke. The resistance in both directions should be smooth throughout the stroke. If the shock absorber has obvious flat spots in the resistance to movement in either direction, the unit is defective internally and must be replaced.

5. Install the shock spring and secure it in place with the upper spring guide.

Removal/Installation

The cushion lever is a large rocker arm attached to the motorcycle frame through a center pivot supported in needle bearings. The forward point on the cushion lever is connected to the shock absorber while the rear attachment point is connected to the cushion lever rod. The pivot bearings should be serviced any time suspension repairs are performed to maintain proper operation of the suspension system.

Refer to **Figure 63** for this procedure.

1. Remove the swing arm and shock absorber unit as outlined in this chapter.
2. Remove the nut and pivot bolt securing the cushion lever to the shock absorber bracket (**Figure 64**) and remove the cushion lever. Make sure the dust seals on each side of the pivot joint are not damaged or lost.
3. Inspect and lubricate the cushion lever bearing as described in this chapter.
4. Installation is the reverse of these steps. Keep the following points in mind:
   a. Slide the cushion lever carefully into the frame to make sure the center pivot dust seals are not dislodged or damaged.
   b. Lightly grease then install the cushion lever pivot bolt. Tighten the nut as specified in **Table 1**.
   c. Install the shock absorber and swing arm.

Cushion Lever Bearing Inspection and Lubrication

1. Remove the large dust seals and spacers from the center of the cushion lever and from the cushion lever rod (**Figure 65**).
2. Remove the bolt securing the cushion lever rod and separate the components (**Figure 66**).
3. Remove the metal spacers and seals from each end of the cushion lever (**Figure 67**).

NOTE
The metal spacers and seals used on each end of the cushion lever are identical.

4. Clean all components in solvent and dry with a clean rag.
5. Carefully examine both pivot needle bearings (**Figure 68**). Any pits on the needles or signs of rust and corrosion indicate the bearings must be replaced.
6. Slide the spacers into the needle bearings and slowly turn the spacers. If any tight spots or roughness are present the bearings must be replaced.
7. Examine the condition of the seals used on each end of the cushion lever and replace if damaged.

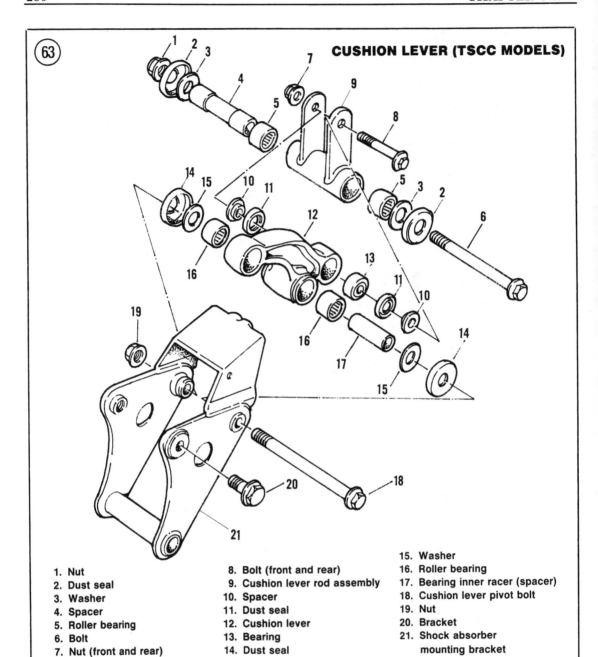

63

CUSHION LEVER (TSCC MODELS)

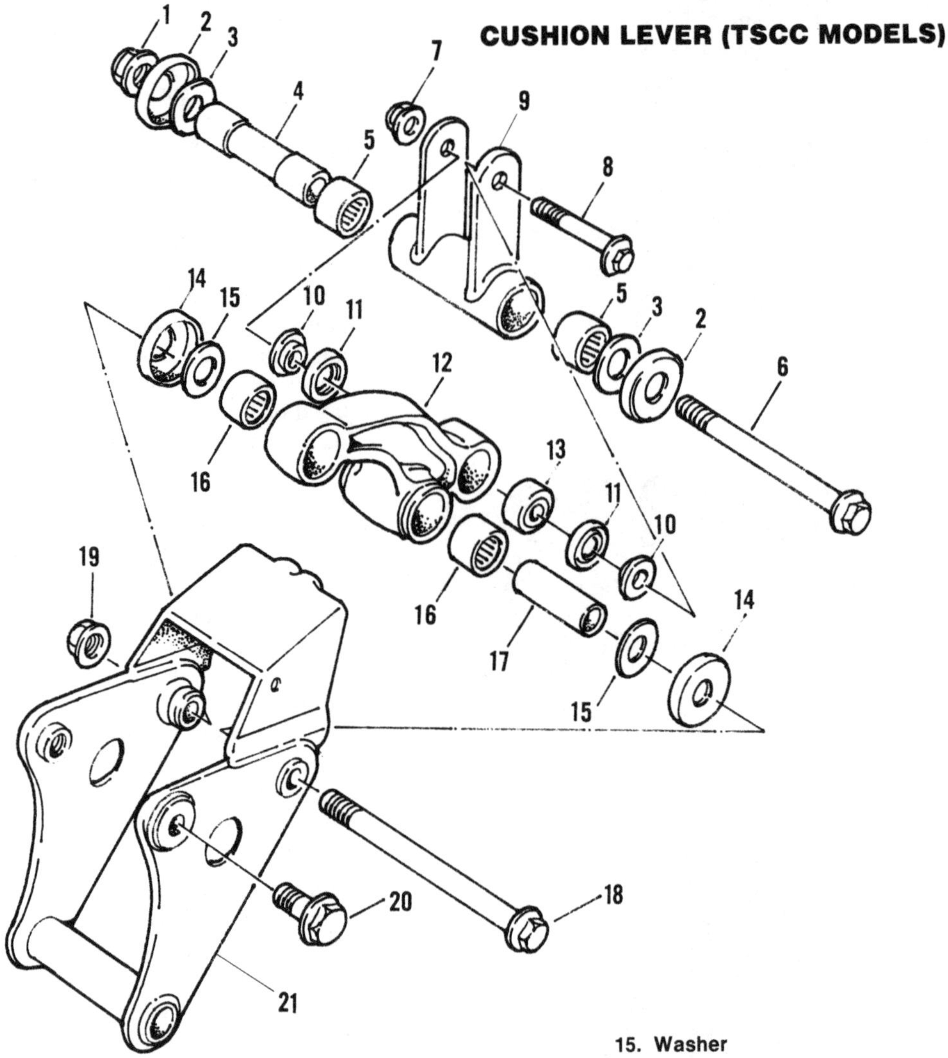

1. Nut
2. Dust seal
3. Washer
4. Spacer
5. Roller bearing
6. Bolt
7. Nut (front and rear)
8. Bolt (front and rear)
9. Cushion lever rod assembly
10. Spacer
11. Dust seal
12. Cushion lever
13. Bearing
14. Dust seal
15. Washer
16. Roller bearing
17. Bearing inner racer (spacer)
18. Cushion lever pivot bolt
19. Nut
20. Bracket
21. Shock absorber mounting bracket

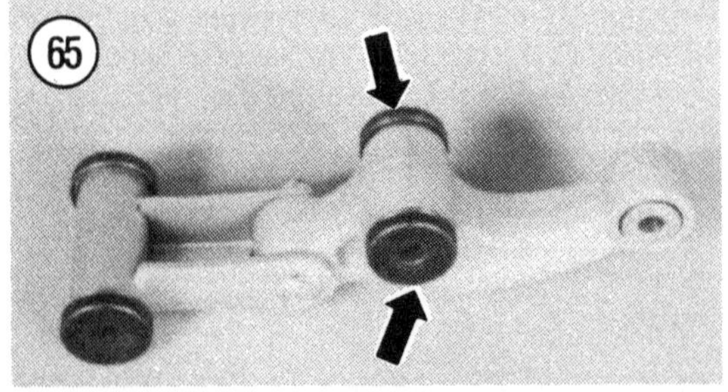

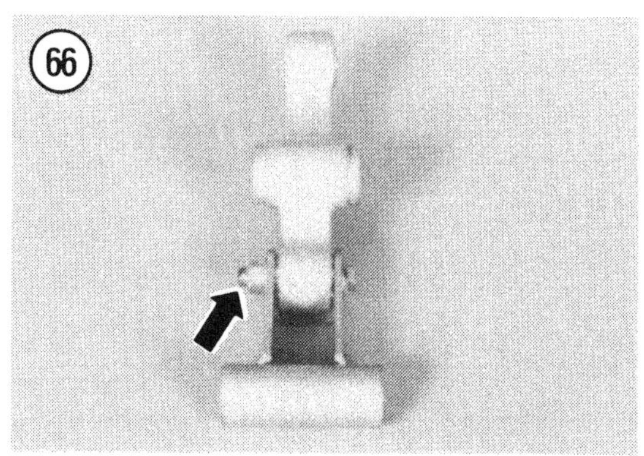

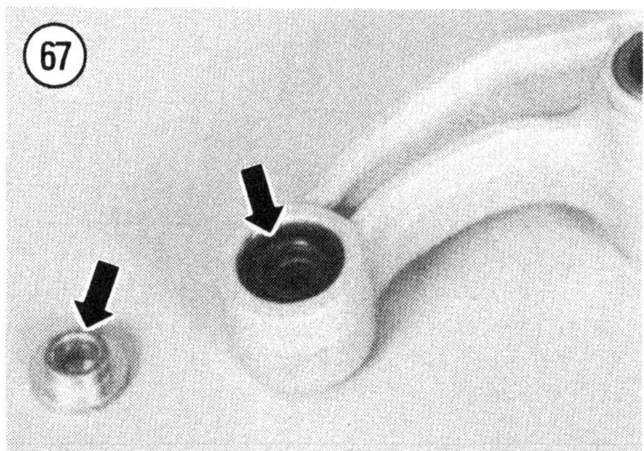

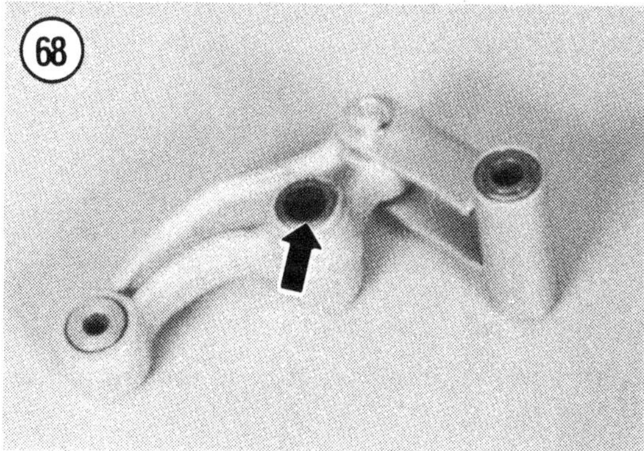

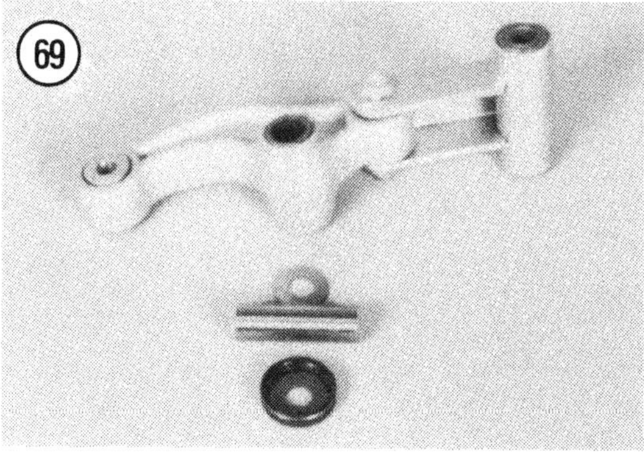

NOTE
The cushion lever seals are very similar to, but different from, the seals used on the lower end of the shock absorber. Do not intermix these seals during suspension servicing and lubrication.

8. Examine the center pivot dust seals and spacers (**Figure 69**). Replace any component that is distorted or damaged in any way. A damaged seal will allow dirt and moisture to enter the pivot needle bearings.
9. If any bearings must be replaced, refer the task to a dealer.
10. Lubricate all the bearings with Moly Lube or a heavy duty waterproof grease such as boat trailer wheel bearing grease.
11. Install the seals on each end of the cushion lever with the seal lips out as shown in **Figure 67**.
12. Assemble the spacers, washers and dust seals as shown in **Figure 65**.

DRIVE CHAIN

Drive chain care is very important. The chain and sprockets should be cleaned, inspected and adjusted at least every 600 miles (1,000 km). If chain or sprocket wear is evident, both sprockets and the chain should be replaced as a set. An excessively stretched chain will cause severe vibration and will be difficult if not impossible to adjust properly.

The drive chain is a pre-lubricated, long-life type with no master link. The lubrication between the rollers and pins in each link is sealed with O-rings as shown in **Figure 70**.

Cleaning and Lubrication

1. Scrub the side plates of the chain with a stiff brush to remove all loose dirt and grit.

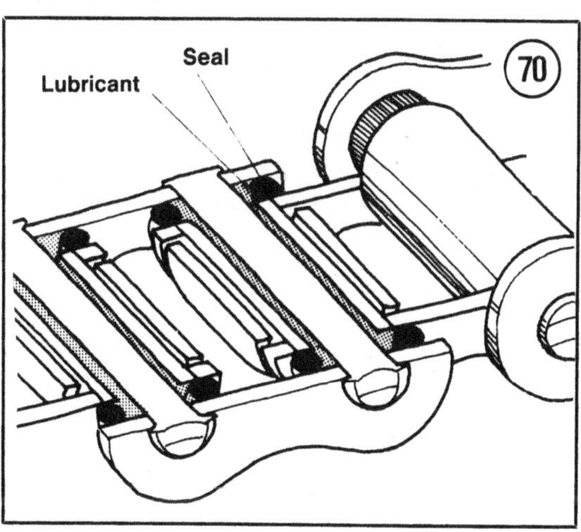

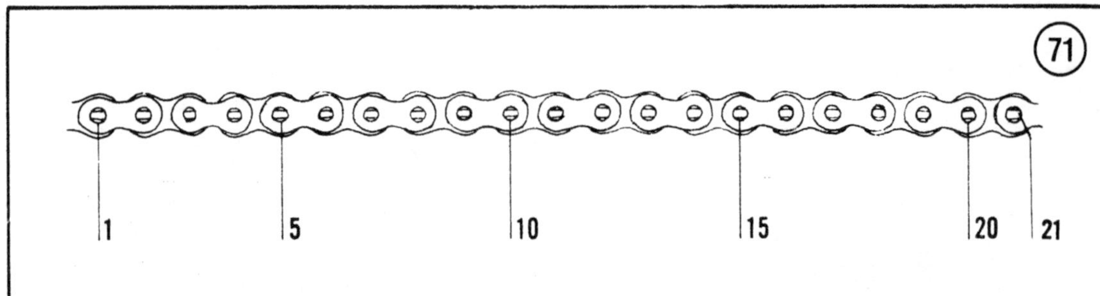

2. Wash the chain with clean kerosene and dry it thoroughly. Use the kerosene sparingly and brush it on the chain side plates, not between the rollers.

CAUTION
Only use kerosene to wash the chain. Do not use gasoline, benzine or similar solvents or the O-rings and permanent lubrication of the chain will be damaged.

3. Lubricate the outside of the chain with motor oil. Do not use specially compounded chain lubricants *unless* they are specifically designated for use on O-ring chains.
4. After the chain has been thoroughly oiled, wipe off the excess with a clean rag.

Inspection

1. Carefully examine the chain for loose pins, damaged rollers, dry or rusty links, kinked links and missing O-rings. The chain must be replaced if any of these conditions exist.
2. To check the stretch of the chain refer to *Rear Wheel Installation* in this chapter and tighten both chain tensioners until all chain slack is removed. Remove the chain guard. With an accurate ruler or a locally improvised measuring gauge, measure the distance between 21 pins on the chain as shown in **Figure 71**. The service limit for all models is 336.5 mm (13.25 in.). The chain must be replaced if it is stretched beyond the service limits.

WARNING
Do not attempt to shorten the chain by removing links and installing a master link; the chain could easily fail. Such a chain failure could cause the rear wheel to lock up, resulting in a serious accident.

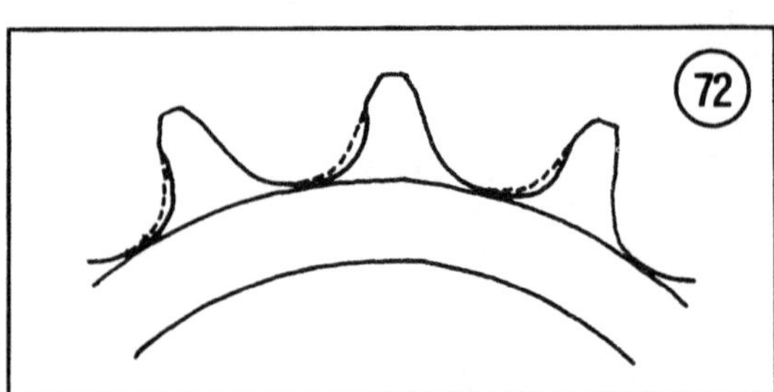

3. Check the sprockets for excessive side wear or undercutting of the teeth as shown in **Figure 72**. If the sprocket is worn, replace both sprockets and the drive chain as a set.

CAUTION
Always replace both sprockets as a set if either is worn excessively or when installing a new drive chain. Never run a new chain on old sprockets or an old chain on new sprockets. Rapid and uneven wear will result and seriously damage the new components.

4. Readjust the chain slack as outlined under *Rear Wheel Installation.*

Removal/Installation

To remove the drive chain it is necessary to remove the swing arm. Perform *Swing Arm Removal* as outlined in this chapter.

Table 1 REAR SUSPENSION TORQUE SPECIFICATIONS

Item	mkg	ft.-lb.
Rear sprocket nut		
1977-1982	4.0-6.0	29-43
1983-1984	2.5-4.0	18-29
Swing arm pivot bolt		
1977-1982 and LD models	5.0-8.0	36-58
All others	5.5-8.8	40-64
Shock absorber nut (1977-1982)	2.0-3.0	15-22
Rear axle nut		
1977-1982	8.5-11.5	62-83
1983-1984	5.0-8.0	36-58
Torque link nut	2.0-3.0	15-22
Rear caliper mounting bolt	2.5-4.0	18-29
Brake disc bolt	1.5-2.5	11-18
Single shock rear suspension components		
Shock absorber bolts	4.8-7.2	35-52
Cushion lever center pivot	8.4-10.0	61-73
Cushion lever rod to cushion lever	4.8-7.2	35-52
Cushion lever rod to swing arm	8.4-10.0	61-73
Upper rear engine mount bolt	6.7-8.0	49-58

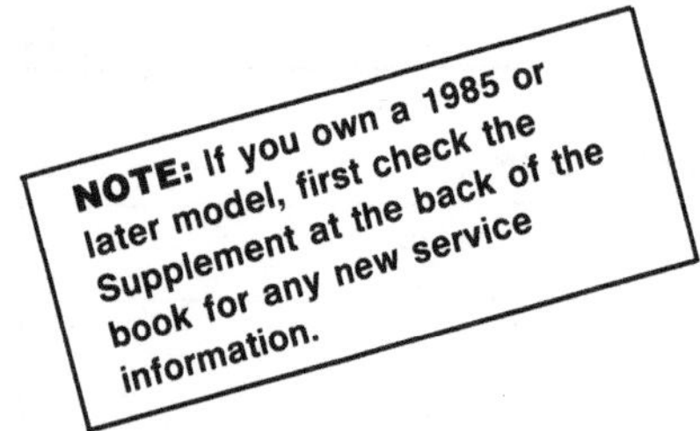
NOTE: If you own a 1985 or later model, first check the Supplement at the back of the book for any new service information.

CHAPTER TEN

BRAKES

All GS550 models are equipped with a hydraulic disc front brake. The rear brake may be either mechanical drum or hydraulic disc, depending on the model.

DRUM BRAKE

The rear drum brake is a single leading shoe type that is mechanically actuated by the brake pedal.

Disassembly/Assembly

1. Remove the rear wheel.
2. Remove the brake backing plate from the drum.
3. Remove the brake shoes by spreading the brake shoes against the spring pressure and rolling the shoes off the backing plate (**Figure 1**).
4. Assembly is the reverse of these steps. Connect both shoes together with the springs before installing the shoes on the backing plate. Adjust the rear brake as outlined in Chapter Three.

Inspection

1. Check the brake shoes for wear and the presence of foreign matter. If the brake drum is grooved deeply enough to snag a fingernail, the drum should be turned down on a lathe and new shoes fitted.
2. Inspect the brake linings for oil, grease or dirt. Replace any linings that are contaminated with oil or grease. Dirt can usually be removed from the linings with a wire brush.
3. Measure the thickness of the linings at the thinnest place. Replace both shoes as a set if any lining is worn to 1.5 mm (1/16 in.).
4. Check the return springs for signs of fatigue or damage. If the springs are weak the brake shoes will drag, causing premature wear and lack of power.
5. When inspecting brakes or installing new shoes, always clean and lube the brake cam and pivot with high-temperature grease. Use only a small amount of grease to avoid contaminating the brake linings.

DISC BRAKES

Three types of front brake calipers and two types of rear calipers are used. On the front, 1979 and earlier models use a round pad style, while

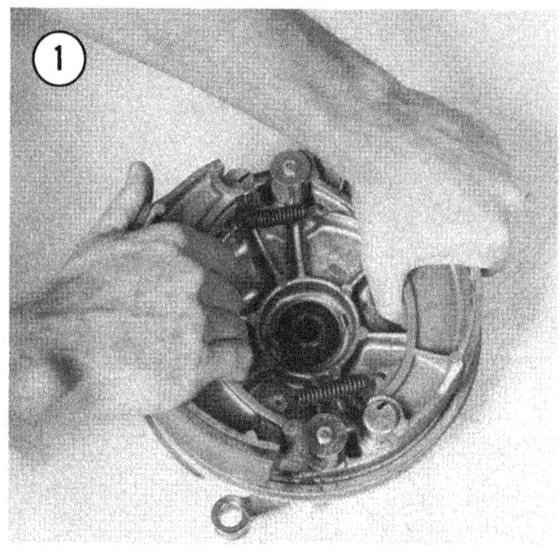
1

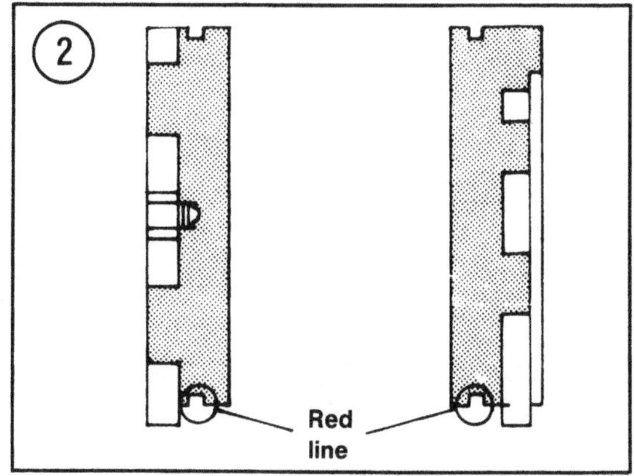

1980-1982 models are fitted with a square pad style caliper. The rear calipers are the same on all models prior to 1983. The front and rear brake calipers on 1983 and later TSCC models are nearly identical, with both units using the same brake pads.

WARNING
If necessary to top off either master cylinder reservoir, only use brake fluid from an unopened container marked DOT 3 or DOT 4. All models use a glycol-based brake fluid. Mixing a glycol-based fluid with a petroleum-based or silicon-based fluid may cause brake component damage leading to brake failure.

Front Brake Pad Replacement (1979 and Earlier Models)

Replace both front pads as a set when they are worn down to the red line as shown in **Figure 2**.

Refer to **Figure 3** for this procedure.

1. Remove the bolts securing the front caliper to the fork leg (**Figure 4**) and slide the caliper off the disc.

NOTE
Do not pull the front brake lever while the caliper is removed or the caliper piston may be pushed completely out of the caliper body.

2. Remove the screw securing the pad lock plate (**Figure 5**) and remove the plate.
3. Press out and remove the stationary pad (**Figure 6**).
4. Pry up and remove the sliding pad (**Figure 7**).
5. Remove the cover from the front master cylinder reservoir. Wrap a rag around the reservoir to catch any brake fluid spills.
6. Slowly press the caliper piston back into the caliper as far as it will go.
7. Apply a *light* film of PBC brake pad grease (part No. 99000-25110) to the *back* of the sliding pad and to the surface of the caliper piston.

NOTE
Suzuki recommends a light film of PBC base (copper-colored) Brake Pad Grease (part No. 99000-25110) be applied between the pad and piston when new pads are installed. The grease the acts as a cushion and helps prevent brake squeal due to metal-to-metal contact.

CAUTION
Do not allow any grease to get on the pad friction material or the pad will be ruined.

8. Install the sliding pad into the caliper body. Make sure that the notch in the pad engages the locating tab in the caliper.
9. Install the stationary pad and secure it with the pad lock plate.
10. Install the caliper. Torque the caliper mounting bolts as specified in **Table 1**. Top up the master cylinder reservoir, if necessary.
11. Spin the front wheel and apply the front brakes a few times to make sure the brakes operate properly and the pads adjust correctly.

Front Pad Replacement (1980-1982 Models)

Replace both front pads as a set when they are worn down to the red line as shown in **Figure 2**.

Refer to **Figure 8** for this procedure.

NOTE
Suzuki recommends the use of a small amount of silicon based (colorless) Caliper Axle Grease (part No. 99000-25100) on the caliper axles when a caliper is disassembled for pad replacement.

NOTE
If front brake pad squeal is a problem, a ***thin*** *film of Suzuki PBC Grease (part No. 99000-25110) can be applied to the back of the pad. The grease acts as a cushion between the pad and the caliper piston to help eliminate brake noise.*

WARNING
Always apply Caliper Axle Grease or PBC grease sparingly or the grease may ooze out and contaminate the pad friction surface and the disc resulting in the loss of brakes.

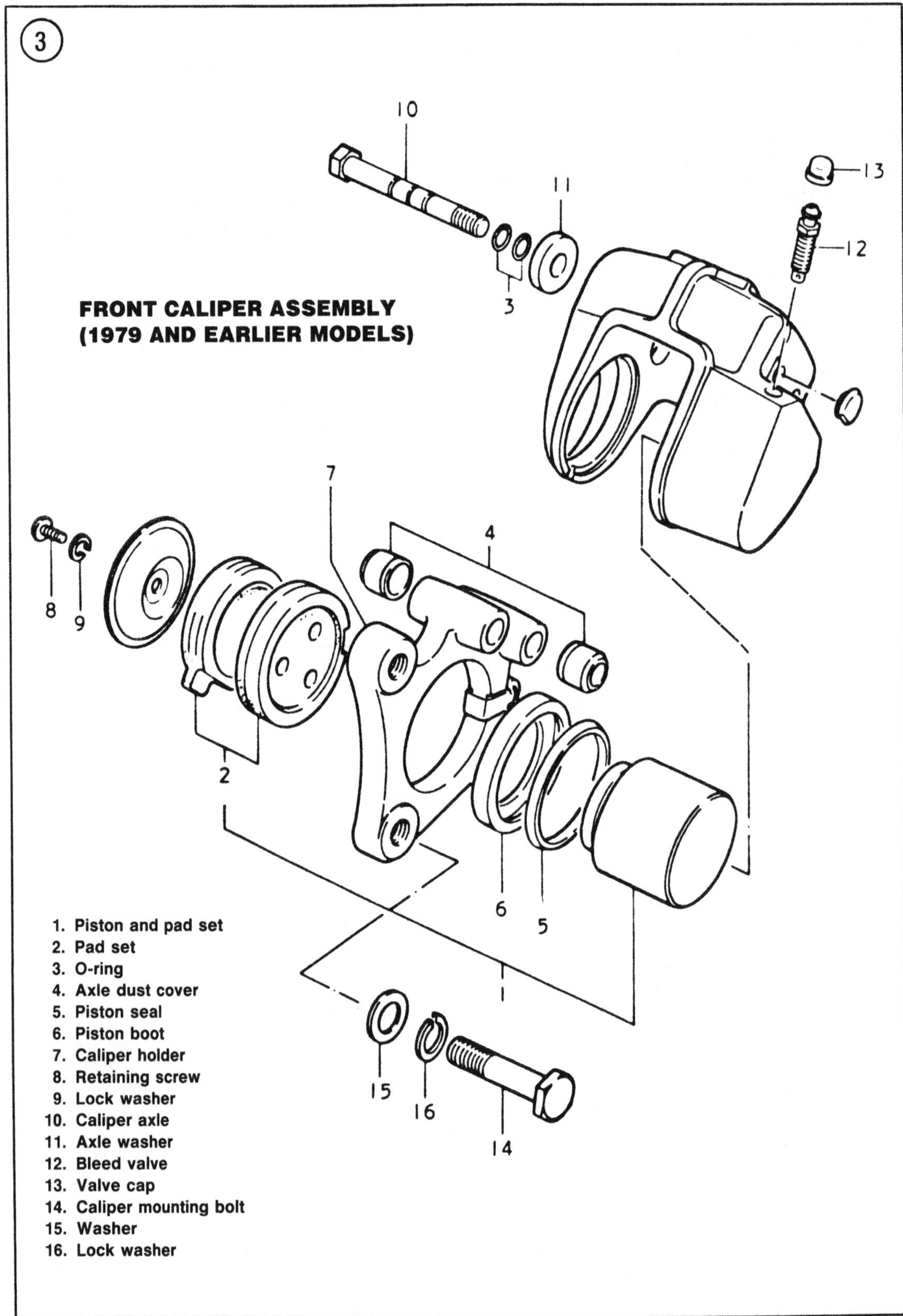
3
FRONT CALIPER ASSEMBLY
(1979 AND EARLIER MODELS)
10
11
13
12
3
7
4
8
9
2
6
5
15
16
14
1. Piston and pad set
2. Pad set
3. O-ring
4. Axle dust cover
5. Piston seal
6. Piston boot
7. Caliper holder
8. Retaining screw
9. Lock washer
10. Caliper axle
11. Axle washer
12. Bleed valve
13. Valve cap
14. Caliper mounting bolt
15. Washer
16. Lock washer

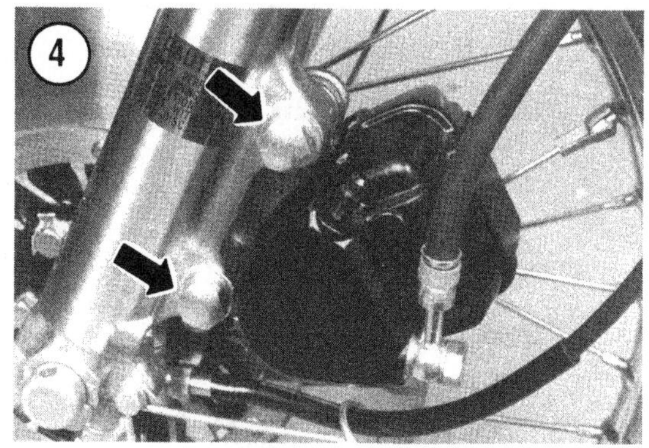

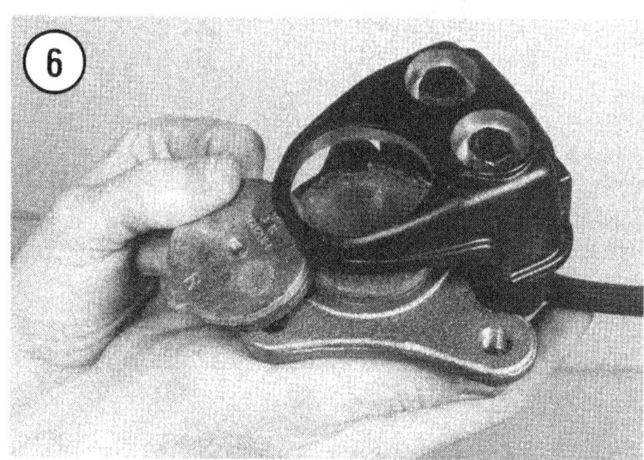

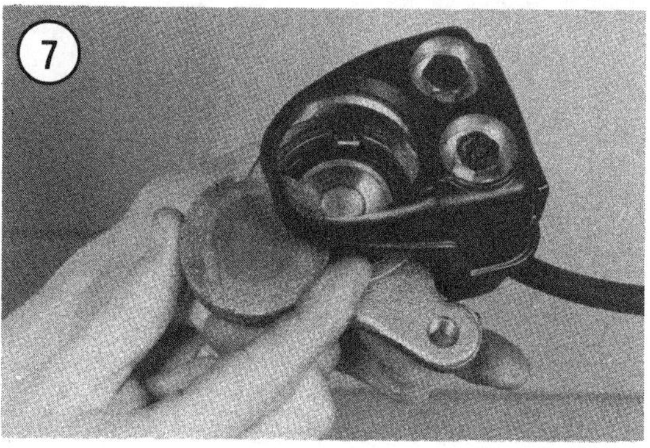

1. Remove the caliper axle bolts securing the outer caliper body to the caliper mounting bracket (**Figure 9**).
2. Carefully remove the caliper body from the fork leg (**Figure 10**).
3. Slide out and remove the outside brake pad (**Figure 11**).
4. Remove the inside brake pad (**Figure 12**).
5. Use a clean rag to carefully wipe the pad sliding surfaces on the caliper mounting bracket (**Figure 13**) and the pad spring in the caliper body (**Figure 14**).
6. Install new inner and outer brake pads. Make sure each pad fits properly in the caliper mounting bracket.
7. Remove the cover from the front master cylinder reservoir. Wrap a rag around the reservoir to catch any brake fluid spills.

NOTE

If the reservoir is full, brake fluid may overflow slightly when the caliper piston is pushed completely back into the caliper.

8. Apply a *light* film of colorless Caliper Axle Grease (part No. 99000-25100) to both caliper axle bolts.

CAUTION

Do not allow any grease to get on the pad friction material or the pad will be ruined.

9. Position the flat portion of each caliper axle nut horizontally as shown in **Figure 15**.

WARNING

The caliper axle nuts must be positioned correctly as shown in ***Figure 15*** *or the caliper body will not fit correctly, resulting in faulty brake operation.*

10. Slowly press the caliper piston back into the caliper as far as it will go. The edge of the piston must be even with the edge of the caliper body as shown in **Figure 16**.
11. Make sure the lower ends of both pads are properly positioned against the pad spring. Hold both pads in position and carefully slide the caliper body onto the caliper mounting bracket (**Figure 10**).
12. Install the caliper axle bolts and torque the bolts to 4.0-5.5 mkg (29-40 ft.-lb.).
13. Top up the master cylinder reservoir with approved brake fluid, if necessary, and install the reservoir cap.

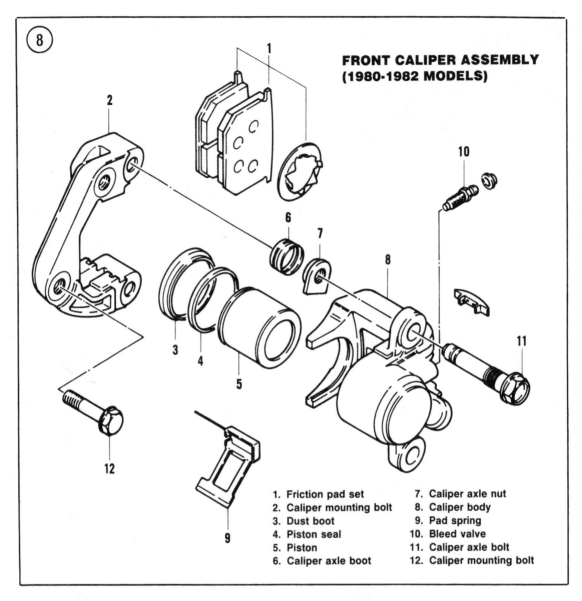

8

FRONT CALIPER ASSEMBLY (1980-1982 MODELS)

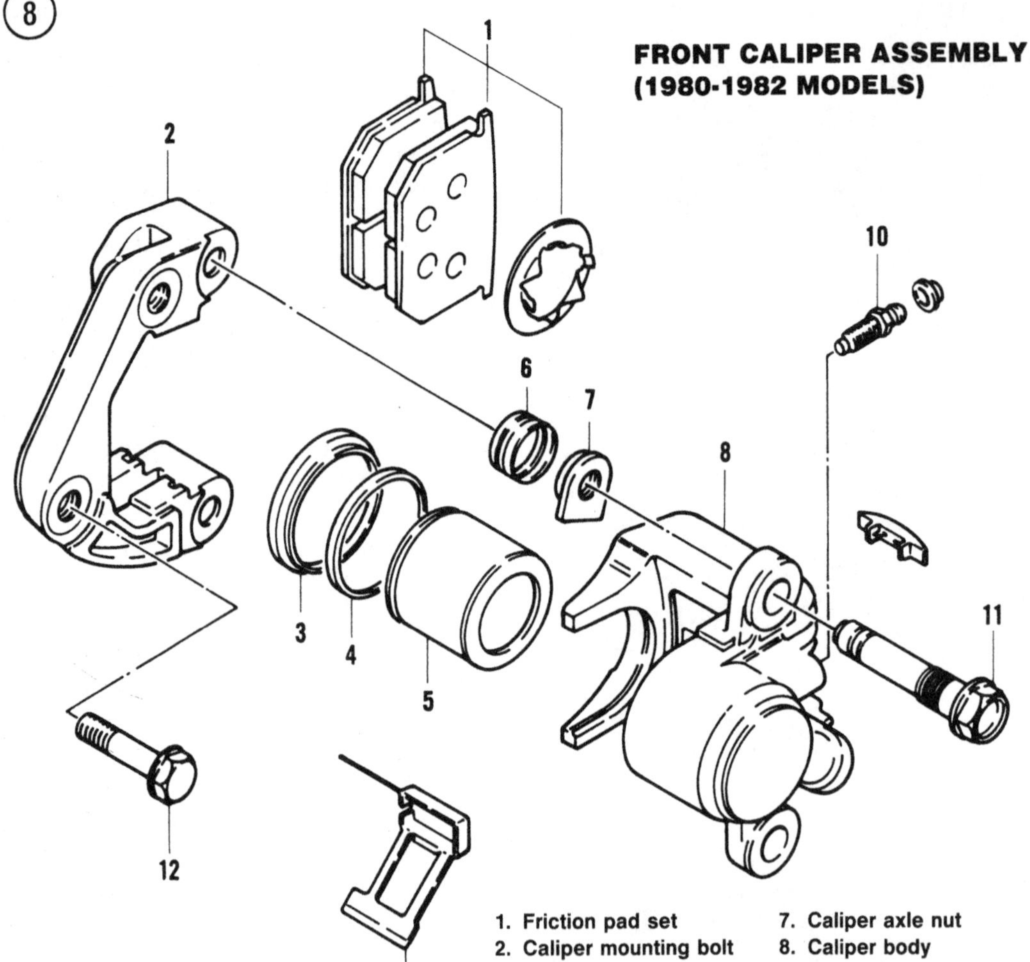

1. Friction pad set
2. Caliper mounting bolt
3. Dust boot
4. Piston seal
5. Piston
6. Caliper axle boot
7. Caliper axle nut
8. Caliper body
9. Pad spring
10. Bleed valve
11. Caliper axle bolt
12. Caliper mounting bolt

9

10

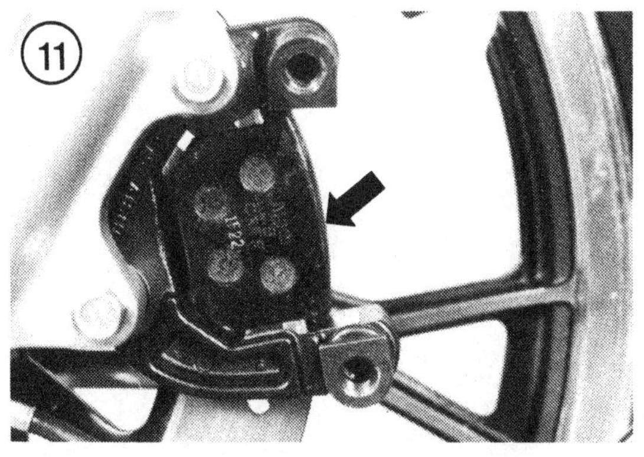

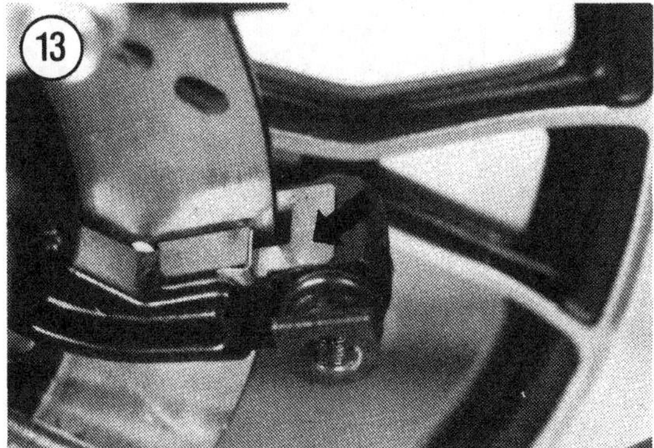

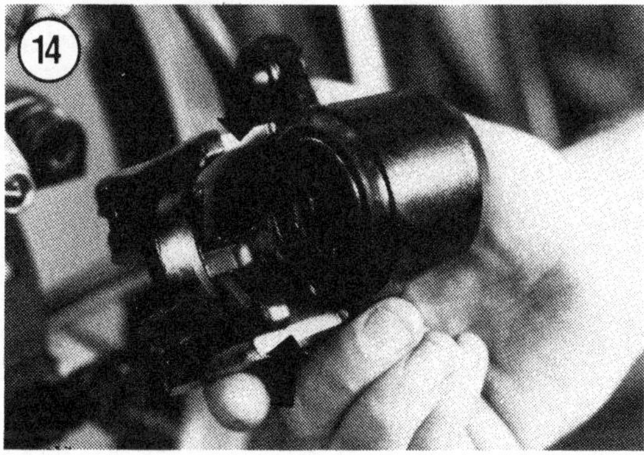

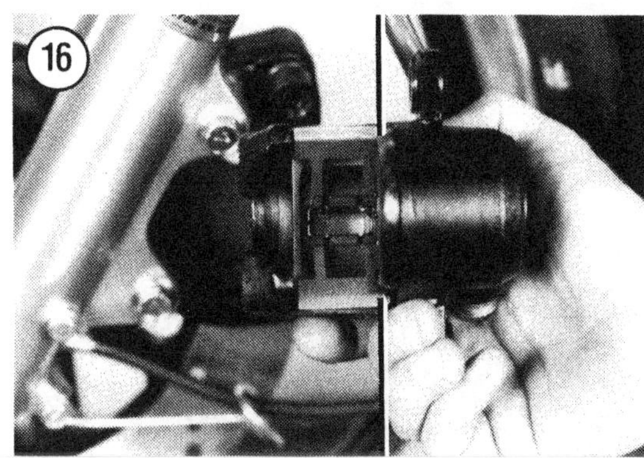

14. Spin the front wheel and apply the front brake a few times to make sure the brakes operate properly and the pads adjust correctly.

Rear Pad Replacement (1977-1982 Models)

Replace the rear brake pads as a set when the shoulder on either pad is worn down (**Figure 17**).

Refer to **Figure 18** for this procedure.

1. Use a screwdriver to gently pry off the plastic inspection cover on the rear caliper (**Figure 19**).
2. Remove the snap clips securing the pad retainer pins (**Figure 20**).
3. Use a small punch or needlenose pliers to push the retainer pins back out of the caliper (**Figure 21**). Do not lose the pad springs positioned over each brake pad.
4. Pull one brake pad up and out of the caliper body as shown in **Figure 22**. Note that the diamond-shaped cut-out on the pad shim faces forward.
5. With a wooden dowel or wedge, slowly push the caliper piston back into the caliper body as far as possible to make enough room for the new pad. The edge of the piston must be even with the edge of the caliper body (**Figure 23**).

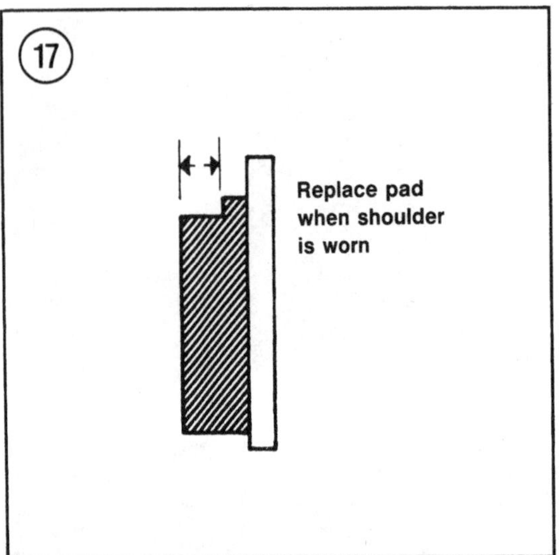

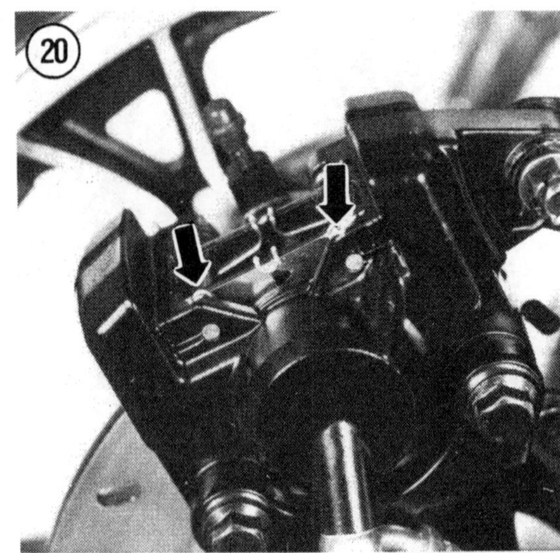

CAUTION

Never use a screwdriver or any metal tool to push the caliper piston back into the caliper body or damage may result to the caliper or the brake disc.

6. Slide in one new brake pad. Install the pad shim so the diamond-shaped cut-out on the shim points forward as shown in **Figure 23**.

NOTE

If the new pad does not slide easily into the caliper body, the piston has not been pushed back far enough.

7. Repeats Steps 4-6 for the other pad.
8. Install the retainer pins and secure with the snap clips. Make sure the ends of the pad springs are hooked under each retainer pin and positioned over the pads as shown in **Figure 24**.
9. Install the plastic inspection cover.

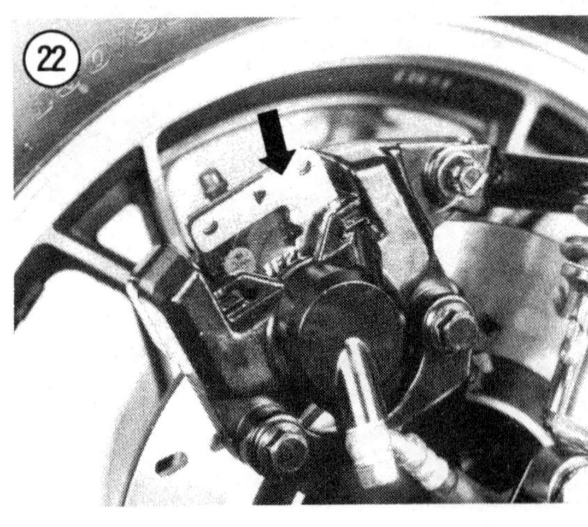

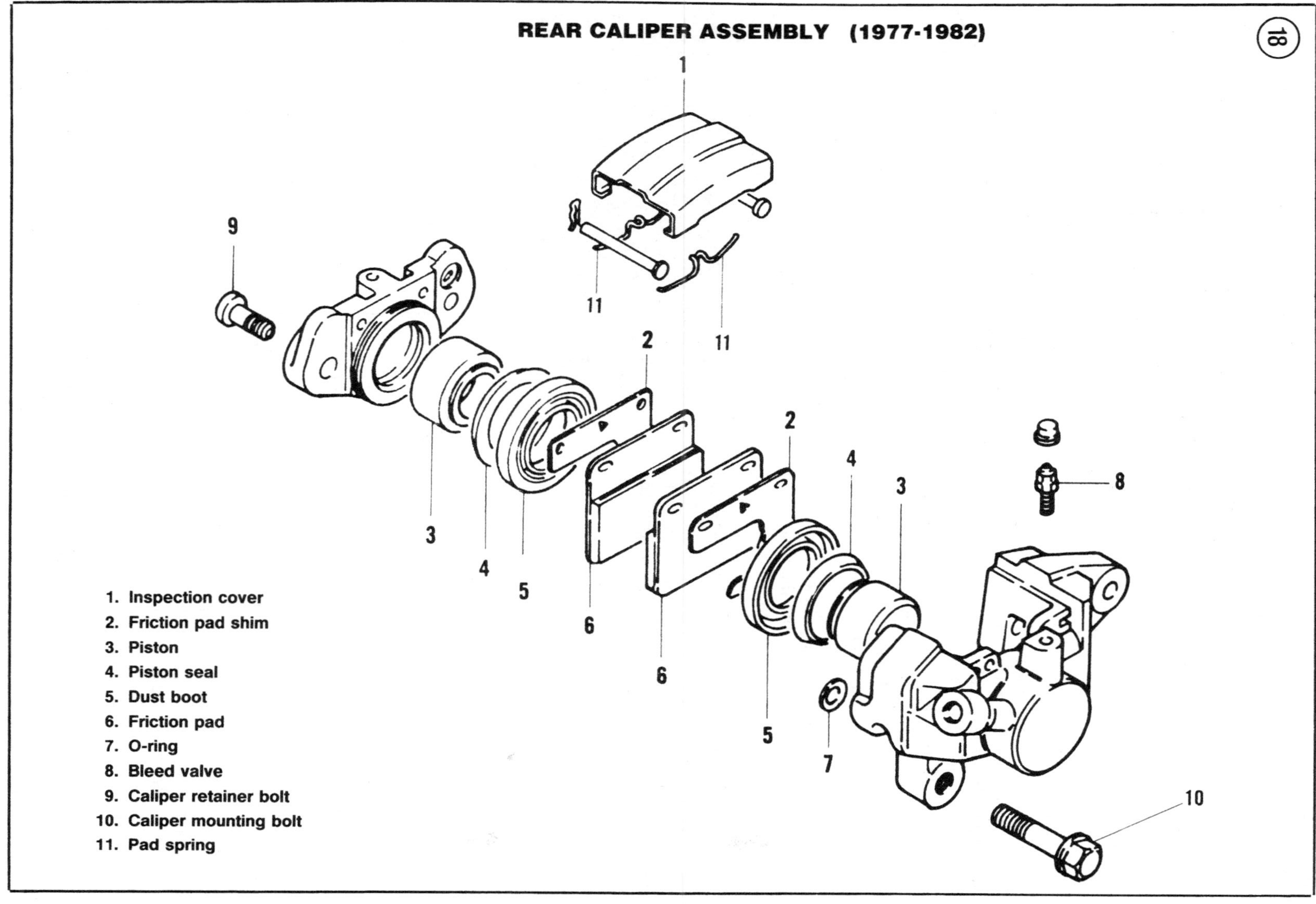
18
REAR CALIPER ASSEMBLY (1977-1982)
1. Inspection cover
2. Friction pad shim
3. Piston
4. Piston seal
5. Dust boot
6. Friction pad
7. O-ring
8. Bleed valve
9. Caliper retainer bolt
10. Caliper mounting bolt
11. Pad spring

Front and Rear Pad Replacement (TSCC Models)

The front and rear brake calipers on TSCC models are nearly identical, with both units using the same brake pads. The pad replacement procedure is the same for both calipers.

Replace the brake pads as a set when they are worn down to the red line as shown in **Figure 25**.

Refer to **Figure 26** or **Figure 27** for this procedure.

1. Use a screwdriver to pry off gently the plastic inspection covers. See **Figure 28** for rear calipers and **Figure 29** for front calipers.
2. Remove the snap clips securing both pad retainer pins (**Figure 30**).
3. Use needlenose pliers to slide both retainer pins back out of the caliper (**Figure 31**). Remove both pins and the pad springs positioned over each brake pad.
4. Pull one brake pad up and out of the caliper body as shown in **Figure 32**. Note the position of the shim behind each pad. Remove the second pad.
5. With a wooden dowel or wedge, slowly push the caliper pistons back into the caliper body as far as possible to make enough room for the new pads. The edge of the pistons must be even with the edges of the caliper body (**Figure 33**).

CAUTION
Never use a screwdriver or any metal tool to push the caliper piston back into the caliper body or damage may result to the caliper or the brake disc.

6. Slide in the new outside brake pad and install the shim between the back of the pad and the caliper piston. Install the first retainer pin just enough to hold the pad and shim in place (**Figure 34**).

NOTE
If the new pad does not slide easily into the caliper body, the piston has not been pushed back far enough.

7. Install the inner pad and shim. Slide the first retainer pin in completely to hold the inner pad and secure the retainer pin with the snap clip.
8. Hook the ends of both pad springs under the first retainer pin and over the edge of the pads as shown in **Figure 35**.
9. Hold down the ends of the pad springs and install the second retainer pin. Secure the pin with the snap clip.

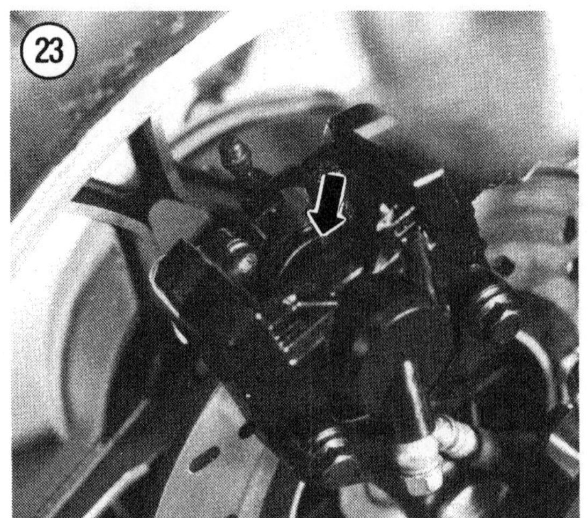

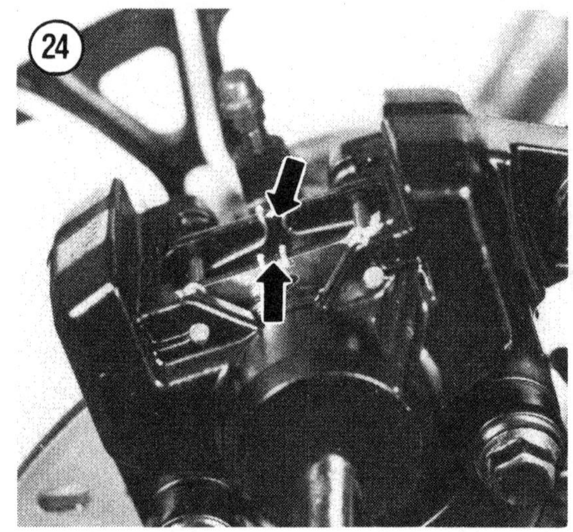

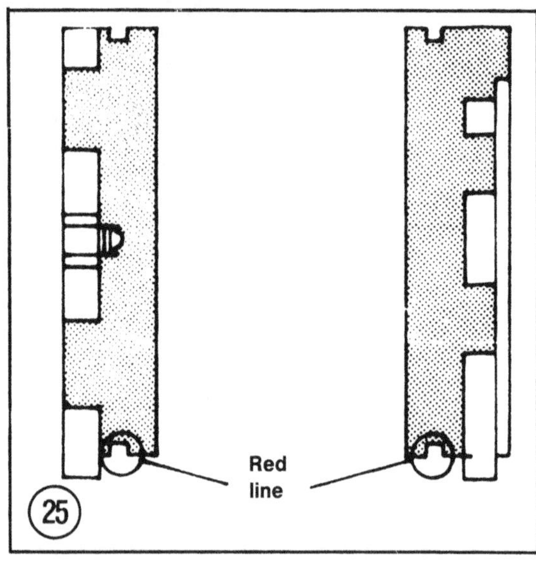

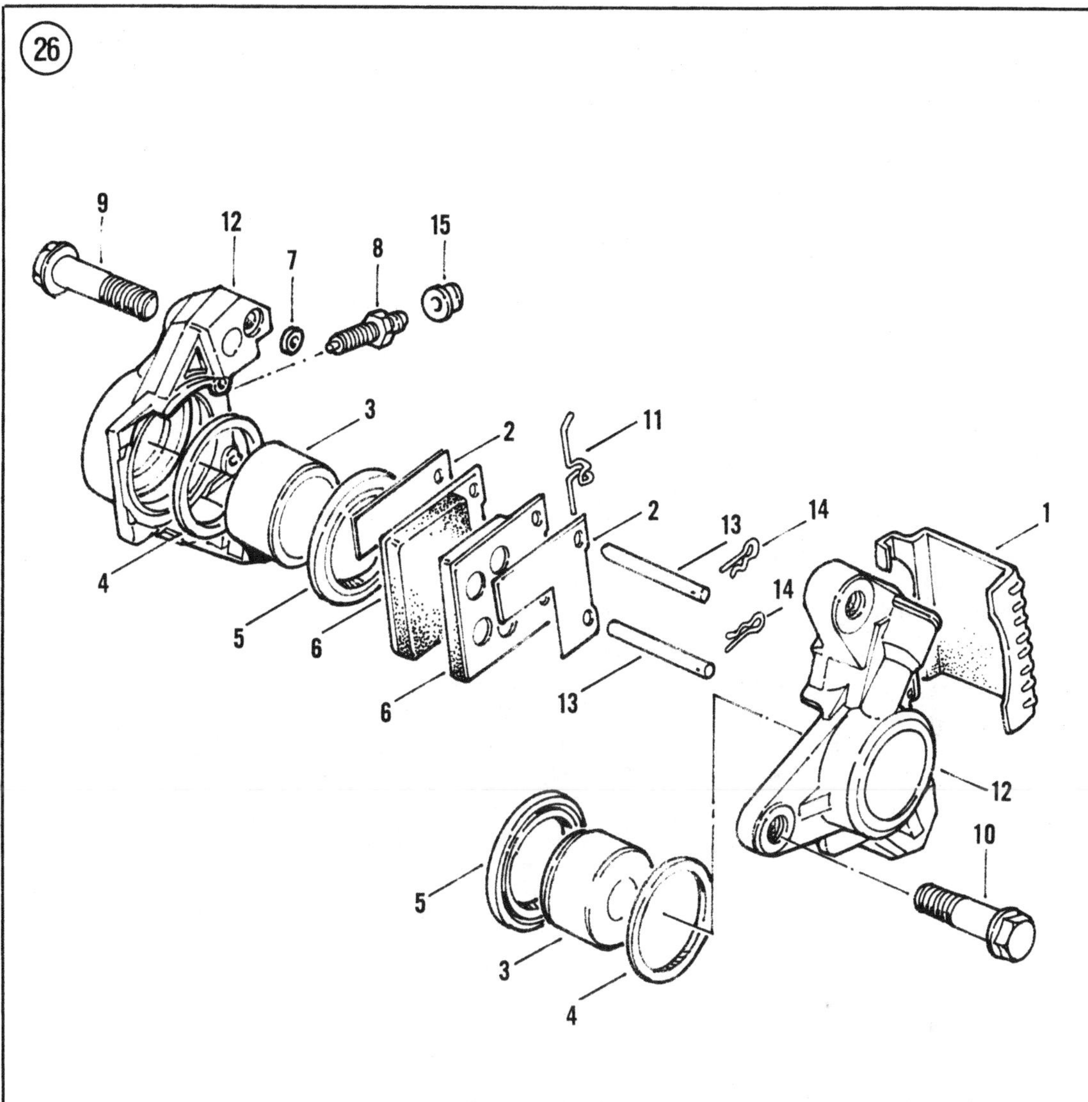

FRONT BRAKE CALIPER (TSCC MODELS)

1. Inspection cover
2. Friction pad shims
3. Piston
4. Piston seal
5. Dust boot
6. Friction pad
7. O-ring
8. Bleed valve
9. Caliper housing bolt
10. Caliper mounting bolt
11. Pad spring
12. Caliper housing
13. Retainer pin
14. Snap clip
15. Bleed valve cap

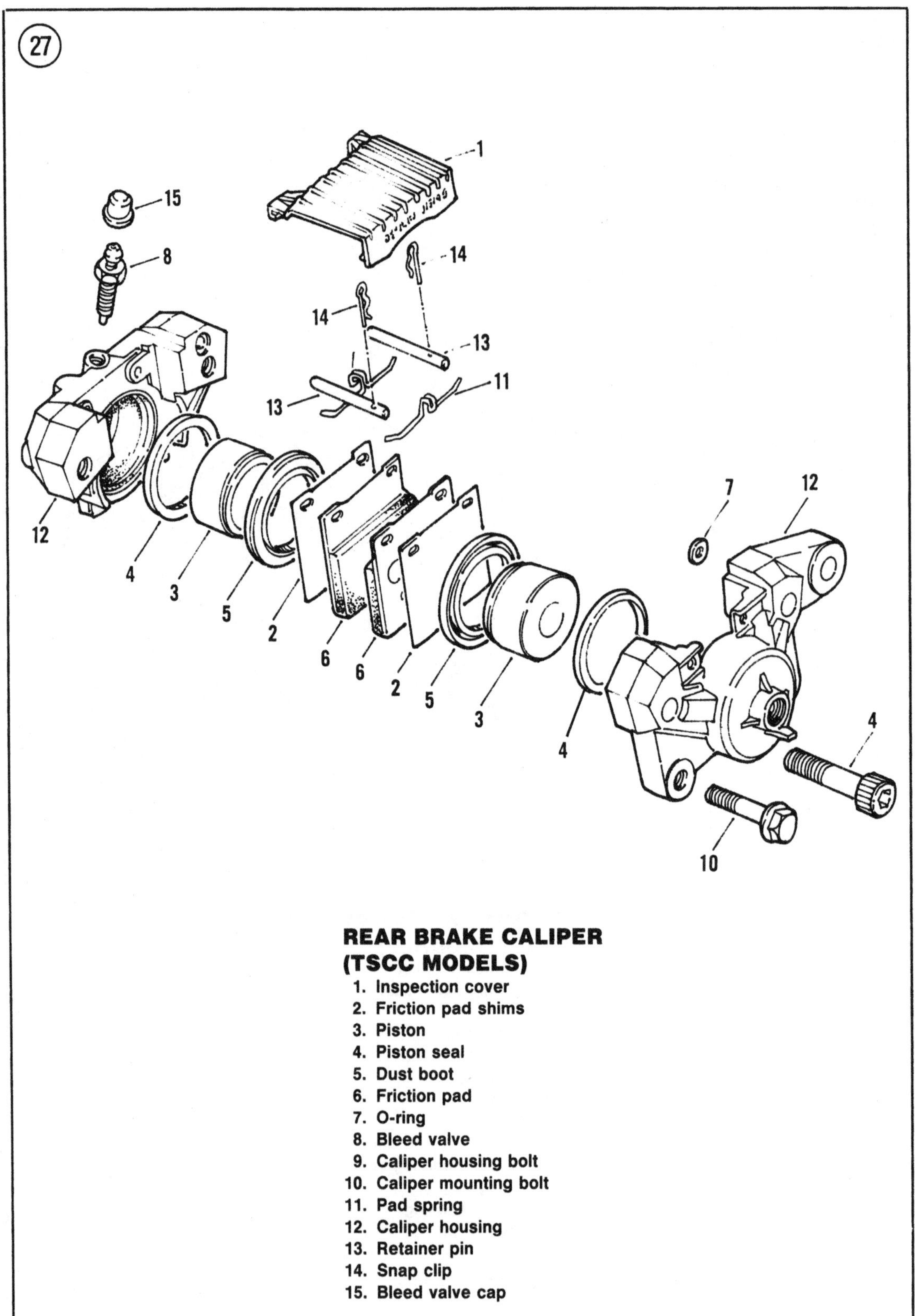

REAR BRAKE CALIPER (TSCC MODELS)

1. Inspection cover
2. Friction pad shims
3. Piston
4. Piston seal
5. Dust boot
6. Friction pad
7. O-ring
8. Bleed valve
9. Caliper housing bolt
10. Caliper mounting bolt
11. Pad spring
12. Caliper housing
13. Retainer pin
14. Snap clip
15. Bleed valve cap

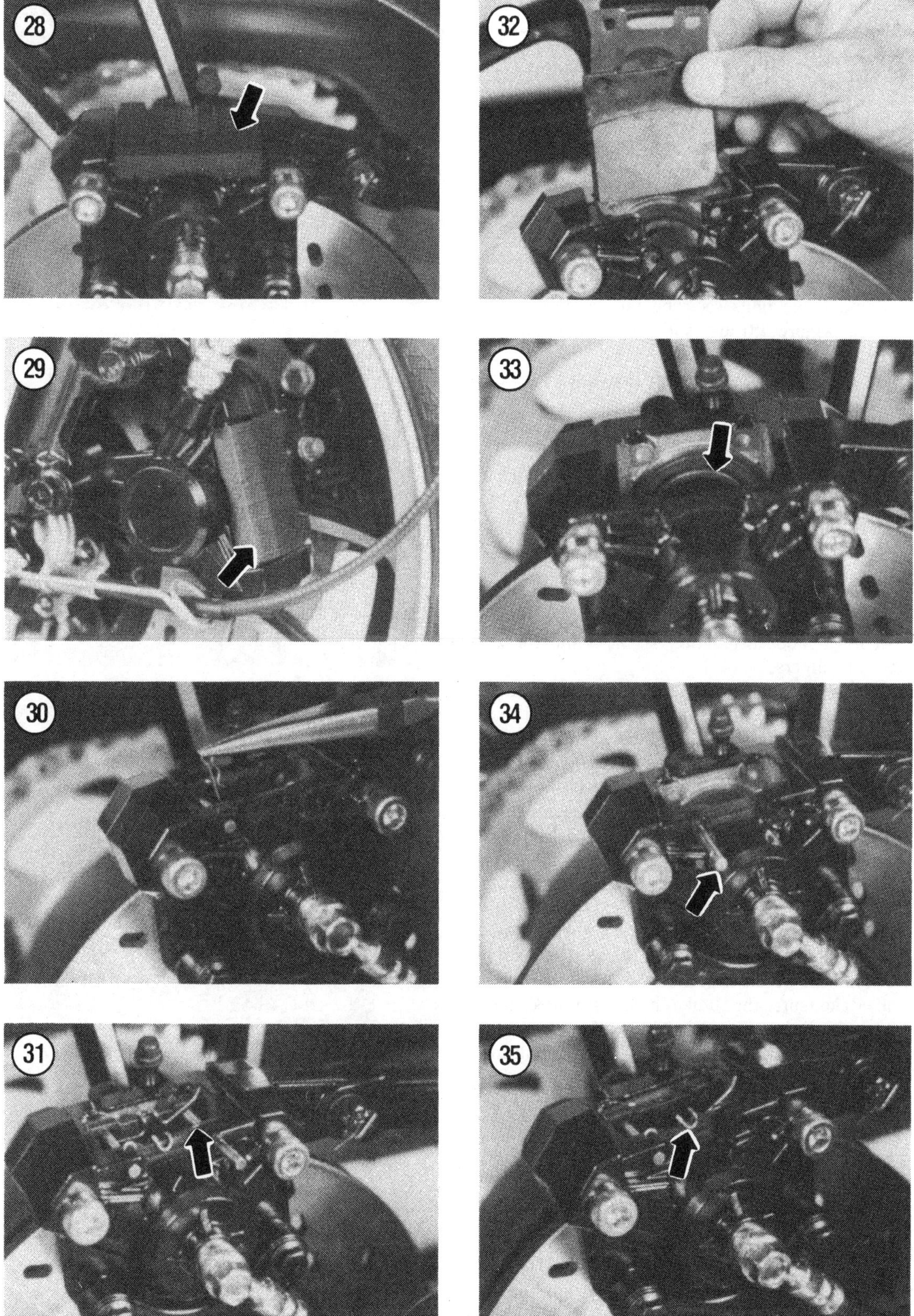
28
32
29
33
30
34
31
35

10. Make sure the ends of the pad springs are hooked under each retainer pin and positioned over the pads as shown in **Figure 36**.
11. Install the plastic inspection covers.

Front Caliper Removal/Installation

Removal and installation is the same for all types of calipers.

1. If the caliper is to be disassembled, remove the brake hose from the caliper (**Figure 37**). Have a container ready to catch any dripping brake fluid.
2. Remove the bolts securing the caliper to the fork leg (**Figure 38**) and slide the caliper off the brake disc.
3. Installation is the reverse of these steps. Keep the following points in mind:
   a. If the brake hose was removed, bleed the brake system as outlined in this chapter.
   b. On TSCC models, make sure the brake hose is positioned as shown in **Figure 39**.
   c. Torque the caliper mounting bolts and the brake hose banjo bolt as specified in **Table 1**.

Rear Caliper Removal/Installation

Removal and installation is the same for all types of calipers.

1. Remove the cotter pin securing the torque link nut (A, **Figure 40**). Remove the bolt and nut securing the torque link to the caliper and disconnect the end of the torque link.
2. If the caliper is to disassembled or must be removed from the motorcycle, remove the banjo bolt securing the brake hose to the caliper (B, **Figure 40**).
3. Remove the bolts securing the caliper to the mounting bracket (C, **Figure 40**) and carefully lift the caliper off the mounting bracket and brake disc.
4. Installation is the reverse of these steps. Keep the following points in mind:
   a. Make sure the brake hose is routed and positioned as shown in **Figure 39**.
   b. Torque the banjo bolt and caliper mounting bolts as specified in **Table 1**.
   c. If the brake hose was disconnected, bleed the brake system as outlined in this chapter.

MASTER CYLINDERS

A separate hydraulic master cylinder is used on the front and rear brake systems. If malfunctions exist in the either master cylinder, refer the defective cylinder to a dealer for rebuilding or repair.

36

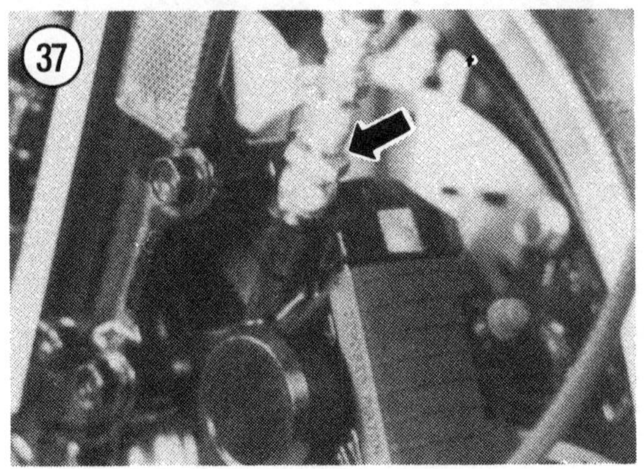
37

38

CAUTION
While performing the following procedures, do not allow brake fluid to contact any painted surfaces or the paint will be damaged.

Front Master Cylinder Removal/Installation

1. Remove the banjo bolt securing the brake hose to the master cylinder (**Figure 41**). Have a few rags or a container ready to catch any fluid drips.

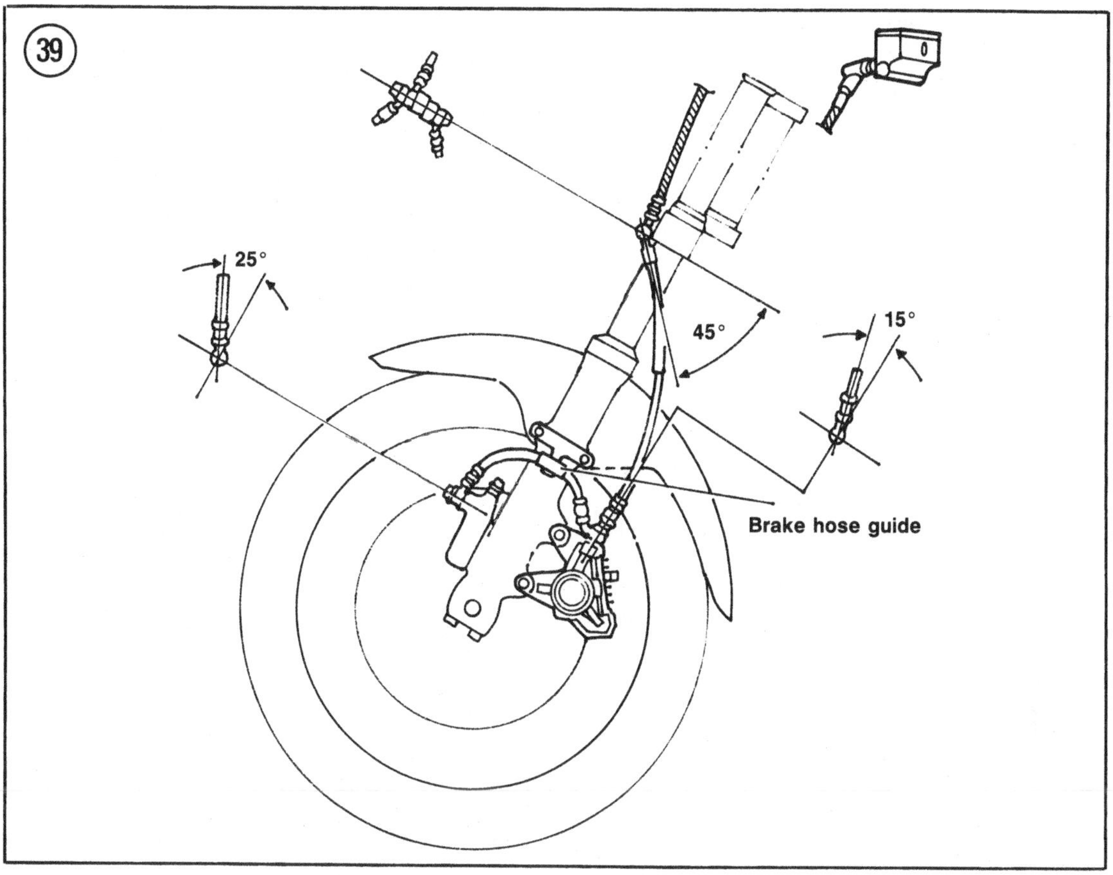

39

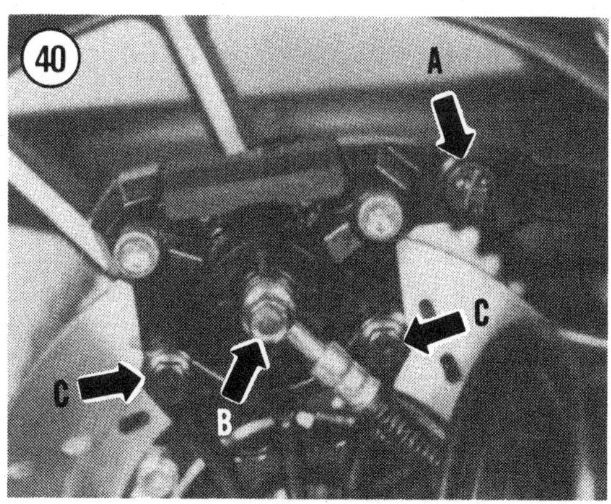

2. Remove the bolts securing the master cylinder to the handlebar (**Figure 42**). Carefully remove the master cylinder.
3. Installation is the reverse of these steps. Keep the following points in mind:
   a. Make sure there is at least 2 mm (3/16 in.) clearance between the master cylinder and the handlebar switch assembly (**Figure 43**).
   b. On all except L models and TSCC models, tighten both clamp bolts gradually so there is an equal clearance between the upper and lower portion of the mount (**Figure 44**).
   c. On TSCC models and L models, tighten the upper clamp bolt first as shown in **Figure 45**.
   d. Torque the mounting bolts and banjo bolt as specified in **Table 1**.
   e. Bleed the brake system as outlined in this chapter.

Rear Master Cylinder Removal/Installation

Refer to **Figure 46** for a typical example of a rear master cylinder.

1. On all but TSCC models, remove the cotter pin and clevis pin securing the brake pedal linkage to the master cylinder (**Figure 47**).
2. On TSCC models, perform the following:
   a. Remove the rear wheel as outlined in Chapter Nine.
   b. Remove the cotter pin and clevis pin securing the pedal linkage to the master cylinder (A, **Figure 48**).
   c. Disconnect the pedal spring and the brake light spring (B, **Figure 48**).
   d. Remove the bolt securing the brake pedal and remove the pedal (**Figure 49**).
   e. Remove the Allen bolts securing the muffler mounting bracket and remove the bracket.
3. Remove the banjo bolt securing the brake hose to the master cylinder (A, **Figure 50**). Have a few rags or a container ready to catch any fluid drips.
4. Remove the bolt securing the fluid reservoir to the frame (**Figure 51**).
5. Remove the bolts securing the master cylinder to the frame and remove the cylinder (B, **Figure 50**).
6. Installation is the reverse of these steps. Keep the following points in mind:
   a. Torque the mounting bolts and banjo bolt as specified in **Table 1**.
   b. Secure the linkage clevis pin with a new cotter pin.
   c. Make sure the brake hose is routed as shown in **Figure 39**.
   d. On TSCC models, install the muffler bracket, brake pedal and rear wheel.
   e. Bleed the brake system as outlined in this chapter.

BRAKE PEDAL ADJUSTMENT (DISC BRAKES)

CAUTION
The brake pedal free play must be properly adjusted or the rear brake pads may drag causing excessive friction and wear.

1. Loosen the locknut on the rear master cylinder pushrod (**Figure 52**).
2. On all but TSCC models, loosen the locknut securing the pedal stopbolt (**Figure 53**) and back off the stopbolt a few turns. A pedal stopbolt is not installed on TSCC models.

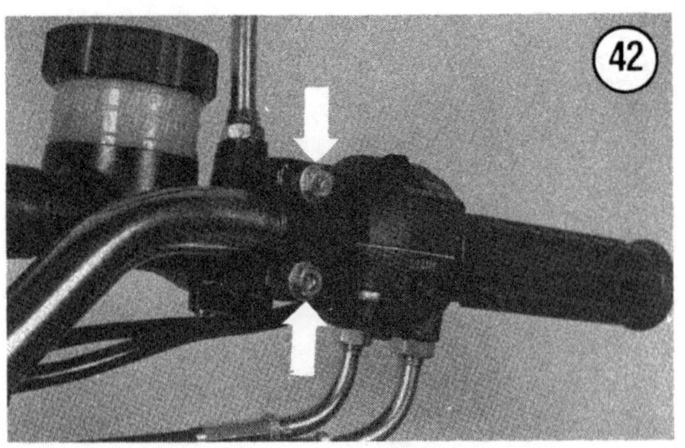

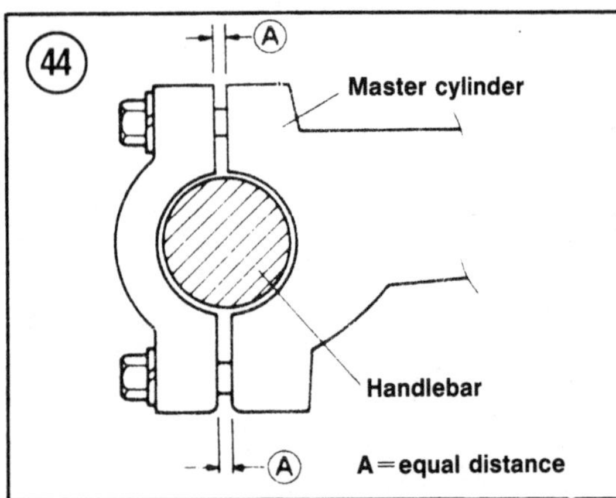

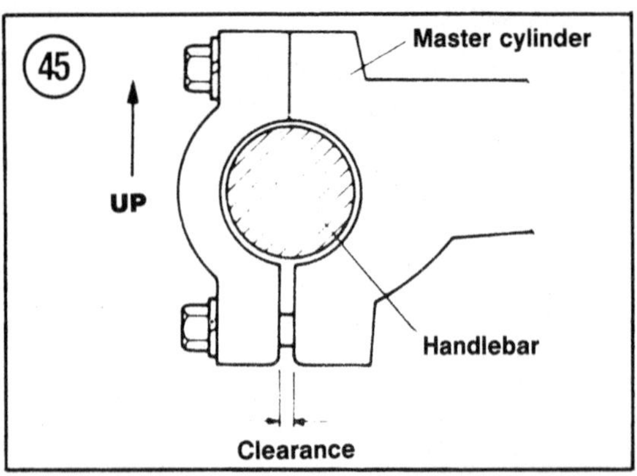

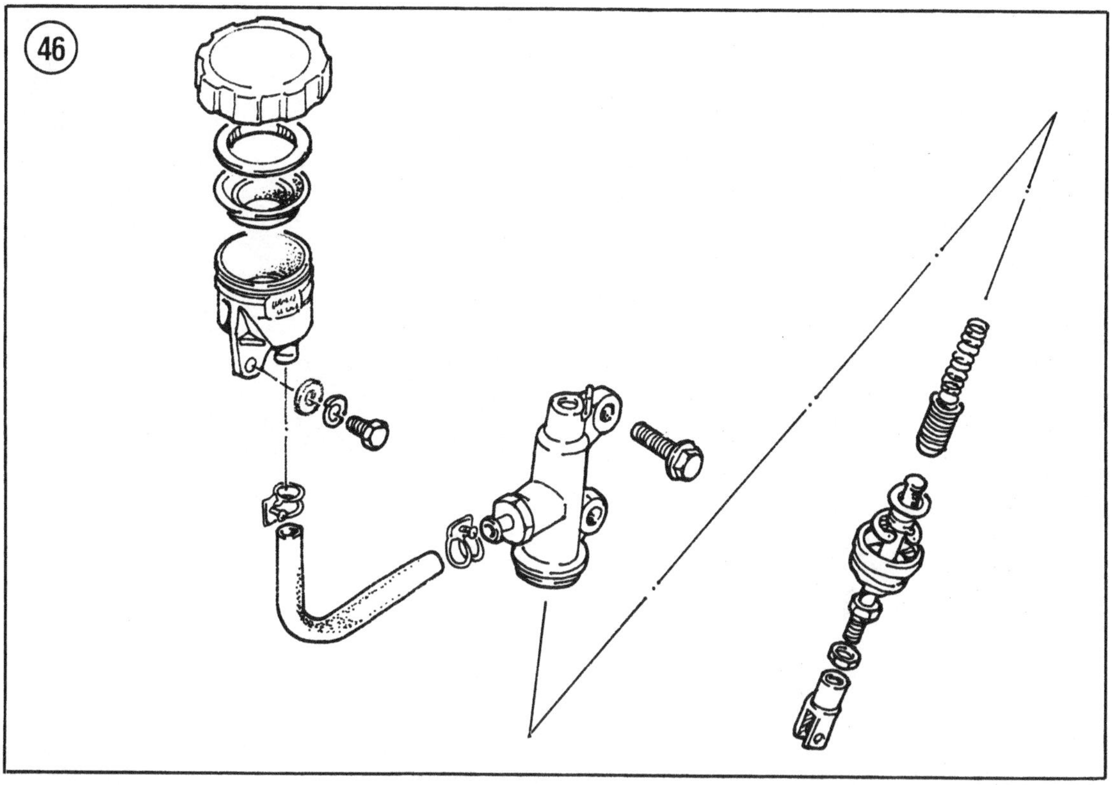

46

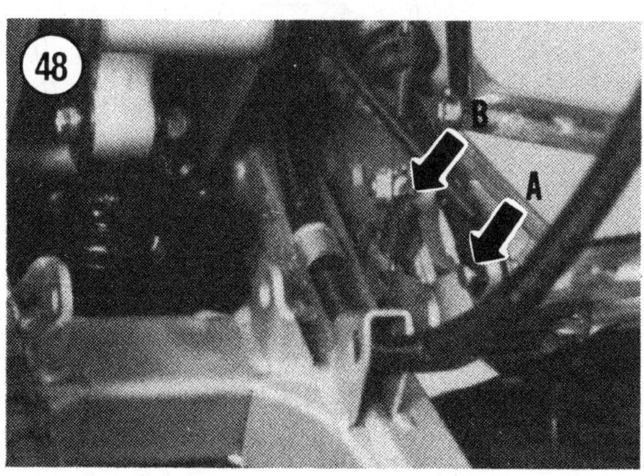

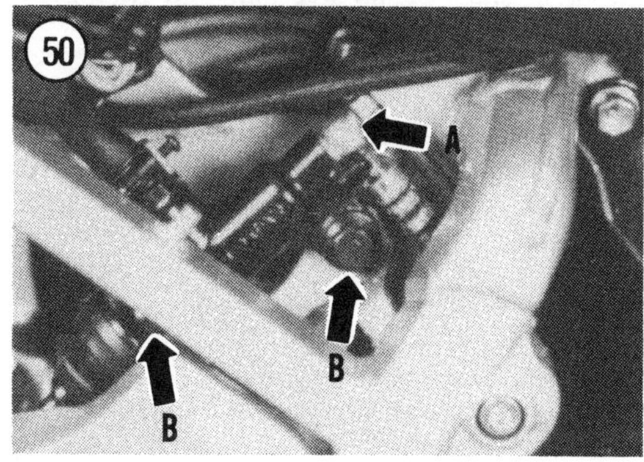

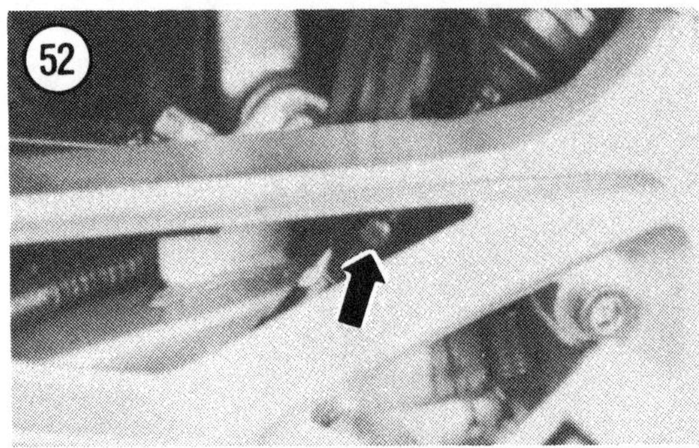

3. Refer to **Table 2** and adjust the master cylinder pushrod until the top of the brake pedal is the specified amount below the footrest (**Figure 54**). Tighten the locknut to secure the pushrod adjustment.
4. On models with a pedal stop bolt, slowly turn down the bolt until it just contacts the tab on the frame. There should be no clearance between the stopbolt and the frame tab (**Figure 53**).

CAUTION
Make sure the stopbolt is not adjusted too tightly or the rear brakes will ride against the brake disc causing premature wear and heat build-up.

5. Secure the stopbolt with the locknut. Recheck the pedal and stopbolt free play and readjust if necessary.

BRAKE DISC

The brake discs should be routinely inspected for scoring, abrasion and runout. Replace any disc that is scored or grooved deep enough to snag a fingernail.

Runout Inspection

NOTE
This inspection procedure can be performed with the wheels still installed on the motorcycle.

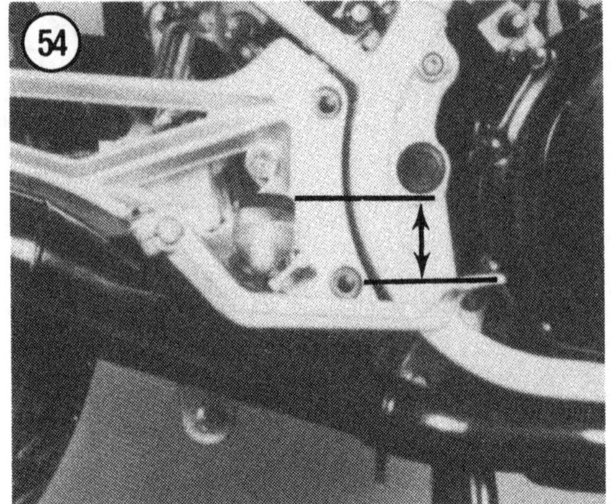

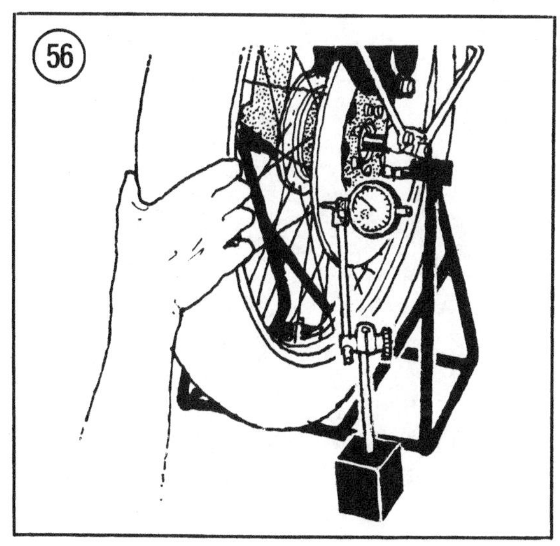

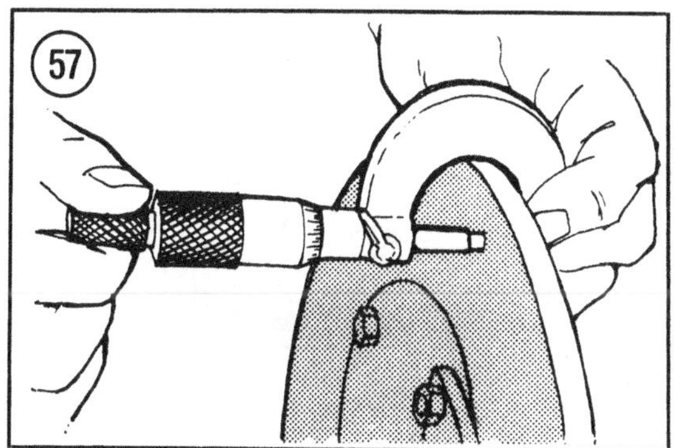

1. Raise the wheel being checked and position a dial indicator against the surface of the disc as shown in **Figure 55** or **Figure 56**.
2. Slowly rotate the wheel and check the runout on the dial indicator. If the runout exceeds the limit specified in **Table 3**, the disc is warped and must be replaced.
3. Measure the thickness of the disc in at least 8 places with a micrometer (**Figure 57**). If the disc thickness is not as specified in **Table 3**, the disc must be replaced.

Removal/Installation

Refer to *Front Wheel Disassembly* in Chapter Eight or *Rear Wheel Disassembly* in Chapter Nine to remove the brake discs.

BLEEDING AND CHANGING BRAKE FLUID

Bleeding

The hydraulic brake systems must be bled to remove all air and contamination. Bleeding the

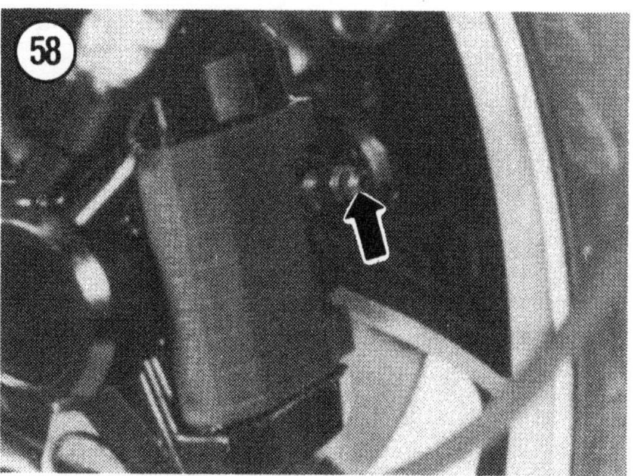

system is necessary any time a line or hose is disconnected, a cylinder or caliper is removed and disassembled, or when the brake feel in the lever or pedal is spongy, indicating the presence of air in the system.

1. Fill the master cylinder reservoir with fresh brake fluid to the upper line. Install the reservoir cap.

WARNING
When adding brake fluid to either master cylinder reservoir, only use brake fluid from an unopened container rated DOT 3 or DOT 4. All models use a glycol-based brake fluid. Mixing a glycol-based fluid with any other type of fluid, whether petroleum-based or silicon-based, may cause brake component damage leading to brake failure.

2. Refer to **Figure 58** for the location of the front bleed valve and **Figure 59** for the rear bleed valve. On 1980 and earlier models, two bleed valves on fitted on the rear caliper (**Figure 60**).
3. Remove the dust cap from each bleed valve and connect a 2-foot length of clear plastic tubing to the

10

valve as shown in **Figure 61**. Place the other end of the tubing in an empty can.

4. Pump the brake lever or pedal several times until resistance is felt. Hold the lever or pedal and open the bleed valve about 1/4 turn. Continue to squeeze the lever or pedal until it reaches the limit of travel. Hold it in this position and close the bleed valve.

5. Release the pedal or lever and repeat the bleeding procedure as necessary until the fluid passing through the tubing is clean and free of air bubbles.

WARNING

Never reuse the fluid that has been drained or bled through the brake system. Fluid that has passed through the brake system is contaminated with air and moisture and considered used fluid. Always discard used fluid.

NOTE

Do not allow the reservoir to empty during the bleeding process or more air will be drawn into the system. Always keep the reservoir topped off.

6. When the brake fluid is clean and free of air, tighten the bleed valve and remove the tubing. Install the dust cap on the valve.

7. On TSCC models fitted with anti-dive forks, bleed the brakes and anti-dive modulator in the following sequence:
   a. Left anti-dive modulator valve (**Figure 62**).
   b. Left brake caliper.
   c. Right anti-dive modulator valve.
   d. Right brake caliper.

8. Top up the reservoir to the upper limit line. Hold the pedal or lever down and check all the brake line connections for leaks. Correct any leaks immediately.

Changing Fluid

Each time a fluid reservoir cap is removed, a small amount of contamination and moisture enter the reservoir. The same thing occurs if there is a leak or any part of the system is loosened or disconnected. Dirt can clog the system and moisture can lead to corrosion of internal brake components.

To keep the brake system as clean and free of contamination as possible, completely change the brake fluid at least every 2 years.

To change the fluid, perform *Bleeding* and continue adding new fluid until the fluid bled out is visibly clean and without air bubbles.

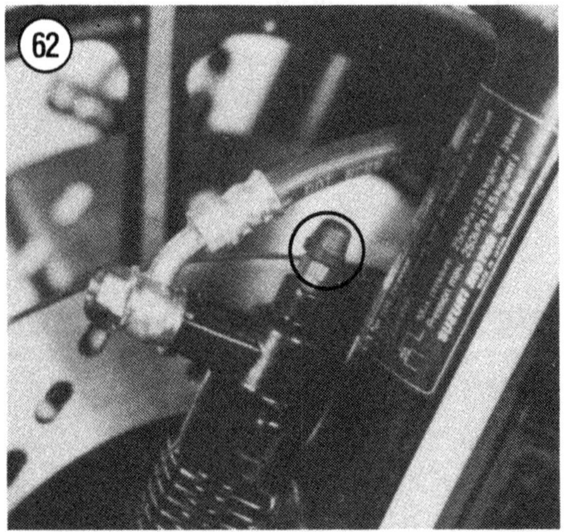

Table 1 BRAKE COMPONENT TORQUE SPECIFICATIONS

Item	mkg	ft.-lb.
Caliper mounting bolts	2.5-4.0	18-29
Front caliper axle bolts (1977-1982)	4.0-5.5	29-40
Caliper housing bolts (1983-1984)		
Front caliper	3.0-3.6	22-26
Rear caliper	2.8-3.2	20-23
Brake disc bolts	1.5-2.5	11-18
Brake hose union bolts	2.0-2.5	15-18
Front master cylinder clamp bolts	0.5-0.8	4-6
Rear master cylinder mounting bolts	1.5-2.5	11-18
Caliper bleeder valves	0.7-0.9	5-7
Anti-dive components (1983-1984)		
Modulator valve bolt	0.6-0.8	5-6
Modulator plunger bolt	0.4-0.5	3-3.5
Torque link nuts	2.0-3.0	15-22
Brake pedal bolt	1.5-2.5	11-18

Table 2 BRAKE PEDAL HEIGHT ADJUSTMENT

Model	mm	in.
TSCC (hydraulic rear)	35	1-3/8
TSCC (drum rear)	5-15	1/4-9/16
MZ models	40	1-1/2
All others	20	3/4

Table 3 BRAKE DISC SPECIFICATIONS

	Standard	Service limit
Disc runout	0.10 mm (0.004 in.)	0.3 mm (0.012 in.)
Front disc thickness		
ET, LT models	6.5-6.9 mm (0.256-0.272 in.)	6.0 mm (0.236 in.)
TX, LX, LZ models	5.8-6.2 mm (0.252-0.268 in.)	5.5 mm (0.22 in.)
MZ, ESD, LD, ESE models	4.8-5.2 mm (0.189-0.205 in.)	4.5 mm (0.17 in.)
Rear disc thickness		
LZ models	5.8-6.2 mm (0.252-0.268 in.)	5.5 mm (0.22 in.)
All others	6.5-6.9 mm (0.256-0.272 in.)	6.0 mm (0.236 in.)

10

SUPPLEMENT

1985 AND LATER SERVICE INFORMATION

The following supplement provides procedures unique to the GS550E and GS550L since 1985. All other service procedures are identical to earlier models.

The chapter headings in this supplement corrospond to the those in the main body of this book. If a change is not included in the supplement, there are no changes affecting models since 1985.

CHAPTER THREE

LUBRICATION, MAINTENANCE AND TUNE-UP

PERIODIC MAINTENANCE

Front Fork Oil (GS550E, GS550L Models)

The procedure for changing the fork oil is the same as on previous models. Recommended quantity and oil level have changed.

Recommended fork oil capacity in each fork leg is as follows:

a. GS550E: 345 cc (11.6 oz.).
b. GS550L:
   1985: 276 cc (9.3 oz.).
   1986: 248 cc (8.4 oz.).

Recommended fork oil level in each fork leg is as follows:

a. GS550E: 114 mm (4.5 oz.).
b. GS550L:
   1985: 179 cc (7.05 in.).
   1986: 181 cc (7.1 in.).

CHAPTER SIX

FUEL AND EXHAUST SYSTEMS

EVAPORATION EMISSION CONTROL SYSTEM (CALIFORNIA MODELS ONLY)

NOTE
Due to manufacturing dates, the 1985 GS550L is exempt from the evaporative emission control system.

Fuel vapor from the fuel tank is routed into a charcoal canister at the rear of the bike. Refer to **Figure 1** for 1985-on GS550E models or **Figure 2** for 1986 GS550L models. The vapor is stored in the canister when the engine is not running. When the engine is running, the vapor is drawn through the purge hoses and pipe and into the carburetors to be burned.

Make sure all hose clamps are tight. Check all hoses for deterioration and replace as necessary. Prior to removing any hoses, mark all hoses and fittings with a piece of masking tape to identify their attachment points. This is necessary to ensure proper installation. All vapor hoses are black with a red stripe and all purge hoses are black only.

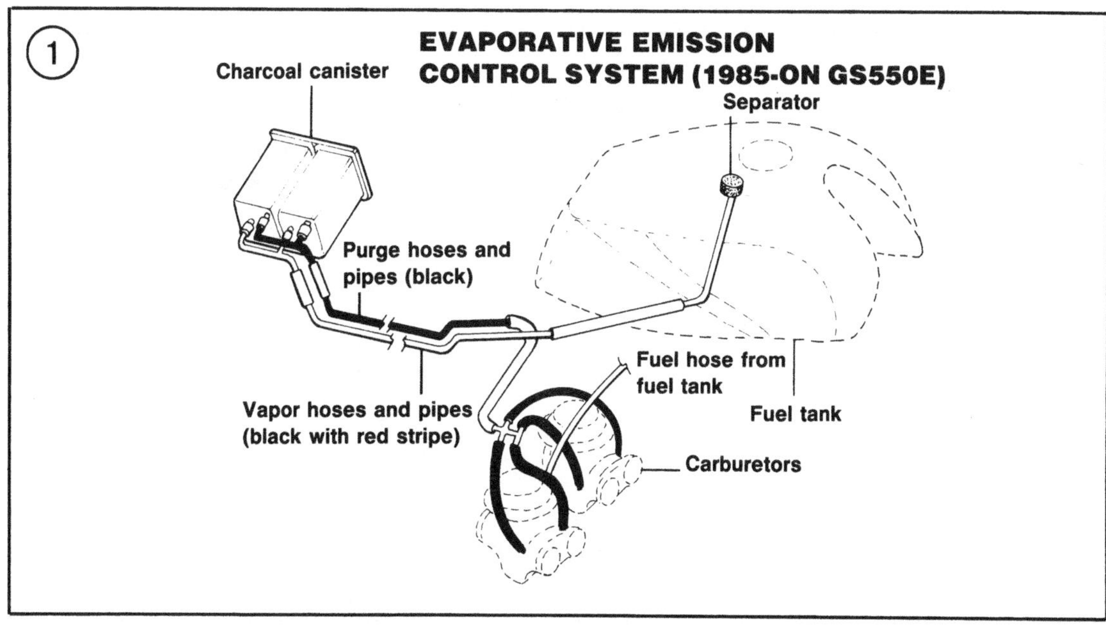

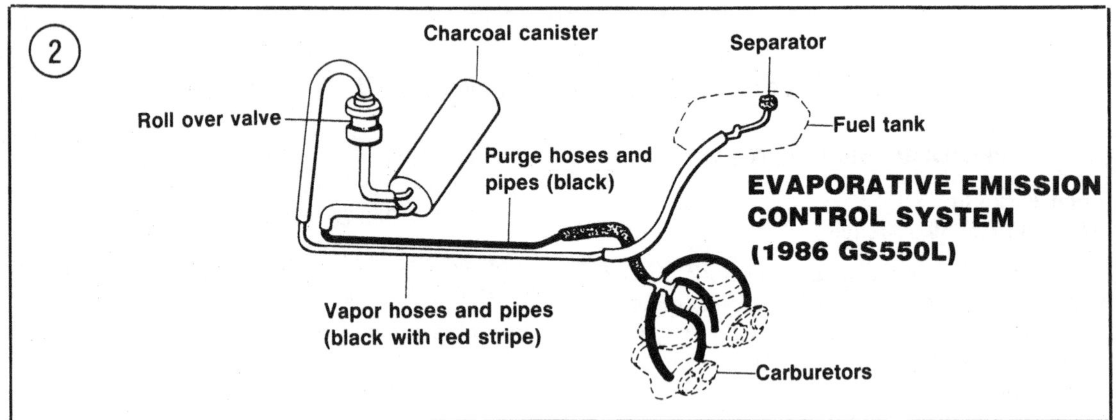

CHAPTER EIGHT

FRONT SUSPENSION AND STEERING

FRONT WHEEL

Disassembly/Assembly

The disassembly and assembly procedures are the same as on previous models. The appearance of the wheel and some components are slightly different as shown in **Figure 3**.

FRONT FORK (GS550E MODELS)

Removal/Installation

Removal and installation of the front fork is the same as on previous models with the exception of the anti-dive modular valve unit. The anti-dive modular valve unit is no longer tied in with the hydraulic brake system so there is no brake hose attached to the unit.

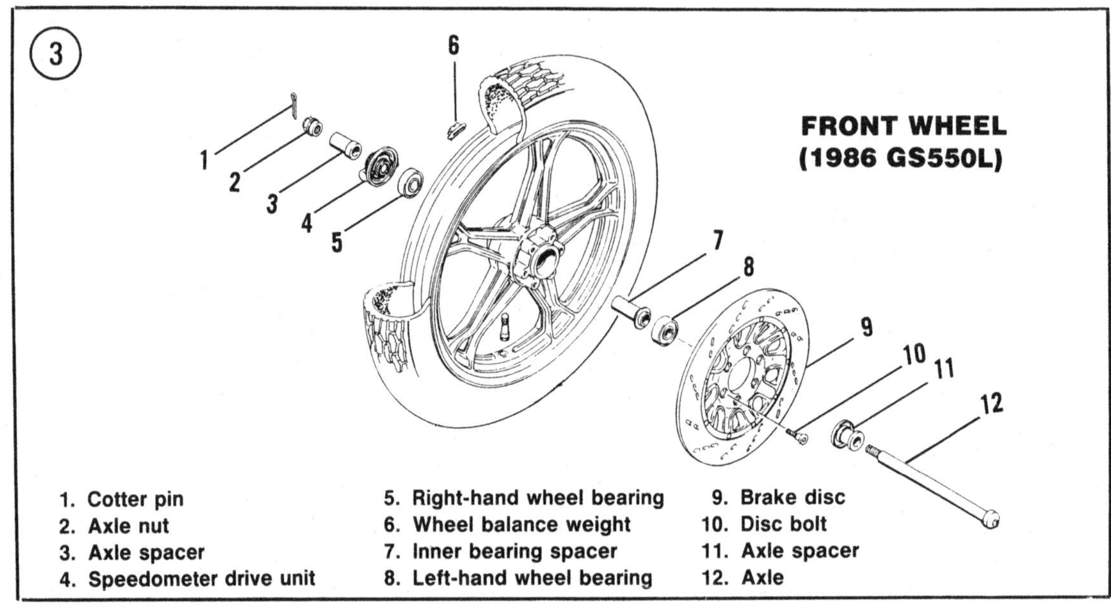

1. Cotter pin
2. Axle nut
3. Axle spacer
4. Speedometer drive unit
5. Right-hand wheel bearing
6. Wheel balance weight
7. Inner bearing spacer
8. Left-hand wheel bearing
9. Brake disc
10. Disc bolt
11. Axle spacer
12. Axle

Disassembly/Assembly

Refer to **Figure 4** for this procedure.

Disassembly and assembly of the front fork is the same as on previous models. Even though the anti-dive modular valve unit attached to the exterior of the fork slider is different, all internal fork components are the same.

ANTI-DIVE MODULAR VALVE REMOVAL/INSTALLATION (GS550E MODELS)

Removal/Installation

Refer to **Figure 4** for this procedure. The anti-dive modular valve unit cannot be serviced and if defective must be replaced as a unit.

1. If the fork leg has not been removed, drain the fork oil as described in Chapter Three in the main body of this book.
2. Remove the Allen bolts securing the anti-dive modular valve unit to the fork slider.
3. Remove the anti-dive modular valve unit and the O-ring seals.
4. Inspect the O-rings for damage or deterioration; replace as a pair if either is damaged.
5. Install the anti-dive modular valve unit and O-rings onto the fork slider.
6. Apply blue Loctite Lock N' Seal to the threads of the Allen bolts. Install the Allen bolts and tighten to
0.6-0.8 mkg (4.5-6 ft.-lb.).
7. Refill the fork with fork oil as described in Chapter Three in the main body of this book.

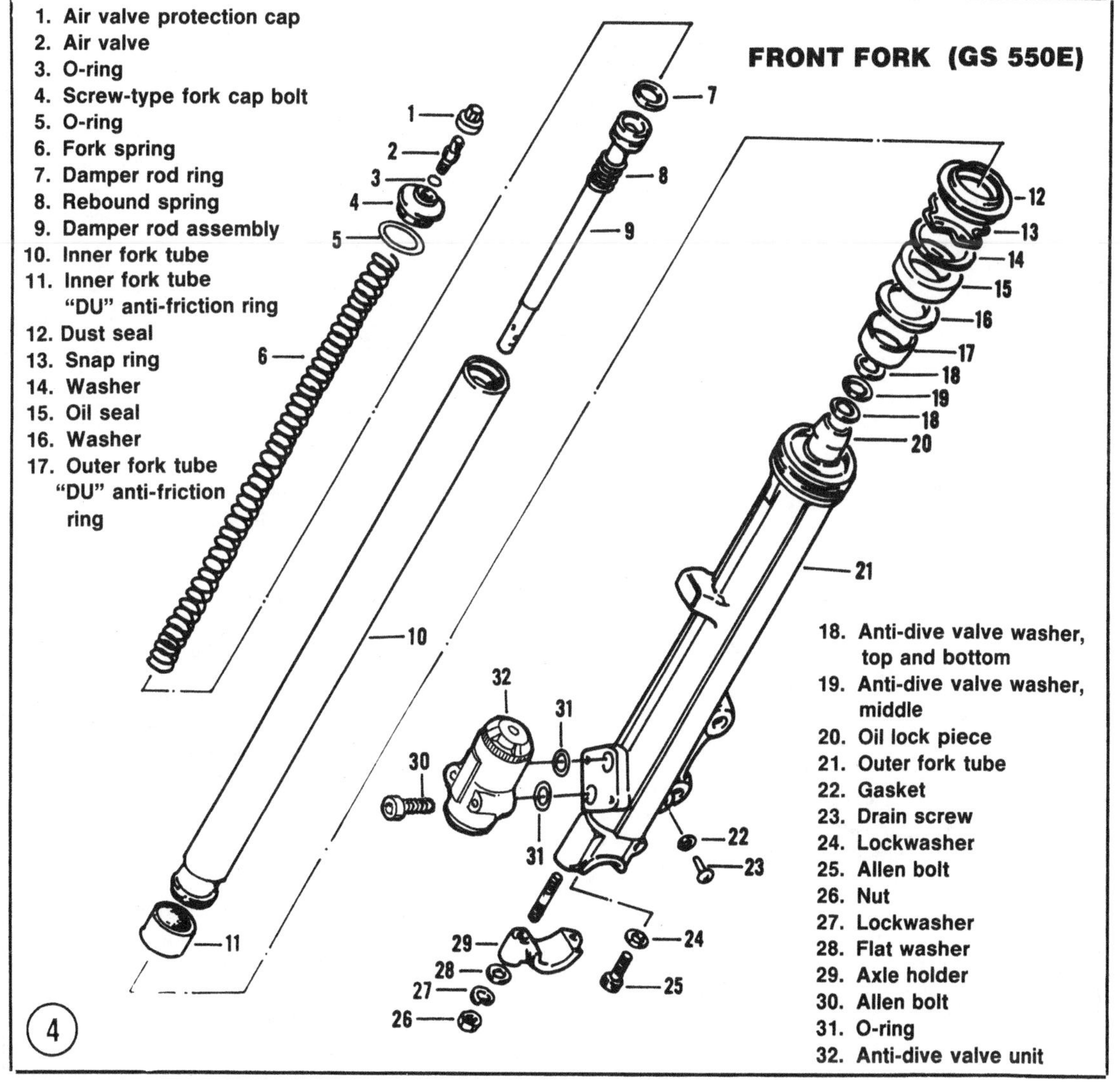

FRONT FORK (1986 GS550L MODELS)

Removal/Installation

The removal and installation procedures are the same as on previous models.

Disassembly/Assembly

Refer to **Figure 5** for this procedure.

1. Clamp the outer fork tube in a vise with soft jaws with the lower end facing up.

2. Use an impact tool and loosen the Allen bolt (**Figure 6**) in the bottom of the outer fork tube. Some fork oil may drip out at this time.

NOTE
This bolt has been secured with Loctite and is often very difficult to remove because the damper rod will turn inside the outer fork tube. It sometimes can be removed with an air impact driver. If you are unable to remove it, take the fork tubes to a dealer and have the bolts removed.

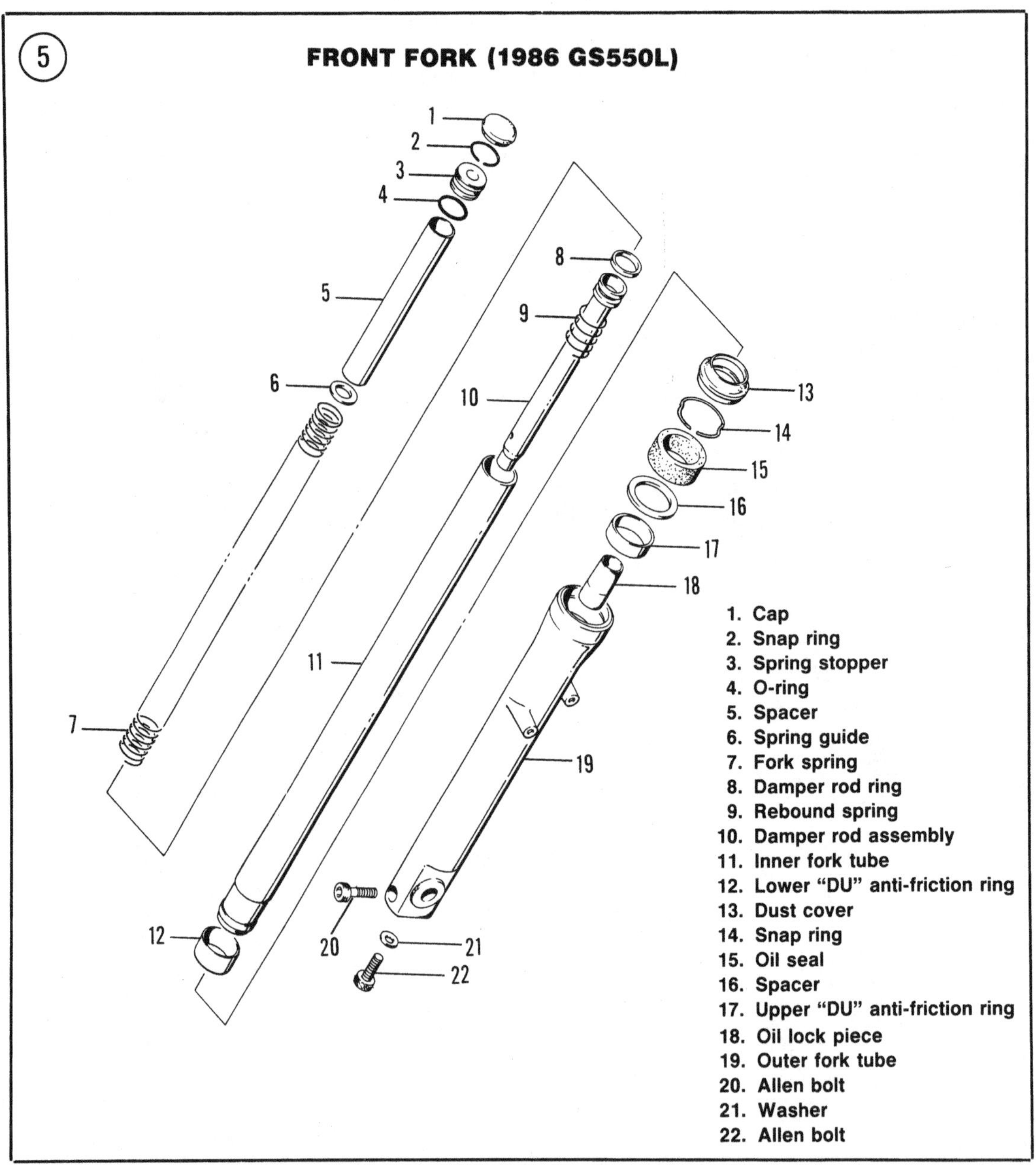

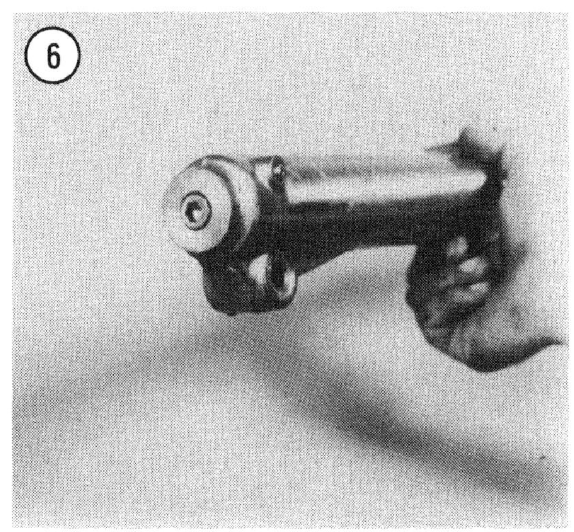
6

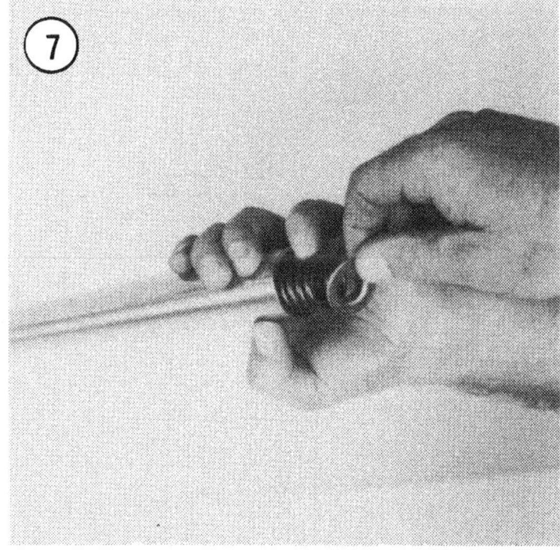
7

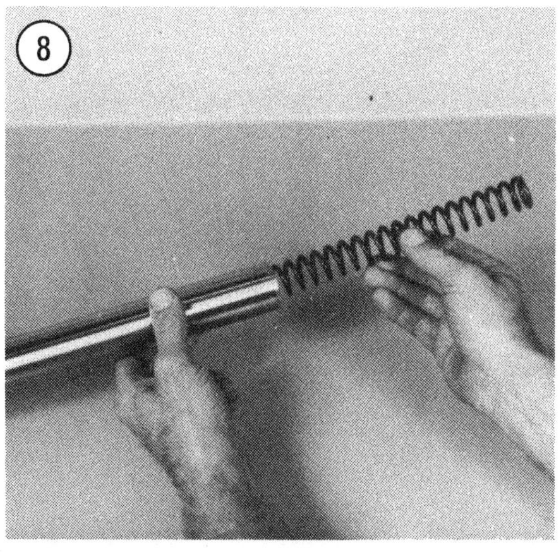
8

3. Remove the cap from the top of the inner tube.

WARNING
Be careful when removing the spring stopper as the fork spring is under pressure.

4. Press down on the spring stopper and remove the snap ring securing the spring stopper.
5. Remove the spring stopper and O-ring seal.
6. Remove the spring spacer, spring guide (**Figure 7**) and fork spring (**Figure 8**).
7. Remove the Allen bolt and washer.
8. Tip up the inner tube and completely drain the fork oil. Stroke the fork several times over a drain pan to pump out any remaining oil. Stand the fork tube (upside down) in a drain pan and allow the tube to drain for several minutes.
9. Remove the dust seal and the snap ring (**Figure 9**) from the outer fork tube.

NOTE
On this type of fork, force is needed to remove the inner tube from the outer fork tube.

10. Install the outer fork tube in a vise with soft jaws and clamp the vise securely on the brake caliper mounting lugs as shown in **Figure 10**.
11. There is an interference fit between the "DU" ring in the inner tube and the"DU" ring on the outer fork tube. In order to remove the inner tube from the outer fork tube, pull hard on the inner tube using quick in and out strokes. Doing this will withdraw the "DU" ring, spacer and oil seal from the outer fork tube (**Figure 11**).

NOTE
It may be necessary to slightly heat the area on the outer fork tube around the oil seal prior to removal. Use a rag soaked in hot water; do not apply a flame directly to the fork outer fork tube.

12. Withdraw the innner tube from the outer fork tube and remove the oil lock piece (**Figure 12**).
13. Turn the inner tube upside down and slide off the oil seal, spacer and upper "DU" ring from the fork tube.

14. Tip up the fork tube and slide out the damper rod assembly complete with the rebound spring (**Figure 13**).
15. If replacement is necessary, use a screwdriver blade and carefully spread open and remove the "DU" ring from the end of the inner tube (**Figure 14**).
16. Perform *Inspection and Seal Replacement* as described in Chapter Eight in the main body of this book with the following exception. The service limit on the front fork spring is 449 mm (17.7 in.). Replace the spring if it has sagged to this dimension or less.
17. Assembly is the reverse of these steps. Keep in mind the following:

a. Make sure all fork components are clean and dry. Wipe out the seal bore in the outer fork tube.
b. If removed, carefully install a new "DU" ring on the end of the inner fork tube (**Figure 14**). Take care not to damage the Teflon surface of the "DU" ring.
c. Apply a light film of grease to the outer edge and lips of each fork seal.
d. Slide the lower "DU" ring, seal spacer and oil seal on the inner fork tube as shown in **Figure 11**.
e. Lightly oil the inner and outer fork tubes and damper rod assembly with clean fork oil before assembling the parts.
f. Make sure the rebound (top out) spring is installed on the damper rod and install the damper rod assembly into the inner fork tube (**Figure 13**).

NOTE
Temporarily install the fork spring, spring guide, spacer, spring stopper and snap ring. The tension of the fork spring will help keep the damper rod extended through the end of the upper fork tube and ease the assembly process.

g. Slide the oil lock piece over the end of the damper rod assembly as shown in **Figure 12**.
h. Carefully install the inner fork tube with the damper rod assembly into the outer fork tube as shown in **Figure 15**.
i. Clean the thread of the Allen bolt thoroughly with solvent or spray contact cleaner. Make sure the washer is fitted to the Allen bolt and apply Suzuki Bond No. 1207B or equivalent to the first threads next to the washer. Apply a

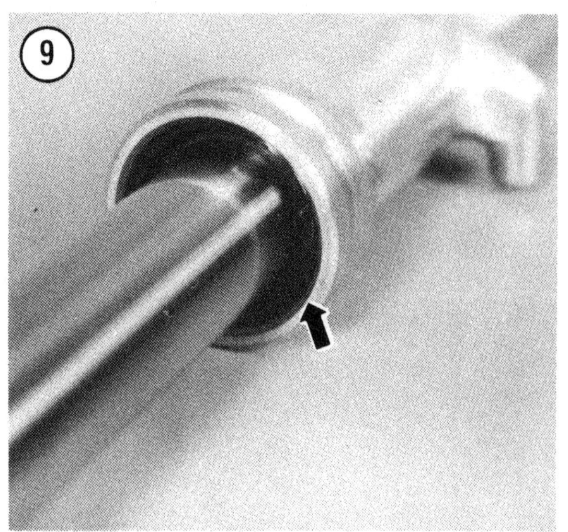
9

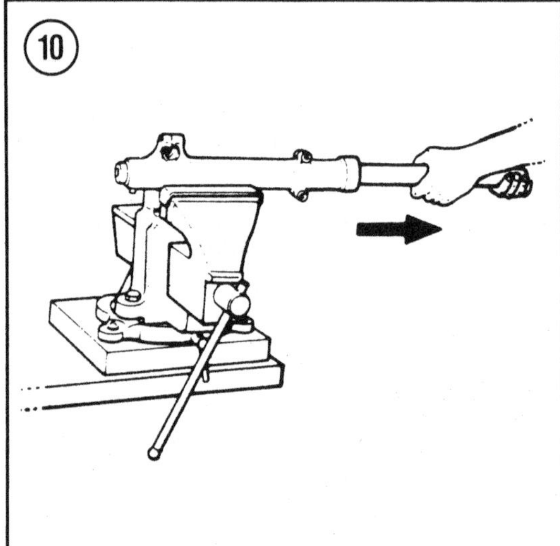
10

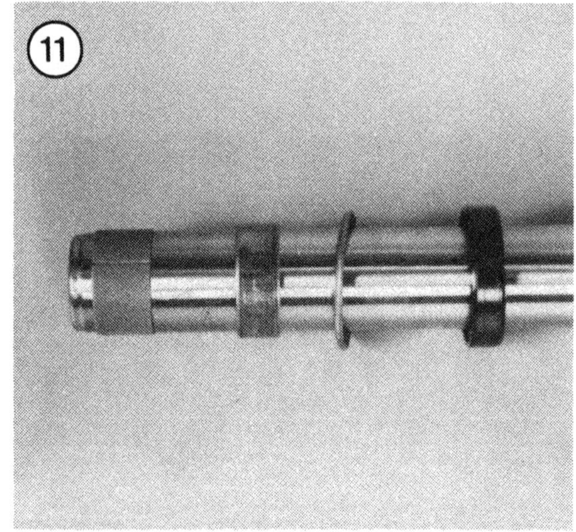
11

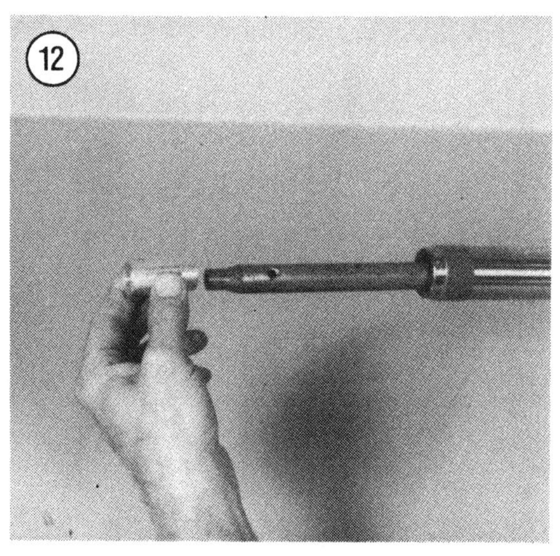

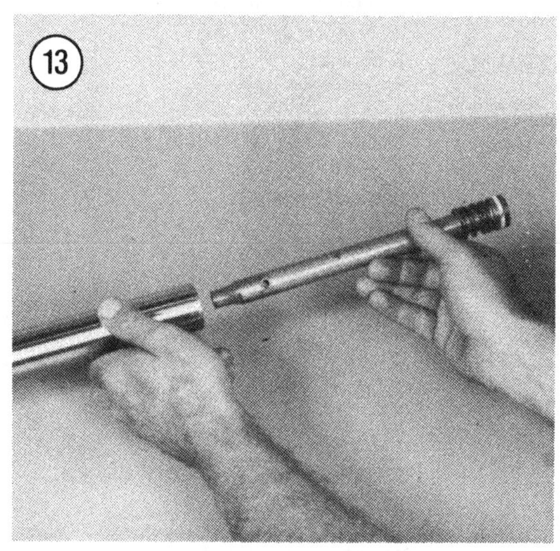

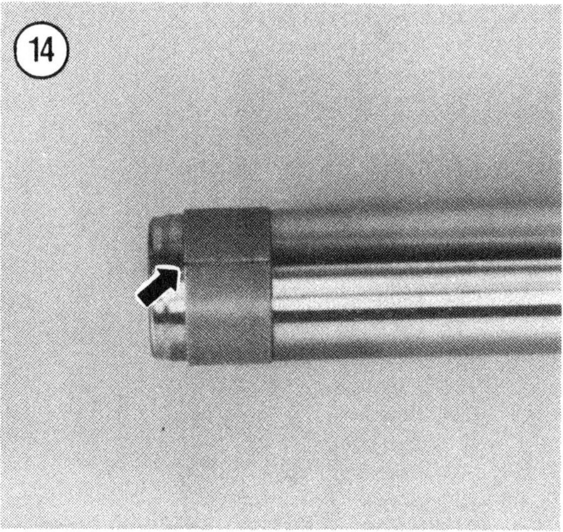

couple of drops of blue Loctite (Loctite 242) to the remaining threads on the bolt. Install the bolt and tighten using an impact driver or Suzuki holding tool (as described in Chapter Eight in the main body of this book). Tighten the bolt to 15-25 N•m (11-18 ft.-lb.).

j. Install the upper "DU" ring, spacer and oil seal into the outer fork tube. Use a piece of pipe over the inner fork tube or a seal installation tool to carefully tap the oil seal into place. Make sure that the seal is fully seated into the outer fork tube. Secure the seal with the snap ring (**Figure 9**). Make sure the snap ring is locked into the groove in the outer fork tube. Install the dust cover over the top of the outer fork tube.

18. Press down on the spring stopper and remove the snap ring securing the spring stopper.

WARNING
Be careful when removing the spring stopper as the fork spring is under pressure.

19. Remove the spring stopper and O-ring seal.
20. Remove the spring spacer, spring guide and fork spring.
21. Add 248 cc (8.4 oz.) of SAE 15 fork oil to each fork tube. Use a graduated baby bottle to make sure the oil amount is correct for each fork tube.
22. The fork oil can also be measured from the top of the fork tube. Use an accurate ruler or the Suzuki oil level gauge (Suzuki part No. 09943-74111) to make sure the oil level is correct (181 mm/7.1 in.). The oil level must be measured with the fork completely compressed and without the spring in place.

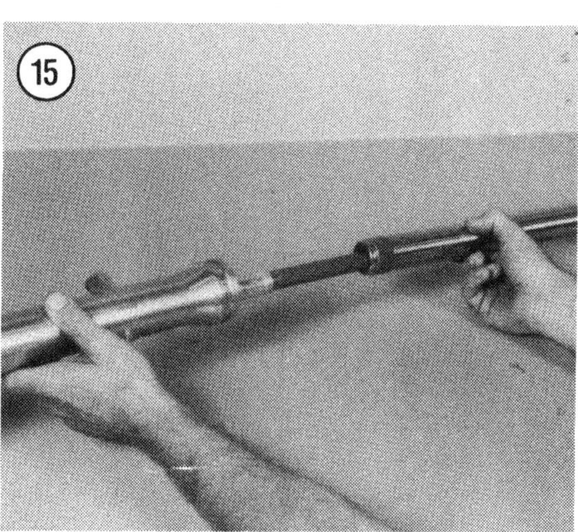

11

23. Install the fork spring with the closer wound coils toward the top.
24. Install the spring guide and spacer.
25. Make sure the O-ring seal is in good condition (**Figure 16**). Replace if necessary.
26. Install the spring stopper and snap ring. Make sure the snap ring is completly seated in the groove in the inner fork tube.
27. Install the cap.

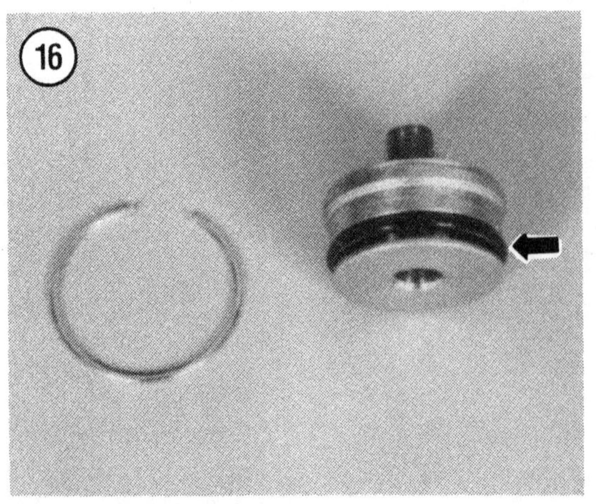

STEERING HEAD

Disassembly/Lubrication/ Assembly (GS550L Models)

Refer to **Figure 17** for this procedure.

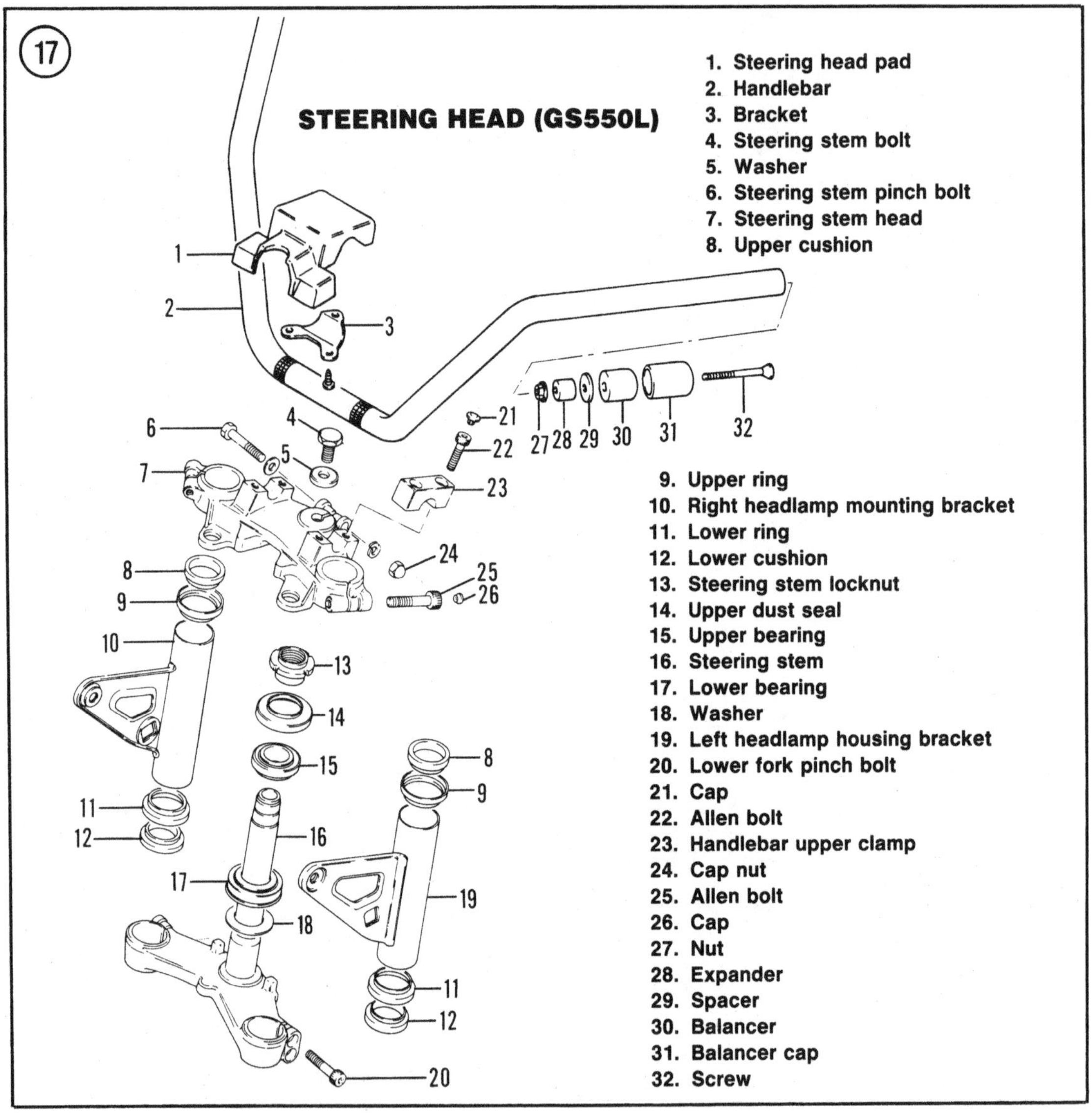

17

STEERING HEAD (GS550L)

1. Steering head pad
2. Handlebar
3. Bracket
4. Steering stem bolt
5. Washer
6. Steering stem pinch bolt
7. Steering stem head
8. Upper cushion
9. Upper ring
10. Right headlamp mounting bracket
11. Lower ring
12. Lower cushion
13. Steering stem locknut
14. Upper dust seal
15. Upper bearing
16. Steering stem
17. Lower bearing
18. Washer
19. Left headlamp housing bracket
20. Lower fork pinch bolt
21. Cap
22. Allen bolt
23. Handlebar upper clamp
24. Cap nut
25. Allen bolt
26. Cap
27. Nut
28. Expander
29. Spacer
30. Balancer
31. Balancer cap
32. Screw

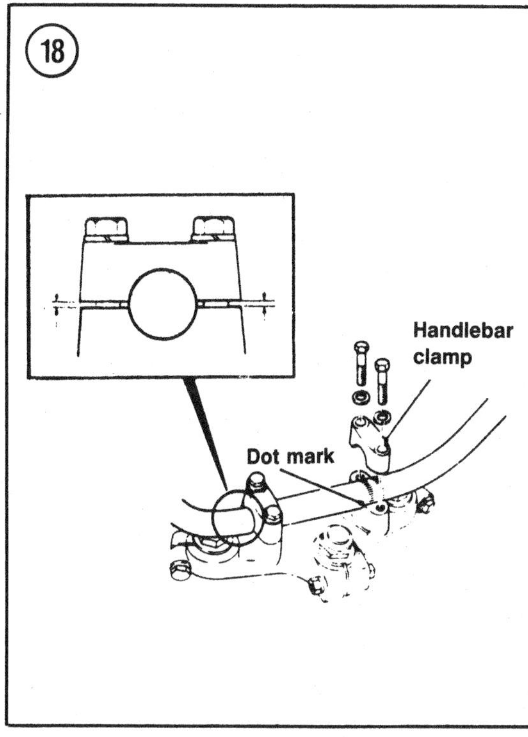

Disassembly, lubrication and assembly are the same as on TSCC models with the exception of some bolt locations and the 1-piece handlebar design.

Handlebar Removal/ Installatiton (GS550L Models)

Refer to **Figure 17** for this procedure.

1. If the handlebar is to be replaced, it is necessary to remove the clutch lever, front master cylinder and throttle grip. Refer to Chapter Ten in the main body of this book to remove the front master cylinder.
2. Remove the screws securing the steering head cover and remove the cover.
3. Remove the caps from the Allen bolts on the handlebar clamps.
4. Remove the Allen bolts securing the handlebar clamps and remove the handlebar.
5. Install the handlebar with the dot and the handlebar clamps positioned as shown in **Figure 18**. Tighen the clamp bolts to 1.2-2.0 mkg (8.5-14.5 ft.-lb.). Install the caps into the Allen bolts.
6. Install the clutch lever, front master cylinder and throttle grip if removed.

CHAPTER TEN

BRAKES

DISC BRAKES

Front Caliper Removal/Installation (GS550E and GS550L Models)

The anti-dive modular valve unit is no longer tied-in with the hydraulic brake system, so there is no brake hose attached to the unit from the front caliper assembly.

INDEX

1977 GS550B
1978 GS550C & EC

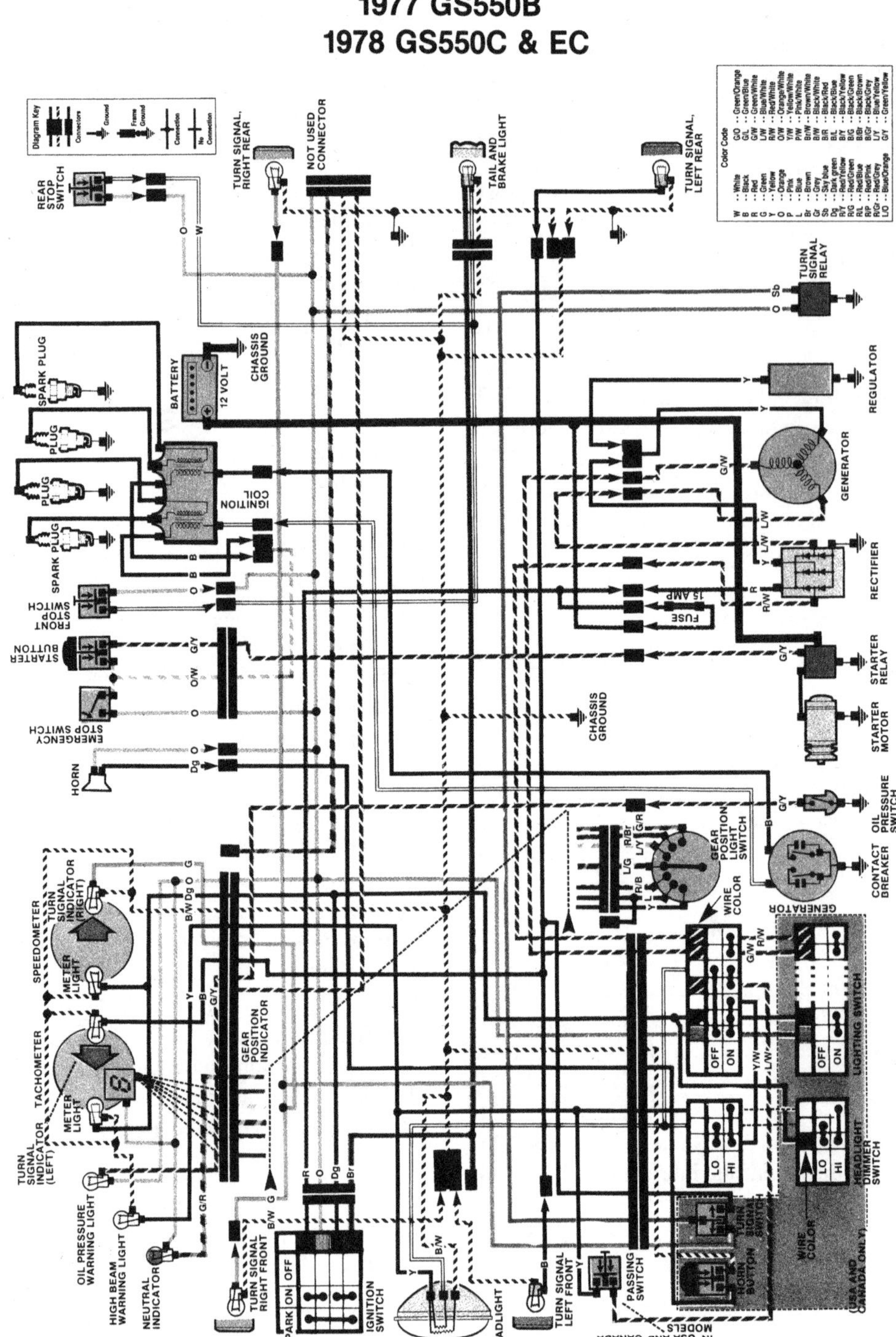

1979 GS550N & EN

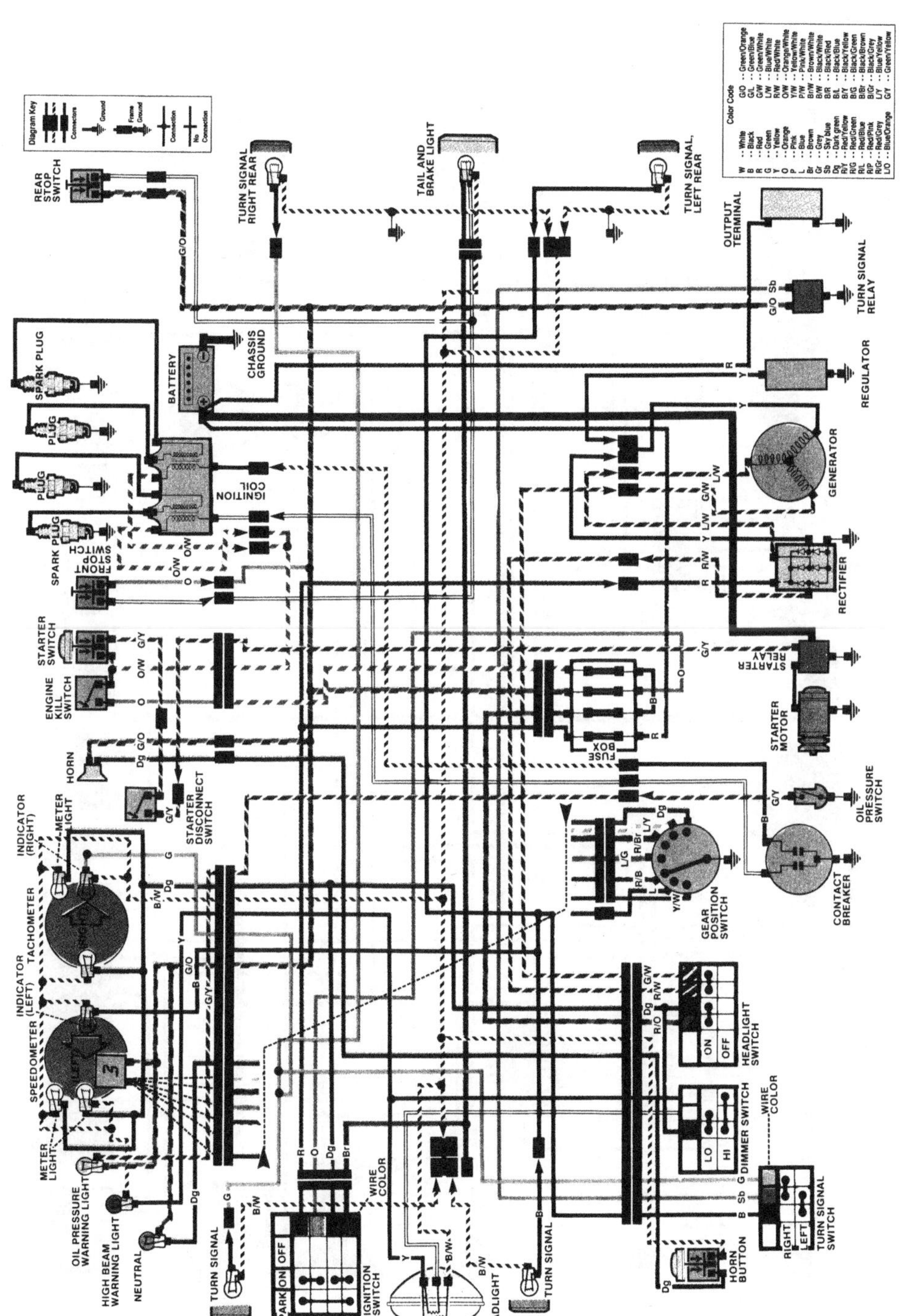

1979 GS550LN

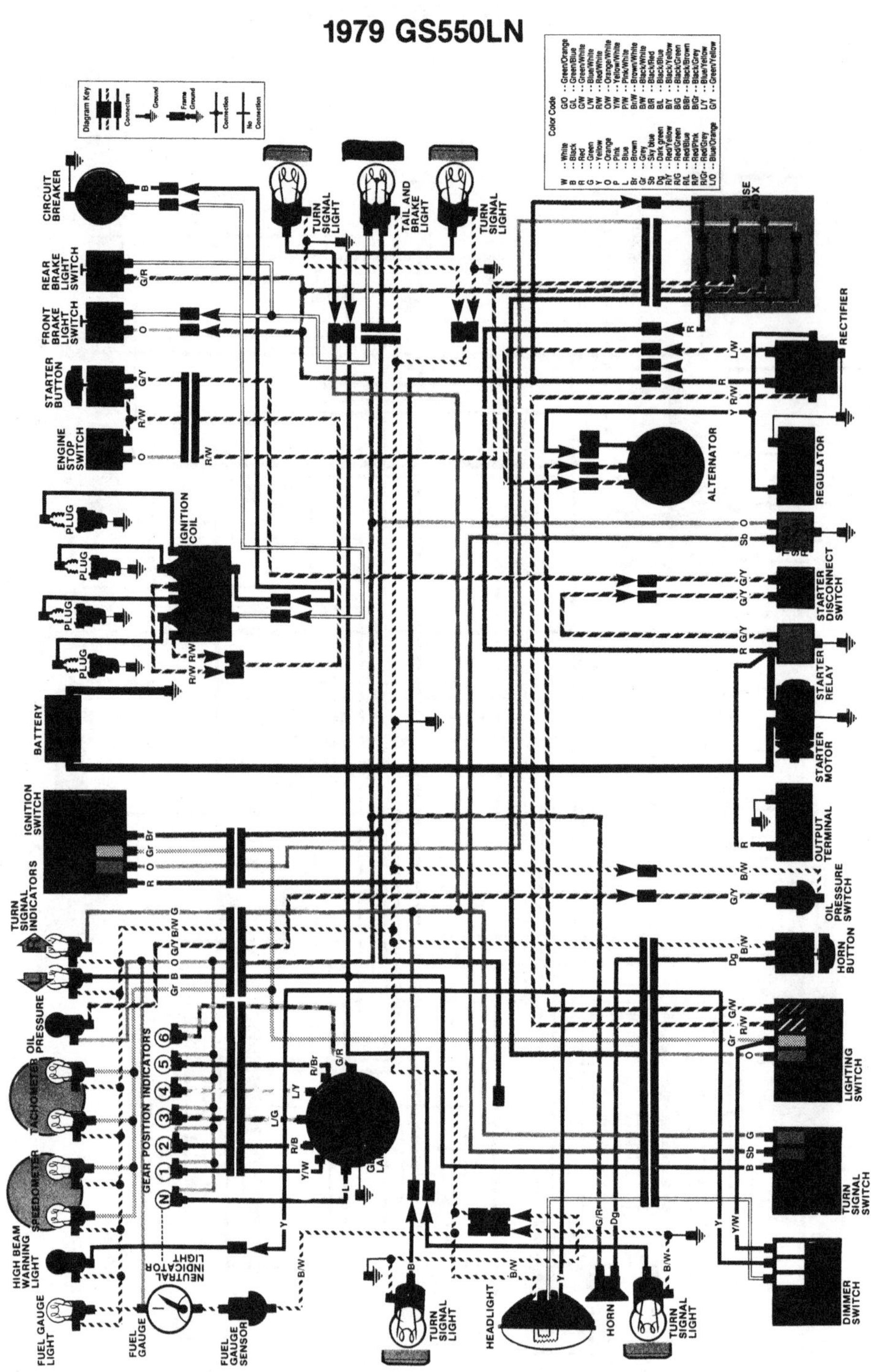

1980 GS550ET

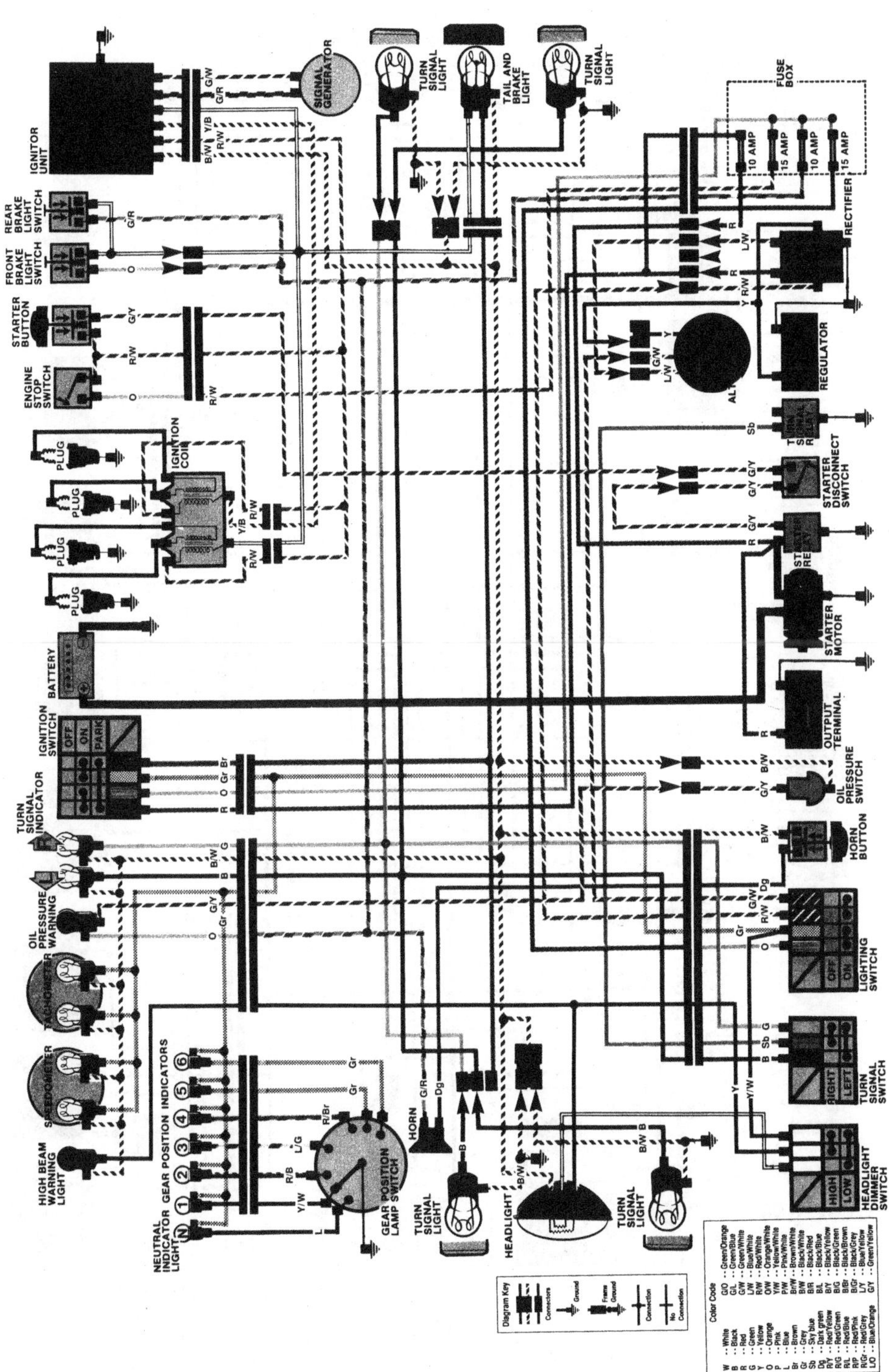

1980 GS550LT

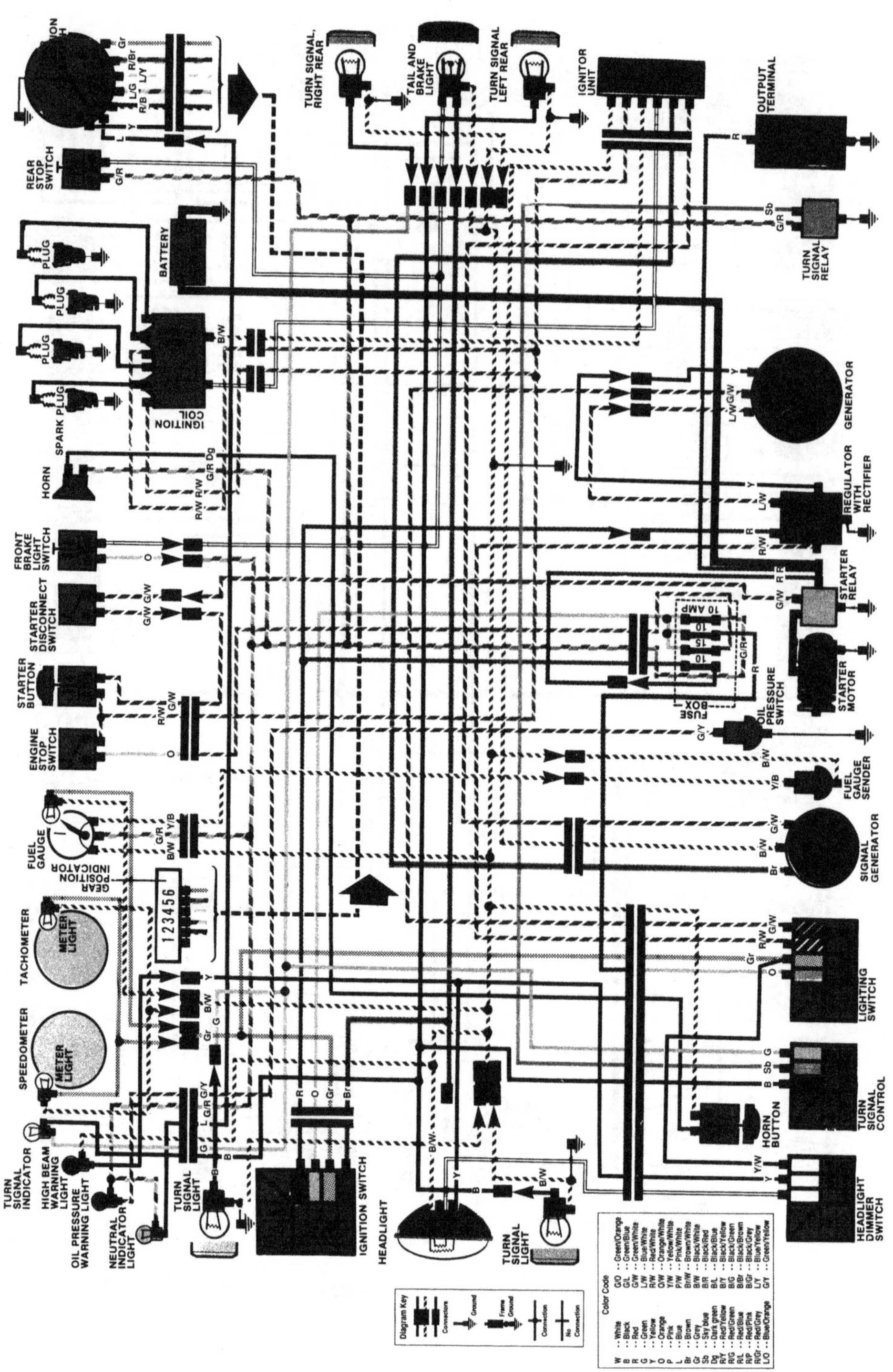

1981 GS550LX

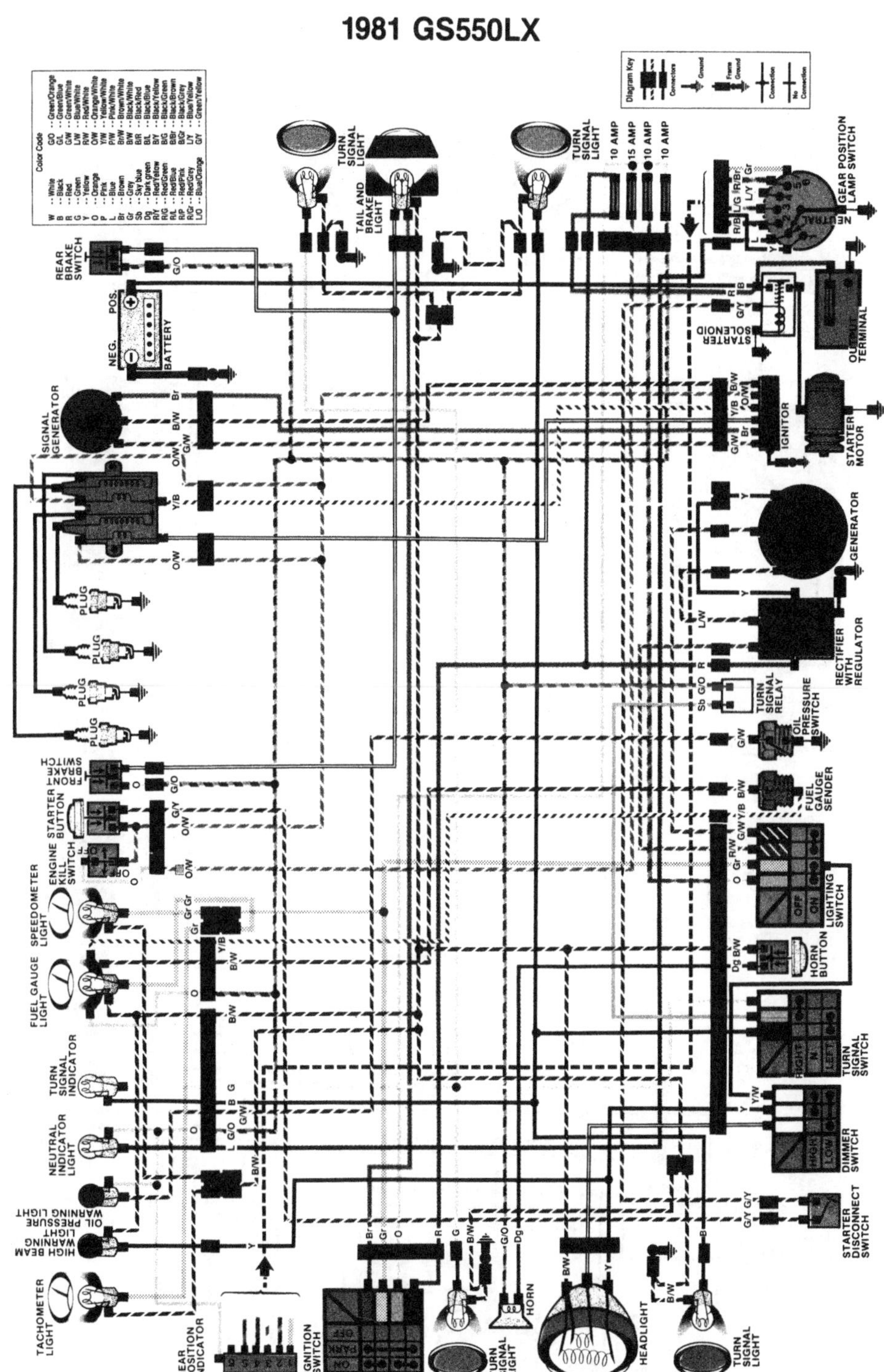

1981 GS550TX

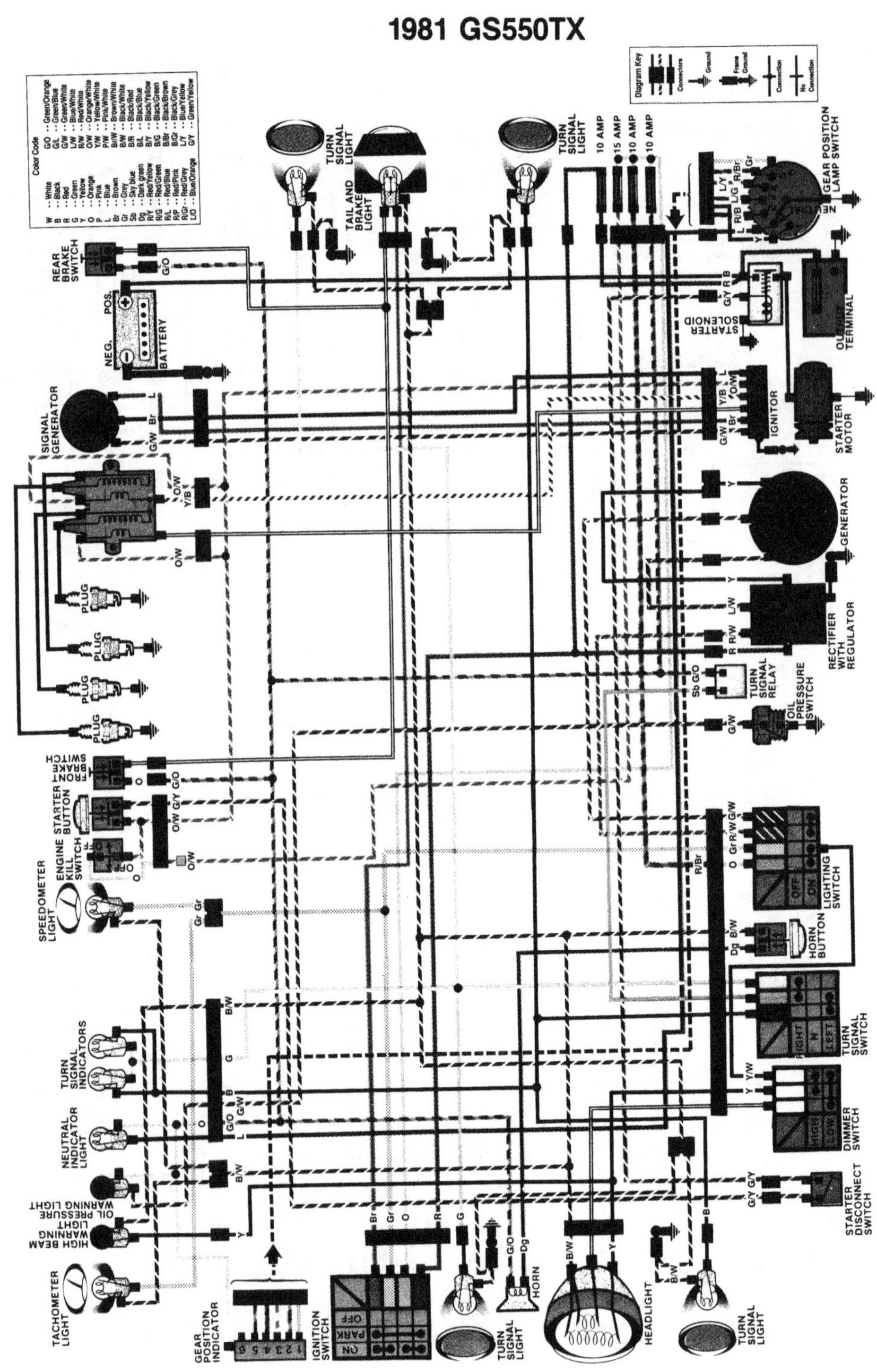

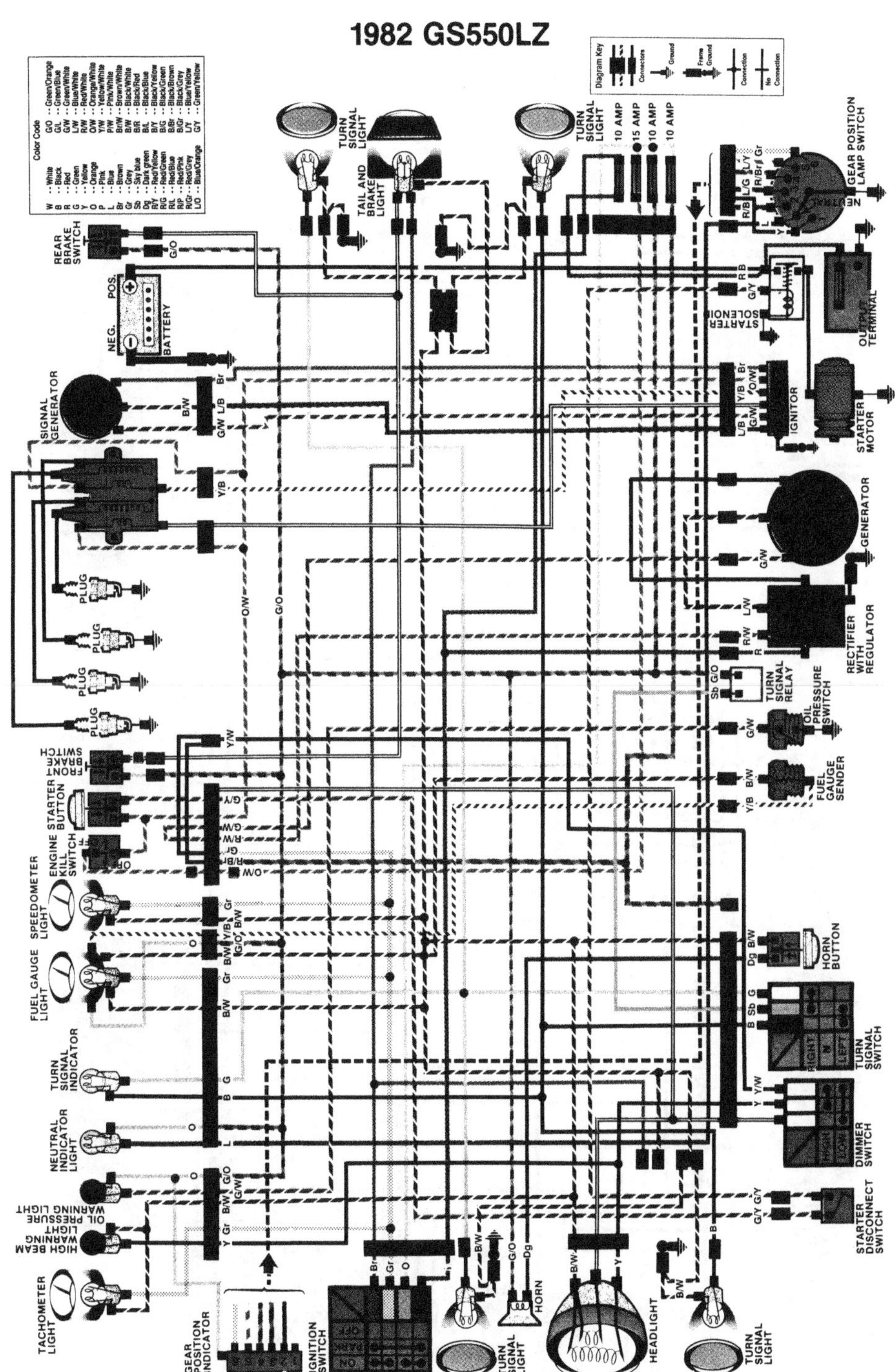
1982 GS550LZ
TURN SIGNAL LIGHT
TAIL AND BRAKE LIGHT
TURN SIGNAL LIGHT
10 AMP
15 AMP
10 AMP
10 AMP
GEAR POSITION LAMP SWITCH
REAR BRAKE SWITCH
BATTERY
POS.
NEG.
STARTER SOLENOID
OUTPUT TERMINAL
SIGNAL GENERATOR
IGNITOR
STARTER MOTOR
GENERATOR
PLUG
PLUG
PLUG
PLUG
RECTIFIER WITH REGULATOR
TURN SIGNAL RELAY
OIL PRESSURE SWITCH
FRONT BRAKE SWITCH
FUEL GAUGE SENDER
STARTER BUTTON
ENGINE KILL SWITCH
SPEEDOMETER LIGHT
FUEL GAUGE LIGHT
HORN BUTTON
TURN SIGNAL SWITCH
TURN SIGNAL INDICATOR
NEUTRAL INDICATOR LIGHT
DIMMER SWITCH
OIL PRESSURE WARNING LIGHT
HIGH BEAM WARNING LIGHT
STARTER DISCONNECT SWITCH
TACHOMETER LIGHT
GEAR POSITION INDICATOR
IGNITION SWITCH
TURN SIGNAL LIGHT
HORN
HEADLIGHT
TURN SIGNAL LIGHT

13

1982 GS550MZ

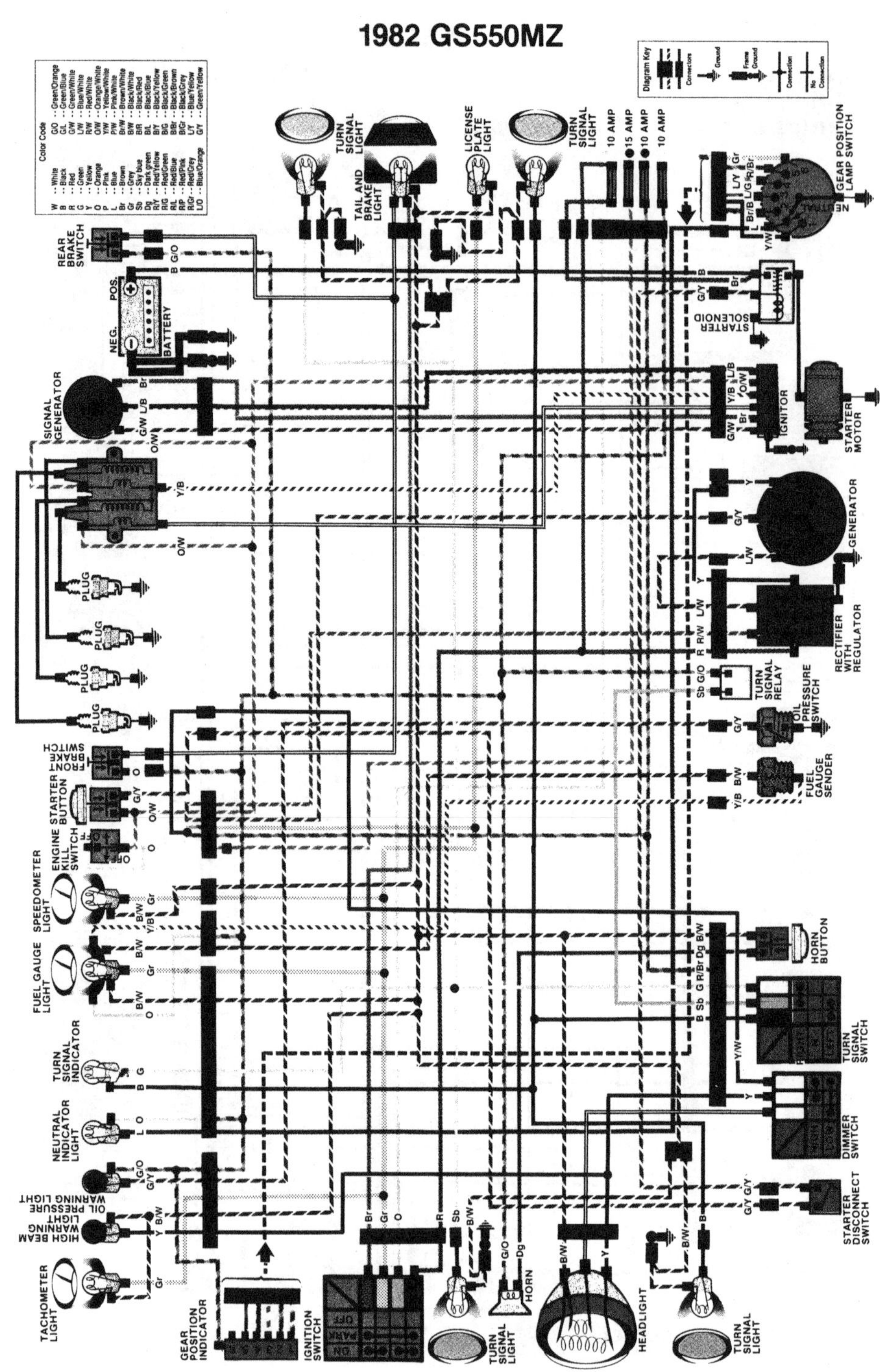

1983 GS550ED

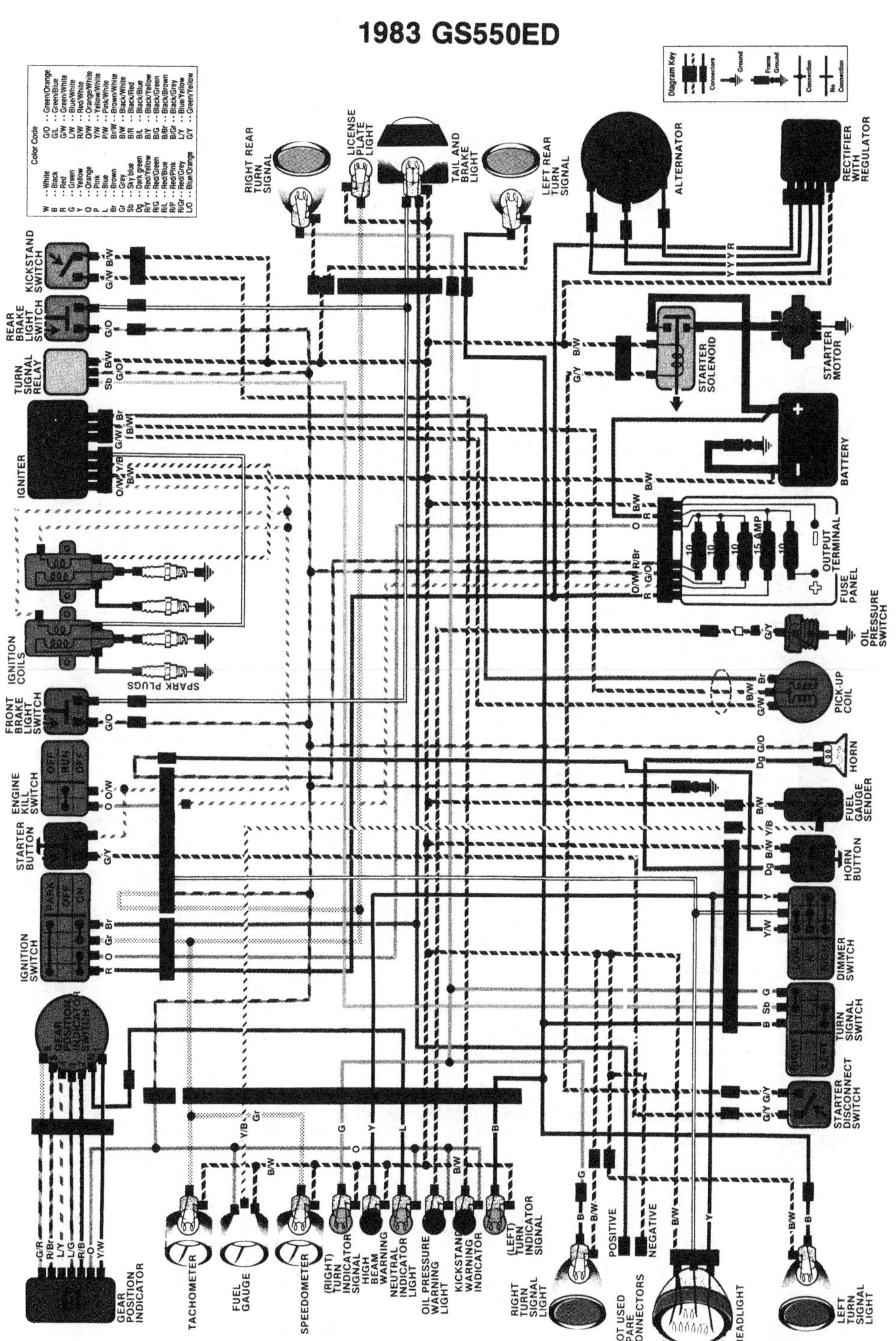

1983 GS550LD

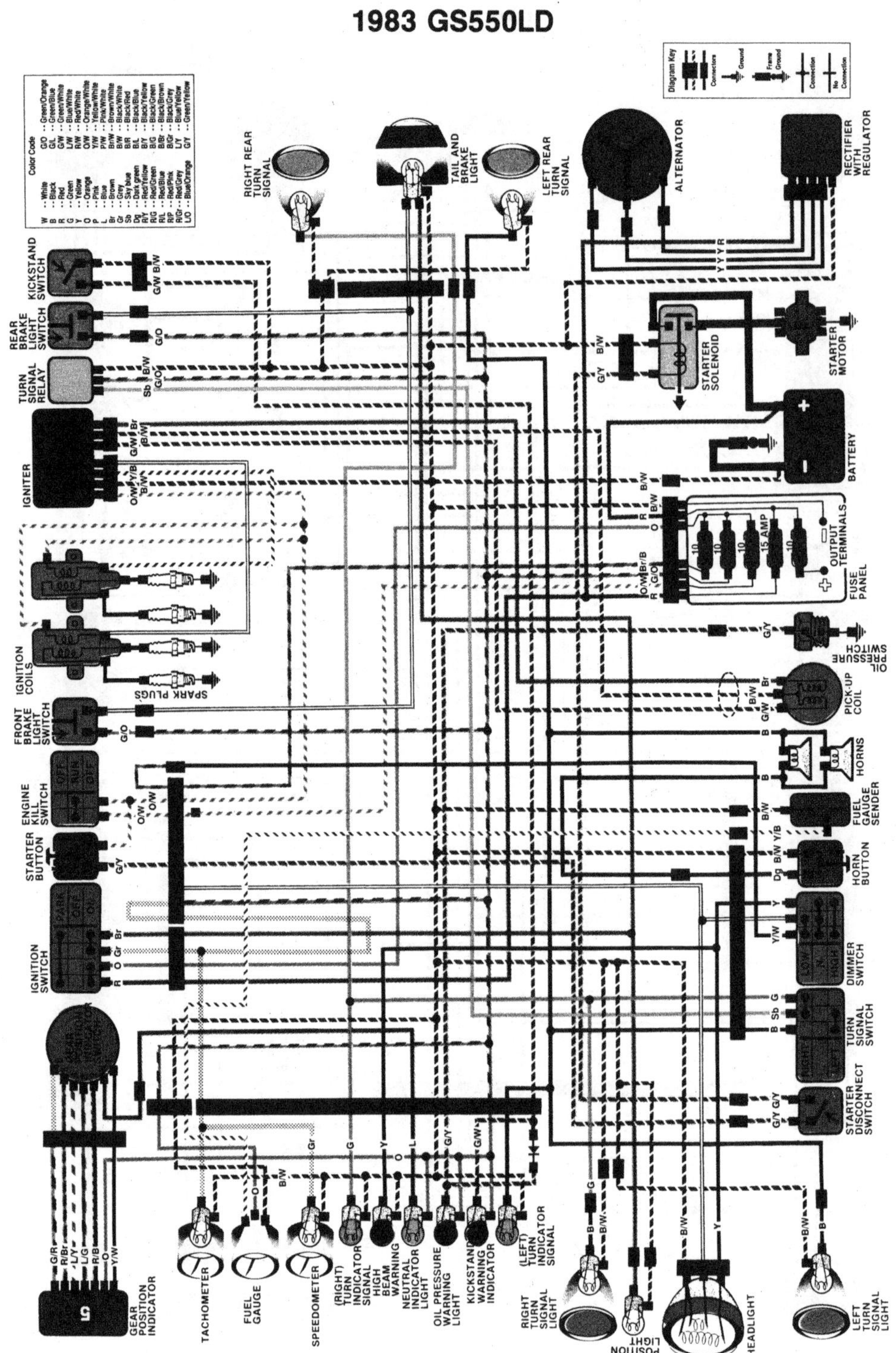

1983 GS550ESD, 1984 GS550ESE, 1985 GS550ESF & 1986 GS550ESG

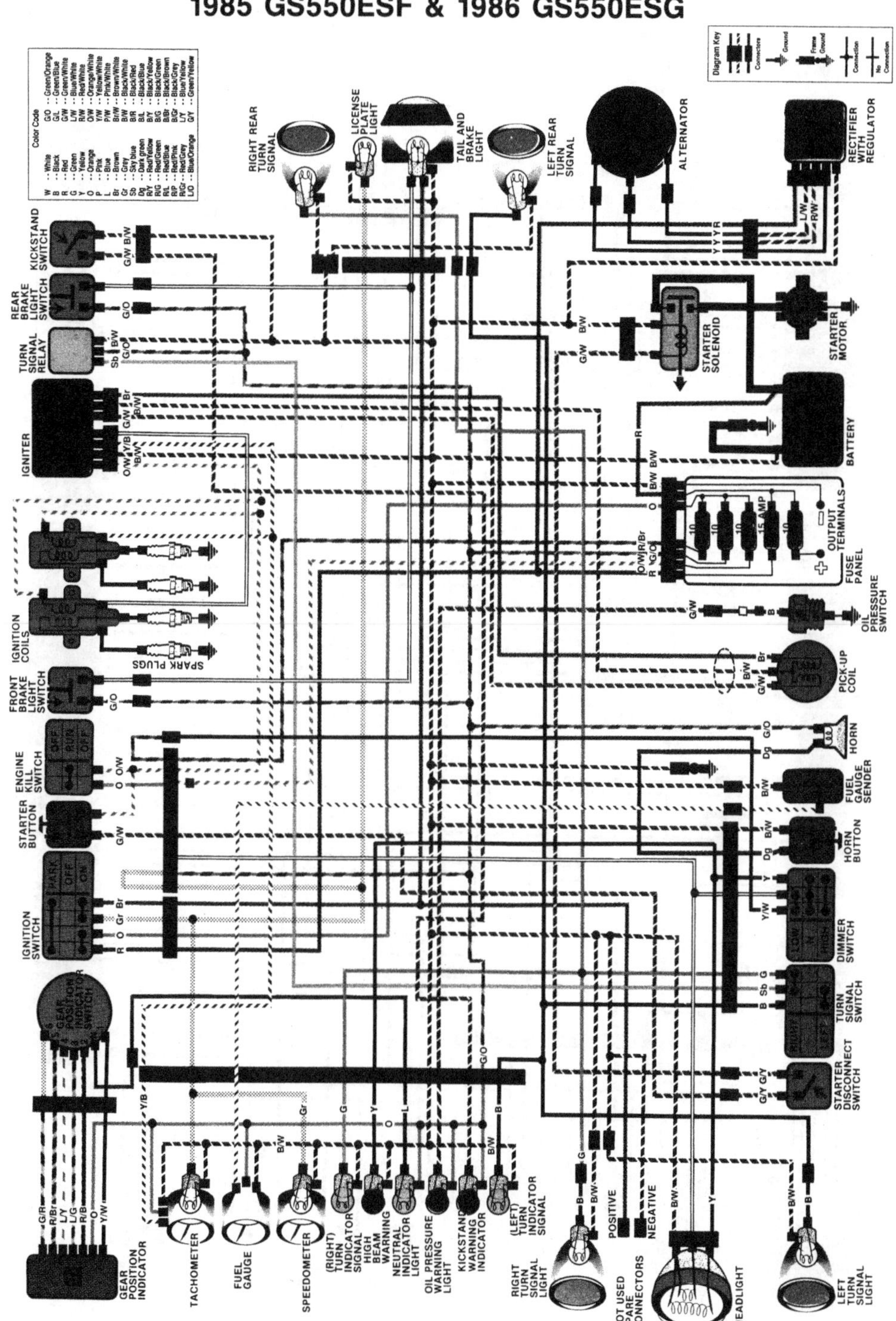

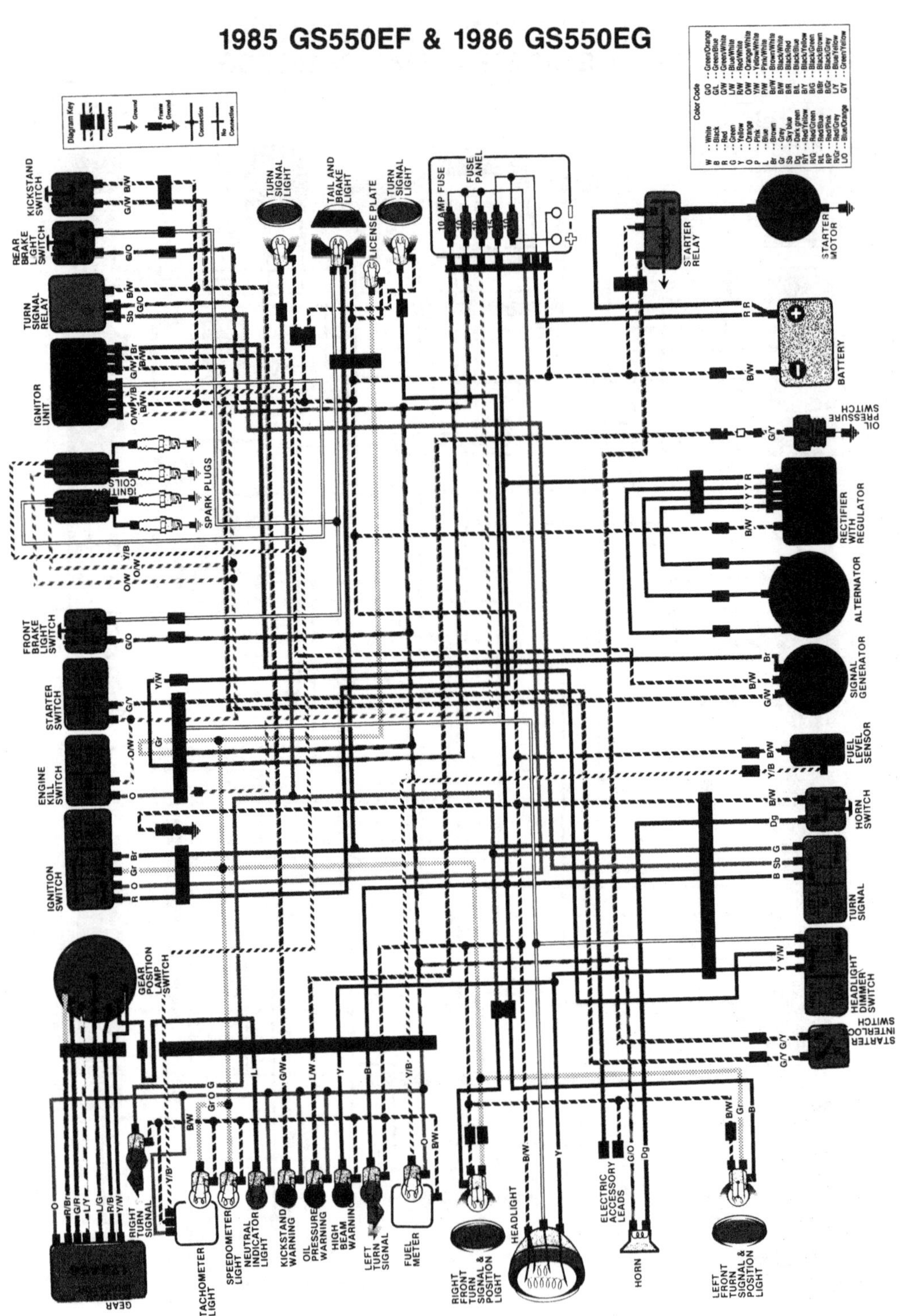
1985 GS550EF & 1986 GS550EG

1985 GS550LF & 1986 GS550LG

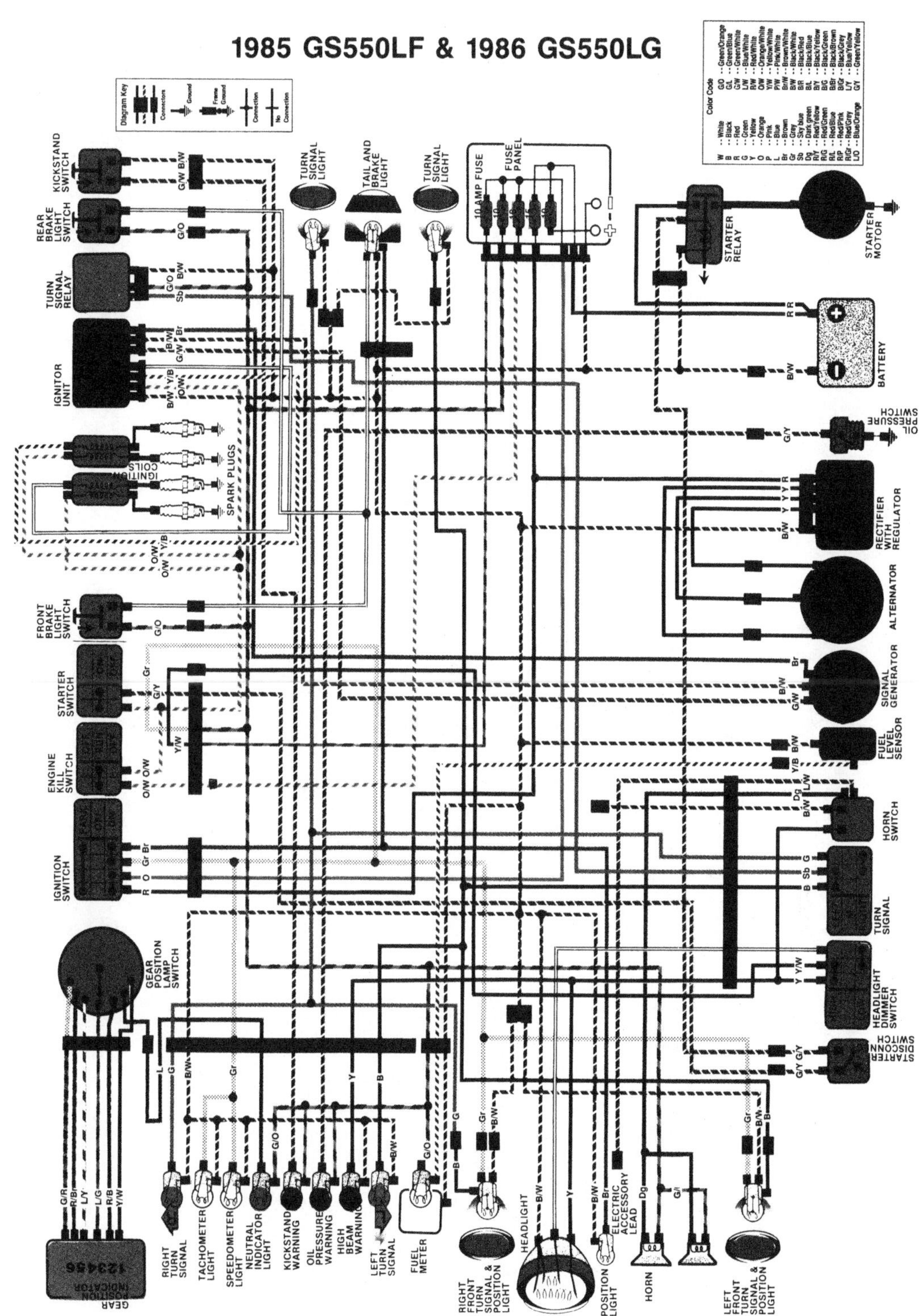

NOTES

NOTES

NOTES

NOTES

NOTES

MAINTENANCE LOG

Date	Miles	Type of Service

Check out *clymer.com* for our full line of powersport repair manuals.

BMW

- M308 500 & 600cc Twins, 55-69
- M502-3 BMW R50/5-R100GS PD, 70-96
- M500-3 BMW K-Series, 85-97
- M501-3 K1200RS, GT & LT, 98-10
- M503-3 R850, R1100, R1150 & R1200C, 93-05
- M309 F650, 1994-2000

HARLEY-DAVIDSON

- M419 Sportsters, 59-85
- M429-5 XL/XLH Sportster, 86-03
- M427-3 XL Sportster, 04-11
- M418 Panheads, 48-65
- M420 Shovelheads,66-84
- M421-3 FLS/FXS Evolution,84-99
- M423-2 FLS/FXS Twin Cam, 00-05
- M250 FLS/FXS/FXC Softail, 06-09
- M422-3 FLH/FLT/FXR Evolution, 84-98
- M430-4 FLH/FLT Twin Cam, 99-05
- M252 FLH/FLT, 06-09
- M426 VRSC Series, 02-07
- M424-2 FXD Evolution, 91-98
- M425-3 FXD Twin Cam, 99-05

HONDA

ATVs

- M316 Odyssey FL250, 77-84
- M311 ATC, TRX & Fourtrax 70-125, 70-87
- M433 Fourtrax 90, 93-00
- M326 ATC185 & 200, 80-86
- M347 ATC200X & Fourtrax 200SX, 86-88
- M455 ATC250 & Fourtrax 200/250, 84-87
- M342 ATC250R, 81-84
- M348 TRX250R/Fourtrax 250R & ATC250R, 85-89
- M456-4 TRX250X 87-92; TRX300EX 93-06
- M446-3 TRX250 Recon & Recon ES, 97-07
- M215 TRX250EX, 01-05
- M346-3 TRX300/Fourtrax 300 & TRX300FW/Fourtrax 4x4, 88-00
- M200-2 TRX350 Rancher, 00-06
- M459-3 TRX400 Foreman 95-03
- M454-4 TRX400EX 99-07
- M201 TRX450R & TRX450ER, 04-09
- M205 TRX450 Foreman, 98-04
- M210 TRX500 Rubicon, 01-04
- M206 TRX500 Foreman, 05-11

Singles

- M310-13 50-110cc OHC Singles, 65-99
- M315 100-350cc OHC, 69-82
- M317 125-250cc Elsinore, 73-80
- M442 CR60-125R Pro-Link, 81-88
- M431-2 CR80R, 89-95, CR125R, 89-91
- M435 CR80R &CR80RB, 96-02
- M457-2 CR125R, 92-97; CR250R, 92-96
- M464 CR125R, 1998-2002
- M443 CR250R-500R Pro-Link, 81-87
- M432-3 CR250R, 88-91 & CR500R, 88-01
- M437 CR250R, 97-01
- M352 CRF250R, CRF250X, CRF450R & CRF450X, 02-05
- M319-3 XR50R, CRF50F, XR70R & CRF70F, 97-09
- M312-14 XL/XR75-100, 75-91
- M222 XR80R, CRF80F, XR100R, & CRF100F, 92-09
- M318-4 XL/XR/TLR 125-200, 79-03
- M328-4 XL/XR250, 78-00; XL/XR350R 83-85; XR200R, 84-85; XR250L, 91-96
- M320-2 XR400R, 96-04
- M221 XR600R, 91-07; XR650L, 93-07
- M339-8 XL/XR 500-600, 79-90
- M225 XR650R, 00-07

Twins

- M321 125-200cc Twins, 65-78
- M322 250-350cc Twins, 64-74
- M323 250-360cc Twins, 74-77
- M324-5 Twinstar, Rebel 250 & Nighthawk 250, 78-03
- M334 400-450cc Twins, 78-87
- M333 450 & 500cc Twins, 65-76
- M335 CX & GL500/650, 78-83
- M344 VT500, 83-88
- M313 VT700 & 750, 83-87
- M314-3 VT750 Shadow Chain Drive, 98-06
- M440 VT1100C Shadow, 85-96
- M460-4 VT1100 Series, 95-07
- M230 VTX1800 Series, 02-08
- M231 VTX1300 Series, 03-09

Fours

- M332 CB350-550, SOHC, 71-78
- M345 CB550 & 650, 83-85
- M336 CB650,79-82
- M341 CB750 SOHC, 69-78
- M337 CB750 DOHC, 79-82
- M436 CB750 Nighthawk, 91-93 & 95-99
- M325 CB900, 1000 & 1100, 80-83
- M439 600 Hurricane, 87-90
- M441-2 CBR600F2 & F3, 91-98
- M445-2 CBR600F4, 99-06
- M220 CBR600RR, 03-06
- M434-2 CBR900RR Fireblade, 93-99
- M329 500cc V-Fours, 84-86
- M349 700-1000cc Interceptor, 83-85
- M458-2 VFR700F-750F, 86-97
- M438 VFR800FI Interceptor, 98-00
- M327 700-1100cc V-Fours, 82-88
- M508 ST1100/Pan European, 90-02
- M340 GL1000 & 1100, 75-83
- M504 GL1200, 84-87

Sixes

- M505 GL1500 Gold Wing, 88-92
- M506-2 GL1500 Gold Wing, 93-00
- M507-3 GL1800 Gold Wing, 01-10
- M462-2 GL1500C Valkyrie, 97-03

KAWASAKI

ATVs

- M465-3 Bayou KLF220 & KLF250, 88-10
- M466-4 Bayou KLF300, 86-04
- M467 Bayou KLF400, 93-99
- M470 Lakota KEF300, 95-99
- M385-2 Mojave KSF250, 87-04

Singles

- M350-9 80-350cc Rotary Valve, 66-01
- M444-2 KX60, 83-02; KX80 83-90
- M448-2 KX80, 91-00; KX85, 01-10 & KX100, 89-09
- M351 KDX200, 83-88
- M447-3 KX125 & KX250, 82-91; KX500, 83-04
- M472-2 KX125, 92-00
- M473-2 KX250, 92-00
- M474-3 KLR650, 87-07
- M240-2 KLR650, 08-12

Twins

- M355 KZ400, KZ/Z440, EN450 & EN500, 74-95
- M360-3 EX500, GPZ500S, & Ninja 500R, 87-02
- M356-5 Vulcan 700 & 750, 85-06
- M354-3 Vulcan 800 & Vulcan 800 Classic, 95-05
- M357-2 Vulcan 1500, 87-99
- M471-3 Vulcan 1500 Series, 96-08
- M245 Vulcan 1600 Series, 03-08

Fours

- M449 KZ500/550 & ZX550, 79-85
- M450 KZ, Z & ZX750, 80-85
- M358 KZ650, 77-83
- M359-3 Z & KZ 900-1000cc, 73-81
- M451-3 KZ, ZX & ZN 1000 &1100cc, 81-02
- M452-3 ZX500 & Ninja ZX600, 85-97
- M468-2 Ninja ZX-6, 90-04
- M469 Ninja ZX-7, ZX7R & ZX7RR, 91-98
- M453-3 Ninja ZX900, ZX1000 & ZX1100, 84-01
- M409 Concours, 86-04

POLARIS

ATVs

- M496 3-, 4- and 6-Wheel Models w/250-425cc Engines, 85-95
- M362-2 Magnum & Big Boss, 96-99
- M363 Scrambler 500 4X4, 97-00
- M365-4 Sportsman/Xplorer, 96-10
- M366 Sportsman 600/700/800 Twins, 02-10
- M367 Predator 500, 03-07

SUZUKI

ATVs

- M381 ALT/LT 125 & 185, 83-87
- M475 LT230 & LT250, 85-90
- M380-2 LT250R Quad Racer, 85-92
- M483-2 LT-4WD, LT-F4WDX & LT-F250, 87-98
- M270-2 LT-Z400, 03-08
- M343-2 LT-F500F Quadrunner, 98-02

Singles

- M369 125-400cc, 64-81
- M371 RM50-400 Twin Shock, 75-81
- M379 RM125-500 Single Shock, 81-88
- M386 RM80-250, 89-95
- M400 RM125, 96-00
- M401 RM250, 96-02
- M476 DR250-350, 90-94
- M477-3 DR-Z400E, S & SM, 00-09
- M384-4 LS650 Savage/S40, 86-07

Twins

- M372 GS400-450 Chain Drive, 77-87
- M484-3 GS500E Twins, 89-02
- M361 SV650, 1999-2002
- M481-5 VS700-800 Intruder/S50, 85-07
- M261-2 1500 Intruder/C90, 98-09
- M260-2 Volusia/Boulevard C50, 01-08
- M482-3 VS1400 Intruder/S83, 87-07

Triple

- M368 GT380, 550 & 750, 72-77

Fours

- M373 GS550, 77-86
- M364 GS650, 81-83
- M370 GS750, 77-82
- M376 GS850-1100 Shaft Drive, 79-84
- M378 GS1100 Chain Drive, 80-81
- M383-3 Katana 600, 88-96 GSX-R750-1100, 86-87
- M331 GSX-R600, 97-00
- M264 GSX-R600, 01-05
- M478-2 GSX-R750, 88-92; GSX750F Katana, 89-96
- M485 GSX-R750, 96-99
- M377 GSX-R1000, 01-04
- M266 GSX-R1000, 05-06
- M265 GSX1300R Hayabusa, 99-07
- M338 Bandit 600, 95-00
- M353 GSF1200 Bandit, 96-03

YAMAHA

ATVs

- M499-2 YFM80 Moto-4, Badger & Raptor, 85-08
- M394 YTM200, 225 & YFM200, 83-86
- M488-5 Blaster, 88-05
- M489-2 Timberwolf, 89-00
- M487-5 Warrior, 87-04
- M486-6 Banshee, 87-06
- M490-3 Moto-4 & Big Bear, 87-04
- M493 Kodiak, 93-98
- M287 YFZ450, 04-09
- M285-2 Grizzly 660, 02-08
- M280-2 Raptor 660R, 01-05
- M290 Raptor 700R, 06-09

Singles

- M492-2 PW50 & 80 Y-Zinger & BW80 Big Wheel 80, 81-02
- M410 80-175 Piston Port, 68-76
- M415 250-400 Piston Port, 68-76
- M412 DT & MX Series, 77-83
- M414 IT125-490, 76-86
- M393 YZ50-80 Monoshock, 78-90
- M413 YZ100-490 Monoshock, 76-84
- M390 YZ125-250, 85-87 YZ490, 85-90
- M391 YZ125-250, 88-93 & WR250Z, 91-93
- M497-2 YZ125, 94-01
- M498 YZ250, 94-98; WR250Z, 94-97
- M406 YZ250F & WR250F, 01-03
- M491-2 YZ400F, 98-99 & 426F, 00-02; WR400F, 98-00 & 426F, 00-01
- M417 XT125-250, 80-84
- M480-3 XT350, 85-00; TT350, 86-87
- M405 XT/TT 500, 76-81
- M416 XT/TT 600, 83-89

Twins

- M403 650cc Twins, 70-82
- M395-10 XV535-1100 Virago, 81-03
- M495-6 V-Star 650, 98-09
- M281-4 V-Star 1100, 99-09
- M283 V-Star 1300, 07-10
- M282-2 Road Star, 99-07

Triple

- M404 XS750 & XS850, 77-81

Fours

- M387 XJ550, XJ600 & FJ600, 81-92
- M494 XJ600 Seca II/Diversion, 92-98
- M388 YX600 Radian & FZ600, 86-90
- M396 FZR600, 89-93
- M392 FZ700-750 & Fazer, 85-87
- M411 XS1100, 78-81
- M461 YZF-R6, 99-04
- M398 YZF-R1, 98-03
- M399 FZ1, 01-05
- M397 FJ1100 & 1200, 84-93
- M375 V-Max, 85-03
- M374-2 Royal Star, 96-10

VINTAGE MOTORCYCLES

Clymer® Collection Series

- M330 Vintage British Street Bikes, BSA 500–650cc Unit Twins; Norton 750 & 850cc Commandos; Triumph 500-750cc Twins
- M300 Vintage Dirt Bikes, V. 1 Bultaco, 125-370cc Singles; Montesa, 123-360cc Singles; Ossa, 125-250cc Singles
- M305 Vintage Japanese Street Bikes Honda, 250 & 305cc Twins; Kawasaki, 250-750cc Triples; Kawasaki, 900 & 1000cc Fours